WORD
BIBLICAL
COMMENTARY

WORD
BIBLICAL
COMMENTARY

VOLUME 26

Jeremiah 1-25

PETER C. CRAIGIE[†]
PAGE H. KELLEY
JOEL F. DRINKARD, JR.

WORD BOOKS, PUBLISHER • DALLAS, TEXAS

Word Biblical Commentary
JEREMIAH 1–25
Copyright © 1991 by Word, Incorporated

Library of Congress Cataloging-in-Publication Data
Main entry under title:

Word biblical commentary.

   Includes bibliographies.
   1. Bible—Commentaries—Collected works.
BS491.2.W67   220.7'7   81-71768
ISBN 0–8499–0225–8/ (vol. 26) AACR2

Printed in the United States of America

Scripture quotations in the body of the commentary marked RSV are from the Revised Standard Version of the Bible, copyright 1946 (renewed 1973), 1956, and © 1971 by the Division of Christian Education of the National Council of the Churches of Christ in the USA and are used by permission. The authors' own translation of the text appears in italic type under the heading "Translation."

6 7 8 9 10 11 12 — 03 02 01 00

In memoriam

Peter C. Craigie

(1938–1988)

Contents

Foreword   x
Editorial Preface   xi
Abbreviations   xii

GENERAL BIBLIOGRAPHY   xxiii
  Commentaries on Jeremiah
  Monographs and Other Books
  Articles

INTRODUCTION   xxx
  Form and Structure of the Book of Jeremiah   xxxi
  The Prophet Jeremiah   xxxvii
  The Hebrew and Greek Texts of Jeremiah   xli
  Historical Background for the Book of Jeremiah   xlv

TEXT AND COMMENTARY
    I. Preface to the Book of Jeremiah (1:1–3)   1
   II. Call and Commission (1:4–10)   6
  III. An Account of Two Visions (1:11–19)   13
  IV. Jeremiah's Early Oracles (2:1–6:30)   19
      A. Oracles concerning Judah's Evil (2:1–37)   20
          The Lost Love of Youth (2:1–3)   22
          A Lawsuit against People and Prophets (2:4–13)   25
          Defection and Slavery (2:14–19)   30
          The Indictment for Evil (2:20–28)   34
          Israel's Rebelliousness (2:29–32)   39
          The Way of Evil (2:33–37)   42
      B. The Prophetic Plea for Repentance (3:1–4:4)   46
          Repentance: Introduction and Elaboration (3:1–5)   48
          The Failure of Israel and Judah (3:6–11)   53
          An Invitation to Repentance Addressed to Israel (3:12–13)   56
          An Invitation to Repentance Addressed to Judah (3:14–18)   58
          Repentance and Forgiveness (3:19–4:2)   62
          Repetition of the Call to Repentance (4:3–4)   66
      C. The Declaration of Divine Judgment (4:5–6:30)   69
          The Declaration of Disaster (4:5–10)   70
          The Winds of War (4:11–18)   74
          The Prophetic Anguish (4:19–22)   78
          A Vision of Chaos (4:23–28)   80
          A Lament for Zion (4:29–31)   83
          A Dialogue concerning Judgment (5:1–9)   85
          The Theme of Judgment Renewed (5:10–19)   89

           Poems on Evil and Judgment (5:20–31)   93
           A Call of Warning (6:1–8)   97
           Dialogue: Comprehensive Judgment (6:9–15)   101
           Warning, Refusal, and Judgment (6:16–21)   104
           An Oracle and Concluding Dialogue (6:22–30)   107
     V.   The Temple Sermon (7:1–8:3)   113
    VI.   Miscellaneous Sayings concerning National Evil and
               Its Consequences (8:4–10:25)   129
           A. Unrepentant People and Unwise Wise Men (8:4–12)   130
           B. Judgment and Despair (8:13–23 [8:13–9:1])   135
           C. The Sorrow of God (9:1–10 [9:2–11]   140
           D. The Rationale of Judgment (9:11–15 [9:12–16])   145
           E. A Call to Lament (9:16–21 [9:17–22])   148
           F. Judgment upon All (9:22–25 [9:23–26])   151
           G. Idols and the True God (10:1–16)   154
           H. Vicarious Suffering (10:17–25)   161
   VII.   Why Judgment? (11:1–13:27)   165
           A. Jeremiah and the Covenant (11:1–17)   166
               Excursus: Jeremiah's Confessions   172
           B. The First Confession: Jeremiah and the Men
                   of Anathoth (11:18–12:6)   174
           C. The Sorrow of God (12:7–17)   181
           D. Symbolism and Sin (13:1–27)   186
  VIII.   Judgment and Ostracism (14:1–16:21)   194
           A. Drought and Destruction (14:1–15:9)   195
           B. A Second Confession: Jeremiah's Ostracism (15:10–21)   205
           C. Jeremiah's Life and Related Sayings (16:1–21)   213
    IX.   Sin and Its Consequences (17:1–13)   220
           A. Judah's Sin and Its Consequences (17:1–4)   221
           B. The Two Ways (17:5–8)   224
           C. The Deceitful Heart (17:9–10)   227
           D. The Partridge and the One Gaining Wealth
                   Unjustly (17:11)   228
           E. Judgment on Those Forsaking God (17:12–13)   229
     X.   Oracles (17:14–20:20)   233
           A. A Third Confession of Jeremiah: Heal Me,
                   Destroy Them (17:14–18)   233
           B. Sabbath Observance (17:19–27)   237
           C. The Potter's Shop (18:1–12)   240
           D. A Horrifying Thing (18:13–17)   246
           E. Jeremiah's Fourth Confession (18:18–23)   250
           F. The Broken Decanter (19:1–13)   254
           G. Another Temple Sermon and Its Results (19:14–20:6)   263
           H. A Final Confession (20:7–13)   268
           I. Cursed Was the Day (20:14–18)   276
    XI.   Oracles against Zedekiah and Jerusalem (21:1–10)   282
   XII.   Oracles against the Kings of Judah (21:11–23:8)   290
           A. Oracle against a King and Jerusalem (21:11–14)   290

B. Oracle against an Unnamed King (22:1–5)   294
C. Another Oracle against an Unnamed King (22:6–7)   299
D. Why Was This City Destroyed? (22:8–9)   302
E. Weeping for the Dead or the Living? (22:10)   304
F. An Oracle against Shallum (22:11–12)   305
G. An Oracle against Jehoiakim (22:13–19)   307
H. Oracle against Jerusalem (22:20–23)   313
I. Oracle against Coniah (22:24–27)   317
J. Another Oracle against Coniah (22:28–30)   320
K. Judgment on Present and Future Shepherds
      and a Blessing (23:1–4)   324
L. A Future King (23:5–6)   328
M. The Return (23:7–8)   331
XIII. Oracles concerning Prophets and Prophecy (23:9–24:10)   334
A. An Oracle concerning the Prophets (23:9–12)   334
B. Samaria's Prophets and Jerusalem's Prophets (23:13–15)   338
C. Further Words against False Prophets (23:16–22)   341
D. The Preeminence of God (23:23–24)   345
E. Dreamers of Dreams and Yahweh's Word (23:25–32)   347
F. The "Burden" of the Lord (23:33–40)   351
XIV. A Vision and Judgment Oracles (24:1–25:38)   356
A. Two Baskets of Figs (24:1–10)   356
B. Judgment on Judah (25:1–11)   361
C. Judgment on Babylon (25:12–14)   367
D. Judgment on the Nations (25:15–29)   368
E. Oracles against the Nations (25:30–38)   372

Indexes   377

Foreword

The untimely death of Peter Craigie cut short his work on this commentary. At the time of his death in 1988, he had completed the first seven chapters of Jeremiah and proceeded as far as verse 4 of chapter 8. In consultation with his wife, Elizabeth, the editors decided to assign the balance of Jeremiah 1–25, and the second volume—Jeremiah 26–52—to writers among the faculty of The Southern Baptist Seminary, where Old Testament Editor John Watts serves.

Dr. Craigie's work in this volume, including the Introduction, is presented essentially as it left his pen. The commentary on Jeremiah 8:4 through chapter 16 is the work of Page Kelley, and the commentary on chapters 17 through 25 has been prepared by Joel Drinkard. Gerald Keown has updated and expanded Dr. Craigie's bibliography, Gerald Morris has gathered the list of ancient commentaries, and Thomas Smothers has written The Historical Background for the Book of Jeremiah. The division of labor will undoubtedly result in different emphases in parts of the book, but it has allowed for the specialization of interest by the writers that bears fruit in these pages.

The authors and editors will be grateful if this volume may serve in its own way to perpetuate the memory of and display appreciation for Peter Craigie.

> He wed learning to piety,
> clothed brilliance in humility,
> joined service in the academy with fruitfulness in the church.
> More than most of his peers, he mastered
> the high art of doing many things well:
> scholarship in matters Hebraic and Semitic,
> collegiality with teachers older and younger,
> vitality in the learned societies to which he was pledged,
> effectiveness in his ministry and as dean
>   and provost of the University of Calgary,
> affection and care for his wife and family,
> congeniality with a host of friends, and
> adoration of his Maker and Redeemer.

Peter Craigie's contributions to this and other series of commentaries, his monographs and technical studies, and his popular expositions all combine to remind us of the huge debt owed him by students of the Bible. The prodigious output in a relatively brief time makes us both grateful for his discipline and eager to learn with him the psalmist's prayer:

> So teach us to number our days
> that we may get a heart of wisdom.
>   Psalm 90:12

JOHN D. W. WATTS
DAVID A. HUBBARD

Editorial Preface

The launching of the *Word Biblical Commentary* brings to fulfillment an enterprise of several years' planning. The publishers and the members of the editorial board met in 1977 to explore the possibility of a new commentary on the books of the Bible that would incorporate several distinctive features. Prospective readers of these volumes are entitled to know what such features were intended to be; whether the aims of the commentary have been fully achieved time alone will tell.

First, we have tried to cast a wide net to include as contributors a number of scholars from around the world who not only share our aims, but are in the main engaged in the ministry of teaching in university, college, and seminary. They represent a rich diversity of denominational allegiance. The broad stance of our contributors can rightly be called evangelical, and this term is to be understood in its positive, historic sense of a commitment to Scripture as divine revelation, and to the truth and power of the Christian gospel.

Then, the commentaries in our series are all commissioned and written for the purpose of inclusion in the *Word Biblical Commentary*. Unlike several of our distinguished counterparts in the field of commentary writing, there are no translated works, originally written in a non-English language. Also, our commentators were asked to prepare their own rendering of the original biblical text and to use those languages as the basis of their own comments and exegesis. What may be claimed as distinctive with this series is that it is based on the biblical languages, yet it seeks to make the technical and scholarly approach to a theological understanding of Scripture understandable by—and useful to—the fledgling student, the working minister, and colleagues in the guild of professional scholars and teachers as well.

Finally, a word must be said about the format of the series. The layout, in clearly defined sections, has been consciously devised to assist readers at different levels. Those wishing to learn about the textual witnesses on which the translation is offered are invited to consult the section headed *Notes*. If the readers' concern is with the state of modern scholarship on any given portion of Scripture, they should turn to the sections of *Bibliography* and *Form/Structure/Setting*. For a clear exposition of the passage's meaning and its relevance to the ongoing biblical revelation, the *Comment* and concluding *Explanation* are designed expressly to meet that need. There is therefore something for everyone who may pick up and use these volumes.

If these aims come anywhere near realization, the intention of the editors will have been met, and the labor of our team of contributors rewarded.

General Editors: *David A. Hubbard*
Glenn W. Barker †
Old Testament: *John D. W. Watts*
New Testament: *Ralph P. Martin*

Abbreviations

PERIODICALS, SERIALS, AND REFERENCE WORKS

AAS	*Acta apostolicae sedis*
AASF	Annales Academic Scientarum Fennicae
AASOR	Annual of the American Schools of Oriental Research
AB	Anchor Bible
AbrN	*Abr-Nahrain*
AcOr	*Acta orientalia*
ADAJ	Annual of the Department of Antiquities of Jordan
AfO	*Archiv für Orientforschung*
AGJU	Arbeiten zur Geschichte des antiken Judentums und des Urchristentums
AHW	W. von Soden, *Akkadisches Handwörterbuch*
AJA	*American Journal of Archaeology*
AJAS	*American Journal of Arabic Studies*
AJBA	*Australian Journal of Biblical Archaeology*
AJSL	*American Journal of Semitic Languages and Literature*
AJT	*American Journal of Theology*
ALBO	Analecta lovaniensia biblica et orientalia
ALUOS	Annual of Leeds University Oriental Society
AnBib	Analecta biblica
ANEP	J. B. Pritchard (ed.), *Ancient Near East in Pictures*
ANESTP	J. B. Pritchard (ed.), *Ancient Near East Supplementary Texts and Pictures*
ANET	J. B. Pritchard (ed.), *Ancient Near Eastern Texts*
AnOr	Analecta orientalia
ANQ	*Andover Newton Quarterly*
AOAT	Alter Orient und Altes Testament
AOS	American Oriental Series
APOT	R. H. Charles (ed.), *Apocrypha and Pseudepigrapha of the Old Testament*
ARG	*Archiv für Reformationsgeschichte*
ARM	Archives royales de Mari
ArOr	*Archiv orientální*
ARW	*Archiv für Religionswissenschaft*
ASSR	*Archives des sciences sociales des religions*
ASTI	*Annual of the Swedish Theological Institute*
ATAbh	Alttestamentliche Abhandlungen
ATANT	Abhandlungen zur Theologie des Alten und Neuen Testaments
ATR	*Anglican Theological Review*
AusBR	*Australian Biblical Review*
AUSS	*Andrews University Seminary Studies*

BA	*Biblical Archaeologist*
BANE	G. E. Wright (ed.), *The Bible and the Ancient Near East*
BAR	*Biblical Archaeologist Reader*
BASOR	*Bulletin of the American Schools of Oriental Research*
BAT	Die Botschaft des Alten Testaments
BCSR	*Bulletin of the Council on the Study of Religion*
BDB	F. Brown, S. R. Driver, and C. A. Briggs, *Hebrew and English Lexicon of the Old Testament*
BeO	*Bibbia e oriente*
BETL	Bibliotheca ephemeridum theologicarum lovaniensium
BEvT	Beiträge zur evangelischen Theologie
BFCT	Beiträge zur Förderung christlicher Theologie
BGBE	Beiträge zur Geschichte der biblischen Exegese
BHH	B. Reicke and L. Rost (eds.), *Biblisch-historisches Handwörterbuch*
BHK	R. Kittel, *Biblia hebraica.*
BHS	*Biblia hebraica stuttgartensia*
BHT	Beiträge zur historischen Theologie
Bib	*Biblica*
BibB	Biblische Beiträge
BibIll	*Biblical Illustrator*
BibLeb	*Bibel und Leben*
BibOr	Biblica et orientalia
BibS(F)	Biblische Studien (Freiburg, 1895–)
BibS(N)	Biblische Studien (Neukirchen, 1951–)
BIES	*Bulletin of the Israel Exploration Society*
BIFAO	*Bulletin de l'institut français d'archéologie orientale*
BJRL	*Bulletin Bulletin of the John Rylands University Library of Manchester*
BK	*Bibel und Kirche*
BKAT	Biblischer Kommentar: Altes Testament
BLit	*Bibel und Liturgie*
BMik	*Beth Mikra*
BN	*Biblische Notizen*
BO	*Bibliotheca orientalis*
BR	*Biblical Research*
BSac	*Bibliotheca Sacra*
BSO(A)S	*Bulletin of the School of Oriental (and African) Studies*
BSS	*Bibliotheca Sanctorum*
BSt	Biblische Studien
BT	*The Bible Translator*
BTB	*Biblical Theology Bulletin*
BTS	*Bible et terre sainte*
BVC	*Bible et vie chrétienne*
BWANT	Beiträge zur Wissenschaft vom Alten und Neuen Testament
BZ	*Biblische Zeitschrift*
BZAW	Beihefte zur ZAW
CAD	*The Assyrian Dictionary of the Oriental Institute of the University of Chicago*
CAH	*Cambridge Ancient History*

CAT	Commentaire de l'Ancien Testament
CB	*Cultura bíblica*
CBQ	*Catholic Biblical Quarterly*
CBQMS	Catholic Biblical Quarterly—Monograph Series
CCath	Corpus Catholicorum
CJT	*Canadian Journal of Theology*
CleM	*Clergy Monthly*
CML	G. R. Driver, *Canaanite Myths and Legends* (Edinburg, 1956); rev. ed. J. C. L. Gibson (Edinburgh, 1978)
ConB	Coniectanea biblica
COT	Commentaar op het OT
CQ	*Church Quarterly*
CQR	*Church Quarterly Review*
CRAIBL	*Comptes rendus de l'Académie des inscriptions et belles-lettres*
CSCO	Corpus scriptorum christianorum orientalium
CTA	A. Herdner, *Corpus des tablettes en cunéiforms alphabétiques*
CTM	*Concordia Theological Monthly*
CurTM	*Currents in Theology and Mission*
DACL	*Dictionnaire d'archéologie chrétienne et de liturgie*
DBSup	*Dictionnaire de la Bible, Supplément*
DD	*Dor le Dor*
DISO	C.-F. Jean and J. Hoftijzer, *Dictionnaire des inscriptions sémitiques de l'ouest*
Div	*Divinitas*
DJD	Discoveries in the Judaean Desert
DOTT	D. W. Thomas (ed.), *Documents from Old Testament Times*
DTT	*Dansk teologisk tidsskrift*
Ebib	Etudes bibliques
ECarm	*Ephemerides Carmeliticae*
EHAT	Exegetisches Handbuch zum Alten Testament
EHO	Cross and Freedman, *Early Hebrew Orthography*
EI	*Eres\Israel*
EncJud	*Encyclopaedia judaica* (1971)
EnchBib	*Enchiridion biblicum*
EngSt	*English Studies*
EstBib	*Estudios bíblicos*
ET	*Église et Théologie*
ETL	*Ephemerides theologicae lovanienses*
ETR	*Etudes théologiques et religieuses*
EuntDoc	*Euntes Docete*
EvK	Evangelische Kommentare
EvQ	*Evangelical Quarterly*
EvT	*Evangelische Theologie (EvTh)*
Exp	*The Expositor*
ExpTim	*Expository Times*
FrancSt	*Franciscan Studies*
FRLANT	Forschungen zur Religion und Literatur des Alten und Neuen Testaments

GAG	W. von Soden, *Grundriss der akkadischen Grammatik*
GKB	Gesenius-Kautzsch-Bergsträsser, *Hebräische Grammatik*
GKC	*Gesenius' Hebrew Grammar,* ed. E. Kautzsch, tr. A. E. Cowley
GTJ	*Grace Theological Journal*
HALAT	W. Baumgartner et al., *Hebräisches und aramäisches Lexikon zum Alten Testament*
HAR	*Hebrew Annual Review*
HAT	Handbuch zum Alten Testament
HDR	Harvard Dissertations in Religion
Hen	*Henoch*
HeyJ	*Heythrop Journal*
HibJ	*Hibbert Journal*
HKAT	Handkommentar zum Alten Testament
HS	*Hebrew Studies*
HSAT	*Die Heilige Schrift des Alten Testament,* 2 vols.; ed. E. Kautzsche and A. Bertholet (Tübingen: ⁴1922–23)
HSM	Harvard Semitic Monographs
HTR	*Harvard Theological Review*
HTS	Harvard Theological Studies
HUCA	*Hebrew Union College Annual*
HUCM	Monographs of Hebrew Union College
IB	*Interpreter's Bible*
ICC	International Critical Commentary
IDB	G. A. Buttrick (ed.), *Interpreter's Dictionary of the Bible*
IDBSup	Supplementary volume to *IDB*
IEJ	*Israel Exploration Journal*
IndJTh	*Indian Journal of Theology*
Int	*Interpretation*
ISBE	G. W. Bromiley (ed.), *International Standard Bible Encyclopedia,* rev.
ITQ	*Irish Theological Quarterly*
ITS	*Innsbrucker theologisches Studien*
JA	*Journal asiatique*
JAAR	*Journal of the American Academy of Religion*
JAC	Jahrbuch für Antike und Christentum
JANESCU	*Journal of the Ancient Near Eastern Society of Columbia University*
JAOS	*Journal of the American Oriental Society*
JAS	*Journal of Asian Studies*
JB	A. Jones (ed.), *Jerusalem Bible*
JBC	R. E. Brown et al. (eds.), *The Jerome Biblical Commentary*
JBL	*Journal of Biblical Literature*
JBR	*Journal of Bible and Religion*
JBS	Jerusalem Biblical Studies
JCS	*Journal of Cuneiform Studies*
JDS	Judean Desert Studies
JEA	*Journal of Egyptian Archaeology*
JEOL	*Jaarbericht . . . ex oriente lux*
JETS	*Journal of the Evangelical Theological Society*

JJS	*Journal of Jewish Studies*
JMES	*Journal of Middle Eastern Studies*
JNES	*Journal of Near Eastern Studies*
JNSL	*Journal of Northwest Semitic Languages*
JPOS	*Journal of Palestine Oriental Society*
JPSV	Jewish Publication Society Version
JQR	*Jewish Quarterly Review*
JQRMS	Jewish Quarterly Review Monograph Series
JR	*Journal of Religion*
JRAS	*Journal of the Royal Asiatic Society*
JRelS	*Journal of Religious Studies*
JSOT	*Journal for the Study of the Old Testament*
JSOTSup	Supplement to *JSOT*
JSS	*Journal of Semitic Studies*
JSSR	*Journal for the Scientific Study of Religion*
JTC	*Journal for Theology and the Church*
JTS	*Journal of Theological Studies*
Judaica	*Judaica: Beiträge zum Verständnis . . .*
KAI	H. Donner and W. Röllig, *Kanaanäische und aramäische Inschriften*
KAT	E. Sellin (ed.), Kommentar zum Alten Testament
KB	L. Koehler and W. Baumgartner, *Lexicon in Veteris Testamenti libros*
KD	*Kerygma und Dogma*
KIT	Kleine Texte
KTU	*Die Keilalphabetischen Texte aus Ugarit,* I, ed. M. Dietrich, O. Loretz, and J. Sammartin, AOAT 24 (1976)
LCC	Library of Christian Classics
LCL	Loeb Classical Library
LD	Lectio divina
Les	*Lesonénu*
LLAVT	E. Vogt, *Lexicon linguae aramaicae Veteris Testamenti*
LQ	*Lutheran Quarterly*
LR	*Luterische Rundschau*
LSJ	Liddel-Scott-Jones, *Greek-English Lexicon*
LTK	*Lexicon für Theologie und Kirche*
LumVit	*Lumen Vitae*
LUÅ	Lunds universitets årsskrift
MBA	Y. Aharoni and M. Ari-Yonah, *Macmillan Bible Atlas,* rev. ed. (New York: Macmillan, 1977)
McCQ	*McCormick Quarterly*
MDOG	Mitteilungen der deutschen Orient-Gesellschaft
MelT	*Melita Theologica*
MGWJ	*Monatsschrift für Geschichte und Wissenschaft des Judentums*
MScRel	*Mélanges de science religieuse*
MTZ	*Münchener theologische Zeitschrift*
MUSJ	*Mélanges de l'université Saint-Joseph*
MVAG	Mitteilungen der vorder-asiatisch-ägyptischen Gesellschaft
NedTTs	*Nederlands theologish tijdschrift*
NGTT	*Nederduits Gereformeerde Teologiese Tydskrif*

NHS	Nag Hammadi Studies
NICOT	New International Commentary on the Old Testament
NKZ	*Neue kirchliche Zeitschrift*
NorTT	*Norsk Teologisk Tidsskrift*
NovT	*Novum Testamentum*
NRT	*La nouvelle revue théologique*
NSH	Kuhnigk, *Nordwestsemitische Studien zum Hoseabuch* (Rome: Biblical Institute Press, 1974)
OBO	Orbis biblicus et orientalis
OIP	Oriental Institute Publications
OLP	Orientalia lovaniensia periodica
OLZ	*Orientalische Literaturzeitung*
Or	*Orientalia* (Rome)
OrAnt	*Oriens antiquus*
OrChr	*Oriens christianus*
OrSyr	*L'orient syrien*
OTL	Old Testament Library
OTS	*Oudtestamentische Studiën*
OTWSA	*Die Outestamentiese Werkgemeenskap in Suid-Afrika*
PAAJR	*Proceedings of the American Academy of Jewish Research*
PCB	M. Black and H. H. Rowley (eds.), *Peake's Commentary on the Bible* (London: Thomas Nelson and Sons, 1963)
PEFQS	*Palestine Exploration Fund, Quarterly Statement*
PEQ	*Palestine Exploration Quarterly*
PG	J. Migne, *Patrologia graeca*
PJ	*Palästina-Jahrbuch*
PL	J. Migne, *Patrologia latina*
PRU	*Le Palais royal d'Ugarit*
PSTJ	*Perkins (School of Theology) Journal*
PW	Pauly-Wissowa, *Real-Encyclopädie der classischen Altertumswissenschaft*
PWSup	Supplement to PW
QDAP	*Quarterly of the Department of Antiquities in Palestine*
RA	*Revue d'assyriologie et d'archéologie orientale*
RAC	*Reallexikon für Antike und Christentum*
RArch	*Revue archéologuique*
RB	*Revue biblique*
RCB	*Revista de cultura biblica*
RE	*Realencyklopädie für protestantische Theologie und Kirche*
RechBib	Recherches bibliques
REJ	*Revue des études juives*
RelS	*Religious Studies*
RelSRev	*Religious Studies Review*
RES	*Répertoire d'épigraphie sémitique*
ResQ	*Restoration Quarterly*
RevExp	*Review and Expositor*
RevistB	*Revista biblica*
RevQ	*Revue de Qumran*
RevScRel	*Revue des sciences religieuses*

RevSém	*Revue sémitique*
RGG	*Religion in Geschichte und Gegenwart*
RHPR	*Revue d'histoire et de philosophie religieuses*
RHR	*Revue de l'histoire des religions*
RivB	*Rivista biblica*
RR	*Review of Religion*
RSO	*Revista degli studi orientali*
RSP	*Ras Shamra Parallels*, ed. L. R. Fisher, AnOr 49 (Rome: Pontifical Biblical Institute, 1972)
RSPT	*Revue des sciences philosophiques et théologiques*
RSR	*Recherches de science religieuse*
RTL	*Revue théologique de Louvain*
RTP	*Revue de théologie et de philosophie*
RUO	*Revue de l'université d'Ottawa*
SANT	Studien zum Alten und Neuen Testament
SAOC	Studies in Ancient Oriental Civilization
SAT	Die Schriften des Alten Testaments in Auswahl übersetzt und erklärt, ed. Herman Gunkel
SAYP	Cross and Freedman, *Studies in Ancient Yahwistic Poetry*
SB	Sources bibliques
SBB	Stuttgarter biblische Beiträge
SBFLA	*Studii biblici franciscani liber annuus*
SBLASP	Society of Biblical Literature Abstracts and Seminar Papers
SBLDS	SBL Dissertation Series
SBLMasS	SBL Masoretic Studies
SBLMS	SBL Monograph Series
SBLSBS	SBL Sources for Biblical Study
SBLSCS	SBL Septuagint and Cognate Studies
SBLTT	SBL Texts and Translations
SBM	Stuttgarter biblische Monographien
SBS	Stuttgarter Bibelstudien
SBT	Studies in Biblical Theology
ScÉs	*Science et esprit*
Scr	*Scripture*
ScrB	*Scripture Bulletin*
SD	Studies and Documents
SEÅ	*Svensk exegetisk årsbok*
Sef	*Sefarad*
SEHM	Stuart, *Studies in Early Hebrew Meter*
Sem	*Semitica*
SJT	*Scottish Journal of Theology*
SOTP	H. H. Rowley (ed.), *Studies in Old Testament Prophecy*
SOTSMS	Society for Old Testament Study Monograph Series
SPAW	Sitzungsberichte der preussischen Akademie der Wissenschaften
SR	*Studies in Religion / Sciences religieuses*
SSS	Semitic Study Series
ST	*Studia theologica*
STÅ	*Svensk teologisk årsskrift*

STDJ	Studies on the Texts of the Desert of Judah
STK	*Svensk teologisk kvartalskrift*
StudOr	Studia orientalia
SVTP	Studia in Veteris Testamenti pseudepigrapha
SWJT	*Southwestern Journal of Theology*
TBl	*Theologische Blätter*
TBT	*The Bible Today*
TBü	Theologische Bücherei
TD	*Theology Digest*
TDOT	G. J. Botterweck and H. Ringgren (eds.), *Theological Dictionary of the Old Testament* (Grand Rapids: Eerdmans, 1974–)
TextsS	Texts and Studies
TF	*Theologische Forschung*
TGl	*Theologie und Glaube*
TGUOS	*Transactions: Glasgow University Oriental Society*
ThLife	*Theology and Life*
ThSz	*Theologiai Szemle*
ThV	*Theologisches Versuche* (Berlin)
TLZ	*Theologische Literaturzeitung*
TP	*Theologie und Philosophie*
TQ	*Theologische Quartalschrift*
TRev	*Theologische Revue*
TRu	*Theologische Rundschau*
TS	*Theological Studies*
TSK	*Theologische Studien und Kritiken*
TT	*Teologisk Tidsskrift*
TTKi	*Tidsskrift for Teologi og Kirke*
TToday	*Theology Today*
TTZ	*Trierer theologische Zeitschrift*
TU	Texte und Untersuchungen
TV	*Theologia Viatorum*
TWAT	G. J. Botterweck and H. Ringgren (eds.), *Theologisches Wörterbuch zum Alten Testament*
TWOT	R. L. Harris, et al. (eds.), *Theological Wordbook of the Old Testament* (Chicago: Moody Press, 1980)
TynBul	*Tyndale Bulletin*
TZ	*Theologische Zeitschrift (ThZ)*
UF	*Ugarit-Forschungen*
USQR	*Union Seminary Quarterly Review*
UT	C. H. Gordon, *Ugaritic Textbook*
UUÅ	Uppsala universitetsårsskrift
VC	*Vigilae christianae*
VD	*Verbum domini*
VF	*Verkündigung und Forschung*
VSpir	*Vie spirituelle*
VT	*Vetus Testamentum*
VTSup	Vetus Testamentum, Supplements
WBC	Word Biblical Commentary

WDB	*Westminster Dictionary of the Bible*
WHAB	*Westminster Historical Atlas of the Bible*
WMANT	Wissenschaftliche Monographien zum Alten und Neuen Testament
WO	*Die Welt des Orients*
WTJ	*Westminster Theological Journal*
WuD	*Wort und Dienst*
WUNT	Wissenschaftliche Untersuchungen zum Neuen Testament
WZKM	*Wiener Zeitschrift für die Kunde des Morgenlandes*
WZKSO	*Wiener Zeitschrift für die Kunde Süd- und Ostasiens*
ZA	*Zeitschrift für Assyriologie*
ZAW	*Zeitschrift für die alttestamentliche Wissenschaft*
ZDMG	*Zeitschrift der deutsche morgenländischen Gesellschaft*
ZDPV	*Zeitschrift der deutschen Palästina-Vereins*
ZEE	*Zeitschrift für evangelische Ethik*
ZKG	*Zeitschrift für Kirchengeschichte*
ZKT	*Zeitschrift für katholische Theologie*
ZNW	*Zeitschrift für die neutestamentliche Wissenschaft*
ZRGG	*Zeitschrift für Religions- und Geistesgeschichte*
ZTK	*Zeitschrift für Theologie und Kirche*
ZWT	*Zeitschrift für wissenschaftliche Theologie*

HEBREW GRAMMAR

abs	absolute	hithp	hithpael
acc	accusative	hoph	hophal
act	active	impf	imperfect
adv	adverb / adverbial	impv	imperative
aor	aorist	ind	indicative
apoc	apocopated	inf	infinitive
c	common	juss	jussive
coh	cohortative	masc, m	masculine
conj	conjunction	niph	niphal
consec	consecutive	obj	object
const	construct	pass	passive
conv	converted	pf	perfect
dittogr	dittography	pl	plural
fem, f	feminine	poss	possessive
fut	future	prep	preposition
gen	genitive	pronom	pronominal
haplogr	haplography	ptcp	participle
hiph	hiphil	sg	singular
		stat	stative
		subj	subject / subjective
		suff	suffix
		voc	vocative

NOTE: Hebrew שׂ (*sin*) is differentiated by pointing from שׁ (*shin*) only when ambiguity might otherwise result.

Textual Notes

Akk.	Akkadian	OL	Old Latin
Arab.	Arabic	Q	Qere (Masoretic suggested pronunciation)
Aram.	Aramaic		
C	Codex of the Prophets from Cairo	2Q Jer	Jeremiah from Qumran Cave 2
Eg.	Egyptian	4Q Jer	Jeremiah from Qumran Cave 4
Eng.	English		
Eth.	Ethiopic	Syr	Syriac Peshitta
EVV	English versions	Syrh	Syrohexapla
Gk.	Greek	Tg	Targum
Heb.	Hebrew	*tiq. soph.*	*"tiqune sopherim,"* corrections of the Scribes
Hex.	Hexapla		
K	Kethib (consonantal text)		
		Ug.	Ugaritic
L	Leningrad Codex	Vg	Vulgate
LXX	The Septuagint	α'	Aquila
LXX^A (etc.)	Alexandrinus Codex of the Septuagint (etc.)	θ'	Theodotion
		σ'	Symmachus
MT	Masoretic Text	>	mutated/transformed to
OG	Old Greek	<	from

1	first person
2	second person
3	third person

Biblical and Apocryphal Books

			Solomon
		Isa	Isaiah
		Jer	Jeremiah
		Lam	Lamentations
Gen	Genesis	Ezek	Ezekiel
Exod	Exodus	Dan	Daniel
Lev	Leviticus	Hos	Hosea
Num	Numbers	Joel	Joel
Deut	Deuteronomy	Amos	Amos
Josh	Joshua	Obad	Obadiah
Judg	Judges	Jonah	Jonah
Ruth	Ruth	Mic	Micah
1–2 Sam	1–2 Samuel	Nah	Nahum
1–2 Kgs	1–2 Kings	Hab	Habakkuk
1–2 Chr	1–2 Chronicles	Zeph	Zephaniah
Ezra	Ezra	Hag	Haggai
Neh	Nehemiah	Zech	Zechariah
Esth	Esther	Mal	Malachi
Job	Job	Sir	Ecclesiasticus or The Wisdom of Jesus Son of Sirach
Ps(s)	Psalm(s)		
Prov	Proverbs	Matt	Matthew
Eccl	Ecclesiastes	John	John
Cant	Canticles, Song of		

Acts   Acts
Rom   Romans
Phil   Philippians
Heb   Hebrews
Rev   Revelation

MISCELLANEOUS

ANE — Ancient Near East
AV — Authorized Version
b. — *breve* (metrically short poetic line)
B.C. — Before Christ
c. — circa
chap(s). — chapter(s)
cols. — columns
diss. — dissertation
E — Elohist (supposed biblical literary source)
ed(s). — edition; edited by; editor(s)
esp. — especially
ET — English translation
FS — Festschrift
hap. leg. — *hapax legomenon* sole occurrence

J — Yahwist (supposed biblical literary source)
JB — Jerusalem Bible
KJV — King James Version
l — *longum* (metrically long poetic line)
lit. — literally
MS(S) — manuscript(s)
n. — note
NAB — New American Bible
NEB — New English Bible
NIV — New International Version
NJV — New Jewish Version
n.s. — new series
NT — New Testament
obv. — obverse
OT — Old Testament
p. — page
Pers. — Persian
pl. — plate
rev. — reverse
RSV — Revised Standard Version
tr. — translated; translator
UP — University Press
v(v) — verse(s)
viz. — by alteration

General Bibliography

In the bibliography that follows, there have been listed (i) commentaries, both general and technical, on the Book of Jeremiah, (ii) other studies pertaining, for the most part, to the book as a whole or general issues related to the book, and (iii) reviews of current scholarship. As there is a vast body of secondary literature associated with the Book of Jeremiah, the bibliography is limited to fairly recent works on the book; a few older and classical works have been included. The bibliography has excluded particular items pertaining to the detailed study of a chapter or verse; these items are all listed separately in the detailed bibliographies that precede each section of the commentary. For studies pertaining to Jeremiah's so-called Confessions, see the bibliography in the *Excursus* ("The Confessions of Jeremiah").

Commentaries
(referred to in the text by authors' names only)

CHURCH FATHERS

Origen. *Homilias in Jeremiam.* Origenis opera omnia, III. *PG* 13. Paris: 1857. Col. 256–534. [Greek. Third century. Only covers Jer 1–20.] **Chrysostom.** *Commentarium in Jeremiam prophetam.* S. P. N. Joannis Chrysostomi opera omnia quae extant, xiii. *PG* 64. 1860. Col. 739–1038. [Greek. Fourth century.] **Ephraim of Syria.** *Commentarium in Jeremiam.* Opera Syriaca et Latina, 2. Rome: 1740. Col. 98–162. [Fourth century.] **Cyrill of Alexandria.** *Fragmenta ex Catenus in Jeremiam.* S. P. N. Cyrilli opera quae reperiri potuerunt omnia, III. *PG* 70. 1859. Col. 1451–58. [Greek. Fifth century. Very short and fragmented.] **Theodoret of Cyrene.** *Beati Theodoreti, in divini Jeremiae prophetam interpretatio.* Theodoreti opera omnia, III. PG *81.* 1859. Col. 495–760. [Greek. Fifth century.] **Jerome.** *S. Eusebii Hieronymi, Commentarium in Jeremiam prophetam libri sex.* Sancti Eusebii Hieronymi opera omnia, IV. *PL* 24. Col. 706–936. [Latin. Fifth century. Only covers Jer 1–32.]

MEDIEVAL CHURCHMEN

Maurus. *Beati Rabani Mauri, Expositionis super Jeremiam prophetam libri viginti.* B. Rabani Mauri opera omnia, V. *PL* 111. 1852. Col. 793–1182. [Latin. Ninth century.] **Rupert of Deutz.** *In Jeremiam prophetam commentarium liber unus.* R. D. D. Ruperti opera omnia, I. *PL* 167. 1854. Col. 1363–1420. [Latin. Twelfth century.] **Thomas Aquinas.** *In Jeremiam prophetam expositio.* Opera, 13. Rome: 1570. Venice: 1594. Antwerp: 1612. [Latin. Thirteenth century. Only covers Jer 1– 42.]

MEDIEVAL JEWISH COMMENTATORS

Rashi (Solomon ben Isaac). *Commentary on the Latter Prophets.* Venice: 1608. [A Latin version edited by Johann Fr. Breihaupt, Gotha: 1713. Rashi lived 1040–1105.] **David Kimchi.** *Commentary on the Latter Prophets.* Pesaro: 1515. Paris: 1556. [Also included in Moses Frankfurter's larger Bible, Amsterdam: 1724–1727. Kimchi's dates: 1160?–1235?.] **Arama**

(Meir ben Isaac). *Urim ve-Tummim.* Venice: 1603. [A commentary on Isaiah and Jeremiah. Included in Moses Frankfurter's larger Bible, Amsterdam, 1724–1727. Arama lived in Spain, 1460?–1545?]

REFORMATION AND COUNTER-REFORMATION

Calvin, J. *Commentaries on the Book of the Prophet Jeremiah and Lamentations.* Trans. and ed. J. Owen. 5 vols. Grand Rapids: Eerdmans, 1950. [Originally Latin. 1589. Can be found in Latin as vols. 37–39 of the Opera omnia, Corpus reformatorum, 65–67.] **Zwingli, U. D.** *Huldrichi Zwingli, annotationes in Genesim, Exodum, Esaiam & Jeremiam Prophetas.* Zurich: 1581. [Also in Opera omnia, 14. Corpus reformatorum, 101.] **Melanchthon, P.** *Argumentam in Jeremiam Prophetam.* Opera omnia, 13. Corpus reformatorum, 13. Col. 804–14. [Very short and fragmentary. Not really commentary.] **Capella, A.** *Commentaria in Jeremiam prophetam, in cartusia Scalae Dei.* Rome: 1586. [Latin. Roman Catholic.] **Christoph a Castro.** Paris: 1609. [Latin. Jeremiah, Lamentations, Baruch.] **Maldonatus, J.** Lyon: 1611. [Latin. Jeremiah, Baruch.] **Sanctius (Sanchez), G.** Antwerp: 1611. Lyon: 1618. [Latin.] **Ghislerius, M.** Lyon: 1623. [Latin.]

ENLIGHTENMENT THROUGH NINETEENTH CENTURY

Lowth, W. *Commentary upon the Prophecy and Lamentations of Jeremiah.* London: 1718. **Michaelis, J. D.** *Observationes philologicae et criticae in Jeremiae vaticinia.* Göttingen: 1743. **Cheyne, J. K.** *Jeremiah.* The Pulpit Commentary. London: 1883. **Keil, C. F.** *Biblischer Commentar über den Propheten Jeremia.* Leipzig: 1872. ———. *Jeremiah.* Biblical Commentary. Edinborough, 1880. **Naegelsbach, C. W. E.** *The Book of the Prophet Jeremiah, Theologically and Homiletically Expounded.* New York: Scribner's, 1886.

TWENTIETH CENTURY

Achtemeier, E. *Deuteronomy, Jeremiah.* Proclamation Commentaries. Philadelphia: Fortress, 1978. **Aeschimann, A.** *Le prophète Jérémie: Commentaire.* Neuchâtel: Delachaux and Niestlé, 1959. **Blackwood, A. W.** *Commentary on Jeremiah.* Waco: Word Books, 1977. **Boadt, L.** *Jeremiah 1–25.* Old Testament Message 9. Wilmington: Glazier, 1982. ———. *Jeremiah 26–52.* Old Testament Message 10. Wilmington: Glazier, 1983. **Bright, J.** *Jeremiah.* AB Garden City, NY: Doubleday, 1965. **Brueggemann, W.** *A Commentary on the Book of Jeremiah 1–25: To Pluck Up, to Tear Down.* International Theological Commentary. Grand Rapids: Eerdmans, 1988. **Carroll, R. P.** *Jeremiah.* OTL. Philadelphia: Westminster, 1986. **Clements, R. E.** *Jeremiah.* Interpretation. Atlanta: John Knox, 1988. **Condamin, A.** *Le Livre de Jérémie.* Ebib. Paris: Gabalda, 1936. **Cornill, C. H.** *Das Buch Jeremia.* Leipzig: Tauchnitz, 1905. **Craigie, P. C.** *The Book of Deuteronomy.* The New International Commentary on the Old Testament. Grand Rapids, MI: Eerdmans, 1976. ———. *Psalms 1–50.* WBC 19. Waco, TX: Word Books, 1983. **Cunliffe-Jones, H.** *The Book of Jeremiah: Introduction and Commentary.* The Torch Bible Commentaries. London: SCM, 1960. **Dalglish, E. R.** *Jeremiah, Lamentations.* Layman's Bible Book Commentary 2. Nashville: Broadman, 1983. **Davidson, R.** *Jeremiah, Volume I.* The Daily Study Bible. Philadelphia: Westminster Press. 1983. ———. *Jeremiah, Volume II.* The Daily Study Bible. Philadelphia: Westminster, 1985. **Driver, S. R.** *The Book of the Prophet Jeremiah.* London: Hodder & Stoughton, 1906. **Duhm, B.** *Das Buch Jeremia.* Kurzer Hand-Commentar zum Alten Testament. Tübingen/Leipzig: Mohr (Siebeck), 1901. **Feinberg, C. L.** *Jeremiah: A Commentary.* Grand Rapids: Zondervan, 1982. **Fohrer, G.** *Die propheten des Alten Testament 3. Die Propheten des Fruhen 6 Jahrhunderts.* 1975. ———. *Die symbolische Handlungen der Propheten.* 2nd ed. ATANT 4. Zurich: Zwingli Verlag, 1968. **Freedman, H.** *Jeremiah: Hebrew Text and English Translation with an Introduction and Commentary.* London: Soncino, 1949. **Freehof, S. B.** *Book of Jeremiah: A Commentary.* The Jewish Commentary for Bible Readers. New York: Union of American Hebrew Congregations, 1977. **Giesebrecht, F.** *Das Buch*

Jeremia. HKAT 3, 2. Göttingen: Vandenhoeck & Ruprecht, 1907. **Green, J. L.** "Jeremiah." In *The Broadman Bible Commentary.* Nashville: Broadman, 1971. *VI,* 1–202. **Haag, E.** *Das Buch Jeremia,* vols. 1 and 2. Geistliche Schriftlesung, 5/1 & 2. Düsseldorf: Patmos Verlag, 1971, 1977. **Harrison, R. K.** *Jeremiah and Lamentations: An Introduction and Commentary.* Tyndale Old Testament Commentaries. London: Tyndale, 1973. **Heschel, A. J.** *The Prophets.* New York: Harper, 1962. **Holladay, W. L.** *Jeremiah 1.* Hermeneia. Philadelphia/Minneapolis: Augsburg Fortress, 1986. ———. *Jeremiah 2.* Hermeneia. Philadelphia/Minneapolis: Augsburg Fortress, 1989. **Hyatt, J. P.** "Introduction and Exegesis, Jeremiah." In *IB.* Nashville: Abingdon, 1956. V, 775–1142. **Kuist, H. T.** *Jeremiah.* Layman's Bible Commentaries. London: SCM, 1961. **Lamparter, H.** *Prophet wider Willen: der Prophet Jeremia.* BAT 20. Stuttgart: Calwer Verlag, 1964. **Leslie, E. A.** *Jeremiah: Chronologically Arranged, Translated, and Interpreted.* New York: Abingdon Press, 1954. **Martens, E. A.** *Jeremiah.* Believers Church Bible Commentary. Scottdale, PA: Herald, 1986. **McKane, W. A.** *Critical and Exegetical Commentary on Jeremiah, I.* ICC Edinburgh: T. & T. Clark, 1986. **Neil, W.** *Prophets of Israel (2). Jeremiah and Ezekiel.* Bible Guides 8. Nashville: Abingdon, 1964. **Nicholson, E. W.** *The Book of the Prophet Jeremiah.* The Cambridge Bible Commentary on the New English Bible. Cambridge: Cambridge University, 1973, 1975. **Nötscher, F.** *Das Buch Jeremias.* Die Heilige Schrift des Alten Testaments 7, 2. Bonn: Hanstein, 1934. *Peake's Commentary on the Bible.* Ed. H. H. Rowley. London/New York: Nelson, 1962. **Rudolph, W.** *Jeremia.* HAT. Tübingen: Mohr (Siebeck), 1968. **Schreiner, J.** *Jeremia 1–25:14.* Die Neue Echter Bibel. Würzburg: Echter Verlag, 1981. **Sekine, M.** *Eremiya-sho chūkai Joū* (ET: "A Commentary on the Book of Jeremiah"). The Works of M. Sekine, vol. 14. 1962. Reprint. Tokyo: Sinchi-Shobo, 1981. **Selms, A. van.** *Jeremia.* Deel 1 (Jer. 1–25). De Predeking van het Oude Testament. Nijkerk: G. F. Callenbach, 1972. *Starý zákon: překlad s výkladem: 12. Jeremjáš - Plač.* Prague: Kalich, 1983. [A commentary in modern Czech on Jeremiah and Lamentations.] **Strobel, A.** *Trauer um Jerusalem: Jeremia-Klagelieder-Baruch.* Stuttgarter Kleiner Kommentar AT 11. Stuttgart: KBW Verlag, 1973. **Thompson, J. A.** *The Book of Jeremiah.* NICOT. Grand Rapids: Eerdmans, 1980. **Volz, P.** *Der Prophet Jeremia.* KAT. Leipzig: Deichert, 1928. **Wambacq, B. N.** *Jeremias, Klaagliederen/Baruch, Brief van Jeremias vit de grondtekst vertaald en uitgelegd.* De Boeken van het Oude Testament. Roermond: Romen and Zonen, 1957. **Weiser, A.** *Das Buch des Propheten Jeremia.* Das Alte Testament Deutsche. Göttingen: Vandenhoeck & Ruprecht, 1969. **Woods, J.** *Jeremiah.* Epworth Preacher's Commentaries. London: Epworth, 1964.

Monographs and Other Books
(referred to in the text by authors' names and shortened titles)

Andersen, F. I., and **Forbes, A. D.** *A Linguistic Concordance of Jeremiah: Hebrew Vocabulary and Idiom.* 2 volumes. The Computer Bible, 14 and 14a. Wooster, OH: Biblical Research Associates, 1978. **Baumgartner, W.** *Die Klagegedichte de Jeremia.* BZAW 32. Giessen: Topelmann, 1917. ———. *Jeremiah's Poems of Lament.* Trans. D. E. Orton. Sheffield: Almond, 1988. **Berridge, J. M.** *Prophet, People and the Word of Yahweh: An Examination of Form and Content in the Proclamation of the Prophet Jeremiah.* Zurich: EVZ-Verlag, 1970. **Blank, S. H.** *Jeremiah: Man and Prophet.* Cincinnati: HUC, 1961. **Bogaert, P. M.**, ed. *Le Livre de Jérémie. Le prophète et son milieu, les oracles et leur transmission.* BETL 54. Leuven: UP, 1981. **Bonnard, P. E.** *Le Psautier selon Jérémie.* LD 26. Paris: Les Éditions du Cerf, 1960. **La Bonnardière, A.-M.** *Le Livre de Jérémie.* Biblia Augustiniania. Paris: Études Augustiniennes, 1972. **Briend, J.** *Le Livre de Jérémie.* Cahiers Evangile 40. Paris: Les Éditions du Cerf, 1982. **Bright, J.** *Covenant and Promise: The Future in the Preaching of the Pre-exilic Prophets.* London: SCM, 1977. **Carroll, R. P.** *From Chaos to Covenant: Prophecy in the Book of Jeremiah.* New York: Crossroad, 1981. ———. *When Prophecy Failed: Cognitive Dissonance in the Prophetic Traditions of the Old Testament.* New York: Seabury, 1979. **Diamond, A. R.** *The Confessions of Jeremiah in Context: Scenes of Prophetic Drama.* JSOTSup 45. Sheffield: JSOT Press, 1986. **Durham, J. I.**, and **Porter, J. R.**, eds. *Proclamation and Presence: Old Testament Essays in Honour of Gwynne Henton Davies.* Richmond: John Knox

Press, 1970. **Efird, J. M.** *Jeremiah: Prophet under Siege.* Valley Forge: Judson, 1979. **Hillers, D. R.** *Treaty-Curses and the Old Testament Prophets.* BibOr 11. Rome: Pontifical Biblical Institute, 1964.**Holladay, W. L.** *Jeremiah: Spokesman Out of Time.* New York: Pilgrim, 1974. ———. *The Architecture of Jeremiah 1–20.* London: Associated University Presses, 1976. **Hyatt, J. P.** *Jeremiah: Prophet of Courage and Hope.* Nashville: Abingdon, 1958. **Johnson, A. R.** *The Vitality of the Individual in the Thought of Ancient Israel.* Cardiff: University of Wales, 1949. **König, E.** *Historisch-Comparative Syntax der hebräischen Sprache.* Leipzig: Hinrichs, 1897. **Kraus, H.-J.** *Prophetie in der Krisis: Studien zu Texten aus dem Buche Jeremia.* Neukirchen-Vluyn: Erziehungsverein, 1964. **Lundbom, J. R.** *Jeremiah: A Study of Ancient Hebrew Rhetoric.* SBLDS 18. Missoula, MT: Scholars Press, 1975. **McKane, W.** *Prophets and Wise Men.* SBT 44. Naperville, IL: Allenson, 1965. **Melchert, J.** *Jeremia als Nachricht. Prophetische Texte im Religions-unterricht-Reflexionen und Unterrichtsplanungen.* Düsseldorf: Patmos Verlag, 1977. **Meyer, I.** *Jeremia und die falschen Propheten.* OBO 13. Göttingen: Vandenhoeck & Ruprecht; Fribourg: Universitatsverlag, 1977. **Miller, J. W.** *Das Verhältnis Jeremias und Hesekiels sprachlich und theologisch untersucht, mit besonderer Berücksichtigung der Prosareden Jeremias.* Assen: Van Gorcum, 1955. **Neher, A.** *Jérémie.* Paris: Librairie Plon, 1960. **Nicholson, E. W.** *Preaching to the Exiles: A Study of the Prose Tradition in the Book of Jeremiah.* New York: Schocken Books, 1970. **O'Connor, K. M.** *The Confessions of Jeremiah: Their Interpretation and Role in Chapters 1–25.* SBLDS 94. Atlanta: Scholars Press, 1988. **Overholt, T. W.** *The Threat of Falsehood: A Study in the Theology of the Book of Jeremiah.* SBT 2nd ser. 16. Naperville, IL: Allenson, 1970. **Perdue, L. G.,** and **Kovacs, B. W.,** eds. *A Prophet to the Nations: Essays in Jeremiah Studies.* Winona Lake, IN: Eisenbrauns, 1984. **Pohlmann, K.-F.** *Studien zum Jeremiabuch.* Göttingen: Vandenhoeck & Ruprecht, 1978. **Polk, T.** *The Prophetic Persona: Jeremiah and the Language of the Self.* JSOTSup 32. Sheffield, 1984. **Raitt, T. M.** *A Theology of Exile: Judgment/Deliverance in Jeremiah and Ezekiel.* Philadelphia: Fortress, 1977. **Reventlow, H. G.** *Liturgie und prophetisches Ich bei Jeremia.* Gütersloh: Gerd Mohn, 1963. **Ridouard, A.** *Jérémie, l'épreuve de la foi.* Paris: Éditions du Cerf, 1983. **Schneider, D.** *Der Prophet Jeremia.* Wuppertaler Studienbibel. Wuppertal: Brockhaus Verlag, 1977. **Schultes, J. L.** *Umkehre ist immer moglich. Ein Arbeitsheft zum Buch Jeremia.* Gesprache zur Bibel 6. Klosterneuburg: Osterreichisches Katholisches Bibelwerk, 1978. **Seierstad, I. P.** *Die Offenbarungserlebnisse der Propheten Amos, Jesaja und Jeremia.* 2nd ed. Norwegian Research Council: Universitetsvorlaget, 1965. **Seitz, C. R.** *Theology in Conflict: Reactions to the Exile in the Book of Jeremiah.* New York: de Gruyter, 1989. **Skinner, J.** *Prophecy and Religion: Studies in the Life of Jeremiah.* Cambridge: Cambridge UP, 1922. **Smith, M. S.** *The Laments of Jeremiah and Their Contexts: A Literary and Redactional Study of Jeremiah 11–20.* SBLMS 42. Atlanta: Scholars Press, 1990. **Stulman, L.** *The Other Text of Jeremiah.* New York: Lanham, 1985. **Thiel, W.** *Die deuteronomistische Redaktion von Jeremia 1–25.* WMANT 41. Neukirchen-Vluyn: Neukirchener Verlag, 1973. ———. *Die deuteronomistische Redaktion von Jeremia 26–45. Mit einer Gesamtbeurteilung der deuteronomistischen Redaktion des Buches Jeremias.* WMANT 52. Neukirchen-Vluyn: Neukirchener Verlag, 1981. **Thompson, J. G. S. S.** *The Word of the Lord in Jeremiah.* Tyndale Old Testament Lecture. London: Tyndale Press, 1959. **Wanke, G.** *Untersuchungen zur sogenannten Baruchschrift.* BZAW 122. Berlin: de Gruyter, 1971. **Weippert, H.** *Die Prosareden der Jeremiabuches.* BZAW 132. Berlin: de Gruyter, 1973. ———. *Schöpfer des Himmels und der Erds. Ein Beitrag zur Theologie des Jeremiabuches.* SBS 102. Stuttgart: Katholisches Bibelwerk, 1981. **Wisser, L.** *Jérémie, critique de la vie sociale: justice sociale et connaisance de Dieu dans la livre de Jérémie.* Geneva: Labor et Fides, 1982. **Wolff, C.** *Jeremia in Frühjudentum und Urchristentum.* Texte und Untersuchungen zur Geschichte der Altchristlichen Literatur, 118. Berlin: Akademie Verlag, 1976.

Articles

(referred to in the text by authors' names and journal citations)

Ackroyd, P. R. "Aspects of the Jeremiah Tradition." *IndJTH* 20 (1971) 1–12. ———. "Biblical Classics, I: John Skinner: Prophecy and Religion." *ExpTim* 89 (1978) 356–58. **Augustin, F.**

"Baruch und das Jeremia." *ZAW* 67 (1955) 50–56. **Avigad, N.** "Jerahmeel and Baruch: King's Son and Scribe." *BA* 42 (1979) 114–18. **Barker, K. L.** "Jeremiah's Ministry and Ours." *BSac* 127 (1970) 223–31. **Berger, K.** "Hartherzigkeit und Gottes Gesetz: die Vorgeschichte des antijudischen Vorwurfs in Mc 10:5." *ZNW* 61 (1970) 1–47. **Berridge, J. M.** "Jeremia und die Prophetie des Amos." *TZ* 35 (1979) 321–41. **Blank, S. H.** "The Confessions of Jeremiah, and the Meaning of Prayer." *HUCA* 21 (1948) 331–54. **Briggs, C. R.** "Prophets and Traditions: the Relations between Jeremiah and the Traditions of Northern Israel." *AusBR* 20 (1972) 1–15. **Bright, J.** "Book of Jeremiah: Its Structure, Its Problems, and Their Significance for the Interpreter." *Int* 9 (1955) 259–78.———. "The Date of the Prose Sermons in Jeremiah." *JBL* 70 (1951) 15–35. ———. "The Prophetic Reminiscence: Its Place and Function in the Book of Jeremiah." In *Biblical Essays, Proceedings: Die Ou Testamentiese Werkgemeenskap* (1966) 11–30. ———. "Jeremiah's Complaints." In *Proclamation and Presence*. FS G. H. Davies. Ed. J. I. Durham and J. R. Porter. Richmond: John Knox, 1970. 189–214. **Broughton, P. E.** "The Call of Jeremiah: The Relation of Dt. 18:9–22 to the Call and Life of Jeremiah." *AusBR* 6 (1958) 39–46. **Brueggemann, W.** "Jeremiah's Use of Rhetorical Questions." *JBL* 92 (1973) 358–74. **Buchanan, G. W.** "The Word of God and the Apocalyptic Vision." SBLASP 14 (1978) 183–92. **Busch, R. J. Vanden** "Jeremiah: A Spiritual Metamorphosis." *BTB* 10 (1980) 17–24. **Carlson, E. L.** "The World of Jeremiah." *SWJT* 4 (1961) 57–68. **Cassuto, U.** "The Prophecies of Jeremiah Concerning the Gentiles." In *Biblical and Oriental Studies, I: The Bible.* Trans. I. Abrahams. Jerusalem: Magnes, 1973. 178–226. **Childs, B. S.** "The Enemy from the North and the Chaos Tradition." *JBL* 78 (1959) 187–98. **Corré, A. D.** "ʿelle, hēmma = sic." [pronouns in Jeremiah] *Bib* 54 (1973) 263–64. **Crenshaw, J. L.** "YHWH Sᵉbaʾot Shᵉmo: a Form-critical Analysis." *ZAW* 81 (1969) 156–75. **Cummins, P.** "Jeremias Orator." *CBQ* 11 (1949) 191–201. **Dahood, M. J.** "Two Textual Notes on Jeremia." *CBQ* 23 (1961) 462–64. **Davidson, R.** "Orthodoxy and the Prophetic Word: a Study in the Relationship Between Jeremiah and Deuteronomy." *VT* 14 (1964) 407–16. **Dobbie, R.** "Jeremiah and the Preacher." *CJT* 4 (1958) 37–45. **Driver, S. R.** "Linguistic and Textual Problems: Jeremiah." *JQR* 28 (1937–38) 97–129. **Eichler, U.** "Der Klagende Jeremia. Eine Untersuchung zu den Klagen Jeremia und ihrer Bedeutung zum Verstehen seines Leidens." *TLZ* 103 (1978) 918–19. [Summary of 1968 Heidelberg dissertation.] **Eissfeldt, O.** "Voraussage-Empfang, Offenbarungagewissheit und Gebetskraft-Erfahrung bei Jeremia." *NovT* 5 (1962) 77–81. **Ellison, H. L.** "Prophecy of Jeremiah." *EvQ* 31 (1959) 143–51, 205–17; 32 (1960) 3–14, 107–13, 212–23; 33 (1961) 27–35, 148–56, 220–27; 34 (1962) 16–28, 96–102, 154–162; 35 (1963) 4–14, 160–67, 196–205; 36 (1964) 3–11, 92–99, 148–56; 37 (1965) 21–28, 100–109, 147–54, 232–41; 38 (1966) 40–51, 158–68, 233–40; 39 (1967) 40–47, 165–72, 216–24. **Elliot, R. H.** "Old Testament Prophecy." *RevExp* 58 (1961) 407–16. **France, R. T.** "Herod and the Children of Bethlehem." *NovT* 21 (1979) 98–120. **Frank, R. M.** "Jeremias of Pethion ibn Ayyub al-Sahhar." [with Arabic text of chaps. 1–6] *CBQ* 21 (1959) 136–70. ———. "'Citation' from the Prophet Jeremias in Ibn Qutaiba and Tabari." [with Arabic texts and ET] *CBQ* 17 (1955) 379–402. **Gerstenberger, E.** "Jeremiah's Complaints." *JBL* 82 (1963) 393–408. **Gordon, T. C.** "A New Date for Jeremiah." *ExpTim* 44 (1932–33) 562–65. **Granild, S.** "Jeremia und das Deuteronomium." *ST* 16 (1962) 135–54. **Grelot, P.** "Soixante-dix Semaines d'Annees." *Bib* 50 (1969) 186. **Habel, N. C.** "Appeal to Ancient Tradition as a Literary Form." *ZAW* 88 (1976) 25–72. ———. "The Form and Significance of the Call Narratives." *ZAW* 77 (1965) 297–323. **Herrmann, S.** "Forschung am Jeremiabuch. Probleme und Tendenzen ihrer neueren Entwicklung." *TLZ* 102 (1977) 481–90. **Hobbs, T. R.** "Some Remarks on the Structure and Composition of the Book of Jeremiah." *CBQ* 34 (1972) 257–75. ———. "Some Proverbial Reflections in the Book of Jeremiah." *ZAW* 91 (1979) 62–72. **Hoffken, P.** "Zu den Heilszusatzen in der Volkerorakelsammlung des Jeremiabuches." *VT* 27 (1977) 398–412. **Holladay, W. L.** "Prototype and Copies: A New Approach to the Poetry-Prose Problem in the Book of Jeremiah." *JBL* 79 (1960) 351–67. ———. "The Background of Jeremiah's Self-Understanding." *JBL* 83 (1964) 153–64.———. "A Fresh Look at 'Source B' and 'Source C' in Jeremiah." *VT* 25

(1975) 394–412. ———. "The Book of Jeremiah." IDBSup, 470–72. ———. "Jeremiah and Women's Liberation." *ANQ* 12 (1972) 213–23. ———. "Jeremiah in Judah's Eyes and Ours: Musing on Some Issues in Old Testament Hermeneutics." *ANQ* 13 (1972) 115–32. ———. "Jeremiah's Lawsuit with God: a Study in Suffering and Meaning." *Int* 17 (1963) 280–87. ———. "Recovery of Poetic Passages of Jeremiah." *JBL* 85 (1966) 401–35. ———. "Style, Irony, and Authenticity in the Book of Jeremiah." *JBL* 81 (1962) 44–54. **Honeycutt, R. L.** "Jeremiah and the Cult." *RevExp* 58 (1961) 464–73. **Horwitz, W. J.** "Audience Reaction to Jeremiah." *CBQ* 32 (1970) 555–64. **Hyatt, J. P.** "The Beginnings of Jeremiah's Prophecy." *ZAW* 78 (1966) 204–14. ———. "The Deuteronomic Edition of Jeremiah." *Vanderbilt Studies in the Humanities* 1 (1951) 71–95. ———. "Jeremiah and Deuteronomy." *JNES* 1 (1942) 156–73. ———. "Torah in the Book of Jeremiah." *JBL* 60 (1941) 381–96. **Janzen, J. G.** "Double Readings in the Text of Jeremiah." *HTR* 60 (1967) 433–47. **Jeremias, J.** "Die Vollmacht des Propheten im Alten Testament." *EvT* 31 (1971) 305–22. **Jobling, D. K.** "The Quest of the Historical Jeremiah: Hermeneutical Implications of Recent Literature." *USQR* 34 (1978) 3–12. **Kapelrud, A. S.** "Jeremia—en landsskiver?" *Kirke og Kultur* 83 (1978) 28–39. **Keller, B.** "Langage de Jérémie." *ETR* (1978) 53, 360–65. **Kelley, P. H.** "Jeremiah's Concept of Individual Religion." *RevExp* 58 (1961) 452–63. **Klein, W. C.** "Commentary on Jeremiah." *ATR* 55 (1963) 121–58, 284–309. **Kuist, H. T.** "Book of Jeremiah." *Int* 4 (1950) 322–41. **Kurichianil, J.** "Jeremiah, the Prophet of Prayer." *ITS* 18 (1981) 34–46. **Kutsch, E.** "Das Jahr der Katastrophe: 587 V Chr. Kritische Erwagungen zu Neueren Chronologischen Versuchen." *Bib* 55 (1974) 520–45. **Laberge, L.** "Le drame de la fidélité chez Jérémie." *ET* 11 (1980) 9–31. **Long, B. O.** "Prophetic Authority as Social Reality." In *Canon and Authority,* ed. G. W. Coats and B. O. Long. Philadelphia: Fortress, 1977. 3–20. **Lörcher, H.** "Das Verhältnis der Prosareden zu Erzahlungen im Jeremiabuch." *TLZ* 102 (1977) 395–396. [Summary of 1974 Tübingen dissertation.] **Ludwig, T. M.** "Law-gospel Tension in Jeremiah." *CTM* 36 (1965) 70–79. **Malamat, A.** "Jeremiah and the Last Two Kings of Judah." *PEQ* 83 (1951) 81–87. **Manahan, R. E.** "A Theology of Pseudoprophets: A Study in Jeremiah." *GTJ* 1 (1980) 77–96. ———. "An Interpretive Survey: Audience Reaction Quotations in Jeremiah." *GTJ* 1 (1980) 163–83. **Marböck, J.** "Jeremia." *BLit* 50 (1977) 85–95. **Martin-Achard, R.** "Esaie et Jérémie aux prises avec les problèmes politiques." *RHPR* 47 (1967) 208–24. **May, H. G.** "Towards an Objective Approach to the Book Jeremiah: the Biographer." *JBL* 61 (1942) 139–55. ———. "The Chronology of Jeremiah's Oracles." *JNES* 4 (1945) 217–27. ———. "Jeremiah's Biographer." *JBR* 10 (1942) 195–201. **Milgrom, J.** "Concerning Jeremiah's Repudiation of Sacrifice." *ZAW* 89 (1977) 273–75. **Muilenburg, J.** "The Terminology of Adversity in Jeremiah." In *Translating and Understanding the Old Testament.* Ed. H. T. Frank and W. L. Reed. Nashville: Abingdon Press, 1970. 42–63. **Orlinsky, H. M.** "Nationalism-Universalism in the Book of Jeremiah." In *Understanding the Sacred Text.* Ed. J. Reumann. Valley Forge: Judson, 1972. 61–84. **Overholt, T. W.** "Remarks on the Continuity of the Jeremiah Tradition." *JBL* 91 (1972) 457–62. ———. "Jeremiah and the Nature of the Prophetic Process." In *Scripture in History and Theology: Essays in Honor of J. Coert Rylaarsdam.* Ed. A. Merrill and T. Overholt. (1967) 129–50. ———. "Some Reflections on the Date of Jeremiah's Call." *CBQ* 33 (1971) 165–84. **Pilch, J. J.** "Jeremiah and Symbolism." *TBT* 19 (1981) 105–11. **Reid, D. P.** "Prophet Wanted—No Coward Need Apply." *TBT* 18 (1980) 11–16. **Roche, M. de.** "Contra Creation, Covenant and Conquest (Jer. viii 13)." *VT* 30 (1980) 280–90. **Rowley, H. H.** "The Early Prophecies of Jeremiah in Their Setting." *BJRL* 45 (1962) 198–234. **Schehr, T.** "Jeremiah: the Power of God's Word." *TBT* 19 (1981) 87–92. **Schreiner, J.** "Ja sagen zu Gott-Der Prophet Jeremia." *TLZ* 90 (1981) 29–40. **Schutzinger, H.** "Die arabische Jeremia-Erzahlungen und ihre Beziehungen zur judischen religiosen Uberlieferung." *ZRGG* 25 (1973) 1–19. **Sturdy, J. V. M.** "The Authorship of the 'Prose Sermons' of Jeremiah." In *Prophecy.* Ed. J. A. Emerton. BZAW 150. Berlin: de Gruyter, 1980. 143–50. **Tambasco, A.** "Jeremiah and the Law of the Heart." *TBT* 19 (1981) 100–104. **Telcs, G.** "Jeremiah and Nebuchadnezzar, King of Justice." *CJT* 15 (1969) 122–30. **Urbock, W. J.** "Jeremiah: A Man for Our Seasoning." *CurTM* 5 (1978) 144–

57. **Vermeylen, J.** "Jérémie: le prophète et le livre." *ETL* 58 (1982) 140–44. **Weinfeld, M.** "Jeremiah and the Spiritual Metamorphosis of Israel." *ZAW* 88 (1976) 17–56. **Weisman, Z.** "Stylistic Parallels in Amos and Jeremiah: Their Implications for the Composition of Amos." *Shnaton* 1 (1975) 129–49. **Weften, P.** "Leiden und Leidenserfahrung im Buch Jeremia." *ZTK* 74 (1977) 123–50. **Whitley, C. F.** "The Date of Jeremiah's Call." *VT* 14 (1964) 467–83.

Introduction

Although the Book of Jeremiah is only one of more than a dozen prophetic books that have survived from ancient Israel, in many ways it stands out above the others as the book of prophecy *par excellence*. First, it is the largest of the books of the prophets; despite the greater number of chapters in Isaiah, Jeremiah is longer with respect to both the number of words and the number of verses. But length alone does not necessarily contribute to greatness; it is also the substance of this book that has contributed to its stature and continuing appeal down through the centuries. Whereas the message emerges distinctively from each of the prophetic books, the messenger is commonly concealed or remains virtually anonymous. In the Book of Jeremiah, the figure of the prophet himself emerges as a truly human character. It may be a weakness in most modern readers, but it is commonly the case that we can identify more readily with the message when the character of the messenger is known to us. It is true that in the changing currents of contemporary scholarship, the biography of the prophet is considered by some writers to be virtually inaccessible; but even to the skeptical, something of the stature of an extraordinary man is revealed in the book that has been named after Jeremiah.

The English language has been influenced by one aspect of the personality of this prophet from ancient times. The word *jeremiad,* according to the *Oxford English Dictionary,* means "lamentation, doleful complaint"; it is derived from the prophet's name, though its meaning may be misleading with respect to the substance of the Book of Jeremiah. There is indeed a theme of lament running through the prophet's book, not least in the so-called Confessions of Jeremiah, but the message of the book as a whole is rich, its mournful notes offset by some of the purest expressions of hope that are to be found anywhere in the OT.

A further aspect of the greatness of the Book of Jeremiah emerges from the historical context in which it is set. The world of the late seventh and early sixth centuries B.C. was going through a time of extraordinary change. Old and established empires were beginning to crumble, new and threatening world powers were emerging on the horizons of history, and the ordinary citizens of that world were gripped by fear and tossed about by the uncertain waves of a new era that was dawning. Judah, the small state to which Jeremiah belonged, was not invulnerable to the currents of international change; its days of survival as a state, during the prophet's youth, were already numbered. Yet Jeremiah stood out among the citizens of that uncertain world as a man of vision; where most people saw only turmoil and uncertainty, to him had been revealed an understanding, in part, of the chaos of his age. He spoke not only of the nations at large but also of his own small nation; he perceived the hand of God at work in the crises of his world and delivered a message, at once moral and spiritual, that addressed both the travail of his own age and yet also transcended his immediate world to continue to speak with urgency to subsequent generations.

From a Christian perspective, there is an additional dimension to the greatness of the Book of Jeremiah that cannot be overlooked. The prophet spoke of a new covenant, a new work of God in the world; he was not the first of the prophets so to speak, yet the clarity of his message and the power of his words were to capture the faith and imagination of subsequent generations. Later, in the history of the early church, the Christians were to label the two parts of their Scriptures as the "Old Covenant" and "New Covenant," respectively (*covenant* being the literal translation of the term commonly rendered in English by the word *testament*). In so doing, they gave expression to their self-understanding; they believed themselves to be the people of the New Covenant of God, whose existence had been anticipated centuries earlier in the words of Jeremiah (31:31).

For these and many other reasons, the Book of Jeremiah deserves special recognition and careful study. It brings to us first a message from the most critical turning point in the history of the Hebrew people. It was preserved as a national treasure in the Jewish canon of Scripture. It was inherited as a part of the Scripture of the earliest Christian Church. It is a book that has survived the ravages of time and continues to speak to us in the latter part of the twentieth century. And yet, for all its greatness and importance, it is well for the reader to recognize at the outset that this is not an easy book to read. Some of the difficulties associated with reading and understanding the Book of Jeremiah may become clear if first we examine the form in which the book has survived.

THE FORM AND STRUCTURE OF THE BOOK OF JEREMIAH

Bibliography

Augustin, F. "Baruch und das Buch Jeremia." *ZAW* 67 (1955) 50–56. **Carroll, R. P.** *From Chaos to Covenant: Prophecy in the Book of Jeremiah.* New York: Crossroad, 1981. **Herrmann, S.** "Forschung am Jeremiabuch. Probleme und Tendenzen ihrer neueren Entwicklung." *TLZ* 102 (1977) 481–90. **Hobbs, T. R.** "Some Remarks on the Structure and Composition of the Book of Jeremiah." *CBQ* 34 (1972) 257–75. **Holladay, W. L.** "Prototype and Copies: A New Approach to the Poetry-Prose Problem in the Book of Jeremiah." *JBL* 79 (1960) 351–67. ———. "A Fresh Look at 'Source B' and 'Source C' in Jeremiah." *VT* 25 (1975) 394–412. ———. *The Architecture of Jeremiah 1–20.* London: Associated University Presses, 1976. **Lörcher, H.** "Das Verhältnis der Prosareden zu den Erzählungen im Jeremiabuch." *TLZ* 102 (1977) 395–96. **Overholt, T. W.** "Remarks on the Continuity of the Jeremiah Tradition." *JBL* 91 (1972) 457–62. **Pohlmann, K.-F.** *Studien zum Jeremiabuch. Ein Beitrag zur Frage nach der Entstehung des Jeremiabuches.* Göttingen: Vandenhoeck & Ruprecht, 1978. **Sturdy, J. V. M.** "The Authorship of the 'Prose Sermons' of Jeremiah." In *Prophecy,* ed. J. A. Emerton. BZAW 150. Berlin: de Gruyter, 1980. 143–50. **Thiel, W.** *Die deuteronomistische Redaktion von Jeremia 1–25.* WMANT 41. Neukirchen-Vluyn: Neukirchener Verlag, 1973. ———. *Die deuteronomistische Redaktion von Jeremia 26–45. Mit einer Gesamtbeurteilung der deuteronomistischen Redaktion des Buches Jeremias.* WMANT 52. Neukirchen-Vluyn: Neukircher Verlag, 1981. **Weippert, H.** *Die Prosareden des Jeremiabuches.* BZAW 132. Berlin: de Gruyter, 1973.

The modern reader of the Book of Jeremiah is faced at the outset with a difficult task. What has survived is not a *book,* in the normal sense of that word; it does not move from beginning to end, following a clear logic and inner development. Indeed, the major portion of the substance of this "book" was never designed for the literary context in which it has survived; the stuff of which Jeremiah's book is constructed started life in various contexts, ranging from public proclamation to private diary. What we are dealing with, then, in reading the Book of Jeremiah, is a work that is essentially an anthology, or more precisely an anthology of anthologies. And the collection of anthologies brings together a number of sayings and writings that were associated with the prophet, binding them together in a single volume. But whereas a modern anthology provides guidance to its readers by the extensive use of titles, notes, and headings, only a few such aids to reading have survived in Jeremiah. Furthermore, the logic by which this collection of anthologies was compiled can be only partially reconstructed, so that the reader cannot always determine the reason for the sequence and arrangement of the materials that comprise the whole.

The data that provide the clues to the character of the book are contained within the text itself; a few examples follow. (i) 25:1–14 contains a narrative which suggests strongly that it is a conclusion to a collection of oracles, yet clearly the extant book continues for many more chapters. (ii) 30:1–2 is in the form of an introduction to another "book," probably chaps. 30–33. (iii) 46:1 appears to be the introduction to a further anthology, namely a collection of oracles addressed to foreign nations (46–51). These three points are merely clues to the smaller anthologies within the larger anthology. Yet within each of these subunits, it is clear that a further anthological character can be determined. Jeremiah's book, in other words, is a collection of other anthologies, the smaller units in turn containing collections of sayings and various types of written materials.

Furthermore, there is considerable variety in the literary forms of the various parts of the book that constitute the whole. Traditionally, three principal types of material have been distinguished, labelled Types A, B, and C, respectively. (The three types were recognized as early as B. Duhm, *Das Buch Jeremia*, 1901, and designated A, B, and C by S. Mowinckel, *Zur Komposition des Buches Jeremia* [Kristiania: J. Dybwad, 1914]). (i) The prophet's oracles, recorded in poetic form, are designated *Type A* material. (ii) Prose narratives, which are essentially biographical and historical in character, written with references to Jeremiah in the third person, are designated *Type B* material. (iii) Speeches or discourses, which are in prose rather than poetic form, and which have a distinctive literary style, are designated *Type C* material. This threefold classification of the principal literary forms of Jeremiah is useful, though not comprehensive; some materials (e.g., the so-called Confessions, commonly labeled Type A) do not easily fit into any one of the classifications.

These preliminary indications as to the character of the Book of Jeremiah are confirmed partially by the substance of the book itself. Chapter 36 contains an account of the prophet dictating to Baruch, his scribe, the substance of his early oracles. When the scroll containing this early compilation was destroyed, a further scroll was compiled, this time with additions (36:32). It is not possible to determine the content of either of these scrolls, beyond the reasonable supposition that it is contained within chaps. 1–25, but we know that considerable later additions have been added to that initial collection. The significance of the story in Jer 36 is that it provides partial insight into the process of the compilation of materials. Prophecies that were delivered in the first instance orally were later recorded in writing; whether they were recorded from memory or from notes cannot be known.

It is not our intention at this point in the Introduction to volume 1 of the commentary on Jeremiah to provide a full hypothesis of the form and structure of the Book of Jeremiah and the process by which the book came into being. The data for such a hypothesis are contained in the notes under *Form/Structure/Setting* throughout the two volumes of the commentary. In the chapters that follow, the reader will find detailed notes on the form of each literary unit and on its relationship to the larger literary context. However, it is necessary to provide some general directions to the reader, in order to set an overall framework of understanding within which to read the book.

It is clear that the book assumed its present form either very late in the prophet's lifetime, or more probably after his death. It is also clear that the process of compiling the book involved many stages of editorial collection and arrangement; the incident described in Jer 36 is but one, and not necessarily the first, of numerous stages in a complex process. It is also perhaps wise to recognize from the beginning that insufficient data have survived from which to reconstruct accurately the process of the composition and compilation of the book. With these precautions in mind, it is nevertheless possible to proceed cautiously with an attempt to understand how the book reached its present form.

The beginning point for such an inquiry, however, immediately presents us with a dilemma. Ideally one might wish to start with the book in its finished form and then work gradually backwards, trying to identify the origin and setting of each unit of the anthology, either in the life and ministry of the prophet, or in the editorial and redactional process that went into the making of the book. But in practice, we cannot easily start with the finished form of the book precisely because we are not sure of what that finished form was. The surviving form of the Masoretic Text differs from that on which the Septuagint was based in several radical ways, and both textual traditions have survived in the MS evidence from Qumran: see further "The Hebrew and Greek Texts of Jeremiah" (below). If we cannot start with the finished product, neither can we start with the initial units, for they are in a sense the object of the inquiry! We must begin, then, with a review of certain known factors and then attempt to move cautiously from there to formulate a hypothesis.

The starting point of the investigation is the observation that Jeremiah was a prophet; as such, he was engaged in public oratory, declaring God's word to the people of Judah. The prophetic word was necessarily delivered orally in the first instance, for its message was addressed in public to the prophet's contemporaries; what we cannot know for certain is whether the message was also written and, if written, whether it was written down before or after delivery. In some cases, it was clearly written down after the event, and after a considerable passage of time (Jer 36), though again the details are vague. Furthermore, when the process of writing entered into the preservation of the message, we are told that Baruch, Jeremiah's scribe, was involved as a recorder, but we do not know the extent to which Jeremiah himself may have been engaged in the activity of writing.

The message itself is also the subject of some difficulty. Taking the text at face value, the prophet's sayings have survived in two forms; some are poetic oracles, and some are prose narrative discourses. The uncertainty concerns, in part, the difficulty of knowing whether the prophet addressed the people in two modes, poetic and prosaic, or whether the different modes or forms of the oracles in the book simply reflect the manner of recording the prophet's message (assuming for the moment that either or both types of message are authentic to the prophet).

Various possibilities are open; it is possible that the prophet employed two different forms of language in public proclamation, either because of the nature of the message he received, or because the occasion on which the message was given demanded a different and appropriate kind of delivery. A second possibility is that the prophet spoke only in poetic oracles; in the recording, or recollecting, of the oracles, some were recorded in their original poetic form, whereas others were recorded in prose, in which an attempt was made simply to record the substance (not the original form) of the message. (The reverse possibility is also open, though improbable, namely that the prophet spoke only in prose form, but that the message was subsequently reworked into poetic form for ease of memorization.) In dealing with this second possibility, there are numerous difficulties. If some credence is given to the role of Baruch, as described in Jer 36, then it is possible that the dictation process resulted in the prose accounts of the prophet's messages, and that the poetic oracles were written, or remembered, or recorded earlier (and closer to the time of delivery) by the prophet himself.

Still a third possibility is that one may be able to distinguish between authentic and nonauthentic prophetic utterances on the basis of their form. Those who pursue this line of reasoning tend to view the poetic oracles as being the genuine proclamations of the prophet, whereas the prose accounts, given their different literary style, are considered to be later productions—not of the prophet, but of those standing in the tradition of the prophet who sought to apply his message to other, or later, generations (e.g., those in the Babylonian exile).

The resolution of the various difficulties associated with each of these possibilities is not an easy task; indeed, a complete resolution is probably impossible, given the paucity of evidence, and at best we may hope for a reasonably persuasive hypothesis. If we begin once again with the prophet's initial ministry, we must ask whether it is likely that he used only one mode of language (the poetic) or two (both prose and poetry)? While there is no certain answer to this question, the evidence of the other prophetic and historical books would suggest that two forms of address were open to the prophet, the poetic and the prosaic. With respect to poetic discourse, one might suppose that the form would continue to be preserved at the point at which that discourse was reduced to writing, since the poetic form was an essential part of the message. One might also suppose that the poetic messages were remembered and transmitted initially in oral form, for in part the purpose of poetic speech was to render its substance more memorable in a society that was not dependent on books and writing to the same extent that most modern societies are. On the other hand, if a speech were delivered in prosaic form, the form as such is less critical than the substance. If it were reduced to writing, the extent to which the written record reproduced accurately the spoken address would depend on numerous factors, such as the time span between delivery and recording, the identity of the person doing the recording, and the purpose for which the record was made.

That the poetic oracles in the Book of Jeremiah are essentially authentic seems to be a fairly certain starting point. The prose discourses, however, are much more difficult to assess, for though one may reasonably suppose that Jeremiah could have employed a prose form of delivery in addition to the poetic form, we cannot be sure that he did so. Nor can we be sure, if there were some oracles delivered in prose, as to the extent of the differences between the form of delivery and the form of recording. If, for example, the prose discourses were among those dictated to Baruch, we do not know the extent to which Baruch's own hand stamped them with a peculiar and distinctive character. But an even more serious difficulty is that proposed in the hypothesis that the prose discourses, Type C material, do not come from the prophet, but are the product of later tradition.

Those who propose this line of interpretation commonly argue that the language of the prose discourses reflects a later development of tradition, in which original sayings of the prophet have been developed and applied to new life situations, notably the life of those in exile. Thus E. W. Nicholson's cogent study, *Preaching to the Exiles* (1970), traces the prose discourses for the most part to a second stage in the development of the Book of Jeremiah, in which the deposit of Jeremiah's preaching was further amplified and applied to the lives of those in exile who gathered for worship and instruction. Despite the cogency of such a hypothesis, clearly it is based upon the assumption that the text of the extant Book of Jeremiah contains sufficient data, of a redactional and stylistic nature, to enable such considerable reconstruction of the life situations in which the prose discourses may be interpreted. J. V. M. Sturdy has argued rather persuasively that the literary criteria on which much of Nicholson's hypothesis is based are open to alternative interpretation ("Authorship of the 'Prose Sermons,'" 143–50). Indeed, Sturdy's own position is that a group of Jeremiah's disciples were responsible for the creation of the prose sermons.

Proposals of this kind concerning the nature and origin of the prose discourses introduce the difficulty of the so-called deuteronomic language in the text of Jeremiah. The views of Nicholson, Pohlmann, Thiel, and many others are based on the detection of supposedly deuteronomic influence on the final form of the book, and they advance varieties of hypotheses to explain such distinctive style. Thus, Thiel's two-volume study of the deuteronomistic redaction of Jeremiah contains an attempt to distinguish between the original Jeremianic core and the extensive two-stage deuteronomistic revision of the book ([i] 1–25 and [ii] 26–45), which is thought to have been concluded in Judah c. 550 B.C. But despite the scope and ingenuity of such analyses, there is not even agreement amongst scholars as to the existence and/or extent of D-language in Jeremiah. Thus, in addition to Sturdy's study (above), Bright (*Jeremiah*, lxxi–lxxiii, and "The Date of the Prose Sermons of Jeremiah," *JBL* 70 [1951] 15–35) is not persuaded that the prose of the discourse narratives can be properly called "deuteronomistic" at all. And H. Weippert's recent study (*Die Prosareden des Jeremiabuches*, 1973) comes to a similar conclusion; she argues that the language of the speeches is sixth-century prose, that the peculiarities of the language are typical of Jeremiah's period, and that there is no difficulty in supposing that the prophet used both poetry and prose in his speeches.

When such fundamental differences of opinion exist among various scholars, it is at the very least clear that the data are insufficiently precise and permit at best only hypotheses. The general perspective assumed in this commentary is that of Bright and Weippert. It should be stressed, however, that to work within the somewhat conservative tradition of Bright, Weippert, and others, is no less hypothetical than it would be to develop the commentary within the perspective of E. W. Nicholson. The data are of such a nature as to require a working hypothesis of some kind. R. P. Carroll *(From Chaos to Covenant, 19)* has recently been critical of the approach taken by Weippert and others:

> The flatness of the view of the book produced by these approaches does not contribute very much to the understanding of the complexities of the subject or the period, and the attempt to make Jeremiah a Carlylean hero is rather backward looking. However, it is a view that will appeal to biblicist positions and, though out of sympathy with it, I note it as an alternative approach to the analysis of this book.

Carroll's own interpretation of the book is expressed largely in terms of the development of later tradition, going considerably beyond the perspectives presented by Nicholson. But what is crucial is that Carroll's observations on the alternative approach fail to express clearly the hypothetical nature of any approach. Whether our final view of the book is flat or the opposite (lumpy?), whether Jeremiah emerges as a Carlylean hero or is lost entirely in the mists of time and ancient imaginations, such alternative possibilities as these are essentially irrelevant. The relevant factors are the data, and thence the hypotheses that may reasonably be constructed upon them. The rather condescending observation that a view such as that of Weippert will appeal to the "biblicist" is equally irrelevant. What Weippert has done is to examine in detail the prose and literary characteristics of the narrative discourses, and she has formulated her hypotheses on the nature of the discourses in the light of the evidence. It is true, of course, that Weippert may have been "conditioned" in her examination by certain assumptions or presuppositions, but such is also true of Carroll's examination of the data and his subsequent interpretation. Finally, though it may well be true that the more conservative approach to the prose discourses may be "flat," by Carroll's definition, it is also true that such an approach involves considerable speculation and complexity in the attempt to understand the present form of the narrative that comprises the Book of Jeremiah. But it should be repeated that the conservative approach to the prose discourses in Jeremiah is no less hypothetical than are other, more tradition-oriented approaches to interpretation.

There remains a further difficulty in formulating an understanding of the Book of Jeremiah in its present form. It has been argued so far that in the prose discourses and in the poetic oracles, we have two different, yet essentially Jeremianic, traditions concerning the prophet's ministry. We have refrained from forming any precise proposals at this stage as to the respective roles of Jeremiah, Baruch, and others in the reduction of these traditions to writing, though various possibilities have been noted. Finally, it is suggested that the third type of material (namely, Type B, biographical and historical narratives) may have been compiled and added by Baruch and/or a subsequent scribe (or scribes) in the tradition of Baruch, who committed to writing certain incidents in the prophet's life and in Judah's history. These narratives, for the most part, are related to the prophet's speeches and interpret them in particular contexts (for one complex approach to the relationship between the speeches and their accompanying narratives, see H. Lörcher, *TLZ* 102 (1977) 395–96). Eventually, and perhaps in a series of different stages, the Book of Jeremiah gradually assumed the present shape in which it has been preserved in the Hebrew text (a different form of the text being preserved in the tradition reflected by the Septuagint). At a number of places, these final stages in the compilation of the book can be observed, sometimes simply in the arrangement and editing of the material as such, and sometimes in editorial or redactional additions. These matters are discussed in detail under the heading *Form/Structure/Setting* in the body of the commentary.

There remain certain issues that require further discussion, though they are no more free from the uncertainties of hypothesis than the matters summarized above. Certain questions, in particular, require attention. Why was the Book of Jeremiah compiled? When was the Book of Jeremiah compiled? And where was the Book of Jeremiah compiled? An attempt to answer these questions will be made after assessing some of the difficulties associated with coming to an understanding of the prophet himself.

THE PROPHET JEREMIAH

Bibliography

Blank, S. H. *Jeremiah: Man and Prophet.* Cincinnati: Hebrew Union College Press, 1961. **Carroll, R. P.** *From Chaos to Covenant: Prophecy in the Book of Jeremiah.* New York: Crossroad, 1981. 5–30. **Holladay, W.** *Jeremiah: Spokesman Out of Time.* Philadelphia: United Church Press, 1974. **Hyatt, J. P.** *Jeremiah; Prophet of Courage and Hope.* Nashville: Abingdon Press, 1958. **Jobling, D. K.** "The Quest of the Historical Jeremiah: Hermeneutical Implications of Recent Literature." *USQR* 34 (1978) 3–12. **Muilenburg, J.** "Baruch the Scribe." In *Proclamation and Presence: Old Testament Essays in Honour of Gwynne Henton Davies.* Ed. J. I. Durham and J. R. Porter. Richmond: John Knox Press, 1970. 215–38. **Neher, A.** *Jérémie.* Paris: Librarie Plon, 1960. **Reventlow, H. G.** *Liturgie und prophetisches Ich bei Jeremia.* Gütersloh: Gerd Mohn, 1963. **Skinner, J.** *Prophecy and Religion: Studies in the Life of Jeremiah.* 3rd ed. Cambridge: Cambridge University Press, 1930.

Although it is not an easy task simply to read the Book of Jeremiah, given the form in which its subject matter has survived, nevertheless it is an indisputable fact that, taken at face value, a partial but striking picture of the prophet emerges from the pages of the book named after him. Unlike many of the biblical prophets, who remain perpetually as figures in the shadows of history, Jeremiah stands out as a truly human figure. He is torn between faith and doubt, he is deeply involved in the contemporary affairs of his time, and, in the pages of his book, he passes from youth to old age against the backdrop of the history of his era. Yet any such picture of the prophet, in all its heroic and tragic dimensions, is clearly dependent upon one's interpretation of the book named after Jeremiah, and, as we have already observed, the interpretation of the many sources that comprise the book is encompassed by immense difficulties.

In recent scholarship, the trend towards interpreting the sources (especially the narrative discourses and accompanying stories) as the product of later tradition has had a natural corollary, namely that the biography of a historical Jeremiah has receded more and more from view, almost to be lost in the shades of remote antiquity. This withdrawal of the figure of Jeremiah from historical view is a natural consequence of trends in the literary analysis of the book, not merely a perversity of modern scholarship. Clearly the extent to which a historical Jeremiah might be known cannot be determined independently of a resolution to the literary problems associated with the Book of Jeremiah. Nevertheless, some observations on the characteristics of this trend in

Jeremiah studies are appropriate in order to provide a context for the commentary which follows.

Jobling, amongst others, has suggested a parallel between the "quest" for the historical Jeremiah and that for the "historical Jesus" (*USQR* 34 (1978) 3–12). Noting the differences that have come about in Jeremiah research since Skinner's *Prophecy and Religion* (1920), Jobling has proposed that at most we can find beliefs *about* Jeremiah in the book named after him, rather than historically reliable narrative. And Carroll, also noting a parallel with the "quest for the historical Jesus," has pushed the matter still further. "What is being asserted is that this story (about Jeremiah) represents the construction of the traditionists during, and possibly after, the exile (sixth century) and that this tells us more about the development of thought in that period than about the historical Jeremiah. Just as we cannot construct the historical Jesus from the church's theological views about him, so we cannot reconstruct Jeremiah from the highly developed theological presentations in the Book of Jeremiah (only more so!)" (*From Chaos to Covenant*, 25–26). The radical nature of such positions with respect to the "historical Jeremiah" is especially evident in the quotation from Carroll. And though to some extent the possibility of such views must be admitted, given the complexity of the evidence in the book, the probability of such views about the historical (or nonhistorical) Jeremiah needs to be assessed in a wider context.

First, it should be stressed that the analogy of Jeremiah studies with those of the historical Jesus (and especially the synoptic Gospels) is not very precise and not very helpful. In whatever manner one resolves the problems of the "quest for the historical Jesus," one should note that the problems are real ones. Precisely because Jesus, the Christ, became a figure worshiped in the earliest Christian community, there arises the difficulty of discerning the historical from that which is the substance of faith. And we know from the narratives of the earliest church (outside the Gospels) that the basic beliefs of the earliest Christian community focused upon the *person* of Jesus Christ. Hence there is a natural difficulty for the historian of Jesus, which can be resolved in various different ways, in attempting to distinguish the original, or authentic, narratives concerning Jesus from the later possible accretions of the community of faith. But all these difficulties arise in the study of the Gospels precisely because the person of Jesus was the object of faith. It is at this crucial point that the parallel with Jeremiah breaks down. No doubt subsequent generations "believed" (rightly or wrongly) certain things about Jeremiah, but the person of Jeremiah was not the object of faith. Nor is there any need to suppose that the authority of certain beliefs (e.g., concerning the destruction of Jerusalem and the judgment of God) could only gain acceptance if placed in the mouth of such an authoritative (though essentially unknown!) prophet as Jeremiah.

Indeed, one of the most persuasive arguments for the authenticity of the historical recollections concerning Jeremiah is that they are not, in the last resort, crucial or essential to the substance of his message. That is to say, there is no firm evidence outside the Book of Jeremiah that the figure of the prophet ever became the object of beliefs or veneration of any kind. Nor is it clear why the figure of Jeremiah might have been chosen as a kind of clotheshorse upon which the traditionists of a later age should seek to hang their own theological beliefs. But the main point is simply that the evidence concerning the Hebrew prophets as a whole is such that one need not suppose that a record of any part of the life of a prophet was necessary, in addition to the words of the message. Thus, among the eighth-century prophets, we know virtually nothing of Micah beyond the words of his message, but brief incidents in the lives of Hosea and Amos have survived, supplementing to an extent our knowledge of the words of their prophecies. Ezekiel's life is known in a few details, in part because his ministry contained not only words but also actions. But there are not, in our judgment, clear analogies to the proposal that later traditionists, following after "original" prophets, created biographical and historical narratives to convey their own teachings. Indeed, one of the striking aspects of Jeremiah, when examined beyond the confines of his book, is the relative lack of interest in him in OT times (cf. 2 Chr 36:20–22 and Dan 9:2, 24–27) and even beyond the biblical period (see further C. Wolff, *Jeremia im Frühjudentum und Urchristentum* [Berlin: Akademie Verlag, 1976]).

It must certainly be granted that in the investigation of any figure in ancient history, the inquiry is beset on every side by uncertainties and the necessity of hypotheses. And it must also be admitted that the complexities involved in understanding Jeremiah's book make difficult any attempt at reconstructing the history of the life of Jeremiah. Even where narratives about the prophet's life are accepted, after critical examination, as containing reasonably reliable historical data, there remain vast periods of the prophet's life and ministry concerning which we have no historical or biographical information at all. But the admitted difficulties in finding the "historical Jeremiah" are even more grave if one turns to the quest for the later traditionists who "created" the Jeremiah that has survived. For them, no explicit evidence has survived, beyond the allusions and inferences that may perhaps be detected in the book. Nor is there any external record of their existence, or precise external parallel for their supposed activities. These observations do not disprove their existence, yet they serve as a reminder that if Jeremiah himself is lost in the mists of history, the clouds of time that shroud the traditionists are no less dense.

The observation that elements of history and biography have survived with respect to such prophets as Hosea, Amos, and Ezekiel, suggests a reason for the survival of similar elements in the Book of Jeremiah. Sometimes a prophetic message can continue to hold meaning and power, whether or not we know the time and circumstance in which it was delivered. Sometimes, however, the clarity of a message is more intimately related, with respect to its initial meaning, to a particular life situation. And with respect to Jeremiah, it may be that elements of history and biography have survived precisely in order to illuminate the message and ministry as a whole. In this sense, the historical and biographical portions of the book have an important, but supplementary, role; they serve to provide sufficient background for a better understanding of the message.

It is certainly clear that whoever assembled the Book of Jeremiah in its present form did not do so in order to provide us with a life of the prophet. Viewed as biography, the Book of Jeremiah would be incomplete, inadequate, unchronological, and generally unsatisfactory. But when the biographical and historical narratives are seen in their rightful place, supplementing the prophetic word to make possible a deeper understanding, then one is not being too uncritical in accepting with caution the historical implications of the ancient text.

One may reasonably suppose that, apart from a few autobiographical notes from the prophet himself, the tradition of supplementing the record of the prophet's word began with Baruch. The narrative contained in Jer 36 is the basis for such a view. Carroll has argued that the narrative concerning the role of Baruch cannot be taken as a historical account and that it is "a literary creation designed to incorporate the scribal influence into the Jeremiah tradition" (*From Chaos to Covenant*, 15). But such a view is unnecessarily skeptical. The role of Baruch, as described in Jer 36, need not be removed from the realm of history, and one may postulate that he continued to have an influential role in the prophet's life and in the recording of his ministry, even down to the time at which both the prophet and Baruch were taken into exile in Egypt (43:6–7). Whether Baruch, or a later scribe, was responsible for the Book of Jeremiah as it has survived, cannot be known. It is certainly probable that Baruch, under the influence of Jeremiah, played a significant role in bringing the book to its present form. But one must also suppose that if the foundational work were done by Baruch, some final editing and arranging were done at a later date, probably after the death of both Jeremiah and Baruch.

In the light of these observations on the historical nature of the prophet Jeremiah, we must return to certain questions about the book named after him. Why was it compiled? When was it compiled? Where was it compiled? None of the questions can be answered with certainty, but it is possible to propose some general hypotheses.

As to why the book was compiled, the principal reason lay beyond the book itself in a tradition that had been established in Judah more than a century earlier. Beginning at least in the eighth century B.C., the sayings of certain influential and great prophets had been preserved in writing; the tradition perhaps began because of the recognition of the inherent worth of their prophetic oracles, together with the recognition that they addressed the continuing history and fate of the chosen people. And Jeremiah's oracles, apart from their inherent religious worth, addressed the history of Judah in its last days as an independent nation. Yet the initiative in compilation appears to have begun during the prophet's lifetime, with the assistance of Baruch (Jer 36); it may be that this incident prompted a continuing literary activity, supplementing the prophetic ministry, so that in an unusually comprehensive fashion we have a record of Jeremiah's prophetic ministry. But by the end of the ministry, a further reason for the recording of the oracles and the compiling of the book had emerged; insofar as the prophet, especially in the latter part of his ministry, declared a message of hope for future generations, it was imperative that the message be preserved. In summary, the initial initiative in the compilation of the book no doubt occurred during the prophet's lifetime, and the work was brought to a conclusion shortly after his death. From this observation, it follows that no single time can be specified for the process of compilation. The process had begun by 605 B.C., if not earlier, and it may have continued for a short time after the unknown date of the prophet's death. The basic substance of the book was no doubt complete by 550 B.C., though the subsequent manuscript traditions (discussed in the section that follows) indicate that there continued to be differences in the precise shape and form of the book. And likewise, the place of compilation is uncertain; the process began in Judah, continued no doubt in Egypt (during Jeremiah's exile), and may have then developed independently in the different locations in which the tradition was preserved: Judah, Egypt, and Babylon. To understand the difficulties of knowing what was the final form of the book, we must now turn to a brief review of the differences between the textual traditions represented in the MT and the LXX, respectively.

(*Note:* the details of the life and vocation of the prophet, within the general perspectives specified above, and the historical circumstances in which he ministered, are described in detail in the body of the commentary. On the general historical context, see especially the *Comment* and *Explanation* on 1:1–3.)

THE HEBREW AND GREEK TEXTS OF JEREMIAH

Bibliography

(a)   Texts: **Rudolph, W.**, ed. *Liber Jeremiae. BHS* 8, 1970. **Ziegler, J.** *Jeremias, Baruch, Threni, Epistula Jeremiae. Septuaginta. Vetus Testamentum Graecum*, vol. 15. Göttingen, 1976.

(b)   *Studies:* **Althann, R.** *A Philological Analysis of Jeremiah 4–6 in the Light of Northwest Semitic.* BibOr 38. Rome: Biblical Institute Press, 1983. **Brockington, L. H.** *The Hebrew Text of the Old Testament.* Oxford: Oxford UP, 1973. **Cross, F. M.** *The Ancient Library of Qumran.* Garden City, NY: Doubleday, 1958. 186–94. **Dahood, M.** "The Metaphor in Jeremiah 17:13." *Bib* 48 (1967) 109–10. ———. "Hebrew-Ugaritic Lexicography II." *Bib* 45 (1964) 393–412. ———. "Philological Notes on Jer 18:14–15." *ZAW* 74 (1962) 207–9. ———. *Ugaritic-Hebrew Philology.* BibOr 17. Rome: Pontifical Biblical Institute, 1965. **Ehrlich, A. B.** *Randglossen zur hebraischen Bibel.* Vol. 4. Leipzig: Hinrichs, 1912. **Janzen, J. G.** *Studies in the Text of Jeremiah.* HSM 6 Cambridge, MA: Harvard University Press, 1973. **Rossi, G. B. de.** *Variae Lectiones Veteris Testamenti.* Vol. 3. Parma: Bodoni, 1786. **Stulman, L.** *The Other Text of Jeremiah.* Lanham, MD: UP of America, 1985. ———. "Some Theological and Lexical Differences between the Old Greek and the MT of the Jeremiah Prose Discourses." *HS* 25 (1984) 18–23. **Talmon, S.** and **Tov, E.** "A Commentary on the Text of Jeremiah. I. The LXX of Jer 1:1–7." *Textus* 9 (1981) 1–15. **Tov, E.** *The Septuagint Translation of Jeremiah and Baruch: A Discussion of an Early Revision of the LXX of Jeremiah 29–52 and Baruch 1:1–3:8.* HSM 8. Missoula, MT: Scholars Press, 1976. ———. "L'incidence de la critique textuelle sur la critique littéraire dans le livre de Jérémie." *RB* 79 (1972) 189–99. ———. "Exegetical Notes on the Hebrew Vorlage of the LXX of Jeremiah 27 (34)." *ZAW* 91 (1979) 73–93. ———. *The Text-Critical Use of the Septuagint in Biblical Research.* JBS 3. Tel Aviv: Simor, 1981. **Ziegler, J.** *Beiträge zur Jeremias-Septuaginta.* Göttingen: Vandenhoek & Ruprecht, 1958). **Zlotowitz, B. M.** *The Septuagint Translation of Hebrew Terms in Relation to God in the Book of Jeremiah.* New York: Ktav, 1981.

The Hebrew text of the Book of Jeremiah, in the Masoretic tradition, is for the most part reasonably clear and straightforward. There are a few places where either the vocalization of the text, or on occasion the consonantal text itself, is difficult to comprehend and where some kind of corruption of the text may have occurred. These cases are examined in the *Notes* following the translation, throughout the commentary. But in general, the principal difficulty for the translator, especially in dealing with the poetic passages in Jeremiah, is the problem of catching the literary force and power of the poetry, while at the same time remaining faithful to the fundamental meaning of the text.

Nevertheless, despite the relative clarity of the Hebrew text in its received form, the surface calm almost certainly veils a long and complex prehistory of a text tradition which has undergone a considerable degree of modification and change.

The clues to the prehistory of the text are provided by the evidence of the Greek text of the LXX, on the one hand, and the fragments of Hebrew text of Jeremiah that were found near Qumran, on the other hand. That the Greek text of Jeremiah poses problems for the approach to the Hebrew text has long been recognized. In general terms, the Greek text is approximately one-eighth shorter than the Hebrew text, sometimes omitting a word or phrase found in MT and sometimes omitting entire passages (e.g., 33:14–26; 39:4–13). Furthermore, the sequence and arrangement of material differ between the two text traditions, most notably in the location of the "Foreign Nation Oracles," occurring as chaps. 46–51 in Hebrew but located after 25:13 in the Greek version (and, in addition, the oracles occur in a different sequence in the respective texts). It is clear that the Hebrew tradition represented by the LXX translation differed from that of the MT on which most modern English translations of the Bible are based. But having recognized the difference, it is much more difficult to provide a coherent account of the reasons for it, or to know with certainty whether the MT or the *Vorlage* of the LXX represents the most ancient and original textual tradition. The task is complicated further by the fact that the Greek text itself is uneven, an unevenness which in the past has led scholars to posit that the two parts of the LXX (1–28 and 29–52) were prepared by two different translators. Recently it has been proposed, with persuasive arguments, that the second half of the Greek translation is a revision of an earlier translation, the so-called Old Greek text, the latter having survived only in the first half of the text of the LXX (see further, E. Tov, *The Septuagint Translation of Jeremiah and Baruch*, 1976).

The Qumran evidence for the Hebrew text of Jeremiah is relatively slender, comprising four manuscripts. Three of these (2Q Jer, 4Q Jer^a, 4Q Jer^c) represent the standard Hebrew textual tradition that has survived in the MT. A fourth fragment (4Q Jer^b), however, is of particular interest in that it appears to contain a portion of the text that constituted the *Vorlage* of LXX, or the "Old Greek" text of Jeremiah. 4Q Jer^b is a fair-sized fragment, containing Jer 9:22–10:18, although only the lefthand portion of the column of text has survived, so that the beginnings of the lines must be reconstructed. In several ways, 4Q Jer^b corresponds to the LXX version of 9:22–10:18, rather than to the MT version: (i) 10:6–8, 10 (MT) are omitted, as they are in LXX; (ii) v 5 (MT) follows v 9, as it does in the LXX; (iii) word order in 10:4 parallels that of the LXX, rather than of the MT. In summary, 4Q Jer^b would seem to provide a small piece of evidence for the Hebrew recension lying behind the LXX text of Jeremiah, and it is of interest to note that samples of both recensions, that is the textual traditions represented in both the MT and the LXX, were found in a single cave (4Q), indicating a continuing state of fluidity with respect to the text of the Book of Jeremiah.

In theory, one might suppose that the discovery of fragments of Jeremiah in the caves in the vicinity of Qumran would help to resolve the difficulties. In practice, the new data have certainly provided the basis for the further development of hypotheses concerning the history and provenance of Hebrew recensions, as has been done by F. M. Cross, and worked out in some detail with respect to Jeremiah by J. G. Janzen (*Studies in the Text of Jeremiah*). But, without wishing to criticize in any way the detailed and meticulous work of Janzen, his hypothetical reconstructions inevitably must leave one with a sense of unease. If, as he proposes, the Hebrew *Vorlage* of the LXX is generally superior to the MT and has undergone less recensional development, and if indeed the MT has undergone much secondary expansion, then the tendency would be to prefer the Hebrew text underlying the LXX. But the unease remains, for two reasons: (i) Janzen inevitably is dealing with hypotheses; he argues his case well, but the data are susceptible to alternative reconstruction or, perhaps more realistically, to the recognition that there are simply insufficient data to reconstruct a coherent history of the recensions of the Hebrew text of Jeremiah. (ii) Despite the persuasiveness of Janzen's hypothesis, the fact remains that the Hebrew text underlying the LXX has not survived, with the exception of the small Qumran fragment.

If, however, one espouses a position of agnosticism with respect to the early recensional history of the Hebrew text of Jeremiah, urging the paucity of the evidence, one is left with a practical problem. Which textual tradition should be the basis of translation and commentary, that represented by the MT or that presupposed by the LXX? A canonical approach to Scripture does not help entirely in the resolution of this dilemma. In theory, one might raise the question from a Christian understanding of the canon: Does the Hebrew or the Greek text claim recognition with respect to canonicity? To this question, there is no simple answer. On the one hand, it is clear that the OT of the earliest Christian church was the LXX. On the other hand, following the influence of Jerome in the fifth century, and the essential espousal of his perspectives by Reformers such as Martin Luther, it is the Hebrew text (MT) which has become the basis of modern English (and other) Bibles. (On these issues, see further B. Vawter, "Prophecy and the Redactional Question," in *No Famine in the Land: Studies in Honor of John L. McKenzie*, ed. J. W. Flanagan and A. W. Robinson [Missoula, MT: Scholars Press, 1975] 127–39.) Indeed, despite the tradition of the earliest church, one could hardly but agree with the principle of accepting the primacy of the Hebrew text, for in many places the LXX represents a thoroughly inadequate translation of the Hebrew original. But while that perspective may hold true in general, it leaves a peculiar problem with respect to Jeremiah: given the possibility that the Septuagint may represent a better text, should it not be preferred?

Let us return to the problem of the differences between the MT and the LXX: Does the evidence, particularly that from Qumran, really establish the superiority of the Greek text, or more precisely its Hebrew antecedent? In general terms, one could take several different approaches toward the explanation of the discrepancies and differences between the two textual traditions for which evidence has survived. (i) The longer Hebrew text (MT) is original; the Greek translators abbreviated the text and rearranged its contents into what they considered to be a more appropriate sequence. (ii) The Greek text (more precisely, its Hebrew *Vorlage*) represents the original Hebrew tradition, which was later expanded and rearranged into the form of the extant MT. (iii) There were, from an early date, different traditions of the text of Jeremiah in circulation, and no effort was made initially to produce a standard and authoritative text; hence, different versions coexisted (as at Qumran).

The issues are more complex, however, than this threefold classification of potential solutions might suggest. If either the first or second approach could be proved, then one could proceed to work with either the Hebrew (MT) or the Greek (LXX) text as the best witness to the original book of Jeremiah. The third option leads to much greater uncertainty, for if there were several editions of the text from an early date, of which only two have survived, then (unless one could establish the superiority or antiquity of one tradition over another) one would be wisest to accept *both traditions* as constituting part of the evidence for the earliest development of the text. In other words, there may have been several "Jeremiahs" from an early date, representing different forms of the book that were produced in different regions (Babylon, Palestine, Egypt). To search for the original Jeremiah would therefore be missing the point, for there may have been several "originals," relatively independent of each other. Alternatively, the different textual traditions may be thought to reflect different stages in the redaction of the "original Jeremiah." Tov, for example, proposes that the textual tradition represented in the LXX reflects a first major redaction of the book, whereas the tradition in the MT reflects a second and expanded redaction of the book (E. Tov, "L'incidence de la critique textuelle sur la critique littéraire dans le livre de Jérémie," *RB* 79 (1972) 189–99).

As has already been indicated, the work of Cross and Janzen has culminated in the proposal that the Hebrew text represented in the LXX may be the older and better textual tradition, and therefore it should be preferred to the MT, which is considered to contain later expansions. The practical difficulty of this approach, if it could be sustained, has already been noted: if the LXX represents the best tradition, then the commentator is forced to work "at arm's length" from the original and best text, for with the exception of the single (and incomplete) fragment from Qumran, the proposed better textual tradition has survived only in translation. The position of Cross and Janzen, however, is by no means certain even on theoretical grounds, as has been indicated by some recent research on the Hebrew text represented by the MT.

Robert Althann has undertaken a detailed study of Jer 4–6, in which he has given particular attention to the poetic nature of the MT in the light of the evidence of Northwest Semitic poetry (*A Philological Analysis of Jeremiah 4–6 in the Light of Northwest Semitic*, 1983). One significant aspect of Althann's study is that he concludes that the MT of Jeremiah is not expansionistic, but rather that the LXX translators tended to condense the larger (poetic) forms of the original Hebrew text. Thus, the failure of the Greek translators to appreciate the canons of Hebrew (and Semitic) poetry led them to eliminate what they considered to be repetitious parts of their original text, thereby failing to recognize the essential character of repetitive parallelism in Hebrew poetry. With these, and similar, arguments Althann presents a persuasive case for the primacy (or at least authenticity) of the Hebrew text (MT), without denying that different textual traditions may account for some of the divergences between MT and LXX.

Althann's views, it may be responded, are based on a very limited analysis of the Hebrew text (namely chaps. 4–6). While this must be acknowledged, it should also be recognized that all views of the ancient textual history of Jeremiah are based on limited evidence. The Qumran evidence, for example, which plays a significant role in the alternatives to Althann's hypothesis, is equally slender. It would probably be wisest simply to take the view that there are insufficient data to provide a comprehensive and adequate account of the early textual history of Jeremiah. Thus, while it cannot be assumed that the MT is the best witness to the "original Jeremiah," from a strictly historical perspective, nor is it clearly established that the LXX contains a better witness to the original text, assuming that there was a single "original text."

The resolution to the problems which has been adopted in this commentary is essentially a practical one. The commentary is one in a series of commentaries on the Hebrew text of the Bible, which in turn is the basis of the majority of modern translations of the Bible. And, of course, even when one prefers in theory the text represented in the translation of the LXX, the fact remains that that text survives only in translation, with the minor exception of the Qumran fragment. Hence, the translation in this book and the accompanying commentary are based on the MT. In the *Notes*, the significant variations from the MT that occur in the LXX are cited. But very rarely have these variations been used as a the basis of emending the MT; if the *Vorlage* of the LXX represents a different recensional tradition, emendation becomes too precarious a business to undertake, with the possible exception of its assistance in places where the Hebrew text appears to be incomprehensible.

HISTORICAL BACKGROUND FOR THE BOOK OF JEREMIAH

Bibliography

Aharoni, Y. *The Land of the Bible: A Historical Geography.* Philadelphia: Westminster, 1967. **Bright, J.** *A History of Israel.* 3rd ed. Philadelphia: Westminster, 1981. **Hayes, J. H.** and **Miller, J. M.**, eds. *Israelite and Judean History.* Philadelphia: Westminster, 1977. **Herrmann, S.** *A History of Israel in Old Testament Times.* 2nd ed. Philadelphia: Fortress, 1981. **Malamat, A.** "The Last Kings of Judah and the Fall of Jerusalem." *IEJ* 18 (1968) 137–56. **Noth, M.** *The History of Israel.* 2nd ed. New York: Harper and Row, 1960. **Pritchard, J. B.**, ed. *Ancient Near Eastern Texts Relating to the Old Testament.* 2nd ed. Princeton: Princeton UP, 1955. **Wiseman, D. J.** *Chronicles of Chaldean Kings (626–556 B.C.) in the British Museum.* London: The Trustees of the British Museum, 1956.

The life and preaching career of Jeremiah clearly fall within the context of the years 627–587 B.C. (or perhaps a little later). The data available are sufficient to chart the course of events in Judah during those years and to relate them to the actions of the more powerful nations of Egypt, Assyria, and Babylon. The attempts to integrate the life and deeds of Jeremiah into the larger national history may be found in the appropriate sections of this commentary. What is offered here is a historical summary of the major persons and events against which the career of Jeremiah is to be viewed.

Josiah came to the throne of Judah in 640 when he was eight years old (1 Kgs 22:1; 2 Chr 34:1). His thirty-one-year reign was to see a radical shift in the international power structure of the Middle East. Asshurbanipal of Assyria (668–627) inherited a vast empire from his father Esarhaddon (680–669), but in the course of his reign external and internal pressures so weakened his hold that by the time of his death Assyria was on the verge of collapse. Egypt under Psammetichus I (664–610) declared its independence from Assyria, probably about 665 (J. Bright, *A History*, 313). On the northern border of Assyria the Medes and their allies, the Lydians and the Cimmerians, exerted steady pressure. In 652 Babylon revolted and was pacified only after a four-year struggle. Asshurbanipal's struggles to maintain his empire enjoyed a large amount of success, but the decades-long efforts drained the Assyrian resources and made collapse inevitable.

Assyria's problems with larger foes made it possible for Josiah to pursue a plan of national renaissance. Josiah is remembered for his religious or cultic reform, but it must be remembered that the reform had its political side. There are two traditions about Josiah's reforms. According to the Chronicler (2 Chr 34:3–7) the reform began in 628 with the move to eliminate the high places and all vestiges of foreign cults in Judah, followed by a similar campaign in Manasseh, Ephraim, and Simeon, as far as Naphtali. Then in 622 with the discovery of the book of the law during the renovation of the temple in Jerusalem, the reform took on a new phase, reforming the cult in Jerusalem with emphasis on the observance of the Passover (2 Chr 34:8–35:19).

The parallel account in Kings (2 Kgs 22:3–23:5) gives the impression that Josiah's religious reform was directly related to the discovery of the book of the law in 622, and that the reform was carried out wholly according to its precepts. Both accounts of Josiah's reign indicate that he was able to do as he wished in much of the territory of the former state of Israel. This was made possible by the increasingly precarious position of Assyria under Sin-shar-ishkun (629–612). In 626 Nabopolassar took Babylon from Assyria and assumed the kingship (D. J. Wiseman, *Chronicles*, 6–7, 50–51). In 614 the Medes under Cyaxeres captured Asshur, the old capital of Assyria, and in 612 Nineveh fell to the combined Babylonian and Median forces (*ANET*, 304–5). What was left of the Assyrian army retreated to Haran, where, in 610, they were routed (*ANET*, 305).

The following year (605), fearing the rapid rise of Babylonian power, Egyptian forces under Neco II (610–594) marched north again to aid the Assyrian attempt to regain Haran. Josiah interposed his forces to try to block the Egyptian advance at Megiddo and there lost his life (2 Kgs 23:29–30; 2 Chr 35:20–24). Judah's brief experience of political independence and a quasi-united kingdom was at an end. Although details of the campaign are sketchy, the combined Egyptian-Assyrian forces were not successful against the Babylonians. The Assyrian empire was finally destroyed.

For the next four years (609–605) Egypt was in control of Palestine and Syria. The Judeans placed Jehoahaz on the throne in Jerusalem, but after a reign of only three months, the Egyptians replaced him with Jehoiakim (609–598, 2 Kgs 23:30–37). In his reign Josiah's reform lapsed, and foreign cults were reinstituted. Jehoiakim was a compliant vassal, more concerned with personal aggrandizement (Jer 22:13–19) than with responsible rule.

In 605 Nebuchadnezzar decisively defeated the Egyptians at Carchemish (D. J. Wiseman, *Chronicles*, 25–26, 66–69) (Jer 46), pursuing them as far as Hamath in Syria. After his installation as king in Babylon (604) Nebuchadnezzar consolidated his gains, destroying Ashkelon and receiving tribute from all the kings of the Hatti land (Syria-Palestine, D. J. Wiseman, *Chronicles*, 69), including Jehoiakim (2 Kgs 24:1). In the following two years Nebuchadnezzar conducted two more campaigns in Syria-Palestine, details of which are unknown.

In 601 Nebuchadnezzar and Neco fought a bloody but indecisive battle near the Egyptian frontier. In laconic fashion the Babylonian Chronicle reports that the Babylonian forces returned to Babylon and that Nebuchadnezzar spent the next year replenishing his forces (D. J. Wiseman, *Chronicles*, 29–30, 71). It was in this context that Jehoiakim in 601 rebelled against Babylon (2 Kgs 24:1).

In 598 Nebuchadnezzar again marched into the Hatti land, this time intent on dealing with rebellious Jerusalem. He besieged the city, captured it on the second day of Adar (March 15/16, 597 [D. J. Wiseman, *Chronicles*, 33, 72–73] 2 Kgs 24:10–17), deposed the king, Jehoiakin, the successor of Jehoiakim, who had died shortly before, and installed Mattaniah (Zedekiah) as the new king. Jehoiakin was exiled to Babylon together with the royal family and several thousands of the leaders and people with special skills (2 Kgs 24:10–16; 2 Chr 36:9–10). Jehoiakin continued to be regarded as the legitimate ruler by both Judeans and Babylonians (J. Bright, *A History*, 328). Ration tablets from Babylon list commodities supplied to Jehoiakin and other deposed rulers from the west (*ANET*, 308).

Zedekiah's reign (597–587) was a time of turbulent political intrigue in Judah, with pro-Egyptian, pro-Babylonian, and pro-independence parties jockeying for position. In 595/594 there was an abortive internal insurrection at Babylon which had to be suppressed (D. J. Wiseman, *Chronicles*, 36, 72–73). Apparently the news of the uprising was the occasion of a meeting of foreign ministers in Jerusalem in 594, including representatives from Edom, Moab, Ammon, Tyre, and Sidon, to consider throwing off the yoke of Babylon (Jer 27:1–3). The intrigue, for whatever reasons, came to nothing. But by 589 Judah had finally decided firmly on a course to seek independence. In 588 Nebuchadnezzar laid Jerusalem under siege again (2 Kgs 25:1) and began the systematic destruction of strong points in Judah. The Lachish Letters offer some insights into the stresses and strains on the Judean forces (*ANET*, 321–22). A brief surge of hope occurred when news arrived in Jerusalem that Egyptian forces were marching against the Babylonians (Jer 37:5), but the threat was quickly dealt with and the siege of Jerusalem was continued. In 587 the Babylonian forces breached the walls of Jerusalem. Zedekiah managed to escape toward the Jordan River, but he was caught near Jericho and marched before Nebuchadnezzar at Riblah in Syria. There Zedekiah's sons were slain before his eyes, and then his own eyes were put out and he was carried away to Babylon (2 Kgs 25:5–7). The city of Jerusalem was demolished.

Nebuchadnezzar appointed Gedaliah to be the civil administrator of the province with headquarters at Mizpah, just north of Jerusalem (2 Kgs 25:22–23; Jer 40:5). Gedaliah had had the office of chamberlain at the court of Zedekiah. Gedaliah counseled submission on the part of those remaining in the land in the hope that further tragedy could be avoided (2 Kgs 25:24). Many of the Judeans who had managed to escape to the Transjordan had confidence in Gedaliah and returned (Jer 40:11–12). But some of the Judean officers who had made good their escape from the Babylonians rejected Gedaliah's leadership, killed him along with the residents of Mizpah and the Babylonian garrison stationed there, and fled to Ammon (2 Kgs 25:23–25; Jer 40:7–41:15). Many of the remaining residents in the land soon fled for refuge to Egypt, apparently in order to escape the expected Babylonian retribution, taking Jeremiah and Baruch with them (2 Kgs 25:26; Jer 42:1–43:7). Jer 52:30 tells of a third deportation from Judah in 582, the twenty-third year of Nebuchadnezzar.

I. Preface to the Book of Jeremiah (1:1–3)

Bibliography

Levin, C. "Noch einmal: die Anfänge des Propheten Jeremia." *VT* 31 (1981) 428–40.
Overholt, T. W. "Some Reflections on the Date of Jeremiah's Call." *CBQ* 33 (1971) 165–84.
Tucker, G. M. "Prophetic Superscriptions and the Growth of the Canon." In *Canon and Authority*. Ed. G. M. Coats and B. O. Long. Philadelphia: Fortress, 1977. 56–70. **Vogt, E.** "Verba Jeremias Filii Helciae." *VD* 42 (1964) 169–72.

Translation

[1] *The words of Jeremiah,[a] son of Hilkiah, one of the priests at Anathoth in the territory of Benjamin,* [2] *to whom the LORD's word came in the time of Josiah, son of Amon, the King of Judah, in the thirteenth year of his reign.* [3] *And it continued in the time of Jehoiakim, Josiah's son, King of Judah, until the end[a] of the eleventh year of Zedekiah, son of Josiah, King of Judah; that is, until the deportation of the people of Jerusalem in the fifth month.*

Notes

1.a. LXX has a longer text: "The word of God which came to Jeremiah."
3.a. Heb. םֹח, "end, completion," is omitted in LXX, perhaps because it was thought to be inconsistent with the reference to the "fifth month." But the regnal year was probably different from the calendar year (lunar) indicated in the reference to the month.

Form/Structure/Setting

The opening three verses of the Book of Jeremiah may be entitled loosely a *preface*. With respect to modern conventions in the production of books, they fall somewhere between the title page and the preface, being longer than the title page (though incorporating the title) and shorter than many modern prefaces.

Within the biblical prophetic books, there are certain common elements in all such prefaces; there are degrees of variation between them, however, and they are not structured rigidly but adapt the general framework to the particular character of the book. In general terms, the four following elements may be present in a preface to a prophetic book: (i) the specification that it contains a word or vision from the Lord (thereby defining the substance as prophecy); (ii) the name of the person or prophet through whom the word was delivered; (iii) the time and place at which the word was given, or the period during which the prophet ministered; and (iv) the subject or theme of the prophetic word. Of these four points, the first two are common to all the prophetic books, though they may occur with more or less specific detail (possibly the only exception being Malachi, which may provide the title, not the name, of the prophet). The occurrence of the latter two elements, namely chronology and subject matter, varies considerably from one prophetic book to another. The preface to Jeremiah contains three of the four conventional elements. (i) The book is entitled "the Words of Jeremiah" (1:1), though it is specified that it was the Lord's word which came to him (1:2). (ii) The person through whom the word was delivered is specified in more detail than is the case with some prophetic books; we are provided with his name, his father's name and profession, and the place in which his family lived. (iii) The historical period is specified from three perspectives, namely the regnal year in which the prophetic ministry began (1:2), the reigns of the kings through which it continued, and the approximate close of the prophetic ministry (1:3). (iv) No specific information is provided as to the subject matter of the divine word, as is done in some other prophetic prefaces (e.g., Isa 1:1; Amos 1:1).

The comprehensive chronological perspective indicates that the preface was written and added to the collection of oracles after the major activity of collecting the material together in the form of a book had taken place. That is, the latest date specified (the "deportation") is the date after which the preface was written, though how long afterwards it was written is not known. Nor can there be absolute certainty whether the preface was written after the completion of the whole book of Jeremiah as we now know it, or after the collection of one or more of the smaller "books" which now form a part of the whole.

Comment

1   *The subject matter.* The principal subject matter of the book is defined as "words"; they are the words of Jeremiah, but Jeremiah in turn spoke the Lord's word which he received as a prophet. Thus the book contains prophecy, for prophecy is none other than the word of God addressed to the people of God through a prophet, the Lord's spokesman. Defined as such, the authority of the substance of the book becomes clear. It does not contain simply the social and religious critique of a remarkable man who lived during the seventh and sixth centuries B.C.; rather, his message has its source and origin in God, even though the message itself comes through the medium of a human speaker. Jeremiah, as a prophet, gives the message its distinctive form, couching it in his own words which are inevitably colored by his personality and character, but the message comes from God and has the authority of its divine source.

The content or specific focus of the words is not given in summary form, as it is in the prefaces to certain other prophetic books, perhaps because the length of the ministry and diverse objects of the message were too large to encapsulate in a summary statement.

The prophet. The prophet's name is Jeremiah; the name is not uncommon in Hebrew, though its precise significance is uncertain. It probably means "the Lord exalts" (see V. Maag, "Jeremia," *BHH* 2, 812–14), though the sense could be "the Lord loosens." His father, Hilkiah, is described as one of the priests who lived in the small village of Anathoth in the territory of Benjamin. (The implications of Jeremiah's priestly background are examined in more detail in the *Comment* on the following section: 1:4–10.)

Anathoth, Jeremiah's home town, was situated about three miles northeast of Jerusalem. The name survives in the modern village of ʿAnata, though the site of the original Anathoth was in all probability just southwest of ʿAnata at Ras el-Kharrubeh (see C. E. DeVries, *ISBE* I, 121–22). Though Anathoth was situated close to Jerusalem, it was located nevertheless at the very edge of the wilderness; to the east of Anathoth, the land falls away into the desert of the great rift valley in which the Dead Sea is located. And, if we are to judge by the language of the prophet, that wilderness region had exerted its influence on the mind and personality of the prophet. "The vision of that desert maze was burnt into the prophet's mind, and he contrasted it with the clear, ordered Word of God" (Sir George Adam Smith, *The Historical Geography of the Holy Land* [1894, repr. London: Collins, 1966] 212–13). In this respect, there are certain parallels between Jeremiah's home and that of his predecessor Amos, who had lived in Tekoa, further south than Anathoth, but also bordering the great wilderness region.

2–3 *The chronological framework.* Three specific pieces of information are then provided with respect to the period of history in which Jeremiah undertook his prophetic ministry: (i) the ministry began in the thirteenth year of King Josiah; (ii) it continued through the reign of King Jehoiakim; and (iii) it lasted until the eleventh year of King Zedekiah. Each of these chronological statements must be examined in more detail.

As Josiah's reign extended from 640 to 609 B.C., the initial date in the preface refers to the year 627 B.C. as the beginning point of the prophet's ministry. Following the death of Josiah, King Jehoahaz reigned for three months (in 609 B.C.), but, perhaps because of the brevity of his reign, no reference is made to him in the dating process which goes by regnal years.

King Jehoiakim ruled in Judah from 609 to 598 B.C., and the prophet's ministry continued throughout his reign. Jehoiakim died in 598 B.C., and was succeeded, for about three months, by his eighteen-year-old son, Jehoiachin, but no reference is made to him in the preface to Jeremiah.

Jehoiachin was replaced as King by Zedekiah (Mattaniah), who reigned from 597 to 587 B.C. as the last king of Judah prior to its ultimate and total defeat by the Babylonian armies in 587 B.C.

The chronological references in Jer 1:1–3 set the broad framework of history within which the prophet's ministry is to be interpreted; there remain however a number of problems with respect to the significance of the chronological framework. The first pertains to the precise significance of the year 627 B.C. as the beginning of the prophet's ministry; the second pertains to the difficulty of forming an assessment of the extent of the prophet's ministry *after* the chronological period specified in the preface.

The year 627 B.C. is specified as the year in which the Lord's word came to Jeremiah. In view of the statement that Jeremiah was set aside for a prophetic ministry even before his birth (1:4; see the *Comment* on the following passage), there have been a few scholars who interpret the year 627 B.C. as the year of the Jeremiah's birth. For an analysis and critique of such views, see particularly J. A. Thompson, *Jeremiah*, 50–56. With respect to the text under consideration, such a view is highly unlikely; the words of the preface would more naturally imply the point at which Jeremiah became conscious of the divine vocation and message. Thus, we may suppose that 627 B.C. was the year of the prophet's awareness of vocation, and perhaps also the year in which his ministry began. Since we do not know precisely his age at the time of vocation, the most we can assume is that the prophet was born sometime before 640 B.C.

Though the preface indicates that the prophet's ministry extended to the year of the deportation (587 B.C.), it is clear that in a limited fashion, the prophet continued to exercise some kind of ministry in Egypt (Jer 42–44). Although the absence of any reference to this period of the prophet's life in the preface may indicate that the preface was written and added to the book before the addition of sections concerning the Egyptian sojourn, it is equally likely that the purpose of the preface was simply to specify the period of the prophet's *national ministry.* The last part of his life in exile may have been viewed merely as an appendix to the principal period of prophetic ministry.

Thus, the prophetic ministry of Jeremiah extended over a period of more than forty years (627–587 B.C.). There has not survived a complete record of that ministry in the book named after the prophet, but rather excerpts from various periods in the ministry. The book contains portions of oracles and sermons delivered during the ministry, though precise dating of each passage is not possible; hence, while the general historical background to the prophet Jeremiah is well known, the specific background to the respective portions of his book cannot always be determined precisely. The historical and biographical narratives in the collection can normally be dated rather more precisely, and hence the background can be reconstructed more fully with the aid of other biblical and Near Eastern texts.

Explanation

The preface to a book merely sets the stage; it rarely has a dramatic character but rather provides the fundamental data that are necessary for reading what follows. The preface to Jeremiah certainly provides these fundamental data; the book contains the words of Jeremiah of Anathoth, who in turn was a prophet speaking the word of the Lord. But, although it contains only fundamental data, there is an element of drama in the preface, which may elude us, given our separation in time from that period of history; the drama is provided by the references to the kings during whose reigns the prophet ministered.

Jeremiah's long ministry extended through a period of human history in which radical and violent changes were taking place. When he began his ministry, Josiah was king. On the surface, it was a bright time in history for the Hebrew people. The great Assyrian Empire, remembered in later history for the violence of its militarist policies, was in a state of decline; for centuries, it had been a threat on the northern horizon, sometimes a conqueror and sometimes a restless neighbor. Assyria's decline, which was complete with the defeat of its capital Nineveh in 612 B.C., could be taken as a source of encouragement to the Hebrews, who had frequently suffered at Assyria's hands. Indeed, it was precisely the decline of Assyria during the early part of Josiah's reign that made so much change seem possible. Judah became independent again; it freed itself of foreign religious influences and reformed its worship; it expanded its land holdings, retaking some of the lands that had belonged long ago to the northern state of Israel, but which Assyria could no longer control. Jeremiah began his ministry in a period of buoyancy and hope, though he perceived more clearly than did others that it was a false hope.

The decline of Assyria from imperial power not unnaturally left a vacuum in international politics of the time. Judah's brief prosperity early in Josiah's reign was a consequence of that vacuum of power, but it was only a matter of time until new (and renewed) superpowers emerged to engage in a struggle for the supremacy once held by Assyria. Egypt, which at the beginning of the seventh century B.C. had been little more than a vassal of Assyria, began to flex its muscles again; under the Pharaohs Psammetichus (663–609 B.C.) and Necho (609–593 B.C.), it began to reassert its influence in the Near East. But in the east, two other imperial powers also had their goal set on imperial supremacy, though initially they acted as allies: the Medes, under Cyaxeres (c. 625–585 B.C.), and the Neo-Babylonian Empire, under the leadership of Nabopolassar (626–605 B.C.) and later Nebuchadnezzar (605–562 B.C.), were both gaining strength and influence. With Egypt growing powerful in the southwest, and the Medes and Neo-Babylonians growing in the east, the tiny state of Judah was caught between the great powers of the time that sought imperial control of the Near Eastern world. Things were briefly bright at the beginning of Josiah's reign, but, from the larger perspective, the small state of Judah was but a pawn in the game of power played out through the decades of Jeremiah's ministry. With the decline of Assyria, Egypt took control; with the weakness of Egypt, Babylon gained ascendancy. And through it all, the citizens of Judah were tossed now this way, now that, until at last in 587 B.C. their holy city was destroyed by the Babylonians and great numbers of citizens were taken into exile.

Thus, from one perspective, Jeremiah lived through a period of momentous international change, when old authorities were declining and new powers were emerging. All these external forces had their impact on the life and politics of the nation of Judah, and inevitably Jeremiah was drawn into the current events of his time. But Jeremiah, as a prophet, saw beyond the immediate historical events of his age; he read the handwriting of God in the events of his nation's history. And the true crisis, he perceived clearly, lay not in external matters but in the inner national and religious life of his people. It was less the strength of external enemies than the weakness at the core of his own nation that he felt and proclaimed.

We only begin to understand the power of Jeremiah's book if we grasp something of the chaos of his world. In a time of radical change in international affairs and the brokerage of power, the prophet also saw, and experienced before his death, that a radical change was occurring in this history of the kingdom of God and the divine purpose in the world.

II. Call and Commission (1:4–10)

Bibliography

Ahuviya, A. "I have set you for a prophet for the Gentiles." *BMik* 29, 98 (1983) 249–54 (Heb). **Bach, R.** "Bauen und Pflanzen." *Studien zur Theologie der alttestamentlichen Ueberlieferungen.* Ed. R. Rendtorff and K. Koch. Neukirchen: Neukirchener Verlag, 1961. 7–32. **Balzer, K.** "Considerations Concerning the Office and Calling of the Prophet." *HTR* 61 (1968) 567–81. **Berridge, J. M.** *Prophet, People.* 26–62. **Bewer, J. A.** "Historical Criticism of Jeremiah 1:4–19." *AJT* 6 (1902) 510–18. **Boer, P. A. H. de.** *Jeremia's Twijfel.* Leiden: Brill, 1957. **Brodie, L.** "Creative Writing: Missing Link in Biblical Research." *BTB* 8 (1978) 34–39. **Broughton, P. E.** "The Call of Jeremiah: The Relation of Deut. 18, 9–22 to the Call of Jeremiah." *AusBR* 6 (1958) 37–46. **Clements, R. E.** *Prophecy and Tradition.* Atlanta: John Knox, 1975. **Cornill, C. H.** "Die literarhistorische Methode und Jeremia Kap. 1." *ZAW* 27 (1907) 100–10. **Childs, B. S.** *The Book of Exodus.* OTL. Philadelphia: Westminster, 1974. 53–60 [Comparison with call of Moses]. **Dahlberg, B. T.** "The Typological Use of Jeremiah 1:4–9 in Matthew 16:13–34." *JBL* 94 (1975) 73–80. **Garcia Moreno, A.** "Vocación de Jeremiás." *EstBib* 27 (1968) 49–68. **Gilula, M.** "An Egyptian Parallel to Jeremiah 1:4–5." *VT* 17 (1967) 114. **Gouders, K.** "Siehe, ich lege meine Worte in deinem Mund. Die Berufung des propheten Jeremias (Jer. 1:4–10)." *Bib* 12 (1971) 162–86. ———. "Zu einer Theologia der prophetischen Berufung." *Bib* 12 (1971) 79–93. ———. *Die prophetischen Berufungsberichte Moses, Isaias, Jeremias und Ezechiel. Auslegung, Form- und Gattungsgeschichte, zu Theologie der Berufung.* Ph.D. diss., Bonn, 1971. **Gunneweg, A. H. J.** "Ordinationsformular oder Berufsbericht in Jeremia 1." FS Ernst Benz, *Glaube, Geist, Geschichte.* Ed. G. Mueller and W. Zeller. Leiden: Brill, 1967. 91–98. **Habel, N. C.** "The Form and Significance of the Call Narratives." *ZAW* 77 (1965) 297–323. **Henry, M.-L.** *Prophet und Tradition. Versuch einer Problemstellung.* BZAW 116. Berlin: de Gruyter, 1969. **Holladay, W. L.** "The Background of Jeremiah's Self-Understanding: Moses, Samuel, and Psalm 22." *JBL* 83 (1964) 153–64. ———. "Jeremiah and Moses, Further Observations." *JBL* 85 (1966) 17–27. ———. "Prototype and Copies: A New Approach to the Poetry-Prose Problem in the Book of Jeremiah." *JBL* 79 (1960) 351–67. **Jong, C. de.** *De Volken bij Jeremia. Hun plaats in zijn prediking en in het boek Jeremia.* 2 vols. Ph.D. diss., Theological Academy, Kampen, 1978. **Kilian, R.** "Die prophetischen Berufungsberichte." *Theologie im Wandel.* FS zum 150-jährigen Bestehen der Katholisch-Theologischen Fakultät an die Universität Tübingen. Tubinger Theologische Reihi 1. Munich: Wewel, 1967. 356–76. **Kraus, H.-J.** *Worship in Israel.* Richmond: Knox, 1966. 108–11. **Lewin, E. D.** "Arguing for Authority: A Rhetorical Study of Jer. 1:4–19 and 20:7–18." *JSOT* 32 (1985) 105–19. **Marks, J.** "The Imagery of Jeremiah's Call." *McCQ* 16 (1963) 29–38. **Mehl, L.** "A Call to Prophetic Ministry: Reflections on Jeremiah 1:4–10." *CurTM* 8 (1981) 151–55. **Michaud, H.** "La vocation du prophète des nations." In *Maqqél Shaqqédh, La Branche d'Amandier, Hommage à Wilhelm Vischer.* Montpellier: Causse, Graille, Castelnau, 1960. 157–64. **Mosis, R.** "Ich lege mein Wort in deinem Mund: Geistliche Impulse aus Jeremiah (1:4–10)." *FrancSt* 62 (1980) 89. **Mottu, H.** "Aux sources de notre vocation: Jérémie." *RTP* 114 (1982) 105–19. **Muilenburg, J.** "The 'Office' of the Prophet in Ancient Israel." In *The Bible in Modern Scholarship.* Papers Read at the 100th Meeting of the Society of Biblical Literature, Dec. 28–30, 1964. Ed. J. P. Hyatt. Nashville: Abingdon, 1965. 74–97. **Olmo Lete, G. del.** *La Vocación del lider en el antiguo Israel. Morfologia de los ralatos biblicos de vocación.* Ph.D. diss., Universidad Ponteficia Salamanca, 1973. **Overholt, T. W.** "Some Reflections on the Date of Jeremiah's Call." *CBQ* 33 (1971) 165–84. **Plöger, J. G.** "Zum Propheten berufen. Jer. 1:4–10 in Auslegung u. Verkundigung." In *Dynamik in Wort.* Stuttgart: Katholisches Bibelwerk, 1983. 103–18. **Reventlow, H. G.** *Liturgie,* 24–77. **Richter, W.** *Die sogenannten vorprophetischen Berufsberichte.*

FRLANT 101. Göttingen: Vandenhoeck & Ruprecht, 1970. **Ross, J. F.** "The Prophet as Yahweh's Messenger." In *Israel's Prophetic Heritage.* FS J. Muilenburg. Ed. B. W. Anderson and W. Harrelson. New York: Harper, 1962. 98–107. **Schreiner, J.** "Prophetsein im Untergang. Aus der Verkundigung des Propheten Jeremias: Jer. 1:4–19." *BibLeb* 7 (1966) 15–28. **Schultes, J. L.** "Gott nimmt ganz in seinem Dienst. Bibel Meditation zu Jer. 1:4–10." *BLit* 48 (1975) 180–83. **Stade, B.** "Emendationen—Jer. 1:4 (sic for 1:5)." *ZAW* 22 (1902) 328. **Vermeylen, J.** "La redaction de Jeremie 1:4–19." *ETL* 58 (1982) 252–78. **Vischer, W.** "Vocation of the Prophet of the Nations: An Exegesis of Jer. 1:4–10." *Int* 9 (1955) 310–17. **Voeglin, E.** *Order and History I: Israel and Revelation.* Baton Rouge: Louisiana State UP, 1956. 467–70. **Vogels, W.** "Les recits de vocation des prophètes." *NRT* 95 (1973) 3–24. **Vogt, E.** "Vocatio Jeremiae." *VD* 42 (1964) 241–51. **Weippert, H.** *Die Prosareden des Jeremiabuches.* BZAW 132. Berlin: de Gruyter, 1973. 193–99. **Zimmerli, W.** *Ezekiel I.* Hermeneia. Philadelphia: Fortress, 1979. 97–100.

Translation

[4]*And the LORD's word came to me:*[a] [5]*"Before I formed*[a] *you in the belly, I knew you; before you came forth from the womb, I set you aside. I appointed you to be a prophet to the nations."*

[6]*But I said, "Oh master, LORD! Look, I don't know how to speak, because I'm only a youth."*[a]

[7]*But the LORD said to me, "Don't say* '[a]*I'm only a youth,' because wherever*[b] *I send you, you will go, and whatever I command you, you will speak.* [8]*Don't be afraid of them, because I am with you to look after you. It is the LORD's word!"*

[9]*And the LORD stretched out his hand*[a] *and touched*[b] *my mouth. Then the LORD said to me, "Look, I have put my words in your mouth.* [10]*See! This very day, I have given you authority over the nations and over the kingdoms, to pluck out and to pull down,* [a]*to destroy and to demolish,*[a] *to build and to plant."*

Notes

4.a. LXX πρὸς αὐτόν, "to him," implies a Heb. אליו. But the first person form of the MT אלי is preferable, as indicated by the context (vv 6, 7).

5.a. MT K אצרך < יצר, qal "formed you." Q אצורך < צור may also mean "formed you." M. Dahood (*Psalms 51–100*, AB 17 [Garden City, NY: Doubleday, 1966] 225–26) suggests a meaning like "summon" in Ps 77:3. But perhaps there is an intentional play on the meanings "form" and "summon" as in Isa 49:1, 5. See also the related noun צרה in 4:31 which Holladay (I, 20) suggests should be translated "beckon."

6.a. נער may mean "a child, a boy, or a youth."

7.a. A few MSS of LXX and Syr add "for."

7.b. Or, perhaps, "to whomever" (על and אל are frequently interchanged in Jeremiah).

9.a. LXX adds πρός με, "to me."

9.b. Reading וינע, qal "touched," for MT's hiph "caused to touch," as indicated by LXX and Vg.

10.a-a. MT ולהאביד ולהרוס, "to destroy and to demolish," are often thought to be additions to the text influenced by 18:7, 9. See Volz, Rudolph, and Holladay (I, 21). Tg, Syr, and Vg follow MT. LXX has five verbs in this sentence instead of the six of MT (two of three in 18:7 and four of six in 31:28) LXX 38:28. See Janzen, *Text of Jeremiah*, 35. This variation in the versions is not enough to change MT.

Form/Structure/Setting

The prophet's vocation is described in this short narrative; the form employed is that of a dialogue between the Lord and Jeremiah, written in the manner of a first-person account of the experience. As such, the passage has numerous similarities to other prophetic narratives of vocation (e.g., Isa 6:1–13; Ezek 1–3), and the experience of vocation as it is described here has parallels to other prophetic experiences (notably that of Samuel). Consequently, the passage has been studied extensively both from a strictly form-critical perspective (see, e.g., N. Habel and K. Gouders) and from various other literary perspectives (e.g., G. del Olmo Lete, A. Garcia Moreno, J. Vermeylen, and R. P. Carroll, *From Chaos to Covenant*, 31–58).

The form-critical approach, in the narrow sense, is not entirely satisfactory with respect to the call narrative. For while a general *Gattung* of call narratives may be posited, with several common characteristics, the actual differences between the three most fundamental call narratives in prophetic books (Isaiah, Jeremiah, Ezekiel) undermine any confidence that there was a clearly delineated literary type. And further, insofar as the narratives may be taken as reflecting genuine religious experience, the commonality of themes in the narratives may reflect more the commonality of experience than the existence of a distinctive literary type. (In Habel's analysis [*ZAW* 77 (1965) 297–323], however, the call narratives are seen more as the product of theological reflection than autobiographical recollection; if such were the case, and if there were indeed a firm *Gattung* of call narrative, one might expect a much greater degree of similarity in literary structure, sequence, and content than is actually the case in the few call narratives that have survived.)

Thus, appropriate perspectives are required for the interpretation of the substance of this narrative and for understanding the reason for its location at this point in the collection of Jeremiah's oracles. First, it is not unreasonable that any collection of oracles of a prophetic nature would be prefaced by an account of the vocation of the person through whom they were delivered. It is a natural, though not necessary, way of opening the substance of a prophetic book. It is natural in that it provides a perspective from which to read the oracles that follow. It is not in theory necessary, if only because so many of the prophetic books do not provide any detailed account of vocation (e.g., Joel, Obadiah, Micah). Second, it is a distinctive feature of Jeremiah's call narrative (in contrast to those of Isaiah and Ezekiel) that very little circumstantial detail is given; whereas Isaiah was in the temple and Ezekiel by the Chebar Canal, we do not know of the circumstances surrounding Jeremiah's call. The purpose, in other words, is not simply biographical; if the author or editor had intended to provide primarily information about the religious experience and circumstances of the prophet, a more detailed account would be expected. It is therefore probable that the insertion of the call narrative at the beginning of the collection of oracles had other purposes. It established the authority of the prophet; he was not simply declaring his own opinions but was declaring the divine word, in both its destructive and constructive dimensions. Closely related to the first purpose, the call narrative establishes the authenticity of Jeremiah's oracles, in contrast to those of the false prophets who are so frequently denounced in the prophetic ministry that follows.

Whether the call narrative was inserted at the beginning of the collection of oracles and related materials at a final stage in the preparation of the book or at an earlier point in the compilation of the smaller collections that comprise the whole cannot be known with certainty. Schmidt has argued that the narrative comes from an editor in the time of the exile, claiming that the catastrophe of

586 B.C. is presupposed in its substance (*ThV* 13 (1975/76) 182–209). But it is equally possible that the call narrative stems from the time of the scroll compiled in 605 B.C. (see Jer 36). In that initial compilation of oracles, it would have been appropriate to preface the collection with an account of the call and to establish the nature of the message (v 10) which was called into question by the king (36:29). It is therefore probable, though not certain, that the literary location of the call narrative reflects the period 605 B.C. And if there is any merit in viewing 1:1–25:13 as an initial collection of oracles, then the introductory call narrative (1:4–10) may balance the concluding and summary statements pertaining to the collection (25:1–13).

There is little reason to doubt the authenticity of the substance of the call narrative. Although written down some twenty years after the call (according to the hypothesis summarized above), it reflects, no doubt, the prophet's recollection of the profound spiritual experience that changed the course of his life. It is thin on historical detail, but eloquent in terms of the spiritual struggle which it conveys. Although written essentially in prose, the elements of poetry typical of the divine oracle can still be perceived in the account of the Lord's word to Jeremiah (see vv 5, 7, 10).

It is commonly claimed that the call narrative has been given its present form by a Deuteronomic author or editor (see E. W. Nicholson, *Preaching to the Exiles*, 114–15, and *Jeremiah 1–25*, 23–26; R. P. Carroll, *From Chaos to Covenant*, 44–46). To take only one of several items of evidence for such a proposal, it is noted that God's promise to put his words in Jeremiah's mouth (v 9) is strikingly similar to the words concerning the coming prophet in Deut 18:18. But this and other similar items to the Deuteronomic tradition (e.g., the youthfulness of Jeremiah and that of the prophet Samuel, 1 Sam 2:18) do not necessarily establish Deuteronomic authorship or editorial revision. The real issue concerns the fundamental notion of prophecy in Israel, and its source. One of the clearest statements of the nature of prophecy in Israel is that contained in Deut 18:15–22, and one may assume that such a statement had influenced the nature and practice of prophecy in a fundamental manner. Furthermore, however one interprets the origin and nature of Deuteronomy, it is clear that the book had something of a renaissance in Judah during the early part of Jeremiah's ministry (see further Craigie, *The Book of Deuteronomy*, 46–49). One would assume that Jeremiah was familiar with the substance of the book, and it might also be assumed that his self-understanding as a prophet was influenced by such passages as Deut 18:15–22 and 34:10–12. Thus, the occurrence of Deuteronomic-like material in 1:4–10 and elsewhere in Jeremiah, while it cannot be denied, poses for the interpreter several possibilities, not the least of which is that the prophet himself was profoundly influenced by the substance of Deuteronomy. And with respect to 1:4–10, it is far from clear that the passage has any Deuteronomic origin or editing (though the presence of Deuteronomic influence elsewhere in Jeremiah is by no means to be denied).

Comment

4 The call narrative begins with a familiar statement: "the LORD's word came to me" (1:4). Elsewhere in the book, this expression prefaces the declaration of the prophetic oracle (e.g., 2:1), but here it introduces not an oracle but an experience.

And whereas the oracle, on receipt, would be publicly declared, the narrative beginning here is a description of a private event. As in the general exercise of prophetic office, a direct encounter with God is stated to have taken place; but whereas normally that encounter involved the receipt of God's word for transmission to God's people, in this instance dialogue occurs. For in this narrative, Jeremiah is not the messenger but the one to whom the message is addressed. And the narrative is essentially in prose form, rather than the poetic form common to oracles, because a description of encounter and dialogue is presented. Though the call is described in terms suggesting a straightforward conversation between God and Jeremiah, one may suppose that the dialogue form is merely a vehicle for giving expression to the profoundly religious experience of vocation.

The account of the vocation is extremely concise, but it conveys nevertheless the dynamics of the dialogue and the struggle of the prophet. Jeremiah is told first of all that before he was born, indeed before he was conceived, he had been set aside for the role of prophet. The language is similar to that in the "Hymn to Wisdom" (especially Prov 8:22–30), but the similarity may be incidental; Brodie has proposed an interrelationship (*BTB* 8 [1978] 34–39), though on rather tenuous grounds. Although the verse may imply some form of theological determinism or predestination, that is hardly its purpose. From one perspective, the initial divine words to Jeremiah seem to present him with a *fait accompli:* he was set aside before he was born. Yet, in the dynamics of the dialogue, the opening words present Jeremiah with an overwhelming sense of God's purpose, but they still require a response from him and subsequent acts of obedience. In fact, despite the deterministic tone of the opening statement, the undertones throughout the narrative are those of human freedom and the capacity to respond to the divine call. Yet the response, once it is freely and positively given, will be immensely strengthened by this opening statement of the dialogue; the call to be a prophet was not simply the consequence of divine whim but the expression of firm purpose. And although in freedom Jeremiah could have resisted the call, it is equally clear that he could only discover the meaning of his birth and mortal existence in responding to the call.

6–8   Not unreasonably, Jeremiah attempted initially to step politely away from the overwhelming announcement of his God. He posed two reasonable excuses, both, he must have thought, offering sufficient grounds for turning aside the divine call. First, he didn't know how to speak (or perhaps, what to say); second, he was clearly too young for the task. Since he had been told that he was to be a "prophet to the nations" (v 5; see also v 10), his excuses were in fact sound reasons for refusal. With respect to subject matter, he had no particular message at that point in his life for his own nation, much less other nations. And the second excuse was closely related: How could such a young person perform such a formidable task? (We do not know exactly what age Jeremiah was at the time; see note 1:6.a. We may reasonably suppose he was in his late teens or early twenties.)

The precise nature of the office to which he was called, namely to be "a prophet to the nations," has been the source of much discussion. From one perspective (in the light of the rest of the book), he was to become a "prophet to Judah," and in a broader sense to Israel as a whole (even though, in his time, the northern state no longer survived). But the expression "prophet to the nations" need not imply any direct address of prophetic oracles to foreign nations as such; rather, the substance of the prophetic oracles would address not only the nation of Judah, but also other foreign nations, for all had a role to play within the divine purpose. Thus, the reference to "nations" does not refer only to foreign nations (e.g., nations from the north, as argued by de Jong in volume 1 of his *De Volken bij Jeremia*), but includes Judah and Israel (some of Israel's territory had been regained from Assyria during the early part of Josiah's reign). The call, in other words, was to be a prophet in an international setting; though the primary message was to Judah, its implications involved no less Assyria, Babylon, Egypt, and other states. It may be that this part of the call narrative presupposes all the oracles that compose the Book of Jeremiah, including the "foreign nation" oracles (Jer 46–51); but it is equally possible that the primary reference may be to the initial collection (1:1–25:13), which clearly has an international component (cf. 36:29).

Jeremiah's two objections were overruled. If he were worried about the substance of his message on the basis of lack of experience, he need have had no concern, for he would be told what to say at the appropriate time (v 7). And if his fears were based on his youthfulness, he could be assured of God's protection (v 8), although the assurance has an ominous tone to it. The assurance does not say that there will be no grounds for fear, only that protection will be provided. Thus, the excuses of Jeremiah were overruled, as were the objections of the youthful Moses in his encounter with vocation in an earlier period (Exod 3:11–4:12).

9 The narrative then states that the Lord stretched out his hand and touched Jeremiah's mouth; although up to this point the call narrative has been presented strictly as dialogue, these words may indicate a visionary quality to the experience of vocation. In Isaiah's visionary experience of vocation, his lips were touched with a burning coal as a symbol of cleansing (Isa 6:6–7). In this context, however, the divine touch does not symbolize cleansing but rather the imparting of the divine word: "Look, I have put my words in your mouth" (v 9). As Ezekiel, in his visionary experience, ate the scroll (3:1–3) and thus made the divine word a part of his very being, so too the divine word becomes a part of Jeremiah's being. This divine act, the implanting of the prophetic word, renders useless Jeremiah's claimed incapacity to speak.

10 Finally, a statement is made concerning the authority of Jeremiah's prophetic ministry to the nations. The authority in part is simply a consequence of the divine origin of the message, but it is particularly crucial that the authority be recognized, given the negative nature of much of the message he is to deliver. Of the six verbs used in v 10b, four are negative and destructive and only two are positive and constructive. Immediately, the unpleasant nature of the new prophet's task becomes clear; it is one thing simply to declare a prophetic word, but when most of that word is negative and destructive, it is bound to elicit a hostile response. These themes of destruction and construction recur frequently throughout the remainder of the book (see further 12:14–17; 18:7–9; 24:6 in this volume of the commentary); here in the vocation, they set down the lines and character of the prophetic ministry that will follow.

Curiously, we are not provided with an account of Jeremiah's response and obedience to the divine call, as we are in Isaiah (6:8). In part, the reason is to be found in the purpose of the call narrative; it is not intended to be a full account but only to establish the authority and authenticity of the ministry that is to follow. In another sense, a description of Jeremiah's response is unnecessary, for the entire substance of his book provides eloquent testimony to the young man's affirmative response.

Explanation

In this brief account of Jeremiah's vocation, one can find insight into one in a long series of divine vocations and responses: Moses, Samuel, Isaiah, Ezekiel, Hosea, Amos, to name only a few. And the tradition of call and response stretches beyond the period of the OT; indeed, when Paul later writes of his experience of vocation, he employs language that appears to have been directly influenced by the vocation of Jeremiah (Gal 1:15–16). In all these accounts, despite their variety, the initiative is taken by God; the response is invited from human beings. And in that sequence of divine initiative and human response one can find an insight into the manner in which God works in his world.

In the expression of God's will for his people, no less than his purposes for the world as a whole, he employs the instrumentality of human servants and prophets to make himself known to his people. Jeremiah, more than most, was aware of the fragility and incompetence of the human instrument. He was too young for such a task, he thought, though he could scarcely have known that he would be an old and experienced man before his task was complete! Yet the mystery of the divine *modus operandi* was that it expressed divine strength through the weak vessel of a human servant. The message of God, transmitted through a human messenger, did not overwhelm the intended audience but presented those who heard it with a choice and an opportunity to respond. And since human beings rarely like to be faced with the truth and concomitant demand for choice and decision, the task of the divine messenger was rarely a pleasant one.

But the very essence of the call narrative is to be found in the authority given to the one who responded positively to the vocation (v 10). Later, Jesus was to give his disciples authority (Matt 16:13–19), as described in a passage that may well have been influenced by Jeremiah (see Dahlberg, *JBL* 94 [1975] 73–80). The messenger of God speaks with the authority of God, not simply with the force of his own personality. That authority, of course, is rarely recognized by those to whom the authoritative word is addressed, but it is there all the same. And if the proclamation of the authoritative word often leaves the messenger with a sense of frustration and failure, that messenger has nevertheless been faithful in the appointed task.

III. An Account of Two Visions (1:11–19)

Bibliography

Berridge, J. M. *Prophet, People.* 63–201. **Bode, E. L.** "The Seething Cauldron—Jer. 1:13." *TBT* 42 (1969) 898–903. **Cazelles, H.** "Zephaniah, Jeremiah and the Scythians in Palestine." In *A Prophet to the Nations, Essays in Jeremiah Studies.* Ed. L. G. Perdue and B. Kovacs. Winona Lake, IN: Eisenbrauns, 1984. 129–49. [ET of "Sophonie, Jeremie, et les Sythes en Palestine." *RB* 74 (1967) 24–44.] **Childs, B. S.** "The Enemy from the North and the Chaos Tradition." *JBL* 78 (1959) 187–98. **Cogan, M.** "Sentencing at the Gate in Jeremiah 1:15–16." *Gratz College Annual* 1 (1972) 3–6. **Harris, S. L.** "The Second Vision of Jeremiah: Jer. 1:13–15." *JBL* 102 (1983) 281–82. **Horst, F.** "Die Visionsschilderungen der alttestamentlichen Propheten." *EvT* 20 (1960) 193–205. **Irwin, W. A.** "The Face of the Pot, Jeremiah 1:13b." *AJSL* 47 (1930–31) 288–89. **Jungling, J.-W.** "Ich mache dich zu einer ehernen Mauer. Literarkritische Ueberlegungen zum Verhaltnis von Jer. 1:18–19 zu Jer. 15:20–21." *Bib* 54 (1973) 1–24. **Lauha, A.** *Zaphon: der Norden und die Nordvölker im Alten Testament.* AASF 49. Helsinki: Standerhuset, 1943. **Lindblom, J.** "Der Kessel in Jer i, 12f." *ZAW* 68 (1956) 223–24. **Long, B. O.** "Reports of Visions among the Prophets." *JBL* 95 (1976) 353–65. **Loretz, O.** "Die Spruche Jeremias in Jer. 1.17–9.25." *UF* 2 (1970) 109–30. **Marx, A.** "A propos des doublets du livre Jérémie. Réflexions sur la formation d'un livre prophétique." In *Prophecy.* Ed. J. A. Emerton. BZAW 150. Berlin: de Gruyter, 1980. 106–20. **Niditch, S.** *The Symbolic Vision in Biblical Tradition.* HSM 30. Chico, CA: Scholars, 1983. 41–52. **Reventlow, H. G.** *Liturgie.* 77–87. **Sauer, G.** "Mandelzweig und Kessel in Jer. 1:11ff." *ZAW* 78 (1966) 56–61. **Talmon, S.** "An Apparently Redundant MT Reading—Jeremiah 1:18." *Textus* 8 (1973) 160–63. [Vaggione, R. P. "Over All Asia? The Extent of the Scythian Domination in Herodotus." *JBL* 92 (1973)523–30.] ———. "Scythians." IDBSup. 797–98. **Williams, W. G.** "Jeremiah's Vision of the Almond Rod." In *A Stubborn Faith:* FS W. A. Irwin. Ed. E. C. Hobbs. Dallas: Southern Methodist University, 1956. 90–99. **Wood, P. S.** "Jeremiah's Figure of the Almond Rod." *JBL* 61 (1942) 99–103. **Zimmerli, W.** "Visionary Experience in Jeremiah." In *Israel's Prophetic Tradition:* FS P. R. Ackroyd. Ed. R. J. Coggins. Cambridge: Cambridge UP, 1982. 95–118.

Translation

[11]*And the LORD's word came to me: "What do you see, Jeremiah?"[a] And I said, "I see a branch of an almond tree."*

[12]*And the LORD said to me, "You have seen correctly, for I am watching my word, to carry it out."*

[13]*And the LORD's word came to me a second time: "What do you see?"[a]*
And I said, "I see a pot[b] being boiled, with its top turned away from the north."

[14]*And the LORD said to me, "Disaster shall blow down[a] from the north upon all the land's inhabitants. [15]For look, I am summoning all the clans[a] and kingdoms of the north—it is the LORD's word!*

'They will come and each will set up his throne
by the access to the gates of Jerusalem;
and against all her walls round about,
and against all the cities of Judah.'

[16]*And I will declare my complaints against them,[a] concerning all their evil in forsaking me, in making burnt offerings to foreign gods, and in worshiping the products[b] of their*

own hands. [17]*But as for you, brace yourself like a man!*[a] *Stand up and tell them every-thing that I am commanding you.*[b] *Don't be terrified because of their presence, or else I may terrify you in their presence.* [18]*But today I have made you a fortified city, an iron pillar,*[a] *a bronze wall*[b] [c]*against the whole land, against the kings of Judah*[c] *and*[d] *its princes,* [e]*against priests and the people of the land.* [19]*And they will fight against you, but will not prevail over you, for I am with you to deliver you"—it is the LORD's word!*

Notes

11.a. LXX lacks "Jeremiah." Read MT.

13.a. LXX and MT agree in omitting "Jeremiah," which appeared in MT. See note 11.a. above. But one MS of C inserts "Jeremiah" to parallel 11.a.

13.b. MT סיר has two meanings (BDB, 696): "a pot" when fem or masc, but "a kindled thorn(bush)" when masc (see Eccl 7:6 and others). See S. L. Harris. Here the word is apparently masc, as indicated by the following pronom suff. LXX λέβητα reads "pot."

14.a. MT תפתח (niph), "be let loose." But the translation in LXX suggests a Heb. form derived from נפח (which is used in the previous verse), probably תפח, "blow." Either reading makes sense.

15.a. MT משפחות ממלכות, "tribes of the kingdoms." LXX has only τὰς βασιλείας, "the kingdom." Janzen (*Text of Jeremiah*, 10) calls the two Heb. words parallel variants. Read MT with "and" between.

16.a. MT אותם, "them," with the sign of the acc. Many MSS read אתם, "with them," the pronoun with prep. The issue is whether a prep is needed in this usage as in 39:5 and 52:19, or whether only the sign of the acc will do as in 4:12 and 12:1.

16.b. MT is pl. Many MSS, Vg, and Syr favor a sg.

17.a. Lit., "Gird up your loins."

17.b. MT אנכי אצוך MT points the verb as piel impf, which makes the pronoun redundant. Some MSS read אנכי מצוך, "I am commanding you." The ptcp would require the pronoun (see Syr, Tg, and Vg *praecipio*, a present tense that may translate the ptcp). Read the variant.

18.a. Or perhaps "iron bolt." The phrase is missing in LXX but fits the context admirably and should be retained as an original part of the text. See Talmon, *Textus* 8 (1973) 160–63.

18.b. The sg const form is read (חמת), with good MS support (cf. LXX).

18.c-c. MT על כל הארץ למלכי יהודה, "against all the land of the kings of Judah." LXX πασι τοῖς βασιλεῦσιν Ἰούδα, "to the kings of Judah." This phrase with על, "against," comes between two groups with ל The latter is ambiguous. Before the phrase with על, it means "to" or "into," or does not need to be translated at all. Afterward, it continues the meaning "against." Read MT.

18.d. MT omits "and." Add it with some MSS, LXX, and Syr.

18.e. Some MSS and Syr add "and." LXX omits the entire phrase. A comma is sufficient to render MT.

Form/Structure/Setting

The account of Jeremiah's call (1:4–10) is now supplemented by a further narrative in which there are described two visions and a further charge pertaining to the call. In the editorial formation of the book, the entire passage (vv 4–19) forms a whole, in which the different dimensions of the vocation are elaborated. But the component parts of the chapter, and of vv 11–19 in particular, were in all probability drawn from different periods in the prophet's early ministry.

The passage begins with an account of two visions, the first concerning the almond branch (vv 11–12), the second being the vision of the boiling pot (vv 13–15). The experiences of vocation that are described in Isaiah and Ezekiel lead one to expect visions to be associated with a prophetic call. But with respect to Jeremiah's call, there is no reason to suppose that the two visions described here were contemporaneous with the initial experience of vocation. The visions themselves appear to be quite distinct and may have been separated in the prophet's experience by the passage of time (as may be implied by the expression "a second time" in v 13). And indeed both visions may have occurred at a time later than that described in 1:4–10. They are nevertheless appropriately placed after the narrative in 1:4–10 in the editorial arrangement of the book. The call narrative continues a retrospective account of the vocation from the vantage point of a later period in the prophet's ministry; from that same later perspective, the account of two visionary experiences has been added, appropriately supplementing the initial experience. From an editorial perspective, the visions supplement the call and provide the whole picture that the reader requires to understand the chapters that follow. From the perspective of prophetic experience, one may perhaps perceive how the prophet's initial awareness of vocation and purpose was deepened and sharpened by these later visionary experiences. Having proposed that the visions postdate the vocation, it is nevertheless difficult, if not impossible, to date the visions to a particular period in the prophet's life. The first vision, some have proposed, may presuppose a period of ministry followed by disappointment, to which the vision offers encouragement. And the second vision might be dated precisely if the enemy from the north could be identified accurately. But neither of these lines of inquiry lead to assured results; see further the *Comment* that follows. It is safer simply to recognize that vocation, while its starting point can be identified sometimes in a particular experience, is nevertheless a continuing theme in ministry; an initial call may subsequently be strengthened in the course of the ministry by further understanding and further clarification of the divine purpose.

The last part of the passage (vv 16–19) resumes the themes of the call narrative; indeed 1:4–10 and 1:16–19 may originally have formed a single call narrative, which has subsequently been split by the insertion of the visionary accounts (1:11–15). If such were the case, then the original narrative may have been abbreviated, for v 16 seems to presuppose a reference to Judah (Israel), whereas v 10 is addressed to the nations as a whole. But whether or not vv 16–19 originally belonged with 1:4–10, the verses certainly supplement the earlier call narrative, containing an account of the divine charge to the prophet and a renewed promise of protection. A number of scholars have noted the similarity in language between 1:18–19 and 15:20 (see particularly the studies of H. W. Jungling, *Bib* 54 [1973] 1–24; A. Marx, "A propos des doublets," 106–20), but the interpretation of the parallel language is far from clear. It may be a consequence of the repetition of a similar theme or of similar circumstances (Marx), or it may be that the literary character of the collection can be determined by fixing the literary sequence of the parallel passages, and thus postulating the initial and developed use of the language (Jungling). It is certainly striking, as Jungling notes, that the recurrence of the language appears in one of Jeremiah's so-called confessions, with which 1:4–19 naturally has close affinities, given its association with Jeremiah's initial religious experience. Without being able to determine precisely the relationship between 1:18–19 and 15:20, the explanation is most likely to be found in experiential, rather than strictly literary, terms. In the prophet's later spiritual struggles and in his attempt to cope with the continuing reality of vocation, the words of God addressed to him at the beginning of his ministry return to haunt him, yet also to encourage him in the continuation of his task.

Comment

11–12 *The first vision.* The vision of the branch of an almond tree is slender
in substance, but significant in meaning. What the prophet sees is simply a branch
of an almond tree; presumably the branch was a living limb on a flourishing tree.
The prophet is asked what it is that he sees; after responding, he is given a divine
word that is at first rather perplexing: "I am watching my word, to carry it out." In
the interpretation of the vision and the accompanying oracle, it is necessary first
of all to recognize the Hebrew word play, which cannot be captured in translation.
In response to the initial question, Jeremiah says he sees a *shaqed* (almond); God
responds that he is *shoqed* (watching). In other words, the word play indicates that
the tree and the divine watching are intimately interrelated.

The visionary account is so concise and short in detail that a degree of imagination must be employed in seeking to grasp the full significance of the vision
and its accompanying word. Either, we may suppose that the prophet saw a
branch in bud: soon the beautiful almond blossom would break forth from the
bud in splendid flower. Or, it is possible that the branch was already in flower, an
incontestable sign of the advent of spring. In the first instance, the vision would
indicate to Jeremiah that the divine word he was to proclaim was like the blossom
in bud: it was about to break forth. In the second instance, the proclamation of
the word was itself a sign of the advent of God's action in bringing about the
substance of the prophetic word. In both approaches, there is a sense of certainty
and inevitability; the prophetic word declared by Jeremiah would necessarily be
fulfilled.

The substance of the vision and its interpretive word is too general to enable it
to be related to a particular point in the prophet's ministry. Such a visionary experience would be significant at the very beginning of the prophet's ministry, in
response to the reluctant prophet's hesitancy about proclaiming a word concerning the substance of which he had no guarantee of fulfillment. But equally,
the vision could have come after several years of the early prophetic ministry,
when Jeremiah must have wondered from time to time about the authenticity of
the word he proclaimed.

The vision of the almond tree, as is commonly the case with such visionary
experiences, was rooted no doubt in the prophet's life in Anathoth. As Thompson (153) has noted, to this day almond trees grow and flourish in the vicinity of
the village of ʿAnata as no doubt was also the case in the prophet's time. And the
almond tree (*prunus dulcis*) was the first to bloom in spring, sometimes as early as
January, making it a particularly striking tree among the various species that grew
and flowered in Judah in Jeremiah's time (for an illustration, see *IDB*, III, 1587).

13–15 *The second vision.* To envisage the second scene that met Jeremiah's eyes,
one must imagine an open fire, with a cooking pot resting on its coals or logs. Perhaps
because of the unevenness of the base, the pot was tipped to one side; the tipped
pot faced towards the south. The wind, blowing from the north, fanned the embers
into fierce flame, causing the pot to boil, so that its liquid contents overflowed
and trickled in a southerly direction.

As the prophet described the scene that met his eyes in the vision, a common
enough domestic scene, he was again given a divine word that verbalized the
substance of the vision. Disaster, like a strong north wind, would blow upon Judah;

these winds of war would bring trouble to the very gates of Jerusalem, emptying the city of part of its inhabitants.

The identification of the foe from the north is not specified in the divine word. Working on the assumption that the oracle could be dated to the beginning of the prophet's ministry, it used to be assumed that the northern foe was a reference to the Scythians, a marauding people from the steep country of what is now southern Russia; such a specific reference is most unlikely (cf. Vaggione, *JBL* 92 [1973] 523–30). The plural reference in v 15 ("clans" and "kingdoms") makes it likely, if the prophetic word was indeed from the early ministry, that various or many enemies were envisaged; during the early period of Jeremiah's ministry, international affairs to the north were characterized by numerous military movements, of which that of the Scythians was merely one (see M. Noth, *The History of Israel*, 270). Nevertheless, by the time that the account of the vision had been incorporated into the opening chapter of the book, the northern enemy would have been identified clearly with Babylon, whose armies were later to fulfill the disaster anticipated in v 15b.

16–19 *The prophetic charge.* The word *them* in v 16 has no immediate antecedent (grammatically) in the literary context, though it would appear to refer to the citizens of Judah as a whole (the actual antecedent may have been contained in a part of the original passage omitted in the editorial process of collection). The substance of the verse indicates some of the themes of the prophet's later preaching; he would declare God's complaints against the chosen people, based on their forsaking of the true faith, their adoption of foreign religious practices, and their adulation of homemade idols.

Jeremiah is then given his charge and instructed to carry out his ministry; in the most basic terms, it is to "tell them everything that I command you" (v 17), which in turn is a reiteration of the basic call (1:7). There then follows a further reiteration: the command not to be afraid and the promise of protection (1:8) are restated, though in longer and more elaborate form (1:17–19). Employing a variety of metaphors, the Lord informs Jeremiah that he will have the strength of a fortified city, an iron pillar, or a bronze wall; perhaps ironically, the guarantee of strength and protection carries with it the certainty of attack. For all that, the language contrasts with that of the word accompanying the second vision. Jerusalem, that impregnable fortress that had stood for so many centuries, would have an army encamped at its gates and would succumb (v 15); Jeremiah, who was to be as a fortified city, would survive all attacks, though there were to be occasions in his future life when that survival seemed severely in doubt. Finally, his launching into the ministry of the prophet was given a firm foundation: "I am with you to deliver you" (v 19).

Explanation

With its elaboration of the preceding account of the call (1:4–10), this passage illuminates still further the dimensions of vocation. First, there is the call, which Jeremiah was unable to resist. Now we are provided with an account of two visions, assuring the prophet of the authenticity of his mission, despite any doubts he may have entertained, and of the awesome and judgmental substance of his message. Finally he is told to get on with the task, to proclaim the divine word and be fearless in the face of the opposition that his message was bound to evoke.

With the vocation and response now complete, Jeremiah found himself in a virtually impossible position. On the one hand, he was assigned to a task that no right-thinking person would desire to have, given its enormous dimensions and the inevitably negative response to its undertaking. On the other hand, as God's prophet, he had been given a task that was not only an honor but also an extraordinary responsibility. Moses Maimonides, the great Jewish scholar of the twelfth century A.D., grasped powerfully the essence of the dilemma:

> Thus, we find prophets that did not leave off
> speaking to the people until they were slain;
> it is this divine influence that moves them,
> that does not allow them to rest in any way,
> though they might bring upon themselves great
> evils by their action. Thus, when Jeremiah was
> despised, like other teachers and scholars of his
> age, he could not, though he desired it, withhold
> his prophecy or cease from reminding the people
> of the truths which they rejected. (*The Guide for the Perplexed,* chap. xxxvii)

We begin to perceive that while vocation comes at the beginning of a ministry, just as it comes at the beginning of the book, it is also something that continues and pervades the entire ministry. Jeremiah's vocation not only set him on the path of the prophet but continued to be with him throughout his ministry. At every experience of hardship, he would recall this occasion that had set him on the path; in one sense, it would be a sorrowful remembrance, as he perceived the grief it had brought, but in another sense it would be a source of encouragement, as he recalled the promise and protection offered at the very beginning of this new juncture in life.

The account of the vocation in Jer 1 has set the stage for reading with understanding the chapters of the book that follow. But now that the stage has been set, the reader must be careful not to forget this account of vocation, for its memory will return to haunt the prophet in later years (and subsequent chapters). The memory will emerge openly in the "Confessions" that ensue from later trials, but still its shadow is felt in the last years of the prophet's life as a refugee in Egypt, cut off from the land in which the call came.

IV. Jeremiah's Early Oracles (2:1–6:30)

Bibliography

Albertz, R. "Jer 2–6 und die Fruhzeitverkundigung Jeremias." *ZAW* 98 (1982) 20–47. **Carroll, R. P.** *From Chaos to Covenant.* 59–83. **Hall, G. H.** *The Marriage of Imagery of Jeremiah 2 and 3: A Study of Antecedents and Innovations in a Prophetic Metaphor.* Ph.D diss., Union Theological Seminary, 1980. **Holladay, W. L.** "The Identification of the Two Scrolls of Jeremiah." *VT* 30 (1980) 452–67. ———. *The Architecture of Jeremiah 1–20.* 30–101. **Paterson, R. M.** "Repentance or Judgment: The Construction and Purpose of Jer. 2–6." *ExpTim* 96 (1984–85) 199–203. **Thiel, W.** *Die deuteronomistische Radaktion des Buches Jeremia.* Ph.D. diss., Humboldt-Universitat, Berlin, 1970.

Chaps. 2–6 form a relatively coherent literary unit in the larger collection of materials that comprise the Book of Jeremiah; it is possible that at an early stage in the development of the book, this collection of prophetic oracles was brought together as a kind of summary of the prophet's early ministry.

With respect to style, almost all of these chapters are poetic in form; their subject matter is Type A material, namely prophetic oracles coming from the prophet Jeremiah. There are only a few short prose passages in this literary unit, some of which have an autobiographical character, and some of which may provide clues to the process of redaction; the details are examined in the commentary that follows.

The principal difficulty of interpreting these chapters as a whole lies in the problem of determining the boundaries of the individual oracles that make up the collection. In some cases, clues are provided by the conventional oracular *formulae* (e.g., 2:1 and 2:4), but in other cases, the prophetic oracles appear simply to be set alongside each other, with no clear introductory *formulae*. In the analysis of the chapters and the delineation of the component oracles, there is inevitably a degree of subjectivity involved, particularly as the logic of relationship between the oracles includes commonality of theme. When two or three oracles developing a similar theme are set side by side, it is inevitable not only that the boundaries between them will be difficult to determine but also that they may appear to have a greater degree of unity than is actually the case.

Some scholars have proposed that the collection of oracles in Jer 2–6 is to be related to the description of two scrolls given in Jer 36. Thus Holladay (*VT* 30 [1980] 452–67) attempts to identify large portions of 2–6 (and subsequent chapters) with the substance of the two scrolls later dictated by the prophet to Baruch. While the details of his analysis (and the distinctions between what was contained in the first scroll and what was added to the second) must inevitably remain uncertain, given the nature of the evidence, the general perspective is doubtless correct. Thus Jer 36 provides some further insight into the manner in which a collection such as 2–6 came into being; its component parts were originally delivered separately but were subsequently brought together into an ordered collection of the prophet's sayings. The particular occasions and settings in which each of the prophetic oracles was originally delivered can rarely be determined with any certainty. Sometimes the form and substance of an oracle may provide clues, but they are at best elusive clues. To some extent, the inability to determine the original setting may not matter; it is clear from Jer 36 that the reading of the scroll containing collected oracles conveyed as powerfully their inner meaning as did the original proclamation.

While there are a number of common themes linking together the literary unit as a whole, the collection of oracles can be subdivided into three smaller collections, each mini-collection being linked to the following collection by a progressive logic and inner movement: (i) the indictment of Judah for evil (2); (ii) the prophetic plea for repentance (3:1–4:4); and (iii) the declaration of divine judgment (4:5–6:30). Each of these three units is in turn a collection of shorter oracles, placed side by side, and developing from different perspectives the central themes of the subunit.

The description of 2–6 as Jeremiah's "early oracles" can be used only with caution. The word *early* in this context covers the period from Jeremiah's call and initial prophetic ministry during the reign of King Josiah (c. 627 B.C.) down to the period of 605 B.C., namely the fourth year of King Jehoiakim's reign in which the scrolls were dictated (Jer 36). But even this broad chronological framework, while in general correct, must be employed with sufficient flexibility to recognize that a number of short oracles may come from a time later than 605 B.C. Albertz has argued that chaps. 2–6 fall into two units: (i) 2:4–4:2 (excluding 3:6–18) from Jeremiah's earlier ministry (627–609 B.C.), and (ii) 4:3–6:30, from the period 609–605 B.C. Such an analysis is attractive but not entirely persuasive. The substance of the oracles, the probability that many have survived only in summary form, and the thematic arrangement of 2–6 suggest that such a chronological analysis may not be possible, though it should be added that the study of Albertz (*ZAW* 98 [1982] 20–47) is instructive with respect to the historical background of the oracles.

A. Oracles concerning Judah's Evil (2:1–37)

Form/Structure/Setting

The chapter as a whole contains a penetrating indictment of Israel's sin. In its present form, it is made up of a series of oracles (or portions of oracles) which have been woven together to form a coherent narrative. The setting and structure of the component oracles are difficult to determine, principally because there can be no certainty that the whole of each oracle has survived, or has been used in the editorial rearrangement; these matters are discussed under *Form/Structure/Setting* following the translation of each portion of the chapter.

The chapter can be divided into its component parts, with some difficulty, using as criteria (i) subject, (ii) internal literary criteria, and (iii) the number and gender of forms of address, as follows:

2:1–3	(2nd person feminine singular)
2:4–13	(2nd person masculine plural)
2:14–19	(2nd person feminine singular)
2:20–28	(2nd person feminine singular)
2:29–32	(2nd person masculine plural)
2:33–37	(2nd person feminine singular)

The reason for different number and gender in the originally independent oracles can only be speculated upon. The singular form implies an address to the nation as a whole; the plural form might imply an address to a crowd or congregation in particular. It is possible, in other words, that the singular form might presuppose a formal and national context and the plural form an informal and public context. But such logic is dangerous, for even within sections there is further change (e.g., Israel is "he," masculine singular, in v 14 but "you," feminine singular, in v 18).

Some of the sections that now stand independently of each other may originally have formed parts of a single oracle. Thus vv 1–3 and 14–19 may have originally formed a single oracle, and indeed vv 20–28 and 33–37 could also have belonged to it. Likewise, vv 4–13 and 29–32 might once have belonged together. But such attempts at reconstruction, principally on the basis of the number and gender of forms of address, are thoroughly speculative. What must be recognized is that the editorial arrangement of the chapter has been undertaken with great care, so that there are links between originally independent sections, and the usage of common language throughout the sections, without respect to the number and gender of the form of address.

The following points provide some indication of the language and themes binding together the chapter as a whole, to form an intricate mosaic: (i) a key expression הלך אחרי, "go after," designating Israel's apostasy, and linking originally separate units: vv 2, 5, 8, 23, 25; (ii) the frequent use of אמר, "say," followed by quoted speech, evoking the legal context of the original sayings: vv 6, 8, 20, 23, 25, 27, 31, 35; (iii) the frequent use of various interrogative particles (e.g., מדוע איה), again indicating a legal, or "lawsuit," context: e.g., vv 6, 8, 14, 28, 31; (iv) in addition, some units are linked by key words: e.g., עבד, "slave," v 14 and אעבד, "I will (not) serve," v 20; and (v) other uses of key terms are examined in more detail under *Form/Structure/Setting* following the translation of each of the sections.

The foregoing observations make it important to stress that the chapter should be read as a literary unity, despite the originally disparate origins of its sources. The prophet's original messages, their settings and audiences, must remain the subject of conjecture; what we have been given is a carefully developed literary construction, and it is important to read it as such. It is probable that the chapter (as a part of Jer 2–6) took on substantially its present form as a result of the process of writing and expansion described in Jer 36.

The Lost Love of Youth (2:1–3)

Bibliography

Fox, M. V. "Jeremiah 2:2 and the 'Desert Ideal.'" *CBQ* 35 (1973) 441–50. **Roche, M. de.** "Jeremiah 2:2–3 and Israel's Love for God during the Wilderness Wanderings." *CBQ* 45 (1983) 364–76. **Schottroff, W.** "Jeremia 2:1–3. Erwägungen zur Methode der Prophetenexegese." *ZTK* 67 (1970) 263–94. **Watson, W. G. E.** "Symmetry of Stanza in Jeremiah 2.2b–3." *JSOT* 19 (1981) 107–10. **Wiener, C.** "Jeremie ii, 2: 'Fiancailles' ou 'Epousailles'?" *RSR* 44 (1956) 403–7.

ON ḤESED:

Glueck, N. *Ḥesed in the Bible.* Cincinnati: Hebrew Union College, 1967. **Sakenfeld, K. D.** *The Meaning of Ḥesed in the Hebrew Bible.* HSM 17. Missoula, MT: Scholars, 1978. **Stoebe, H.-J.** "Die Bedeutung des Wortes ḥäsäd im Alten Testament." *VT* 2 (1952) 244–54. **Zobel, H.-J.** "חסד." *TWAT* 3, cols. 48–71.

Translation

> [1] *Then the LORD's word came to me:* [2] *"Go and proclaim in Jerusalem's hearing the following:*
>
> *'Thus said the LORD:* [a]
>
> | | |
> |---|---|
> | *What I remember about you is the devotion of your youth,* | (3+2) |
> | *the love at the time of your betrothal,* | |
> | *how you followed me* [b] *in the wilderness,* | (3+2) |
> | *in an unsown land.* [b] | |
> | [3]   *Israel was holy for the LORD,* | (3+2) |
> | *the first-fruit of his harvest.* [a] | |
> | *All that eat it are guilty;* | (3+3) |
> | *evil shall overtake them.'"* | |
>
> *The LORD's oracle!*

Notes

2.a. In LXX, the introduction to the oracle is shorter: "And he said, 'Thus says the Lord. . . ,'" combining the substance of vv 1–2.

2.b-b. LXX omits "in the wilderness, in an unsown land" and replaces it with: "following the Holy One of Israel."

3.a. תבואתה is written as if with a fem suff, ה, ; see the discussion of the MS evidence in de Rossi, III, 65. Given the uncertain antecedent of the fem suff, it is better to read תבואתו, "his harvest," following Q, with some support from Heb. MSS as noted by de Rossi. GKC, § 7c, 91a contends that ה sometimes occurs for the masc suff.

Form/Structure/Setting

At first appearance, vv 1–3 appear to constitute a self-contained oracle, beginning with an introductory formula (vv 1–2a) and being followed by a formula introducing the next oracle (v 4). Yet it is probable that the original oracle comprised vv 1–3 and 14–19 (at least); in the editing of the collection, the original unity has been separated by the insertion of an additional oracle (vv 4–13). The difference in style is more evident in Hebrew than in English, for the first oracle (vv 1–3, 14–19) employs second feminine singular suffixes, whereas the inserted text (vv 4–13) employs the second person masculine plural form. Nevertheless, while recognizing the division of the original text, the verses (1–19) should be read in their present order. Bright (9–18) rearranges them (translating vv 14–19 immediately after v 3), to restore the unity of the original oracle, but to do this is to overlook the editorial purpose in rearranging the verses in the first place (unless, as is possible, the rearrangement was purely accidental). It is probable that the editorial arrangement is deliberate. The initial verses (2–3) set the positive note which, in different ways, is to be developed and contrasted in the sayings and portions of sayings that follow in the remainder of the chapter. The latter part of the opening verses (v 3b) introduces the negative note that is developed in the remainder of the chapter.

There is no reason to doubt that the geographical location of the original oracle's proclamation was Jerusalem (v 2), despite the absence of the reference to place in LXX. But what the specific setting or occasion might have been cannot be determined. The political overtones of the message as a whole (especially vv 14–19) suggest a public proclamation to the people in general, the message being relevant to the religious implications of the then current foreign policy. If it is correct that this oracle was a part of the collection contained in Baruch's scroll, then the later setting and occasion are clarified in Jer 36. Conversely, the reaction of the king, as described in Jer 36, might imply that initially the oracles had a general public proclamation, rather than being delivered in some formal, or royal, context.

While the date of the passage cannot be determined precisely, a time in the reign of King Josiah is probable. Whether the substance of the oracle related to Josiah's religious reform in general, or his foreign policy in particular (cf. vv 18–19), is uncertain. Yet it is clear that Jeremiah's ministry, as exemplified in these verses, was clearly pertinent to the key religious and international concerns of Josiah's time.

Watson (*JSOT* 19 [1981] 107–10) has proposed with respect to the poetic structure of vv 2–3 that the passage contains a type of synonymous parallelism characterized by gender-matched parallel terms, providing a common element to both poetic stanzas. While the data upon which the hypothesis is based are clear, it remains uncertain whether this is indeed a characteristic of the poetic structure, or merely coincidence in the collocation of words.

Comment

Jeremiah is called upon to go to Jerusalem and proclaim the divine word; while the principal intent was that the message be declared to the citizens of Jerusalem, it may also be implied by v 2 that Jeremiah was to travel to Jerusalem from his home in Anathoth to undertake the divine command. He was to introduce his proclamation with "Thus says the Lord" (v 2), thereby establishing the source and authority of his message, and his role as a prophet, in the presence of his audience. Whether the message that follows was in fact his first prophetic speech, following his vocation (chap. 1), cannot be known with certainty, though doubt-less the following words do provide an insight regarding the themes of the prophet's preaching in the early part of his ministry.

The portion of the oracle contained in vv 2–3 contains three parts: a recollec-tion of youthful love (v 2), Israel in the metaphor of the harvest (v 3), and a declaration of the fate of those who undermined Israel's holiness.

2 *Youthful love.* The prophet begins by referring to the Lord's memory, spe-cifically a positive memory of better times, which (before the chapter concludes) will be contrasted terribly with the awful reality of the present. In language that may have been influenced by Hosea (especially 1–3), and that has certain simi-larities to Ezek 16, the prophet describes God's wistful recollection of the early days of love and bliss. The focus of the language is not so much the evocation of the "desert ideal" (see the discussion in Fox, *CBQ* 35 [1973] 263–94) as it is an elaboration upon the Sinai Covenant. The covenant, metaphorically speaking, has been the marriage of Israel and God, born and nourished in youthful love that could not be diminished or weakened by the experience of wilderness. The wilderness was not a positive ideal but a place of hardship, yet the difficulties of that early period had easily been conquered by love. As with young people in love, the beauty of relationship may make poverty and hardship seem of no con-sequence; so had it been in God's memory of the early marriage.

The later expansions of the theme of love, both in this chapter and elsewhere in Jeremiah, will make it clear that love and marriage are more than metaphors in v 2. The essence of the Sinai covenant had been a relationship of love between God and Israel, but that relationship had implications for both religion and politics. With respect to religion, a nation that loved God could not practice love for other gods, for example, the fertility cults whose worship was permeated with sexual activity. And with respect to politics, a nation bound in contract to the Lord could not also join itself by treaty to other nations as its lord and master. The divine memory was of pure love, before the religious and political perversions of love had arisen in later times to spoil the continuing relationship.

3a *Israel, the harvest.* The metaphor now changes from that of the love sealed in the covenant of Sinai to the birth of Israel as a nation in the promised land. The gift of a constitution at Sinai was matched now by the gift of a land; the youthful people were to become a mature nation. And Israel, as a nation, is de-scribed as the "first-fruit of his harvest," namely, the first nation among all the nations that were to be God's harvest. As in the agricultural world the first-fruits were to be set aside from common use and dedicated totally to God, so too Israel was to be set aside as God's special possession among the nations of mankind.

The first two portions of the prophet's statement, elaborating upon the divine memory of distant and better days, set up the positive perspective, both of God's love and of Israel's early history; they form a backdrop to the mournful con-demnations that dominate the rest of the chapter. The relationship began well, but then one of the partners, namely Israel, failed, and the idyllic world of love began to collapse.

3b *The destruction of Israel's holiness.* The judgmental tone that is introduced continues to employ the metaphor of harvest. The first-fruits of the harvest were to be set aside for God, not to be put to common use (e.g., as food), which would profane them. So too Israel, the "First-Fruits" of the world of nations, was to be kept separate for God, devoted only to God's purpose. The expression "all that eat it," in continuation of the metaphor, refers to all those who would put the nation to common use, making it like any other nation, and forgetting the special divine purpose for which Israel was to be set aside. In context, it is not to foreigners that reference is made, but to all those members of the nation who participated in the perversion of national purpose. All such were guilty and their punishment would eventually overtake them.

Israel's failure and coming judgment are here expressed extremely succinctly; the following oracles elaborate in greater detail both the nature of the failure and the form of the judgment. Thus, vv 1–3, though originally a part of an independent oracle, serve as an appropriate introduction to chaps. 2–6 as a whole.

Explanation

See the *Explanation* following 2:33–37.

A Lawsuit against People and Prophets (2:4–13)

Bibliography

Barstad, H. M. "HBL als Bezeichnung der fremden Götter im Alten Testament und der Gott Huba." *ST* 32 (1978) 57–65. **Milgrom, J.** "The Date of Jeremiah, Chapter 2." *JNES* 14 (1955) 65–69. **Naef, H.-D.** "Gottes Treue und Israels Untreue: Aufbau und Einheit von Jer 2:2–13." *ZAW* 99 (1987) 37–57. **Overholt, T. W.** "Jeremiah 2 and the Problem of 'Audience Reaction.'" *CBQ* 41 (1979) 262–73. **Roche, M. de.** "Israel's 'Two Evils' in Jeremiah II 13." *VT* 31 (1981) 369–72. **Williams, P.** "The Fatal and Foolish Exchange; Living Waters for 'Nothing': A Study of Jeremiah 2:4–13." *Austin Seminary Bulletin.* Faculty Edition 81 (1965) 3–59.

ON COVENANT LAWSUIT (*rîv*):

Gemser, B. "The *rîb-* or Controversy-Pattern in Hebrew Mentality." *Wisdom in Israel and in the Ancient Near East.* FS H. H. Rowley. Ed. M. Noth and D. W. Thomas. VTSup 3. Leiden: Brill, 1955. 120–37. **Harvey, J.** "Le Riv-Pattern: Requisitoire prophetique sur las rupture de l'Alliance." *Bib* 43 (1962) 172–96. **Huffmon, H. B.** "The Covenant Law Suit in the Prophets." *JBL* 78 (1959) 285–95. **Limburg, J.** "The Root ריב and the Prophetic Lawsuit Speeches." *JBL* 88 (1969) 291–304. **Nielsen, K.** *Yahweh as Prosecutor and Judge: An Investigation of the Prophetic Lawsuit (Rîb-Pattern).* JSOTSup 9. Sheffield: Sheffield University, 1978. **Ramsey, G. W.** "Speech Forms in Hebrew Law and Prophetic Oracles." *JBL* 96 (1977) 45–58. **Roche, M. de.** "Yahweh's *rîb* against Israel: A Reassessment of the So-Called 'Prophetic Lawsuit' in the Preexilic Prophets." *JBL* 102 (1983) 563–74. **Suganuma, E.** "The Covenant Rib Form in Jeremiah 2: A Form Critical Study." *Journal of the College of Dairy Agriculture* 4 (Nopporo, Hokkaido, Japan, 1972) 121–54.

Translation

⁴*Hear the LORD's word, House of Jacob, and all families of the house of Israel.*
5   *Thus said the Lord:*

    "What fault did your fathers find in me,   (4+3)
       that they became remote from me?
    Then they pursued vanity,   (3+1?)
       becoming vain in the process.

6   And they did not say: 'Where is the LORD   (4+4+3)
       who brought us up from the land of Egypt,
       who led us in the wilderness,
    in a land of desert and pit,   (3+3)
       in a land of dryness and darkness,[a]
    in a land through which no man passed   (4+3)
       and where humans did not dwell.'

7   But I brought you to a garden land,   (4+3)
       to eat its fruit and its good produce;
    yet you went in and defiled my land   (3+3)
       and turned my inheritance into an abomination.

8   The priests did not say: 'Where is the LORD?' (4+3)
       and those skilled in the Torah did not know me.
    And the pastors transgressed against me,   (3+3+3)
       and the prophets prophesied by Baal
       and pursued what does not profit.

9   Therefore I shall still contend with you,"   (4+3)
           the LORD's oracle!
    "and I shall contend with your grandchildren.[a]

10   For cross to the coastlands of Cyprus[a] and see, (4+4+4)
       or send to Kedar and reflect with great care
       and see if there was ever anything like this!

11   Has a nation ever changed its gods?   (3+3)
       And they are not even real gods!
    But my people have exchanged their glory[a] (3+2)
       for that which does not profit.

12   Be horrified, O heavens, at this!   (3+3+4)
       Let your hair bristle! Be absolutely amazed!"[a]
           The LORD's oracle.

13   "For my people have committed two crimes.
    They have rejected me, a fountain of living waters, (4?+3)
       to dig cisterns for themselves,
    broken cisterns   (2?+3)
       that don't hold water!"[a]

Notes

6.a. On Hebrew צלמות, "(deep) darkness," see D. W. Thomas, "*slmwt* in the Old Testament," *JSS* 7 (1962) 191–200; P. C. Craigie, *Psalms 1–50,* 207. LXX has ἀκάρπῳ, "barren," implying a Heb. reading גלמודה, "barren." The similarity of two Heb. words is such that one could have been mistakenly written for the other, but which one was original remains uncertain. Following LXX, the translation "barren" might seem to balance more appropriately the preceding word "dryness." But "darkness" is also appropriate to the context. Given the disparities between the text of LXX (Jeremiah) and the Heb. text, it is safest to retain the translation "darkness."

9.a. A few Heb. MSS (de Rossi, III, 65) and Vg omit "sons of" and render simply: "your children." Though this is a possible reading, it is best to stick to the Heb. text (supported by LXX).

10. a. On the meaning of כתיים, "Cyprus," see H. E. del Medico, "L'identification des Kittim avec les Romains," *VT* 10 (1960) 448–53.

11.a. An original text, with first-person suff "*my* glory," in effect "me," has been modified by the scribes (*tiq. soph.*) to circumvent what seemed to be a direct expression of a divine title.

12.a. חרבו, "be amazed," is interpreted as the third in a sequence of imperatives, from חרב (II). LXX implies a reading חרבה, implying repetition, and is followed by Bright (11) and Thompson (166); but the figurative usage of חרב provides acceptable sense and the change (after LXX) is unnecessary.

13.a. The metrical analysis of v 13 as a whole remains somewhat speculative.

Form/Structure/Setting

For the larger literary context in which this prophetic oracle is set, see the preceding notes on Jer 2–6 and on 2:1–3. The literary unity of vv 4–13, in which the second person masculine plural (in suffixes, etc.) is employed, is clearly distinguished from the preceding (vv 1–3) and the following section (vv 14–19). It is possible, however, that vv 4–13 are only part of an originally longer poetic unit, which may have included in addition vv 29–32 (see below).

The prophetic oracle contains a number of elements that suggest a literary link between it and the so-called lawsuit form (see further Limburg, *JBL* 88 [1969] 291–304; Huffmon, *JBL* 78 [1959] 286–95; and Thompson, 159–61). There is clearly some degree of relationship, as is implied by the use of the verb ריב, "contend, bring suit" (v 9), the call to the nation to listen (v 4–5), the recollection of God's past provision and the nation's failure, and the summoning of "heaven" as a witness (v 12). Yet all the elements of the lawsuit pattern are not present in the oracle in its present form (viz. vv 4–13), nor do the extant elements appear in the expected sequence. Hence, in the interpretation of the present literary form of the passage, the possibility of a lawsuit background must be taken into account, but it cannot be the principal guide to interpretation.

The structure of the oracle may be set forth as follows:

(i) *Question:* "What fault. . . ?" (v 5a–b). The question, while introducing the passage, also alludes back to the preceding narrative (vv 1–3). Everything started well, but what went wrong?

(ii) *The analysis* (vv 5c–8): The fault, for which there was no excuse, lay not in God but in the people as a whole. This passage has a careful structure, set off by a chiastic inclusio.

A   הלך אחרי, "go after" (v 5b)
     B   איה יהוה, "where is the Lord?" (v 6)
     B'   איה יהוה, "where is the Lord?" (v 8)
A'   הלך אחרי, "go after" (v 8)

(iii) *The announcement of lawsuit* (v 9): it is introduced by "therefore," thus linking the following charges to the preceding sins.

(iv) *The substance of the suit* (vv 10–11): Israel has changed its God.

(v) *The address to the legal witness* (vv 12–13): "heaven," a witness to the original covenant, is invited to observe Israel's "two crimes."

The original sermon, prior to its adaptation to the present context, no doubt made flexible use of the covenant/treaty lawsuit model. Just as, in the case of the treaty-analogy, the great king would send a messenger to the subservient ruler pointing out the disruption of treaty relationships, so too the prophet was God's messenger to the covenant people. He pointed to the failure in the people's relationship to their covenant God, announced God's declaration of a lawsuit, and specified the crimes for which charges were laid. In the original sermon, the prophet would have continued to a declaration of God's judgment on Israel, but that has not survived in vv 4–13. One may suppose that the original sermon or oracle, to which this passage belonged, was delivered at an early point in Jeremiah's ministry; it may have been delivered before Josiah's reformation, and it may reflect, in part, Judah's vassal status to a foreign power (Assyria: see further vv 14–19).

In its present form, however, the editor has placed the passage after vv 1–3, employing the verses to demonstrate what happened to cause the dreadful change between the fresh love of the "youth" of the covenant relationship and the present sad state of affairs in Judah. The words are also addressed to the former state of Israel; though it no longer existed as an independent nation, its very failure was a consequence of the decline elaborated in these verses. The edited form of the passage may be dated from 605 B.C., or even later.

Comment

The prophetic message begins, as before, with the declaration that its substance is God's word. The message is directed, in a theoretical sense, to Israel as a whole, both the northern and southern states; that is, the prophet envisages all of Israel as his audience, even though the northern state had been defeated in war a century earlier and he was preaching in Jerusalem, the capital city of the southern state.

The message begins with a rhetorical question. In general terms, the underlying question is: "What went wrong to spoil the love of earlier times?" But it is phrased differently, perhaps ironically: "What fault did your fathers find in me?" Clearly, there was no fault in God, but in the forefathers themselves, yet the phrasing of the question in this manner enables the prophet not only to elaborate on the fault of the people but also to bring out the faultless behavior of God.

5c–8 The prophet immediately proceeds to answer his own question pinpointing where the true failure in the ancient relationship of covenant lay. Having once become remote in their relationship with God, the people pursued "vanity," or a "worthless goal" (הבל). The literary structure of the passage reveals that the essence of failure lay in this false pursuit, of "vanity" (v 5) and of what does not profit (v 8). Barstad (*ST* 32 [1978] 57–65) has suggested that the word "vanity" might actually be a term for a particular god, or type of god, and refers to a later pre-Islamic Arab deity named Hubal. While the sentiment of his observation is correct, the specific proposal is not persuasive; the Hebrew noun should simply be taken to mean "vanity" in a general sense. Yet, in practice, the essence of the vanity of the fathers was that they had abandoned faith in the true God; it had been replaced by false faith, notably (in this context) faith in the cult of the Canaanite deity Baal (v 8). And the failure of the forefathers had been comprehensive: all the people are implied by "they" in v 6, but in addition priests, scholars, pastors, and prophets had failed (v 8).

The failure in part was a consequence of the loss of spiritual memory (cf. Deut 8). When they were in the promised and plentiful land, they no longer recalled the faithful God who had redeemed them from Egypt and led them safely through the inhospitable and uninhabited wilderness. But the question "Where is the

Lord?" (vv 6, 8) may imply more than that. Neither the people nor the priests had continued to seek the Lord in worship or prayer, and all had been fellow-conspirators in the fall from faith. If God had guarded his people in the wilderness (v 6), how much more should they have recognized his presence in the land of plenty (v 7)? But all had failed: the nation that was to have been holy (cf. v 3) had polluted its promised land.

The substance of v 8 makes clear that the failure lay not only with the people as a whole but also with the religious and national leaders. The "priests" failed in their task. "Those skilled in the Torah" were probably Levites, some of whom were entrusted with the business of religious education. They, too, had failed; they knew their "bible," but they did not know, in a personal and intimate fashion, their God. The "pastors" (literally "shepherds") were not religious leaders but national leaders, responsible for the government and welfare of the people; as they were themselves engaged in transgression, they could neither set a good example nor rule the people with integrity. The "prophets," who should have spoken only in God's name, prophesied in the name of Baal, the Canaanite fertility god; thus the word of God never reached the people through their ministry.

9 Given such comprehensive failure, God declares his intention to "contend" with his people. The word "contend" has the sense "bring a suit against someone" or "bring a person to trial." The specific charges are stated in the following verses and bring to focus the elaboration of evil and failure in the preceding verses. But the statute under which the charges would be laid was none other than that of Israel's covenant with God, first formed at Sinai and renewed in different forms through subsequent generations. Israel, in committing itself to God in covenant, had sworn itself to total allegiance and accepted the consequences if it should fail in that allegiance. Now the failure had come to pass, and Israel must answer to God for its loss of allegiance. Jeremiah is the messenger through whom the divine declaration of the legal suit is declared.

10–11 The crime of which the people are charged is stated: "they have exchanged their glory" (viz. God). The charge is introduced, however, with a series of flourishes, which serve to emphasize the gravity of the crime. You could take a tour to Cyprus and visit the Phoenician colony there, or you could go eastwards and camp in Kedar, where the desert bedouin lived, and you could observe such foreigners, with their pagan religious practices. But for all the folly of such faiths, devoted to gods without real substance, you would observe that the residents of Cyprus and Kedar were at least faithful to their gods. Not so Israel! Israel was the only nation to have worshiped once the single true God, and the only nation ever to have exchanged faith in the true God for the vain pursuit of foreign and empty deities.

12 The last portion of the oracle is addressed to the "heavens." In the initial forming and renewal of God's covenant with Israel, heaven and earth had been the "witnesses" called upon to observe the solemn conclusion of the covenant relationship (cf. Deut 4:26 and Craigie, *Deuteronomy*, 138). Heaven's horror would be elicited because it had observed (in the past) the solemn declaration of allegiance to God but perceived now the terrible faithlessness in Israel, which made mockery of all those past commitments.

13a The crime, in the address to heaven, is shown in its twofold aspect: the people had rejected God and chosen a useless alternative. In view of de Roche (*VT* 31 [1981] 369–72), these two crimes are to be interpreted as a marital metaphor, the rejection of the wife (the Lord) and consorting with other lovers (Baalim). But this interpretation, based on such passages as Prov 5:15–18, is somewhat far-fetched; in the conventional use of such imagery, especially in covenant contexts, the Lord is husband and Israel is the wife, as is also implied, in Jer 2, by the use of feminine suffixes in 2:2 and elsewhere. Rather, the central metaphor is that of water, which is one of the staples of life. Israel had rejected God, from whom "water" always flowed, and sought to replace God with cracked and leaky cisterns, which would always be empty.

Explanation

See the *Explanation* following 2:33–37.

Defection and Slavery (2:14–19)

Translation

<table>
<tr><td>14</td><td>Is Israel a slave?</td><td>(2?+3)</td></tr>
<tr><td></td><td>Or is he a household servant?^a</td><td></td></tr>
<tr><td>15</td><td>Why has he become an object of prey</td><td>(3+3+2)</td></tr>
<tr><td></td><td>over whom lion cubs roar^a</td><td></td></tr>
<tr><td></td><td>and squabble noisily?</td><td></td></tr>
<tr><td></td><td>For they have made his land a wasteland,</td><td>(3+3?)</td></tr>
<tr><td></td><td>his cities aflame,^b devoid of inhabitants.</td><td></td></tr>
<tr><td>16</td><td>Even the people of Noph and Tahpanhes</td><td>(2+2)</td></tr>
<tr><td></td><td>will fracture^a your forehead.</td><td></td></tr>
<tr><td>17</td><td>Have you not brought this upon yourself</td><td>(3+3)</td></tr>
<tr><td></td><td>by leaving the LORD your God</td><td></td></tr>
<tr><td></td><td>(at the time he was leading you in the way)?^a</td><td></td></tr>
<tr><td>18</td><td>So what is the point now in your going to Egypt</td><td>(4+3)</td></tr>
<tr><td></td><td>to drink the water of the Nile?^a</td><td></td></tr>
<tr><td></td><td>And what is the point in your going to Assyria</td><td>(3+3)</td></tr>
<tr><td></td><td>to drink the water of the Euphrates?</td><td></td></tr>
<tr><td>19</td><td>Your crime will cripple^a you,</td><td>(2+2)</td></tr>
<tr><td></td><td>and your defections will rebuke you.</td><td></td></tr>
<tr><td></td><td>So know and see how evil and bitter</td><td>(4+3+3)</td></tr>
<tr><td></td><td>is your leaving the LORD your God</td><td></td></tr>
<tr><td></td><td>with no fear^b of me in you."</td><td></td></tr>
<tr><td></td><td>The LORD's oracle, the LORD of Hosts.^c</td><td></td></tr>
</table>

Notes

14.a. Lit., "one born of the house," namely a slave or servant, not bought, but born and raised, in the household.

15.a. A pf tense שָׁאֲגוּ, "roared," is expected in the grammatical context; there is no MSS evidence, however, to support changing the text.

15.b. נצתה, "burn," is fem sg in the consonantal text, but the antecedent is pl; it is better to read the pl form נצתן. A few MSS (de Rossi, III, 65) suggest the root is נתץ, "broke down," but this alternative (presumably the result of accidental metathesis) is not entirely persuasive, though it is possible.

16.a. ירעוך is difficult: as vocalized, it would appear to be a form of רעה, "graze." LXX implies the verb ידע, "know," but also replaces the following word, "forehead," with "mocked you"; LXX is probably not a sure guide in this context. The most satisfactory solution, with some support from Syr, is to read יִרְעֻוּך (from רעע II, BDB, 949), meaning "break, fracture."

17.a. The third line of v 17 should probably be deleted in its entirety. It does not make a great deal of sense and is probably a dittogr (slightly changed) of the first line of v 18. Both lines have twelve consonants, of which eight are common and in the same sequence. (But see Holladay, I, 51–52.)

18.a. LXX translates "Geon," rather than "Nile," but there is no support for such a reading in MT.

19.a. Lit., "discipline, chastise."

19.b. The line is rendered in LXX: "I have taken no pleasure in you," but this is of little help. The problem lies in the vocalization and interpretation of פחדתי. As it stands, פַּחְדָּה (noun fem.) is a *hap. leg.*: "dread" (the masc form being normal). The appropriate solution may be supplied by Syr suggesting the reading לֹא פָחַדְתִּי אֵלַי (de Rossi, III, 66), "neither did you fear me" (which has the support of one Heb. MS). Alternatively, the verb could be vocalized as an internal passive (פֻּהְדְתִּי), "I was not feared by you," as suggested by Dahood, *Ugaritic-Hebrew Philology*, 21.)

19.c. The concluding oracular formula is long and somewhat unusual; LXX suggests "oracle of the Lord your God," which is possible.

Form/Structure/Setting

Vv 14–19 are a continuation of the oracle with which the chapter began: see further the comments under *Form/Structure/Setting* at 2:1–3. Because the passage is a continuation, it does not begin with a customary oracular introduction. The concluding phrase in v 19, "the Lord's oracle," may mark the end of this prophetic passage (as suggested by Thompson, 175), but this is uncertain, partly because such phrases appear to occur in the middle of prophetic oracles (e.g., in 2:9), and partly because a further section of this chapter may belong with vv 14–19. In 2:33–37, second person feminine singular suffixes are again employed, as in the passage under discussion. Hence, it is possible that the original oracle, prior to its present editorial arrangement, included vv 1–3, 14–19, and 33–37. See further the comments on *Form/Structure/Setting* at 2:33–37.

The substance of vv 14–19 provides further information pertaining to the original setting of the oracle and the possible date of its composition. The historical data are nevertheless elusive. The Egyptian reference in v 16 is sometimes linked to Judah's defeat by Egypt in 609 B.C. (Bright, 14; Thompson, 173–74). The verb "fracture" should probably be translated by an English future tense, however (cf. NEB), which would undermine such historical identification. The references to Egypt and Assyria in v 18 may be taken to imply a date early in Jeremiah's ministry; the Assyrian decline was already in process when Jeremiah began to be a prophet and the end for Assyria came c. 612 B.C. Hence, a date prior to 612 B.C. would be implied. The real difficulty, however, is whether either of these poetic verses can provide hard evidence as to dating. The prophet (beginning in vv 2–3) is addressing all Israel, both the Northern (no longer surviving) Kingdom and the Southern Kingdom, and reflecting upon the tragic course of history. For much of that historical past, Israel had vacillated in its external politics between Egypt and Assyria (and later Babylon). Thus, though the evidence is uncertain, a date prior to 612 B.C. (including v 16) for the passage is probable, but precision in dating is impossible. Given such a provisional dating, these verses (along with vv 1–3) should be interpreted in the context of King Josiah's reign.

The inner structure of this part of the larger oracle may be set forth as follows. A question is raised (vv 14–15b) and elaborated (vv 15c–16) regarding Israel's sad estate. An answer is provided (v 17), affirming that Israel's disaster is its own fault. The answer is of such a kind that it is no use turning to others for help (vv 18–19).

Comment

14   The passage begins with a question: "Is Israel a slave?" The question must be contrasted to an affirmation in the original introduction to the oracle: "Israel was holy for the Lord" (v 3). Israel's first estate was that of a special relationship to God in covenant, in a privileged bond of love. The "slavery" of Egypt had been exchanged for the "service" of God (in both cases, forms of the Hebrew word עבד, "slave, servant," being used: see further Craigie, *Deuteronomy*, 82–83.) But now, the free service of God had been exchanged once more for slavery, as it is implied by the question. The two expressions employed in v 14, "slave" and "household servant," are parallel terms in the poetic context; they imply a degree of progression, nevertheless. The slave was commonly purchased or acquired in warfare; the household servant was born to slaves already belonging to a household. Israel, in the metaphor, had not only become a slave, but after a generation or more had become a household servant, one for whom even the memory of freedom had been lost. But the statement of Israel's slavery in the form of two questions implies that slavery should never have come to pass. Israel, in its covenant, had been granted freedom.

The covenant context of the metaphor clarifies a further dimension of the language. The word עבד, "slave," in addition to its household usage, could designate a vassal state, bound by treaty to a sovereign power. Israel's "treaty" with God should have eliminated such alliances, but Israel's history, in Jeremiah's time, was one of constant servitude to a foreign power, to a greater or lesser extent. In other words, the issue of Israel's slavery was not merely a metaphor but a comment on the actual historical experience of international relationships.

14b–15   The metaphor changes; now Israel, like a wounded beast, is portrayed as being at the mercy of the young lions, hungry and competing for their dinner. The picture is one of abject weakness, where there should have been strength. And the metaphor is in striking contrast to other uses of similar language. In Ps 34:11, the young lions are described as going hungry, while the faithful servant of the Lord lacks nothing (see further Craigie, *Psalms 1–50*, 280). But in this prophetic word, those who have not been faithful have become an appetizer for the young lions. Moving out of the metaphor (v 15c–d), Israel's land has been devastated and depopulated by the depredations of enemies; whether the words should be taken to refer to the wasteland that was once the Northern Kingdom, or whether in more general poetic terms they refer to the covenant people as a whole, is not certain.

The Egyptians are referred to indirectly in v 16, in which two Egyptian cities are mentioned as being among those foreign enemies who would bring grief to

Israel. Noph (Egyptian *mn-nfr-pypy*) is better known by its later name, Memphis. It was situated on the Nile (whence the name of the modern city in Tennessee, which was named in 1819 on the basis of its similar location by the River Mississippi) and had been the capital city of Egypt in the days of the Old Kingdom. Indeed, the modern English word *Egypt* comes from one of the names used of Memphis, namely Hi-ku-ptah (literally, "the mansion of Ptah's soul," a temple located in Memphis). In biblical times, and during the later Greek period, Memphis was one of the greatest cities of Egypt; today, virtually nothing of importance remains at the site, some twelve miles south of Cairo. But the importance of the city in biblical times was such that the reference to Noph might be taken to imply Egypt as a whole.

Tahpanhes, on the other hand, presents a different kind of problem. Referred to as Daphnae in the Greek period, the site is known now as Tell Defenneh; it is located about twenty-two miles south-southwest of the modern Port Said. Sir William Flinders Petrie, excavating at Tell Defenneh during 1885–86, uncovered beneath the soils of a mound the remains of what had once been a military fortress (W. M. F. Petrie, A. S. Murray, and F. L. Griffith, *Tanis, Part II: Nebesheh (Am) and Defenneh (Tahpanhes)*, Egyptian Exploration Fund [London, 1888]). As a military installation, Tahpanhes was thus designed to guard the northeastern approach to Egypt on the road that extended eastwards from Tahpanhes, through approximately 150 miles of desert to the region of Gaza (W. M. F. Petrie, *Egypt and Israel* [London: S.P.C.K., 1911] 86–90). In addition to the military colony, there were also settlements of foreigners in the region of Tahpanhes; in the sixth century B.C., Greek smiths settled there and introduced iron-working into Egypt (J. R. Harris, *The Legacy of Egypt* [Oxford: Clarendon Press, 1971] 90). One may suppose, therefore, that Tahpanhes, though by no means a city as important as Memphis from the Egyptian perspective, was nevertheless a key Egyptian city, or town, from the Hebrew perspective; it would be the first significant place one came to on a journey from Judah to Egypt. (Later, Jeremiah and other Hebrew refugees were to settle there: 43:7–9.) In summary, Noph and Tahpanhes were two significant places from a Hebrew perspective, representing the might of Egypt and its metaphorical "fracturing" of Israel's head (2:16).

17 The prophet declares that the grief that had befallen Israel could be blamed on no external source; the people had brought it upon themselves. Having deserted God and the faith of the covenant, they had by implication invited the covenant curses to fall upon their own heads. And so it was pointless to turn either to Egypt or Assyria for help (see *Form/Structure/Setting*, above, for the chronological implications of these references). When the treaty with God had been broken, no treaty with Egypt or Assyria could mend the damage.

18 In the immediate context, the reference to the "water" of the two great rivers, Nile and Euphrates, is probably to be interpreted as a metaphor of refreshment. As their own land had become a parched "wasteland," Israel might naturally think of turning to other sources for refreshing water. But in the editorial rearrangement of chap. 2 as a whole, the metaphor of water takes on further significance. Israel had exchanged the "fountain of living water" for "leaky cisterns"; now, with cisterns empty, it would seek water from Egypt or Assyria, but yet would fail to return to the source of "living waters." Thus, the editorial rearrangements of the original messages had heightened the power and effectiveness of the prophet's word in written form.

19 The coming judgment of Israel was not a random act of God but a direct consequence of the nation's sin. Israel's own crimes would return to haunt it; its "defections" from the treaty stipulations would rebuke the nation in its self-induced judgment. To desert God brings with it the experience of evil and bitterness; nothing can avert the consequence other than a penitent return to the God of covenant, a theme that is developed in the next chapter.

Explanation

See the *Explanation* following 2:33–37.

The Indictment for Evil (2:20–28)

Bibliography

Bailey, K. E., and **Holladay, W. L.** "The 'Young Camel' and 'Wild Ass' in Jer. 2:23–25." *VT* 18 (1968) 256–60. **Ceresko, A. R.** "The Function of Antanaclasis (mṣ᾽) 'to find'/mṣ᾽ 'to reach, overtake, grasp') in Hebrew Poetry, Especially in the Book of Qoheleth." *CBQ* 44 (1982) 551–69. **Fishbane, M. A.** "Revelation and Tradition: Aspects of InnerBiblical Exegesis." *JBL* 99 (1980) 343–61, esp. 351–52. **Holladay, W. L.** "On Every High Hill and Under Every Green Tree." *VT* 11 (1961) 170–76. **McKane, W.** "Jeremiah II 23–25: Observations on the Versions and History of Exegesis." *OTS* 17 (1972) 73–88. **Nicholson, E. W.** "Blood-Spattered Altars?" *VT* 27 (1977) 113–17. **Olyan, S. M.** "Cultic Confessions in Jer 2:27a." *ZAW* 99 (1987) 254–59. **Soggin, J. A.** "A proposito di sacrifici di fanciulli e di culto dei morti nell Antico Testamento." *OrAnt* 8 (1969) 215–17.

Translation

20	*"For long ago I* [a] *broke your yoke,*	(3+2+3)
	I shattered your shackles;	
	but you said: 'I will not serve.' [b]	
	So on every high hill	(3+3+3)
	and under every flourishing tree,	
	you lay prone, as a prostitute.	
21	*Yet I planted you as a fine domestic vine*	(3+3)
	of completely [a] *pure stock.*	
	So how have you become alien to me,	(3+3)
	warped as the tendrils [b] *of a wild vine?*	
22	*For if you should wash in detergent* [a]	(3+3+3)
	and use great quantities of soap,	
	your stain would remain ingrained [b] *before me."*—	
	The Lord GOD's oracle. [c]	
23	*"How can you say: 'I am not defiled,*	(4+4)
	I have not chased the Baals'?	
	Look at your trail in the valley, [a]	(3+3)
	know what you have done!	

	A swift young camel,	(2+2)
	crisscrossing her tracks!	
24	*A wild ass,*[a] *wise in the wilderness way,*	(3+3?+3)
	sniffing the wind in hot desire[b]—	
	who can restrain her lust?	
	None of her mates need stir themselves;	(3+2)
	in her mouth,[c] *they will find her.*	
25	*Never let your foot be bare*	(3+2)
	or your throat[a] *be parched.*	
	But you said: 'It's no good! No!	(3+3+2)
	For I have loved strangers	
	and I will pursue them.'	
26	*As the shame of a thief entrapped,*	(4+4)
	so have they shamed Israel's house.[a]	
	They—their kings and their princes,	(3+2)
	their priests and their prophets—	
27	*They say to the wood: 'You are my father!'*	(4+3)
	and to the stone: 'You gave me birth!'	
	For they have turned their back to me,	(3+2)
	not facing me,	
	yet whenever they are in trouble they say:	(3+2)
	'Rise up and save us!'	
28	*But where are the gods you made for yourself?*	(4+4)
	Let them rise up, if they can save you in your trouble.	
	For as numerous as your cities[a]	(3+3)
	were your gods, O Judah!''[b]	

Notes

20.a. LXX implies that the first two verbs of v 20 should be pointed as 2 masc sg: "you broke . . . you shattered . . ."; cf. Bright, 11; RSV, etc. The reading is possible, but the first-person form suits the context (see *Comment,* below); hence the vocalization of MT is retained.

20.b. Several MSS have the word אעבר, "I will (not) cross, transgress" (de Rossi, III, 66); but it is probably an erroneous copying of MT (rather than vice versa).

21.a. Q כלו (masc) for the apparently fem form in MT (K), the antecedent being the "vine" (masc). Or, the consonantal text may reflect the old orthographic form of the masc suffix (Thompson, 176).

21.b. סורי, "tendrils," is a speculative translation, supposing a participial formation of סור, "turn." Others resolve the problem of the uncertain meaning of the text by redividing the consonants: לסוריה גפן, "foul-smelling vine"; e.g., Bright, 11.

22.a. Heb. נתר is probably a solution of sodium carbonate, functioning as a simple detergent.

22.b. Or perhaps "inscribed": see Craigie, *Psalms 1–50,* 154 (note 1.a.).

22.c. Lit., "oracle of the Lord, Yahweh."

23.a. LXX reads: ἐν τῷ πολυανδρείῳ, "in the burial ground," for MT's "in the valley."

24.a. פרה, "wild ass," more commonly spelled פרא (for which there is support in the Heb. MSS of v 24; de Rossi, III, 66). The assumption of corruption here, and therefore the proposed alternate reading in the note in *BHS,* is probably unnecessary, though it is clear that the translators of LXX had difficulty. Bright (12) thinks "wild ass" disturbs the figure; but see the *Comment* below.

24.b. נפשׁו: read (Q) נפשׁה (fem) to agree with the subject of the verb.

24.c. LXX translated a different Heb. text: "at the time of its humiliation" (probably Heb. בענלה), but MT is to be preferred.

25.a. Reading (Q) "throat" (not "threshing floor," K), from Heb. גרון, "neck, throat."

26.a. For בית, "house," LXX has υἱοί (בני, "sons of [Israel]").

28.a. The marginal note in NEB renders עָרִים as "blood-spattered altars," influenced no doubt by LXX. R. Driver, *CML*[1], 142, who so interpreted Ugaritic *ģr* and related it to a supposed Heb. עָרֹה in Jer 2:28. But the translation should certainly be rejected. In the two texts cited by Driver (*ģr* in *CTA* 5.vi.17 and 6.i.2), the term should be translated "skin"; see Gibson, *CML*[2], 155; A. Caquot et al., *Textes Ougaritiques*, I, 250–51; E. W. Nicholson, "Blood-spattered Altars?" *VT* 27 (1977) 113–17.

28.b. LXX adds: "according to the number of Jerusalem's streets, they sacrificed to Baal."

Form/Structure/Setting

This passage, though continuing to employ the second person feminine singular form of address, appears nevertheless to be quite distinct from the preceding section (2:14–19). It has, however, a number of literary links with 2:4–13, even though the latter passage employs the second person masculine plural form of address. (i) The expression הלך אחרי is employed again (vv 23, 25; see vv 5, 8). (ii) There is frequent usage of quoted speech after אמר (vv 20, 23, 25, 27) as there was in the previous passage (vv 6, 8). (iii) There is repeated usage of certain key terms: טמא (vv 7, 23); Baal (vv 8, 23); רעה (vv 13, 27, 28).

Nevertheless, for all the links between this passage and 2:4–13, it is linked also, in the editorial rearrangement, to the preceding section, 2:14–19, principally by the use of the root עבד. The preceding passage began with the rhetorical question: "Is Israel a *slave* [עבד]?" This passage puts contrasting words in Israel's mouth: "I will not *serve*" (אעבד, v 20).

The structure of the passage as a whole is dominated by the quoted words of Israel (vv 20, 22, 25, 27), followed by the prophetic (divine) response. The words of Israel are not intended to be literal *quotations* but are words placed in the mouth of the prophet's audience to exemplify their actions (see further, Overholt, *CBQ* 41 [1979] 262–73). In its original and complete form, the oracle must have used, or adapted, the language of the covenant lawsuit against Israel to convey its message. In this passage, however, it is not the political breach of covenant that is the focus of the message (as it was in 2:14–19) but rather the religious breach; in scathing language, the pursuit of fertility religion is denounced as an act of covenant unfaithfulness. Thus the passage alludes back to beginnings of Israel's covenant introduced at the beginning of the chapter but develops in a contrasting fashion the early love (2:2) that has now become debased. A period early in Josiah's reign may be supposed, perhaps close to the beginning of his religious reformation.

An unusual literary device is used in vv 24–25, called *antanaclasis*, namely, the repetition of the same word, with a different meaning. (i) Ceresko (*CBQ* 44 [1982] 558–59) identifies the phenomenon in the use of מצא, "find," in v 24, and מצא, "catch," in v 26, accentuated still further by the word play on מצמאה, "parched," in v 25. (ii) It is possible that a further example occurs in v 26. בשת, "shame" (from בוש), is contrasted with הביש, which has been translated "they shamed," but could be derived from יבש, "to wither," thereby linking the line further to the enigmatic v 25. In any case, it is clear in this passage that a number of aspects of the poet's art may be observed.

Comment

The passage begins with Israel's declaration "I will not serve" (v 20c), but there is some uncertainty as to the proper translation and interpretation of the

two preceding lines. Most interpreters, after LXX, translate "*you* broke your yoke
. . . *you* shattered your shackles . . ."; in this translation, the lines describe Israel's
rebellion. Like a wild ox, breaking the restraining yoke, Israel shucked off all
responsibility to God and defiantly announced that it would not serve. But it is
more likely that the text should be translated: "*I* broke your yoke, *I* shattered your
shackles" (see note 20.a.). Translated in this fashion, the verse depicts a striking
contrast. Israel had been "slaves" (עבדים) in Egypt, but God had broken that yoke
of slavery in order that his people might become the "servants" (עבדים) of the Lord
in the covenant relationship; despite that act of liberation, ungrateful Israel still
proclaimed, "I will not *serve*" (אעבד). The thrust of the prophetic declaration thus
highlights not only rebellion but also the profound ingratitude reflected in that
rebellion.

The nature of the rebellion in the latter part of v 20 is depicted in terms of
Israel's abandonment of the true faith and its resort to the coarse practices of the
fertility religion associated with the Canaanite deity Baal. The "high hill" was no
doubt a typical location for a country shrine of Baal, its altitude pointing to the
heavenly home of Baal from where came the rains that made the land fertile.
And shrines would also be located under particular "flourishing trees," themselves
symbols of the fertility that was the central concern of the Baal religion. The
practices associated with these country shrines were essentially sexual. It was believed that the fertility of the land depended upon the fertility of the gods,
illustrated most powerfully in the impregnation of a female deity by Baal. And
the fertility of the gods, in turn, was believed to be influenced, as by imitative
magic, by the sexual activities of the worshipers. Thus a central act of worship in
a fertility religion was the sexual union of male and female, the earthly act believed to be influential in the heavenly sphere. Hence, when Jeremiah says: "you
lay prone, as a prostitute," he is not using metaphorical language: the language is
literal, though the use of the term "prostitute" clearly colors the act with Jeremiah's
moral and spiritual perspective. An act that the participants persuaded themselves
was "holy" was in fact none other than a debased act of prostitution.

The perversion of Israel's religion is elaborated in v 21 in terms of the metaphor
of the vine. Israel had been planted as "fine domestic vine," specifically the *Sorek*
vine, growing in the vine-country east of Jerusalem and producing a fine red fruit.
Being of pure stock, this vine should have produced a pure harvest. But, going
against the laws of nature, the vine had somehow become warped and twisted,
producing only wild grapes of little value. Jeremiah's use of the metaphor is
striking. In the original and positive use of the metaphor, Israel was like a vine,
taken from Egypt and planted in the promised land to flourish and be fruitful
(Ps 80:8–11). Jeremiah develops the negative aspects of the metaphor; the pure-
stock vine becomes wild and produces worthless fruit. And later, after the
destruction of Jerusalem, Ezekiel developed the theme even further in a parable;
as the vine did not produce the intended good fruit, its wood was only good for
burning (Ezek 15:1–8).

There is a further change of metaphor in v 22; now the language of hygiene is
introduced. Israel's sin, in practicing the fertility religions, was like a deeply in-
grained stain. It is not entirely clear whether an ingrained garment is imagined,
from which the mark cannot be removed despite the frequent usage of some
wonderful detergent. Or the metaphor may be the filth on the body, which no

amount of vigorous scrubbing can eliminate. But the emphasis is on the stain of sin that remains clearly in God's sight.

Once again, as if set in a court of law, Israel's protestation of innocence is captured in the quotation of v 23, "I am not defiled, I have not chased the Baals." The language flows directly from the preceding metaphor; the one whose in-grained filth is evident for all to see proclaims hypocritically, "I am not defiled." The one for whom the hill-top shrines and woodland bowers had become a second home (v 20) declares, "I have not chased the Baals." The word *Baals* is used in the plural (in contrast to the singular in v 8), implying not several gods, but the multitude of country shrines dedicated to the fertility god Baal.

The folly and hypocrisy of Israel's declaration is elaborated still further in vv 23c–24. It is possible, though not certain, that the reference to the "valley" (v 23) is an indirect reference to the Valley of ben-Hinnon, southwest of Jerusalem, in which pagan rituals were practiced. It was there that pagan rituals to foreign deities were undertaken (2 Kgs 23:10); hence there may be an allusion here to child sacrifice (cf. Soggin, *OrAnt* 8 [1969] 215–17). But it is perhaps more probable that the reference to the valley is intended in a more general sense as a part of the metaphor of the young camel in the later part of the verse.

As Bailey and Holladay have demonstrated clearly (*VT* 18 [1968] 256–60), the metaphor of the camel illustrates unreliability, whereas that of the wild ass illustrates lust-debased passion. The camel metaphor focuses on the young beast, which is fast and skittish, unpredictable and totally unreliable. It runs in this direction and then that, apparently with no rhyme or reason, leaving behind it in the sand of the valley floor a crisscrossing network of tracks. The young camel was in constant and speedy motion, but going nowhere; so too was Israel without direction and purpose in its unpredictable movements and actions.

The metaphor of the wild ass, however, brings out a further dimension of Israel's behavior, expressed in coarse language, but bringing out vividly the nature of its folly in succumbing to the fertility religion. The female ass, in heat, becomes desperate to find a male, rubbing its nose in the dust and sniffing the wind in search of a male ass. Then it charges about, seeking a partner with whom to fulfill its urgent and animal passions. So too Israel had become the servant of its own lewd passions, driven in its pursuit of those with whom it might fulfill its lustful desires. The picture is a tasteless one, especially to those who were all too familiar with the frenetic activities of the wild ass in heat, but it brought home powerfully the animal-nature of Israel's false religion that is so roundly condemned in the prophet's preaching.

The words of Israel in the quotation of v 25 reveal a different perspective in the self-understanding of the accused. Whereas before a degree of innocence had been proclaimed, albeit falsely (v 23), now a sense of resignation appears: "It's no good! No! For I have loved strangers and I will pursue them." The beloved strangers were no doubt the fertility gods whose foul cults held such strong attraction; like one addicted, but with a self-knowledge of that addiction, Israel is portrayed as resigned to the folly of its ways. But lest such resignation should sit too lightly upon Israel, the prophet illuminates the dimensions of its folly.

Israel's leaders (kings and princes, priests and prophets, v 26; cf. 2:8) have brought shame upon Israel. Just as a sneak thief, loving the darkness and trapped in the light of discovery, is filled with shame, so too the discovery and revelation of the evil acts of Israel's national leaders brings ignominy and shame on Israel as a whole. The prophet's use of language portrays sharply the idiocy of their shameful acts. What folly to say to a sculpted stone, the symbol of a fertility deity, "you gave me birth," or to say to the carved lump of wood, "you are my father!" Yet the stone pillars and wooden poles of the fertility cults were precisely the symbols of birth and parenthood; they were phallic symbols, representing the powers of creativity considered to be so central to existence in the fertility religions. Jeremiah, though, brings out the weakness of those symbols of power in his mocking question. When times of trouble come, it is no good to pray to standing stones and protruding pillars of wood; they can offer no help, for despite their symbolism, they have no real life. Israel had as many gods as it had cities, but with every new god, it became weaker, not stronger. For true strength lay in one God, who was alive, rather than in the multitude of deities symbolized in stone and wood.

Explanation

See the *Explanation* following 2:33–37.

Israel's Rebelliousness (2:29–32)

Bibliography

Bergman, J., Ringgren, H., and Tsevat, T. "B^ethulah." *TDOT* II (1975) 338–43. **Hoffmann, Y.** "Jeremiah 2:30." *ZAW* 89 (1977) 418–20. **Kahler, L.** "Jeremiah 2:31." *ZAW* 44 (1926) 62. **Loewenclau, I. von.** "Zu Jeremia ii 30." *VT* 16 (1966) 117–23.

Translation

29   *"Why do you contend against me?*   (3+3)
    Every one of you has rebelled against me."[a]
      The LORD's oracle.

30   *"I have stricken your sons to no avail;*   (3+3)
    they have not accepted correction.[a]
  Your sword has devoured your prophets   (3+2)
    as would a rampaging lion.[b]

31   *(You are the generation! Observe the LORD's word.)*[a]   (2+3)
  Have I become a wilderness to Israel,   (3+3)
    or a land of total darkness?
  Why do my people say: 'We have taken control![b]   (3+3)
    We will no longer come to you.'

32   *Does a young woman*[a] *forget her jewelry,*   (3+2)
    a bride her sashes?
  But my people have forgotten me   (2+2)
    for days beyond counting."

Notes

29.a. LXX has a longer line: "Why do you speak [implying תדברו for MT's תריבו] to me? You have all been ungodly, and you have all transgressed against me."

30.a. Various attempts have been made to emend the text of the first part of v 30; see the note in *BHS* and the proposals of Hoffmann, *ZAW* 89 (1977) 418–20. Yet the problem of the verse lies in its interpretation (see below), and there are not sound reasons for doubting the integrity of the text. Therefore, the translation reflects MT without emendation.

30.b. LXX adds: "but you were not afraid."

31.a. This line has the appearance of an editorial addition, being apparently additional to the poetic structure; it may refer back to v 30, by way of applying the meaning of that verse to the later readers of the text of Jeremiah. LXX apparently had a different text and reads: "Hear the Lord's word; thus said the Lord. . . ."

31.b. רדנו is interpreted as from רדה, "rule, dominate, take control." Alternatively, the text might be read (assuming haplogr) מרדנו, "we have rebelled."

32.a. "Young woman" seems the appropriate translation for בתולה in this context, rather than "virgin"; see *TDOT* 2 (1975) 338–43.

Form/Structure/Setting

In this passage, second person masculine plural suffixes are employed again, as in 2:4–13, with which passage the present section may have belonged originally. In the preceding section, the Lord declared his intention to "contend" (ריב) with Israel (2:9); in this context, the question is raised as to why Israel "contends" with God (2:29). A further link between the two sections may be seen in the use of the word "wilderness" (מדבר); in the preceding section, the people were reminded of how God had led them through the "wilderness" (2:6), whereas now he asks if he has become a "wilderness" to his people (2:31). In summary, it is probable that both passages belonged originally to a single oracle, though the original oracle was probably greater than the sum of the two surviving parts. (For further information on the original setting of the oracle, see the discussion at 2:4–13.)

Comment

"Why do you contend with me?" (v 29); the use of the verb "contend" (ריב) indicates that Israel, in its folly, wanted to bring suit against God for the failure in the covenant relationship. Presumably Israel (in the prophet's representation of its position) was working on the basis that the best defense was attack; as God had declared his intention to bring suit (2:9), Israel would bring a countersuit. But such a course of action was foolish, for the very basis of the covenant relationship was obedience, yet the essence of all Israel's actions was rebellion (v 29b).

The precise sense of the words "I have stricken your sons" (v 30) remains uncertain. The general reference is clearly to a divine act of correction, or chastisement, which had been to no avail; that is, it had not turned the people back from their rebellious ways. The word "sons" should probably not be interpreted literally; the general sense is the "people" of Israel. Nevertheless, the affliction of sons may imply the judgment of God passing from one generation to another (cf. Deut 5:9 and 28:59). Hence, the reference here would be to God's acts of chastisement, always intended to turn the people back to their true faith, throughout Israel's history.

Given this general interpretation of v 30a–b, it is probable that v 30c–d should also be interpreted in general terms, although it is possible to interpret the verse with respect to particular acts of violence against the true prophets (cf. 26:20–23). Interpreted in general terms, the verse forms a contrast with 2:8, where the false prophets of Baal apparently prophesied without constraint. In contrast, the true prophets, bringing God's word, were sometimes slain for their efforts (which was almost to be the experience of Jeremiah, later in his ministry).

The reference to the "rampaging lion" (v 30) may perhaps be understood as a simple and effective simile. Alternatively, the simile may allude to the ancient practice of engraving an animal's head on the top of a sword blade, the blade in turn being envisaged as the beast's devouring tongue (Thompson, 183).

The note inserted in brackets at the beginning of v 31 may be an editorial addition (see the note 31.a.). Its purpose, in part, would be to apply the message of Jeremiah's original sermon to subsequent generations of readers of that sermon. But, in addition, it is possible that what prompted the insertion of the note in the first place was the enigmatic reference to "sons" in v 30a (see above). Perhaps the editor's intention was to imply that the "sons" were none other than subsequent generations, and that therefore readers of the passage should take particular note of the implication of the message.

The divine statement in the form of a rhetorical question ("Have I become a wilderness?" v 31b) is stated in deliberate contrast to 2:6. The Lord, with whom Israel contends, is none other than the One who led them through the wilderness and the land of darkness; now they treat him as if he were a "wilderness" and "land of total darkness," offering neither succor nor light. The contrast is brought out all the more vividly by the quoted words of the people: "We have taken control." In the wilderness travels, the people were dependent on God as guide and provider of food and water. Now, in arrogant self-sufficiency, they think they can do without God and treat him not as the great provider but as if he were a barren wasteland.

The incongruity of Israel's folly is illustrated in v 32. A "young woman" (perhaps one preparing for marriage) would not forget her jewelry, nor would a "bride" forget the sashes of her bridal gown on the day of her wedding. Yet Israel, for longer than anyone could remember, had forgotten God. The metaphor at the beginning of the verse alludes to the language at the beginning of Jer 2: "the love at the time of your betrothal" (v 2). That love should have been lasting, the perpetual hallmark of the covenant relationship. Yet it had been a fleeting emotion, soon forgotten; love and commitment had been replaced by arrogance and an overweening sense of self-sufficiency. Such was Israel's rebellion.

Explanation

See the *Explanation* following 2:33–37.

The Way of Evil (2:33–37)

Bibliography

Fishbane, M. A. "Revelation and Tradition." *JBL* 99 (1980) 351–52. **Holladay, W. L.** "Jeremiah II 34b." *VT* 25 (1975) 221–25. **Soggin, J. A.** "Einige Bemerkungen über Jeremia ii 34." *VT* 8 (1958) 433–35. **Srobel, A.** "Jeremia 2, 34 im Rahmen des Gedichtes 2, 29–37." In *Kirche und Bibel*. FS E. Shick. Paderborn: Schoningh, 1979. 449–58.

Translation

33   *"How carefully you planned your way*   (2+2)
          of seeking love,
        so that even to the wicked women   (2?+2)
          you have taught [a] *your ways.*

34   *There was even found* [a] *on the hems of your robes* [b]   (3+3+2)
          the lifeblood of the innocent poor,
          not caught in an act of crime. [c]
    But in addition to all these things, [d]   (3+3+3)

35   *still you said: 'I am innocent!*
          surely his anger has turned from me.'
    I will certainly contend with you on that point,   (3+3)
          given your statement: 'I have not sinned.'

36   *Why do you take so very lightly* [a]   (2+2)
          the changing of your way?
    You shall be disappointed even by Egypt,   (3?+3)
          just as you were by Assyria

37   *You will only get out of this*   (3?+3)
          with your hands upon your head,
    for the LORD has rejected those whom you trusted,   (3+3)
          so that you will find no success with their help." [a]

Notes

33.a. The verb is written as 1 sg, "I taught," but (following Q) should be translated, as above, 2 sg, "you."

34.a. The pl form of the verb is translated indefinitely; the expected subject is "blood," which is, however, grammatically sg.

34.b. כנפיך, "hem, skirts." LXX translates: "in your hands," implying Heb. כפיך, which is a possible reading, though MT is more likely.

34.c. מחתרת: lit., "act of burglary, housebreaking" (see Exod 22:1, Heb.).

34.d. This line is difficult; for various proposals of emendation or revocalization, see Holladay, *VT* 25 (1975) 221–25. Holladay proposes to redivide the consonants and revocalize as follows: כִּי עֻלֵּךְ לְאָלָה, "indeed, your yoke has become execrable," which is possible, but not entirely persuasive in context. LXX, obviously finding the line difficult, understands אֵלֶּה as אֵלָה, "oak," but this is improbable. The translation above is an attempt to make sense of the line as it stands, but it is by no means certain, and the following *waw*-consec (in v 35) is improbable following such a construction. Bright (13) simply states that the line cannot be translated, which might be the wisest course!

36.a. The verb is interpreted as an impf form of זלל (II), "to take lightly," rather than being a de-fectively written form from אזל (as in AV). See further LXX and L. H. Brockington, *The Hebrew Text of the Old Testament*, 199.

37.a. MT להם, "to them." But one Heb. MS (de Rossi, III, 67) reads בהם (translated "with their help" above), with some support from Syr.

Form/Structure/Setting

This portion of an oracle, inserted into the fabric of the chapter as a whole, has the closest literary links to 2:20–28 (more precisely vv 23–26), to which it probably belonged in the pre-editorial state of the text. Both passages use the second person feminine singular form of address, but the more distinctive points of linkage between the two passages may be observed in the following data. (i) A key word in 2:33–37 is דרך, "way," in v 33 (twice) and v 36; see also the double usage of the term in v 23. (ii) The theme continues to be that of "love" (אהבה); see v 25 and v 33. (iii) The word בקש, "seek," is used in both passages (see v 24 and v 33). (iv) The word מצא, "find," is used twice in v 34, echoing the earlier occurrences in v 24 and v 26. (v) The root בוש, "shame, disappoint," is used twice in v 36, echoing the earlier double occurrence in v 26. It may be supposed, therefore, that originally vv 33–37 followed on directly from v 28, prior to the editorial insertion of vv 29–32. (On the possible setting of the whole passage, see *Form/Structure/Setting* at 2:20–28.)

Comment

The indictment of the nation continues with a scathing denunciation of its pursuit of "love" (v 33). The contrast, again, is with the word "love" at the beginning of the chapter (2:2), where it was used to describe Israel's first love for God at the "time of betrothal." The pure emotion of the early days of covenant relationship has been exchanged for lewd passion, namely, the nation's dedicated pursuit of the base forms of love that are given expression in the faith and practice of the fertility religion of Baal. Israel's misdirected planning of the life of love had become so debased that, in the sarcastic language of the prophet, the action could teach a few tricks to the common prostitutes (the "wicked women," v 33). But the power of the indictment is also emphasized by the opening expression "how carefully"; Israel's faithfulness had not temporarily lapsed, but the people had consciously dedicated themselves to a new "way," and had become expert in it.

The decline in spirituality and pursuit of false love inevitably had moral consequences; first, there came the immoral practices of the new religion, and from that all the rest began to follow. For the pursuit of a new kind of love meant the abandonment not only of the old love of the covenant relationship but also of the law of the covenant relationship within which that first love was to have found its expression. Hence, those dedicated to a new kind of love are quickly found to have innocent blood on their garments (v 34). The covenant concern for the "innocent poor" no longer belongs to the new ethic associated with fertility love. The poor may be exploited for personal benefit, their lives being of no particular consequence. Under the old covenant law, it was possible that a burglar, caught in the act of housebreaking, might be killed by the homeowner in self-defense (Exod 22:2–3, EVV). But such controlled conditions under which death might occur no longer survived under the new ethic; the blood on the garments was that of the innocent, who had committed no such criminal act.

Despite this wholesale exchange of faith, and the moral decline which accompanied it, still the nation had the gall to claim, "I am innocent" (v 35). The language is a continuation of the legal (lawsuit) overtones of the chapter as a whole; in spite of all the evidence presented to the contrary, the nation still declares its innocence. And the depth of the ignorance of the guilty party appears to be emphasized in its next words: "surely his anger has turned from me." Many are the criminals in court who have proclaimed with a straight face "not guilty," knowing full well their guilt but seeking nevertheless to avoid conviction. Yet here the proclamation of innocence seems to be genuinely ignorant. The true faith had been left so far in the past, the new faith had been so warmly embraced, that the voice of conscience had died completely, and the guilty party really believed that nothing would happen. Yet such innocent and ignorant hope is to be rudely awakened: "I will certainly contend with you on that point" (v 35). The language again points to a disputation in law; God would not simply accept at face value the statement "I have not sinned," but would bring out in rebuttal the full falsity of the declaration.

In part, the rebuttal is contained in v 36. Given Israel's actions, followed by the statement "I have not sinned," it was clear that the nation did not take seriously its ancient covenant commitment. Thus, in giving up the way of covenant and pursuing the way of fertility faith, the people considered it to be a matter of no great consequence. But all too soon, the folly of its way would become evident, as the foreign allies and masters upon whom Israel had come to depend turned out to be a total disappointment. Treaties with foreign states, like the covenant with God, implied commitments on the part of partners to the treaty; yet Israel, unfaithful in its covenant commitment, would discover that those foreigners to whom it was bound in treaty could also be unfaithful. Just as they had been disappointed by Assyria in the past, so too would they be disappointed in any future relationship of commitment with Egypt. Whether these international references allude to specific circumstances cannot be determined with certainty. It might be suggested that the words reflect a date c. 605 B.C., by which time Assyria has fallen from power and Egypt was a significant power on Judah's political horizons. But equally, if the oracle were from the earliest part of Jeremiah's ministry, the words could simply reflect the nation's typical tendency to vacillation, turning now to Assyria and now to Egypt. And, ironically, the let-down from foreign allies would be a breach of treaty no different in principle from Israel's failure in covenant relationship with God.

V 37 uses an expression of uncertain meaning: "with your hands upon your head." Thompson (186) suggests that the words indicate a sign of grief, citing 2 Sam 13:19. The end-panel of King Aharim of Byblos shows women in a mourning dance, their hands held over their heads (cf. J. Gray, *The Canaanites* [New York: Praeger, 1964] pl. 57 and p. 255). But equally, the words may imply that the nation, in turning to Egypt for aid, would find not help but captivity. In Egyptian reliefs depicting warfare, Egypt's enemies are frequently shown holding their hands above their heads, either as prisoners of war (in which case the hands are tied above the head) or else prior to being killed, when the upheld arms appear to be in a position of self-protection. Prisoners with hands tied above their heads are depicted on a limestone relief from as early as the fifth dynasty; persons with upstretched hands, about to be slain, may be observed in the famous Karnak relief, from the temple of Amon, dating to the time of Thutmosis III (Dynasty XVIII). See further K. Michalowski, *Art of Ancient Egypt* (New York: Abrams, n.d.), 367 (pl. 235) and 387 (pl. 363). Egypt's aid, in other words, might result in captivity and death; the covenant with God, which had been rejected, was a covenant of freedom and life. When the true covenant had been abandoned, there could be no hope for success elsewhere.

Explanation (2:1–37)

The literary form of Jeremiah's sayings in chaps. 2–6 presents first an indictment of Israel's evil, followed by a call for repentance (3:1–4:4) and a concluding declaration of judgment (4:5–6:30). From an awareness of this larger perspective, it follows that the prophet's message in chap. 2 is only a partial message; before he invites repentance, he must first establish beyond doubt the reality of the evil from which he will ask his people to turn. Chap. 2 thus contains an anatomy of evil, documented with evidence of past and present sins; its purpose, though, is not simply to serve as a record of failure but rather to prod the consciences of listeners and readers to the recognition of the need for repentance. Only when the full extent of present evil is recognized is a complete and wholehearted repentance possible.

The perspective from which the indictment of evil is presented is that of covenant; though the word "covenant" is not employed, the chapter abounds with the language of covenant and allusions to that fundamental relationship between Israel and God. Israel's failure in covenant is demonstrated from two different, but related, perspectives, each of which is interlaced throughout the chapter, creating the closely knit fabric of the whole. One perspective is that of religious apostasy; Israel had abandoned the exclusive faith in the one covenant God and had participated in a syncretistic fashion in the fertility cult of Baal. The second perspective is political and international: instead of recognizing the single suzerainty of the Lord, the nation vacillated between dependence on Assyria and on Egypt, both foreign and pagan powers.

The two perspectives are developed in different ways, yet it is clear that the fundamental failure in all of Israel's history was a failure in relationship; the evil analyzed here with such penetrating perception is an evil that flows from the loss of an intimate relationship with God. Religiously, the primary relationship of trust has been broken, and so the language of prostitution is employed by the prophet to illustrate the people's unfaithfulness. Nationally, the independent state has lost its confidence and turned to foreign powers for help, and so the language of international relationships is employed to illustrate national failure.

What binds all these perspectives together is the notion of covenant. Israel had been joined to God in covenant but had failed in all its covenant responsibilities. That failure led to further covenants of a false kind, the covenant to the fertility faith of Baal, depicted as a prostitution of the true faith, and treaties (which in Hebrew is the same word as covenant) with foreign nations, tantamount to a national rejection of the true faith.

Though the language of the chapter is interrupted occasionally by the anticipation of judgment, it is the failure in relationship that is foremost in the prophet's
mind. And the nation that has failed in relationship is on trial, submitted to cross-
questioning with respect to its faith. The nation's response, expressed rhetorically
in the prophet's sermons, illuminates its guilt for the imaginary members of the
court to see and hear. The responses alternate between denial of failure and protestation of innocence, on the one hand, to admission of guilt coupled with
arrogant and insolent affirmations of self-sufficiency, on the other hand. No doubt
the prophet's technique in this use of the language of the courtroom was to create insight and self-awareness. If they could only grasp it, they would be able to
repent, for true repentance may only follow upon the recognition of the nature
and extent of the fundamental failure in relationship.

With the benefit of hindsight, we can see the crucial significance of these themes
from the prophet's early preaching. Israel's national existence, as a covenant
people, depended upon their maintenance of a loving and faithful relationship
with God. When that relationship was lost, there could be no sure ground for the
continuing existence of Israel as a nation. Its raison d'être would have gone. And
that, in essence, is what the prophet is saying in his indictment of Israel's sin. Yet
his sole purpose in this dismal chapter is to change the state of affairs that he
perceived to exist. He exposed sin in its reality only as a precursor to this call for
repentance. He felt in his innermost being that the end of his nation must be
very close, unless drastic and radical action were taken. Like a marriage coun-
selor dealing with an unfaithful partner to a relationship, he perceived all too
clearly that the relationship would collapse entirely unless immediate and radical
measures were undertaken.

Later in his life, he saw that he had failed, for the end of the nation came
while he was still a prophet. Perhaps he could have done none other than fail, yet
the genius of his book is that the message remains true. Before the call to repentance can be heeded, the full extent of evil must be exposed, and at bottom the
root of evil in Israel was the loss and perversion of its ancient covenant love for
God.

B. The Prophetic Plea for Repentance (3:1–4:4)

Bibliography

Holladay, W. L. *Architecture.* 45–54. **Jobling, D.** "Jeremiah's Poem in III.I.–IV.2." *VT* 28 (1978)
45–55. **Muilenburg, J.** "A Study of Hebrew Rhetoric: Repetition and Style." *VTSup* I. Leiden:
Brill, 1953. 97–111. **Raitt, T. M.** "The Prophetic Summons to Repentance." *ZAW* 83 (1971)
30–49.

Form/Structure/Setting

This passage comprises the second principal unit in the collection of Jeremiah's
early oracles contained in chaps. 2–6 (see above); following the indictment of

Israel for its sin (Jer 2), there is now stated a passionate plea for repentance (3:1–4:4), followed in section three of the collection (4:5–6:30) by a declaration of the advent of divine judgment. As in the preceding section of this collection of prophetic oracles, the unit has been constructed, in its present literary format, from originally independent oracles (or portions thereof). And as before, the parts of the new whole have been carefully welded together; whereas some of the textual joints are evident (e.g., between the prose and poetic sections), in other places it is not easy to determine what were the original constituent parts from which the whole has been fashioned. The points summarized below attempt to provide a perspective on the chapter as a whole; the conjectural issues are dealt with in greater detail in the discussion of the individual parts of the chapter.

Introduction: 3:1. Although v 1 is commonly interpreted as poetry and as a part of the opening section (vv 1–5), it is better to understand it as prose, serving as an introductory theme for the key theme of the chapter, namely "repentance" (for which various forms of the root שוב are employed). This verse also provides an introduction to the central language of the chapter, namely, marriage/unfaithfulness/ prostitution, by which the theme is to be developed in the remainder of the chapter. Structurally, it is parallel to 2:2–3 in the preceding section. In 2:2–3, the fundamental perspective (namely youthful love) is established against which the indictment of Israel's evil is to be presented; likewise, in 3:1, the fundamental folly from which the call to repentance will be issued is established.

> *Poetry: 3:2–5.* The people's unfaithfulness.
> *Prose: 3:6–11.* The failure of Israel and Judah.
> *Poetry: 3:12–13.* Invitation to Israel to repent.
> *Prose: 3:14–18.* Invitation to Judah to repent.
> *Poetry: 3:19–4:2.* Forgiveness and repentance.
> *Summary (poetry): 4:3–4.* Repetition of call to repentance.

This summary of the material contained in the section as a whole provides only an analysis of the material in its present form but does not yet address the more vexing question of the relationship between the parts or the integrity of the whole. In turning to these issues, there are numerous problems, including the interrelationship of the poetic sections, if any, and the place and role of the prose units in the larger context.

Most scholars have argued that the principal poetic sections originally formed a single poem. Thus Bright (25) states that 3:1–5, 19–25, and 4:1–4 were a single unit. And Jobling, in a rhetorical study, has proposed that the original poem consisted of 3:1–5, 19–20, 12b–13, and 3:21–4:2. Although there is some disagreement between these and other scholars concerning what was in the poem, and the sequence of the parts, it is nevertheless doubtful that one can conclude that there was ever a single poem underlying the chapter, for a number of reasons. (i) There is inconsistency in the number and gender of forms of address (specifically the second person, "you") in the various poetic units: second person feminine singular (vv 2, 13, 19); second person masculine plural (vv 12, 19, 20, 22); second person masculine singular (4:1). While the reason for such inconsistency cannot be determined with certainty, it should certainly be noted (in contrast to chap. 2) that the forms militate against original poetic unity. (ii) The commonality of theme, on the basis of which the chapter was brought together in the first place, suggests greater unity between the component parts than may actually be the case. (iii) The editorial process (as observed in chap. 2) was such that in all probability only portions of oracles were employed in the construction of the literary unit, and even if one or two of the poetic elements of Jer 3 may originally have belonged together, we can have no assurance that anything like a single or complete poem ever lay behind the chapter as it now stands.

The interpretation of the prose units in this section is equally difficult. They may originally have formed a whole, having been separated by the insertion of the poetry (vv 12–13), or the poetic unit may have been part of the whole, or the two prose units may have been drawn from separate sources.

There is thus enormous uncertainty with respect to the prehistory of the units that make up this section of the book as a whole; detailed issues are examined under *Form/Structure/Setting* in the discussion of each passage. Yet to some extent, the obsession with seeking the antecedent parts from which this section of Jer 2–6 has been constructed may be misleading, for it may blind us to the extraordinary unity of theme in the present literary form of the whole passage. The key theme, extending throughout, is that of repentance, highlighted by various uses of the root שוב, which occurs in every unit except 4:3–4 (which is a summary and transitional passage) as follows: 3:1 (twice), 7 (twice), 8, 10, 11, 12 (twice), 14 (twice), 19, 22 (thrice), 4:1 (twice). But there are also many other key words, occurring in both the poetic and prose passages; while on the one hand, these common words and themes provided the editorial criteria for the selection of units in the construction of the whole, they also provided an extraordinary degree of literary unity to the whole text, despite its character as a kind of literary mosaic. It should be stressed that these interlocking words and themes provide not only a degree of unity to the poetic elements but also firmly establish the prose units as a part of the whole. And likewise, the prose units contribute substantially to the development of the theme of the whole chapter and its movement toward climax. However one is to resolve the complex question of the relationship between prose and poetry, it is clear that in this section prose and poetry go closely together to form an integral whole. The prose was certainly not a loose addendum to an originally poetic unit; rather, the editor has worked both prose and poetry into the literary mosaic, and if indeed the collection of material in Jer 2–6 represents not only the prophet's early oracles but also an early collection of oracles (viz. c. 605 B.C.), then one must suppose that some prose elements formed a substantial part of the Book of Jeremiah from an early point in the process that led to its compilation. The question whether the prose can be described as Deuteronomic is addressed in the notes that follow.

Repentance: Introduction and Elaboration (3:1–5)

Bibliography

Fishbane, M. A. "Torah and Tradition." In *Tradition and Theology in the Old Testament.* Ed. D. Knight. Philadelphia: Fortress Press, 1977. 284–86. ———. "Revelation and Tradition." *JBL*

99 (1980) 351. **Hobbs, T. R.** "Jeremiah 3:1–5 and Deuteronomy 24:1–4." *ZAW* 86 (1974) 23–29. **Jöuon, P.** "Le sens du mot Hebreu SPY." *JA* 7 (1906) 137–39. **Long, B. O.** "The Stylistic Components of Jeremiah 3:1–5." *ZAW* 88 (1976) 386–90. **Martin, J. D.** "The Forensic Background to Jeremiah III.1." *VT* 19 (1969) 82–92. **McKane, W. A.** "SPY(Y)M with Special Reference to the Book of Jeremiah." In *Mélanges bibliques et orientaux en l'honneur de M. Henri Conzelles.* Ed. A. Caquot and M. Delcor. AOAT 212. Neukirchen-Vluyn: Neukirchener Verlag, 1981. 319–35. **Wurz, H.** "Die Möglichtheit der Umkehr nach Jer 3, 1." *Erbe als Auftrag.* FS J. Pritz. Wiener Beitrag zur Theologie 40 (1973) 259–73. **Zakowitch, Y.** "The Woman's Rights in the Biblical Law of Divorce." *JLA* 4 (1981) 28–46.

Translation

1   *A saying:*
"If a man should divorce his wife, and she should go from him and marry [a] *another man, can the first man return to her* [b] *again? Would not that land* [c] *be defiled? But you have acted as a whore with a multitude of companions—yet you return to me?"*
The LORD's oracle.

2	*"Raise your eyes to the open country* [a] *and look!*	(3+3)
	Where have you not been laid?	
	By the highways you sat in wait for them,	(3+2)
	like a Bedouin [b] *in the wilderness,*	
	and you have defiled the land	(2+2)
	by your prostitution and your perversity.	
3	[a] *So the showers were withheld,*	(2+2)
	and there was no springtime rain; [a]	
	but you had the brazenness of a prostitute, [b]	(4?+2)
	refusing to be humiliated.	
4	*Didn't you then call me, 'My father!*	(4+3)
	you are the close friend of my youth!	
5	*Will he hold a grudge for ever*	(2+2)
	or keep watch in perpetuity?'	
	See how you spoke and acted,	(3+2)
	doing all the evil you could!"	

Notes

1.a. Lit., "and she should belong (or be) to another man."

1.b. Lit., "can he return to her?" LXX reverses the notion, translating "may she return to him?" Hobbs (*ZAW* 86 [1974] 23) and others think that LXX may be original here and that the Heb. text may reflect a later attempt to align the passage with Deut 24:1–4. But this is far from certain, and the differences between LXX and MT (which continue in the next line) more probably reflect the varieties between two textual traditions.

1.c. LXX translates "would not that woman be defiled?" whereas the Heb. reference to land fits in with the law of Deut 24:1–4. The Heb. text is more probable, reflecting knowledge of the legal tradition (see further the *Comment*), whereas the LXX reflects an attempt to continue the surface logic of the preceding lines.

2.a. The precise meaning of Heb. שפים is uncertain, both here and in other places in Jeremiah (3:21; 4:11; 7:29; 12:12; 14:6) and Isaiah (41:18; 49:9). The various ways in which the word is rendered in the versions, and the lexical and philological background to the Heb., are examined in great detail by W. McKane (in *Mélanges bibliques*, 319–35). Though he comes to no positive conclusion, McKane demonstrates clearly that "hill tops, high places" is an inappropriate translation; perhaps the closest we can come to the meaning is "open country, countryside." The same difficulty is encountered in Ugaritic, where the word *špm* occurs twice, once fairly clearly (*CTA* 23.4) and once in a broken text (*CTA* 1.ii.11). In the first of these texts, it is associated with "wilderness," *bmdbr.špm* (in a fashion similar to Jer 4:11 and 12:12), and is commonly translated "(sand) dunes": Gibson, *CML*, 123; Caquot et al., *Textes Ougaritiques* I, 369; G. del Olmo Lete, *Mitos y Leyendas de Canaan* (Madrid: Cristiandad, 1981) 631. The suggestion seems to go back to Driver (*CML*, 149), who followed Virolleaud (*Syria* 14 [1933] 137), but proposed an etymology on the basis of Arab. (*safiyatu*, "sand dunes") and Syriac (*šapya*, "plain"). For further discussion of the possible meaning of Ug. *špm*, see P. Xella, *Il Mito di ŠHR e ŠLM* (Studi Semitici 44, University of Rome, 1973) 43–44. J. C. de Moor, however, interprets the word as ptcp from *šwp*, "to adorn" (*New Year with Canaanites and Israelites*, II [Kampen, 1972] 19, n. 67); the suggestion is unlikely, but if it were to prove correct, then the Heb. term would appear to be totally unrelated. Finally, there remains the possibility that Ug. *špm* is a place name; see the discussion by M. C. Astour in *RSP* II, 332–33 (with bibliography). In summary, though the meaning of Heb. שְׁפִם and Ug. *špm* remain uncertain, the translation of both terms by "open country, countryside" would seem to fit best the lexical background and the contextual usage.

2.b. "Bedouin" is a translation of Heb. עֲרָבִי; the word suggests a translation "Arab" (cf. NEB), though the modern semantic range of that term makes the translation quite inappropriate. The general sense is of a person who dwells in the desert, hence "Bedouin"; on the meaning of the simile, see the *Comment* below. LXX translates with the word κορώνη, "crow, raven," implying Heb. עֹרֵב, "raven," which is possible, if the gentilic *yodh* were to be omitted from the consonantal text of MT.

3.a. LXX has a quite different text for the first two lines of v 3: "and you kept many shepherds as a stumbling block for yourself." The difference reflects a quite different textual tradition, of uncertain meaning, though "shepherds" are referred to again in v 15 (in both MT and LXX).

3.b. Lit., "the forehead of a female prostitute."

Form/Structure/Setting

These verses contain in effect two parts, which have been joined nevertheless so that both together serve to function as an introduction to 3:1–4:4.

The first part consists of v 1, which would appear to be written in normal Hebrew prose, despite being set out as poetry in both *BHS* and most modern translations (e.g., RSV, NEB). The first part of the verse is essentially a paraphrase of the substance of the law also known in Deut 24:1–4; the second part of the verse applies the paraphrase to the theme about to be elaborated in the section that follows. There is no clear parallelism within the lines, which simply summarize the substance of the law and its application. The paragraph is introduced by "A Saying" (לֵאמֹר), which is presumably an abbreviated form of the familiar prophetic introduction (cf. 2:1) and is concluded by "the Lord's oracle," indicating perhaps the original integrity and independence of the verse. The verse is probably not a "didactic question" (or part thereof), as proposed by Hobbs (*ZAW* 86 [1974], 23–29); it is perhaps better classified, with Long (*ZAW* 88 [1976], 386–90), as a "disputation." Yet, in its immediate literary context, it is important rather to observe its introductory role with respect to the section on repentance that follows. Several key words and themes in this verse will be constantly repeated and elaborated in the following units: שָׁלַח (cf. v 8); שׁוּב (throughout); חָנֵף (cf. vv 2, 9); הִנֵּה (v 5); and others.

Immediately following the prose introduction is a poetic passage, closely linked to the introduction, in which the basic theme is elaborated. It draws upon the language of the prose introduction (e.g., in the use of הִנֵּה and חָנֵף), but also sets out further words and themes which eventually will be worked into the larger mosaic of the chapter as a whole (e.g., the repetition of שְׁפִים, v 2, in v 21; the reference to "my father," v 4, [see also vv 18 and 19]; and various other themes). There is no further reference to repentance in vv 2–5, which has been in introduced rhetorically in v 1, for at this stage the purpose is to create an awareness of the need for repentance, concurrently with the apparent futility of it, before establishing later that repentance is not only possible but also essential.

Comment

1 *Introduction.* The opening verse contains a much condensed paraphrase of the legislation pertaining to marriage, divorce, and remarriage in Deut 24:1–4. In essence, when a man has divorced a woman, who then remarries and is subsequently divorced, the original husband may not remarry her (see further Craigie, *Deuteronomy,* 304–6). The law clearly pertains to marital affairs, not to the convenant faith, but the synopsis of the law is provided at the beginning for two reasons: (i) the language of marriage (and unfaithfulness) continues the metaphor of the relationship between God and Israel that has already been extensively employed in Jer 2; (ii) the law here uses the word שׁוּב (of the husband "returning" to the former wife), a word which may also denote "repentance." Beyond these general points, it would be unwise to press the opening analogy of marital law, for as the prophet develops the theme, he freely adapts it to his immediate purpose. (Thus, though the legal summary indicates that the original husband cannot *return* to the original wife, in the development of the theme, the concern is with the return of Israel, the wife, to the Lord, the husband. But the purpose of the chapter is not legal; the summarized legislation merely provides the starting point for the elaboration of unfaithfulness and the invitation to return to God that follow.) In this development of the law of remarriage and divorce with respect to Israel's relationship to God, Jeremiah is standing in the tradition of Hosea (1–3); nevertheless, Jeremiah develops the theme differently from its appearance in the Book of Hosea. The remarriage of which Hosea writes (3:1–5) is an anticipation of the new covenant; here, in Jeremiah, the law is adapted and developed with specific emphasis on the possibility and necessity of *repentance,* which (given the nation's failure) might at first seem to be impossible or "illegal." The quite different ways in which the marital law is developed make improbable any dependence of Jeremiah on the earlier work of Hosea in this context.

The second part of the introductory verse makes clear the way in which the legal analogy is to be applied. The nation had "acted as a whore with a multitude of companions"; that is, it had abandoned the covenant relationship of faithfulness to the one God and freely experimented with the practices of false faiths. In effect, by her actions, the nation had deserted God. While her new estate could hardly be dignified by the word marriage, it was a series of marital-type relationships, none of which was lasting or characterized by any degree of faithfulness. Given such behavior, how could the nation possibly return to its first relationship of marriage, even if it desired to do so? Had such actions not rendered impossible the restoration of relationship? That is the dilemma. But the introduction is powerful as a means of grasping attention. To the reader who has not even pondered the possibility of repentance, the opening statement in this section on repentance suggests that it might not be possible! That, certainly, is the legal perspective presupposed by the opening analogy, but before the chapter is complete, the requirements of law will have been overwhelmed by the compassion of grace.

2–5 *Elaboration.* The prophet now develops his theme in lines of poetry; the language might at first seem offensive, but the real offense lies in the behavior that is described. Those to whom the prophet addressed his message need only turn their eyes to the landscape round about them; there was not a place where they had not offended. The sexual nature of the description is not merely a development of the opening legislation; rather, it is the prophet's way of reducing to its basic character the actions of the citizens in their participation in the sexual frolics that marked certain types of fertility cult. They could not claim to have been seduced or forced into such actions; indeed, they were out there in the highways and byways searching for opportunities. The simile of the Bedouin (v 2d) does not imply any moral criticism of the desert dwellers; rather, as the Bedouin could be seen on the wilderness highways offering certain wares for sale, so too the chosen people sat out in public places looking for lovers. They were active pursuers of evil, not merely passive recipients; by their action, they had defiled their holy and promised land.

The reference to the withholding of rain in v 3 seems at first somewhat incongruous in context, but the meaning is to be found in the nature of the fertility cults in which the people were engaged. The rituals of fertility were designed in part to ensure that Baal, the great God of fertility, continued to send the rains upon which the fertility of the land depended. God's withholding of the rains should have indicated clearly enough to the people that their fertility rites ensured nothing; the God of covenant was as much Lord of the natural world as he was of the events of history. But even the withholding of rains and consequent drought was of no avail; with remarkable obduracy, the people continued in their foul practices, showing not the least sense of humiliation or understanding.

Indeed, the hypocrisy of the syncretistic religion of Jeremiah's day is stated clearly in vv 4–5; the people wanted it both ways—the assurances that came from the old covenant faith, coupled with the newly found joys of fertility worship. And so those who defiled the land by their actions of prostitution could still address God as "father" and glibly refer to the friendship of youth. God remembered that youthful devotion with fondness and sorrow (cf. 2:2), but the glib statement of v 5 suggests no deep understanding by the nation of the words that are used. The people's words in v 5a–b seem to be in the form of an aside; no sooner had they said "my father" than they went on to say (to reassure themselves) that God would not hold a grudge. They not only insulted God by their words and actions but lied to themselves, thereby bolstering false confidence and keeping at bay the qualms of a conscience almost dead. But the prophet's words (v 5c–d) reveal again precisely those home-truths that the people did not want to know.

Explanation

See the *Explanation* following 4:3–4.

The Failure of Israel and Judah (3:6–11)

Bibliography

Erlandson, S. "בגד." *TDOT.* I, 470–73. **Holladay, W. L.** *The Root šûbh in the Old Testament.* Leiden: Brill, 1958. ———. "The Recovery of Poetic Passages of Jeremiah." *JBL* 85 (1966) 401–35. **McKane, W.** "Relations between Poetry and Prose in the Book of Jeremiah with Special Reference to Jeremiah 3:6–11." VTSup 32 (1980) 220–37. **Rowley, H. H.** "The Early Prophecies of Jeremiah in Their Setting." *BJRL* 45 (1962–63) 198–234.

Translation

[6]*And the LORD said to me during the reign of King Josiah, "Have you seen what apostate Israel has done? She went up every high hill and under every flourishing tree and there she behaved as a prostitute.[a]* [7]*But I said to myself: 'after she has done all these things, she will return to me.' But she did not return, and Judah, her faithless sister, observed it.* [8]*And she[a] observed that, on the basis of all the occasions that apostate Israel committed adultery, I divorced her and gave to her the divorce document.[b] But her sister, faithless Judah, had no fear and she too went and acted like a prostitute.* [9]*And by the very frivolity of her prostitution, she defiled the land[a] and committed adultery with standing stone and wooden pillar.[b]* [10]*And even with all this happening, Judah, her faithless sister, has not returned to me wholeheartedly, but only deceitfully." The LORD's oracle.* [11]*So the LORD said to me, "Apostate Israel has justified herself more than faithless Judah."*

Notes

6.a. The 3 fem sg form of the verb is read (with *BHS*), rather than the 2nd person implied by the consonantal text.
8.a. MT's 1st person form is read as 3 fem sg, with some support from Heb. MSS (de Rossi, III, 68), Syr, and some Gk. MSS.
8.b. LXX has slightly longer text, indicating that the bill of divorce was placed "into her hand" (with which compare Deut 24:1, the passage on which the legal analogy is based).
9.a. The clause "she defiled the land" is omitted in LXX.
9.b. Lit., "with stone and wood," which in turn were fertility cult objects (cf. 2:27 and *Comment*).

Form/Structure/Setting

This prose passage is introduced as a word of the Lord addressed to Jeremiah (though there has survived no accompanying word to indicate that it was to be addressed in public to Judah); it is in the form of a monologue. The language is normal prose, having many affinities with the surrounding poetry; it would appear to be an integral part of the literary structure of 3:1–4:4. In other words, along with the poetry in the larger section, this prose passage has been employed in the editorial arrangement as an essential "building block"; it is not merely an editorial addendum. E. W. Nicholson (44) and many others have claimed that this passage is "in the characteristic prose style of the book and is probably the work of a Deuteronomic editor." But the evidence for such a view is far from clear, and much of what might appear to be Deuteronomic in this context is a

natural corollary of the theme of the whole section, which develops the paraphrase of Deut 24:1–4 provided in 3:1.

Just why the passage is in prose and not poetry is not known: see the general
discussion in the *Introduction* and the detailed studies of this passage in McKane
(VTSup 32 [1980] 220–37) and Holladay (*JBL* 85 [1966] 401–35). On the one
hand, the discourse may originally have been in prose; on the other hand, an
originally poetic discourse may have been reduced to prose (e.g., in the context
of Baruch's scribal activity). But it is more important to recognize the affinities of
this prose passage with its literary setting and also its related poetic narratives. In
particular, the prose passage continues to develop the theme of 3:1 and the poetry of 3:2–5, notably in the following language: (i) שׁוּב, "return," in vv 6, 7, 8, 10,
11 (developing the usage in 3:1); (ii) זנה, "to behave as a prostitute," in vv 6, 9 (cf.
3:1, 2, 3); (iii) שׁלח, "divorce," in v 8 (cf. v 1); (iv) חנף, "defile," v 9 (cf. vv 1, 2). There
is thus little reason to doubt that the language of the passage is Jeremianic prose.

The oracle is introduced with a general statement of date, namely, that it came
from Josiah's period. There is little reason to doubt the general dating, though it
would be difficult to be more precise in dating, given the general state of affairs
that it describes. It is possible, but by no means certain, that the oracle could
date to the earliest period of Jeremiah's ministry (viz. before Josiah's reform),
but in that it may contain a perspective of general retrospect, namely, a review of
the nation's history since the fall of Samaria and Israel, such precise dating cannot be assured. That the oracle comes from Josiah's period, however, need not
be doubted (cf. Rowley, *BJRL* 45 [1962–1963] 198–234).

It is possible, though by no means certain, that this passage originally formed a
part of a larger narrative to which 3:14–18 also belonged. The monologue character
of the text under examination, and the absence of a specific word to be declared,
would be nicely balanced by the call to repentance contained in 3:14–18.

Comment

The monologue begins with an account of the evil behavior of the then defunct
state of Israel, which was conquered by the Assyrians in 722 B.C. The citizens of the
Northern Kingdom had indulged in the gross practices of the fertility religions at a
multitude of country shrines. It had been the divine hope that once these foul practices had run their course, Israel would return to the true faith; the very practice
of false faiths should have made it clear to the participants in those rituals that
they were not only wrong but also futile with respect to their goals pertaining to the
fertility of the land. Yet such was not the case; Israel did not return to the true
faith, and all the time Judah, the southern neighbor, was watching what was going on. The consequence of the nation of Israel's folly was that it was destroyed;
the failure in the life of faith led to the termination of the covenant, and to the
defeat of the nation. In the language of the monologue, the termination of Israel's
national existence is described in terms of adultery, followed by divorce. But Judah,
all the while observing from the south, learned nothing from Israel's fate in history; Judah continued to act in precisely the same manner that had culminated
in its neighbor's demise. And the very frivolity of Judah's actions, and the consequent defilement of the holy land, implied that Judah too must be divorced; her
adulterous associations with false fertility faiths (on "stone" and "wood" in v 9; cf.

the *Comment* on 2:27) provided the grounds for such a divorce. Perhaps v 10 implies that there was a superficial change of heart, a temporary return to the relationship of covenant, in the nation of Judah; if so, it is possible that the allusion is to the reforms undertaken in the reign of King Josiah. But even such reform, as the prophet indicates firmly, would be to no avail; they were not profound, they did not reflect a wholehearted change of life, but merely covered deceitfully a fundamentally unfaithful character that had not been transformed.

This section of the message concerning repentance goes beyond the introductory presentation of the theme (3:1–5), though in doing so it develops further the general theme. The opening verses of the chapter had set forth the analogy of marriage and covenant; as Judah had failed in its marriage, or covenant, with God and forged new covenants with foreign deities, it could not expect the automatic right of returning to God. But in this prose narrative, the culpability and folly of Judah are heightened in the comparison with Israel,, and the two are presented as sisters. Judah had failed in faithfulness, but it could hardly claim the excuse of ignorance or inexperience. It had watched carefully its sister Israel tread the path of failure, and it had seen clearly the consequences of such failure. But Judah had been too foolish, or too perverse, to learn the lessons of history. Jeremiah's contrast here is developed even more fully in the lewd tale of Oholah and Oholibah (Ezek 23). But there is no reason to assume any interdependence of the two passages. As the narrative under examination appears to be Jeremianic, not Deuteronomic, we need not assume that it has been stamped by the influence of Ezekiel. While it is possible (given the relative chronology of the two texts) that Ezekiel's allegory of the two sisters was influenced either by Jeremiah's preaching or writing, such a possibility is at best distant. Once the notion of marital unfaithfulness had been applied to the covenant relationship, notably by Hosea with reference to Israel, the later adaptation of the same notion to Judah must naturally have evoked the parallel between two sisters.

The key words in this prose oracle are the various forms of שׁוּב; the theme develops the initial use of the term in 3:1. As Holladay has shown (*The Root šûbh in the Old Testament*), the word has many different nuances; in this passage, the different aspects of the word are contrasted for striking effect. The basic sense of the word is to "turn," but it may have the nuance "turn to," "turn from," and various other developed senses. In the initial usage (3:1), it was used of the "return" of a man to a woman after divorce and remarriage, and of the "return" (in effect, "repentance") of Judah to God. Throughout the narrative, the Northern Kingdom is called "*Apostate* [מְשֻׁבָה] Israel," that is, a nation that has *turned* from God to evil. God thought that after Israel's folly, the nation would *return* (v 7, in effect, "repent"), but she did not *return* (לֹא שָׁבָה). Likewise Judah (v 10), despite an apparent change of heart, had not *returned* to God. The power of the language, apart from its contrast of turning "to" and "from," is to be seen also in its applicability to the relationships of both marriage and covenant. But the climax of the whole theme is to be found in the impassioned plea for the repentance, for a *return* to God, presented in 4:1.

Closely related to "apostate Israel" is the expression "faithless Judah." The word בָּגוֹדָה, "faithless," a form of which is employed again later in the chapter (cf. 3:20), may also apply to both covenant and marriage. In the context of marriage, it denotes such acts as desertion and the establishing of a relationship with another person; in the context of covenant, it denotes the failure to maintain the responsibilities of relationship. And, as the basic designation of Judah in this passage, it points to the nation's fundamental flaw: it was not so much a breaking of the divine *law*, as it was a failure in *relationship* with God, from which all other calamities flowed.

Explanation

See the *Explanation* following 4:3–4.

An Invitation to Repentance Addressed to Israel (3:12–13)

Bibliography

Cazelles, H. "Israël du nord et arche d 'alliance (Jér. III 16)." *VT* 18 (1968) 147–58. **Petersen, D. L.** *Late Israelite Prophecy.* SBLMS 23. Missoula, MT: Scholars, 1977. 32. **Turner, P. D. M.** "Two Septuagintalisms with στηρίζειν." *VT* 28 (1978) 481–82.

Translation

12	"Go and proclaim these words to the north, saying,	
	'Repent, apostate Israel!'	(3+3)
	The LORD's oracle.	
	'I will no longer frown[a] on you.	
	For I am perpetually loving!'	(2+2)
	The LORD's oracle.	
	'I will not keep a grudge forever.	
13	But you must acknowledge your iniquity,	(3+3)
	that you have rebelled against the LORD your God,	
	that you have scattered your tracks toward strangers	(3+2?)
	(under every flourishing tree)[a]	
	and not obeyed[b] my voice.'	
	The LORD's oracle."	

Notes

12.a. Lit., "I will not make my face fall on you." LXX has στηριῶ, "I will not *set* (my face)." On the use of the verb στηρίζειν in LXX (cf. Jer 21:10; 24:6), cf. Turner, *VT* 28 (1978) 481–82.

13.a. This line may be an addition to the original text (cf. *BHS*), specifically a duplication of the same expression in 3:6, but this is uncertain, and the phrase is found in both the Heb. MSS and LXX.

13.b. The pl form of the verb is unexpected (after the preceding sg forms), and probably 2 sg should be read (with LXX).

Form/Structure/Setting

On the possible relationship of this short unit to its immediate literary context, see 3:1–4:4, *Form/Structure/Setting*. In summary, while the verses may originally have

belonged to a larger poem (Jobling, *VT* 28 [1978] 45–55), or may have simply been
an integral part of the surrounding prose narrative, it is more probable that they
are a fragment of an originally larger poetic oracle addressed to Israel.

The language of this short passage linked it to both the preceding prose section and the introductory poetic section. (i) Links with the introductory poetic
section are seen in the common usage of the verb נטר in conjunction with לעולם
(v 12; cf. v 5) and in the notion of "ways" (דרכיך, v 13; cf. v 2). (ii) Links with the
preceding prose section are to be seen in the use of "apostate Israel" (v 12; cf. vv
6, 8, 11) and perhaps, if the text is sound (see note 13.a.), in the repeated use of
the phrase: "under every flourishing tree" (v 13; cf. v 6). The theme linking all
three sections is that of the word שוב, "turning, repentance."

Given the brevity of the unit, the original setting of the verses and their date
cannot be determined. But the introductory prophetic formula (v 12a) specifies
that the words were to be addressed to the north, and the substance of the verses
refers to Israel; these two items together strongly suggest a prophetic oracle explicitly addressed to the north, not Judah, in the first instance. The northern focus
does not necessarily imply an address to those in exile from the Northern Kingdom;
more probably, one may suppose that a part of Jeremiah's ministry was exercised
in the territory that formerly belonged to the northern state, but came under
the control of Judah in Josiah's time (2 Kgs 23:15–20) with the decline of Assyrian
power. Thus, the original oracle to which this fragment belonged was probably
addressed to that remnant in the north who still survived in the land. But in the
new literary context into which these verses have been arranged, they serve a
slightly different purpose. Following the comparison of the two sisters (3:6–11),
there is first an invitation to the northerners to repent, who in a sense were less
evil than their southern neighbors (3:11), which is then followed by an invitation
addressed to Judah (3:14–18).

Comment

The initial invitation has an effective play on words: literally, "Turn (back), O
turned (aside) Israel." And this invitation to repentance is made possible by God's
covenant character, which is "perpetually loving" (חסיד). Beyond all the requirements of the covenant regulations, God continued to love those who had long
since ceased to love him and earnestly desired their return to him. If it is correct
that the words were initially declared in the context of a northern ministry of the
prophet, they held the potential of enormous comfort to those who heard them.
For the inhabitants of the Northern Kingdom had long since lost their independence; for approximately a century, they and their predecessors had had time to
reflect on the dreadful end to which the apostasy of a previous age had led. And
yet now, in the midst of a time of hopelessness, the divine word comes again; still
it addresses sin, but it offers also the gracious invitation to repentance, beyond
which lay the possibility of a new relationship.

But if there was to be a response of repentance, there must also be a recognition of what made it necessary. Only after the full recognition and acknowledgment
of evil was a true turning back to God possible (v 13). Verse 13 contains a strange
metaphor: "you have scattered your tracks towards strangers." In general terms,
it indicates the manner in which Israel had turned from the "path" (דרך) of the

true faith, and pursued the "tracks" (דרכים) that led to the worship of foreign deities. All such tracks led in the opposite direction from the covenant faith, which road was a way of obedience. Obedience to the divine voice was crucial, not only because it led into the path of full life (cf. Ps 1) but also because it sprang from the love which was at the heart of the covenant relationship.

Explanation

See the *Explanation* following 4:3–4.

An Invitation to Repentance Addressed to Judah (3:14–18)

Bibliography

Cazelles, H. "Israel du nord et Arche d'Alliance (Jer III 16)." *VT* 18 (1968) 147–58. **Grech, P.** "Interprophetic Re-interpretation and Old Testament Eschatology." *Augustinianum* 9 (1969) 235–65. **Haran, M.** "The Disappearance of the Ark." In *Israel Exploration Quarterly Reader 1*. New York: Ktav, 1981. 262–74; *IEJ* 13 (1963) 46–58. **Soggin, J. A.** "The Ark of the Covenant, Jeremiah 3.16." In *Le Livre de Jérémie. Le prophete et son milieu, les oracles et leur transmission.* Ed P. M. Bogaert. 215–21. **Spencer, A. B.** "שרירות as Self-reliance." *JBL* 100 (1981), 247–48. **Weinfeld, M.** "Jeremiah and the Spiritual Metamorphosis of Israel." *ZAW* 88 (1976) 17–56.

Translation

[14] *"'Turn back, backsliding children'* [a] *—the LORD's oracle—'for I am your master;* [b] *and I will take you, one from each city and two from each district,* [c] *and restore you to Zion.'* [15] *And I shall appoint for you rulers* [a] *who share my mind,* [b] *and they shall govern you with knowledge and understanding.* [16] *Then, when you increase and are fruitful in the land, in those days—the LORD's oracle—they will no longer say, 'The Ark of the Covenant of the LORD!' The thought will not arise,* [a] *for they won't remember it* [b] *and they won't miss it, and one will not be constructed again.* [17] *At that time, they will call Jerusalem 'The LORD's Throne.' And all the nations shall be gathered to it (to the LORD's name, to Jerusalem),* [a] *and they will no longer walk after the self-reliance* [b] *of their evil heart.* [18] *In those days, the House of Judah shall walk alongside the House of Israel, and from a northern country they shall enter into the land* [a] *together, which I have given to your* [b] *fathers as an inheritance."*

Notes

14.a. This translation, which attempts to capture the word play on the root שוב, is based on Bright, 22.

14.b. בעלתי could also be translated "I was (your) husband"; see further the *Comment*.

14.c. Alternatively, משפחה could be translated "clan." On the translation "district," parallel to the preceding city, see Bright, 22.

15.a. Lit., "shepherds." Cf. 2:8 (and *Comment*).

15.b. Lit., "according to my heart."

16.a. Lit., "it will not come up upon (the) heart."

16.b. Some MSS replace בו, "it," with עוד, "again," and a few MSS add עוד after בו (de Rossi, III, 68).

17.a. The phrase set off in brackets is omitted in LXX and has the appearance of an explanatory gloss after אליה, "to it."

17.b. שררות is traditionally rendered "prompting" (cf. NEB). The translation "self-reliance" (with negative implications) follows the study of Spencer (*JBL* 100 [1981] 247–48).

18.a. The expression is על־הארץ. It is probably better to read אל for על with a few Heb. MSS (de Rossi, III, 68), though the interchange of these two prepositions is not uncommon in Jeremiah.

18.b. LXX and Syr presuppose a 3 pl suff, "*their* fathers," but the 2 pl suff of MT provides acceptable sense.

Form/Structure/Setting

The attempt to understand the form and setting of 3:14–18 is rendered more difficult than usual by the identification of a number of complex issues to which there is no easy solution. (i) The uncertain relationship between 3:14–18 and the two preceding units, namely, 3:12–13, 6–11, has already been specified in the preceding notes. (ii) Though 3:14–18 have been designated prose, the literary character of the text is disputed. Thus, by way of example, RSV renders v 14 in poetry and Thompson (198) takes vv 14–15 as poetry. (iii) The possibility of poetry in vv 14–15 makes more complex the relation between these verses and vv 12–13. Do they begin the prose section or end the poetic section? Holladay takes v 14a to belong to the preceding poetic section (*Architecture*, 46–48), but others would interpret v 14a as the opening announcement of the prose section. (iv) The section, in its present form, is almost certainly made up of two or more parts. Verses 14–15, whether prose or poetry, form a unit (in which second person pronouns are used), vv 16–17 seem to form an independent unit, and v 18 may be an editorial addition (the third person is used in vv 16–17, but there is uncertainty with respect to v 18; see note 18.b.). (v) Of all the units that comprise the larger section (3:1–4:4), this passage (vv 14–18) has the least commonality of language and theme with the surrounding narrative. It begins with a key word (שובו, v 14), but after that the key words and themes that permeate the remainder of 3:1–4:4 are essentially absent. (vi) Finally, there is considerable difficulty in interpreting the meaning of several of these verses, and that difficulty in turn makes for uncertainty in the interpretation of the setting and possible date of the literary unit, or its component parts. In the interpretation that follows, the essence of the view is provided which will be elaborated in the *Comment*.

The passage appears to have gone through two stages of development before reaching its present form. The original unit, integral to the larger context concerning repentance, consists of vv 14–15, to which have been added first vv 16–17, and later v 18. Clearly such a view is hypothetical, but the following are the details of the hypothesis. (i) Verses 14–15 belong to the original section on repentance (3:1–4:4). The opening line (v 14a) contains an invitation to repentance, balancing the similar invitation in the opening line of the preceding poetic oracle (v 12b). Originally, v 15 would have been followed by vv 19ff., in which the key words are taken up again: note שובו, (v 14) and תשובו, "turn back" (v 19); בנים, "children" (vv 14, 19, 22); שובבים, "backsliding" (vv 14, 22); and probably also the verb נתן (vv 15, 19). The invitation to repentance is followed by a promise, not of return from exile, but of the restoration of good government (see *Comment*). (ii) Verses 16–17 are Jeremianic, and probably also relatively early (see Weinfeld, *ZAW* 88 [1976] 19–26), and have been added as an expansion of the notion of good government. Though the substance of these verses has little in common with the immediate literary context, it has a great deal in common with other Jeremianic passages (see Weinfeld, and from a different literary perspective, P. Grech, *Augustinianum* 9 [1969] 235–65). (iii) Finally, v 18 was added, perhaps as an editorial addition reflecting the exilic period and amplifying certain aspects of the substance of the preceding verses. The details of this analysis will now be elaborated with respect to the substance of the verses.

Comment

14–15 *The call to repentance.* The opening two verses of the unit, integral to the larger passage on repentance (3:1–4:4), balance the two immediately preceding verses. Thus, vv 12–13 offer repentance to Israel, and vv 14–15 offer repentance to Judah. Though the present form of vv 14–15 would seem to be prose, there is indeed a semipoetic character to them, perhaps indicating that they were originally poetic but have been reduced to the prose of their present form.

The opening invitation to repentance precisely balances that given to Israel (v 12b), but whereas Israel is addressed by name in the preceding passage, here the address is simply to "backsliding children," by which is apparently meant the citizens of Judah (perhaps an allusion back to "children" in 2:30, and the same word is used again in 3:19). The expression "I am your master" fits well with the general character of the larger context, though it is employed only here. Translated "I am you master," it provides the appropriate nuance for the theme of good government immediately following. But it could equally be translated "I am your *husband*" (בעלתי), thus developing in a different direction the theme of divorce and remarriage established in 3:1; repentance could indeed be followed by a renewal of the marriage relationship. And the nuance goes further; "I am your *ba'al* (husband)" implies that no longer would Judah be bound to the Baals of the fertility faith to which she had so easily fallen away from the true covenant faith.

The statement that people would be taken from city and country and restored to Zion may seem at first to indicate a restoration of Judean exiles (if late) or Israelite exiles (if early) to the holy city. But such is probably not the intent, and the words must be interpreted in conjunction with v 15. Verses 14b–15 indicate that repentance would be followed by a restoration of proper government in Zion (Jerusalem), in contrast to the evil government that held control in the land at the time Jeremiah delivered the oracle (see further the indictment of government in 2:8, where reference is made to evil "rulers" or "shepherds," the same word that is employed here in 3:15). In summary, the restoration was promised, if only the people and would repent, and would include good government, with the cities and districts properly represented and the rulers wise and godly men. (The details of administration and government during the period in question are not well known; for a general survey, see R. de Vaux, *Ancient Israel,* 2nd ed. [London, 1965] 133–38.)

16–17 *The ark of the covenant.* These two verses supplement the notion of good and restored government. They anticipate a government of a world kind, in which the central place of Jerusalem and God is recognized by all nations. Though the verses are supplementary in their present context, there is no good reason for denying that they are Jeremianic; indeed, Weinfeld presents strong arguments not only for the authenticity of the verses but also for their dating in the reign of Josiah (*ZAW* 88 [1976] 23). The verses clearly have a future, indeed eschatalogical focus. In this, they do not reflect the period after 586 B.C. but develop on older prophetic tradition in Israel, in which the transformation described here is already anticipated (cf. Isa 2:2–4; Mic 4:1–4). In this sense, the actual location or condition of the ark in Josiah's time of Jeremiah's time is irrelevant (see further the studies of Soggin and Haran with respect to the ark's history in the period); the verses imply nothing with respect to the actual location of the ark in the late seventh or early sixth centuries B.C. but rather anticipate a future age in which the ark would no longer have a function.

Thus, Jeremiah anticipates a future time; in the introductory, and perhaps redactional statement of v 16a, it would happen after the prosperity and increase that would follow upon the restoration of good government, which in turn was contingent upon repentance. The expression "The Ark of the Covenant of the Lord" was presumably a ritual statement, employed in some liturgical context associated with the ark; such a statement would no longer be used, for the ark would cease to have any important role in the faith of this future Israel. The reason is clarified in v 17; the ark, which was God's throne, would cease to be important, because Jerusalem itself would become God's throne on earth. And whereas the ark had symbolized God's presence in Israel, in the future, Jerusalem itself would symbolize God's presence in the larger context of the world of nations. The anticipated transformation, in other words, would extend beyond the chosen people to incorporate the nations of the world as a whole, whose self-reliance would be exchanged for reliance upon God. In this vision of a distant future, Jeremiah sees beyond the catastrophe of his time, at which the chosen people's calling is on the verge of collapse, to a future period in which the ancient call to Israel to serve as a nation of priests (Exod 19:5–6) would be fulfilled. The general theme introduced in these verses is expanded in much greater detail later in the Book of Jeremiah (see particularly 31:31–34).

18 *The restoration of Israel and Judah.* This verse would appear to be an editorial addition. It is prompted by the earlier references to both Judah and Israel, and the immediately preceding reference to a distant future. From the later perspective of exile, the precursor to the splendid anticipation of vv 16–17 would be the restoration of Israel and Judah to the promised land, the land from which they had been exiled in the divine acts of judgment. Though a late addition to the basic narrative, the substance of the verse is consonant with Jeremiah's thought (see Thompson, 203–4); whether it comes from Jeremiah, or Baruch, or some later scribe, cannot be determined.

Explanation

See the *Explanation* following 4:3–4.

Repentance and Forgiveness (3:19–4:2)

Bibliography

Ellison, H. L. "The Prophecy of Jeremiah." *EvQ* 32 (1960) 214–15. **Paul, S. M.** "לשנות אימוץ" (Adoption Formula)." *Ereṣ Israel* 14 (1978) 31–36. [Heb; English summary, 123.] **Seebass, H.** "בוש." *TDOT*, II, 50–60.

Translation

19	*"I used to think*	(2+2?)
	how I would like to make you sons[a]	
	and give you a pleasant land,	(3+3)
	the most beautiful[b] *inheritance of the nations.*	
	And I used to think you[c] *would call me 'My father'*	(3+3)
	and not turn[d] *back from following me.*	
20	*Yet as surely as a wife has been faithless to her partner,*	(4+4)
	so you have been faithless to me, O House of Israel."	
	The LORD's oracle.	
21	*A sound is heard over the countryside,*[a]	(3+3)
	the weeping entreaties of Israel's children,	
	for they have perverted their path,	(3+3)
	they have forgotten the LORD their God.	
22	*"Turn back, backsliding children;*	(3+3)
	let me heal[a] *your backsliding!"*	
	"Here we are! We have come to you,	(3+3)
	for you are the LORD our God.	
23	*Surely the hill-shrines*[a] *are a sham,*	(3+2)
	and the murmurings on the mountains.	
	Surely in the LORD our God	(3+2)
	is Israel's salvation!	
24	*But shame has devoured*	(2+3?)
	our fathers' toil from the time of our youth,	
	their flocks and their herbs,	(2+2)
	their sons and their daughters.	
25	*Let our shame be our bed,*[a]	(2+2)
	and let our humiliation be our blanket,[b]	
	for we have sinned against the LORD our God,	(3+3)
	we and our fathers from the time of our youth;	
	and up to this day we have not obeyed	(3?+3)
	the voice of the LORD our God."	
4:1	*"If you turn, O Israel"*	(2+2)
	—the LORD's oracle—	
	"turn to me!	
	And if you put aside from me your sinful things	(3+2)
	and[a] *do not waver,*	

2   *and take in integrity the oath The LORD lives*   (3+2)
          in justice and in righteousness,
       Then nations shall bless themselves by him   (3+2)
          and in him shall they exult."

Notes

19.a. LXX has a slightly different text: "Amen, Lord, for I will set . . . ," implying כִּי יְהוָה אָמֵן. The variation appears to reflect a different textual tradition.

19.b. צְבִי צִבְאוֹת is interpreted as a superlative expression; LXX again differs, presupposing a text אֱלֹהֵי צְבָאוֹת, "God of hosts."

19.c. The consonantal text, in both cases, implies 2 pl (followed by LXX and Syr); but the Q and many Hebrew MSS (de Rossi, III, 68d) render the verb as sg, which would be more appropriate given the sg suffixes earlier in the verse. But in v 20, the pl form of the verb reappears, with no evidence in the Heb. MSS for the sg.

19.d. Reading with the LXX, Syr, and Tg בוּ־ (pl), "and they will not turn back." Q reads בִ־י (sg), "and she will not turn back."

21.a. On the meaning of שְׁפָיִים, see note 3:2.a.

22.a. אֶרְפָּה, "heal"; one would expect אֶרְפָּא, for which there is abundant evidence in the Heb. MSS (cf. de Rossi, III, 69), but the form here is interpreted as a conflated form of the coh: אֶרְפָּאָה.

23.a. Lit., "hills."

25.a. Lit., "Let us lie in our shame."

25.b. Lit., "our humiliation shall cover us."

4:1.a. The conj could perhaps be omitted (with C, LXX, and Syr), but the evidence of the Heb. MSS tradition favors its retention.

Form/Structure/Setting

This poetic section, though it has a number of distinct components, would appear to be a unity, perhaps drawn from an originally longer prophetic oracle, or perhaps linked initially to other poetic unity in the larger section (see further comments on the *Form/Structure/Setting* of 3:1–4:4 as a whole). The poetry appears to extend throughout, though the poetic analysis is particularly difficult in vv 24–25 (cf. RSV, which renders these verses as prose, in contrast to NEB).

The internal structure of the unit may be analyzed as follows:

God's disappointment with Israel (vv 19–20)
Change of heart and the invitation to return (vv 21–22b)
A psalm of penitence (vv 22c–25)
The consequence of repentance (4:1–2)

Though the passage as a whole has considerable unity of theme, some parts may have had independent origin, notably the psalm (or extract of a psalm) of penitence (vv 22c–25).

The interrelationship between this passage and the larger literary context (3:1–4:4) may be noted particularly in the usage and repetition of the following words and themes. (a) בָּנִים (vv 19, 22; cf. v 14); (b) נָחַל (v 19, cf. v 18); (c) קָרָא אָבִי (v 19; cf. v 4); (d) בָּגַד (v 20; cf. vv 7, 8, 11); (e) שְׁפִי (v 21; cf. v 2); (f) דֶּרֶךְ (v 21; cf. vv 2, 13); (g) שֶׁקֶר (v 23; cf. v 10); (h) נָעוּר (vv 24, 25; cf. v 4; 2:2); (i) כְּלִם (v 25; cf. v 3); (j) שָׁמַע בְּקוֹל (v 25; cf. v 13), and (k) various forms of שׁוּב throughout. While a few of these repetitions may be coincidental (and the list is far from comprehensive), the overall unity of theme between 3:19–4:2 and the larger context is impressive.

Though it is impossible to be precise, one may suppose that the original oracle to which this passage belonged was delivered at some point during the reign of King Josiah.

Comment

19–20   *God's disappointment with Israel.* These verbs provide insight into the divine nostalgia and disappointment over the chosen people. All along, it had been God's intention to give his people the status of "sons"; as such, they would have received as an inheritance a wonderful land, they would have called God "My father," and they would not have turned back from walking in his ways. The nostalgia lies in that he had indeed made his people sons and given them a land as an inheritance; the disappointment is to be found in the failure of the people to respond to that sonship, for they had been consistently unfaithful toward God.

The metaphor of faithfulness is expressed once again in marital language (v 20), resuming the principal theme of the chapter (cf. 3:1–5). As a wife had been faithless toward her husband, so too had the "House of Israel" (here apparently embracing both the Northern and Southern Kingdoms) been totally unfaithful. Both metaphors, that of God as parent and God as husband, reveal different dimensions of the covenant faith. The notion of God as father is the dominant one in Deuteronomy: see further Deut 1:31; 8:5; and Craigie, *Deuteronomy*, 41–42. It is that notion of father and son that is developed in v 19, but the sadness is mixed with irony. While God had hoped to be addressed lovingly by his people as "My father," the reality of history had been that the expression was only used in hypocrisy, in times of temporary trial (cf. 3:3). The reflective nature of these verses illuminates the warmth and love that lie permanently in the heart of God. He is disappointed at failure but still loves and still desires repentance (3:22). It is important to retain memory of this deep compassion when we read the prophet's declarations of judgment (4:5ff.); in judgment, the compassion is still present, hoping beyond the judgment for a restoration of the relationship of love.

21–22b   *Israel's change of heart and the invitation to repentance.* The prophet's words in v 21 reflect more wishful thinking than historical reality. That is, he does not describe an event that has happened; he describes what he wishes to happen, hoping thereby to communicate his vision to his audience and thus to stimulate them towards action. His words conjure up the sound of lament, issuing from a nation that has at last perceived the error of its ways; having forgotten God, their paths through life have become the twisted byways of evil, away from the true source of their existence. In anguish, perceiving the error of their ways, the people turn back to God in entreaty and repentance—or such was the prophet's desire.

But even if such a situation arose, would it be futile? Was a return to God any longer possible? That was the frightening question introduced at the very beginning of this discourse on repentance (3:1). Now the prophet firmly answers that question by announcing the divine invitation to repent (v 22a–b). And in the light of the preceding narrative, the very offer of the invitation is seen to be an extraordinary act of divine grace. Could a divorced woman, remarried and then divorced again, return to her husband? Under the law, no (3:1). And under law, such would surely also hold true for Israel. Having abandoned the covenant and taken up false covenants, could there be a return to the first covenant relationship? The law of covenant clearly indicated the contrary. Yet though covenant was characterized by law, it was initiated in love (Deut 7). And above all, the invitation to repentance expressed here is an act of love and an illumination of the nature of God's love.

22c–25 *A psalm of penitence.* These words of penitence are used by the prophet as if they were the words of the people. That is, the rhetorical device of the preceding verses is continued; in the prophet's ideal, the people would indeed take such words on their lips and turn back to God in repentance, leaving their folly behind them. But it is an ideal not yet achieved; indeed, it was one goal of the prophet's ministry, which he hoped in part to attain through the use of the words.

Seen in their immediate literary context, the words have the form of one part of a liturgy of penitence. First, God (through the presiding priest or cult-prophet) declares the invitation to repentance (vv 22a–b). Here, the people declare the words of repentance (vv 22c–25) as their response to that invitation. Then, in the following verses (4:1–2), there is a further response from God through the priest/prophet. But the words as such do not form a liturgy in context (though they may have been drawn from some liturgy familiar to the people); the liturgical form has been adapted to stress the divine invitation to repentance and the ideal response required from the people.

The words, if they had been used and understood by the people, would have reflected the appropriated stages in the return to God. First, in coming to God, the people declare their recognition: "you are the Lord our God." This simple statement was crucial, for the root of past errors lay in their failure to recognize the Lord as their one and true God, and their consequent resort to the false gods of the fertility cults. Having declared their recognition of God, they would immediately pass on to a denunciation of the false gods to whom they had resorted. The hillside shrines of the fertility faith, for all their attraction and appeal, were in reality a sham; the words spoken there, for all their promise of fertility and prosperity, were essentially no more than "murmurings," words without true substance (v 23a–b). For Israel, "salvation" (victory, deliverance) could only be found in the one true God of the covenant.

The recognition of the true source of salvation was colored by the recognition of all that had been lost during the days of false faith: "shame has devoured our fathers' toil. . . ." (v 24). It is possible that the word "shame" here is a circumlocution for the name of Baal, as it is elsewhere in Jeremiah and in the OT (cf. 11:3), in which case the sense is that the years devoted to Baal have made a mockery of the work and striving of former generations (cf. Thompson, 209–10). But such an interpretation is not necessary (cf. Seebass, *TDOT,* II, 55), and the prophet's words may simply indicate how the folly of former years has made mockery of all that was done.

At the end of the statement of penitence (v 25), there is a clear and unambiguous confession of sin. The people, if they were to respond to Jeremiah's preaching, would recognize clearly that they had sinned against God, and that such actions had their consequences. Sin would be their bed, humiliation their blanket, but they could not claim that someone else had done this to them. They had made their own bed and must lie in it. The only possibility of a new life lay in recognition of sin, and the words of confession, here stated, opened the door of exit from the bedroom of shame. The nature of the sin, as it is specified at the end of v 25, is the failure to obey God's voice: that is, the failure to obey the covenant stipulations for the faith of Israel. Obedience to the divine voice should have sprung from love for the God of covenant; when love had been turned aside from God to the deities of the hillside shrines, true obedience was no longer possible, for the promptings of the divine voice were drowned out by the murmurings on the mountains.

4:1–2   *The consequences of repentance.* The words of penitence, if they had been spoken by the people, would have been followed by the words of God once more: "If you *turn . . . turn* to me." Once again, there is a play on the root שׁוּב, which dominates this section (3:1–4:4) as a whole. The essence of failure had been "turning"; it began when the people turned from God to the faith in fertility gods, and turned from good to the practice of evil. The prophet's plea throughout is that a people that has turned away might turn back, and in these words (a response to the preceding words of penitence) there is a plea for a genuine turning to the only direction in which life might be found, namely, a turning toward God. A true turning to God, and a concurrent putting aside of the sinful practices associated with the past, would make possible new life if the integrity of the covenant community could be employed again: "The Lord lives!" These words could only be used with integrity, justice, and righteousness, if they were believed; and belief in them necessarily involved the abandonment of the cult of Baal. The worshipers of Baal also had a cultic cry: "Baal lives." Those words would have to be put aside forever, and the words recognizing the life of the Lord used in their place. When all these things had taken place—a turning back to God, a putting aside of sin, and a new recognition of the Living God—only then could God's ancient purpose for the chosen people be fulfilled, namely, that blessing should come to all nations, by virtue of their recognition of God through the ministry of Israel (4:2; cf. Exod 19:5–6). Thus, it becomes clear that the purpose of the call to repentance is not for the sake of the chosen people alone but also for the sake of God's larger purpose in the world, namely, the blessing of all nations through the instrumentality of Israel.

Explanation

See the *Explanation* following 4:3–4.

Repetition of the Call to Repentance (4:3–4)

Bibliography

Althann, R. *"mwl,* 'Circumcise' with the *lamedh* of Agency." *Bib* 62 (1981), 239–40. **Berridge, J. M.** *Prophet, People.* 77. **Déaut, R. le.** "Le Thème de la Circoncision du Coeur (Dt. xxx 6; Jer iv 4) dans les Versions anciennes (LXX et Targum) et à Qumrân." VTSup 32. Leiden: Brill, 1981. 178–205.

Translation

3   For thus has the LORD said to the citizens[a] of Judah and to Jerusalem:[b]
    "Till the untilled ground,   (3+3?)
       but do not plant among thorns.
4   Be circumcised by[a] the LORD   (2+3)
       and set aside the foreskins[b] of your heart,
    citizens of Judah   (2+2)
       and inhabitants of Jerusalem.
    Or else my fury will go forth like a fire: (3+3+3)
       it will burn with none to extinguish it,
       because of the evil of your actions."

Notes

3.a. Lit., "man": the sense is collective.
3.b. Alternatively, "to the inhabitants of Jerusalem," with the support of a few Heb. MSS, LXX, Syr, and Tg (cf. v 4).
4.a. The *lamedh* attached to the divine name designates agency, as proposed by Althann (*Bib* 62 [1981] 239–40), thus providing a notion parallel to that in Deut 30:6.
4.b. Many Heb. MSS, LXX and Syr employ a sg noun.

Form/Structure/Setting

The two concluding verses in the section of repentance appear to have been originally independent from the preceding literary unit; their current location serves both as a conclusion to the preceding narrative and as a transition to the long section on judgment which will follow. The short oracular introduction (in prose) may either indicate the separate oracle from which the verses were drawn, or may serve to narrow the focus of the preceding verses, which had incorporated both Israel and Judah; now, in the concluding statement, the focus is specifically on Judah and Jerusalem, for in this context the tradition was preserved and to Judah the message (in its literary form) was addressed.

The language and imagery of this short unit are for the most part quite distinctive and differ in various ways from the main theme of repentance in 3:1 to 4:2. It is linked to the immediately preceding section by the repeated use of the verb סור, "set aside" (v 4; cf. 4:1), but other than that there is no significant overlap in language and theme with the preceding passage. But the general theme of repentance (vv 3–4a) and the threat of judgment (v 4b) indicate clearly the transitional role of the verses, and thus the editor's purpose, in the arrangement of Jer 2–6 as a whole.

Comment

In the summary statement concerning repentance, the first metaphor to be employed is drawn from the agricultural world. "Untilled ground" (or virgin soil) is to be broken up, so that a good harvest can be planted and can grow in a place that was formerly a wilderness of weeds. The essence of the first part of this metaphor is the notion of hardness. The hard ground cannot be penetrated by the scattered seeds, and so cannot give place to the new life contained within the seeds. Only when that hardness is broken up can the seed find a place in which to grow. But the metaphor is expanded; some seeds do grow in the hard untilled soils of the wilderness, those of the thornbush. The seeds of new life must be planted in the broken soil, but away from the thorns that would suffocate and inhibit growth. Thus, in the prophet's first metaphor, he is developing an older theme, already employed in the eighth century B.C. by an earlier prophet, Hosea (10:12). The hardness of the heart, like virgin soil, must be broken up, so that the seeds of righteousness and new life might flourish. And as Jeremiah, in these words, stands in the tradition of Hosea, so later we see another teacher take up the same theme and develop it still further in the "Parable of the Sower and the Seed" (Mark 4:1–9).

The second metaphor seems at first to be entirely different, yet it continues the theme of hardness. The external sign of the covenant, in Israel's religion, was that of circumcision, an ancient practice going back to the time of Abraham (Gen 17:10–14). But the prophet here employs the practice in a metaphorical manner: it is the heart that must be circumcised. And whereas the literal sign of the covenant was inflicted by human agency (v 4a), the life of the covenant, despite its multitude of external manifestations, at base was a relationship of the heart (here referring to the whole inner life) between a person and God. Those with a hard heart could not have a deep relationship with the living God. And thus, just as hard ground was to be broken up, so too hardness of heart must be cut away and removed if there was to be a true and lasting turning back to God in repentance.

Failure to break up the hard ground of formerly sterile lives would lead inevitably to judgment. Briefly, the prophet indicates the alternative of judgment; as a fire in the country could quickly burn up the dry stubble and thornbushes (to continue the agricultural metaphor), so would God's wrath consume Judah in its evil. But this theme is developed in greater detail in the next section.

Explanation for 3:1–4:4

The prophet's declaration of God's indictment of national evil (Jer 2) is now followed by a passionate plea for repentance. The plea can only follow the indictment, for repentance is an act of turning. If it is to be undertaken clearly and consciously, there must be knowledge in the minds of those who repent both of that from which they turn, namely the perpetual practice of evil, and the One to whom they turn, namely the God of the covenant.

The essence of repentance, as this portion of the Book of Jeremiah makes so clear, is turning. The introduction of one of the ancient prayers of St. Augustine captures the spirit of the message: "O Thou, from whom to be turned is to fall, to whom to be turned is to rise." For the key to life is to be found in the direction in which one faces; if that direction is wrong, one must turn to seek the true direction and walk in that path of life. Thus, the prophet is engaged in a formidable task: he must not only demonstrate to his people that they have turned in the wrong direction in their path through life, but he must also persuade them consciously to turn to a new direction, that which leads toward God.

But although repentance is a human action, a conscious turning, it cannot be undertaken easily and lightly; thus, before the prophet delivers the invitation to repent, he calls the very possibility of repentance into question. Granted that from a human perspective repentance is essential, is it nevertheless permissible to turn back to the God who has, for so long, been so shamelessly ignored? All the analogies of law would suggest that repentance from so comprehensive a history of rejection was impossible. You cannot simply reject a relationship of love for a long period of time and then, when inclination takes you, casually return to it. Yet the prophet makes clear that the analogy of law is inadequate; because law is always subservient to the divine love, repentance is possible. But because love has been rejected, repentance can never be a casual matter; it must involve radical change and the appropriate penitence of attitude in returning.

It is also clear in the prophet's words that repentance is not simply a turning away from evil deeds. Much more than that is required, for evil actions are but the consequence of a deeper problem, namely, a fundamental dislocation of relationship. This dimension of repentance is brought out clearly in the prophet's use of the language of marriage and marital unfaithfulness. In marriage, an act of unfaithfulness is critical by virtue of that which it designates, that is, a failure in the commitment of love by one partner to the relationship. And Israel's catalogue of crimes, detailed at such length by the prophet, is critical because it points to a deeper fault lying beneath the surface. At root, Israel had lost sight of its love and faithfulness toward God in the relationship of covenant. And by virtue of the vacuum created in the absence of love, every form of evil was sucked into the life of the nation. If there was to be repentance, there would have to be extensive housecleaning; a multitude of false friends would have to be cut off, but above all the true relationship with God must be restored.

Although the goal of repentance is the restoration of the relationship with God, that too can easily become a selfish goal unless it is retained in its proper perspective. Jeremiah's impassioned plea for repentance was addressed to the chosen people; he desired to see them turn aside from their collision course with disaster. Yet the prophet's vision was wider than that; he had not forgotten God's larger purpose of the world, to be achieved through the instrumentality of God's people. And, thus, part of his passion in seeking to turn the people back to God was related to the desire that all nations might be blessed by God through Israel (4:2). And that is a healthy perspective to retain in all thinking about repentance. The focus must not be only upon those called upon to repent but also upon the larger world that God desires to reach through the transformed lives of the repentant and forgiven.

C. The Declaration of Divine Judgment (4:5–6:30)

Bibliography

Althann, R. *A Philological Analysis of Jeremiah 4–6 in the Light of Northwest Semitic.* Ph.D. diss., University of Zimbabwe, 1980 [BibOr 38. Rome: Biblical Institute, 1983]. **Castellino, G. R.** "Observations on the Literary Structure of Some Passages in Jeremiah." *VT* 30 (1980) 398–408.

Gailey, J. G., Jr. "The Sword and the Heart, Evil from the North—and Within, An Expo-
sition of Jeremiah 4:5–6:30." *Int* 9 (1955) 294–309. Odajima, T. "Prophetic Speeches of
Jeremiah on the Foe from the North." *Shangaku-Ronshu* 12 (1977) 84–123 [in Japanese].
Reventlow, H. G. *Liturgie und prophetisches Ich bei Jereia.* Gütersloh: Gerd Mohn, 1963. *Rizzi,
G. Sermoni poetici Geremiani appartenenti al ciclo del pericolo dal nord: Uno studio sul genere
letterario di Ger. 4:5–6:30 & Ger. 8:4–9:25.* Jerusalem: Franciscan Publishing House, 1980.

Form/Structure/Setting

This composite passage forms the third and final portion of the collection of
Jeremiah's early oracles; see further the introductory comments at 2:1 and 3:1.
The indictment of Judah's evil (chap. 2) and the plea for repentance (3:1–4:4)
are now followed by a series of declarations pertaining to the divine judgment, its
source, role, and consequences. As in the preceding sections of the collection,
the passage is composite, drawn from a variety of sources, but once again the end
result is a carefully constructed artistic whole, so that, as before, it is not easy to
determine the limits, original interrelationships, and origins of the component
parts.

The form-critical and literary details of the parts are examined more closely in
the notes entitled *Form/Structure/Setting* that follow each subsection. The passage
as a whole is principally poetic, with only a few prose portions (which Althann
has argued can be translated and interpreted in poetic terms). In form, there is
considerable variety in the component parts, including poems, oracles of various
kinds, and dialogue. Though various attempts have been made to define the parts
in precise literary or form-critical terms, from "stanzas" (Castellino) to "poetic
sermons" (Rizzi), in general the literary unity of the whole, which in turn must
be seen in the larger context of chaps. 2–6, impresses the reader; despite disparate sources and origins and a composite text, we are dealing overall with a finely
crafted and finished product, and it is important not to lose sight of the whole in
the examination of the parts.

(*N.B.*: the section entitled *Explanation* follows the commentary of 6:22–30 and
embraces the theological and religious issues of 4:5–6:30 as a whole.)

The Declaration of Disaster (4:5–10)

Bibliography

Berridge, J. M. *Prophet, People.* 91–113. Boer, P. A. H. de. *Jeremia's Twijfel.* Leiden: Brill, 1957.
Buffs, Y. "His Majesty's Loyal Opposition: A Study in Prophetic Intercession." *Conservative
Judaism* 33/3 (1980) 25–37. Christensen, D. L. *Transformations of the War Oracle in Old Testament Prophecy.* HDR 3. Missoula, MT: Scholars, 1975. 188–90. Reventlow, H. G. *Liturgie.*
94–121. Thomas, D. W. "מלאו in Jeremiah iv.5: A Military Term." *JJS* 3 (1952) 47–52.

Translation

5	*"Announce it in Judah*	(2+2)
	and in Jerusalem spread the word,[a]	
	and sound the trumpet in the land;	(3+2)
	proclaim it, confirm it,	
	and say: 'Get together and let us enter	(3+2)
	the fortified cities.'	
6	*Hoist the signal: 'To Zion!'*	(2+2)
	Make for safety. Don't stand about!	
	For I am about to bring disaster from the north	(4?+2)
	and devastating destruction.	
7	*A lion has leaped forth from his lair,*	(3+3)
	a destroyer of nations has decamped.	
	He has set out from his den[a]	(2+3)
	to make your country a wasteland;	
	your cities will be reduced to ruins,	(2+2)
	devoid of inhabitants.	
8	*So put on sackcloth,*	(3+2)
	wail and howl,	
	for the LORD's fierce wrath	(3+2?)
	has not turned from us.[a]	

[9] *And on that day"—the LORD's oracle—"the King's courage will fail, and that of the princes too, and the priests will be horrified, and the prophets will be speechless."* [10] *So I said,*[a] *"Lord GOD, surely you have totally deceived this people, and Jerusalem too, in saying 'You shall have peace,' when a sword is pricking*[b] *their throat!"*[c]

Notes

5.a. ואמרו, "and say," is omitted from the end of this line, being probably a dittogr derived from the same word later in the verse. Alternatively, the first two lines may be addressed to the prophet, and then ואמרו (standing outside the metrical arrangement) may introduce the oracle as such, which would begin: "Sound the trumpet!"

7.a. Lit., "from his place."

8.a. It may be that there has been some dislocation of word order in this verse, the ממנו perhaps originally following שב; but of this there can be little certainty (cf. *BHS*).

10.a. *BHS*, referring to 14:13 from which they think the present form of the verb (1 sg) may have come, suggests reading: ואמרו, "and they will say," for which there is some support in LXX^A. But the first-person form of the verb is well supported in the Heb. MSS (and other traditions of LXX) and should be retained; see further the *Comment*.

10.b. Lit., "touches."

10.c. On נפש, "throat," in Heb. and Ug., see Craigie, *Psalms 1–50,* 97–98.

Form/Structure/Setting

The third section (4:5–6:30) in this collection of Jeremiah's early oracles (2:1–6:30), in which the theme of coming judgment is developed, opens with a passage that establishes the theme, which will be portrayed in different ways in the sections that follow. The opening passage, a composite literary unit, introduces the theme with a declaration of the coming of fatal conflict.

The message is for the most part poetic in form. The basic prophetic oracle comprises the poetic v 5–7, which are expressed as God's word, to which the prophet has added his own word of exhortation (v 8), also in poetry and integral to the preceding verses. (It should be noted that even the opening words of v 5, which are sometimes translated into prose, as in the RSV, are poetic in character, having a distinctive internal chiastic structure.) The form of the last two verses is debatable (vv 9–10); both have been translated as prose (cf. RSV), though some translators have attempted to find poetic structure in both verses (e.g., Bright, 28–29), and some translate v 9 as poetry and v 10 as prose (cf. NEB).

With respect to the development of the text in its present form, vv 5–8 form the basic unit, to which vv 9 and 10 have been added, in all probability from separate sources. Yet all the verses would appear to be Jeremianic, and it is reasonable to suppose that the editorial process, bringing together vv 9 and 10 with vv 5–8, was a part of the larger editorial process by which chaps. 2–6 as a whole were compiled. The opening verses (vv 5–8) are in the general form of a "call to alarm" (H. G. Reventlow, *Liturgie und prophetisches Ich bei Jeremia*), though precision in the form-critical analysis is difficult, for in all probability these verses originally belonged to a larger prophetic oracle. The judgment portion of the oracle is employed here, in keeping with the theme of the immediate literary context, but the original oracle may have contained in addition such features as the indictment of sin and the call to repentance (such as appear in 2:1–4:4). The verses added to the basic poetic oracle develop its substance from different perspectives; see further the *Comment*.

The date of the verses that compose this passage cannot be determined with certainty. The anticipation of disaster coming from the "north" (v 6) is of little assistance; if the oracle were originally delivered in the early period of Josiah's reign, various northern enemies are possible (see further the *Comment* on 1:13–15), but by the time these verses were incorporated within their present literary context (c. 605 B.C.), the northern foe was almost certainly indentified as the Babylonian Empire. While the sense of urgency and the imminence of threat breathed in these verses have suggested to some commentators a later date, perhaps even 597 or 587 B.C., such a conclusion is a fragile one to draw from the dramatic and colorful nature of the poetry. The words could have been delivered in a time of peace (as may be implied at least for v 10) or alternatively on the eve of battle; their urgency does not necessarily reflect the proximity of the danger but rather its real nature and the necessity of repentance. The prophet's own words (v 8) may perhaps reflect a period in which a false sense of security has emerged, which he sought to shatter with his declaration.

Comment

The third part of this collection of Jeremiah's early oracles concerns judgment; it begins, however, not with an explicit reference to judgment, in any religious sense, but rather with an announcement concerning the advance of a powerful and destructive enemy. The language, though its theme is religious, is drawn directly from the nation's experience of warfare and invasion. When the armies of a foreign power approached, trumpets would be sounded throughout the cities and towns of the land. Like the air raid sirens, whose doleful drones became so familiar during the Second World War, the sounded trumpets throughout ancient Judah warned the citizens to take cover and prepare for an attack. God's message, through this prophet, is that such an attack was coming. The imagined scene is developed further: people in the countryside and outlying hamlets are urged to retreat to the supposed safety of the fortified cities, in which at least the semblance of resistance to the advancing foe might be offered. The "signal" (v 6) may have been a flag of some kind, hoisted on a high place, so that all could see it and take its warning; the message, "To Zion," was that the people should retreat to the fortress in Jerusalem, seeking a safe place in the time of crisis.

The elaborate proclamation of warning is followed by a statement of the reason, which may be viewed from two perspectives. (i) Essentially, the warning of danger was to be announced because the forces of a devastatingly powerful foe were approaching Judah from the north. The identity of the foe is not specified, but the geographical orientation is significant. The north was a direction from which danger constantly threatened. From the north, Israel had been defeated in 722 B.C., and throughout the decades of Jeremiah's life, northern foes threatened, most significantly the Babylonian Empire by the last decade of the seventh century B.C. But in addition to the literal foe that might come from the north, the direction might have held various threatening connotations in the popular consciousness of the time. In the religious conceptions of Syria-Palestine, especially those of Baal religion, the north was not only a home of the gods but perhaps also a place associated with destructive powers (cf. A. Lauha, *Zaphon. Der Norden und die Nordvolker im Alten Testament*. AASF [Helsinki: Vetenskakliga Samfundens Forlagsexpedition, 1943] 49–52). And there may be an element of irony in the prophet's message. One of Israel's great hymns of praise explicitly associated Zion with the north (Ps 48:2), but now the people were to flee to Zion, for a foe approached from the north (see further Craigie, *Psalms 1–50*, 353).

(ii) The second perspective from which the announcement of warning may be viewed is that of its source. The prophet does not simply declare that an enemy is coming, but (quoting God's word) he says, "I am about to bring . . ." The source of the threat is to be found in the divine initiative and that initiative in turn would make it perfectly clear to the prophet's audience that he was not simply predicting invasion but rather was proclaiming judgment. By means of a foreign power, as voracious and destructive as the fierce lion, the sovereign God would exercise his judgment on his people.

Having declared the divine word, the prophet adds an exhortative and explanatory word of his own (v 8); he encourages the people to lament, in recognition of the fact that the Lord's righteous wrath has not yet been turned aside. The injunction to don sackcloth, the symbolic dress of mourning and lamentation, and concurrently to "wail and howl," has implicit within it a last-minute plea for repentance. After disaster, they would indeed lament, but to no avail; before the event, there remained always a ray of hope that the enemy tide might be turned aside by an act of national repentance. But for such an event to happen, the people would first have to recognize that the source of external threat was not the foreign enemy as such but rather their own God who had been rejected by the nation.

The supplementary statement of v 9 seems to be expressed from a slightly later perspective in time. While v 8 might be taken to imply that there was yet the possibility of averting disaster, the judgment day seems to be inevitable in v 9. All the nation's leaders would horrified and incapacitated when the judgment day finally came, unable to perform the tasks to which they were appointed.

The concluding verse (v 10) is not a prophetic declaration, addressed to the people; rather, it is an aside that affords a brief glance into the private dimension of the prophet's life and ministry. Whether this verse was added in the editorial process at the direction of the prophet or it was drawn from a private source of the prophet's writings cannot be known. Yet the sentiment seems genuinely Jeremianic; the prophet, having declared the word of judgment, is personally horrified by the implications of what he has said. What prompts the saying (or its insertion at this point in the text) is probably the reference to "prophets" in v 9. The prophets in general, specifically the false prophets (a theme to be developed in greater detail later in the book: cf. 6:13–14), have created the illusion of peace amongst the people. Jeremiah attributes this dangerous illusion directly to God, describing it as a deceit; it is thus attributed, presumably, not in the sense that God directly instructed the false prophets to declare peace but rather in the sense that he permitted them so to prophesy. Alternatively, as de Boer has proposed (*Jeremia's Twijfel*), the prophet may be expressing his misgivings. The divine word for one situation is not necessarily the same for another situation, for the passage of time overtakes events, and in the process the people are deceived.

While the words of v 10 may appear on the surface simply to be a statement addressed to God, lying beneath the surface of the words is an element of supplication (see Muffs, *Conservative Judaism* 33 [1980] 25–37). The prophet, quite independently, is acting as an intercessor, protesting the awfulness of the divine wrath and seeking to present mitigating circumstances, namely, the deception to which his people have fallen prey. And in these few words of the intercessory protest, we begin to see a little more of the character and internal struggle of the prophet. His commission was to declare God's word to the people, yet he also heard that word and saw clearly its consequences. So the prophet who proclaimed judgment also engaged in prayer that the judgment be averted. In the last resort, he was not successful, yet his compassion for the people to whom he ministered is evident in this brief aside in the midst of a terrible flow of proclamation of disaster. And the integrity of the prophet of judgment emerges from the knowledge that his task was undertaken, not in malicious glee, but rather in painful compassion.

Explanation

See the Explanation following 6:22–30.

The Winds of War (4:11–18)

Bibliography

Althann, R. "Jeremiah IV 11–12: Stichometry, Parallelism, and Translation." *VT* 28 (1978) 385–91. **Baly, D.** *The Geography of the Bible.* New York: Harper, 1974. 51–53. **Healey, J. F.**

"Syriac *NṢR*, Ugaritic *NṢR* II, Hebrew *NṢR* II, Akkadian *NṢR* II." *VT* 26 (1976) 429–37. **Holladay, W. L.** "Structure, Syntax and Meaning in Jeremiah IV 11–12a." *VT* 26 (1976) 28–37. **Meyer, I.** *Jeremia und die falsche Propheten.* Göttingen: Vandenhoeck & Ruprecht, 1977. 81–85. **Rabin, C.** "Noṣerim." *Textus* 5 (1965) 44–52. **Robinson, T. H.** "Note on the Text of Jer. iv 11." *JTS* 23 (1922) 68. **Soggin, J. A.** "Zum wiederentdeckten altkanaanäischen Monat ṣh." *ZAW* 77 (1965) 83–86. ———. "Nachtrag zu *ZAW* 77 (1965) S. 83–86." *ZAW* 77 (1965) 326.

Translation

¹¹*At that time it will be said to this people and to Jerusalem, "A withering wind from the desert's dunes*ᵃ *directly against the daughter of my people*ᵇ—*but not to winnow and not to purify!* ¹²*A wind too full for this*ᵃ *blows*ᵇ *for me. Now it is I myself who shall declare judgment on them."*

¹³ *Look! Like clouds he rises,*	(3+2)
and like the whirlwind his chariots.	
Swifter than eagles are his horses—	(3+3)
"Woe to us, for we are ruined!"	
¹⁴ *Wash out your heart of wickedness*	(3+3?)
so that you might be saved, O Jerusalem.	
How long will you harbor within you	(3+2)
your devilish designs?	
¹⁵ *For a voice is declaring from Dan,*	(4+4)
and someone proclaims ill from Mount Ephraim:	
¹⁶ *"Remind the nations of those things,*ᵃ	(3+2)
*proclaim against*ᵇ *Jerusalem:*	
*Criers*ᶜ *are coming from a distant land*	(4+4)
and raising their voice against Judah's cities.	
¹⁷ *Like estate guards, they are against her from every side,*	(4+2?)
for she rebelled against me."	
The Lord's oracle.	
¹⁸ *Your way and your deeds*	(2+2)
will have brought these things upon you.	
this is your own wickedness that is so bitter,	(3+3?)
that has pierced your very heart.	

Notes

11.a. שְׁפָיִם, "dunes": cf. R. Althann, 388–89. Alternatively, translate "bare heights (of the desert)"; K. Elliger, "Der Sinn des hebräischen Wortes *šᵉpî*," *ZAW* 83 (1971) 317–29.

11.b. Alternatively, the Heb. words could be interpreted as standing in apposition: "(my) daughter, my people" (Bright, 32).

12.a. Lit., "these things." Alternatively, מֵאֵלֶּה could perhaps be deleted on the grounds of dittogr.

12.b. Lit., "comes."

16.a. Reading הַנֵּה for הִנֵּה, "behold"; cf. NEB and L. H. Brockington, *The Hebrew Text of the Old Testament*, 199. For further discussion, see Bright, 29 (note).

16.b. לְ is translated "against," on the basis of the two similar uses of the prep in the following lines (vv 16–17). Alternatively, translate "to" (cf. RSV).

16.c. To translate נֹצְרִם "criers," on the basis of a root נצר, II (cf. Healey, *VT* 26 [1976] 429–37) is preferable to a translation "besiegers" (based on an unusual nuance of נצר, I) or emending to "enemies" (with possible support from LXX).

Form/Structure/Setting

The declaration of judgment in this composite passage describes further the coming of the enemy that will be God's instrument of punishment.

The section consists primarily of two units: (i) a prose oracle (vv 11–12), in which the coming enemy is likened to the scorching wind from the desert; (ii) a poetic oracle (vv 13–17), elaborating still further the nature and devastating power of the approaching enemy. In all probability, both units belonged originally to larger oracles, from which these portions have been extracted to develop the theme of coming judgment that is central to chaps. 4–6. The notion linking the two units together in their present literary structure is the metaphor/simile of "wind" (v 11) and "whirlwind" (v 13). A third section has been added (v 18), in which the prophet has contributed his own interpretive comment regarding the cause of the coming disaster.

There is considerable debate whether v 11–12 should be rendered as prose (cf. RSV) or set out as poetry. The articles by Althann (*VT* 28 [1978] 385–91) and by Holladay (*VT* 26 [1976] 28–37) present lengthy arguments for the interpretation of the verses as poetry. For all the value of such arguments, they are not entirely persuasive with respect to defining the parallelism of the lines in question. In places, there may remain remnants of a parallel structure (e.g., the last four words of v 11), but the verses as a whole appear to be mosaic in character. It must probably be supposed that we are dealing with a prose summary of what was originally a poetic oracle.

The setting of the oracles was no doubt Jerusalem (vv 11, 14, 16), but the date is not determinable. On the one hand, the sense of imminence and urgency might suggest a late date. On the other hand, the second oracle in the larger context contains a call to repentance and cleansing, implying that a time yet remains before the judgmental end will come.

Comment

The declaration of divine judgment continues, first with the use of wind as a metaphor of God's instrument of destruction. It is the *sirocco* to which the prophet refers, the hot dry wind that blows through the land from time to time, usually coming from the desert regions lying to the east and south of the promised land. Sir George Adam Smith penned a memorable description of the desert wind in his diary for April 26, 1891:

> Atmosphere thickening. At 1.45 (p.m.) wind rises, 93°; 2.30, gale blowing, air filled with fine sand, horizon shortened to a mile, sun not visible, grey sky, but a slight shadow cast by the tents. View from tent-door of light grey limestone land under dark grey sky, misty range of hills a mile off, and one camel visible . . . (*The Historical Geography of the Holy Land,* 25th ed., [1931] 65).

This hot and oppressive wind is of no use to either land or farmer. It blows too strongly to be used for winnowing the cut harvest; it is too dry, sucking moisture from the soil, to enrich the land. And such a wind of judgment will blow "for me" (v 12: viz. to serve God's purpose). Like the sirocco, the wind of judgment would blow in quickly, irresistible in its power, oppressive in its effect, draining all color from the nation's life and leaving a drab gray world in its wake. But here, as the wind represents the invading enemy already referred to in the preceding verses, it is clear that it blows only at the divine behest.

In the poetic oracle, the message begins with a simile, now that of the storm with its accumulating clouds and whirling winds. The phenomena of storm represent the formidable size and power of the advancing enemy, its host or horses likened in speed to that of the soaring eagles. The effect of the advent of this army of judgment is highlighted by the exclamation of v 13d, wrung out from the inhabitants of Jerusalem as they see their doom draw near: "Woe to us, for we are ruined." The plea that the people repent and purge themselves of their impurity (v 14) follows directly upon the exclamation of v 13. They would be able to see disaster drawing near. Would they be able to see also that its roots lay within themselves, that a turning from sin might yet avert that which seemed to be irresistible?

But the prophet does not dwell upon his call to repentance and salvation; rather, he emphasizes still more the urgency of the situation in vv 15–16. Dan and Mount Ephraim lay to the north of Jerusalem, the direction from which the prophet had already indicated judgment would come (4:6). The city of Dan (modern Tell el-Qadi) lay to the north of Lake Chinnereth (Galilee), by the headwaters of the Jordan. It was in the northernmost region of the territories that had once belonged to Israel, and it lay directly on the route by which a northern enemy might be expected to approach. The "voice from Dan" was an intimation that the enemy was on the way; the ill-news from Mount Samaria, the mountainous region lying to the north of Jerusalem, indicated that the threatening enemy was quickly drawing closer. The clamorous "criers" (v 16) for a distant land soon would be shouting out their war-cries against the cities of Judah, then surrounding Jerusalem. They would encircle the capital city much as guards surrounded an estate to protect its pastures from enemies, but the foe from the north would be guarding the capital city only in order to destroy it themselves.

The root of this coming conflict, portrayed in almost cosmic proportions, lay not in some international plot, nor even in the greed of Judah's enemies. The root of it all lay in the chosen people's rebellion against God (v 17). It was not to be fate or bad luck; judgment, when it came, would be a *consequence*, specifically a consequence of the nation's rejection of its divine mission and its God. This consequence is elaborated in the personal and reflective word that Jeremiah adds to the oracle (v 18). A terrible thing was about to happen, but it was simply the fruit of Jerusalem's own history. A nation has sown the wind; now it must reap the whirlwind.

Explanation

See the *Explanation* following 6:22–30.

The Prophetic Anguish (4:19–22)

Bibliography

Berridge, J. M. *Prophet, People* 169–70. **Kumaki, F. K.** "A New Look at Jer 4:19–22 and 10:19–21." *Annual of the Japanese Biblical Institute* 8 (1982) 113–22. **Malamat, A.** "A Mari Prophecy and Nathan's Dynastic Oracle." In *Prophecy. Essays presented to Georg Fohrer on his Sixty-fifth Birthday.* Ed. J. A. Emerton. Berlin: de Gruyter, 1980. 68–82. **McKane, W.** *Prophets and Wise Men.* 88–89.

Translation

19	*O my anguish,[a] my anguish! I writhe![b]*	(3+2)
	O, the walls of my heart!	
	My heart is palpitating within me,	(3+2)
	I cannot keep silence!	
	For you[c] have heard the trumpet-blast,	(4+3)
	O my soul, the warning of war!	
20	*Disaster upon disaster[a] is announced,*	(3+3)
	that the entire land is devastated.	
	Suddenly my tents are devastated,	(3+2)
	in an instant, my tent-flaps!	
21	*How long must I see the standard,*	(3+3)
	must I hear the trumpet-blast?	
22	*"For my people are foolish,*	(3+3)
	they know me not.	
	They are stupid children,	(3+3)
	and they have no understanding.	
	They are wise in the ways of wickedness	(3+3)
	but know not how to do good."	

Notes

19.a. Lit., "intestines, bowels" (the seat of emotions).

19.b. The translation is based on K אחולה, meaning "I writhe," for which there is extensive MSS support (de Rossi, III, 70–71; cf. LXX). Q indicates a hiph form of יחל, "wait, tarry."

19.c. שמעתי is interpreted as the archaic 2 fem sg form of the verb, of which נפשי is subject (cf. Q; see Bright, 30).

20.a. The syntactic structure "x upon x" (here, "disaster upon disaster") is quite common in extrabiblical writings; see Malamat, "A Mari Prophecy," 72.

Form/Structure/Setting

(i) Vv 19–21 contain a unit in the "confessional" style of Jeremiah; see further the discussion of Jeremiah's "confessions" at 11:18–23. (ii) The confessional unit is intimately related to a portion of an oracle (v 22) in which God laments the stupidity of his chosen people. The oracular verse is (or has become) an integral part of the preceding confession, providing in part the basis of the prophet's expression of anguish.

These verses, though incorporated within the larger context of material that was once employed in public declaration, no doubt are drawn originally from a private setting in the prophet's life, in which he reflected upon the meaning and apparent inevitability of his public message. The date of the verses within the prophet's career cannot be determined precisely, but it is not necessary to assume that these words are provoked by the actual invasion and the beginning of disaster. They seem to stem rather from the prophet's imagination, from his mental re-creation of the reality of which he spoke. Thus he has "heard the trumpet-blast" (v 19) in his "soul," that is, his innermost being. To the audience, Jeremiah's public proclamations were addressed to future disasters and judgment; to the prophet himself, the reality of his message converted the substance of the future into the anguish of the present.

Comment

A public figure such as Jeremiah has two faces: that which is seen by the general public, and that of the private life. Jeremiah's public face was a stern one, for he spoke of God's coming judgment and the future devastation of his nation and land. But the private thoughts of a man cannot be read from the public face, nor can the internal anguish be discerned from the severity of external appearance. The preceding sections, describing the advance of God's instrument of judgment, are stern and almost ruthless in substance. These verses of confession illuminate the internal torment of a man who is torn, precisely because he is himself so gripped by the urgency of his public preaching. He is not stern in public because he is heartless; it is because he loves his nation and people so dearly that he speaks the severe word, but it takes a terrible toll on his own emotional life.

The description begins with language in the form of a lament; the anguish is physical, but its roots lie in the mind that has grasped the coming terror. The word translated "anguish" is literally "bowels"; he is "sick to the stomach" as he envisages his nation's judgment. Like an unstable cardiac patient, his heart flutters and palpitates, creating what seems to be a voice he cannot control. With the inner ear, he has already heard the trumpet-blast of which he spoke; he already sees the armies of chaos on the march. The envisaged disaster of the land seems to penetrate his own immediate world of experience; his "tents" are devastated in the disaster, for he will be involved in the judgment as much as the people to whom he ministers.

The words of the divine oracle (v 22) serve both to emphasize the inevitability of the coming judgment and to contrast the public apathy with the prophet's private anguish. They emphasize the inevitability of judgment in that the ignorance and stupidity of the nation has become so fundamental to its character that it cannot perceive its plight. The same folly that invited the impending judgment is so deep-seated that there is no hope of sudden wisdom, no prospect of a dawning understanding that might turn the people to repentance. But the public apathy also contrasts with the prophet's anguish. The prophet has declared the message; the people have heard it. The prophet is horrified by the substance of what he has said; the people blithely accept it or ignore it. The prophet, seeming externally to be so stern, is torn internally with grief. The people, critical no doubt of this apparently harsh prophet, have lost their capacity for any inner feelings at all.

Explanation

See the *Explanation* following 6:22–30.

A Vision of Chaos (4:23–28)

Bibliography

Berridge, J. M. *Prophet, People.* 191–93. **Eppstein, V.** "The Day of Yahweh in Jeremiah 4, 23–28." *JBL* 87 (1968) 93–97. **Fishbane, M.** "Jeremiah *IV* 23–26 and Job *III* 3–13." *VT* 21 (1971) 151–67. **Holladay, W. L.** "The Recovery of the Poetic Passages of Jeremiah." *JBL* 85 (1966) 404–6. ——— "Style, Irony and Authenticity in Jeremiah." *JBL* 81 (1962) 44–54. **Lindblom, J.** *Prophecy.* 126–27. **Soggin, J. A.** "The 'Negation' in Jeremiah 4:27 and 5:10a, cf 5:18b." In *Old Testament and Oriental Studies.* BibOr 29 (1975) 179–83. **Weippert, H.** *Schöpfer des Himmels und der Erde.* 50–54.

Translation

23   *I looked at the world—behold, emptiness and void—*   (4+3)
        at the heavens, and their light was no more!

24   *I looked at the mountains—behold, they are quaking,*   (4+3)
        and all the hills rocked back and forth.

25   *I looked—behold, mankind was no more,*   (4+3)
        and every bird of the heavens had fled.

26   *I looked—the garden land was wilderness,*   (4+3?)
        with all its cities shattered,[a]

    because of the LORD,   (2+3)
        because of his fierce wrath.

[27]*For thus said the LORD:*

    "The entire world shall be wasteland,   (3+3)
        but I will not[a] *yet have brought the end.*

28   *For this, the world shall mourn,*   (3+3)
        and the heavens above grow black.

    For[a] *I have spoken and have not relented;*[b]   (3+3)
        I have considered but will not turn back. "

Notes

26.a. Many MSS (cf. LXX) have the reading נִצְּתוּ (niph of יצת), "were burned."

27.a. MT clearly has a negative particle (לֹא); the suggestion to read לֹה (cf. *BHS*, note) is in many ways persuasive, but is without support in Heb. MSS and the versions.

28.a. The introductory על is anomalous. The suggestion in *BHS* that it be deleted as dittogr is probable. Alternatively, read על כן, "therefore," for כי על, for which there is some support in Heb. MSS (de Rossi, III, 72).

28.b. זמתי, "I have considered," is transposed to follow נחמתי, following LXX and is implied by the poetic structure.

Form/Structure/Setting

Verses 23–26 contain a poetic account of a vision of chaos, the horror of the subject matter highlighted by the extraordinary beauty and force of the poetry. There are affinities with the language of the creation story in Gen. 1:1–2:4a, though this poem is in reverse, describing the emergence of chaos from order (Fishbane, *VT* 21 [1971] 151–67). But there are also affinities with the second creation story (Gen. 2:4b ff.), both in the absence of and reference to the primeval waters and in the allusion to wilderness (see further Weippert, *Schöpfer des Himmels und der Erde*, 51). The prophet adapts the ancient traditions of creation to give expression to his fearful vision of chaos.

It is possible that vv 23–26 are drawn from a collection of the prophet's "confessional" saying or writings, as in the preceding section (4:19–21). As before, the confessional words are followed by a portion of an oracle, with which they are closely related in substance. On the basis of this parallel structure, the oracular section (vv 27–28) should be recognized as being integrally related to the preceding poem rather than being, for example, a sort of "mitigating gloss" (cf. Nicholson, 56) designed to relieve the terrible note of finality in the poem (see further the *Comment*). The interrelationship between oracle and poem is reinforced by the reference to divine "speech" (v 28), which is an important part of the narrative of creation (Gen 1) adapted in the poem.

The literary interrelationship between Gen 1 and vv 23–28 can be seen in the following tabulation of the parallels between the passages (for which there are also parallels in Job 3:3–13, as noted by Fishbane),

CHAOS (Jeremiah)	*CREATION* (Genesis)
"emptiness and void" (v 23)	"emptiness and void" (1:2)
"light" (v 23)	"light" (1:3)
"heavens" (v 23)	"heavens" (1:8)
"earth" (v 23)	"earth" (1:10)
"bird" (v 25)	"bird" (1:20)
"mankind" (v 25)	"mankind" (1:26)

The parallels and contrasts are taken further in the notion of "speech": creation begins because God speaks, and chaos comes because God has spoken (Jer 4:28). And perhaps a further contrast is implied, as suggested by Fishbane; the Sabbath is the climax of God's creation, but his chaos is a consequence of divine "wrath" (v 26).

The original setting of the verses cannot be specified. Although a public recounting of the vision and the accompanying oracle is possible, the "confessional" character of the vision suggests more the private and contemplative aspect of the prophet's life. The poem may have been created in reflection upon the substance of the oracle, which in turn probably belonged to a larger oracle, declared originally as a part of the prophet's public ministry.

Comment

The prophet's vision is cosmic in scope, escaping the national boundaries of the immediate context of judgment and embracing the entire universe. In the vision, the coming chaos that will overwhelm Israel, cancelling the nation's status as God's special creation (see Deut 5:15, when Israel's "creation" is specified as a ground for observing the Sabbath day), is portrayed poetically as a return to primeval chaos. But the language is poetic; Israel's judgment will be *like* a return to primeval chaos, but the language is only indirectly apocalyptic, for the end of the cosmos will not yet come about, as stated so clearly in the oracle (v 27b).

The undertones of the poetry are evocative of the various themes of order and chaos. In creation, order emerged from chaos; in Israel's creation, an ordered covenant people emerged from the chaos of Egyptian slavery. But chaos, in the prophet's view, is not banished in creation; it is merely held at bay, ever threatening to return. And Israel's behavior, inviting judgment, has released again in the cosmos the terrible forces of chaos. They are forces controlled by God alone, and only God can release them; hence, as so often in the prophet's words, the return of chaos is at the divine permission, but it is instigated by a nation's evil. That which releases chaos is the divine "wrath"; as it was God's love which moved him to bring forth creation and an ordered world, so love's other face, wrath, may release the return to chaos.

There are the seeds of apocalyptic thought in this visionary account, nourished by the imagery of creation employed in the communication of the message of judgment. The immediate sense of the passage and the immediate context confine the thrust of the words to Judah's coming judgment at the hands of a pagan foe. But the imagery of creation, the *Urzeit*, when it is converted to speak of a return of primeval chaos, necessarily evokes the end. The end, in context, is Israel's end, yet the cyclical pattern of the process implies that if the nation of the chosen people can progress from creation and ultimately back to chaos, so too may the cosmos as a whole. And if the nation's return to chaos is a consequence of evil, then so too may the eventual disintegration of cosmos into chaos be a moral consequence within the history of creation. Thus, the "it is good" of the series of steps towards creation in Gen 1 can no longer be stated; when it must be said of either cosmos or creature, "it is evil," then the return to chaos has begun and the age of apocalypse has dawned.

Explanation

See the *Explanation* following 6:22–30.

A Lament for Zion (4:29–31)

Bibliography

Beer, G. "Miscellen: 4. Zu Jeremiah 4:31." *ZAW* 31 (1911) 153–54. **Efros, I.** "An Emendation of Jer. 4:29." *JAOS* 41 (1921) 75. **Levitan, I. S.** "Dr. Efros' Emendation of Jer. 4:29." *JAOS* 41 (1921) 316.

Translation

29	*At the sound of rider and archer,*	(4+3)
	the whole city[a] flees.	
	They enter[b] the thicket[c]	(2+2)
	and ascend the rocks;	
	The whole city is forsaken,	(3+3?)
	none remaining within it.	
30	*But you, [a]what are you doing,*	(2?+2)
	dressing in scarlet,	
	bedecking yourself with golden bangles,	(3+3)
	highlighting your eyes with eyeliner?[b]	
	You beautify yourself in vain,	(2+2+2)
	your lovers despising you,	
	seeking your life!	
31	*For I have heard a sound like a woman in labor,*	(3+2)
	distress like the birth of a firstborn,	
	the sound of daughter Zion gasping,	(3+2)
	her hands outstretched:	
	"Ah, I'm fainting,	(3+2)
	the killers have possessed my life."	

Notes

29.a. LXX renders, "the whole *land*" (viz. הָאָרֶץ), implying that הָעִיר here is an accidental duplication of הָעִיר later in the verse. But it is best to retain *city*, which seems to be the central theme of the poem as a whole.

29.b. LXX has a longer text here: "They entered the caves, and they hid themselves in the groves, and they ascended the rocks." LXX is followed by NEB, but it is best to remain with the Heb. text.

29.c. עָב, normally "cloud," is here "thicket" or "bush." See also 1 Kgs 7:6 and G. Garbini, "Note linguistico-filologiche," *Hen* 4 (1982) 163–73.

30.a. שָׁדוּד, "desolate one," is tentatively deleted, after LXX (cf. NEB); the masc form is anomalous in the grammatical context.

30.b. פוּךְ, lit., "antimony, stibnite." The metallic substance was crushed, blended with soot, and used as an eyeliner to heighten the beauty and brightness of the eyes.

Form/Structure/Setting

This poetic passage from Jeremiah contrasts the inevitability of Jerusalem's judgment with the obtuseness of its citizens in failing to perceive the finality of their plight, seeking always a final escape from their doom. It is not clear whether (i) this portion of a poem belonged originally to a larger oracle, or (ii) the first person references imply the prophet, and thus contain his own poetic reflections on Zion's plight. The setting is Jerusalem and the words were initially delivered in public ministry to the people (as implied by the direct form of address in v 30). The date cannot be specified beyond the general chronological perspectives of the larger narrative to which this poem now belongs. The metaphorical language implies that this portion of the prophet's preaching was initially part of a critique of Jerusalem's treaties and alliances with various foreign powers (the "lovers" of v 30).

Comment

The prophet begins with a description of what would be the normal reaction of a city faced with crisis (v 29). There follows a description of the abnormal reaction that would be Jerusalem's, in which the metaphor of prostitution is skillfully employed by the poet (vv 30–31).

Normally, if citizens of an undefended city heard of the advent of a powerful army ("rider and archer," v 29), they would take to the hills or seek some security in the impenetrable bush, leaving behind the forsaken city in the path of the enemy. Their city might be destroyed, but in any case they could not have defended it; flight would at least secure their lives. They would not be cowards, but realists; it is not particularly courageous to remain at home, with no defense, to face an overwhelmingly superior enemy.

But the citizens of Jerusalem would have no such wisdom when God's army of judgment advanced on its walls. Jeremiah draws on the metaphor of the prostitute to convey his message of Jerusalem's future folly. Jerusalem would dress herself up for the occasion, donning a bright scarlet dress, decking herself with gold bangles, highlighting her eyes to increase her seductive allure. But the whole exercise would be in vain, for clothes and bangles do not substitute for beauty; Jerusalem no longer knew that her beauty had long since fled, exchanged for a haggard countenance framed by a courtesan's costume. She did not know that her hoped-for lovers were haters, wanting only her death.

The language of childbirth is introduced in v 31; at first it appears as if the metaphor has been changed, but it has only been developed. The prostitute of v 30 is also pregnant; Jerusalem's demise would be like that of a prostitute giving birth to a firstborn bastard. The language is not pretty, but it was designed to catch attention, to evoke reaction, and thus perhaps to penetrate the dull minds of those to whom it was addressed. It may be that the prophet implies in v 31 not merely death in the course of child-delivery (in metaphorical terms), but death in pregnancy at the hands of the ruthless soldiers, a practice that was not uncommon in the ancient Near East.

Explanation

See the *Explanation* following 6:22–30.

A Dialogue concerning Judgment (5:1–9)

Bibliography

Berkovitz, E. "The Biblical Meaning of Justice." *Judaism* 18 (1969) 188–209. **Berridge, J. M.** *Prophet, People.* 77–80, 83. **Carroll, R. P.** "Theodicy and Community: The Text and Subtext of Jeremiah 5:1–6." *OTS* 23 (1984) 19–39. **Dahood, M.** *Ugaritic-Hebrew Philology.* 74. **Holladay, W. L.** *Architecture,* 85–86. **Jastrow, M.** "Jeremiah 5:8." *AJSL* 13 (1986/7) 216–17. **Lundbom, J. R.** *Jeremiah.* 75–78. **May, H. C.** "Individual Responsibility and Retribution." *HUCA* 32 (1961) 115–16. **Sutcliffe, E. F.** "A Note on Jer. 5:3." *JSS* 5 (1960) 348–49. **Wisser, L.** *Jérémie, Critique de la vie sociale: justice sociale et connaissance de Dieu dans le livre de Jérémie.* Geneva: Labor et Fides, 1982. 31–33. **Wittstruck, T.** "The Influence of Treaty Curse Imagery on the Beast Imagery of Daniel 7." *JBL* 97 (1978) 100–102.

Translation

1 "Stroll through the streets of Jerusalem (3+2)
   and observe and take notes!
   And search her public concourses (2+2)
   to see if a man can be found,
   if anyone is acting justly, (3+2+2)
   seeking truth—
   and I will forgive her!"
                    The LORD's oracle.[a]
2 "Though they say, 'As the Lord lives,' (3+3)
   surely[a] they swear falsely."
3 "Your eyes, O LORD, (2+2)
   do they not look for truth?
   You struck them, (2+2)
   but they were not weakened;
   you took them to the limits—they refused (2+2)
   to accept correction!
   They made their faces harder than rock; (3+2)
   they refused to repent!
4 Then I said, "They are only the poor! (3+2)
   They[a] behave as fools,
   for they don't know the LORD's way, (4?+2)
   the manner[b] of their God.
5 I will go to the noblemen (2+2)
   and will address them,
   for they know the LORD's way, (4?+2)
   the manner of their God."
   But they too had broken the yoke, (4?+2)
   had ripped apart the reins,
6 Therefore a forest-lion will slaughter them, (4+3)

> a desert wolf will devastate them;
> a leopard stalks their cities—   (3+3)
>   all leaving them will be torn to shreds.
> For their sins have been many,   (3+2)
>   their backslidings numerous. "
> 7 "Why should I forgive you this?   (3+2+3)
>   Your children have forsaken me
>   and sworn by 'no-gods.'
> Though I provided[a] fully for them, they committed adultery;   (3+3)
>   they patronize[b] a prostitute's place!
> 8 They are stallions, hot[a] and lusty[b],   (4+4)
>   each one neighing for his neighbor's wife.
> 9 Should I not punish for these things?"   (2+2)
>   The LORD's oracle.
> "And with a nation like this,   (3+3)
>   should I not take vengeance?[a] "

Notes

1.a. The phrase נאם־יהוה is added on the basis of LXX; it was probably omitted accidentally on the basis of the similarity with the opening words of v 2.

2.a. Reading אך, "surely," with many Heb. MSS (de Rossi, III, 72) and Syr, for MT's לכן, "therefore."

4.a. הם, "they," is taken to introduce the second line of the verse, and the *athnah* is moved to the preceding word (cf. *BHS*).

4.b. On the translation of משפט (commonly, "justice") by "manner," see Berkovitz, *Judaism* 18 (1969) 188–209.

7.a. "Provide" is from שׂבע; a few MSS indicate the root is שׁבע, "swear," already employed in the preceding line (cf. de Rossi, III, 72). It is best to retain MT's distinction, the similar roots serving to heighten the poetic contrast.

7.b. The normal sense of the hithp of גדד would be "lacerate themselves," which is a possible translation here; the reference would be to the pagan practice associated with the fertility cult. The translation "patronize" assumes a denominative sense related to גדוד, "group, troop." Alternatively, read יתגוררו (hithp of גור), "seek hospitality with," but this too is a rare verb.

8.a. מיזנים. The sense of the word is uncertain, the translation above being suggested by context. If the root is יזן (here a pual ptcp), it is a hap. leg. BDB suggests a hoph ptcp of זון, "feed," also a hap. leg. (though a noun מזון, "food," is known).

8.b. משכים. The meaning of this word is also uncertain. It is apparently a hiph ptcp of שׁכה, but this root is of uncertain meaning. Dahood (*Ugaritic-Hebrew Philology*, 74) attempts to establish the meaning "lustful" on the basis of Ug. *ntk* (in *UT* 54:14–15). But the normal sense of Ug. *ntk* is "bite"; in the text cited, the form is *ntkp* (itself of uncertain meaning). Thus, though Dahood appears to be correct in identifying the sense of the Heb. word, little support is offered by Ug.

9.a. Lit , "should not my soul avenge itself?"

Form/Structure/Setting

This passage, a part of the continuing mosaic descriptive of coming judgment, is set in the form of a dialogue between the Lord and his prophet. The literary structure suggests that the dialogue should be viewed as an integrated literary unit; whether it was composed from various oracles for insertion at this point in the text or drawn from some private source of the prophet's reflections, remains uncertain. Only v 7, addressed directly to Jerusalem (or Judah), is in the form of direct address to the people, and may have been drawn from the prophet's publicly declared oracles. Verse 7 may indeed be the nucleus around which this dialogue has grown, although as we shall see, the dialogue has the form of a closely knit literary unit. The structure of the dialogue may be set out as follows.

(i) The Lord's word to Jeremiah (vv 1–2).
(ii) The prophet's response (vv 3–6).
(iii) The Lord's word:
  (a) Quotation from public oracle (v 7).
  (b) Response to Jeremiah (vv 8–9).

The parts of the dialogue are interlocked by the repetition of common words and roots. Note in particular the following: (i) God's reference to "truth" (אמונה) in v 1 is taken up in the prophet's response (v 3). (ii) The possibility of forgiveness (סלח, v 1) in God's opening words is resumed in the divine oracle (סלח, v 7). Note also the repeated use of the verb שבע, "swear," in vv 1 and 7. (iii) Within the prophet's statement (vv 3–6), forms of the verbs הכה and שוב are repeated (in vv 3 and 6), separated by the repetitive contrast between the "poor" and the "noblemen" (vv 4b and 5b), thus forming a kind of chiastic structure to the prophet's discourse.

This setting, both of the public oracle (v 7) and of the complete dialogue, is Jerusalem. The date of the parts and the whole is more difficult to determine. The oracle which seems to form the nucleus of the composition (v 7), with its reference to idolatrous religious practices, may come from the very earliest period of the prophet's ministry (during King Josiah's reign). The dialogue as a whole, however, seems to reflect a later period, in which idolatry has been replaced by more general concerns of a social nature; it is, in some ways, a kingdom of theodicy (cf., Feinberg, 55–57), precipitated perhaps by the change in character of Jerusalem's evil from a cultic to a social nature. Thus the date of the dialogue might be set in the later years of Josiah's reign, or the earliest part of Jehoiakim's reign.

Comment

The dialogue is reminiscent of Abraham's prayer for Sodom (Gen 18:23–33), but the initiative lies entirely with God (though it may presuppose a question from Jeremiah concerning the harshness of the coming judgment). The prophet is invited to traverse the streets of Jerusalem and observe what is taking place in the capital city. He is told specifically to search for people who might be living according to the divine principles of justice and truth; if such persons could be found, then on their behalf the Lord would forgive the city's sin. But the invitation to search is followed by a warning; he may find people superficially orthodox, who use the proper formula of oaths ("As the LORD lives," v 2), but their language is false, a hypocritical veneer covering the lies within.

This is dialogue, and so Jeremiah reflects on Jerusalem and his experiences there (rather than literally walking the city's streets). Ultimately, he concludes that when the criterion is divine truth, there are no honest people left. Even the acts of divine chastisement had failed to bring people back to their spiritual senses;

they simply hardened their faces, stubbornly refusing to repent and to return to the true faith (v 3).

But Jeremiah does not want to let go of the loophole provided in God's opening words, the possibility that the city might be spared. He says, perhaps to himself (vv 4–5), that he has looked to the wrong people: the "poor" (v 5) probably refers simply to the ordinary citizens, the people in the streets. If he were to turn to Jerusalem's elite citizens, then surely he would find persons who knew the Lord's way and lived accordingly. (Note the repetition of *mišpat* ["justice, manner"] in vv 1, 4, 5.) But the prophet's plan was in vain, for the noble were no different from the common people; they too had broken free from the divine constraint to pursue their own evil path.

And so the prophet concludes that despite the divine loophole—forgiveness if a few righteous persons could be found—the reality was that judgment was fully deserved. The judgment is described in a series of animal metaphors: Jerusalem and its citizens would be ravaged by the lion, the wolf, and the leopard (v 6). The language, however, is more than metaphorical and probably alludes to the divine curses, contingent upon covenant obedience, being brought into effect. The eighth-century-B.C. Sefire treaties speak of the ravaging of lion and leopard as the fulfillment of a treaty curse (Wittstruck, *JBL* 97 [1978] 100–102). Hosea 13:7–8 also uses similar language. The treaty-curse background clarifies the nature of the divine judgment; it is not merely a coming disaster, but it is specifically a disaster elicited by Jerusalem's disobedience and evil actions: "their sins have been many, their backslidings numerous" (v 6).

In the Lord's response to Jeremiah's words, the opening portion (v 7) appears to be drawn from what was once a public oracle addressed to the people of Jerusalem/Judah (see *Form/Structure/Setting* above); the words are addressed to the people, not the prophet. There can be no forgiveness, for the people *en masse* have embraced idolatry, the "no-gods" of alien cults. The language of adultery and prostitution indicates that the particular forms of idolatry were those associated with the fertility cult, specifically that of Baal.

In v 8 the dialogue continues (following the quotation of v 7). The people are likened to stallions, neighing for a mate. As this portion of the dialogue may be later in time than v 7, it is uncertain whether the allusion is still to the fertility cult or more generally to the adultery that characterized Jerusalem's social life. In either case, the consequence is the same: the dialogue that began with the possibility of repentance closes on a negative note. The door of forgiveness seems to be slammed shut; such rampant evil as that of Jerusalem positively begs for the onset of divine judgment.

The movement of the dialogue is thus from the dangled possibility of divine forgiveness (v 1) to its final removal (v 9). It is a kind of theodicy in that it establishes, by means of dialogue and searching questions, the divine right to judge as a response to a city's evil. If, as is probable, the dialogue reflects a period after Josiah's reform, the starting point for the prophet's questions may be found in the (superficial) changes that have taken place in society. On the surface, many of the former abuses of worship in Jerusalem had been cleaned up. So was it right for the prophet still to preach the same harsh message of judgment? But the prophet, in the course of his dialogue with God, is instructed to look beneath the surface, to see whether truth and justice have become the hallmark of his society. When he cannot persuade himself that such a transformation has really taken place, his problem of theodicy disappears. Jeremiah joins his voice with God's in declaring that judgment must come.

Explanation

See the *Explanation* following 6:22–30.

The Theme of Judgment Renewed (5:10–19)

Bibliography

Dahood, M. *Ugaritic-Hebrew Philology.* 50. **Fohrer, G.** *Die Propheten des Alten Testament 3. Die Propheten des Fruhen 6 Jahrhunderts.* **Grover, M.** "The Ten Commandments' Change of Names." *BMik* 27 (1981) 16–21 [in Heb.]. **Long, B. O.** "The Effect of Divination upon Israelite Literature." *JBL* 92 (1973) 489–97. **Lundbom, J. R.** *Jeremiah.* 39–41. **Meyer, I.** *Jeremia und die falschen Propheten.* 85–93. **Schmuttermayr, G.** "Beobachtungen zu Jer 5,13." *BZ* n.s. 9 (1965) 215–32. **Skweres, D. E.** "Das Motiv der Strafgrunderfragung in biblischen und neuassyrischen Texten." *BZ* 14 (1970) 181–97. **Sutcliffe, E. F.** "A Note on לא הוא Jer 5:12." *Bib* 41 (1960) 287–90. **Westermann, C.** *Basic Forms of Prophetic Speech.* Philadelphia: Westminster, 1967. 169–76.

Translation

10	*"Go up into her vine-rows and destroy,*	(3+2)
	but do not[a] *yet make a full end.*	
	Strip away her tendrils,	(2+3)
	for they do not belong to the LORD.	
11	*For they have acted in a totally faithless manner toward me,*	(4+4)
	both the House of Israel and the House of Judah.	
12	*They have behaved deceitfully against the LORD,*	(2+2)
	and said, 'He'll do nothing!	
	Nothing bad will happen to us,	(3+3)
	nor shall we see either sword or famine.	
13	*The prophets are windbags,*	(3+3)
	and the prophetic word[a] *is not in them!'"*[b]	
14	*Therefore, thus said the LORD, the God of Hosts:*	
	"Thus shall it be done to them,	(3+3?)
	because they[a] *have spoken this word.*	
	I'm going to make my word fire in your mouth,	(5+4)
	and this people are firewood, so it will consume them.	
15	*Lo, I am bringing against you*	(3+4)
	a nation from far away, O House of Israel;	
	it is an enduring nation,	(3+3)
	it is a nation from ancient times,	

> *a nation whose language you don't know*   (3+3)
> *and whose speech you cannot comprehend.*

16 *Its quiver is like an open grave;*   (3+2)
> *all within it* [a] *are warriors.*

17 *And it shall consume your harvest and your food;*   (3+3)
> *it* [a] *shall consume your sons and your daughters.*

> *It shall consume your sheep and your cattle;*   (3+3)
> *it shall consume your vines and your fig trees.*

> *It will destroy* [b] *by the sword* [c] *your fortified cities*   (4+4)
> *in which you place your trust.*"

18 "*But even in those days*"—the LORD's oracle—"*I will not bring about your complete end.* 19 *But when you (people)* [a] *say, 'For what reason has the LORD our God done all these things to us?' Then you (Jeremiah)* [a] *shall say to them: Just as you have rejected me and served foreign gods in your land, so shall you serve strangers in a land that is not your own.*'"

Notes

10.a. אל (both here and in the similar clause in v 18) is translated as a negative, "not." However, it is possible to translate it, in both instances, as an asseverative particle, "surely"; see Dahood, *Ugaritic-Hebrew Philology*, 50, after J. A. Soggin, *Bib* 46 (1965) 57–58. The sense is radically altered, depending upon the choice of translation. The negative has been retained on the basis of context; the notion of pruning (v 10b) and the notion of exile (v 19) seem to support the notion that "*not* a final end" is in the prophet's mind, but only a terrible act of judgment that will seem like the end.

13.a. הדבר. The word could be vocalized simply הַדָּבָר, "the word," for which there is slender MS support. Alternatively, accepting MT's vocalization, דִּבֶּר could be rendered "prophetic revelation (word)" (see Grover, *BMik* 27 [1981] 16–21), which might find some support in LXX: λόγος κυρίου, "word of the Lord."

13.b. The final phrase of v 13 in MT has been transposed and appears as the second line of v 14, where it more naturally fits the context. The displacement may have been a consequence of the repetition of כה, "thus."

14.a. MT has 2nd person "you." Context strongly implies a 3 suff (as above), though there is no support from the Heb. MSS.

16.a. Lit., "all of them." The translation "all within it" is an attempt to clarify, by expansion, the simile of the quiver (first line), which is continued in this allusion to the "arrows" (warriors) contained in the quiver.

17.a. The sg form of the verb is read יאכל; there is support from one Heb. MS, Syr, and Vg (de Rossi, III, 73), and the sg is implied by the three other sg forms of the same verb in the immediate context.

17.b. ירשש is translated "destroy," a poel form of רשש, but the verb is very rare in the Heb. Bible and the sense is uncertain. LXX implies "threshing" (corn).

17.c. בחרב, "by the sword," is tentatively transposed to the first line, as implied by sense and meter. NEB omits the phrase (cf. Brockington, *The Hebrew Text of the Old Testament*, 200), though without good grounds.

19.a. "People" and "Jeremiah" have been added (in parentheses) to clarify that the address "you" in this verb is pl in its first use and sg at its second occurrence.

Form/Structure/Setting

A collection of poetic fragments, together with a short prose passage, have been knitted together to form this section, which is unified by the theme that the coming judgment, for all its severity, will not be a *final end*. The component parts of the section are as follows.

(i) *Vv 10–13:* a portion of a poetic oracle intimating the coming of the enemy, an instrument of judgment, as a consequence of the people's evil behavior. (It is possible that this passage could be further subdivided: (a) vv 10–11 and (b) 12–13.) The words are addressed, poetically, to the foreign agent of judgment, and the justification of that judgment is established by the quotation of the people's words (vv 12–13), which are self-condemning.

(ii) *V 14:* a portion of a prophetic oracle addressed to Jeremiah, descriptive now of the "burning word" or judgment.

(iii) *Vv 15–17:* a portion of a poetic oracle addressed to the "House of Israel" (Judah in this context?), describing the coming of the enemy and the totality of its destruction.

(iv) *Vv 18–19:* a prose oracle, resuming the theme of section (i) and introducing the subject of exile. It is addressed to both nation and prophet, both of whom are spoken to in the second person (see *Notes,* 19.a. and 19.b.). (Note, however, that Althann, *Jeremiah 4–6,* 304–5, provides a strong argument for interpreting this section as poetry.)

The mosaic nature of the component parts of the oracle should not blind us to the literary unity of the whole in its present form. The parts have been woven together to form a thematic unity, both with respect to subject matter (see *Comment*) and by the use of particular words and phrases. The structure of the whole can be set out as follows, to indicate the interrelationship and inner development.

A   *Judgment:* but not a final end (vv 10–13) (v 10b; cf. v 18b in A').
B   *The word to the prophet* (v 14): linked to A by (i) עשה (v 14, note 13.b.; cf. v 10), and (ii) דבר (v 14; cf. v 13).
C   *Judgment against Israel* (vv 15–17): linked to B by אכל (v 17; cf. v 14).
A' *Judgment:* but not a final end (vv 18–19) (v 18b; cf. v 10b in A).

There is no good reason to doubt the Jeremianic nature of the three poetic sections, though the prose section (vv 18–19), with its reference to exile, is commonly attributed to an unknown prophet of the exilic period (e.g., Fohrer, *Die Propheten des Alten Testaments,* 3) or to a Deuteronomic editor (Nicholson, 62). The careful literary structure of the passage (above) and its setting in Jeremiah 4–6 as a whole tend to militate against the view that the prose narrative should be identified as a Deuteronomic editorial addition. The parallel with Deut 29:22–28 and 1 Kgs 9:8–9 (cited by Nicholson) is general rather than specific. The background to the prose section is rather to be found in the question-answer schema, rooted originally in prophetic practice of divination, but becoming a literary form (or perhaps motif) in and of itself, and by necessity being prosaic in form rather than poetic. (See further Long, *JBL* 92 [1973] 489–97; Skweres, *BZ* 9 [1965] 215–32). It seems reasonable to conclude, therefore, that the prose section, along with the poetic units, is Jeremianic.

Although the setting of these units is to be identified with Jerusalem and Judah, it is not easy to specify precise dates. Verses 12–13 may be taken to imply that the threat of judgment is not imminent, though equally they may merely reflect the nation's self-confidence. The distant nation (vv 15–17) is sometimes identified with Babylon (e.g., Thompson, 242) and thus taken to imply a date early in Jehoiakim's reign. While such a view is in all probability correct, the text itself does not establish clearly the identity of the enemy.

Comment

10–13 *The coming judgment.* Judgment is here described in the metaphor of pruning a vineyard, with the clarification (v 10b) that while pruning is an act of judgment, it nevertheless has a constructive purpose and should not be seen as a final and terminal act of God. The pagan power, to whom these words are addressed, are to prune, but not to cut down the vines altogether. It is a radical metaphor, indicating the severe cutting that would take place and implying the gathering and burning of the useless tendrils. But for all its severity, it is not a metaphor implying finality. It is a means to the end of clearing away the faithlessness that had come to typify the chosen people's relationship with God (v 11), but its ultimate goal was to restore faithful relationship.

The judgment is presented here as being, in effect, invited by a people who had become so self-confident that they did not really believe that anything bad could happen to them. Their overweening confidence in their own eternal security was accompanied by a casual dismissal of the message of the prophets (v 13). A word play is employed here, to heighten the literary effect. They call the prophets "windbags" (רוח: literally "wind"), but of course the word רוח may be translated not only "wind," but also "spirit." The essence of true prophecy was the *spirit* of God, but such was their blindness, or willful ignorance, that they could not discern between *wind* and the true *spirit* of prophecy. Such unwarranted self-confidence, accompanied by the rejection of the divine word through the prophets, would be the ground of the judgment of pruning described in vv 10–11.

14 *The word of the prophet.* Though originally part of a separate oracle, these words develop naturally the substance of the preceding verses. The people had rejected the prophet's words as "wind"; what they would experience, therefore, was the prophet Jeremiah's word as "fire" in the time of their judgment. They would be as a bundle of kindling, easily ignited by the fire of the divine word.

15–17 *Judgment against Israel.* The metaphor of being *consumed* (the verb is אכל) by the word of fire is now developed in another direction; the coming enemy would "consume" (אכל) Judah's supplies and its citizens (v 17).

The enemy nation that would serve as God's instrument of judgment is described in such a way as to heighten its power and alien character. It would be an "enduring" and "ancient" nation (v 15), perhaps indicating its existence and history were much longer and more impressive than that of Judah. Its speech would be unintelligible, alien in the cultural context of Jerusalem. Its force would be overwhelming, every citizen a fighting soldier (v 16). And, the final blow, this pagan power would destroy every basis of false confidence in which the people had come to place their trust (v 17). The judgment would be devastating in its extent.

18–19 *The end—but not quite.* Perhaps because of the air of finality evoked by v 17, it is emphasized again that the coming time of judgment would not be the absolute end. The language anticipates the kind of dialogue that would take place after the judgment (indeed the kind of dialogue found in Ezekiel, prophet of Exile: e.g., Ezek 14:1–5). The people will ask why all this happened, and the prophet, on God's behalf, will answer. Their rejection of the true God for foreign gods would result in God's rejecting their special status and sending them to serve in a foreign land. (It should be repeated that such references to exile do not necessarily presuppose that the exile has already occurred. A multitude of historical examples, including Israel's fate in 722 B.C., indicated that exile could be one of the forms assumed by divine judgment.) But like the "pruning" of v 10, the reference to exile leaves open the door of possibility. The end of the nation in its land would come about in the judgment here anticipated. Nevertheless, this was not a final end, for there yet remained those people of God who could ask of his prophet: "Why has all this happened to us?" Thus, we perceive in Jeremiah, even before the exile, an anticipation of the thought of Ezekiel and the later prophets, namely, that beyond the immediate horizon of judgment, there remained yet a more distant prospect of hope.

Explanation

See the *Explanation* following 6:22–30.

Poems on Evil and Judgment (5:20–31)

Bibliography

Corré, A. D. "*ʾēlle, hēmma* = sic." *Bib* 54 (1973) 263–64. **Dahood, M.** "Jer. 5:31 and *UT* 127.32." *Bib* 57 (1976) 106–8. **Emerton, J. A.** "Notes on Some Problems in Jeremiah V 26." In *Mélanges bibliques et orientaux en l'honneur de M. Henri Cazelles*. Ed. A. Caquot and M. Delcor. AOAT 212. Neukirchen-Vluyn: Neukirchener Verlag, 1981. 125–33. **Gaster, T. H.** "Jeremiah v. 28." *ExpTim* 56 (1944/45) 54. **Holladay, W. L.** *Architecture*, 88–90. ———. "'The Priests scrape out on their Hands.' Jer. 5:31." *VT* 15 (1965) 111–13. **Meyer, I.** *Jeremia*. 93–99. **Overholt, T. W.** *Falsehood*. 73–74. **Rendsburg, G.** "Hebrew RHM—'rain'." *VT* 33 (1983) 357–62. **Tawil, H.** "Hebrew הצלח/צלח, Akkadian *eṣēru/šūṣuru*: A Lexicographical Note." *JBL* 95 (1976) 405–13. **Thomas, D. W.** "Jeremiah v.28." *ExpTim* 57 (1945/46) 54–55.

Translation

20	"Declare this in the House of Jacob and proclaim it in Judah, saying:	(4+3)
21	'Now hear this, O foolish and heartless people.	(2+2?)
	You have eyes, but don't see.	(2+2)
	You have ears, but don't hear.	(2+2)
22	Have you no reverence for me?' The LORD's oracle.	(2+2)
	'Will you not tremble because of me? It is I who set the sand as the sea's boundary, a perpetual limit which it cannot pass.	(4+3)

It tosses back and forth, but is powerless; (3+3)
and its waves roar, but cannot pass it.
23 *But this nation has* (3+3+2)
a stubborn and rebellious heart;
they have turned outside and gone beyond.
24 *And they did not say in their heart* (3?+3)
"Let us revere the LORD our God,
the One who provides rain, (2+3)
both fall and spring rain in season;
the weeks appointed for harvest (3+2)
he guarantees for us."
25 *Your iniquities have turned these things*[a] *aside,* (3+4)
and your sins have kept the rain[b] *from you.*
26 *For wicked men are found among my people;* (3+3)
they watch, as in a fowler's hide.[a]
They set a trap, (2+2)
they catch men.
27 *Like a basket full of birds,* (3+3)
so are their households full of treachery;
and thus they became great and rich; (3+2)
28 *they grew fat and became smooth!*[a]
They have even overlooked words of wickedness; (3+2)
they have not tried a case properly.
The orphan's case they do not deal with properly,[b] (3+3)
nor do they do justice in the judgment of the poor.
29 *Should I not punish for these things?'* (2+2)
The LORD's oracle.
'And with a nation like this, (3+3)
should I not take vengeance?'[a]
30 *An awful and horrible thing* (2+2)
has happened in the land!
31 *The prophets prophesy falsely,* (3+3)
and the priests rule on their own authority,[a]
and my people love it so! (3+3)
But what will you do when it ends?"

Notes

25.a. אלה, "these things." Corré (*Bib* 54 [1973] 263–64) has proposed that the word functions as does *sic* in English, indicating that the preceding text has been copied correctly, despite appearances. In this context, however, the suggestion is improbable, and the standard translation (above) is preferable.

25.b טוב, RSV "good." In context (v 24), the sense "rain" is to be preferred (cf. Rendsburg, *VT* 33 [1983] 357–62).

26.a. This line has long been a source of difficulty; the translation above is based on Emerton's meticulous examination of the text (*Mélanges bibliques*, 125–33). The reading is כְּשָׂךְ (cf. Lam 2:6), "as (in) a blind." The simile compares evil-doers to bird-hunters concealed in a blind, waiting to catch their game.

28.a. The sense of עשתו, translated "they became smooth" is uncertain and suggested by context עשת (I) is a *hap. leg.* in this verbal sense. The clause is omitted in LXX.

28.b. This translation is based on the study of Tawil (*JBL* 95 [1976] 405–13) and the proposal that הצלח may have the sense "see that justice is done" (based on the usage of Akk. *ešeru šušuru*).

29.a. See note 5:9.a.

31.a. Lit., "the priests rule (?) upon their hands." Dahood (*Bib* 57 [1976] 106–8) has made the attractive proposal that the line should be translated "the priests lower their hands into mischief." This assumes that על should not be interpreted as a prep but as a noun על, "mischief," based on Ug. *ġlt*, "mischief" (*UT* 127.32). However, the sense of the Ug. term is not well defined. Gordon proposes "inactivity" (*UT*, 464), Gibson suggests "weakness" (*CML*, 155), Gray translates "miscalculation" on the basis of an Arab. cognate (*THE KRT Text in the Literature of Ras Shamra*. 2nd ed. [Leiden: Brill] 1964, 28), and Caquot et al. translate "malheur" (*Textes ougaritiques*, I, 596). In summary, the sense of the Ug. term is too insecure to strengthen Dahood's translation concerning the Heb. text. If the literal sense is taken, it is best to assume that the Heb. is idiomatic, perhaps implying that priests do nothing (in the Eng. idiom, "they sit upon their hands").

Form/Structure/Setting

Three poems are here set together, unified by the theme of "people" (note the use of עם: [i] vv 21, 23; [ii] v 26; [iii] v 31). Each poem elaborates upon different aspects of the people's failure and hence the inevitability of their judgment.

The people's perversity (vv 20–25). The poem begins with a conventional oracular formula (v 20). The words are in the form of direct divine address (via the prophet) to the nation as a whole and are drawn no doubt from an originally longer oracle employed in Jeremiah's public ministry in Judah (v 20). The contents do not enable specific dating of the larger oracle from which this poem is drawn, although if vv 24–25 contain an allusion to drought (cf. 3:3), the passage may have been employed originally early in the prophet's ministry.

The people's injustice (vv 26–29). The language in the principal section of this poem (vv 26–28) describes the people in impersonal terms. Verse 29, which duplicates v 9 as a kind of refrain, employs the first person of God, though the people are still described rather than addressed. It is possible that these verses should be understood as belonging originally to the dialogue from which 5:1–9 are drawn, in which case the refrain (vv 9, 29) would have provided some overall structure to the dialogue as a whole. On the setting, see further *Form/Structure/Setting* at 5:1–9.

The people's leaders (vv 30–31). These two verses seem to be independent from the preceding poems. The reference to prophecy might suggest a link to the poetic fragment in 5:12–13.

In summary, for all the diversity of sources from which the three poems are drawn, they are unified in their present literary context by their elaboration upon the theme "people" (עם).

Comment

20–25 *The people's perversity.* This portion of a poetic oracle begins with a call addressed to the people, inviting them to hear the divine word. But the opening words of the address are phrased in such a way as to echo both condemnation and desperation. "Hear this . . . you who have ears, but don't hear" (v 21); the people thus addressed have persistently failed to hear the divine address in the past, yet despite their record of deafness they are implored once again to hear. They have suffered equally from blindness, having seen God's world but having failed to perceive the divine hand in its movements and structures. Thus the people are "foolish and heartless," the latter term implying in context "ignorant." The consequence of ignorance was lack of reverence (v 22). As they did not hear the divine voice or see correctly the divine world, they could not revere God. In fact, they had reversed the divine order of things. In the biblical tradition of wisdom, "the reverence of the LORD is the beginning of wisdom" (Prov 1:7). Failing to see or to hear correctly, they did not fear the Lord, and thus were fools.

There follow two aspects of God's world which, if understood, should have elicited reverence from the people, and might yet have such an effect as the prophet declares them. (i) The mighty ocean (deified as *Yam*, god of chaos, in certain Canaanite religions) seemed in storm to typify the restless chaos of the created world, yet its sandy beaches established a limit beyond which the sea could not pass. For all its power, for all the pounding of its waves, the sea was controlled by the "perpetual limit" established by God, the sand on the seashore. Yet Israel, though its "beaches" had been divinely ordained by the stipulations of covenant, constantly went beyond those limits; the chaos that was its life had gone out of control.

(ii) Furthermore, Israel had also failed entirely to perceive that the rains upon which their land, and therefore their life and harvest, depended were a part of the provision of God. The implication in these words is that Israel had come to depend upon the alien faith in Baal, whom so many of the Canaanites believed to be the purveyor of rain and the provider of harvest.

The section as a whole is primarily descriptive of Israel's failure; it implies that if the people would even now hear the divine word and understand, repentance and a new future might be possible. It might also imply that there had been a recent experience of drought (v 25), understood as judgment but also as a heaven-sent warning. But the section does not develop fully the nature of divine judgment, only the kind of folly and irreverence that would contribute to the coming of judgment.

26–29 *The people's injustice.* Whereas the preceding section had focused on the people's failure to see God's hand in nature, and hinted at their participation in alien faiths, the focus now shifts to the area of social justice. As has been noted, these verses may originally have belonged to the dialogue of which we have already read a portion in 5:1–9. The words are spoken by God, addressed to the prophet, and they describe the folly of the people upon whom judgment must come.

The evil actions of the people are described in the simile of the fowler. In the bird-hunt, a net would be hidden, perhaps in the water of a pond, or perhaps in the shrubbery of trees and bushes. (Both types of bird-hunt are illustrated in Egyptian art: see plates 17 and 19 in K. Michalowski, *Art of Ancient Egypt* [New York: Abrams, n.d.] The hunters would then hide, secreting themselves in a constructed hiding place, until the birds returned. At a signal from a watcher, the net would be released and pulled tight, ensnaring the birds in its meshes. The simile is an effective one for describing the people's evil. They deliberately planned their evil actions, secreting themselves to catch unaware the innocent and the weak. And like the fowler returning home with a basketful of birds, they filled their homes with the loot stolen from their weaker prey. They became rich at the expense of the poor, strong at the expense of the weak.

The lawcourts, too, which should have been the domain in which integrity was preserved, had become corrupt in Judah. "Words of wickedness" (v 28) were probably the lies told in court, overlooked by the judges for a fee, whereby the rich and powerful subverted justice to their own ends and to the disadvantage of the poor. The orphan, a traditional symbol of one without power and influence, and the poor were vulnerable even in the courts, the places where their cases should have been upheld and ruled on in justice.

And so the refrain, echoing the earlier statement of the words (v 29; cf. v 9), is repeated again: such evil and injustice invite the Lord's punishment, which must surely come in the form of judgment. Jeremiah here echoes Amos.

30–31 *The people's leaders.* Even the spiritual leaders of the people had been corrupted by the ethos of the age. The prophets, whose responsibility it was to declare God's word to the people, prophesied falsely; instead of speaking the divine word, they proclaimed their own words, offering comfort to the oppressors and disillusionment to the oppressed. The prophets no doubt benefited financially from their false message, being rewarded by those doers of evil who desired to hear no uncomfortable message. But the proclamation of falsehood by the prophets was a further terrible evil; when the word of prophecy had become falsehood, who any longer knew the truth? Indeed, the task of one like Jeremiah must have been infinitely more difficult in a time when false prophets proliferated; how was he to establish that his word was the truth when the majority of his colleagues were saying something entirely different?

Not only the prophets but also the priests had failed in their tasks. They continued, no doubt, to fulfill their formal functions in worship, but they made a mockery of their own activities by condoning evil. And their role of teaching the true faith must have been abandoned, because they no longer knew the truth in their own lives. But perhaps worse than the failure of prophet and priest was the fact that the people as a whole loved the miserable state of affairs into which their nation had sunk. To those for whom evil had become a daily diet, there was great consolation in not being reproved by a prophet or reproached by a priest. And yet, the message ends on an ominous note, not developed in any detail, yet pregnant with the threat of judgment. "What will you do when it ends?" (v 31). When the era of evil finally terminated and judgment came, an entire nation would discover that it had based its way of life on folly.

Explanation

See the *Explanation* following 6:22–30.

A Call of Warning (6:1–8)

Bibliography

Berridge, J. M. "Jeremia und die Prophetie des Amos." *TZ* 35 (1979) 321–41. **Christensen, D. L.** *Transformations of the War Oracles in Old Testament Prophecy.* HDR 3. Missoula, MT: Scholars Press, 1975. 190–92. **Holladay, W. L.** *Architecture.* 90–91. **Lundbom, J. R.** *Jeremiah,*

78–79. **Soggin, J. A.** "Der Prophetische Gedanke über den heiligen Krieg, als Gericht gagen Israel." *VT* 10 (1960) 79–83 = "The Prophets on Holy War as Judgement against Israel." In *Old Testament and Oriental Studies.* BibOr 29. Rome: Biblical Institute, 1975. 67–71.

Translation

1	"Seek safety, O people of Benjamin, (3+2)

1   "Seek safety, O people of Benjamin,   (3+2)
       from Jerusalem's center!
       Toot the trumpet in Tekoa[a]   (3+3?)
       and set a signal[b] on Beth-hacherem,
       for evil glares from the north,   (3+2)
       and terrible destruction!
2   I thought of Daughter Zion as pasture land, a thing of beauty,[a]   (4+4)
       to whom shepherds come with their flocks;
3   they pitch their tents around her,   (4+3)
       they graze, each in his own section.
4   'Prepare for war against her!   (3+3)
       Up, and let's attack at noon!
       Damn![a] The daylight declines,   (3+3)
       the evening shadows lengthen!
5   Up, and let's attack at night   (3+2)
       and let's shatter her strongholds!'"
6   For thus said the LORD of hosts,
       "Cut down her trees and pour out soil   (3+2)
       for a siege-mound against Jerusalem.
       Oh, city of deception![a]   (3+3)
       All is oppression within her!
7   Just as a well[a] keeps fresh its water,   (3+3)
       so she keeps fresh her evil.
       'Violence! Destruction!' is heard within her;   (4+4)
       sickness and wounds are perpetually before me.
8   Be warned, O Jerusalem,   (2+3)
       lest I should be entirely alienated from you,
       lest I should make you a desolation,   (2+2)
       a land devoid of inhabitants."

Notes

1.a. The translation attempts to catch the assonance of the Heb. text: ובתקוע תקעו.

1.b. Again (see note 1.a.), there is assonance in the Heb. text: שאו משאת. The word משאת is used in the Lachish letters (4:10) to denote a "fire-signal" (*ANET*, 322). On the use of fire-signals in Mesopotamia, see G. Dossin, "Signaux lumineux au pays de Mari," *RA* 35 (1938) 174–86.

2.a. The translation of v 2, as vocalized in MT, is difficult; LXX presupposes a different text: "and your pride, O Daughter of Zion, shall be taken away." נָוֶה should be understood as "pasture" (BDB, 627), as implied by the reference to "shepherds" in the following line. דמיתי is interpreted as piel of דמה (I).

4.a. Lit., "woe to us"; assuming these to be the words of the enemy (as punctuated above), they express frustration, but determination to attack despite the time of the day. Alternatively, this and the following line could be set off in quotation marks to represent the fear of those attacked, rather than the determination of the attackers.

6.a. RSV translates, "This is the city which must be punished" (cf. *AV* et al.); but if this were the sense, a fem form of הָפְקַד, "punish," would be expected. LXX renders, "O false city," ὦ πόλις ψευδής, implying a Heb. text, הוֹי עִיר הַשֶּׁקֶר, which is the basis of the translation above. But the text remains uncertain.

7.a. Q בְּאֵר is followed (for K בור).

Form/Structure/Setting

The structure of this poetic warning oracle may be set out as follows. (i) A portion of a "call to alarm" (v 1; cf. 4:5–8). (ii) A brief pastoral scene (vv 2–3), converted into a battle scene (vv 4–5), characterized by a note of urgency. (iii) A divine oracle (vv 6–8), in which an enemy is instructed to lay siege to Jerusalem, but a final warning to Jerusalem (v 8) is also issued. The theme of the poem as a whole is similar to that in 4:5–10, although it is developed in a new direction. (Note also the common usage of הָעֵזּוּ, "seek safety," in v 1 and 4:6.)

Although parts of this poem may have been drawn originally from separate sources, in its present form it is an effective poetic unity. The structure of the whole is bound together by the use of assonance, word play, and repetition. Note, in particular, the following characteristics of the poem, which give the whole a sense of literary unity.

(i)   Assonance/word play on תקע:

v 1 תקוע	"Tekoa"
v 1 תקעו	"toot, blow"
v 3 תקעו	"pitch"
v 8 תקע	"be alienated," from

(ii)   Assonance/word play on רעה:

v 1 רעה	"evil"
v 3 רעים	"shepherds"
v 3 רעו	"graze"
v 7 רעתה	"her evil"

(iii)   Repetition:

(a) קרב	(vv 1, 6)
(b) קומו ונעלה	(vv 4, 5)

The original setting of the prophetic words was almost certainly Jerusalem (vv 1, 2, 6); the references to Benjamin, Tekoa, and Beth-hacherem must be interpreted in the context of Jerusalem (see below). The date cannot be determined with any precision. On the one hand, the poem breathes an atmosphere of urgency and imminence, but the warning note at the end (v 8) suggests there is still time before the city's collapse.

Comment

The poem begins with a call to flee to safety from the city of Jerusalem, which is the object of the enemy's anticipated attack. The perspective is thus different from, and perhaps later than, that continued in 4:5–6, which implies that Jerusalem was still considered a place of refuge in time of danger. The alarm call is addressed to the "people of Benjamin," namely the tribe to which Jeremiah belonged, but the expression in this context seems simply to designate the city of Jerusalem (located on the Benjamin-Judah territorial border) and the inhabitants of its environs. The reference to Tekoa is partly literary (see note 1.a.), partly geographical. Tekoa, which had once been the home of Amos, lay about twelve miles south of Jerusalem, bordering the great wilderness area that extended east, down into the great depression and the shores of the Dead Sea. Facing a foe from the north, citizens of Jerusalem might be expected to flee south to Tekoa, and from there eastwards into the comparative safety of the wilderness.

The reference to Beth-hacherem (v 1) is not easy to interpret, in part because the ancient site cannot be fixed with absolute certainty. It is possible that Beth-hacherem should be identified with ʿAin Karim, about three miles west of Jerusalem. If this identification were correct, then some cairns found on top of the hill, Jebel ʿAli, adjoining the village of ʿAin Karim, might be identified with the signal fires referred to by Jeremiah (see J. F. Prewitt, *ISBE*, I, 468). The more probable identification of Beth-Hacherem, however, is with the tell at Ramat Rahel, about two miles south of Jerusalem, just east of the main road to Bethlehem. Here, Jehoiakim apparently built a fortress/palace (perhaps alluded to in Jer. 22:13–19), of which the remains have been excavated (cf. Y. Aharoni, *The Land of the Bible* [Philadelphia: Westminster, 1967] 341, 351). If this poetic passage were late (which is far from certain), then there may be a degree of irony in the reference to Beth-hacherem, for the town of the new fortress from Jehoiakim's time would be the place in which the signal of disaster would be seen. But the more general interpretation is the safer one; in the face of disaster, people should flee south from Jerusalem via Beth-hacherem and Tekoa.

There follow in vv 2–5 two vignettes in which the poet has sharply contrasted the pastoral scene of Jerusalem, as it might have been, with the raucous preparations for battle that soon would become reality. Jerusalem (referred to as Daughter Zion) could have been the center of a pastoral setting in which shepherds, men of peace, tended their flocks. But the imagery is changed abruptly; the shepherds are suddenly transformed into military commanders, hastily preparing their "flocks" (viz. soldiers) for an attack on the city. They are so eager to get on with the job that even a nighttime assault (not normally viable) is given consideration. They want to shatter the "strongholds" (v 5), alluding no doubt to both Jerusalem and nearby places such as Tekoa and Beth-hacherem. The sharpness of the contrast between the pastoral and military scenes (vv 2–5) helps to emphasize the sense of urgency conveyed in the initial call to alarm (v 1).

In the divine oracle (vv 6–8), with which the poem ends, a new perspective is added to what precedes. The enemy is actually commanded by God to get on with the preparation for siege (v 6a); the coming events, in other words, will occur at the divine behest, not merely as a circumstance of history. The enemy is instructed to cut down trees and "pour out soil" (viz. scoop up soil in buckets and pour it out to form a mound). The siege-mound thus constructed would provide the enemy with the capacity to breach the city's walls.

The instruction to the enemy to lay siege to Jerusalem is followed by a lament-like passage (vv 6b–7), which contains both condemnation and sorrow. The condemnation concerns Jerusalem's propensity for falsehood and violence, her extraordinary capacity for keeping evil "fresh," just as a well keeps its water fresh! The words illuminate the perpetual tension within God; here, he is presented as the one who orders Jerusalem's destruction because of the city's evil, yet laments the evil that makes such an order necessary. And the final warning (v 8) seems to issue from the lament; the order for destruction has been issued, but the warning suggests there may yet be time for repentance, there may still be a chance of the flood of desolation being turned aside.

Explanation

See the *Explanation* following 6:22–30

Dialogue: Comprehensive Judgment (6:9–15)

Bibliography

Berridge, J. M. *Prophet, People.* 78–79. **Holladay, W. L.** *Architecture,* 91–92. **Meyer, I.** *Jeremia.* 99–110. **Overholt, T. W.** *Falsehood,* 74–79.

Translation

9 *Thus said the LORD of Hosts,*

"Like the vine, they shall thoroughly glean [a]   (3+2)
  Israel's remnant.
Like a grape-cutter, pass your hand   (3+2?)
  over the tendrils." [b]

10 *"Whom shall I address*   (2+2)
  or shall I warn, that they may hear?
Ha! Their ear is uncircumcised,   (3+3)
  and they are unable to pay attention!
Ha! To them the LORD's word was   (4+3)
  a reproach that they took no pleasure in!
11 *But I am filled with the LORD's anger;*   (3+2)
  I am weary with holding it in."

"Pour forth on the child in the street   (3+3)
  and also on the gang of youths.
For they will be taken, together with husband and wife,   (3+3)
  the old along with the extremely ancient.
12 *And their homes shall be turned over to others,*   (3+3)
  their fields and wives as well!
For I will stretch out my hand   (2+2)
  against the land's inhabitants."
         The LORD's oracle.

¹³   *"For from the least of them to the greatest of them,*   (3+3)
     each is greedy for gain.
     And from prophet to priest,   (2?+3)
     each engages in falsehood.

¹⁴   *They have healed my people's wound*   (3+2)
     superficially, saying:
     'Peace, peace,'   (2+2)
     but there is no peace!

¹⁵   *They should have been ashamed in acting abominably,*   (3+2+2)
     but were not in the least ashamed;
     they didn't know how to be humiliated!^a
     Therefore, they shall fall among the fallen;   (3+3)
     they shall be overthrown in the time of their doom."^b
     The LORD has spoken.

Notes

9.a. LXX "Glean, glean . . ." implies an impv sg form of MT's pl impf (cf. *BHS*, note); this translation would create a degree of parallelism with the following impv: "pass your hand . . ." But it is preferable to retain MT. The comparison, basic to the poetic structure, changes from an object (the "vine") to a person (the "grape-cutter"); the address likewise changes from descriptive language of the enemy's action "they shall glean," to words addressed to the prophet in dialogue, "pass your hand."

9.b. "Tendrils" (סלסלות); the Heb. word is a *hap. leg.*, the sense being inferred from context.

15.a. Vv 12–15 are paralleled in 8:10–13. MT here has הכלים (hiph inf const); the niph form (הכלם) in 8:12 is to be preferred and is translated above.

15.b. Again (see note 6:1.a.), the reading of 8:12 is preferred: פקדתם (eliminating the *yodh* in 6:14), "their doom, visitation."

Form/Structure/Setting

The internal structure of this literary unit is that of a dialogue (or portion thereof) between the Lord and his prophet. (i) The Lord speaks (v 9), with instructions to his prophet. (ii) Jeremiah responds (vv 10–11a), with a question and a complaint. (iii) The Lord answers Jeremiah's question (vv 11b–12) and adds some comments on the nation's evil and coming judgment (vv 13–15).

The passage is similar to the dialogue in 5:1–9; it is possible that originally both passages belonged to a larger text in which a more comprehensive record of the dialogue was preserved. The following points of contact between 6:9–15 and the earlier dialogue (5:1–9) are worthy of note.

(i) In each passage, the dialogical sequence is the same: (a) the Lord speaks, (b) Jeremiah responds with question and comment, and (c) the Lord speaks again.

(ii) In both passages, certain key words or themes are repeated (or continued): e.g., (a) The "streets of Jerusalem" (חוצות) may be alluded to again in 6:11 (חוץ). (b) The people's capacity for "falsehood" (5:2, שקר) is repeated in 6:13 (שקר). (c) In both passages, there is reference to the "great, noble" (גדול: see 5:5 and 6:13). (d) Both passages end with the theme of judgment expressed as "punishment" (with the root פקד: 5:9 and 6:15).

The data summarized above provide reasonable grounds for supposing an original link between 6:9–16 and 5:1–9, prior to the editorial arrangement of the passages in their present position. Certain of the themes of the text separating the two dialogues are taken up and developed in this unit (6:9–15), suggesting perhaps reasons for the overall editorial arrangement. Thus the imagery of the vineyard contained in an earlier poetic fragment (5:10) is resumed in the Lord's opening words of the dialogue (6:9). And the prior critique of prophets and priests (5:31) is developed further in the Lord's response to his prophet (6:13–14).

As with the preceding dialogue, the setting of this passage is no doubt Jerusalem, here pictured as a vineyard ready for harvest, though the harvest is a metaphor for judgment. The date cannot be pinned down precisely, though the later years of Josiah's reign are the probable period reflected in these verses. The dialogue represents the personal encounter between the prophet and God; it implies that the prophet's ministry had not been going well, and that he had turned to the Lord for direction and help.

Comment

The words of the opening address are somewhat difficult to interpret, in part because of the difficulty in translating 9 (see notes 6:9.a. and 6:9.b.). The simile is that of the vineyard and the grape-harvest; Israel is likened to the vines in the vineyard, and its coming judgment will be like the cutting down of fruit from the vines. If the verse has been translated correctly, a double instrumentality is expressed with respect to the coming judgment. "They shall glean": the reference is to the enemy hosts, who have already been summoned to the vineyard to act as the instruments of judgment (5:10). But here, the simile is more precise than in 5:10; the use of the word "glean" and the reference to "remnant" imply the totally comprehensive nature of the judgment; in this sense, 6:9 contains a far more devastating word than 5:10, in which a note of caution was expressed and the completeness of the judgment was denied. But while the enemy would do the gleaning, Jeremiah seems to be set in the role of the owner of the vineyard, examining the tendrils of the vine to see whether the fruit was ripe for cutting. It may be that the prophet's role as "inspector of grapes" prompts his question in response to God's opening declaration implying the nearness of judgment.

Jeremiah's question (v 10) reveals in part his understanding of the prophet's role. He has been told of the coming harvest of judgment and desperately wants to warn his people, in the hope of averting disaster. But whom should he warn? More precisely, what person or group could be warned who would actually pay any attention to his words and act in such a way as to turn aside the coming disaster? The prophet had already been preaching with unflagging zeal, but he might as well have addressed sticks and stones for all the response he was getting. The people's ears were "uncircumcised" (v 10); the metaphor indicates that their ears were closed, unable to hear the truth. The divine word caused only discomfort and displeasure; in that sense it could be heard, but the essence of its message did not penetrate to the minds of those who listened. And the result of this ministry with no response was frustrating for Jeremiah. He was filled with the "Lord's anger" (v 11); the sense may be that he was gripped with divine anger at Israel's sin, or else that he was overwhelmed with a godly anger at his people's inability to hear and to respond to the warning of judgment.

The Lord's response to the prophet's question is comprehensive, though not necessarily very encouraging, given the nature of Jeremiah's complaint.

He is to continue to address his message to all his fellow citizens: to the children playing in the streets, to the groups of teenagers, to men and women, to senior citizens, and even to those in the advanced geriatric category (v 11). If Jeremiah could have responded at this point, he would no doubt have complained that he had tried that already, though to no avail, but that was not the point! The message must still be proclaimed, whether or not the people responded. And he was to tell these assorted sections of society that their homes and lands would be lost, not primarily as a consequence of enemy attack, but because the Lord's hand was stretched out in judgment against his own people.

Having commanded Jeremiah to address all sections of his society, the Lord continues to elaborate upon the reason; all sections were equally guilty, "from the least of them to the greatest of them" (v 13). Even the clergy ("prophet and priest," v 13) were responsible for the national crisis in Judah. Having seen the nation's "wound" (viz. that not all was well), they offered only a placebo, with no power to cure. They spoke of peace, when there was no peace. (It is possible they spoke of peace with reference to a period of temporary calm in international affairs, failing to see that there can be no real peace when a nation is sick at heart.) Indeed, the clergy were so far gone in their abominable acts that they no longer knew the shamefulness of what they were doing. When evil is pursued and practiced regularly and devotedly, it produces eventually a moral blindness in the perpetrator. And so, the divine oracle concludes, given the widespread and rampant nature of the whole nation's evil, all would fall in the coming day of judgment.

Explanation

See the *Explanation* following 6:22–30.

Warning, Refusal, and Judgment (6:16–21)

Bibliography

Berridge, J. M. *Prophet, People.* 88–91. **Holladay, W. L.** *Architecture.* 75–83, 93–97.

Translation

[16] *Thus said the LORD,*
   "Stand at the crossroads[a] *and look,*   (3+3)

> *and ask about the ways of antiquity,*
> *about the path of the good: then walk in it*   (4+3)
> *and find rest for your soul."*
> *But they said, "We will not walk in it!"*
> 17 *"I appointed watchmen for you:*   (3+3)
> *'Pay attention to the trumpet blast!'"*
> *But they said, "We will not pay attention."*
> 18 *"Therefore listen, O nations, and know the evidence;*   (5+4)
> 19 *listen, O earth, to what is in them.*[a]
> *Look, I am going to bring evil*   (4+4)
> *to this people, the fruit of their own plots;*
> *for they have not attended to my words,*   (3?+2)
> *and as for my instruction, they have rejected it.*
> 20 *Why do you bring*[a] *me this, frankincense from Sheba,*   (5+4)
> *and finely perfumed oil*[b] *from a distant land?*
> *Your burnt-offerings are unacceptable,*   (3+3)
> *and your sacrifices do not please*[c] *me."*
> 21 *Therefore, thus has the* LORD *spoken,*
> *"Look, I am about to place in front of this people*   (4+3)
> *stumbling-blocks, and they shall stumble over them;*
> *both fathers and sons,*   (3+3)
> *neighbor and friend shall perish!"*

Notes

16.a. Lit., "roads, ways."

19.a. This line and the preceding line are difficult to translate; Bright (45) despairs and leaves the lines untranslated. LXX translates, "Therefore the nations heard and they that feed their flocks . . ." (reading ורעי for ודעי). I have read a pl form (ודעו) for MT's sg, for which there is good MSS evidence (see de Rossi, III, 73), and interpreted עדה as "testimony, evidence" (BDB, 729). It is possible that the two parts of the second line were accidentally reversed, obscuring thereby the original parallelism that is brought out in the translation above. Nevertheless, the translation provided here must be considered tentative.

20.a. The translation is based on the reading תביאו, which is presupposed in LXX.

20.b. Lit., the "stalk/reed of the good." The expression probably relates to *calamus*, a perfumed oil derived from the "sweet flag," a member of the *Araceae* family of plants, which flourish in swampy land in temperate and semitropical climates.

20.c. Lit., "have not passed by me."

Form/Structure/Setting

There is some debate whether this passage is prose or poetry. NEB renders it as prose (with the exception of the last four lines of v 21), but RSV and most other modern versions understand the text as poetry. It is best to classify the text as poetry; it is probable that in places the text has suffered some corruption (see especially vv 18–19a), which in turn has tended to obscure the poetic structure. But taken as a whole, the passage is characterized by the classical parallelism of Hebrew poetry.

The passage appears to be an extract from a longer passage containing a part of the prophet's orally proclaimed message. In its present context, it is probably linked to the preceding dialogue by the key word הקשׁיב, "pay attention," introduced in the dialogue in 6:10 and developed in this context in vv 17 (twice) and 19. Likewise, it may be linked (editorially) with the following passage by the common theme of "walking in the way" (v 16; compare 6:25).

The structure of the passage suggests that it may have belonged to a "mock liturgy," or perhaps a speech that was a parody of the address delivered in a covenant renewal ceremony. The "mock liturgy" is suggested in vv 16–17, in which the Lord's invitation is met by the solemn pseudo-liturgical "We will not." The twofold divine oracle that follows (each part introduced by "therefore," vv 18, 21) indicates the judgment that would follow the two refusals, just as in the covenant background to the parody, the positive affirmations would be followed by statements of blessing.

Thus, with respect to setting and date, it is reasonable to suppose that this passage, in its originally oral proclamation, must be linked to a period of the prophet's ministry in the reign of Josiah. And the specific occasion giving rise to the prophecy was probably a covenant renewal ceremony conducted in Jerusalem. The structure of the oracle, together with its content (v 20), suggests that the prophet was reacting to a formal ceremonial occasion, with liturgical proceedings and the offering of sacrifices, which to Jeremiah seemed to be merely a hypocritical veneer covering a false faith.

Comment

The oracle begins with an invitation from the Lord (v 16). The people are invited to "stand at the crossroads," or perhaps to consider the various ways of life open to them; having considered, they should then choose the right way. The invitation was no doubt reminiscent to the crowd of the similar invitation and injunction that were central to the covenant renewal ceremony (cf. Deut. 30:1–20). They should reflect on the "ways of antiquity," namely the way of life and faith walked in by their ancestors, which was the way of covenant. They should reflect also on the "path of the good," which was the essential description of the covenant way of life (cf. Ps 1). But whereas in the covenant ceremony the people would solemnly respond to the invitation with a positive answer, here in the oracle the veneer of respectability and piety is stripped away: "We will not walk in it."

The second invitation is structured in a similar fashion (v 17). God had appointed "watchmen" for his people, to warn them with the trumpet blast of coming danger. But the people stated they would not heed warnings. The metaphor of the "watchmen" refers to the prophets; it is elaborated, at a later date, in the ministry of Ezekiel (see 3:16–21; 33:1–20).

The nation's express refusal to respond positively to the divine invitations is then followed by two statements of judgment. They are introduced by the summoning of witnesses to observe the proclamation of judgment (vv 18–19a), which is again reminiscent of the witnesses invoked in the covenant renewal ceremony (see Deut. 30:19; 32:1–2). The first judgment is that God will bring evil upon his own people (v 19), because they have rejected his instruction. It is clear from v 20 that they have not rejected the *external* dimension of God's instruction. They have brought to the temple expensive imported goods, frankincense from Sheba (probably South Arabia, which may not have been the place frankincense originated, but merely the region through which it was traded) and *calamus* (perhaps imported from northeast Africa). Furthermore, they have maintained the formal worship of the covenant ceremony, which has precipitated this particular incident in the prophet's ministry. But for all the external manifestations of religion, there was no truth to it, no heart in it, and so judgment must come. The second judgment (v 21) makes perfectly clear that God would be directly instrumental in causing his people's "stumbling." But the stumbling and fall would come only because of the obdurate and perverse blindness of a people who refused to hear properly the gracious invitations of God (vv 16–17).

Explanation

See the *Explanation* following 6:22–30.

An Oracle and Concluding Dialogue (6:22–30)

Bibliography

Dahood, M. "Hebrew-Ugaritic Lexicography, I." *Bib* 44 (1963) 289–303.———. *Ugaritic-Hebrew Philology.* 14, 53. **Driver, G. R.** "Two Misunderstood Passages of the Old Testament: Jeremiah vi.27–30." *JTS* NS 6 (1955) 84–87. **Emerton, J. A.** "A Problem in the Hebrew Text of Jer. 6:23 and 50:42." *JTS* 23 (1972) 106–13. **Gelio, R.** "E possible un 'is relativo/demonstrativo in ebraico biblico?" *RivB* 31 (1983) 411–34. **Holladay, W. L.** *Architecture.* 93–97. **Loretz, O.** "'Verworfenes Silber' (Jer. 6:27–30)." In *Wort, Lied und Gottesspruch* 2. FS J. Ziegler. Wurzburg: Echter, 1972. 231–32. **Robinson, T. H.** "The Text of Jeremiah vi. 27–30, in the Light of Ezekiel xxii. 17–22." *JTS* 16 (1914/15) 482–90. **Soggin, J. A.** "Jeremias 6:27–30." *VT* 9 (1959) 95–98. **Waldman, N.** "A Comparative Note on Exodus 15:14–16." *JQR* 66 (1975/76) 189–92.

Holladay, W. L. has a full bibliography on ancient metallurgy, including:
Forbes, R. J. *Studies in Ancient Technology* 8. Leiden: Brill, 1964. **Gale, N. H.** and **Zofia, S.-G.** "Lead and Silver in the Ancient Aegean." *Scientific American* 244/6 (June, 1981) 176–92. See also **Barrois, A.-G.** *Manuel d'archéologie biblique* I. Paris: Picard, 1939. 372.

Translation

22 *Thus said the* LORD,   (4+4)
    "Behold! A people comes from a northern land;
    a great nation is stirring from earth's remote realms!
23 *They grasp bow and blade;*   (3+3+3)
    they[a] *are cruel and without mercy,*
    their sound, like the sea, roaring.
    And they ride upon horses,   (3+3+3)

>   each in position for battle^b—
>   against you, O Daughter of Zion!"

24   We heard the news—   (2+2)
>   our hands sagged,
>   distress grasped us,   (2+2)
>   pain like that of a woman in labor!

25   Do not venture forth^a into the countryside   (2+2)
>   and do not travel^a on the highway,
>   for the enemy has a sword,   (2+2)
>   and terror is all around.

26   O Daughter of my people, don sackcloth   (2+2)
>   and roll in ashes;
>   mourn as for an only child,   (3+2)
>   the most bitter of lamentations!
>   For he comes suddenly—   (3+2)
>   the destroyer^a is upon us!

27   "I have appointed you a tester of my people, an assayer,^a   (4?+3)
>   so that you may examine and test their mettle.^b

28   All of them are routinely rebellious,^a   (3+2+3)
>   perpetuating slander,
>   all of them wreaking havoc.

29   The bellows^a puff,   (2+2+3?)
>   the fire is ready:^b
>   lead, copper, iron!^c
>   But for naught the refining continues,   (3+3)
>   for the wicked are not removed.

30   They are named 'reject silver,'   (4+4)
>   for the LORD has rejected them."

Notes

23.a. The plural המה, "they," is read, as implied by context, and supported by the parallel passage (50:42) and a number of Heb. MSS (de Rossi, III, 74), Syr, and Vg.

23.b. This line has been the source of some difficulty, in part because the comparison implied by כאיש, "like a man," seems anomalous. On the possibility of a relative pronoun here, see Gelio (*RivB* 32 [1983] 411–34), but this resolution of the problem is improbable. It is preferable, with Emerton (*JTS* 23 [1972] 106–13), to remove the *kaph* as a dittogr and to translate (as above) without the comparison.

25.a. The consonantal text implies fem sg forms for both verbs (the implied subject being, perhaps, the "Daughter of Zion" in v 23), whereas the vocalization (Q) indicates that the verbs should be read as pl forms, or more general admonitions.

26.a. LXX implies Heb. הֹשֵׁד, "ruin, destruction."

27.a. Heb. מבצר, lit., "fortification," is curious in context. Dahood (*Hebrew-Ugaritic Philology*, 53) proposes to translate "assayer," on the basis of Ug. *bsr*, in *UT* 2067.3. But the Ug. evidence in this context is uncertain; the text *UT* 2067 (*KTU* 4.370/*PRU* V. 67) contains a list of names, and it is probably best to understand *bsr* as a personal name (M. Heltzer, *The Internal Organization of the Kingdom of Ugarit* [1982], 10). The older derivation of the sense *assayer*, from Hebrew מְבַצֵּר, "one who searches" (Bright, 49), remains possible, but the word may simply be a gloss (cf. 1:18).

27.b. Lit., "their way."

28.a. סרי, apparently not in the text followed by LXX, may be a dittogr.

29.a. Reading מַפֻּחַ, "bellows," the *mem* being wrongly attached to the following word (see note 29.b.); see Dahood, *Bib* 44 (1963) 298.

29.b. Reading אֵשׁ תָּם for מֵאֲשָׁם (see also note 29.a.), after Thompson, 265 (n. 5).

29.c. "Copper and iron" are added here, moved from the preceding verse, where the phrase seems to be misplaced; see further Thompson, 265, and the discussion in Bright, 49 (n. 27).

Form/Structure/Setting

The long declaration of divine judgment (4:5–6:30) comes to a conclusion in this section with two passages that round out the principal themes: (i) an oracle returning to the theme of the foe from the north (6:22–26), and (ii) a short passage, perhaps a portion of a dialogue, in which Jeremiah's role as God's agent is specified (6:27–30).

(i) The oracle concerning the foe from the north (6:22–26) develops and concludes earlier references to the same theme in the larger context of judgment: see 4:5–18, 23–28; 6:1–8. As with those earlier passages, it is probable that these verses were originally part of a larger oracle, of which only a small section has been used, in which are stressed the certainty of the coming of the enemy and the consequent terror that advent would spread in Judah. There may be irony intended in the language used to describe the people's fear at the coming of the northern enemy, for in effect it reverses the ancient language in which Israel's approach to the promised land struck fear in the hearts of the Canaanites: see Exod 15:14–16 (cf. N. Waldman, *JQR* 66 [1975/76] 189–92).

(ii) Verses 27–30 may be interpreted as a monologue (as it is punctuated in the translation above), in which the Lord addresses Jeremiah, indicating his role as tester, or assayer. Or it may be a dialogue (or, more probably, a portion of an originally longer dialogue), in which first the Lord speaks (v 27), and then Jeremiah declares his "assayer's report" (vv 28–30). The reference to "fire" in these concluding verses may tie this section, in literary terms, to the conclusion of the preceding section on repentance (3:1–4:4), which also concludes with a reference to "fire" (4:4).

The concluding section of this collection of Jeremiah's early oracles also contains echoes of the opening section of the book. The vision of the "boiling pot," with its anticipation of danger from the north (1:13) is balanced here with the oracle of the foe from the north, and the earlier characterization of Jeremiah's prophetic role (1:10) is amplified in the concluding words of dialogue (6:27–30), elaborating on the role of assayer.

Comment

22–26 *The foe from the north.* On the problem of the identity of the northern enemy, see the *Comment* on 1:13. The enemy is described as being armed with "bow and blade," the latter expression (כִּידוֹן) frequently translated "spear," more properly designating the "short sword" (an extremely versatile weapon for both infantry and cavalry), according to Y. Yadin, *The Scroll of the War of the Sons of Light against the Sons of Darkness* [Jerusalem: Mosad Bialik, 1962] 124–31. The enemy troops are cavalry, a form of military might developed as early as the twelfth century B.C. and used very effectively by the Assyrians, Scythians, and other northern enemies of Israel (see A. Buttery, *Armies and Enemies of Ancient Egypt and Assyria* [Goring by Sea: Wargames Research Group, 1974] 50–53; J. Harmand, *La guerre antique de Sumer a Rome* [Paris: Presses universitaires, 1973] 110–14.) Although marauding enemies from the north generally had broad goals of territorial expansion and conquest, the prophet here portrays them as having a single objective, an attack on the "Daughter of Zion" (v 23).

The poetic description of Judah's response to the news of impending attack is described in the short, staccato lines typical of war poetry (vv 24–26). Instead of preparing a defense against attack, the prophet's compatriots ("we," v 24) are so petrified by the news that they issue orders restricting any movement outside the fortified areas. Although the enemy has not yet struck, they prepare to mourn for the disaster that seems unstoppable; thus Jeremiah conveys in dramatic language the inevitability of total and terrible defeat. The simile of pregnancy and labor, bringing its own uncontrollable travail (v 24), is exchanged for that of a mother lamenting the death of an only child (v 26); in both cases, the feminine imagery is determined by the form of address employed for Judah, namely, "Daughter (of Zion)," in vv 23 and 26.

27–30 *The prophet as assayer.* The prophet's role is reaffirmed, and more precisely defined, in the opening divine declaration (v 27); it is that of an assayer, who is to test the people's "mettle" for its purity and content. The imagery is more precise than simply the metaphor of refining and smelting ores to produce pure and workable metals; the prophet's role is specifically that of assayer, the person who tests metals to judge their content and purity. Hence, the reference to the bellows and fire (v 29) is not an allusion to the basic smelting process, usually conducted near the mines where ores were extracted from the earth, nor even to the crucible and fire used by metalworkers. The prophet is a tester: he takes samples of the metals (though note the textual difficulties here: note 29.c.) and melts them down, hoping to separate some silver from the less valuable metals. But the process is unsuccessful, in metaphorical terms, presumably because the silver content is so low that it cannot be extracted and purified (as implied by v 30) or else is nonexistent. The metaphor, however, is poetically employed and not designed to give a precise description of the assayer's task. The conclusion of the process, despite continual refining, is negative; the combined "metals" that constitute Judah, despite the continued and rigorous assaying process, cannot produce pure silver, but only impure and "reject silver" (v 30). That is to say, the imagery is employed not to indicate that judgment would be a refining process but rather to convey its terminal nature; since no purity could be found, no solid silver, the mixture would be cast away as dross.

The employment of this metaphor fits in harmoniously with the larger context of the narrative. The prophet, as assayer, tests the people, but the fire, by implication, which reduces the metals or mixed ores, is the foe from the north, and it is God who requires that the testing be done. The general metaphorical usage in this passage, though applied distinctively to the context, is nevertheless in keeping with a general tradition in prophetic language and imagery that draws upon the various aspects of ancient metallurgy to illuminate the prophet's task: see further Isa 1:25; Ezek 22:18–22; Zech 13:9; Mal 3:3.

Explanation for 4:5–6:30

The prophetic indictment of Judah's sin (chap. 2) and the call for repentance (3:1–4:4) are followed in this section by the proclamation of judgment. This third section of the collection of early oracles is considerably longer and more elaborate than the two that precede it, so that, although it comes last, it seems to overshadow the entire collection, casting over the whole the seeming inevitability of judgment. But how are we to understand this theme of judgment which, judging by the space allocated to it, seems to have dominated Jeremiah's early ministry?

(i) *The purpose and nature of judgment.* (a) One of the purposes served by the extensive proclamation of judgment is that of *warning*; this role was probably more central in the original oral proclamation of the message than it was in the final written form of the message, whether in this collection (chaps. 4–6) or in the book as a whole. A part of the prophetic function in the national life of Judah was that of "warner"; the message flowed from the preceding call for repentance, indicating clearly what the consequence would be of failure to repent. And the dimension of warning also illuminates one dimension of the character of God who appoints the prophet. Judah's God is not content to sit and watch his people pursue relentlessly the path toward their destruction; both compassion and a sense of responsibility compel him to forewarn them of the consequences of their action. (b) A further purpose served in the proclamation of judgment is that of instruction; specifically, the prophet makes clear to his audience that judgment is not merely an exhibition of the wrath of a capricious deity. Rather, judgment is a *consequence* of prior actions; human evil, injustice, disobedience to the law, and like activities, all lead to, indeed invite, the fate which the prophet portrays as divine judgment. Thus, although judgment is in one sense divinely ordained, it is in another sense humanly invited. In this, as in other sections of the prophetic literature, we perceive the "boomerang" character of the understanding of judgment: it is a return of the consequences of evil upon the heads of the perpetrators. (c) In their final setting of the book as a whole, the oracles of judgment take on a slightly different sense; in the light of subsequent history, they evoke an awful sense of inevitability, as if in their first announcement they had been predictions, rather than warnings. In fact, their final form and setting are educational in a religious context: the prophet, on God's behalf, had indicted Judah of its sin, called the people to repentance, and warned them of the consequences of failing to heed that call. When, at a later date, the judgment had come to pass, it illustrated the truth of the original message. It was not a prediction fulfilled, but a warning authenticated; failing to heed the warning culminated eventually in terrible consequences for Judah.

(ii) *The theology of judgment.* The various strands in this composite section of the prophet's message also illuminate the theological dimensions of Jeremiah's understanding of divine judgment. (a) First, he understood contemporary events, indeed the whole passage of human history, in both theological and moral terms. The threat of invasion posed by the northern enemy (whether that enemy was thought to be the Scythians or the Babylonians) was not simply an incidental turn in the passage of human events; the threat posed from the north was specifically understood to be related to the religious and moral chaos in the south, namely in Judah's national life. Furthermore, the notion that the movements of history were tied to Judah's life and fate presupposed in turn an understanding of God as sovereign in the world of human affairs. That is, although human evil invited its own consequences, the consequences as such,

in that they involved alien and pagan nations, demonstrated the sovereignty of
God in history.

(b) In addition to God's sovereignty in history, Jeremiah also reaffirms the
ancient belief in God's sovereignty over the world of nature. The poem in which
the prophet envisions the return of the created world to a state of primeval chaos
(4:23–28) indicates his perception that morality pervades both the historical order
and the natural order of the world in which human beings live. (c) The notion of
God's joint-sovereignty in the realms of history and nature is balanced by the
perception that human beings, in a sense, forge their own future. That is,
human evil culminates in a disaster of its own making; thus, as the prophet sees
it, Judah's evil creates and shapes its own consequences and fate. But this moral
understanding of the results of human actions presupposes, in turn, Jeremiah's
faith in the moral structure of the universe.

(d) Finally, the whole structure of the prophetic message concerning judgment presupposes faith in a God who is passionately involved in human affairs.
The Lord is not uninvolved in his universe, dispassionately observing or distanc-
ing himself from the human scene. The divine involvement is seen in part in his
dispatch of the prophet, in his warning role, to attempt to turn Judah from the
evil of its ways. It is seen further in the divine hatred of evil which, left unchecked,
leads to the destruction of the very purpose for which the universe was created,
and the consequent return to primeval chaos.

In summary, this dominating theme of judgment in the prophetic message is
not entirely bleak. It does indeed provide a bleak view of human nature and the
capacity of even a privileged nation to cast aside its special status and relentlessly
pursue its own destruction. But the judgmental theme also sheds light on a universe that is created in some mysterious sense with an inherent moral structure, a
structure which in turn permeates the panoply of human history. And further it
illuminates the prophetic faith in a passionate God, one who profoundly cares
about human events and the fate of the chosen people. And it is these dimensions
of Jeremiah's faith that still challenge the modern reader of the ancient book;
somehow this vision of a prophet from the ancient world must be grasped and
understood in our modern world.

V. The Temple Sermon (7:1–8:3)

Bibliography

Ballentine, S. E. "The Prophet as Intercessor: A Reassessment." *JBL* 103 (1984) 161–73. **Boer, P. A. H. de.** *De Voorbede in het Oude Testament.* OTS 3. Leiden: Brill, 1943. 157–70. **Caspari, W.** "Jeremia und der Priesterkodex." *TB1* 3 (1924) 66–67. **Cogan, M.** "A Note on Disinterment in Jeremiah." In *Gratz College, Anniversary Volume.* Ed. I. D. Passow and S. T. Lachs. Philadelphia, 1971. 29–34. **Corré, A. D.** "ʿēlle, hēmma = sic." *Bib* 54 (1973) 263–64. **Culican, W.** "A Votive Model from the Sea." *PEQ* 108 (176) 119–23. **Dahood, M.** "La Regina del Cielo in Geremia." *RivB* 8 (1960) 166–68. **Day, J.** "The Destruction of the Shiloh Sanctuary and Jeremiah vii 12, 14." In *Studies in the Historical Books of the Old Testament.* VTSup 30. Leiden: Brill, 1979. 87–94. **Delcor, M.** "Le culte de la 'Reine du Ciel' selon Jér 7:18; 44: 17–19, 25 et ses survivances." In *Von Kanaan bis Kerala.* FS van der Pleog. Ed. W. C. Delsman et al. AOAT 211. Neukirchen-Vluyn: Neukirchener Verlag, 1982. 101–22. **Eichrodt, W.** "The Right Interpretation of the Old Testament: A Study of Jeremiah 7:1–15." *T Today* 7 (1950) 15–25. **Fohrer, G.** "Jeremias Tempelwort 7:1–15." *TZ* 5 (1949) 401–17 [also in *Studien zur alttestamentlichen Prophetie,* BZAW 99 (Berlin: deGruyter, 1967) 190–203]. **Görg, M.** "Das Tempelwort in Jer 7:4." *BN* 18 (1982) 7–14. **Gray, J.** "Queen of Heaven." *IDB* III, 975. **Hadey, J.** "Jérémie et le temple. Le conflit de la parole prophetique et de la tradition religieuse, Jer 7:1–15; 26:1–19." *ETR* 54 (1979) 438–43. **Herrmann, J.** "Zu Jer 22:29; 7:4." *ZAW* 62 (1949–50) 321–22. **Hertzberg, H. W.** "Sind die Propheten Furbitter?" In *Tradition und Situation.* FS A. Weiser. Ed. E. Wurthwein and O. Kaiser. Göttingen: Vandenhoeck & Ruprecht, 1963. 63–74. **Isbell, C. D.** and **Jackson, M.** "Rhetorical Criticism and Jeremiah 7:1–8:3." *VT* 30 (1980) 20–26. **Kumaki, F. K.** *The Temple Sermon (Jer 7:3–15). Jeremiah's Polemic against the Deuteronomists.* Ph.D. diss. Union Theological Seminary, N.Y., 1981. [DissA 41 (1980) 1103-A.] **König, E.** "On the Meaning and Scope of Jeremiah 7:22–23." *Exp* 6th ser. 6 (1902) 135–54, 208–18, 366–77. **Kraus, H.-J.** *Worship in Israel.* Richmond: Knox, 1966. 117–18. **Lorenz, B.** "Bemerkungen zum Totenkult im Alten Testament." *VT* 32 (1982) 229–34. **Macholz, G. C.** "Jeremia in der Kontinuitat der Prophetie." In *Probleme biblischer Theologie.* FS G. von Rad. Ed. H. W. Wolff. Munich: Kaiser, 1971. 306–34. **Milgrom, J.** "Concerning Jeremiah's Repudiation of Sacrifice." *ZAW* 89 (1977) 273–75. **Pákozdy, L. M. von.** "Der Tempelspruch des Jeremia." *Zeichen der Zeit* 12 (1958) 372–81. **Pearce, R. A.** "Shiloh and Jer. 7:12, 14–15." *VT* 23 (1973) 105–8. **Plataroti, D.** "Zum Gebrauch des Wortes *mlk* im Alten Testament." *VT* 28 (1978) 286–300. **Rast, W. E.** "Cakes for the Queen of Heaven." In *Scripture in History and Theology.* FS J. Coert Tylaarsdam. Ed. A. L. Merrill and T. W. Overholt. Pittsburg Theological Monograph Series 17. Pittsburg: Pickwick, 1977. 167–80. **Reymond, P.** "Sacrifice et 'spiritualité' ou sacrifice et alliance? Jér. 7, 22–24." *ThZ* 21 (1965) 314–17. **Reventlow, H. G.** "Gattung und überlieferung in der 'Tempelrede Jeremias.' Jer. 7 und 26." *ZAW* 81 (1969) 315–52. **Rhodes, A. B.** "Israel's Prophets as Intercessors." In *Scripture in History and Theology.* FS J. Coert Rylaarsdam. Ed. A. R. Merrill and T. W. Overholt. Pittsburg Theological Monograph Series 17. Pittsburg: Pickwick, 1977. 107–28. **Robinson, G.** "The Prohibition of Strange Fire in Ancient Israel." *VT* 28 (1978) 301–17. **Schreiner, J.** "Sicherheit oder Umkehr? Aus der Verkündigung des Propheten Jeremias, Jer 7:1–15; 26:1–6 (II. Teil)." *BibLeb* 7 (1966) 98–111. **Schulz, H.** *Das Todesrecht im Alten Testament.* BZAW 114. Berlin: de Gruyter, 1969. 123–27. **Sekine, M.** "Das Problem der Kultpolemik bei den propheten." *EvT* 28 (1968) 605–9. **Smith, E. J.** "The Decalogue in the Preaching of Jeremias." *CBQ* 4 (1942) 197–209. **Soggin, J. A.**

"Child Sacrifice and Cult of the Dead in the Old Testament." In *Old Testament and Oriental Studies*. BibOr 29. Rome: Biblical Institute Press, 1975. 84–87. **Stade, B.** "Miscellen: 13. Die vermeintliche 'Königen des Himmels.'" *ZAW* 6 (1886) 123–32. ———. "Das vermeintliche aramäisch-assyrische Aequivalent der מלכת השמים Jer 7.44." *ZAW* 6 (1886) 289–339. **Stager, L. E.** and **Wolff, S. R.** "Child Sacrifice at Carthage—Religious Rite or Population Control?" *BAR* 10/1 (1984) 31–51. **Stoebe, H.-J.** "Jeremia, Prophet und Seelsorger." *TZ* 20 (1964) 385–409. ———. "Seelsorge und Mitleid bei Jerekia. Ein Exegetischer Versuch." *Wort und Dienst* NF 4 (1955) 116–34. **Strobel, A.** "Jeremias, Priester ohne Gottesdienst? Zu Jer 7, 21–23." *BZ* n.s. 1 (1957) 214–24. **Sturdy, J. V. M.** "The Authority of the 'Prose Sermons' of Jeremiah." In *Prophecy*. FS G. Fohrer. Ed. J. A. Emerton. Berlin: de Gruyter, 1980. 143–50. **Toll, C.** "Die Würzel PRS im Hebraischen." *Orientalia Suecana* 21 (1972) 73–86. **Vaux, R. de.** *Ancient Israel, Its Life and Institutions*. New York: McGraw-Hill, 1961. 441–46. **Weinfield, M.** "The Worship of Molech and of the Queen of Heaven and Its Background." *UF* 4 (1972) 133–54. ———. "Jeremiah and the Spiritual Metamorphosis of Israel." *ZAW* 88 (1976) 17–56. ———. "Burning Babies in Israel: A Rejoinder to Morton Smith's Article in *JAOS* 95 (1975), pp. 477–79." *UF* 10 (1978) 411–13. **Weippert, H.** *Die Prosareden des Jeremiabuches*. BZAW 132. Berlin: de Gruyter, 1973. 26–48. **Whitley, C. F.** "A Note on Jeremia 7:4." *JTS* NS 5 (1954) 57–59. **Wilcoxen, J. A.** "The Political Background of Jeremiah's Temple Sermon." In *Scripture in History and Theology*. FS J. Coert Tylaarsdam. Ed. A. L. Merrill and T. W. Overholt. Pittsburg Theological Monograph Series 17. Pittsburg: Pickwick, 1977. 151–66. **Wright, G. E.** "Security and Faith: An Exposition of Jeremiah 7:1–15." *The Rule of God: Essays in Biblical Theology*. Garden City, NJ: Doubleday, 1960. 77–92. **Wyk, W. C.** "The Translation of MQWM ('land') in the Temple Speech of Jeremiah." *OTWSA* 24 (1981–82) 103–9. **Young, D. W.** "A Ghost Word in the Testament of Jacob (Gen. 49:4)?" *JBL* 100 (1981) 335–42.

Translation

[1] [a]*The word that came to Jeremiah from the LORD:* [2] *"Stand in the gate of the LORD's house, and there you shall proclaim this word and you shall say, 'Hear the LORD's word, all you Judaeans going in through these gates to worship the LORD.'"* [3] *Thus said the LORD of Hosts, the God of Israel, "Amend your ways and your works, and I will make you dwell in this place.* [4] *Do not put your trust in those deceptive words, 'This[a] is the temple of the LORD, the temple of the LORD, the temple of the LORD.'* [5] *But if you really do amend your ways and your works, if you really do enact justice between one person and another,* [6] *you shall not[a] oppress a sojourner, an orphan, or a widow, and do not shed innocent blood in this place, and if you do not go after pagan gods to your own detriment,* [7] *then I will make you dwell in this place, in the land which I gave to your forefathers, from of old and forever.*

[8] *"Look, you are trusting in those deceptive words to no avail!* [9] *Can you steal, murder, commit adultery, swear falsely, burn incense to Baal, and follow after pagan gods whom you have not known,* [10] *and then come in and stand before me in this house, which is called by my name, and say: 'We are delivered,' only to continue doing all these abominable deeds?* [11] *Has this house, which is called by my name, become a den of burglars[a] in your opinion? Behold, I myself have seen it," says the LORD.* [12] *"So go to my place that used to be in Shiloh, where I made my name dwell at first, and see what I have done to it because of the evil of my people, Israel.* [13] *And now, because you have done all these deeds," says the LORD, "and though I have spoken to you persistently,[a] but you did not listen, and I called you, but you did not answer,* [14] *therefore I will do to the house that is called by my name, in which you place your trust, and to the place which I have given to you and to*

your forefathers—precisely what I have done to Shiloh! [15]*And I will cast you out from my presence, just as I cast out your brethren, all the progeny of Ephraim.*

[16]*"As for you, don't offer prayers on behalf of this people, don't raise a cry and a prayer on their behalf, and don't intercede with me, for I will not hear you.* [17]*Can't you see what they are doing in the cities of Judah and in the streets of Jerusalem?* [18]*The children are gathering wood, and the fathers are kindling the fire, and the women are preparing dough to make sweet-cakes*[a] *for the 'Queen of Heaven'; and they are pouring out libations to pagan gods in order to provoke me.* [19]*But are they provoking me?" says the LORD. "Is it not themselves, to their own shame?"* [20]*Therefore, thus said the LORD,*[a] *"Behold, my anger and my wrath will be poured out upon this place, upon mankind, upon animals, upon the trees of the countryside, and upon the fruit of the earth; and it shall burn and it shall not be put out."*

[21]*Thus said the LORD of Hosts, the God of Israel, "Combine your burnt-offerings with your sacrifices and eat meat.* [22]*For at the time that I*[a] *brought them out from the land of Egypt, I did not speak to your forefathers or command them concerning matters of burnt-offering and sacrifice.* [23]*But I did issue them specific orders on this matter: 'Obey my voice, and I will become your God and you will become my people, and you shall walk in the whole way that I command you, so that things may go well for you.'* [24]*But they did not obey, nor did they listen,*[a] *but rather walked according to their own counsels and their own evil self-reliance,*[b] *and thus went backwards and not forwards!* [25]*From the time that your*[a] *forefathers came out from the land of Egypt up to this day, I have persistently*[b] *sent to you*[c] *all my servants, the prophets;*[d] [26]*but they*[a] *did not obey me and did not listen, but they became more stubborn.*[b] *They did more evil than their forefathers.* [27]*So you shall speak all these words to them, but they will not listen to you. And you shall call to them, but they will not answer you.* [28]*And you shall say to them, 'This is the nation that would not obey the LORD its God and would not accept instruction.' Truth has perished and is excised from their lips.*

[29]a*"Cut off your hair and cast it away, and on the bare heights raise a song of lament; for the LORD has rejected and forsaken the generation of his wrath.*[b]

[30]*"For the Judaeans have done evil in my sight," says the LORD. "They have placed their abominable objects in the house that is called by my name, thus defiling it.* [31]*And they have built high-places,*[a] *Topheth which is in the Valley of ben-Hinnom, to burn their sons and their daughters in the fire, a thing that I did not command and that never even crossed my mind.*[b] [32]*Therefore, behold, the days are coming," says the LORD, "when it will no longer be called Topheth and the Valley of ben-Hinnom, but rather the Valley of Slaughter, and they will bury (bodies) in Topheth, for there will be no other place to do it.* [33]*And the carcass of this people shall become food for the birds of the heaven and the beasts of the earth, and no one shall scare them away.* [34]*And from the cities of Judah and the streets of Jerusalem, I will cause the cessation of the sound of laughter and the sound of joy, the voice of the bridegroom and that of the bride, for the land shall become a wasteland.*

[8:1]*"At that time," says the LORD, "they shall bring forth the bones of the kings of Judah, the bones of its princes, the bones of the priests, the bones of the prophets, and the bones of the inhabitants of Jerusalem from their tombs.* [2]*And they shall spread them out before the sun and the moon and the whole host of heaven, whom they loved and served, after whom they walked, to whom they brought inquiries, and whom they worshiped. They will not be gathered up or buried; they shall serve as dung*[a] *upon the surface of the ground.* [3]*Death shall be preferred over life by all that remain, the remnant of this evil family, in all the remaining*[a] *places to which I have driven them," says the LORD of Hosts.*

Notes

1.a. Vv 1–2a are missing in LXX, as is the final clause in v 2b.

4.a. המה, "these," is curious; a sg form of the demonstrative is expected. *BHS* suggests it is an abbreviation, הם (for המקום) and ה (for הזה), "this place" (v 3). M. Görg (*BN* 18 [1982] 7–14) interprets the word as an interjection, functioning to call attention to the temple, and the threefold evocation of the temple is said to be an aspect of Jeremiah's style (cf. 22:29). A more probable explanation is that of A. D. Corré (*Bib* 54 [1973] 263–64), namely, that המה is an abbreviation for המההדברים, "these are the words," indicating that the unusual wording that precedes it is correct, despite its peculiarity.

6.a. MT לא. Many MSS read אל. The meaning is the same.

11.a. On the sense of פרץ, "break in, penetrate," see C. Toll, *Orientalia Suecana* 21 (1972) 73–86.

13.a. "Persistently" lit., "rising early and saying" (omitted in LXX). The use of השכם, "rising early," is common in Jeremiah (BDB, 1014; Thompson, 272, n. 9) and may be a distinctive characteristic of the prophet's style.

18.a. כונים, "sweet-cakes," is a loan-word from Akk.; see D. W. Young, *JBL* 100 (1981) 335–42, and M. Held, *Eres\-Israel* 16 (1982) 76–85.

20.a. Heb. אדנייהוה, "Lord Yahweh;" LXX has simply "Lord" (presupposing יהוה only).

22.a. Q indicates a first-person pronoun suff, which is translated here.

24.a. Lit., "incline their ear."

24.b. Lit., "self-reliance of their evil heart." On the sense "self-reliance" for שררות, see A. B. Spencer, *JBL* 100 (1981) 247–48; of the ten occurrences of the term in the MT, eight are in Jeremiah, suggesting perhaps that the word is typical of Jeremiah's style and vocabulary.

25.a. LXX, Syr, and Vg have a 3 suff, "their forefathers."

25.b. "Persistently," lit., "rising early and sending," the same idiom noted in 13.a., again indicative of Jeremiah's style.

25.c. LXX and Syr again (see note 25.a.) have a 3rd-person suff.

25.d. The Heb. text adds יום, "day," which is anomalous and should probably be omitted as a dittogr (from the preceding word).

26.a. The ambiguity over pronoun suffixes in the preceding verse (notes 25.a. and 25.c.) leads to uncertainty over the implied subject of the verb (the forefathers or the present generation?). The concluding line of this verse, with its comparison, suggests the present generation is intended.

26.b. Lit., "they stiffened their neck."

29.a. LXX, in v 29, presupposes a fundamentally different Heb. text.

29.b. It is possible that this verse is poetic in form, or is an adaptation of a poetic quotation; cf. *BHS*, RSV, etc.

31.a. Alternatively, following LXX and Tg, translate as sg, "the high-place of Topheth."

31.b. Lit., "did not rise upon my heart."

8:2.a. דמן, "dung," occurs four times in Jeremiah (cf. 9:21 [22]; 16:4; 25:33) and rarely elsewhere in the MT (2 Kgs 9:37; Ps 83:11), and may be a further example of Jeremianic style and vocabulary. (Several other Heb. words may be translated "dung," e.g., גלל and פרש, indicating thereby the distinctiveness of Jeremiah's use of דמן).

3.a. *BHS* (after LXX and Syr), suggests deleting הנשארים, "remaining," as a dittogr, two forms of the word occurring in the preceding line. But the duplicative style may be a further example of the prophet's prose style (cf. 7:4).

Form/Structure/Setting

As Jer 7:1–8:3 is the first major block of prose material (specifically Type C, prose sermons) that we encounter in this prophetic book, it is deserving of detailed study with respect to its language and style. The detailed study of this unit will provide an opportunity to examine in the text some of the theoretical questions raised in the introduction to this volume ("The Form and Structure of the Book of Jeremiah"); it will also provide a foundation for the study of subsequent passages of prose (Type C) material. Although 7:1–8:3 is a composite unit, in all probability, with respect to the origin of the parts (examined below), nevertheless a literary unity to the whole is provided by the common prose style (with the possible exception of 7:29), which contrasts with the surrounding poetic context.

The first issue that requires examination is the *language* of this literary unit. Does the language, specifically the vocabulary and style, permit its classification, for example, as Deuteronomic? (For practical purposes, in the paragraphs that follow, I shall use the expression D-language to embrace both Deuteronomic- and Deuteronomistic-language.) Or does the evidence point to some other form of classification for the prose style? In examining these issues, there are essentially three types of evidence that must be taken into account.

(i) *D-language in 7:1–8:3.* The following expressions, generally classified as "D," occur in the text.

(a) "Other (pagan) gods" (vv 6, 18: אלהים אחרים), the expression is common in both Jeremiah's prose narratives and in D-language. (Statistics on the occurrence of this, and some of the other expressions listed below, are given in Bright, *JBL* 70 [1951] 15–35.)

(b) "so that things may go well for you" (7:23); three other occurrences in Jeremiah and nine in D-language.

(c) "my servants, the prophets" (7:25); six examples in Jer-prose, four in D.

(d) "to you and to your fathers" (7:14); twelve examples in Jer-prose, six in D.

(e) "forefathers came out from the land of Egypt" (7:25); nine examples in Jer-prose, and very common in D.

(f) "have done evil in my sight" (7:30); variations of this expression occur eight times in Jer-prose and are extremely common in D.

(g) "Which is called by my name" (7:10); seven examples in Jer-prose and two in D.

This is by no means a comprehensive listing of phrases and words in 7:1–8:3 which are typical of D-language, but it is sufficient to indicate the grounds of the various hypotheses which posit some form of Deuteronomic character to Jeremiah's prose sermons. (It should be added that language and style are not the only grounds employed in positing a Deuteronomic character; issues of substance and ideology will be raised in the discussion that follows.)

(ii) *Distinctively Jeremianic-language in 7:1–8:3.* (N.B. the word *Jeremianic* in context is used with respect to the style of the book, without necessarily implying that the language was peculiar to the prophet per se.) The following words and expressions are distinctively Jeremianic, occurring rarely (and sometimes never) outside the book.

(a) "rising early" and doing something (7:13, 25); there are eleven examples in Jeremiah's prose, but the expression occurs elsewhere only in 2 Chr 36:15; see note 13.a.

(b) "self-reliance" (שררות): 7:24; although common in Jeremiah, only two occurrences exist outside the book (one in Deut 29:18); see note 24.b.

(c) "dung" (דמן); although common in Jeremiah, the word is very rarely used elsewhere: see note 8:2.a.

(d) "Cities of Judah and streets of Jerusalem" (7:17); the phrase occurs eight times in Jer-prose but not elsewhere.

(e) "going in through these gates" (7:2); the phrase occurs three times in Jer-prose but not elsewhere.

(f) "the Lord of hosts, the God of Israel" (7:3); the expression is very common in Jer-prose (approximately thirty occurrences) and very rare elsewhere.

(iii) *Overlap between Jer-prose and Jer-poetry*. The following distinctive Jer-prose expressions in 7:1–8:3 also occur in Jer-poetry; stylistic aspects are also noted.

(a) Threefold repetition (7:4; see *Notes*); see also 22:29 (and note 8:3.a.).

(b) "self-reliance"; see (ii)(c) above; one occurrence is in a poetic context, 23:17.

(c) "accept instruction" (7:28); four occurrences in Jer-prose, two in Jer-poetry, elsewhere only in Proverbs.

(d) "upon mankind, upon animals" (7:20); ten occurrences in Jer-prose, two in Jer-poetry.

(e) "Amend your ways and your works" (7:3); five examples in Jer-prose, two examples of the verb (only) in Jer-poetry.

What conclusion can be drawn from this review of the language and stylistic usage of 7:1–8:3? First, it must be stressed that any preliminary conclusions drawn from this passage alone must be tentative and must be subject to review in the examination of subsequent Type C material. Second, even when the larger context is taken into account, conclusions must remain tentative; we have a relatively limited corpus of material from which to draw definitive conclusions about the style and linguistic usage of either the prose of Jeremiah or that of the Deuteronomic writers. Nevertheless, some preliminary perspectives emerge from the three categories of evidence listed above.

First, it is clear that there is some degree of common ground between Type C material in Jeremiah and the language of the Deuteronomic corpus. Having recognized that common ground, however, it must also be acknowledged that the "Deuteronomic" aspects of Jeremiah are distinctive; Type C material has vocabulary and stylistic expressions which not only distinguish it from D, but which are also, to a large extent, peculiar to Jeremiah (so far as we can tell, within the limited corpus of material available as evidence). Furthermore, certain of the characteristics of Type C material are also found in Type A material (the prophetic and poetic oracles). These different dimensions of the language of 7:1–8:3 are susceptible to various interpretations; for the moment, however, it is sufficient to review them in the light of the preliminary hypothesis presented in the introduction. It is proposed, tentatively, that the so-called D-language in Type C material is to be explained partially in terms of classical Hebrew prose style, as it existed in the late seventh and early sixth centuries B.C.; that style, in turn, may well have been influenced in part by Josiah's religious reformation and the significant role of Deuteronomy. But in addition, the similarity to D-language may also reflect the commonality of interest and subject matter between Jeremiah and the Deuteronomic tradition; although the two traditions differ in focus and emphasis, there is a commonality of interest in the temple, the land, the law, and other matters.

The distinctiveness of Jeremiah's prose is brought out in the second category of evidence noted above. If the author (whether it were Jeremiah, Baruch, or an unknown scribe) wrote in a style with certain similarities to D, then his distinctive characteristics must also be recognized. But the third category of evidence is also of particular importance. In suggesting some degree of common ground between

Type C and Type A material, it indicates that perhaps it is wrong to posit too sharp a distinction between the major blocks of material in Jeremiah, with respect both to chronology and authorship. The substantive issues of Types A and C material must be considered on their own merit; the stylistic and literary issues, however, on the basis of this preliminary assessment, do not require a totally different approach to interpretation. Indeed, Weippert concludes from a study of this passage that its substance is consistent with the prophet's poetic oracles and need not be considered the product of the editorial activities of Deuteronomists in the exilic or post-exilic period (*Die Prosareden des Jeremiabuches*, 46–48).

The long prose section has five component parts; although each is relatively self-contained, they are linked together into a coherent whole both by a common theme and by certain key words. In a few cases, the original form and setting of the parts (or the larger sections from which they have been drawn) may be detected, but for the most part the final form of the sections, welded into the current literary unity, permits only speculation as to their prehistory.

(i) *The Temple Sermon* (vv 7:1–15). This section appears to be a longer form of the sermon referred to, in summary form only, in 26:1–6. The place of proclamation, namely the temple gates, and the common reference to Shiloh establish reasonable grounds for linking the passages. The date of the passage, therefore, in its original proclamation, would be approximately 609–608 B.C., early in King Jehoiakim's reign, although the date at which it was linked to the following sections cannot be determined. On the basis of the introductory words (7:1) and the moral and legal aspects of the substance, the passage is reminiscent of the so-called torah of entrance (see H. G. Reventlow, *ZAW* 81 [1969] 315–51). The substance of the text moves from the proclamation of the Lord's word (vv 2–7) to a declaration of national apostasy (vv 8–12), concluding with an announcement of judgment (vv 13–15). But the classification is not without difficulties; if anything, the passage may have been part of a larger torah of entrance (part of a liturgy associated with the temple entrance; modifications of such texts may be seen in Pss 15 and 24), abbreviated for usage in its present context. But the clues as to form are suggestive that the original setting of this address was a prophetic proclamation at the temple gate; whether it was delivered by the prophet in a formal capacity or he simply seized the occasion of a temple liturgy, perhaps a major festival, to make his delivery cannot be known with certainty.

(ii) *The 'Queen of Heaven'* (vv 16–20). The second section, focusing on one aspect of pagan worship in Jerusalem, is presented in the form of a direct address from the Lord to the prophet, culminating in an oracle for public proclamation (v 20) announcing the coming of divine wrath. Whether this section was originally part of the temple sermon, or associated with the occasion on which the temple sermon was delivered, is uncertain; nevertheless, the theme of the temple (v 20) and Jerusalem links the two sections together.

(iii) *Sacrifice and Worship* (vv 21–28). These verses contain an oracle proclaiming the divine law and intent pertaining to sacrifices and worship. It is possible that this section, too, in its original delivery, was initially related to the same public occasion which prompted the delivery of the temple sermon (7:1–15).

(iv) *The Valley of Slaughter* (vv 29–34). The opening verse of this section, perhaps poetic in form (see note 29.a.), echoes the sound of lament; the lament, in turn, may have served as the "text" for the "sermon" which follows on the religious abuses associated with Topheth and ben-Hinnom.

(v) *Astral Worship* (8:1–3). The prose section concludes with an oracle denouncing yet another abuse of religious worship and intimating the consequent judgment.

In summary, the prose section (7:1–8:3) contains several parts that have been carefully woven into a finished whole. The common theme linking the parts is worship (both what it should be and what it had become) and thence, by implication, the temple. The key word in the text is "place" (מקום) which, although it is used in different ways, provides a literary thread linking the passage as a whole; vv 4, 6, 12, 14, 20, 32, and 8:3 (see further W. L. Holladay, *Architecture*, 102–3). The conjunction of "place(s)" and "Lord of Hosts" (7:3 and 8:3) may constitute an inclusion for the narrative as a whole.

Comment

1–15   *The temple sermon.* The temple sermon, or the portion of it that has survived in these verses, is introduced as an oracle; it is a direct proclamation from God to Judah delivered by and through the prophet Jeremiah. The location in which the sermon was delivered is specified as "gate of the LORD'S house" (v 2), through which the throngs of worshipers would pass on their way to the activities taking place in the temple court. Although it is possible that the place was chosen simply because it provided the prophet access to a large crowd, it is perhaps more probable that Jeremiah had an official function in the temple ritual, or perhaps unofficially assumed such a function to himself; during the pilgrimage festivals in the temple, the pilgrims were greeted at the temple gates by a servant of the institution, who asked them to examine their moral lives prior to passing through the gates and participating in the worship (see Pss 15, 24; Craigie, *Psalms 1–50*, 150–51, 211–12). If Jeremiah assumed his role of "preacher at the gate" in an unofficial capacity, then it is possible that the custom had lapsed at that time (as seems entirely probable from the substance of the sermon) and was consciously resumed by the prophet to his own moral and spiritual ends. The date of the passage is implied in the parallel account (Jer 26), namely, the months following Jehoiakim's accession to the throne. If the occasion could be pinpointed in the fall of 609 B.C. (though such precision would be very hypothetical), then it may have been the Festival of Tabernacles that provided the setting for the sermon. Alternatively, and perhaps more probably, it may have been the Festival of Weeks in 608 B.C. that drew the pilgrim crowds to the temple, whom Jeremiah in turn addressed at the gates.

The first part of the prophet's message was moral in tone, as was befitting for the address delivered at the temple gates (Pss 15:2–5; 24:3–4): "Amend your ways and your works, and I will make you dwell in this place" (v 3). The exhortation to amend the moral life is followed immediately by a plea to abandon a superficial form of religious faith that had been adopted by the people in place of moral integrity. They had come to think that the presence of the temple in Jerusalem was their guarantee of security and continuity. Thus, in a perverse way, the citizens of Judah had twisted the very essence of their religion: they considered the temple to be so important in God's eyes that perforce they must be secure. They did not perceive the secondary role of the temple, nor did they understand that their own moral integrity was of far greater significance to God than simply the physical presence of a building. God was committed first to his people, as Jeremiah understood very well, not to a building assigned for their use. And so the warning about false trust in the temple is followed by another plea, expressed in the form of a series of conditional clauses: *if* the people would really amend their ways (vv 5–6), *then* God would make them dwell in the temple and land (there is ambiguity as to the precise reference of "place," v 7, namely whether it refers to temple or land), in which, in turn, God's presence was symbolized by the temple. The moral demand is now elaborated in greater detail: what was required of the people was justice, the elimination of oppression, respect for innocent and weak persons, and an abandonment of pagan forms of religion. The substance of the prophet's remarks indicates that the practices he describes were rampant in the land; Josiah's reform, which with its emphasis on Deuteronomy had attempted to eliminate precisely these forms of social and religious evil, seems already to have become a thing of the past. In Jehoiakim's reign, the flame of hope that had burned briefly in Josiah's time was flickering and almost extinguished.

The prophet's sermonic assault on the crowds continues forcefully in vv 8–11, as the catalogue of national evil is elaborated in greater detail. The people continue to trust in "deceptive words" (v 8; viz. "the temple of the LORD," v 4), repeated perpetually and piously, all the while undermining their position by a frontal assault on the Ten Commandments (v 9). Theft, murder, adultery, perjury, and the worship of Baal flourished in the land, but at the time of the great festival, the people flocked to the temple, confident that their violations of the divine code were of little moment to the deity and that, as it were, the wonderful temple covered a multitude of sins! "We are delivered," they say (v 10), little realizing the irony of their proclamation, for in effect they have been delivered by God to the consequences of their own evil. The reference to the breach of various commandments in the Decalogue must be related to some component part of the festival as such, in which the commandments would be read out and the people would declare their assent; the prophetic address reminds the crowd, before they participate in that portion of the festival, of their grossly immoral lives and hence their unworthiness to respond to the proclamation of the Decalogue. If they had been able to respond with integrity, then indeed they would have been able to reply to the priest with faith and hope: "We are delivered." The reality, however, was that the sacred temple had become a "den of burglars" (v 11; see further the *Explanation*), in which society's sinners assembled for relaxation and pleasure in the festival season. But this portion of the prophet's address ends on a solemn note: "I myself have seen it, says the LORD." Human evil and hypocrisy are shattered by the statement that nothing escapes the divine vision; and because God has seen, inevitably reaction must follow.

The people are reminded of the fate of the ancient northern sanctuary in Shiloh. It was there, in the time of the Judges and Samuel, that there had been an important shrine at which God had been worshiped (1 Sam 1–4). Shiloh was located in what had once been the territory of the northern state of Israel; it was about thirty miles north of Jerusalem in the territory of Ephraim. Danish archaeological excavations were undertaken at Shiloh (modern *Seilun*) between 1926 and 1929, and then renewed more recently in an excavation conducted in 1963. Apparently Shiloh experienced some destruction late in the eleventh century B.C. (the Philistine period), but it recovered and continued to flourish as a town throughout the period of the two Kingdoms (though the shrine was probably not restored). The final fate of Shiloh is not known with certainty; in all probability it collapsed finally about 722 B.C., when the Northern Kingdom of Israel fell before the advance of the Assyrians. In a rhetorical fashion, the prophet invites the throngs of pilgrims at Jerusalem's temple to take a pilgrimage to Shiloh and see what happened there. It too had been a place where God's presence was established, but now it was in ruins. The reason for ruin was equally clear to the prophet, for its demise was "because of the evil of my people" (v 12). A temple or shrine, in other words, which was the symbolic location of God's presence among his people, provided no absolute security; God could be driven out of his temple by evil, and when that happened, sooner or later the place would collapse in ruin. Thus, Jeremiah drew upon the resources of contemporary "archaeology" to drive home his point; the stones and ruins of Shiloh, only a few miles north of Jerusalem and known no doubt to the prophet's audience, had a story to tell.

The message of Shiloh seems to introduce a note of inevitability into the prophet's proclamation of judgment (vv 13–15). Because of the people's evil, and because of their persistent refusal to heed warnings of the consequences of that evil, the fate of the temple of Jerusalem must be the same as that of Shiloh's shrine. The account of former and unheeded warnings, in the prophet's address, introduces a note of longsuffering and grace into this otherwise gloomy narrative. Certainly it could not be said that God did not give ample warning of his intentions before moving toward final acts of judgment; over and over again the divine plea had been declared, but just as constantly it had gone unheeded. And so the termination of Jeremiah's temple sermon rings with a funereal tone: "I will cast you out from my presence" (v 15), just as he had done before to the people of Ephraim, in whose territory the shrine of Shiloh was located. The very thing which the pilgrim crowds sought, namely, the divine presence symbolized by the temple, would be gone for ever. Clearly a sermon of this sort would win Jeremiah few friends, for it undermined the very foundations of contemporary religious practice, with its hypocritical sense of self-satisfaction and security; the response of the crowd to the prophet's proclamation is described in Jer 26.

16–20 *The "Queen of Heaven."* Although this passage may come from a different period or occasion in the prophet's ministry than that which precedes it, it is nevertheless integrated into its present literary context. It continues the theme of the abuse of worship in Jerusalem, which was already apparent in the preceding section. It is linked, thematically, by the further reference to "place" (v 20). And, more significantly, the substance seems to follow naturally from the temple sermon. At the end of the sermon, the anticipation of judgment in the public proclamation had taken on such a tone of certainty and inevitability that one might expect the prophet to turn to intercession on behalf of his people. In these private words addressed to the prophet, he is prohibited from praying on behalf of the people, the prohibition in turn creating even greater solemnity in the antecedent statement of judgment. The form of address, namely, a statement directed specifically to Jeremiah, is such that we cannot know whether this portion was ever used in a public context or was originally a record of Jeremiah's private religious experience. It culminates, nevertheless, in an oracle designed for public proclamation (v 20), and the private experience may have been used to introduce the public statement. In literary terms, the private statement (vv 16–19) helps to provide a context of understanding for the general wording of the public oracle.

The reason for the prohibition of the prophet's intercession is the sad state of religious affairs existing in Judah and Jerusalem. Pagan religious practices had become so widespread that it was pointless to pray any more—the nation had gone too far on the road to apostasy! The scene of apostasy is presented in colorful and homely terms, evoking an almost easy atmosphere but highlighting thereby the profound religious ignorance of the participants. The children are out gathering sticks, the fathers are kindling the fire for cooking, and the mothers are making the dough for sweet-cakes. The picture is almost that of a summer picnic and barbeque, until the purpose of all this domestic activity is stated: they are preparing for the ritual of the "Queen of Heaven" and the worship of other pagan deities. The cakes would be shaped or imprinted with the symbols of the heavenly goddess; drinks would be poured out upon the earth as libations to other gods.

The crime involved is that of worshiping deities other than the God of Israel, but here it is practiced at the household level, not in the courts of the temple. Thus gradually it becomes clear how widespread the perversion of religion had become in Jeremiah's time; it was not simply the worship in the temple that had been polluted, but even in the nation's family life religious corruption had set in. And whatever the intent of this familiar form of worship, its consequence was simply the degradation and shame of family life in Judah (v 19).

The identity of the "Queen of Heaven" is not easy to specify. Some scholars have suggested that the queen was the Canaanite goddess Anat (F. F. Hvidberg, *Weeping and Laughter in the Old Testament* [Leiden: Brill, 1962] 115–17), who is called in the Ugaritic texts *bʿlt.šmm.rmm*, "queen of the high heavens." Other Canaanite deities that have been suggested include *Ashtaroth* (who in later tradition was identified as the daughter of *Ouranos*, "Heaven," and *Shapash*, the sun-goddess in the Ugaritic texts). However, the reference to *sweet-cakes* (*kawwānîm*, employing an Akkadian loan word) is reminiscent of the Assyrian astral deities referred to in Amos 5:26 (viz. *Sakkut* and *Kewan*), and it may be that the references to the queen here are to a remnant of Assyrian-type astral cults surviving in Judah. If the reference were to Astarte, then recent archaeological evidence may supplement the present text in pictorial terms (see W. Culican, *PEQ* 108 [1976] 119–23). But, in summary, several goddesses were identified with heaven, and the precise identity of the queen in this context cannot be determined.

It may also be the case that Jeremiah's indictment is addressed not only to the worship of pagan deities in this family cultic practice but is also intended to highlight the manner in which the breaking of the first commandment leads to the breach of others. The picture of children gathering sticks evokes an awareness of illegal Sabbath activities (Num 15:32–35), as does the kindling of fires (Exod 35:3), and if the pagan cult were practiced on the Sabbath, it involved the compound fracture of the Decalogue (see further Robinson, *VT* 28 [1978] 301–17). Thus the critique of the worship of the Queen of Heaven ties in still more closely with

the temple sermon, in which context, too, the breaking of the Ten Commandments had been identified (7:9).

The consequence of this perpetuation of evil at the family level is expressed
forcefully in the concluding oracle (v 20). If "this place" refers to the temple, then it
ties in the failure in family worship with consequences upon the temple, but the
"place" may simply refer to the city of Jerusalem and the nation as a whole, in
which case the proclamation of judgment has more general application. That
apostasy in the family is not a light matter is made clear in the judgment saying;
the consequences embrace even the world of nature (animals, trees, and fruit)
and are devastating in nature.

21–28 *Sacrifice and Worship.* The focus now shifts from the false cult of the
"Queen of Heaven" to the abuse of indigenous Hebrew forms of worship, specifically that form of worship associated with "burnt-offerings" and "sacrifices." This
section of Jeremiah has frequently been associated with the so-called cult-polemic
of the prophets (see further Amos 5:25; Ezek 20:25; Hos 2:18–25; M. Sekine, *EvT*
28 (1968) 605–9) in its apparent reaction to the temple's sacrificial cult. Weinfeld
has identified here a "spiritual metamorphosis" in the prophet's message, in which
Jeremiah maintains the supremacy of ethics over ritual (*ZAW* 88 [1976] 18–56).
But, as Milgrom has pointed out, the prophetic critique is concerned not so much
with the sacrificial cult in general, but specifically with the individual voluntary
sacrifices (Lev. 17:8; 22:17–25; J. Milgrom, *ZAW* 89 [1977] 273–75). Jeremiah is
engaged not in a wholesale critique of the temple, but specifically of certain burnt-
offerings and sacrifices that the people brought to the temple, which in turn were
not a part of the specified public ritual established at Mount Sinai. Thus, we begin
to see the links between this section and the preceding one, in the final and edited
form of the passage; the prophet moves from the critique of the *family's* paganism (as witnessed in the cult of the Queen of Heaven) to the critique of the *family's*
private and voluntary participation in the worship of the temple. It is the theme
of family and private, individual religious practices that links the two sections together.

The passage begins with what is, at first sight, a curious command from God:
the people are commanded to combine their burnt-offerings with their sacrifices
and eat them, as if they constituted profane, or ordinary, meat. Normally the
"burnt-offerings" would be totally consumed by fire and the worshiper would
participate in the consumption of a part of the sacrifice. But, according to the
divine injunction, both meats were to be eaten; the implication is that both were
rejected by God, to whom ostensibly they were offered, and thus they might as
well be eaten by the foolish humans offering them. The reason becomes clear in
the following verses; the principal command given to the Hebrews following the
Exodus from Egypt was obedience to God; at Mount Sinai, when the covenant
was established, matters such as private burnt-offerings and sacrifices were not
given primacy and certainly did not supersede the importance of basic obedience
to God. The prophet emphasizes his point by sketching in the lengthy history of
disobedience in the actions of the Hebrew people. Despite the central significance
of obedience to the divine voice, the people had perpetually ignored it, preferring
to accept their own advice, supremely self-confident, yet actually moving backward
with every assured step forward. This national history of retrogression had not

gone unheeded; the prophets had been sent to warn Israel of the consequences of its action, but they had been steadfastly ignored by each generation, so that the nation's backward progress had accelerated to the abysmal state of affairs that existed in Jeremiah's time.

Thus, for all Jeremiah's preaching and prompting, he was met by deaf ears and hardened hearts; the passage of time had done its ossifying task, so that it seemed to Jeremiah that he addressed a people beyond redemption. In any case, the words declared by the prophet in v 28 ring with the echo of an epitaph; the people of Judah had become a nation conditioned to disobedience, perverse in their refusal of instruction, and no amount of offerings, burnt-offerings, and sacrifices could change the miserable future of judgment they were shaping for themselves.

29–34 *The Valley of Slaughter.* The religious abuses described in the preceding sections reach new depths in this passage, in which the terrible cult of child-sacrifice is described. Just south of Jerusalem, in the steep-sided valley of Hinnom, children were burned as sacrifices at a place called *Topheth* (meaning literally "hearth, fireplace"). Perhaps originally it had been the place where the city's rubbish had been burned, but in Judah's sad descent into paganism it became the place in which a child's life, the most precious of all divine gifts, was destroyed.

Perhaps it is the tragic substance of this narrative that led the editor to preface it with a lament (v 29); the words of the lament, referring to the traditional shearing of hair from the head, set the tone for what is to follow; God had rejected this evil generation, and it was their evil acts as much as their demise that were to be the source of grief.

There has been some debate whether the child-sacrifice to which the prophet refers took place in his own time or whether he referred to the earlier practices in the period of Kings Ahaz and Manasseh (2 Kgs 16:3; 21:6). King Josiah, during the course of his religious reformation, had desecrated Topheth and attempted to terminate the terrible rite (2 Kgs 23:10). But it is probable that the ritual had been revived in Jehoiakim's reign, and the references to it in Ezekiel (20:25–26) may indicate how common the practice had become during the last years of Jerusalem prior to its defeat in 586 B.C. The reference to "abominable objects" (v 30) in the "house" (viz. temple) may point to *masseboth*, or pillars, set up in the temple, but associated with the sacrificial rituals in the valley of Topheth.

Child-sacrifice was practiced in a number of places in the Near East (see particularly A. R. W. Green, *The Role of Human Sacrifice in the Ancient Near East* [Missoula, MT: Scholars Press. 1975] esp. 173–87). In the ruins of the Phoenician city of Carthage, in North Africa, the remains of hundreds of children sacrificed to the goddess Tanit and the god Baal-Hammon have been excavated (L. E. Stager and S. R. Wolff, *BAR* 10/1 [1984] 31–51); the practice was apparently introduced in Carthage by Judah's Phoenician neighbors. The cult, as it was practiced in Jeremiah's time, was apparently associated with the god Baal (see Jer 19:5; 32:35), but it is probable that it was syncretistic in form, combining elements of perverted Yahwism with pagan beliefs. The prophet Ezekiel indicates that child-sacrifice had been "rationalized" on the basis of the ancient Mosaic law of Exod 22:29 (see Craigie, *Ezekiel* [Philadelphia: Westminster Press, 1983] 148–50). But in addition to perverted Yahwism and the worship of Baal, the cult in Jeremiah's time may have been related to that of the Queen of Heaven (7:16–20). The goddess Tanit, in Phoenicia and Carthage, was identified with the goddess Astarte, who (as was noted above) is one of the candidates for the title "Queen of Heaven." And the conjunction of Tanit/Astarte is known in a recently discovered inscription from Sarepta, on the Phoenician coast, from the seventh century B.C., contemporaneous in general terms with the prophet's early period (J. B. Pritchard, *Recovering Sarepta, A Phoenician City* [Princeton, NJ: Princeton University Press, 1978] 104–7).

The prophet's comment with respect to God's attitude to child-sacrifice ("a thing that I did not command and that never even crossed my mind," v 31) is probably designed to undercut the claims of those who practiced the cult, namely that they were only carrying out the ancient Mosaic law (Exod 22:29). But such a rationalization, based on the quotation of a law out of context, is firmly squashed by the divine declaration; only a truly perverted mind could claim that child-sacrifice was a divine institution. And so the words are followed by a proclamation of judgment. The place where the atrocities were performed would become known as the "Valley of Slaughter," not for the bodies of the innocent children, but for the bodies of the perpetrators of the terrible holocaust. The judgment is portrayed in terms no less horrifying than the crime that initiated it; the bodies of the criminals would be piled high, as food for carrion birds, but there would be no farmer or scarecrow to frighten the birds away from their grisly feast. The concluding section of the message, describing the departure of joy from Jerusalem's street, is particularly poignant. No more would the joyful sounds of a wedding, the voices of bride and groom, be heard in Jerusalem. The joy of a wedding carries the happy anticipation of the birth of children, but a nation that sacrificed its children forfeited all right for such cheerful occasions. The union of marriage promised only another candidate for the slaughter, and so God, in an act of mercy for generations yet unborn, must act in judgment.

8:1–3 *Astral Worship.* The long prose section, in which the prophet engages in the critique of various abuses of religious life and worship, culminates in this bleak and comprehensive statement of judgment. The conclusion, both of the passage and of the practices described within it, ties together the preceding themes; while it is a statement of judgment, the shape and character of that judgment are related intimately to the forms of religious abuse which led to it. The time of the judgment lies still in the future from the perspective of the time at which the message was first delivered ("at that time," 8:1), yet the urgency of the prophet's message as a whole suggests that the future is not too far distant.

The fundamental form of the coming judgment is the desecration of the dead, undertaken (by implication) at the hands of invaders who would take over the land. At first sight, it may seem strange to describe a form of judgment as being practiced on those who are already dead, but the force of the message comes home in v 3: despite the desecration of the dead, death would be preferred over life by those unfortunate enough to survive, so terrible would the coming invasion be! In Hebrew thought, the grave was considered an appropriate resting place for the dead, whereas those unburied were considered cursed (1 Kgs 16:4); the exhumation of the bones of those already buried indicated that even the apparent "reward" of decent burial after death was no guarantee against future abuse and punishment (see further R. Lorenz, *VT* 32 [1982] 229–34). The statement concerning the exhumation of bones is comprehensive in scope: the skeletons of kings, princes, priests, prophets, and ordinary citizens would be dragged from their tombs on the judgment day.

The ransacking of tombs for bones by the enemy was in part an act of humiliation, a deliberate flaunting of power and an excessive show of scorn for the defeated victims. But in the prophet's message, the judgment takes on an ironic twist. It was Judah's worship of sun, moon, and the stars of heaven that had contributed to the judgment in the first place; thus, as if in fulfillment of the desires of the dead, their bones are laid out upon the earth, exposed to the very astral "powers" whom once the dead had worshiped. And in the humiliation of the dead, their former heavenly masters were uncaring, complacently shining in the heavens, unconcerned about human fate on the face of the earth. Although in life the citizens of Judah had served these astral deities, offering them affection, soliciting their advice and counsel (much as their modern counterparts might read an astrological chart), in human death the futility of their actions was at last made plain.

The judgment has a tone of absoluteness and finality to it. The bones, once exhumed, would not again be afforded a decent burial (8:2), with its suggestion of perpetual rest; rather, they would become "dung upon the surface of the ground." The reference to "dung" might be better rendered, in modern speech, by "fertilizer." The prophet alludes, perhaps, to the ancient practice of using bones (usually animal bones) as a form of fertilizer. Crushed up (as bonemeal) or calcined in the sunlight into bone ash, the broken down bones of Judah's nobility and common people would provide phosphorus and other nutrients for the ground. Against this bleak scenario, in which death offered no prospect of peace and continuing life was unbearable, the power and solemnity of Jeremiah's message are brought home forcefully.

Explanation

This prose sample of Jeremiah's preaching is illustrative both of the social and religious conditions pertaining in his period and of his response and message to his contemporaries. His was not an age in which formal religious practices had ceased; indeed, on the evidence, they prospered, as is implied by the existence of the pilgrim crowds to whom the temple sermon was addressed. But the formal practice of official religion was undermined in two distinct ways: (i) the collapse of national morality made a mockery of the continuity of formal religion, and (ii) the syncretistic fusing of the ancient faith with pagan practices destroyed any possibility of integrity in the worship conducted in the temple. But while the temple provides one of the threads linking together the component parts of this prose narrative, it is the people themselves, especially the ordinary folk and families of the nation, that constitute the prophet's principal focus. They continued to worship in the temple, blindly hoping thereby to secure God's presence, with its guarantee of security, in their midst. But they saw no inconsistency in combining that formal worship with pagan cultic practices that were fundamentally inconsistent with the national religion. Nor does it seem to have occurred to them that the massive decline in personal and familial morality rendered their various kinds of worship into mere sham and hypocrisy.

The modern reader of an exposé, such as that of Jeremiah, is faced with the difficult task of imagining the lives of those who are exposed. The prophetic critique is so sharp and clear that one can hardly imagine the folly and stupidity of those who are so powerfully condemned. And yet it is important to try to stand where those citizens of Judah stood, to imagine living as they lived and believing as they believed, for otherwise we may miss the power of the prophet's critique and hence avoid perceiving its perpetual relevance. If we are to grasp the central meaning of the "temple sermon" (7:1–15), we must imagine our own great religious festivals and ask whether the same gap exists between the moral life and the public worship. And if we are horrified by the thought of child-sacrifice in the Valley of Hinnom, we need to ask whether it is so fundamentally different, in the taking of young life, from some of the casual forms of abortion that characterize many sectors of modern society. The point is that many ordinary citizens, in any age, easily succumb to the accepted standards and mores of their time; the prophet is that rare species in the human race who can see through society's veneer, its rationalizations and convenient explanations, and expose the sickness and corruption within.

In the NT we can perceive some of the ways in which the ancient message of the prophet was given contemporary application. In the "cleansing of the temple," Jesus quotes Jeremiah in his declaration to those in the temple that they have made God's house a "den of robbers" (Jer 7:11; Matt 21:13). And the very notion of "hell," *Gehenna* (from the *Valley of Hinnom*) draws a part of its meaning and substance from the valley where children were burned in the terrible fires, illustrating powerfully the way in which all forms of "judgment" are essentially of human making, the product and consequence of evil. And thus we perceive that Jeremiah's message had lost little of its pertinence by the first century A.D., and it is as relevant in the twentieth century, if we can overcome the stubbornness and blindness of Jeremiah's first audience, which made them so resistant to his teaching.

VI. Miscellaneous Sayings concerning National Evil and Its Consequences (8:4–10:25)

With regard to substance, form, and origin, this collection of sayings is miscellaneous in character. The subsections, though not closely integrated, contain some common and overlapping themes, including the prophetic detailing of Judah's national evil, the consequences of that evil in terms of judgment, and outbursts of lament evoked both by the evil and its anticipated consequence. Most of the section is in poetry, though there are two short prose sections (9:11–15 [9:12–16] and 9:22–25 [9:23–26]) and a single verse in Aramaic (10:11).

It is very difficult to divide this material into coherent subsections; note the variations among the many commentators. The basic unity of the whole is indicated by common themes and catchwords. The collection is treated, largely for convenience, in eight subsections.

8:4–12	Unrepentant People and Unwise Wise Men
8:13–23 [8:13–9:1]	Judgment and Despair
9:1–10 [9:2–9]	The Sorrow of God
9:11–15 [9:10–16]	The Rationale of Judgment
9:16–21 [9:17–22]	A Call to Lament
9:22–25 [9:23–26]	Judgment upon All
10:1–16	Idols and the True God
10:17–25	Vicarious Suffering

Attention to the common themes and catchwords of the various subsections gives meaning to the whole. The first subsection is a general indictment of the people and their leaders. The second subsection, in response to this indictment, details both the sorrow of the people and the sorrow of Jeremiah over the decree of judgment. The third, also in response to the indictment, testifies to the corresponding sorrow of God. The fourth is a brief prose justification of the pronouncement of judgment. The fifth renews the call to mourning over the sin of the people and the resulting judgment. The sixth explains how God will bring judgment not only upon the leaders of Judah but also upon the nations. Subsection seven details the folly of idolatry, a common theme of the Josianic reform. The final subsection is a concluding lament over the coming judgment. The whole section is a tapestry of indictment and lament, which when woven together shows the great tragedy of the situation.

The dates of the subsections vary and are hard to determine, but probably range from about 609 to 597 B.C., or even later. The poetic subsection 10:1–16 (with the Aramaic insert) may be of a different origin, adapted for its present context.

This entire section has many parallels with 4:5–6:30, which can help explain both passages. Besides many shared themes and ideas, there are numerous shared words, phrases, and entire verses. The number of parallels suggests that this section should be analyzed in comparison and contrast with 4:5–6:30. Some examples follow; for a more detailed examination of these and many more parallels see the

individual sections. (i) An almost word-for-word correspondence exists between
6:12–15 and 8:10–12. (ii) A similar word-for-word correspondence exists between 5:9, 29 and 9:8[9]. (iii) The phrase "they refuse to return" (מאנו לשוב) is
found in 5:3 and 8:5 (found elsewhere only at Hos 11:5). (iv) The word "peace"
(שלום), probably related to the oracle of peace pronounced by the false prophets,
is found at 4:10; 6:14; 8:11, 15; and 9:7[8] (on this usage see J. Sisson, "Jeremiah
and the Jerusalem Conception of Peace," *JBL* 105 [1986] 429–42). (v) The "foe
from the north" found in chap. 4 is echoed in 8:16 and 10:22. (vi) The idea of
"harvesting" Israel is found 6:9 and 8:13. (vii) Jeremiah is called an "assayer" and
"tester" in 6:27 and 9:6[7].

Differences in tone and emphasis between 4:5–6:30 and 8:4–10:25, however,
prevent us from equating the two. The emphasis in 4:5–6:30 is indictment and
judgment, while the overwhelming tone of 8:4–10:25 is sorrow and lament. The
similarities suggest the two passages address the same situation. The differences
can be explained by chronology. The tone of lament and suffering would follow
naturally upon the earlier indictment and announcement of judgment.

A. Unrepentant People and Unwise Wise Men (8:4–12)

Bibliography

Berridge, J. M. *Prophet, People.* 171–73. **Brueggemann, W.** "Jeremiah's Use of Rhetorical
Questions." *JBL* 92 (1973) 358–74. **Cazelles, H.** "Jeremiah and Deuteronomy." In *A Prophet
to the Nations.* Ed. L. G. Perdue and B. W. Kovacs. Winona Lake, IN: Eisenbrauns, 1984.
89–112. **Held, M.** "Rhetorical Questions in Ugaritic and Biblical Hebrew." *W. F. Albright
Volume.* Ed. A. Malamat. *Ereṣ-Israel* 9. Jerusalem: Israel Exploration Society, 1969. 71–79.
Hyatt, J. P. "Torah in the Book of Jeremiah." *JBL* 60 (1941) 382–84. **Klopfenstein, M. A.**
Die Lüge nach dem Alten Testament. Zurich: Gotthelf, 1964. **Lindblom, J.** "Wisdom in the Old
Testament Prophets." In *Wisdom in Israel and in the Ancient Near East.* Ed. M. Noth and D.
W. Thomas. VTSup 3. Leiden: Brill, 1955. **McKane, W.** *Prophets and Wise Men.* **Selms, A. van.**
"Motivated Interrogative Sentences in Hebrew." *Semitics* 2 (1971–72) 143–49. **Sisson, J. P.**
"Jeremiah and the Jerusalem Conception of Peace." *JBL* 105 (1986) 429–42.

Translation

> ⁴ᵃ *"And you shall say to them,*ᵃ *the LORD has spoken thus,*
> *When people fall down, do they not rise up again?*   (3+3)
> *When one turns*ᵇ *away, does he not turn back*ᶜ *again?*
> ⁵ *Why has this people turned away?*ᵃ   (4+3)
> *Why is Jerusalem*ᵇ *in perpetual apostasy?*
> *They have grasped deceit firmly;*   (2+2)
> *they have refused to turn back.*
> ⁶ ᵃ*I paid attention and I listened,*ᵃ   (2+2)
> *but they did not speak trustworthily;*

> no one repents of his evil,   (4+3)
>> saying, 'What have I done?'
>
> Every one turns[b] to his own course,[c]   (3+3)
>> like a horse rushing into battle.

7   Even the stork in the sky   (2+2)
>> knows its seasons;[a]
>
> and the turtledove, swallow,[b] and crane[c]   (3+3)
>> observe the time of their coming;
>
> but my people do not know   (3+3)
>> the fixed order of the LORD.[d]

8   How can you say, 'We are wise,   (4+3)
>> the law of the LORD is with us'?
>
> [a]Surely, it has been made into a lie,[b]   (4+3)
>> by the lying pen of the scribes![a]

9   Wise men are put to shame;   (2+2)
>> they are dismayed and captured.
>
> Behold, they have rejected the LORD's word,   (3+2)
>> [a]and so they have no wisdom.[a]

10   [a]Therefore, I shall give their wives to others,   (4+2)
>> their fields to conquerors,
>
> [b]for [c]from the least to the greatest of them[c]   (3+3)
>> each one[d] is greedy for profit;
>
> from prophet to priest,   (2+3)
>> each is practicing falsehood.

11   And they have healed my people[a] superficially,   (4+3+2)
>> saying, 'Peace, Peace,'
>> but there is no peace!

12   Were they embarrassed when they acted abominably?   (4+2+3)
>> They were not in the least embarrassed,
>> nor have they experienced shame.
>
> Therefore, they shall fall among the fallen;   (3+3)
>> [a]when I punish them,[a] they shall stumble."
>>> The LORD has spoken.

Notes

4.a-a. This phrase, as well as the latter part of v 3, is absent from the LXX and Syr, perhaps indicating its editorial nature. The major Heb. MSS, including 4Q Jer[b], include it; the MT is retained.

4.b. LXX and the Q of some Oriental MSS have pl ישובו, "they turn," to agree with the previous phrase. It is best to maintain the sg.

4.c. G. R. Driver ("Linguistic and Textual Problems: Jeremiah," *JQR* 28 [1937/38] 52–72) suggested that another root, not preserved by Hebrew phonology, accounts for the two opposite meanings of שוב, "turn, return."

5.a. Reading שובב (thus 3 masc sg), the ה a dittogr. Cf. Rudolph, 52.

5.b. ירושלם, "Jerusalem," is omitted in LXX. It is best to retain it in apposition to העם הזה, "this people," carrying out the parallelism.

6.a-a. The LXX has pl imperatives, which would require changing the consonantal text (LXX = הקשיבו ושמעו, "Pay attention, listen"). The MT is preferred.

6.b. The Q of many MSS is כלו. The change is not necessary; see GKC § 91e, and J. C. L. Gibson, *Syrian Semitic Inscriptions: Hebrew and Moabite Inscriptions* (Oxford: UP, 1971) 29, n. 1.

6.c. Reading the Q in opposition to Syr and Tg, which follow the K במרוצתם, "when they are determined." במרוצתם, "in his own course," refers to the horse of the next colon, thus paralleling the מועדיה, "seasons," of the stork in v 7; Holladay, II, 274.

7.a. Many MSS and versions read sg.

7.b. Following the Q; see McKane, 185–86, on the identity of the birds.

7.c. ועגור, the identity of the type of bird is uncertain; *crane* is speculation. The conj is absent in the LXX. Cf. Isa 38:14, where this word and the previous one also occur.

7.d. Lit., "the justice of the Lord." See note 5:4.b.

8.a-a. This phrase is lit., "Truly, behold, to falsehood it has done, the false pen of the scribes." The subj and obj of the first part of the phrase are ambiguous, leading to various interpretations. Rudolph (*BHS*) suggests עשׂה, to specify a fem obj and thus the "Law of the Lord." This would give the sense "The false pen of the scribes makes the Law of the Lord false." See further *Comment.*

8.b. On שׁקר, "false," see M. A. Klopfenstein, *Die Lüge.*

9.a-a. The phrase is often read, "Wisdom of what to them?" Rudolph (*BHS*) suggested חכמתם, the ם omitted by haplogr. The passage would then read "What (good) is their wisdom to them?" Dahood ("The Emphatic Double Negative m'yn in Jer 10:6–7," *CBQ* 37 [1975] 458–59) suggested reading וחכמת as a fem abs form ending in *tāw* and followed by the negative מה. This is the reading adopted here.

10.a. From here through v 12 parallels 6:12–15.

10.b. From this point through v 12 is missing from LXX. See further *Form/Structure/Setting.*

10.c-c. See θ′ and the Syr.

10.d. See note 6.b.

11.a. Lit., "daughter of my people."

12.a-a. Lit., "in the time of their visitation."

Form/Structure/Setting

This passage is composed of three separate pieces (vv 4–7, 8–9, 10–12) joined by common words and themes. The middle subsection (vv 8–9) is recognized by most commentators as an independent piece because of the different subject matter; vv 4–7 refer to the people and 8–9 refer to the wise (so McKane, Rudolph, Carroll). The final subsection (vv 10–12) parallels almost word for word 6:12–15, indicating its independent nature; many consider chap. 6 the original context (so Duhm, McKane, Rudolph, Janzen, *Studies,* 95–96).

The formal and structural analysis of the passage is dependent upon determining the speaker's identity. The matter is complicated by the oracular introductory formula in v 4, which presupposes that the Lord is the speaker, by the reference to the Lord in the third person in v 9, which presupposes someone else is the speaker, and by the first person oracle of judgment in v 10–12. Commentators are divided over whether to interpret the Lord as the speaker (so McKane, Holladay, Carroll, Calvin), Jeremiah as the speaker (so Bright, Rudolph, Volz), or a combination of both (see Berridge *Prophet, People,* 171–72). It is better to admit that the Lord could refer to himself in the third person in v 9 than to ignore or remove the oracular introduction in v 4. Identifying the Lord as the speaker, the first two subsections (8:4–7, 8–9) are accusation speeches and the final subsection (8:10–12) is an oracle of judgment.

Both accusation speeches begin with rhetorical questions and proceed from this basis to the accusation. They are further linked by the parallelism of משׁפט יהוה, "the justice of the Lord," in v 7 and תורת יהוה, "the law of the Lord," in v 8 (see further Klopfenstein, *Die Lüge,* 133). Verses 10–12 are linked to their context by small editorial changes such as the use of בת־עמי, "daughter of my people," in v 11. It is interesting that even those commentators who consider 6:12–15 the primary reference and 8:10–12 secondary, and therefore suggest omitting these verses, usually emend 6:12–15 on the basis of these verses.

This passage has many contacts with both 5:1–9 and 6:9–15, even though the dialogue format evident in these two passages is absent from 8:4–12; see *Form/Structure/Setting* on 6:9–15 for the similarities between 5:1–9 and 6:9–15. As noted earlier there is an almost word-for-word parallel between 6:12–15 and 8:10–12. The major contacts with 5:1–9, beside the similarities in theme and contents, are (i) the phrase מֵאֲנוּ לָשׁוּב, "they refuse to return," 5:3 and 8:4; and (ii) the phrase מִשְׁפַּט אֱלֹהִים/יהוה, "the justice of God/the LORD," in 5:4, 5 and 8:7. The similarities among these three passages suggest that they should be interpreted in connection with one another.

As with the parallel passages, the setting of this passage is probably Jerusalem, and it should be dated in the latter years of Josiah's reign.

Comment

4–5 The rhetorical form מַדּוּעַ . . . אִם . . . ה found in vv 4–5 is peculiar to Jeremiah (2:14, 31; 8:4–5, 19, 22; 14:19; 22:28; 49:41). The questions introduced by ה and אִם assume a situation that is contrary to fact. The מַדּוּעַ clause describes a situation questioned or protested on the basis of the preceding questions (see Held, "Rhetorical Questions"; van Selms, *Semitics* 2 [1971–72] 143–49; Brueggemann, *JBL* 92 [1973] 359–61). The rhetorical form is used here to introduce the indictment against the people. The use of the plural in the first question and the singular in the second question has been noted by many. Berridge (*Prophet, People,* 171–72) explained the change by saying that the people were the subject of the first question and the Lord the subject of the second question (cf. the commentaries of Rashi and Kimchi). The sense conveyed would then be, "Since the Lord always returns to the people, why do they not return to him?" The use of the singular in the second question can also be explained as parallel to Jerusalem in the second half of the מַדּוּעַ clause.

The repeated use of the root שׁוּב, "turn, return," is notable in these two verses.

> When one turns* away, does he not turn* back again?
> Why has this people turned* away?
> Why is Jerusalem in perpetual apostasy?
> They have grasped deceit firmly,
>   they have refused to turn* back.

*(See further W. L. Holladay, *The Root Šûbh in the Old Testament* [Leiden: E. J. Brill, 1958] 1–2).

6 The sense of the first part of this verse is difficult, probably explaining the textual variants (see *Notes*). The interpretation followed here is that the Lord had listened intently but had noticed no one repenting and saying "What have I done?" The latter part of v 6 compares the people to a horse rushing into battle heedless of what it is doing.

7 This verse makes use of an analogy from nature by suggesting that even the birds observe the natural order, but the Lord's people do not observe his ordinances concerning their lives (cf. 5:22–23). On the basis of the parallel with

5:1–9 and the connection with the following verses, "the fixed order of the LORD" (מִשְׁפַּט יהוה) should be understood as the ethical, moral order of the Lord, rather than the natural order.

8–9 The major interpretive crux of these two verses is the identification of the "law of the LORD" which the pen of the scribes had falsified. Duhm (88) identified it with Deuteronomy and used this text as evidence that Jeremiah was opposed to the Deuteronomic reformation. Bright (64) is representative of those who deny that Jeremiah regarded Deuteronomy as a pious fraud or that this text betrays the prophet's attitude toward Josiah's reform. He sees the scribal delusion not in some edition of the law itself but in the notion that possession of the law gave Israel a monopoly on wisdom.

It would be strange indeed to suppose that Jeremiah regarded Deuteronomy as a falsification of the Mosaic law. Perhaps the contrast is between the written law of the Lord and oral distortions of that law by scribes and wise men. McKane (*Prophets and Wise Men*, 102–12) has suggested that this is an attack upon wisdom circles associated with Deuteronomy. Volz, connecting the wise here with "those skilled in the Torah" (תֹּפְשֵׂי הַתּוֹרָה) of 2:8, has suggested that these are the precursors of the scribes we find in later Judaism.

10–12 This oracle of judgment, paralleled by 6:12–15, declares judgment upon everyone, from people to wise man to prophet to priest. As the wisdom of the wise has been shown to be a lie, so are the words of the prophets who declared that everything would be all right and thus proclaimed, "Peace, Peace." The idea of peace is related to Jeremiah's controversy with the cultic prophets throughout the book of Jeremiah. (See Sisson, *JBL* 105 [1986] 429–42; Overholt, *The Threat of Falsehood*.) Jeremiah criticized the prophets for fostering a false sense of security in the people. The prophets were proclaiming that God would protect the people and not allow Jerusalem to fall to the enemy, while Jeremiah was proclaiming approaching doom. This helps to explain Jeremiah's failure to convince the people of their sin and guilt. Because of the failure of the people to listen to Jeremiah's warnings, the same threat of invasion made earlier against the prophets and priests (6:12–15) is now applied to people and wise men. No section of society will be exempt from the visitation of the Lord.

Explanation

The theme of this section is the persistent apostasy and the misplaced values of the people of Jerusalem. This has particular application to the religious leaders, who are characterized by their stubborn refusal to repent (vv 4–6), their sense of religious superiority (v 8), their inordinate greed (v 10), their superficial attention to the hurt of the people (v 11), and their utter lack of shame (v 12).

Such behavior as theirs is compared to the heedless course of the warhorse as it plunges headlong into battle (v 6) and contrasted with the orderly migrations of the stork, the turtledove, the swallow, and the crane (v 7). There is a "fixed order" (מִשְׁפַּט) of the Lord designed to give moral guidance to his people, even as migratory birds are guided in their flight by a sure instinct. Apostasy is contrary to the purpose of God and also to the nature of man. The influence of wisdom thought on the prophet is clearly evident at this point. Elsewhere Jeremiah appeals to the fixed order in the movement of sun, moon, and stars and the orderly progression of day and night as the pattern and pledge of the Lord's continuing preservation of Israel (31:35–36; 33:20–21, 25–26).

This passage is a scathing indictment of the designated spiritual leaders of the people. Scribes are accused of falsifying the law of the Lord with their copying pens (v 8), although the exact nature of their offense is not defined. Wise men have ceased to be truly wise because they have rejected the word of the Lord, the only source of true wisdom (v 9). Prophets and priests have abandoned the high calling of their office and devoted themselves to the pursuit of profit (v 10).

Because of this situation, the doom of both the leaders and the led is sure. Wise men will have no wisdom to escape capture and punishment. Profit-hungry priests and prophets will experience the loss of their wives and fields to invading conquerors. All will share a common fate, stumbling and falling in the day of the Lord's visitation.

B. Judgment and Despair (8:13–23)

Bibliography

Aberbach, D. "*wᵓtn lḥm yᶜrwm* (Jeremiah VIII 13): The Problem and Its Solution." *VT* 27 (1977) 99–101. **Avishur, Y.** "Should a Ugaritic Text be Corrected on the Basis of a Biblical Text?" *VT* 31 (1981) 218–20. **Berridge, J. M.** *Prophet, People.* 170–76. **Ben-Corre, A. D.** *The Daughter of My People: Arabic and Hebrew Paraphrases of Jeremiah 8:13–9:23.* Leiden: E. J. Brill, 1971. **Brueggemann, W.** "Jeremiah's Use of Rhetorical Questions." *JBL* 92 (1973) 358–74. **Dahood, M.** "Hebrew-Ugaritic Lexicography II." *Bib* 45 (1964) 393–412. **Gevirtz, S.** "'Should a Ugaritic Text be Corrected on the Basis of a Biblical Text?' A Response." *VT* 33 (1983) 330–34. ———. "The Ugaritic Parallel to Jeremiah 8:23." *JNES* 20 (1961) 41–46. **Hacohen, D. B.** "*lekā dūmiyyâ tehillâ.*" *BMik* 27 (1981/1982) 109–14. **Held, M.** "Rhetorical Questions in Ugaritic and Biblical Hebrew." *W. F. Albright Volume.* A. Malamat, ed. *Ereṣ-Israel* 9. Jerusalem: Israel Exploration Society, 1969. 71–79. **Holladay, W. L.** "The So-called 'Deuteronomic Gloss' in Jer. VIII 19b." *VT* 12 (1962) 494–98. **Jongeling, B.** "L'expression *my ytn* dans l'Ancien Testament." *VT* 24 (1967) 32–40. **Lindblom, J.** "Wisdom in the Old Testament Prophets." In *Wisdom in Israel and in the Ancient Near East.* Ed. M. Noth and D. W. Thomas. VTSup 3. Leiden: E. J. Brill, 1955. **Loretz, O.** "Jer 8, 23 und KTU 1.16 I 26–28." *Mélanges bibliques et orientaux en l'honneur de M. Henri Cazelles.* Ed. A. Caquot and M. Delcor. AOAT 212. Neukirchen-Vluyn: Neukirchener Verlag, 1981. **McKane, W.** "Poison Trial by Ordeal and the Cup of Wrath." *VT* 38 (1980) 474–92. ———. *Prophets and Wise Men.* **Press, R.** "Das Ordal im Alten Israel I." *ZAW* 51 (1933) 121–40. **Moot, J. C. de.** and **Sprank, K.** "Problematic Passages in the Legend of Kirtu (II)." *UF* 14 (1982) 182. **Rad, G. von.** "The Confessions of Jeremiah." Repr. in *A Prophet to the Nations.* Ed. L. G. Perdue and B. W. Kovacs. Winona Lake, IN: Eisenbrauns, 1984. 339–48. **Reventlow, H. G.** *Liturgie.* 189–96. **Roche, M. de.** "Contra Creation, Covenant and Conquest (Jer. 8:13)." *VT* 30 (1980) 280–90. **Selms, A. van.** "Motivated Interrogative Sentences in Hebrew." *Semitics* 2 (1971–72) 143–49.

Translation

Yahweh:
13 ᵃ"*When I would have harvested them,*"ᵃ (2+3+3)

The LORD's oracle,
"there were no grapes on the vine,
    nor figs on the tree,
and the foliage was withered,
    [b]so I made them a forest stripped bare!"[b]   (2+3)

People:
14   Why do we sit still? Gather together,   (3+4+2)
    let us go into the fortified cities
    and weep[a] there;
For the LORD our God has made us weep,[a]   (4+2+3)
    and given us tears to drink,[b]
    for we have sinned against the LORD.[c]
15   [a]We hoped for peace, but no good came;   (4+4)
    for a time of healing,[b] but saw terror.[a]
16   From Dan we can hear   (2+2)
    the snorting of his horses;
At the sound of the neighing of his stallions,   (3+2)
    all of the land shakes;
They are coming to devour the land and all it contains,   (4+3)
    the cities and those who dwell in them.

Yahweh:
17   "For behold I am sending among you   (4+2)
    serpents, vipers;
Which cannot be charmed,   (3+2)
    and they shall bite you."
                    [a]Oracle of the LORD.[a]

Jeremiah:
18   [a]Sorrow has overwhelmed me;[a]   (3+3)
    my heart is sick within.
19   Listen, the cry[a] of my people[b]   (3+2)
    from throughout the land,[c]
Is the LORD not in Zion?   (3+3)
    Is her King not in her?
[d]Why have they angered me with their idols,   (3+2)
    with their foreign images?[d]
20   The harvest is past, summer has ended;   (4+3)
    but we have not been saved.
21   Because of the breaking of my people,[a] I am broken,[b]   (3+3)
    I mourn, I am gripped with dismay.[c]
22   Is there no balm in Gilead?   (3+3)
    Is there no healer there?
Why[a] then is there no restoration   (4+2)
    of the health of my people?[b]
23 [9:1]   [a]O that my head were waters   (3+3)
    and my eye[b] a fountain of tears,
So that I might weep day and night   (3+3)
    for[c] the slain of my people.[d]

Notes

13.a-a. The exact translation of this passage is unsure; many emendations have been proposed to make sense of it; see Bright, 61. A common translation (so RSV) understands אָסֹף, "to gather," as the inf abs strengthening the verb סוּף, "to bring to an end," which was chosen for assonance even though it is from a different stem; see GKC, 113w, n. 3 and BDB, 692. The option chosen here and supported by LXX revocalizes אָסֹף=אָסֵף, "I gather" (see GKC, 68b), and understands אֲסִיפָם as a noun with the sense of "harvest." Compare to Zeph 1:2, 3.

13.b-b. This line, in its present form, makes little sense (lit., "I gave them, they shall pass over them"); alternate MS readings make little better sense (e.g., עֲבָדוּם, "and they serve them"; de Rossi, III, 75); the LXX omits it entirely. There is general agreement that the verse is corrupt in its present form. De Roche's argument that there is a word play on Gen 12:6–7 (וַיַּעֲבֹר אַבְרָם) is not particularly persuasive (*VT* 30 [1980] 280–90). A more convincing resolution of the problem is made by Aberbach (*VT* 27 [1977] 99–101), that the original text was יַעַר עֵרוֹם, "a forest stripped bare/naked forest," for which he provides a reasonable rationale in terms of the process by which composition took place.

14.a. Understanding דָּמַם as "to mourn or weep"; see Dahood, "Hebrew-Ugaritic Lexicography II," 402. Hacohen (*BMik* 27 [1981/82] 109–14) suggested it is related to the root דּוּם, meaning "to wait or remain" (see further *Comment*).

14.b. For this translation see Dahood, *Bib* 45 (1964) 402.

14.c. The LXX reads αὐτοῦ, "him."

15.a-a. This verse is paralleled in 14:19b.

15.b. Many MSS have the variant spelling מַרְפֵּא, like 14:19b.

17.a-a. Absent from LXX.

18.a-a. The Heb. in this phrase is untranslatable; all translations are based on speculation or emendation. The first word in the MT, מַבְלִיגִיתִי, is the most difficult. Texts from C and numerous other MSS read two words, מַבְלִי גִּיתִי; this reading is supported by the LXX. This phrase would then be translated "without healing" (from the root נגה). A second difficulty concerns the form עֲלֵי.

The most common emendation involves repointing עֲלַי, "upon me," presupposing the prep עַל "upon," but some suggest a verbal form from עלה, "go up"; so *BHS* and Holladay. The final difficulty involves the division of the verse. The LXX omits "Oracle of the Lord"; noting this, many connect מַבְלִי with the last phrase of v 17, resulting in "they shall bite you incurably"; so Volz, Rudolph, Bright, McKane. Usually, v 18 is broken at the *athnaḥ* and considered a bicolon, but Holladay analyzed the verse as a tricolon. The translation adopted here and by most ET accepts the word division מַבְלִי גִּיתִי and considers the verse a bicolon.

19.a. Lit., "Behold, a voice."

19.b. See note 11.a.

19.c. מֶרְחַקִּים occurs elsewhere only at Isa 33:17, where it has a similar meaning. Some translate this as "distant land," presupposing exile. Perhaps because of this, the emendations מֶרְחָבִים, "expanses" (see Hab 1:6), and מֶרְוָחִים, "spacious" (see 22:14), have been proposed, but they are not necessary.

19.d-d. Rudolph, Volz, Bright, and McKane, among others, take this as an insertion or at least a parenthesis, since it interrupts the flow of the passage and presupposes that Yahweh is the speaker. The phrase is attested in the versions and completes the rhetorical form הַ . . . . אִם . . . מַדּוּעַ found exclusively in Jeremiah (2:14, 31; 8:4–5, 19, 22; 14:19; 22:28; 49:1) and should be retained. See Baumgartner, *Klagegidichte*, 73; Reventlow, *Liturgie*, 195; Holladay, *VT* 12 (1962) 494–98; Held, "Rhetorical Questions," 71–79; but see McKane, 193–94; and Thiel, *Redaktion*, 135–36 for the opposite opinion.

21.a. See notes 11.a. and 19.b.

21.b. LXX and Syr omit. See note 21.c.

21.c. LXX adds ὠδῖνες ὡς τικτούσης = חִיל כַּיּוֹלֵדָה, "pain as a woman in travail"; cf. 6:24. MT rendering is preferred.

22.a. LXX and Syr omit כִּי. This form with either כִּי or מַדּוּעַ would mean the same thing; see Held, "Rhetorical Questions," 71–79; and van Selms, *Semitics* 2 (1971–72) 143–49.

22.b. See notes 11.a., 19.b., and 21.b.

23[9:1].a. On the form מִי־יִתֵּן expressing a wish contrary to fact, see Jongeling, "*my ytn*," *VT* 24 (1967) 34.

23[9:1].b. Many MSS and the versions read the more common dual here; the MT is the more difficult reading and is preferred.

23[9:1].c. Many MSS, supported by the Syr and Tg, read עַל, "upon"; the meaning is unaffected.

23[9:1].d. See note 11.a., etc.

Form/Structure/Setting

The composite nature of this section makes it difficult to determine the scope of the component parts and who is speaking in each of these sections. The two problems are intertwined and further complicated by problems of translation and interpretation; few if any commentators agree on all points. The solution offered here can be outlined as follows:

(i) V 13, a divine oracle of judgment, is connected mainly to what follows.

(ii) Vv 14–16 express the lament of the people in response to the previous announcement of judgment.

(iii) V 17, another divine oracle of judgment, prefaces the following lament of Jeremiah.

(iv) Vv 18–23 [9:1] are a lament by Jeremiah concerning the coming judgment.

The problems of translation have compounded the difficulties of understanding v 13 (see *Notes*). Many commentators (e.g., Duhm; Reventlow, *Liturgie*, 190; Hyatt; Holladay) would connect v 13 to the preceding verses, understanding the oracle as continuing the judgment proclaimed in 10–12. The originally independent nature of v 13 is hard to deny. The independence of the preceding verses (10–12) is established by their parallel in 6:12–15; the independence of the following verses is signaled by the obvious change of speaker and tone beginning with v 14. These observations led many to consider the verse as independent and unrelated to its immediate context (so Volz, Carroll, McKane). Simply identifying the independent nature of the verse does not explain why it is included in this passage. We conclude here that this oracle of judgment gives the basis for the following lament (compare Bright).

The word "gather" (אָסֹף) links v 14 to v 13. The speaker in v 16 can be construed to be either God or the people, depending upon how the word נִשְׁמַע is parsed. The different versions reflect this ambiguity. The Vulgate and Syriac understand it to be a niphal perfect third person masculine singular, resulting in the translation "is heard." The other possibility, followed here and assumed by the LXX, reads qal imperfect first person masculine plural, making the translation "we hear." Understanding the verb as first person allows us to link it with the preceding verses of lament.

The connection of v 17, a divine oracle of judgment, to the surrounding verses is largely a matter of interpretation. Very early the obscure מֵי־רֹאשׁ of 8:14 (literally either "bad water" or "water of the head," translated here "tears") was understood to refer to snake venom and was associated with the snakes and adders of this verse; compare the Targums and Rashi. Reventlow (*Liturgie*, 139) suggested a word play of צִפְעֹנִים, "adder," with צָפוֹן, "north," since the preceding verse made allusion to the "enemy from the north" tradition. The position taken here is that this verse is intended as an oracle of judgment to give the context for both the preceding and following laments (see further *Comment*).

The final subsection (18–23 [9:1]) is a lament by Jeremiah in response to the coming judgment. This lament parallels the preceding divine oracle and the lament by the people. The idea of harvest is present in vv 13 and 20. The idea of weeping can be found in vv 14 and 23 [9:1]. The two direct parallels are מִי־רֹאשׁ, "water of the head," in v 14 and רֹאשִׁי מִים, "my head were waters," in v 23 [9:1] and the word "to heal" in vv 15 and 22 (see Holladay, I, 288–89).

These verses reflect approaching invasion. The connection to the "enemy from the north" tradition in v 16 suggests a time shortly after 609 B.C. Both vv 13 and 19 suggest harvest time, perhaps an autumn feast (see *Comment*).

Comment

13 De Roche's attempt (*VT* 30 [1980] 280–90) to interpret this verse as proclaiming the reversal of the promises of creation, covenant, and conquest draws too much on obscure parallels with other passages. The image of harvesting as used in this verse depicts the Lord as coming to his vineyard to harvest the fruit but finding it bare. The image of Israel as a vineyard is found many places in Jeremiah (2:21; 5:10; 6:9) as well as elsewhere in the OT and may be behind the image as used in the NT (cf. especially Luke 13:6–9).

14 The difficulty of translating מִי־רֹאשׁ, "waters of the head," has occasioned many diverse interpretations of this verse. Perhaps the earliest is the interpretation that understands מִי־רֹאשׁ as snake venom in relation to v 17 (reflected in the Targums). Duhm, followed by Rudolph, associates it with the trial by ordeal recorded in Num 5:11–31. McKane associates it with the cup of God's wrath mentioned in Jer 25:15 (see McKane, *VT* 38 [1980] 474–92). The interpretation offered here follows the translation suggested by Dahood (see *Notes*). The idea of weeping fits the context well and allows מִי־רֹאשׁ to be understood as "tears," especially in relation to רֹאשִׁי מִים, "my head were waters," in v 23 [9:1]. The verse can then be understood as a call to mourning.

15 This verse gives the reason for the call to mourning in the previous verse. The people had listened to the promises of peace from the cultic prophets (see *Comment* on 6:12–15), but they had turned out to be false; the threat of invasion is now impossible to ignore.

16 Allusions to the "enemy from the north" (cf. B. S. Childs, "The Enemy from the North and the Chaos Tradition," *JBL* [1978] 187–98), coupled with the allusion to the promises of peace from the cultic prophets in the previous verse, make it clear that the reason for the lament is a threatened invasion.

17 Are the snakes in this oracle to be understood as real snakes (so Volz, Carroll) or as metaphorical of the approaching enemy (so Kimchi, Duhm, Rudolph, McKane)? Two points favor the latter interpretation. Often the reality of the snakes is supported by the understanding of מִי־רֹאשׁ in v 14 in the sense of "snake venom," which is almost universally recognized as wrong (see Holladay for the arguments). Further, the context favors the image of invasion, which would support the metaphorical understanding.

18 This verse begins a lament by Jeremiah over the coming invasion. Some commentators (e.g., Hyatt, Rudolph) have suggested that this lament was a response to some other catastrophe such as famine. The context, however, favors invasion. Compare how a lament also follows the oracle concerning the "foe from the north" in chap. 4.

19–20 As an explanation of his sorrow, Jeremiah offers quotes from the people. "Is the LORD not in Zion? Is her King not in her?" McKane is probably correct that these questions and the following verse have as their background the Autumn New Year Festival when the Lord was enthroned as the King of Jerusalem. The approaching invasion calls the inviolability of Zion into question. The response to the questions makes it clear that the real problem is not the absence of God from Jerusalem but the sin of the people.

21–23 [9:1] Because of the suffering coming upon his people, Jeremiah is gripped with dismay. Once again Jeremiah uses rhetorical questions to express the irony and pathos of the situation as he asks: "Is there no balm in Gilead? Is there no healer there?" The natural answer to these questions would have to be yes but the reality of the situation demands that Jeremiah answer no. The situation elicits weeping and profound sorrow from Jeremiah.

Explanation

Jer 8:4–12 described the almost unheard-of situation of a people perpetually apostate. In these verses we have the response of both the people and Jeremiah to this situation. These verses are written in the shadow of the Babylonian invasion. The people seem unaware of the reason for their punishment and are resigned to their fate. They are content to retreat to their fortified cities and weep over their losses (8:14). They feel they have trusted God to no avail, for the sounds of defeat are closing in upon them (8:15–16). Jeremiah also weeps over the situation. He weeps not just because of the calamity coming upon the people but mainly because of their blindness (8:19–21). They seem oblivious to their sin and attempt to lay all blame upon God. Jeremiah cannot understand why their blindness is incurable (8:22), why they cannot perceive their own sinfulness. The hopelessness of the situation overwhelms him. His heart is broken, and he weeps bitterly.

The NT records an amazingly similar situation involving Jesus and the people of Jerusalem. At the end of his public ministry, we find Jesus approaching Jerusalem for the last time. "And when he drew near and saw the city he wept over it, saying, 'Would that you knew the things that make for peace! But they are hid from your eyes. For the days shall come upon you, when your enemies will cast up a bank about you, and hem you in on every side, and dash you to the ground, you and your children within you, and they will not leave one stone upon another in you; because you did not know the time of your visitation.'" (Luke 19:41–44)

C. The Sorrow of God (9:1–10)

Bibliography

Ben-Corre, A. D. *The Daughter of my People: Arabic and Hebrew Paraphrases of Jeremiah 8:13–9:23.* Leiden: Brill, 1971. **Ben-Reuven, S.** "Buying Mandrakes as Retribution for Buying the

Birthright." *BMik* 28 (1982/83) 230–31. **Berridge, J. M.** *Prophet, People.* 173–76. **Brueggemann, W.** "Jeremiah's Use of Rhetorical Question." *JBL* 92 (1973) 358–74. **Jongeling, B.** "L'expression *my ytn* dans l'Ancien Testament." *VT* 24 (1967) 32–40. **Nötscher, F.** "Zum emphatischen Lamed." *VT* 3 (1953) 372–80. **Overholt, T. W.** *The Threat of Falsehood.* 82–83. **Smith, M. A.** "Jeremiah ix 9—A Divine Lament." *VT* 37 (1987) 97–99. **Snaith, H.** "The Verbs *zābaḥ* and *sāḥaṭ*." *VT* 25 (1975) 242–46. **Soggin, A.** "*Leʾemûnāh* (Jeremiah 9, 2): Emphatic Lamed?" In *Old Testament and Oriental Studies.* BibOr 29. Rome: Biblical Institute Press, 1975.

Translation

1 [2]	a *"O that I had in the wilderness*	(2+2)
	b *a wanderer's dwelling,*b	
	So that I could leave my people,	(2+2)
	and walk away from them;	
	For they are all adulterers,	(3+2)
	a band of traitors.	
2 [3]	*They bend*a *their tongue,*	(2+2)
	*their bow*b *is falsehood,*	
	*and not because of*c *truth*	(2+2)
	*have they prevailed*d *in the land;*	
	for from evil to evil they proceed,	(4+2)
	*and they do not know me."*e	
	f*The LORD's oracle.*f	
3 [4]	*"Beware of your neighbor,*	(3+2)
	and put no trust in any brother;	
	for every brother is a supplanter,	(4+3)
	and every neighbor goes about slandering.	
4 [5]	*Every one deceives his neighbor,*	(3+3)
	they do not speak the truth;	
	they have taught their tongues to speak lies;	(3+2)
	a*being perverted, they are too weak to change.*a,b	
5 [6]	*Oppression*a *upon oppression,*	(2+2+2)
	deceit upon deceit;	
	*they refuse to know me.*b*"*	
	c*The LORD's oracle.*c	
6 [7]	*Therefore, thus says the LORD of Hosts:*	
	"Behold, I will refine them and assay them,	(3+4)
	a*For what else can I do because of my*b *people?*a	
7 [8]	*Their tongue is a deadly*a *arrow,*	(3+3)
	*Deceitful*b *are the words of their mouth;*b	
	Each speaks peace with his neighbor,	(3+3)
	while planning an ambush in his heart.	
8 [9]	*Should I not punish such a nation?"*a	(2+3+3)
	The LORD's oracle.	
	*"On*b *a nation such as this,*	
	Should I not avenge myself?	
9 [10]	*Over the mountains I will weep*a b*and wail,*b	(4+3)
	over the pastures of the wilderness I will lament;	

> For they are laid waste[c] so no one passes through,　(4+4)
> 　nor do they hear the sound of cattle;
> From the birds of heaven to the beasts,　(3+2)
> 　they have fled, have gone.
> 10 [11] I will make Jerusalem into ruins,　(3+2)
> 　a lair of jackals;[a]
> And the cities of Judah, I will make　(4+2)
> 　a desolation, without[b] inhabitants."

Notes

1.a. The numbers in brackets are the Eng. verse numbers (MT 9:1–25=ET 9:2–26). We will follow the Heb. versification in the following.

1.b-b. Instead of מלון ארחים, "a wanderer's dwelling," LXX reads σταθμὸν ἔσχατον = מלון אהרון, "a most distant lodge." With no support from the versions, stay with the MT.

2.a. This verse has provoked many emendations, many based upon understanding Jeremiah as the speaker (see following notes). Holladay, II, 296–97, has argued persuasively that the only emendation needed is to change the pointing of this verb from hiph to qal (וַיַּדְרְכוּ to וַיִּדְרְכוּ); see GKC § 53n. Holladay's translation is followed here.

2.b. The first common emendation, supported by the LXX, is to ignore the suff and attach this word to the previous phrase. The translation would then be "They bend their tongue like a bow."

2.c. The second emendation, supported by LXX, is to drop the prep, but see Notscher, VT 3 [1953] 380, and Soggin, "Le'emûnāh (Jeremiah 9, 2): Emphatic Lamed?" in BibOr 29. See next note for translation.

2.d. The third emendation, supported by the LXX, changes the 3 pl verb to 3 sg (גברו to גברה), changing the subj from the people to "falsehood and not truth." The translation resulting from the last two emendations is "falsehood, and not truth, prevails in the land."

2.e. Many suppose ואתי, "and me," is an abbreviation of ואת יהוה, "and the Lord," changing the obj from "me" to "the Lord," and the speaker from the Lord to Jeremiah. The translation would then be "They do not know the Lord."

2.f-f. LXX omits.

4.a-a. This colon makes little sense in Heb. The most common emendation, supported by the LXX, is followed here; see next note. In contrast to GKC § 113d, העוה, "being perverted," should not be understood as an obj.

4.b. The first word of the next verse was divided and split between this verse and the next, reading שב: תך, "to change. Oppression. . . ."

5.a. This presupposes the emendation in the previous note.

5.b. Many read אותי, "me," as the contraction את־יהוה, "the Lord," so as to preserve Jeremiah as the speaker; cf. note 2.e.

5.c-c. LXX omits.

6.a-a. The MT text is questionable as can be seen in the versions. Syr is the only major version which follows the MT. The most common emendation of the text, reflected in the LXX and Tg, reads רעתם, "their evils," in place of בת־עמי, "my people," giving a translation like, "What else can I do because of their evils?" This emendation is followed by Volz, Rudolph, and Bright. Holladay proposed extensive emendations, reading איד, "calamity," for איך, "oppression"; בתה, "fury," for בת, "daughter of"; and revocalizing מפני, "my presence"; but these do not really change the sense of the passage.

6.b. See note 8:11.a., etc.

7.a. Following the K (שוהט) which is supported by the LXX, Syr, and Vg. The Q (שחוט, "sharpened") is supported by many MSS (e.g., 4Q Jer[a]) as well as the Syr and Tg. See further Snaith (VT 25 [1975] 242–46).

7.b-b. Lit., "he speaks with his mouth." The sg breaks the symmetry of this verse, causing suggestions that this phrase is out of place. The emendation followed here (reading דברי פיהם) causes little disruption of the text and preserves the symmetry.

8.a. Cf. 5:9, 29.

8.b. Some MSS read ואם, "and if."

9.a. LXX and Syr read pl impv שאו. The MT is preferred.

9.b-b. LXX omits.

9.c. Root צדה. A few MSS read נצתו, "are destroyed" (root נתץ). LXX, Syr, and the Tg suggest a form from נצה, "are deserted, desolate." All roots have virtually synonymous meanings.

10.a. Cf. 51:37.

10.b. Many MSS read the synonymous מאין.

Form/Structure/Setting

The major interpretive issue in this passage is determining who is speaking. Most recent commentators have understood Jeremiah as the speaker in at least the first five verses (e.g., Rudolph, Bright, McKane; Holladay is the notable exception). In order to do this most have deleted "The LORD's oracle" in vv 2 and 6 (supported by LXX) and have read "the LORD" in place of "me" in the phrases "me they have not known/they refuse to know" (see notes 2.e.; 2.f-f.; 5.b.; 5.c-c.). Some have also omitted "Therefore, thus says the LORD of Hosts" in v 6. According to these commentators the problem with God being the speaker is the anthropocentric viewpoint of the verses. For instance, why would God want to leave his people (v 1)? The text as it stands, however, clearly intends God as the speaker. On the basis of other places in the book of Jeremiah which contain a first person lament by God preceded by a lament of Jeremiah (e.g., 12:7–13 and 15:5–9), we can understand this passage as a divine lament with accompanying oracles (compare Smith, "Jeremiah IX 9—A Divine Lament," *VT* 37 [1987] 97–99).

On the basis of the superscriptions and changes of direction, the passage can be broken into four parts and analyzed as follows.

1–2	Divine Lament
3–5	Oracle about tongue
6–8	Oracle about tongue
9–10	Divine Lament

The chiastic structure is confirmed by the use of "wilderness" (מדבר) in vv 1 and 10, by God wishing to leave his people in v 1, and by his threatening to drive them away in v 10. This chiastic structure is only one device holding the passage together. Holladay, I, 298, has noted the similar manner in which vv 1–2 and 3–5 end, connecting the first and second subsections: both end with the form X-preposition-X (evil to evil; deceit upon deceit) followed by "they do not/refuse to know me" and the superscription, "The LORD's oracle." The use of military language to describe the sins of the tongue in vv 2 and 7 ties the first and third subsections.

The connections of this passage to its context are numerous (see *Comment* for further examples). The first verse, 9:1, is connected to 8:23 by מי־יתן. Many commentators (e.g., McKane, Holladay) consider this merely a catchword link, but the structure found elsewhere in the Book of Jeremiah, of a lament by Jeremiah followed by divine lament (see above), suggests the connection may be more than a mere catchword. A second connection of this section to the larger context can be found in the close parallel of v 8 and 5:9, 29 (see *Introduction*). The connection of the last two verses of this section (9–10) to vv 16–21, noted by many commentators (e.g., Volz, Rudolph), links this section with the following verses.

The setting for this passage is not apparent from internal evidence, but on the basis of the larger context we can assume that these oracles address either the latter years of Josiah's reign or the early years of Jehoiakim's reign.

Comment

1   As the lament by Jeremiah concluded with a contrary-to-fact wish, so this divine lament begins with a contrary-to-fact wish. The almost unthinkable idea that God would wish to leave his people and retire to the wilderness is shocking and emphasizes the gravity of the situation. The grammatical form of the wish, however, makes it clear that God has not already left his people; see Jongeling, *VT* 24 [1967] 32–40. This wish is even more shocking in comparison to 8:19, which expresses the people's fear that God has left them ("Is the LORD not in Zion? Is her King not in her?"). Because of the people's sin, their worst fear has become the fantasy of God.

2   The many proposed emendations of v 2 (see *Notes*) reflect various ways of understanding the verse. The difficulties are reflected not only in modern translations but also in the LXX and Targums, Rabbinic commentaries (see Kimchi) and present-day commentaries (e.g., Rudolph). Recognizing these difficulties, the understanding of the verse proposed here makes as few emendations of the MT as possible. The verse reflects God's revulsion at the sin of the people, particularly as manifested in their speech. The tongue is described as a deadly weapon. This military imagery is also reflected in "prevailed" (גברו) and perhaps "go out" (יצאו) (Holladay). The word *falsehood* (שקר) is common throughout Jeremiah and probably has wider allusions (see Overholt, *The Threat of Falsehood*, 82–83).

3   This verse reflects civil unrest at its worst. There is no trust even among brothers. Every social encounter is a trap. Social disintegration is reflected throughout society, both in the narrow circle of family as well as the wider circle of communal relationships (Calvin). The image of "Jacob the cheat" is drawn upon to describe the social decay (see Gen 27). The people are described as "going about slandering" in the last phrase of the verse, reminiscent of 6:28. The idea (also found in 6:28) is used in this verse as well as the first verse of the next subsection (v 6).

4   The very bases of society, trust and truth, have been corrupted. The people intentionally do wrong; they "teach" their tongues to speak falsely. The deliberateness of the people's evil can be found also in 4:22 and 6:7 (Holladay). The people's addiction to evil has robbed them of the moral or spiritual strength to change.

5   Instead of turning from their sin, the people heap sin upon sin and answer deceit with deceit. Holladay has suggested that "deceit" (מרמה) may reflect the Jacob tradition alluded to in v 3 (see Gen 27:35; 34:13). God laments that even though the people have studied evil "they refuse to *know* me" (cf. 5:3; 8:5).

6   In response to the sin of the people, God declares that he will refine them like metal (cf. 6:27–30). The last phrase of this verse has been understood as either a question or an exclamation. At the very least it expresses God's exasperation and perplexity with his people. This expression of exasperation is akin to the wish in v 1.

7   Once again the deadly nature of the people's words is expressed with military imagery: "their tongues are deadly arrows." As the prophets had deceived the people by proclaiming "peace" when attack was close at hand (see 8:11, 15), so the people were deceiving each other.

8   Brueggemann (*JBL* 92 [1973] 358–74) suggested that v 8 answered the question of v 6. The parallels between the structure of this passage and 5:7–9 and 5:20–29 confirm this. All three passages begin with a question expressing God's exasperation with the people, and the previous passages end with a verse almost identical to v 8.

9 Verse 9 begins the final section of the divine lament. The image presented appears to be of invasion and captivity, prompting many commentators to question whether this and the following verse come from a period after the captivity (e.g., Carroll). Smith (*VT* 37 [1987] 97–99) has suggested, on the basis of parallels with Mesopotamian and Ugaritic literary traditions, that God mourns "in the wilderness" and that this is for the loss of his beloved people. This fits well with the pathos expressed in the wish of v 1 and the agonizing question of v 6; God loves his people and goes to the wilderness to mourn their loss.

10 Because of the unrepentant nature of the people, the only alternative left to God is to bring destruction upon the people. They are addicted to evil and unable and unwilling to repent. But instead of God leaving Jerusalem and fleeing to the wilderness (v 1), he will make Jerusalem a wilderness, devoid of people. Perhaps it is in Jerusalem, soon to be a wilderness without sound, that God will mourn for the loss of his people.

Explanation

The concept of a God who suffers is rejected by many because it implies that he is weak and finite. The impossibility of God suffering is a central teaching in some of the great world religions and is even advocated in some Christian circles. However, the notion of a God who cannot suffer, while perhaps making theology more manageable, nevertheless leaves it placid and spiritless. If the love of God is more than an empty metaphor, then the suffering of God must also be regarded as real.

This passage has traditionally been emended in such a way as to make the prophet and not God the sufferer. It seems best, however, to leave the text as it is and to interpret it as the response of God to the unyielding stubbornness of his people.

The grief of God is caused not only by what the people have done to him but more especially by what they have done to each other. They have used their tongues as weapons of war, sacrificing truth and destroying trust, the foundations upon which community must be built. They are so deeply enmeshed in evil that they lack the will to repent. Their evil affects even the natural environment around them (v 9 [10]; cf. 4:24–26). Their rebellion, like that of Adam in Eden, has corrupted their relationship to God, to each other, and to the world around them. God grieves that he must take vengeance on them, even though his ultimate purpose is not to destroy them but to refine and purify them.

D. The Rationale of Judgment (9:11–15)

Bibliography

Bronznick, N. M. "*kî riṣṣaṣ ʿāzab dallîm* (Job 20:19)." *BMik* 27 (1981/82) 220–28. **Castellino, G. R.** "Observations on the Literary Structure of Some Passages in Jeremiah." *VT* 30 (1980)

398–408. **Cazelles, H.** "Jeremiah and Deuteronomy." In *A Prophet to the Nations.* 89–112.
Long, B. O. "Two Question and Answer Schemata in the Prophets." *JBL* 90 (1971) 129–39.
McKane, W. "Poison Trial by Ordeal and the Cup of Wrath." *VT* 30 (1980) 474–92.
Oosterhoff, B. J. "Ein Detail aus der Weisheitslehre (Jer. 9, 11ff.)." In *Travels in the World of the Old Testament.* Ed. M. S. H. G. Herrma van Voos. Assen: Van Gorcum, 1974.

Translation

11 [12] *Who is the man who is wise enough to explain*[a] *this? And to whom has the mouth of* GOD *spoken, that he should declare it?*
    Why is the land ruined,
        and laid waste like a wilderness that no one passes through?
12 [13] *And the* LORD *said,*[a] *"Because they have abandoned my law which I set before them and have not listened to my voice,* [b] *nor walked in accordance with it,*[b] 13 [14] *but have walked after the stubbornness of their own hearts,*[a] *going after the Baals, as their fathers taught them."* 14 [15] *Therefore, thus says the* LORD *of Hosts, the God of Israel,*
    "Behold, I will feed [a] *this people*[a] *wormwood*
        and give them poisonous water to drink.
15 [16] *I will scatter them among the nations whom neither they nor their fathers have known*[a] *and I will send the sword after them until I have consumed them."*

Notes

The numbers in brackets are the Eng. version verse numbers. The Heb. versification is followed here.
    11.a. Reading as a hiph on the basis of context (so Rudolph). It is often read as a qal = "understand."
    12.a. LXX adds "to me" (πρός με).
    12.b-b. LXX omits. Does "it" refer to "law" or "voice"? Janzen, *Studies* 38, argued that "it" refers to "law," and classified this phrase as an expansionist gloss.
    13.a. A few MSS, LXX, and Syr add הרע, "evil." The addition makes no change in meaning.
    14.a-a. LXX omits. Compare to 23:15.
    15.a. A few MSS read ידעום, "known them." The suff is unnecessary and does not affect the meaning.

Form/Structure/Setting

Jer 9:11–15 has often been classified as a late addition coming from the hand of a Deuteronomistic editor; see especially Thiel, *Die deuteronomistiche Redaktion,* 136–38. The basis for this classification is usually the presence of Deuteronomistic language and emphasis in v 12. The emphasis upon the law and the opposition to idolatry are most often cited. However, the matter is not so easily decided. Long (*JBL* 90 [1971] 129–39) classified it as of a mixed scheme, for though he suspected it to be Deuteronomic, he was not willing to classify it as completely Deuteronomistic. The presence of Deuteronomistic language and emphases may be simply one more indication that Jeremiah was sympathetic with the Deuteronomic reform; cf. Cazelles, "Jeremiah and Deuteronomy." Castellino (*VT* 30 [1980] 398–408) included this passage with others in which he attempted to outline a regular literary pattern. He concluded that this passage is the middle section, "intermezzo," of a larger literary unit extending from 9:9 to 9:21. What many commentators (e.g., Rudolph, McKane) consider as evidence that 11–15 constitutes a latter expansion on vv 9–10 (see *Comment* below), Castellino considered part of the regular structure he outlined. Holladay concluded, on the basis of formal parallels with Hos 14:10 and Ps 107:43, that this passage was secondary and late (post-exilic). His parallels, however, are not that close: Hos 14:10 and Ps 107:43 have much more in common with each other than with Jer 9:11–13.

The passage is usually considered prose (so RSV, McKane). The above translation reflects an understanding of 11b and 14b as poetry. Both of these fragments are quotes of poetic material; see further *Comment*.

The setting of the passage is dependent upon whether or not these verses are considered a secondary addition. It is assumed here that they are integral to the Book of Jeremiah. The references to the Deuteronomic reform would place the passage sometime after the reform. The passage reflects invasion (v 11–13), but exile is projected into the future (v 12–15). The date assigned the passage depends upon whether the invasion was already happening or being proleptically experienced by the prophet.

Comment

11 The syntax of this verse is difficult and open to various interpretations. The difficulty is reflected in the various English translations; compare RSV, NEB, and JB, see further Oosterhoff, "Ein Detail." The above translation understands the second clause as a subordinate result clause; thus "Who is the man who is wise enough to explain this?" The two clauses parallel one another and refer to the wise man and the prophet respectively (so McKane). The verse claims that the wise man has been unable to explain the disaster and the prophet has not received a word from God to explain it. The concluding question reflects the latter part of v 9.

12 The answer to the question from the previous verse, "Why is the land ruined, and laid waste like a wilderness that no one passes through," is found here couched in the form of an oracle. The answer is the failure of the people to follow the law. The emphasis upon the wise and the law has been taken by many as proof of Deuteronomic influence (so Thiel, *Die deuteronomistiche Redaktion*), but the wise are also associated with the law in 8:8. The people are described as "abandoning" (עזבם) the law; cf. 8:9, see further Bronznick, *BMik* 27 (1981/82) 220–28. "Abandon" is often used in connection with idolatry; see 5:19, 16:11, 22:9.

13 The people have abandoned God's law and in the stubbornness of their hearts have chosen to follow the Baals (cf. 12:16). Their rebellion resulted in the destruction of their land. The destruction should be understood in the context of the curses pronounced in Deuteronomy against those who fail to follow the law. "Stubbornness" (שררות), found almost exclusively in Jeremiah, is also found in Deut 29:18, which describes the curses on those who reject the law (cf. also Ps 81:13).

14 The nature of the curse along with the references to wormwood and bitter water has occasioned much debate (see McKane, *VT* 30 [1980] 474–92; cf. 8:14 and 23:15). "Wormwood" (לענה) is found eight times in the OT, including Deut 29:17. In light of the connection of the previous verse to Deut 29, perhaps the wormwood is the result of the people's idolatry.

15   The judgment does not end with the destruction of the land; it will only end when the people are uprooted from their land and exiled in a land which they do not know (cf. 5:15). In v 13 the people are condemned for following the Baals "as their fathers taught them" and now they will be exiled in a land "their fathers do not know."

Explanation

Why must judgment fall upon the people of God? Jeremiah's answer could be summed up in one Hebrew word: שְׁרִירוּת, usually translated "stubbornness." Except for two references in Deuteronomy 29:18 and Ps 81:13, usage of this word is restricted to the Book of Jeremiah (cf. 3:17; 7:24; 9:13; 11:8; 13:10; 16:12; 18:12; 23:17). It involves a defiant attitude toward the Lord, a rejection of his law, a preference for other gods, and a refusal to repent.

The threat of "stubbornness" still exists today. It has been described as "atrophy of the will." When people stubbornly refuse to do right, the time comes when they cannot do right. Judgment then comes in the form of living in the prison you have erected for yourself.

E. A Call to Lament (9:16–21)

Bibliography

Cassuto, U. "The Palace of Baal in Tablet II AB of Ras Shamra." In *Biblical and Oriental Studies II.* Jerusalem: Hebrew University, 1975. 113–34. **Castellino, G. R.** "Observations on the Literary Structure of Some Passages in Jeremiah." *VT* 30 (1980) 398–408. **Paul, S. M.** "Cuneiform Light on Jer. 9, 20." *Bib* 49 (1968) 373–76. **Pohl, A.** "Miszellen, 3: Jeremias 9, 20." *Or* 22 (1941) 36–37. **Pope, M. H.** "Mot." IDBSup. 607–8.

Translation

16 [17]a *Thus says the LORD of Hosts,*[a][b] *"Consider this.*[b]

   Call for the mourning women to come,   (3+2)
      send for the skilled women;

17 [18] a*Let them come and make haste,*[a]   (2+3)
      and raise over us a wailing;

   until our eyes run down with tears   (3+2)
      and our eyelids gush with water.

18 [19] *For a sound of wailing*   (3+2)
      is heard from Zion: [a]

   'How we are ruined;   (2+2)
      how utterly ashamed,

   because we have abandoned our land,   (2+3)
      because[b] *they have cast down*[c] *our dwellings.'*

19 [20] *Hear, O women, the word of the LORD,*   (3+3)
    let your ear receive the word of his mouth.
And teach to your daughters a lament,   (3+3)
    and each to her neighbor a dirge.
20 [21] *'Death has come up into our windows;*   (3+2)
    it has entered our palaces,[a]
Cutting off the children from the street   (3+2)
    and the young men from the squares.'
21 [22] *Speak,*[a] [b] *'Thus says the LORD:*[b]
    The dead bodies of men shall fall[c]   (3+3)
    like dung[d] *on the open field,*[e]
    like sheaves behind the reaper,   (3+2)
    which none gather.'"

Notes

The numbers in brackets are the Eng. verse numbers (MT 9:16–21 = ET 9:17–22). The Heb. versification is followed here.

16.a-a. Many commentators omit this phrase. The LXX has λέγει κύριος, "The LORD said."

16.b-b. This word is absent from LXX and Syr.

17.a-a. This phrase is absent from the LXX and Syr. In the MT, "Let them come" is part of v 16. It is placed at the beginning of v 17 here because of meter; compare *BHS*. The LXX reads καὶ φθεγξάσθωσαν, "and let them speak out." The MT is followed here, but the LXX tradition makes equally good sense.

18.a. Some MSS and LXX read בציון, "in Zion." The meaning is not altered.

18.b. Many MSS read וכי, "and because." LXX and Syr read simply ו, "and."

18.c. The Vg and Tg understand this as an impersonal, "our dwellings have been cast down." The LXX has a 1c pl (השלכנו), "we have cast down." Rudolph suggested reading a hoph (הָשְׁלְכְנוּ מִן), "we have been cast from our dwellings." No reading substantially changes the meaning.

20.a. The LXX reads εἰς τὴν γῆν ἡμῶν = באדמתנו, "into our land."

21.a. Absent from the major LXX MSS and Syr. The Gk. texts of Origen, Lucian, and Theodotion read θανάτῳ = דבר, "pestilence."

21.b-b. Absent from LXX.

21.c. LXX reads ἔσονται, "shall be."

21.d. LXX reads εἰς παράδειγμα, "for an example" (cf. Duhm, Volz, Rudolph); cf. 2 Kgs 9:37.

21.e. Many MSS and LXX read האדמה, "the land"; cf. note 20.a.

Form/Structure/Setting

This passage is comparable in form to a lament; indeed the lament meter dominates. The superscription places it in the context of the divine oracle. A major interpretive issue is the extent of the quotations throughout the passage. Most commentators and translators consider the latter part of v 18 a quote, but here the agreement ends. The interpretation of כי in vv 18, 19, and 20 is crucial. The three occurrences of כי in v 18 should be translated as conjunctions "For . . . , because . . . , because . . ." The כי at the beginning of v 19 resumes the second imperative of v 16, "Call the mourning women" (וקראו); it does not appear in the translation. The כי at the beginning of v 20 introduces direct narration and therefore also does not appear in the translation; see BDB, 471 I.1.b.

The passage breaks down easily into two sections 16–18 and 19–21 (cf. Condamin and Holladay). Many interpreters have overlooked the different audiences addressed in these two sections. The commands in the first section are masculine and concern the call for the mourning women. The commands in the second section are feminine and addressed to the mourning women; this is confirmed by the unique feminine "Hear the word of the LORD" in v 19. The final verse, beginning with a second person masculine singular command, is addressed to Jeremiah. Following this analysis the passage can be outlined as follows.

16–17	God's command to call the mourning women.
18	The reason for calling the women.
19	God's command to the mourning women.
20	The dirge to be used by the women.
21	An oracle to be spoken by Jeremiah.

This analysis makes good sense of the MT as it stands, without resorting to emendation or deletion; see further comment on specific verses.

This passage, like the surrounding passages, probably originated on the eve of the siege and deportation of 598/7 B.C. The invasion approaches and Jeremiah can see no hope—it is a time for the mourning.

Comment

16   In response to the preceding pronouncements of judgment the people are instructed to call the professional mourning women to raise a dirge. The appeal for repentance is past; the end has come. This is the only place in the OT that "mourning women" (מְקוֹנְנוֹת) is used and, according to Holladay, the only reference in the OT to professional mourning women (see further E. Jacob, "Mourning," IDB, 3:453–54).

17   The women are commanded to come and raise a great mourning until the people are overcome with grief. The language used to describe the grief is reminiscent of that used in 8:23 [9:1]. Perhaps professional mourners like those mentioned here are implied in the saying of Jesus, "We piped to you, and you did not dance; we wailed, and you did not mourn" (Matt 11:17, RSV).

18   The mourning women are called to add their voices to those from Zion. In the Book of Jeremiah Zion is primarily the dwelling place of God (see e.g., 8:19). The word of lamentation comes because the people have had to "abandon" (עזב) the land. Did they have to "abandon" Zion, God's dwelling place, because they had "abandoned" God's law (see 9:12)?

19   The people had earlier been instructed to call the mourning women (v 16), and in this verse comes God's instruction to the mourning women to lament. The instruction to the women to call their daughters and friends to join them in the lament emphasizes the gravity of the situation.

20   The women's dirge, recorded in this verse, describes how death had invaded all areas of the city; it had invaded the houses of the people and had entered the palaces so that no place was safe. The children would be cut down in the streets and the young men in the squares. This verse has occasioned much debate because of a proposed connection with the Baal epic and the god of death, Môt. Shalom M. Paul (*Bib* 49 [1968] 373–76) has argued persuasively that the proposed connection is not correct. He also rejected some proposed textual emendations based upon the connection. He suggested a better parallel to the

Babylonian demon Lamastu, who preys on children and pregnant women, entering their houses through windows and the cracks around the doors. No parallel is necessary to understand the horror of the image. Death invades the city, filling all its dwellings.

21 In response to the dirge and as a complement to the dirge, Jeremiah is commanded to proclaim an oracle. With graphic language—language so graphic the LXX consistently altered it (see note 21.d.)—the oracle describes the coming destruction. The dead will be so numerous that their bodies will be flung out on the open field like stinking dung. Their bodies will be left in the field to rot like worthless stalks left behind by the reapers.

Explanation

Skinner (*Prophecy and Religion*, 124) called this "perhaps the most brilliant example of the prophetic elegy which the Old Testament contains." For the forcefulness of its language, it should be compared with the shorter elegy in 31:15, where the mother of Israel weeps for her children, refusing to be comforted because they are no more.

War is cruel not only to those who become battlefield casualties but also to those who are left behind to grieve their loss. More often than not these are women—wives, as well as mothers. The scene is reenacted over and over again on our television screens. Black-robed women stand beside open graves in the not-so-holy land, lifting clenched hands toward heaven or beating upon their breasts. What else can they do when the men they love lie dead before them? Why must women always bear an unequal share of the world's sorrow? Why must they teach their own daughters to lament? Why must Rachel grieve over her departed children? Why must Mary weep alone at the cross?

F. Judgment upon All (9:22–25)

Bibliography

Brueggemann, W. A. "The Epistemological Crisis of Israel's Two Histories (Jer. 9:22–23)." In *Israelite Wisdom*. Ed. J. G. Gammie et al. Missoula, MT: Scholars Press, 1978. 85–105. **Kutsch, E.** "Weisheitsspruch und Prophetenwort: zur Traditionsgeschichte des Spruches Jer. 9, 22–23." *BZ* 25 (1981) 161–79. **Rusche, H.** "Zum «jeremiahischen» Hintergrund der Korintherbriefe." *BZ* 31 (1937) 116–19. **Schreiner, J.** "Jeremia 9, 22–23 als Hintergrund des paulinischen 'Sich-Ruhmen.'" In *Neues Testament und Kirche, Fur Rudolf Schnackenburg*. Ed. J. Gnilka. Freiburg: Herder, 1974. 530–42.

Translation

22 [23] *Thus says the LORD:*
    "Let not the wise man glory in his wisdom,
      and let not the mighty man glory in his might,

(3+3+3)

> ^a*let not the rich man glory in his riches.*
> ^{23 [24]} *But let him who glories glory in this:*   (4+3)
>   *that he has understanding and knows me,*
>   *that I am the LORD*   (3+2)
>   *who practices steadfast love,*
>   ^a*justice, and righteousness on the earth;*   (3+2)
>   *for in these things I delight."*
>   *The LORD's oracle.*

^{24 [25]} *"Behold, the days are coming," says the LORD, "when I will punish all the circumcised who are uncircumcised*—^{25[26]}*Egypt, Judah, Edom, the sons of Ammon, Moab, and all the inhabitants of the desert*^a *who cut the corners of their hair;*^a *for all the nations are uncircumcised,*^b *and all the house of Israel is uncircumcised in heart."*^c

Notes

The numbers in brackets are the Eng. version verse numbers (MT 9:22–25 = ET 9:23–26). The Heb. versification is followed here.

22.a. Many MSS and versions add the conj as in the previous cola. This reading probably resulted from misunderstanding the metrical structure.

23.a. The LXX, Syr, and Tg add the conj; cf. note 22.a.

25.a-a. An alternative translation (see KJV, NEB) of this phrase deserves note. Beginning with the Jewish commentators Rashi and Kimchi, this phrase has been translated "fringe of the desert" (קצץ= קצה); cf 25:23 and 49:32.

25.b. The LXX, Syr, and Tg add σαρκί, "of flesh," probably an interpretive addition, but the addition should not be followed because all these nations practiced circumcision; see *Comment.* Rudolph (*BHS*) reads האלה, "these," yielding "all these nations and all the house of Israel."

25.c. The LXX adds αὐτῶν = לבם, "his," another interpretive expansion.

Form/Structure/Setting

These two basically unconnected oracles (vv 22–23; 24–25) should be analyzed separately.

Older commentators have often connected the first oracle (22–23) with the wisdom tradition (e.g., Duhm, Volz; see also Kutsch, *BZ* 25 [1981] 161–79). Recent scholarship, however, has tended to recognize it as related more to the prophetic tradition than the wisdom tradition (e.g., Rudolph, McKane, Holladay; see also Brueggemann, "The Epistemological Crisis," in *Israelite Wisdom*). The earlier commentators tended to characterize the oracle as late and of little importance, but those who have recognized its prophetic character have affirmed its genuineness. The triad of the wise, the mighty, and the rich never occurs in the wisdom literature, and the negative attitude to wealth is foreign to the wisdom tradition. The Masoretic and Greek traditions obviously considered the passage a prophetic oracle as indicated by the messenger formula "Thus says the LORD," and the rubric "The LORD's oracle." However, these could be later additions. The problems of the passage are compounded because there is no direct connection to the immediate context. It is probably placed here on the basis of catchword and common theme. The two words "know" (ידע) and "wise" (חכם) are prominent; on "know" see 8:7; 8:12; 9:2; 10:25, and on "wise" see 8:8–9; 9:11. The oracle itself gives no hint about the setting in which it should be understood. With no compelling evidence to the contrary, the oracle should be understood in the same setting as its immediate literary context and thus in either the latter years of Josiah's reign or the beginning of Jehoiakim's reign.

The second oracle (24–25) is an unconnected oracle concerning circumcision and piety. About the only connection to the larger context is the theme of judgment. Rudolph, on the basis of the list of nations in v 25, has suggested the background of a coalition of nations against the Babylonians. This coalition was headed by Egypt, and all the people practiced circumcision. The Babylonians, who they opposed, did not practice circumcision (so also Bright, Holladay). This setting also fits either the latter years of Josiah's reign or the beginning of Jehoiakim's reign.

Comment

22–23 This short oracle presents two alternative views of life through two triads: wisdom, power, and riches contrast with steadfast love (חֶסֶד), justice, and righteousness. The interpretation of v 23 is crucial in understanding this passage. One view of the passage says that the person who knows God must practice love, justice, and righteousness (e.g., Kimchi). Carroll is probably correct in rejecting this view since, in the Book of Jeremiah, only God practices steadfast love (חֶסֶד), and, besides God, only Josiah (22:15–16) and the future king (23:5) practice justice and righteousness. The godly values, love, justice, and righteousness, put the values of wisdom, power, and riches into proper perspective. Knowledge of the deity is pietistic or confessional in character rather than practical. Brueggemann ("The Epistemological Crisis") probably overstated the case when he analyzed this passage as representative of two major views of life that are in conflict.

Three ambiguous places in v 23 can greatly affect our understanding of the verse. (i) The two verbs used to describe knowing God can be translated in a variety of ways. They may be in parallel (so most ET, Volz, Rudolph, Carroll, McKane), "he has understanding and knows me," or "he understands and knows me." Or the second verb may be subordinate to the first (so Bright, Holladay), "he has the wisdom to know me." (ii) The conjunction כִּי before "I am the LORD" indicates what it means to know the Lord and should be translated as "that" (so Rudolph, RSV) instead of "for" which would indicate the reason for knowing the Lord (so McKane, NEB). (iii) Finally the ambiguous "in these" (בְּאֵלֶּה) could refer either to love, justice, and righteousness (so here) or those people who practice love, justice, and righteousness (Bright, perhaps). The answer depends upon an individual's understanding of the verse.

This verse was perhaps used by Paul in 1 Cor 1:31 and 2 Cor 10:17; it may also have influenced Jas 1:9 and 1 Clem 13:1; see further Kutsch, *BZ* 25 (1981) 161–79; Rusche, *BZ* 31 (1937) 116–19; Schreiner, "Jeremia 9, 22–23."

24–25 The second short oracle is easily misunderstood; see the interpretive additions listed in *Notes*. At the beginning it is necessary to keep in mind that all the nations listed in v 25 practiced circumcision; on circumcision see E. Schürer, *Geschichte des jüdischen Volkes* (Leipzig: Hinrichs, 1901) 1:675–76, and J. M. Sasson, "Circumcision in the Ancient Near East," *JBL* 85 (1966) 473–76. Note also Judah's grouping with the other nations. The punishment coming upon all the circumcised included Judah, because all were uncircumcised of heart. This passage should be understood in the context of two similar passages in Jeremiah (4:4; 6:10) and two passages in Deuteronomy that speak of circumcision (10:16; 30:6). Neither Jeremiah nor Deuteronomy advocate physical circumcision but instead speak of circumcision of the heart (or similarly circumcision of the ears in Jer 6:10). Clearly, only the symbolic meaning of circumcision is considered important. Circumcision was meant to show special status or perhaps to protect from God's anger (Exod 5:24–26?). Calling the people uncircumcised (of heart) declared they had no special status or protection. Judgment would fall upon all.

As with the previous oracle, this oracle or the thought behind it is echoed in the writings of Paul; see especially Rom 2:25–29.

Explanation

What is the measure of true greatness? The world today honors its scholars, especially those in the scientific field, its soldiers, its wealthy aristocrats, and its entertainers. Jeremiah regarded Israel's fascination with wisdom, power, and wealth as ludicrous and idolatrous. When they become one's chief aim in life, they become a hindrance in the search for true greatness.

True greatness, according to the prophet, lies in putting God absolutely first in one's life and seeking to reproduce the qualities he possesses and in which he delights. These are three in number—steadfast love, justice, and righteousness— and they stand in contrast to the three false sources of greatness—wisdom, power, and wealth.

The second oracle (vv 24–25 [25–26]) also enjoins a radical theocentric approach to life. Just as the knowledge of God is more important than wisdom, power, or might, even so faith that springs from the heart is more important than any outward show of religion. To be circumcised in the flesh means absolutely nothing if one is still "uncircumcised in heart." This is as strong a repudiation of empty ritual and formalism as one will find in the OT. In the context of Jeremiah, these oracles declare that neither wisdom, nor power, nor riches, nor circumcision will avail to deliver one from the judgment of God.

G. Idols and the True God (10:1–16)

Bibliography

Ackroyd, P. R. "Jeremiah X. 1–16." *JTS* 14 (1963) 385–90. Andrew, M. E. "Post-Exilic Prophets and the Ministry of Creating Community." *ExpTim* 93 (1982) 42–46. ———. "The Authorship of Jer. 10:1–16." *ZAW* 94 (1982) 20–47. Bogaert, P.-M. "Les mécanismes rédactionnels en Jér. 10, 1–16 (LXX et TM) et la signification des suppléments." *Le Livre de Jérémie.* Ed. P.-M. Bogaert. 228–38. Carmignac, J. "Le Texte de Jérémie 10:13 (ou 51, 16) et Celui de 2 Samuel 23:7; améliorés par Qumran." *RevQ* 7 (1970) 287–90. Dahood, M. "Egyptian ʾIW, 'Island' in Jeremiah 10, 9 and Daniel 10, 5." In *Atti del Secondo Congresso Internazionale di Linguistica Camito-Semitica.* Ed. Pelio Fronzaroli. Quaderni Di Semitistica 5. Firenze: instituto di Linguistica e de Lingue Orientali, 1978. 101–3. ———. "The

Emphatic Double Negative *mᵓyn* in Jeremiah 10:6–7." *CBQ* 37 (1975) 458–59. **Davidson, R.** "Jeremiah X 1–16." *TGUOS* 25 (1976) 41–58. **Deist, F. E.** "Zu *Ktmr Mqsh* in Jer. 10:5." *ZAW* 85 (1973) 225–26. **Dick, M. B.** "Prophetic Poiēsis and the Verbal Icon." *CBQ* 46 (1984) 226–46. **Kissane, E. J.** "Who Maketh Lightnings for the Rain." *JTS* n.s. 3 (1952) 214–16. **Labuschagne, C. J.** *The Incomparability of Yahweh in the Old Testament.* Leiden: Brill, 1966. 68–69. **Margaliot, M.** "Jeremiah X 1–16: A Re-Examination." *VT* 30 (1980) 295–308. **Overholt, T. W.** "The Falsehood of Idolatry: An Interpretation of Jer. X. 1–16." *JTS* 16 (1965) 1–12. **Wambacq, B. N.** "Jérémie, X, 1–16." *RB* 81 (1974) 57–62.

Translation

¹*Hear the word which the LORD has spoken concerning you, O House of Israel!*
²*The LORD has spoken thus:*

"*Do not learn*[a] *the way of the nations,* (3+3+3)
and do not be dismayed at the signs of the heavens,
because the nations are dismayed at them.

3 *For the customs*[a] *of the nations are false;* (4+3+3)
a tree is cut down from the forest,
and worked by the hands of a craftsman with an axe.[b]

4 *With silver and gold they adorn*[a] *it,* (3+2+3)
with [b]*nails and hammers,*[b]
they strengthen it so it cannot move.[c]

5 *Like a scarecrow*[a] *in a cucumber field, they cannot speak;* (4+4)
[b]*they must be carried*[c] *because they cannot walk.*

Do not be afraid of them (3+2+3)
because they cannot do evil;
neither is it in them[d] *to do good.*"

6 [a]*There is absolutely none*[b] *like you, O LORD;* (3+2+3)
You are great,
and your name is great with might.

7 *Who would not fear you,* (3+2+3)
O King of the nations,
for this is your due;[a]
For among all the wise of the nations (3+2+2)
and in all their kingdoms[b]
there is absolutely none like you.[c]

8 *They are both stupid and foolish;* (3+4)
the instruction of idols is wood.[b]

9 *Beaten silver is brought from Tarshish* (4+2)
and gold from the coast of gold;[a]
The work of the craftsman and the goldsmith's hands; (4+3+3)
violet and purple are their clothes,
all the work of skilled men.

10 *But the LORD is the God of truth;* (3+4)
he is the living God, the everlasting King;
At his wrath the earth shakes, (3+3)
and the nations cannot endure his indignation.

¹¹ᵃ *Thus you shall say to them:*

> *"The gods that have not made the heavens and the earth,*   (5+5)
>   *these shall perish from the earth and from under the heavens."*[a]

12   *He*[a] *made the earth with his power;*   (3+3+3)
>   *he established the world with his wisdom,*
>   *and with his understanding stretched out the heavens.*

13   [a]*At the sound of his voice*[a]   (2+3)
>   [b]*the waters of heaven roar,*[b]
>   *and he makes clouds rise*   (2+2)
>   *from the ends of the*[c] *earth.*
>   *He makes lightnings*[d] *for the rain,*   (3+3)
>   *and brings forth the wind*[e] *from his storehouse.*

14   *Every man is stupid and without knowledge,*   (3+3)
>   *and every goldsmith is put to shame by his idols.*
>   *For*[a]*his idol is*[a] *false,*   (3+2)
>   *and there is no breath in them.*

15   *They are worthless,*   (2+2+3)
>   *a work of delusion;*
>   *at the time*[a]*of their punishment,*[a] *they shall perish.*

16   *Not like these is the portion of Jacob,*   (3+3)
>   *for he is the one who formed all things;*
>   [a]*and Israel is the tribe*[a] *of his inheritance;*   (3+3)
>   *the* LORD [b]*of Hosts*[b] *is his name.*

Notes

2.a. Rudolph proposed reading את (sign of the direct obj). This is the only place אל, "to," is used with למד, "learn"; however, it is supported by the LXX. Follow the MT, the most difficult reading.

3.a. חקות is usually translated "statutes." Rudolph suggested reading חתת, "terror," on the basis of Gen 35:5. The emendation is not necessary.

3.b. The only other place this word occurs is Isa 44:12.

4.a. The Syr and Tg suggest reading יצפהו, "cover."

4.b-b. The LXX and 4QJer[b] switch these terms. 4QJer[b] consistently supports the Gk. tradition; it preserves 9:22–10:18. The other Qumran Jer MSS (2QJer, 4QJer[a], 4QJer[c]) usually follow the Masoretic tradition.

4.c. On the basis of the LXX and 4QJer[b], many suggest reading יפיק, "and they cannot move it" (e.g., Rudolph). The MT is acceptable; see GKC § 109g.

5.a. "Scarecrow" occurs only here in OT. The versions disagree. LXX omits it, and Vg and Syr assume תמר, "palm-tree"; Deist (ZAW 85 [1973] 225–26) would read "palm-tree" here also. The MT is confirmed by the Epistle of Jeremiah 69.

5.b. LXX and 4QJer[b] read v 9 here, followed by the rest of v 5 and omitting vv 6, 7, 8, 10.

5.c. Reading ינשאו with some MSS; the MT resulted from scribal error; see GKC § 23i, 47n.

5.d. Reading אתם with some MSS; the MT probably resulted from scribal error.

6.a. LXX omits vv 6–8.

6.b. The מאין here and in v 7 is difficult, lit., "without like you." Rudolph (BHS) suggested deleting the מ in both places, resulting in "none like you." BDB, 35, suggested reading מֵאַיִן, "whence is any like thee." Dahood (CBQ 37 [1975] 458–59) suggested reading מֵאַיִן, thus a double negative built upon מָה resulting in the reading adopted here; see also König, Syntax, 352x. All suggestions mean about the same thing.

7.a. This word occurs only here.

7.b. θ′ reads "kings."

7.c. See note 6.b.

8.b. What does this mean? Rudolph (BHS) suggested reading מעצה, "lacks counsel."

9.a. Following the suggestion of M. Dahood ("Egyptian ʾIW"), the location would be the west coast of Africa; otherwise the place is unknown. Syr and Tg read "Ophir." LXX reads "Mophaz."

11.a-a. The entire verse is Aram. It is usually classified as the Official (Imperial) Aramaic, the *lingua franca* of the civilized world of 700–200 B.C.

12.a. LXX and Syr read "The Lord." Vv12–16 parallel 51:15–19 (LXX 28:15–19).

13.a-a. LXX omits this phrase but includes it at 51:16 (LXX 28:16). The phrase as it stands makes little sense. Duhm proposed reading לְקוֹלוֹ נָתַן, "At his voice pour forth . . ."; thus *BHS.* For the translation here, compare NEB and Driver, G. R., "Linguistic and Textual Problems: Jeremiah," *JQR* 28 (1937–38) 106.

13.b-b. Carmignac (*RevQ* 7 [1970] 287–90) suggested switching this phrase and the previous one on the basis of the Qumran Psalm scroll.

13.c. Q reads the article.

13.d. Kissane (*JTS* n.s. 3 [1952] 214–16) proposed reading בְדָקִים, "Who maketh sluices for the rain," referring to the windows of heaven.

13.e. LXX reads φῶς, "light," both here and in 51:16 (LXX=28:16).

14.a-a. LXX reads "he has poured out" = נָסַךְ. Rudolph suggested נְסָכוֹ, "his images."

15.a-a. 4Q Jerᵇ reads פְּקֻדָּתִים, "when I punish them." Cf. 6:15.

16.a-a. LXX omits.

16.b-b. LXX omits.

Form/Structure/Setting

This highly controversial passage presents problems of authorship and composition, great differences between the LXX and MT, an Aramaic verse (v 11), and consequent interpretation problems. Most modern commentators, beginning with Graf (*Der Prophet Jeremia* [Leipzig, 1862]), have denied that Jeremiah was the author of this passage and have proposed numerous deletions and rearrangements of the text (e.g., Duhm, Volz, Rudolph, Bright). Beginning with Weiser, however, voices against this consensus have arisen. Weiser defended Jeremiah's authorship of the passage but still attempted to rework the text. Building on the work of Weiser, several recent authors have defended both Jeremiah's authorship of the passage and the integrity of the MT (e.g., Ackroyd, *JTS* 14 [1963] 385–9; Overholt, *JTS* 16 [1965] 1–12; Labuschagne, *The Incomparability of Yahweh*, 68–69; Margaliot, *VT* 30 [1980] 295–308). The evidence for the integrity of the MT has convinced many commentators; however, many still deny that Jeremiah was the author of this passage (e.g., Carroll, McKane).

The authorship of this passage has usually been questioned by comparing the similarities of vocabulary and style with Isa 40–48. The similarities of vocabulary are numerous: note idol, image, falsehood, craftsman, wood, goldsmith, gold, silver, axe, hammer, nails, to strengthen, to carry. Different explanations of these similarities have resulted in the different positions: e.g., Rudolph; Margaliot, *VT* 30 [1980] 295–308.

Much disagreement about the composition has resulted from the difficult text and the differences between the LXX and MT (see *Notes*). Many commentators have proposed various deletions and textual rearrangements to address these difficulties. The various proposals concerning the reworking of the text do not agree.

Duhm	1–3a, 5b, 10, 12–16.
Volz	3–5, 10, 12–16.
Rudolph	2–4a, 9, 4b–5, 8, 10, 12–16.
Bright	1–4a, 9, 4b–8, 10–16.

The discovery of 4QJer[b], which agrees with the LXX text, has complicated the situation. The LXX order is 1–5a, 9, 5b, 11–12. None of the various attempts at reworking the text has adequately explained the differences between the LXX and MT, or their relationship.

The Aramaic v 11 is the only instance of a single Aramaic verse within a purely Hebrew passage in the OT. The problem of the verse is complicated by the presence of two orthographic variants of the same word (אַרְקָא, אַרְעָא, "earth"), possibly from two different periods. The verse's presence in the passage requires explanation. The various arguments for and against including it usually hinge upon an analysis of the entire passage: note, for example, the chiasmus at the end of v 11.

Without entering into extensive arguments, the following conclusions have been assumed: (i) Jeremiah is the author of the passage. (ii) The MT of the passage presents a unified text which does not need extensive modification. (iii) The Aramaic v 11 is an integral part of the passage. The interested reader is referred to the articles by Ackroyd, Overholt, and Margaliot and the commentaries of Carroll, Holladay, McKane, and Rudolph.

After the first introductory verse the passage breaks down into four neat sections. Each section is composed of an indictment against the idols, followed by a section showing the superiority of the Lord. The following analysis is dependent upon Margaliot.

Section I.	
2–5	The *weakness* of the idols.
6–7	The *power* of the Lord.
Section II.	
8–9	The *dead* idols.
10	The *living* Lord.
Section III.	
11	The *non-creating* idols.
12–13	The *creator* God.
Section IV.	
14–15	The *foolish* worshipers of idols.
16	The *non-foolish* worshipers of the Lord.

This logical structure makes good sense of the passage. The intent of the passage can be clearly seen as showing the superiority of the Lord over the idols.

Overholt has convincingly shown that all of the ideas presented in this passage have parallels with other portions of the book of Jeremiah. Passages of particular importance for his argument include: 2:8–13, 26–28; 3:1–5; 5:20–25; and 14:22. The similarities between this passage and Isa 40–48 are often noted by those who deny the authenticity of this passage. Margaliot, after an extensive analysis of the similarities and differences between this passage and Isa 40–48, concluded that the differences were so great that a dependence between the two could not be upheld. Overholt and Margaliot would date this passage either during the latter years of Josiah's reign or the early years of Jehoiakim's reign and thus in the same period as the surrounding oracles. According to this argument, it was probably addressed to the northern tribes who had already been taken into captivity and might be subject to the threat of idolatry.

Comment

1   The standard introductory rubric places this passage within the framework of a divine oracle.

2–5   These first four verses make clear the powerlessness of the idols. The first command in v 2, "do not learn," has an unique construction (see note 2.a.), suggesting perhaps a special nuance of meaning. Holladay suggested the translation "become involved with learning." Driver ("Linguistic and Textual Problems: Jeremiah," *JQR* 28 [1937/38] 106) translated it as "addicted to." Dahood ("Hebrew-Ugaritic Lexicography IV," *Bib* 47 [1966] 410) understood אל, "to," as יהוה, "the LORD." The parallelism of "way" (דרך) in v 2 with "customs" (חקות) and the subject matter of this section suggest these two words are referring to the religious practices of the nations. What is the relationship of the last phrase of v 2 ("because the nations . . .") and the first two phrases of v 3 ("For the customs . . . ; a tree is cut down from the forest")? They all begin with כי. Are all three parallel? Most commentators understand the last phrase of v 2 as the response to the immediately preceding command and the two phrases at the beginning of v 3 as the response to the initial command ("Do not learn the way of the nations").

These verses portray the idol-gods as no more than the creations of men. They begin as a tree, are overlaid with precious metals, and are secured so they will stand up. These gods, however, cannot move or speak and are incapable of doing anything, either good or bad. The gods are no more than the materials out of which they are made (Carroll).

6–7   These verses make clear the comparison between the powerlessness of the idols and the power of the Lord. The incomparability of the Lord is emphasized. He is not only greater than idols, but his strength is greater than the power of king or wise man.

8–9   This second comparison between the idol-gods and the Lord contrasts the "living" God and the "dead" idols.

Verse 8 is difficult. The introductory word באחת, "and both," does not relate easily to the following verbs. The second phrase makes even less sense. The verse intends to depict the idols as foolish. In the light of v 10, which describes the vitality of the Lord, the description of the idols as foolish or stupid is intended to show their deficiency. Verse 9 describes the construction of the idols in almost the same terms as vv 3 and 4.

The locations of Tarshish and the "coast of gold" are uncertain. Tarshish is usually considered to be in Spain; see C. H. Gordon, "Tarshish," *IDB* 4:517–18. The "coast of gold," (see note 9.a.), literally "Uphaz," is also unknown. For "Uphaz" the Syr and Tg read "Ophir," located on coast of Africa; see G. W. Van Beek, "Ophir," *IDB* 3:605–6. Wherever their locations, these were places known for their gold and silver. Beside being covered with gold and silver, the idols were clothed in violet and purple. But in spite of the rich adornment, the idol-gods were dead; they were nothing more than the materials out of which they were made.

10   In contrast to the idols, the Lord is the "living" God, the everlasting King. The idol-gods can only shake the earth by falling over, but they are prevented from falling by being nailed down. The earth, however, shakes at the wrath of the Lord, and the nations shake at his anger.

11   The reason for the presence of this Aramaic verse in the midst of the Hebrew has puzzled commentators from the start. Both Rashi and Kimchi accepted the evidence of the Tg as an explanation of the sudden change from Hebrew to Aramaic. The Tg prefaces v 11 with these words: "This is the copy of the letter which the Prophet Jeremiah sent to the leaders of the exile in Babylon: 'If the Chaldeans say to you, worship our idols, then answer them as follows.'" This suggests that v 11 was a shortened version of a letter sent by Jeremiah to Jehoiachin and the other exiles in Babylon between 598 and 587 B.C. (compare 29:1–32).

Modern commentators, when not throwing it out, have classified it as a curse (Overholt, 5) or protective formula (Duhm). The main verb of the verse can be translated either as an indicative (as here) or a jussive ("let them perish"), depending upon how the verse is understood. Whatever its original purpose, its presence here confirms that the passage was addressed to the exiles, for Aramaic was the language of the land where they were exiled. The verse makes it clear that the idol-gods, who had no part in the creation, will perish from the earth, and thus the exiles need not fear them.

12–13   In contrast to the idol-gods who created nothing, the creative acts of the Creator-God are given a threefold description: He made the earth, established the world, and stretched out the heavens (cf. Pss 65:6–8; 77:18; 89:11). This is followed by a fourfold description of God's power over creation. He has power over the rain, the clouds, the lightning, and the wind.

14–15   In this final section the worshipers of the idol-gods are contrasted with the worshipers of the Lord. As the idols were earlier described as foolish (v 8), so here the people who worship the idols are called foolish. The first phrase of v 14 presents problems; compare v 8. Jerome translated the phrase "Every man without knowledge of God is stupid." Many commentators would translate it "Every man is stupid, without knowledge"; e.g., Rudolph. Holladay would translate it "Everyman is too stupid to know." The men who worship idols are stupid, and the maker of idols is put to shame by his idols. In contrast to the Lord who sends forth his "wind" (רוח), v 13, the idols have no "breath" (רוח) in them.

16   The worshipers of the Lord worship the one who formed all things. The Lord is called the "portion" or "possession" of Jacob; compare Num 18:20; Ps 16:5; Lam 3:24; and see G. von Rad, *Old Testament Theology*, vol. 1, trans. D. M. G. Stalker (London: Oliver & Boyd Ltd., 1962) 403–5. Israel is described in traditional language as the Lord's "inheritance"; compare 12:7–9. The verse and the passage end with a concluding hymnic refrain.

Explanation

This section interrupts the message of impending judgment in the surrounding context and warns the people against the folly of idolatry. The satire on idol-making contains many parallels to Second Isaiah (compare Isa 40:18–20; 41:6–7; 44:9–20; 46:5–7). The Lord's superiority to foreign deities is described in the most emphatic manner.

Idolatry is an ever-present threat to the people of God. It involves both a turning away from God and a turning toward something that becomes a substitute for God. It involves rejecting God as Creator and ascribing to created things an authority that belongs to him alone. It is always an evasive maneuver, a subtle form of escapism. How easy it is for us to make idols out of our particular system of ritual, our tradition, a particular place of worship, or even an infallible book. Anything that helps us to avoid the tension and demand of a personal encounter with Almighty God has become for us a form of idolatry. It is not merely as bad as the idolatry that Jeremiah condemned; it is far worse, for we should know better.

H. Vicarious Suffering (10:17–25)

Bibliography

Berridge, J. M. *Prophet, People.* 194–97. **Gelio, R.** "È possibile un ʾîš relative/dimostrativo in ebraico biblico?" *RivB* 31 (1983) 411–34. **Kumaki, F. K.** "A New Look at Jer. 4:19–22 and 10:19–21." *Annual of the Japanese Biblical Institute* 8 (1982) 113–22. **McKane, W.** *Prophets and Wise Men.* 90–91. **Reventlow, H. G.** *Liturgie.* 196–204.

Translation

17	*Gather up*[a] *your bundle*[b] *from the ground,*	(3+2)
	[c]*you who dwell*[c] *under siege.*[d]	
18	*For the* LORD *has spoken thus:*	(3+2)
	"Behold I am casting out	
	the inhabitants of the land	(2+2)
	at this time,[a]	
	[b]*and I will bring distress to them*[b]	(2+2)
	[c]*so that they will find it."*[c]	
19	*Woe is me, because of my breaking;*	(3+2)
	my wound is grievous,	
	and I said, "Surely this is the	(2+4)
	affliction[a] *I must bear."*	
20	*My tent is destroyed and all my cords are broken;*	(4+3)
	my children [a]*are gone from me*[a] *and are no more;*	
	there is no one to spread[b] *my tent again,*	(3+2)
	and to set up[b] *my curtains.*	
21	*Because the shepherds are foolish,*	(3+3)
	and they do not inquire of the LORD.	
	Therefore, they have not prospered,	(3+2)
	and all their flock is scattered.	
22	*The sound of rumor, behold it comes,*	(4+4)
	and a great commotion out of the north	
	to make cities of Judah	(3+3)
	a desolation, a lair of jackals.	

23   *I know,*[a] *O LORD,*   (2+4)
         that a man's way is not his
      and that it is not[b] *for a man*[c] *to walk*   (2+2)
         and to discern[d] *his steps.*
24   *Correct me,*[a] *O LORD, but with justice,*   (3+2)
         not in your anger, lest you destroy me.[a]
25   [a]*Pour out your wrath upon the nations*   (3+2)
         which do not know you,
      and upon the peoples[b]   (2+4)
         that do not call upon your name;
      for they have devoured Jacob,   (2+2+2)
      [c]*they have devoured and consumed him,*[c]
      and laid waste his habitation.

Notes

17.a. LXX reads συνήγαγεν ἔζωθεν, "he has gathered from outside."

17.b. The word occurs here only. LXX has ὑπόστασιν, "substance"; the Vg, "confusion"; the Syr, "shame."

17.c-c. Reading Q יֹשֶׁבֶת, K יֹשַׁבְתִּי רְ, "I dwell"; see GKC § 90n.

17.d. LXX reads ἐκλεκτοῖς = בְּמִבְחָר, "in choice (vessels)"; cf. 22:7; 48:15.

18.a. LXX omits "time" (בַּפַּעַם), reading "this land." Holladay (I, 338) suggested reading "in rage" (בְּזַעַם) on the basis of Hab 3:12.

18.b-b. LXX reads ἐν θλίψει = בְּצָרָה, "with affliction."

18.c-c. LXX and Vg read the passive יִמָּצְאוּ, "they will be found." Driver ("Linguistic and Textual Problems: Jeremiah," *JQR* 28 [1937/38] 107) proposed reading "they will be squeezed dry" (יְמָצוּ). Rudolph (*BHS*) proposed reading "to refuse them exit" (לְמִנֹּעַ מַצָּאָה).

19.a. The versions add 1 sg suff. Omitted in MT by haplogr?

20.a-a. LXX reads και τα πρόβατά = וְצֹאנִי, "and my flocks."

20.b. Rudolph (*BHS*) suggests switching these two verbs.

23.a. Rudolph (*BHS*) suggests reading יָדַעְתָּ, "you know."

23.b. Reading וְלֹא with many MSS (e.g., Reuchlinianus) and versions.

23.c. R. Gelio ("È possibile un ʾiš relativo/dimostrativo in ebraico biblico?" *RivB* 31 [1983] 411–34) suggested that "man" (אִישׁ) should be read as the relative pronoun (equivalent to אֲשֶׁר). It would not significantly change the meaning, and the parallel "man" (אָדָם) in the preceding colon argues against this.

23.d. One MS omits "and"; on הָכִין, "to direct," see GKC § 72z.

24.a. LXX reads "us."

25.a. This verse parallels Ps 79:6–7.

25.b. Many MSS of LXX and Tg read "kingdoms" (מַמְלָכוֹת) following Ps 79:6.

25.c-c. Absent from LXX and Ps 79:7. Cf. M. Dahood, "The Word-pair ʾākal//kālāh in Jeremiah xxx 16," *VT* 27 (1977) 482, n. 2.

Form/Structure/Setting

Two major difficulties confront the interpreter of these verses: the proper grouping of the verses and the speaker in the different subsections. The major commentators do not agree upon these issues and cannot offer a consensus opinion. The following conclusions about the passage are informed by the work of Rudolph, Reventlow (*Liturgie*), Bright, Carroll, and McKane.

The basic forms within the passage are fairly easy to isolate. The first two verses (vv 17–18) announce the invasion in the form of a prophetic oracle. The remainder of the passage (vv 19–25) is in the form of a personal lament. The subject matter of the lament, however, causes many to regard it as a communal lament couched in the first person; see Reventlow, *Liturgie*, 196–204. Jeremiah so identified with the community that he could lament the suffering which would come upon the community, as if it were his own personal suffering. His identification with the community resulted in his pleading for justice for the community. In this passage we see Jeremiah as the cultic intercessor.

The passage can be subdivided upon the basis of subject matter and changes in person, e.g., the use of first person in vv 19–20 and 23–24. The first two verses (vv 17–18) announce imminent invasion in the form of a prophetic oracle. Many commentators connect these verses to 9:21 because of the catchword "gather" (אסף); so Bright, Carroll, Rudolph. Verses 19–20 begin the first-person lament uttered by Jeremiah on behalf of the community concerning the coming invasion. The responsibility for the invasion is laid at the feet of the community leaders in v 21. With echoes of the "enemy from the north" motif, v 22 declares the coming invasion. Verses 23–24, again in the first person, are a prayer for justice. The final verse, echoed in Ps 79:6–7, calls for the wrath of God to be poured out on the nations that have devoured Jacob.

The passage envisions a coming invasion/deportation. This would fit the situation preceding the deportation of either 598 or 586/7 B.C.

Comment

17 Jeremiah characteristically warns the people of the coming invasion by speaking as if the invasion were presently happening. The feminine singular verb makes it clear that Jeremiah is addressing Jerusalem; so McKane, Carroll.

18 In order to strengthen his words, Jeremiah declares the coming invasion in the form of an oracle, perhaps quoting an oracle uttered previously; so Berridge, *Prophet, People*, 176.

19 In the following verses Jeremiah identifies with the community and thus takes upon himself the suffering of Jerusalem and Judah. The second half of the verse describes the inevitability of the coming judgment; so McKane, contra Rudolph.

20 The coming destruction is described in terms reminiscent of the life situation of a Bedouin family; so Carroll. The image of tents, in connection with the coming destruction, is common in Jeremiah; see 4:20 for a similar image of judgment, and 30:18 for the corresponding image of the restoration of tents.

21 Responsibility for the coming invasion/deportation is laid at the feet of the community leaders because they have failed to inquire of the Lord. Kings are described under the common figure of shepherds (cf. 3:15). The shepherds (kings) are accused of failing to seek an oracle from the Lord to help them govern. As a result of their failure, the flock is scattered (an image of deportation); see further McKane, *Prophets and Wise Men*, 90.

22 The prophet's anticipation of the invasion is so intense that he feels it already happening. The news of this event is on its way. The sound of the horses can almost be heard. In language characteristic of the "foe from the north" motif, the prophet described the coming judgment.

23 The "I" of this verse picks up the "I" of vv 19–20, thus continuing the lament. On behalf of the community the prophet pleaded that man cannot direct his own way, implying that only God can (cf. Prov 16:9). On the basis of this traditional wisdom, the prophet pleaded for the Lord to avert the coming disaster.

24 Surprisingly, Jeremiah pleaded for God's justice rather than his mercy in the face of the coming disaster. Had the prophet given up on mercy?

25 This final verse is paralleled by Ps 79:6–7. We have three options to explain this. (i) The psalm is dependent upon Jeremiah. (ii) Jeremiah is dependent upon the psalm. (iii) They both draw from a common tradition. Since no direct evidence informs our decision on this matter, we must decide upon the basis of our presuppositions about the composition of Jeremiah. We have assumed here that they both draw from common tradition. In the preceding verse the prophet pleaded with God to deal with the people according to his justice and not his anger, but in this verse he pleads with God to deal with the nations according to his anger. The Lord's wrath upon the nations would also be an example of his justice, because of what the nations had done to Jacob. This concept of justice runs throughout both the prophetic and the wisdom literature.

Explanation

God had earlier admonished Jeremiah to cease praying for his people (7:16; cf. 14:11–12), since they had placed themselves beyond the reach of prayer. Yet he seems to have continued to intercede on their behalf; he perhaps understood this as an indispensable part of his prophetic ministry. His empathy with his people was such that their suffering became his own. His identification with them was such that when he pleaded for them he was also pleading for himself. In the calamity that threatened Jerusalem he was no mere spectator but one who himself suffered with the people he loved. In this sense his suffering could be termed vicarious.

Another prophetic spokesman, Jesus Christ, also identified himself with Jerusalem and wept over her impending destruction. His identification with his people brought him great distress and eventually led to his death. The pathos of the prophets and of Jesus was an integral part of their ministry and reflected the pathos of God himself.

VII. Why Judgment? (11:1–13:27)

Bibliography

Ahuis, F. *Der klagende Gerichtsprophet. Studien zur Klage in der Überlieferung von den alttestamentlichen Gerichtspropheten.* Calwer Theologische Monographien 12. Stuttgart: Calwer Verlag, 1982. **Baumgartner, W.** *Jeremiah's Poems of Lament.* Trans. D. E. Orton. Sheffield: Almond, 1988. **Diamond, A. R.** *The Confessions of Jeremiah in Context: Scenes of Prophetic Drama.* JSOTSup 45. Sheffield: JSOT Press, 1986. **Hubmann, F. D.** *Untersuchungen zu den Konfessionen Jer. 11, 18–12, 2, und Jer. 15, 10–21.* Forschung zur Bible 30. Zurich: Echter Verlag, 1978. **Thiel, W.** *Die deuteronomistische Redaktion von Jeremia 1–25.* WMANT 41. Neukirchen-Vluyn: Neukirchener Verlag, 1973.

Introduction

The several subsections of this editorial unit joined together provide an explanation for God's judgment upon his people. Besides the rather traditional explanation, that the people broke their covenant with the Lord, the unit contains two sections of lament that graphically portray both the tragedy of the situation and the reluctance of the Lord to bring judgment. The final section, through symbolic action and other means, portrays the horror of the people's sin. As with the other large editorial units in Jeremiah, the section contains diverse units of disparate origin, form, and date. The probable time of compilation was sometime after the fall of Jerusalem, as the exiles attempted to understand their lot.

The superscriptions at 11:1 and 14:1 form the major demarcations for this editorial unit (compare also 7:1 and 18:1); so Rudolph, Hubmann (*Untersuchungen*, 109), and Thiel (*Redaktion*, 106–7). This unit is divided into four major sections on the basis of changes of substance and form. Some of these sections are further subdivided.

11:1–17	Jeremiah and the Covenant
11:18–12:6	Jeremiah and the Men of Anathoth
12:7–17	The Sorrow of God
13:1–27	Symbolism and Sin

The first and perhaps the third subsections are self-contained, while the second and fourth are clearly composite. Each subsection is a mixture of poetry and prose, sometimes dominated by poetry and sometimes by prose. The first subsection, describing how the people have broken their covenant with the Lord as well as the consequences, provides the context for the whole unit. In the second subsection, usually called the first of Jeremiah's *Confessions* (see the Excursus: "Jeremiah's Confessions"), Jeremiah laments the plot against his life as a result of his preaching, perhaps even that recorded in the previous subsection. This lament is multi-faceted, however, and could equally well express the sorrow of the people over their fate at the hands of God. In this lament, questions concerning God's justice dominate: Jeremiah wondered how God could allow this evil to happen to his chosen one. Perhaps in response to this lament, the third subsection contains a lament by the Lord over the sin of his people and what this forces him to do. In this divine lament, we get a rare glimpse of the sorrow that evil causes God. An interesting result of the juxtaposition of these two laments is the picture painted of the devastating effects of sin on both man and God. The final subsection, through symbolic action and prophetic oracle, details the sin of the people, from commoner to royalty, in all of its ugliness. The section taken as a whole is a powerful justification of the Babylonian invasion and resulting exile.

Besides the broad themes that tie the unit together, several minor themes and catchwords confirm the unity. A related complex of catchwords and minor themes, scattered throughout the unit, revolves around the spoiling of the people's pride and their resulting shame. The catchword "pride" (גאון) is found in the second and fourth sections; see 12:5; 13:9. "Spoil" (שחת) is found in the second, third, and fourth sections; see 11:19, 12:10, 13:7, 9, 14. The second and fourth sections are further linked by "prosper" (צלח); see 12:1; 13:7, 10. The idea of shame in connection with idolatry is found in the first and last subsections; see 11:13; 13:26.

A. Jeremiah and the Covenant (11:1–17)

Bibliography

Cazelles, H. "Jeremiah and Deuteronomy." In *A Prophet to the Nations*. 89–112. **Granild, S.** "Jeremia und das Deuteronomium." *ST* 16 (1962) 135–54. **Holladay, W. L.** "Jeremiah and Moses: Further Observations." *JBL* 85 (1966) 17–27. **Hyatt, J. P.** "The Original Text of Jeremiah 11:15–16." *JBL* 60 (1941) 57–60. **Levy, A. J.** "Biblical Note—Jeremiah 11:15." *JAOS* 49 (1929) 363. **Rowley, H. H.** "The Prophet Jeremiah and the Book of Deuteronomy." In *Studies in Old Testament Prophecy*. Ed. H. H. Rowley. Edinburgh: T & T Clark, 1950. 157–74. **Wilhelmi, G.** "Weg Mit den Vielen Altären! (Jeremia XI 15)." *VT* 25 (1975) 119–21.

Translation

[1]*The word that came to Jeremiah from the LORD:* [2]*"Listen*[a] *to the words of this covenant, and speak*[b] *to the men of Judah and to*[c] *the inhabitants of Jerusalem.* [3]*You shall say to them, 'Thus says the God of Israel: "Cursed is the man who ignores the words of this covenant* [4]*which I commanded your fathers when I brought them out of the land of Egypt, from the iron furnace, saying, 'Listen to my voice and do all*[a] *that I command you, and you will be my people and I will be your God';* [5]*that I may confirm the oath which I swore to your fathers, to give to them a land flowing with milk and honey, as at this day".'"* And I answered, "Amen, LORD."*

[6]*And the LORD said to me, "Proclaim all*[a] *these words in the cities of Judah and in the streets of Jerusalem and say, 'Listen to the words of this covenant and do them.* [7a]*For I solemnly admonished your fathers when I brought them up out of the land of Egypt* [b]*and even to this day,*[b] *admonishing them constantly, saying, "Listen to my voice."* [8]*Yet they did not listen or pay attention, but every man walked in the stubbornness of his evil heart, and so I brought upon them all the words of this covenant which I commanded them to do*[a] *and they did not.'"*

⁹*Again the LORD said to me, "There is conspiracy among the men of Judah and the inhabitants of Jerusalem.* ¹⁰*They have turned back to the sins of their forefathers who refused to listen to my words, and*ᵃ *they have gone after other gods to serve them. The house of Israel and the house of Judah have broken the covenant which I made with their fathers."*

¹¹*Therefore thus says the LORD, "Behold I am bringing evil*ᵃ *upon them from which they cannot escape, and when they cry to me I will not*ᵇ *listen.* ¹²*Then the cities of Judah and the inhabitants of Jerusalem will go and they will cry to the gods to whom they are burning incense, but they will not save them at all in the time of their trouble.* ¹³*For your gods have become as numerous as your cities, O Judah; and your* ᵃ*shameful altars,*ᵃ *O Jerusalem, altars to burn incense to Baal, have become as numerous as your streets.* ¹⁴ᵃ*As for you, do not pray for this people or lift up a cry or prayer on their behalf, for I will not listen when they call*ᵇ *to me in the time*ᶜ *of their trouble.*

15	*What is my beloved*ᵃ *doing in my house*	(3+2)
	*when she had done*ᵇ *many vile things?*	
	*Can vows*ᶜ *and sacrificial flesh avert*ᵈ ᵉ*your doom?*ᵉ	(4+4)
	ᶠ *Can you then exult?*ᶠ	
16	*'A green olive tree, beautiful with good fruit,'* ᵃ	(4+3)
	the LORD called you,	
	but ᵇ*with the roar of a great storm*ᵇ	(3+3+2)
	*he will set fire*ᶜ *to it*	
	*and its branches will be burned.*ᵈ	

¹⁷*The LORD of Hosts, who planted you, has pronounced evil against you, because of the evil which the house of Israel and the house of Judah have done, provoking me to anger by burning incense to Baal."*

Notes

11:2.a. The verbs "listen" (שׁמע) and "speak" (דבר) in this verse are difficult. The Leningrad Codex reads "hear" as pl and "speak" as sg; most other MSS read "speak" as pl; see Janzen, *Studies*, 133. Rudolph (*BHS*) avoids the problems by omitting this verse and the first two words of v 3 as expansions. See following notes.

2.b. "Speak" (דברתֶּם) is sg with pl suff in MT. Repoint it pl with no suff (דברתֶם), paralleling "Hear" (שׁמעו), and following most MSS.

2.c. Many MSS, supported by LXX, Syr, and some Tgs read the variant ואֶל, probably to match the previous אֶל.

4.a. Omit אותם, "them," with the LXX, probably added from v 6.

6.a. Omitted in some MSS and LXX; the difference is of little consequence.

7.a.-8.a. Omitted from LXX; some consider this expansionistic; see Janzen, *Studies*, 29–40.

7.b-b. Omitted from many MSS; the meaning is unaffected.

10.a. LXX adds ἰδού = הנה, "behold."

11.a. Some MSS read the variant עליהם; there is no significant difference in meaning or usage.

11.b. Oriental MSS read the variant ואֶל; see GKC § 107p.

13.a-a. Omitted from LXX; Volz, Rudolph omitted it as a secondary gloss from 2:28.

14.a. The first half of this verse is paralleled by 7:16a.

14.b. Rudolph (*BHS*) suggested reading קראֶך, "you call," on the basis of 7:16 and the Tg; the change is not necessary.

14.c. Reading בעת with many MSS and versions; MT resulted from dittogr with previous clause.

15.a. The MT of vv 15–16 is corrupt, and all translations are based upon conjecture and emendation; see Hyatt, *JBL* 60 (1941) 57–60; Wilhelmi, *VT* 25 (1975) 119–21. For this first phrase, Rudolph (*BHS*) proposed reading לי דודֶך, "what to me are your baskets . . . ?"

15.b. Rudolph (*BHS*) proposed reading עשׂית, "you have done," on the basis of many MSS and LXX; this emendation is necessary if the previous one is adopted.

15.c. Reading הנדרים with the LXX (μὴ εὐχαί); MT reads הרבים, "the many."
15.d. Revocalize from qal to hiph with LXX (יעברו > יַעֲבִרוּ); see GKC § 53n.
15.e-e. Lit., "from you because of your evil."
15.f-f. Reading with MT. Many emendations have been proposed; Rudolph *(BHS)* proposed
(ה)אזכה על־זאת, "shall I declare you pure?" *BHS* also proposed transposing 16.b-b. to here.
16.a. LXX omits. *BHS* suggested reading יפיפה, "beautiful in form."
16.b-b. See 15.f-f.
16.c. Rudolph *(BHS)* suggested reading בעלהו, "in its leaves."
16.d. Lit., "break." Read בערו with Rudolph *(BHS)* and Vg.

Form/Structure/Setting

This passage is the second major block of prose material (Type C, prose sermons); refer to *Form/Structure/Setting* on 7:1–8:3 for further discussion of the
problems associated with this type of material. The major interpretive issue for
Type C material is its relationship to "Deuteronomic" material. Many direct parallels with Deuteronomic or Deuteronomistic language and style exist between
Type C material in Jeremiah and Deuteronomy or Deuteronomistic passages
in other biblical books. These parallels can be explained in three basic ways:
(i) Deuteronomy is dependent upon Jeremiah. (ii) Jeremiah is dependent upon
Deuteronomy. (iii) They both come out of the same literary milieu. As with the
previous prose passage (7:1–8:3), this passage is a composite unit with literary
unity provided by the prose style and common words and themes; see below. The
following examples provide the basis for any decision regarding the Deuteronomic
nature of this passage.

Several expressions, generally classified as Deuteronomic or Deuteronomistic,
occur in Jer 11:1–17.

(i) "The words of this covenant" (Jer 11:2, 3, 6) is also found in Deut 29:1 [MT
28:69], 9 [8] and 2 Kings 8:51.

(ii) "Cursed is . . ." (Jer 11:3) is found in Deut 27:26.

(iii) "From the iron furnace" (Jer 11:4) is found in Deut 4:20 and 1 Kgs 8:51.

(iv) "The oath which I swore to your fathers" (Jer 11:5) is found in Deut 7:8;
8:18; 9:5.

(v) "A land flowing with milk and honey" (Jer 11:5; 32:22) is found in Deut
6:3; 11:9; 26:9, 15; 27:3; 31:20; see also Exod 13:5; Josh 5:6.

(vi) "Amen, Lord" (Jer 11:5) is found in Deut 27:15.

(vii) "This covenant which I commanded them to do" (Jer 11:8) is found in
Deut 4:13.

(viii) "To go after other gods" (Jer 11:10) is found in Deut 6:4; 8:19; 11:29;
13:2; 28:14.

This long list of Deuteronomic and Deuteronomistic expressions found in Jer
11:1–7 shows clearly the ground for suggesting a Deuteronomic character to this
passage.

The following expressions from 11:1–17 are characteristic of Jeremianic prose
and seldom occur in Deuteronomy or Deuteronomistic literature.

(i) "Constantly" (Jer 11:7 and seven other times; see 7:13, 25; 25:14; 25:15;
25:19; 29:19; 32:33).

(ii) "Stubbornness of heart" (Jer 11:8 and seven other times; see 3:17; 7:24;
9:13; 13:10; 16:12; 18:12; 23:17). It occurs in Deuteronomy only at 29:18; elsewhere only Ps 81:13.

(iii) "Cities of Judah and streets of Jerusalem" (Jer 11:6) occurs six times and only in Jeremiah; see 7:17; 33:10; 44:6, 17, 21.

(iv) "He has pronounced evil against you" (Jer 11:17) occurs seven times in the OT, six of these times in Jeremiah (16:10; 26:19; 35:17; 36:31; 40:2) and only once elsewhere (1 Kgs 22:23).

The following phrases are common to both Jeremianic prose and poetry.

(i) "Behold I am bringing" (Jer 11:11; see 19:15; 39:16) is absent from Deuteronomy and present only in pre-Deuteronomistic parts of 1 and 2 Kings (see Gray, *I & II Kings,* 2nd ed. [Philadelphia: Westminster Press, 1970] 442–43).

(ii) "Obey my voice" (Jer 11:4, 7; see 3:13; 7:23; 22:21, etc.) is equally common in Deuteronomy and Jeremiah.

This examination of the language and style of Jer 11:1–17, in comparison to the Deuteronomic Corpus, confirms the preliminary conclusion about Type C material arrived at in examining Jer 7:1–8:3. The Type C material in Jeremiah and the Deuteronomic literature both arose out of the same literary milieu: Classical Hebrew prose. The similarities between Type C material and the Deuteronomic literature can be explained on the basis of the common literary milieu and common interests and subject matter; see further *Form/Structure/Setting* on 7:1–8:3.

The passage can be broken down into five subsections on the basis of variations on the messenger formula (vv 1, 6, 9, 11) and the poetic insert (v 15).

11:1–5	The curse of the Covenant
11:6–8	Failure to follow the Covenant
11:9–10	Following other gods
11:11–14	Judgment is coming
11:15–17	Judgment because of idolatry

These subsections are joined together by common themes and an unusual amount of shared language.

Four similar phrases describing the people join the subsections together: (i) "The men of Judah and inhabitants of Jerusalem" is found in subsections 1 and 3 (v 2; v 9). (ii) "The house of Israel and the house of Judah" links subsections 3 and 5 (v 10; v 17). (iii) "The cities of Judah and streets of Jerusalem" joins subsections 2 and 4 (v 6; v 13). (iv) "The cities of Judah and inhabitants of Jerusalem" in subsection 4 (v 12) is a combination of phrases (i) and (iii).

The first four subsections are joined together by a number of common words and themes. The first two subsections speak of the exodus from Egypt (v 4; v 7). "Covenant" is prominent throughout the first three subsections (vv 2, 3; vv 6, 8; v 10). "Listen" (שׁמע) dominates the first four subsections (vv 2, 4; vv 6, 7, 8; v 10; v 14.)

The final three subsections condemn idolatry. The word "gods" is found in subsections 3 and 4 (v 9; vv 12, 13) and the phrase "burn incense to Baal" in subsections 4 and 5 (v 13; v 17).

The common words and phrases tie the first four sections closely together; the final section is only loosely joined to the preceding sections. The poetic nature of vv 15–16, from the last subsection, suggests that these verses are a quote, and the common theme of Baal worship joins this section to the preceding sections.

Verses 7–8 are the beginning point for determining the setting and date of this passage. V 8 says the curse of the covenant has been brought upon the people.

Many commentators understand this curse as the loss of the land and therefore classify this passage as exilic or post-exilic. The following verses, however, speak of judgment as yet in the future; see vv 11–14. Verses 9–10 perhaps reflect Zedekiah's conspiracy against Nebuchadnezzar (see Bright, *A History of Israel,* 3rd ed. [Philadelphia: Westminster, 1981] 328–30). The verses thus could address a period after the time of Josiah when religious apostasy had set in.

Comment

1–2 The sermon begins with a traditional oracular introduction. Verse 2 begins with the word that dominates this entire passage, שׁמע, variously translated as "hear," "listen," and "obey." The people are commanded to "listen to" or "obey" this covenant. Does "this covenant" refer to the covenant renewed during the time of Josiah or more generally the Mosaic covenant? Bright (89) prudently warned against making too sharp a distinction between these two covenants. The Mosaic covenant as recorded in Deuteronomy was reaffirmed in the time of Josiah.

3–5 These verses imitate Deut 27:15–26. They announce the curse upon the man who ignores the covenant. "Covenant" (ברית) is an important concept in OT faith, especially in the Deuteronomic and Priestly traditions; see further Dennis J. McCarthy, *Treaty and Covenant,* AnBib 21A (Rome: Biblical Institute Press, 1978), and George Mendenhall, "Covenant," *IDB* I:714–23. Of the twenty-one verses in Jeremiah that use "covenant," this passage contains five of them (vv 2, 3, 6, 8, 10); Jer 31–34 contains twelve verses which use "covenant."

The passage is composed of numerous phrases invoking images of the covenant. (i) "When I brought them up out of the land of Egypt" evokes images of the original Mosaic covenant; see 7:22 and 34:13. (ii) "Obey the (my) voice" is a common convenantal phrase both in Jeremiah and Deuteronomy; see Jer 3:13; 7:23; 9:12; 11:7; 18:12; 22:21; Exod 19:5; Deut 4:30. (iii) "All I command you," also found in 1:7 and 7:23, is common to both the Deuteronomic and Priestly traditions; see Exod 25:22; Deut 31:5. (iv) "You shall be my people and I will be your God" is a common covenant formula; see Jer 7:23; 30:22; 31:33; Exod 6:7. (v) "A land flowing with milk and honey" is also common in the Deuteronomic and Priestly traditions; see Deut 6:3; Exod 6:3; Josh 5:6.

These words strongly communicate the idea of covenant and the obligation laid upon the people by the covenant. Jeremiah confirmed the validity of the covenant by saying "Amen." He also confirmed the curse, because the people had not kept their obligation.

6–8 On the basis of v 6, many commentators suggest that Jeremiah was sent around as an itinerant evangelist of Josiah's reform. This places too much emphasis upon the phrase "in the cities of Judah and the streets of Jerusalem"; see the many parallels above. Verse 7 updates the words of admonishment and warning concerning the curse of the covenant; as the fathers had been warned, so too had the people of Jeremiah's day. Yet neither the forefathers or the present generation had listened to God; instead they followed their own stubborn, evil hearts (cf. 7:24).

9–10 What is the "conspiracy" mentioned in v 9? In other places "conspiracy" (קשׁר) has a political meaning (see 2 Sam 15:12; 1 Kgs 16:20; 2 Kgs 11:14). As had their forefathers, the people had abandoned the Lord and followed other gods.

Apostasy had political implications. Perhaps Zedekiah's conspiracy against Nebuchadnezzar provides the background for this passage (see Jer 27). The passage suggests a reformation which brought about only a short-lived improvement. The shortness of the reformation is compared to the long history of apostasy which the Josianic reform had attempted to reverse. The allusion to the "house of Israel" suggests that the earlier apostasy and fall of the Northern Kingdom is mentioned as a witness. The failure of the reform consigned Judah to the same fate as Israel.

11–14 The failure of the people to listen to God and obey his words will come back to haunt them. The people will call to the idols they have been worshiping, but the idols cannot hear them. When they cry to the Lord, he will not hear them. The people who would not listen will not be heard. Further, Jeremiah is commanded to refrain from interceding on their behalf. The people have turned to idols from serving the Lord, and the idols cannot help them.

15–17 The prose section is concluded by two poems and a summary verse. The first poem (v 15) questions the people's right to be in the temple. The offerings of the people will have no effect upon the deity, just as their prayers will not reach him. The temple rites are ineffective because of the sin of the people. The irony of the Lord's bringing judgment upon his "beloved" is evident.

The second poem (v 16) compares the people with a green olive tree. The tree will be destroyed by a great storm; it will be burnt to the ground. What was formerly a beautiful tree will become a pile of ashes.

The final verse (v 17) links the preceding poems to their context. The verse begins with a reference to the olive tree of v 16 and ends with mention of burning incense to Baal. Many commentators, noting how the verse links the poems to the preceding sermon, classify the verse as editorial. The language of the verse, however, links it closely to its context; note especially: "Pronounced evil against you," "The house of Israel and the house of Judah," "Burning incense to Baal." The verse links the poems to the sermon, but the language suggests the verse could be original.

Explanation

Jeremiah used traditional materials to weave together this sermon concerning the judgment that would result from the people's failure to keep the covenant. The people had broken the covenant by abandoning their God and worshiping the Baals. Using traditional covenantal language, perhaps even basing his words on Deut 27:15–26, Jeremiah described the curse resulting from the breaking of the covenant. The sermon closely resembles the latter part of the temple sermon recorded in Jer 7. He closes the sermon with two short poems describing the irony and pathos of the situation.

The people were given a second chance with Josiah's reform, but they failed to take advantage of the opportunity. They had the opportunity to renounce their idolatry and perhaps did for a while at the height of the reform, but now they have turned back to the idolatrous ways of their fathers. The covenant has been broken and the people have the gall to think their sacrifices will avert the coming judgment. The disappointment and sorrow of God are evident in the words of Jeremiah, even as he pronounces judgment. God must declare judgment upon the people he has attempted to make his own (v 4), upon his beloved (v 15), upon the tree he has planted (v 16). The Lord has delayed judgment, but because of the persistent rebellion of his people he can delay it no longer. The only solution is the destruction of his people.

Excursus: Jeremiah's Confessions

Bibliography

Ahuis, F. *Der klagende Gerichtsprophet. Studien zur Klage in der Überlieferung von den alttestamentlichen Gerichtspropheten.* Calwer Theologische Monographien 12. Stuttgart: Calwer Verlag, 1982. **Baumgartner, W.** *Die Klagegedichte. Jeremiah's Poems of Lament.* **Behler, G. M.** *Les confessions de Jérémie.* Tournai Casterman: Maredsous, 1959. **Berridge, J. M.** *Prophet, People.* 114–83. **Blank, S. H.** "The Confessions of Jeremiah and the Meaning of Prayer." *HUCA* 21 (1948) 331–54. ———. *Jeremiah: Man and Prophet.* **Bright, J.** "Jeremiah's Complaints: Liturgy, or Expressions of Personal Distress?" In *Proclamation and Presence.* Ed. J. I. Durham and J. R. Porter. London: SCM Press, 1970. 189–214. **Crenshaw, J. L.** "Seduction and Rape: The Confessions of Jeremiah." In *A Whirlpool of Torment: Israelite Traditions of God as an Oppressive Presence.* Overtures to Biblical Theology 12. Philadelphia: Fortress Press, 1984. 31–56. **Diamond, A. R.** *The Confessions of Jeremiah.* **Eichler, U.** "Die klagende Jeremia. Eine Untersuchung zu den Klagen Jeremia und ihrer Bedeutung zum Verstehen seines Leidens." *TLZ* 103 (1978) 918–19. **Fretheim, T.** *The Suffering of God.* Philadelphia: Fortress, 1984. **Herrmann, S.** "Overcoming the Israelite Crisis: Remarks on the Interpretation of the Book of Jeremiah." In *A Prophet to the Nations: Essays in Jeremiah Studies.* Ed. L. G. Perdue and B. W. Kovacs. Winona Lake, IN: Eisenbrauns, 1984. 299–312. **Holladay, W. L.** "The Background of Jeremiah's Self-Understanding." *JBL* 83 (1964) 153–64. [Repr. in *A Prophet to the Nations: Essays in Jeremiah Studies.* Ed. L. G. Perdue and B. W. Kovacs. Winona Lake, IN: Eisenbrauns, 1984. 313–24.] ———. *Jeremiah: Spokesman Out of Time.* Philadelphia: United Church Press, 1974. **Hubmann, F. D.** "Stationen einer Berufung: Die 'Konfessionen' Jeremias—eine Gesamtschau." *TPQ* 132 (1984) 25–39. ———. *Untersuchungen zu den Konfessionen Jer. 11, 18–12, 2, und Jer. 15, 10–21.* Forschung zur Bible 30. Zurich: Echter Verlag, 1978. **Hyatt, J. P.** *Jeremiah, Prophet of Courage and Hope.* New York: Abingdon, 1958. **Ittmann, N.** *Die Konfession Jeremias: ihre Bedeutung für die Verkündigung des Propheten.* WMANT 54. Neukirchen-Vluyn: Neukirchener Verlag, 1981. **Jobling, D. K.** "The Quest of the Historical Jeremiah: Hermeneutical Implications of Recent Literature." *USQR* 34 (1978) 3–12. [Repr. in *A Prophet to the Nations: Essays in Jeremiah Studies.* Ed. L. G. Perdue and B. W. Kovacs. Winona Lake, IN: Eisenbrauns, 1984. 285–98.] **Mihelic, J. L.** "Dialogue with God: A Study of Some of Jeremiah's Confessions." *Int* 14 (1960) 43–50. **Polk, T.** *The Prophetic Persona: Jeremiah and the Language of the Self.* JSOTSup 32. Sheffield, England: JSOT Press, 1984. **Rad, G. von.** "Die Konfessionen Jeremias." *EvT* 3 (1936) 265–76. (Repr. and trans. in *A Prophet to the Nations: Essays in Jeremiah Studies.* Ed. L. G. Perdue and B. W. Kovacs. Winona Lake, IN: Eisenbrauns, 1984. 339–48.) **Reventlow, H. G.** *Liturgie.* **Skinner, J.** *Prophecy and Religion.* **Vermeylen, J.** "Essai de Redaktionsgeschichte des 'Confessions de Jérémie.'" In *Le Livre de Jérémie.* Ed. P.-M. Bogaert. BETL 54. Leuven: UP, 1981. 239–70. **Welten, P.** "Leiden un Leidenserfahrung im Buch Jeremia." *ZTK* 74 (1977) 123–50.

Beginning at 11:18, the Book of Jeremiah records a series of personal complaints. These complaints, which resemble the personal lament in form, have often been called Jeremiah's confessions. Students of these laments have not reached complete agreement about the extent of the laments, but six passages are normally included: 11:18–12:6; 15:10–21; 17:12–18; 18:18–23; 20:7–13; and 20:14–18. Some of the complaints have matching responses by Yahweh. The uniqueness of these laments has occasioned much debate about their nature and purpose. Agreement does not even exist about what they should be called since neutral terminology does not exist; calling them "confessions," "complaints," or "laments" presupposes a different understanding about their nature and purpose. Even though they will be designated confessions in the following discussion, this is only for convenience and is not intended to convey any particular understanding about these passages.

Modern debate about the confessions began with W. Baumgartner (*Die Klagegedichte des Jeremia,* 1917). For Baumgartner the confessions were personal laments modeled after the personal laments of the Psalms. Baumgartner believed the confessions reflected the inner struggle of Jeremiah, and he consequently gave Jeremiah a large role in the creation of the confessions. As a consequence of Baumgartner's view, the confessions were often perceived as merely reflecting the inner struggle of the prophet and therefore not an integral part of his prophetic message; see John Skinner (*Prophecy and Religion,* 1922) for a similar understanding.

Partly in reaction to Baumgartner, but largely under the influence of form critical assumptions, H. G. Reventlow (*Liturgie,* 1963) concluded that the confessions did not represent Jeremiah's inner struggle at all. The confessions were communal laments reflecting the concerns of the community. The prophet identified with the community in his role as cultic intercessor and the prophetic "I" is the prophet's personalization of the community's concerns. Reventlow began with the observation of Baumgartner that the form of the confessions resembled the individual laments of the Psalms. On the basis of the form-critical assumption that all forms of address in the ancient Orient are based on a specific *Sitz im Leben,* Reventlow concluded that the confessions originated in a cultic setting similar to the laments of the Psalms. On the basis of Reventlow's conclusions, the confessions cannot tell us anything about the inner life of the prophet, but are an intimate part of his prophetic message and ministry.

Recent research into the confessions has tended to weld these two view of the confessions together. F. D. Hubmann (*Untersuchungen zu den Konfessionen,* 1978) returned to Baumgartner's view that the confessions do reflect the inner struggle of Jeremiah. He felt that the Lord's responses to the confessions renewed Jeremiah's sense of calling and thus had a direct impact upon his message. N. Ittmann (*Die Konfession Jeremias,* 1981) also concluded that the confessions recorded the inner struggle of the prophet. He distinguished between laments and confessions. Confessions were passages which recorded a confrontation between Jeremiah and the Lord. He emphasized the originality of Jeremiah in the composition of the confessions and concluded that the confessions were integral to Jeremiah's proclamation. F. Ahuis (*Der klagende Gerichtsprophet,* 1982) analyzed the confessions and proposed that they arose in connection with Jeremiah's "oracle of doom," and were therefore not extraneous to his message. The conclusion of these three scholars is that the confessions record the inner struggle of the prophet, while at the same time being an integral part of his message.

The assumptions about the confessions upon which the following study is based are informed by all of the studies surveyed above. In line with Baumgartner and his followers, the confessions are recognized as reflections of the inner life of the prophet. And in agreement with Reventlow, the prophet's role as cultic intercessor is recognized. In some way the sufferings of the prophet, which resulted in his confessions, also reflected the condition of the community and the suffering of God. Jeremiah identified with the community and participated in their suffering. He suffered with particular anguish because it was his inescapable duty to proclaim the approaching judgment. His anguish was real, all the more so because it did not arise from his personal suffering alone but was a reflection of the suffering of his people and the suffering of God.

B. The First Confession: Jeremiah and the Men of Anathoth (11:18–12:6)

Bibliography

Burkitt, F. C. "Justin Martyr and Jeremiah xi 19." *JTS* 33 (1932) 371–373. **Dahood, M.** "Hebrew-Ugaritic Lexicography II." *Bib* 45 (1964) 409. **Diamond, A. R.** *The Confessions of Jeremiah.* **Driver, G. R.** "Difficult Words in the Hebrew Prophets." In *Studies in Old Testament Prophecy.* Ed. H. H. Rowley. Edinburgh: T & T Clark, 1950. 59–61. ———. "Jeremiah xii 6." *JJS* 5 (1954) 177–78. **Ehrman, A.** "Note on בושׁ in Jer. XII. 5." *JSS* 5 (1960) 153. **Gerstenberger, E.** "The Woe-Oracles of the Prophets." *JBL* 81 (1962) 249–63. **Gunneweg, A. H. J.** "Konfession oder Interpretation im Jeremiabuch (Ch. 11, 15, 17, 18, 20)." *ZTK* 67 (1970) 395–416. **Houberg, R.** "Note Sur Jérémie XI 19." *VT* 25 (1975) 676–77. **Hubmann, F. D.** *Untersuchungen zu den Konfessionen Jer. 11, 18–12, 2, und Jer. 15, 10–21.* Forschung zur Bible 30. Zurich: Echter Verlag, 1978. **Kirk, H. E.** "The Hammer and the Anvil: A Subjective Approach to a Pivotal Moment in the Life of a Prophet (Jer. 12:5)." *Int* 1 (1947) 33–40. **McKane, W.** "The Interpretation of Jeremiah xii 1–5." *TGUOS* 20 (1971) 38–48. **Rad, G. von.** "The Confessions of Jeremiah." Repr. and tr. in *A Prophet to the Nations.* Ed. L. G. Perdue and B. W. Kovacs. Winona Lake, IN: Eisenbrauns, 1984. 339–48. **Rowley, H. H.** "The Text and Interpretation of Jer. 11:18–12:6." *AJSL* 42 (1926) 217–27. **Schreiner, J.** *Von Gottes Wort Gefordert; Aus der Verkündigung des Propheten Jeremias.* Düsseldorf: Patmos Verlag, 1967.

Translation

Jeremiah:

18 [a] *The LORD made it known to me,*[b] *and so I knew;*[c]   (3+3)
    then You showed[d] *me their evil deeds.*[e]

19 *But I was like a gentle lamb led to slaughter;*   (5+4)
    I had not known that they devised plots against me:
    [a] *"Let us destroy the tree with its sap,*[a,b]   (3+3+3)
    and let us cut him off from the land of the living,
    that his name be remembered no more."

20 *O LORD of Hosts, who judges righteously,*   (4+3)
    who tries the heart and mind,[a]

    let me see your vengeance upon them,   (3+4)
    for to you I have committed[b] *my cause.*

The Lord:

21 *Therefore thus said the LORD concerning the men of Anathoth, who seek your*[a] *life, and say, "Do not prophesy in the name of the LORD or*[b] *you will die by our hand,"* 22a *Therefore thus says the LORD of Hosts,*[a] *"Behold, I will punish them; the young men shall die by the sword; their sons and their daughters shall die by famine;* 23 *and none of them shall be left, for I will bring evil upon the men of Anathoth, the year of their punishment."*

Jeremiah:

12:1 *Righteous are you, O LORD,*   (3+3+4)
    even when I contend with you,
    nevertheless I would present my case to you.

> *Why does the way of the wicked prosper?*   (4+3)
> *Why do all who are treacherous thrive?*
> 2   *You plant them and they take root;*   (2+3)
> *they grow*ª *and bring forth fruit;*
> *You are near in their mouth*   (3+2)
> *but far from their heart.*
> 3   ª*But you, O LORD,*ª *have known me;* ᵇ*you see me;*ᵇ   (4+3)
> *and you try my heart toward you.*
> ᶜ*Pull them out like sheep for slaughter;*   (3+3)
> *and*ᶜ *set them apart for the day of slaughter.*
> 4   ª*How long will the land mourn?*   (3+3)
> *And the grass and every field wither?*
> *Because of those who dwell in it,*   (2+3)
> *the beasts*ᵇ *and birds are swept away.*ª
> *Because they said,*   (2+3)
> *"He*ᶜ *will not see our latter end."*

The Lord:
> 5   *"If you have raced on foot and they have wearied you,*   (4+3)
> *How will you compete with horses?*
> *And if you trust in a safe land,*   (4+4)
> *How will you do in the jungle of Jordan?*
> 6   *For even your brothers and the house of your father,*   (3+3)
> *even they have dealt treacherously with you.*
> ª*They are in full cry*ᵇ *after you;*ª   (4+2+3)
> *do not believe them,*
> *even though they speak good words to you."*

Notes

11:18.a. The conj is omitted by LXX and Syr, perhaps to link it with the previous verse. It is understood here as a vocative, as in v 20 below.

18.b. Reading with the Syr and LXX γνώρισόν.

18.c. Reading with Rudolph *(BHS)* וָאֵדְעָה = וָאֵדְעָה.

18.d. LXX reads εἶδον = רָאִיתִי, "I saw." Perhaps the MT vocalizations of this and the preceding note arose under the influence of the preceding verse.

18.e. Rudolph proposed transposing 12:6 here to explain what God showed Jeremiah. Bright, Cornill, and *Peake* transpose 12:1–6 before 11:18. Reventlow *(Liturgie,* 240–42) transposed 12:1–4 before 11:18.

19.a-a. LXX reads "Come and let us put wood in his bread" for this phrase.

19.b. Reading בלחו with most commentators; MT reads בלחמו, "with its bread." M. Dahood ("Ugaritic Studies and the Bible," *Gregorianum* 43 [1962] 66) came to much the same conclusion but considered the *mem* in the MT enclitic.

20.a. Rudolph *(BHS)* proposed transposing 12:3 to here.

20.b. Reading גלותי with most commentators for MT גליתי, "revealed."

21.a. LXX has 1 sg.

21.b. LXX reads εἰ δὲ μή = ואם לא.

22.a-a. Omitted in LXX; superfluous here.

12:2.a. Reading ילדו for MT ילכו; supported by LXX.

3.a-a. Rudolph proposed reading simply אתה, "you," mainly on the basis of meter, but there is no textual support for this.

3.b-b. Omitted from LXX.

3.c-c. Omitted from LXX.

4.a-a. Most commentators omit this part of the verse: Volz, Rudolph, Hyatt, etc.

4.b. Many MSS, supported by Syr, Tg, and Vg, read the singular בהמה, "beast," probably in agreement with "bird." Follow MT, the most difficult reading.

4.c. LXX adds ὁ θεός, "God."

6.a-a. Rudolph, following Volz, reads קשרו אחריך כלם, "they have conspired against you." The LXX reading of ἐπισυνήχθησαν, "they have conspired against," somewhat supports this change. Follow MT, the most difficult reading.

6.b. The meaning of the word is uncertain; all versions are interpretive. See Hubmann, *Untersuchungen*, 97–106, for a complete discussion.

Form/Structure/Setting

As with many passages in the book of Jeremiah, this passage presents the exegete with a series of related problems. The resolution of the problems probably depends more upon the exegete's presuppositions than the cogency of the different arguments.

Several problems and inconsistencies in this passage have caused some commentators to suggest rearrangements of the text to surmount these difficulties. These problems include: the rather abrupt manner in which v 18 begins; the unexplained shift from third to second person in v 18; and the amorphous nature of the danger. The following rearrangements of the text are representative:

Bright, *Peake*, Reventlow (rejects v 6): 12:1–6; 11:18–23.
Rowley (*AJSL* 42 [1926] 217–27): 11:18; 12:6; 11:19–20; 12:1–3; 11:21–23; (12:4–5).
Rudolph, Volz: 11:18; 12:6; 11:19–20a; 12:3; 11:20b–23; 12:1–2; 12:4b–5.
Thiel, *Die deuteronomistische Redaktion*, 159: 11:18; 12:6; 11:19–23; 12:1–4a; 12:5

Those who propose such rearrangements of the text justify them as attempts to make better sense of the text. It is debatable, however, whether any attempt to rearrange the text on the basis of a modern conception of meaning is valid. Often the modern exegete assumes that a logical, chronological progression of the text is the basis of meaning and when missing should be supplied. The original editors, who were not averse to emending the text to suit their purposes, apparently perceived adequate meaning in the present arrangement. With the versions in substantial agreement with the MT, the modern exegete must make sense of the received text and not force it into some modern mold.

Another problem in this passage which has plagued commentators is determining which verses are poetry and which are prose. Since this part of Jeremiah is often analyzed on the basis of its identification as either poetry (Type A material) or prose (Type B material), the classification one gives to a particular passage can affect both its date and setting. Holladay, under the influenced of Hubmann, classified the whole passage as poetry thereby supporting his claims for its authenticity. McKane, following Thiel's analysis of Type C material (*Die deuteronomistische Redaktion*, 159), classified 11:20 and 12:1–5 as poetry and the remainder prose. Largely on the basis of this classification, McKane considered 11:21–23 as commentary on 11:18–19 and the poetic fragment in 11:20 as also secondary; likewise he considered 12:6 commentary on 12:1–5. The suggestion followed here and adopted by the majority of commentators classified everything except 11:21–23 as poetry; compare Rudolph, Carroll, RSV.

The basic form used in the passage is the lament as found in the Psalms; for the form of the lament in the Psalms see S. Mowinckel, *The Psalms in Israel's Worship*, trans. D. R. Ap-Thomas (Nashville: Abingdon, 1962), I, 229–39, II, 9–11; for a similar but more detailed analysis of these laments see A. R. Diamond, *The Confessions of Jeremiah in Context*, 22–46, 37–40. The passage contains two separate laments: 11:18–23 and 12:1–6. The basic components of the lament, as reflected in this passage, can be outlined as follows:

Formal Element	1st Lament	2nd Lament
Invocation	11:18	12:1a
Complaint	11:19	12:1b, 2
Prayer	11:20	12:3–4
Divine Response	11:21–23	12:5–6

This formal analysis cannot help us determine whether these are communal or individual laments, since the major difference between communal and individual laments is content; see Mowinckel, *Psalms*, I, 11. Reventlow (*Liturgie*, 244) based his designation of the laments as communal upon the presence of the drought motif (v 4). Carroll (275–79) also considered these laments communal, basing his conclusion partly on the presence of the tree motif (vv 11:19, 12:2), used earlier in the context of the destruction of the nation (v 16). In order to make their theories plausible, both of these commentators must consider 11:21, the reference to Anathoth in 11:23, and 12:6 as secondary, for these verses address concerns of an individual.

These laments are linked to the preceding by the catchword ויהוה (lit., "And the LORD") which begins both v 17 and v 18. The tree motif shared by vv 16–17 and v 19 provides further linkage. See the introduction to this section for the larger thematic unity.

The setting of these laments is difficult to determine because of the use of traditional forms and the lack of historical clues. From the communal point of view, the setting would fit the time before the final deportation, like the surrounding oracles of doom. If we assume that they also speak of the personal experiences of the prophet, we need to identify the plot against him. Perhaps the plot of Hananiah during the reign of Zedekiah (see chap. 37) is the background for this passage, but we have no clear indication that it is.

Comment

This lament begins with obvious abruptness. The context of v 18 is unclear: What does the prophet not know? The abruptness becomes less significant, however, when compared to invocations of other psalmic laments; compare for example Ps 13:1, "How long, O LORD? Will you forget me for ever? How long will you hide your face from me?" See also Ps 28. The abruptness of this verse could also reflect the prophet's initial lack of awareness concerning the plot; see *Comment* on following verse. The Masoretic tradition understands this verse as a simple statement of fact, while the LXX and Syr understand it as vocative.

19 Verse 19 contains the complaint section of the lament. The prophet compared himself to a sheep being led to slaughter (see also 12:3). Like a sheep on the way to slaughter, the prophet was unaware of the threat to his life. The prophet is also described as a tree about to be cut down in the bloom of life (a tree with its sap?), the first of many horticultural metaphors in this and the following lament (see for example the images used in 12:2, 4, 5 in the following lament). The use of the metaphor of the tree has been cited by some as evidence that this is a communal lament, since it was used previously to describe the destruction of the nation (11:16). We understand this as evidence of the broader intent of the complaint; it can be applied to Jeremiah and the nation and may perhaps even mirror the Lord's suffering (see the following lament by God 12:7–17). Jeremiah could complain that his own people plotted his death because they did not want to hear what his prophetic ministry required him to say. Likewise he could complain on behalf of the people that they were being judged by God because of their special status before him. The ambiguity of the passage reflects the ambiguity of the situation in which the prophet found himself. He suffered because of the people and his ministry to them; his announcement of judgment upon the people resulted in his own suffering at the hands of the people. He who had earlier announced to the people that they who had been the Lord's "green olive tree" would be cut down (11:16), now find these same people threatening to cut him down like a green tree. The prophet, who had revealed to the people their fate and the hand of God (11:1–17), has his fate at the hands of the people revealed to him by God. The prophet's fate and the people's fate are intertwined.

20 This verse constitutes the prayer portion of the lament. The prophet pleads for vengeance upon his enemies. The two halves of the verse constitute a twofold basis for the plea. The first half of the verse doxologically describes the Lord as the righteous judge, the tester of men. The second half of the verse contains Jeremiah's actual plea for vengeance upon his enemies. Through the doxological description of the Lord as the righteous judge, Jeremiah implies that the Lord would find Jeremiah righteous if tested (cf. 12:3). The righteous man can naturally expect the Lord to act upon his behalf. In the second half of the verse, Jeremiah claims that he has committed his cause to the Lord; he expects the Lord to punish his enemies.

21 Verse 21 begins the Lord's response to Jeremiah's complaint. Many commentators consider this verse entirely redactional in nature and therefore of only secondary importance. The reasoning behind such a conclusion is a supposed conflict with the preceding verses. The preceding verses are understood by these commentators as describing the plot as hidden from Jeremiah (see for example, Holladay, 374; Hubmann, *Untersuchungen*, 65–72; Thiel, *Die deuteronomistische Redaktion*, 159). An examination of vv 18–20, however, reveals that they describe a plot that was hidden but is now revealed: "then you showed me their evil deeds" (Jer 11:18b). Simply because the preceding verses have not yet delineated the plot against Jeremiah does not mean that it had not been revealed to him. Often the corresponding psalmic laments never specify the evil that prompted the lament (cf. Ps 28). The inclusion of the situation that prompted Jeremiah's lament makes it much more specific and personal. The reference to Anathoth, Jeremiah's hometown (see 1:1), makes it very clear that the lament as it now stands arose out of the situation of Jeremiah's personal life. We must remember, however, that as the Lord's prophet, the fortunes of his personal life were closely linked with the fortunes of the people he served.

This verse also reveals the crux of the enemies' complaint against Jeremiah. They did not want him to continue his prophetic ministry. Surely the background for the enemies' complaint is Jeremiah's many prophecies of doom (e.g., 11:1–17).

22–23 The punishment of Jeremiah's enemies is described in traditional terms in vv 22–23. The enemies are threatened with destruction by sword and famine; the threat of sword and famine (symbolic of invasion?) is common in the prophecies of Jeremiah, especially when linked with "pestilence" דֶּבֶר (chaps 14, 21, 24, 27, 29, 32, 34, etc.). The judgment upon Jeremiah's enemies will come upon them in the "year of their punishment." This phrase occurs two other times, in Jer 23:12; 48:44, both of which are poetic sections. In the first instance it is used in an oracle against the prophets. In the second instance it is found in one of the Oracles against the Nations, against Moab. Judgment is coming upon Jeremiah's enemies and it is described in the same terms as are used to describe the Lord's judgment upon the people for their sins. The complete destruction of a people and their descendants by sword and famine seems an inappropriate punishment for a plot against one man, even if he is a prophet. Once more it is difficult to escape the conclusion that this lament concerns more than just the fortunes of one man.

A note about the destruction of the men of Anathoth: The account of the return from exile recorded in Ezra-Nehemiah states that 128 men of Anathoth returned with the exiles (Ezra 2:23; Neh 7:27), so the destruction was not complete; compare *Comment* on 13:19.

12:1 Chap. 12 begins the second in this series of laments. This lament supplies neither the identity of the speaker or the occasion. Partly because of this, it has been given a wide range of interpretations. In its present position the preceding lament provides both speaker and occasion, but we should be cautious about making assumptions. The two laments have points of contact. The invocation of 12:1, "Righteous are you, O LORD," echoes the prayer of the preceding lament (11:20), "O LORD of Hosts, who judges righteously." The theme of testing is present in 11:20, "who tries the heart and mind," and 12:3, "You try my heart toward you." Both laments use the metaphor of a lamb (11:19; 12:3) and various horticultural metaphors (11:19; 12:2, 4). The mention of Jeremiah's family in 12:6 echoes the reference to the "men of Anathoth" in the preceding lament (11:21–23). The many similarities and points of contact between this and the preceding lament indicate that the two laments address the same situation.

The first verse of this lament is dominated by legal language: "righteous (victorious)" (צַדִּיק), "contend" (רִיב), "case" (מִשְׁפָּט), "wicked" (רֶשַׁע). The first colon is perhaps intentionally ambiguous, "Righteous are you, O LORD . . ." Does it declare the Lord righteous (the righteous judge) or does it declare the Lord innocent of wrongdoing? Is he the one who always gains a favorable decision in a court of law? In context the latter is a real possibility; no matter how strong Jeremiah's case, the Lord always emerges as the winner. The presence of other legal language suggests the use of "contend" (רִיב) in the second colon should be understood in the legal sense of a lawsuit. Holladay (375) noted that in 2:29 Jeremiah uses similar language to declare that Israel does not have a case against the Lord; here Jeremiah claims that while he has a legitimate case against the Lord, he has not the slightest chance of winning a verdict. Still he is determined to have his day in court. In this respect he reminds us somewhat of Job. The third colon uses language that clearly implies the passing of a legal sentence "present my case" (מִשְׁפָּטִים אֲדַבֵּר); it is found only in Jeremiah, see also 1:16; 4:12; 39:5//52:9. The prophet is bold to bring his lawsuit against God.

Jeremiah's complaint begins with the fourth colon of v 1. His statement of the problem is almost classical in formulation: "Why does the way of the wicked prosper? Why do all who are treacherous thrive?" He was confronting the commonly held theory of retribution, which stated that the righteous person would receive good from God's hand and the wicked person would receive evil; on the theory of retribution, see further J. L. Crenshaw, ed., *Theodicy in the Old Testament,* Issues in Religion and Theology 4 (Philadelphia: Fortress Press, 1983). Jeremiah complained that on the contrary the wicked prospered. The complaint is stated in traditional categories and could apply equally well to Jeremiah's personal situation or the fortunes of the nation.

2   The complaint continues in v 2 through the use of a tree metaphor. In 11:19 the threat against Jeremiah's life is described through the image of a green tree being cut down. In this verse Jeremiah describes the prosperity of his enemies with the metaphor of a fruitful tree. Through the metaphor of the tree, Jeremiah not only complains about the inequities of life but also accuses God of complicity in the matter. The enemies are further described as honoring God with their mouths, while being unfaithful in their hearts. This is similar to the indictment of the people in 9:7 [9:8] who speak peace with their mouths but plan ambush in their hearts.

3   The prayer portion of this second lament begins with Jeremiah's protestation of his innocence by urging the Lord to test him, much like the prayer portion of the preceding lament (11:20). It is striking that Jeremiah proclaims his innocence after questioning God's innocence. Jeremiah, who earlier claimed that he was as trusting as a lamb led to slaughter (11:19), now pleads for his enemies to be treated like sheep destined for the slaughter.

4   Instead of continuing with Jeremiah's problems, the first four cola of v 4 change direction and speak of the evil that has come upon the land because of the wickedness of the people: a drought which destroys both plant and animal life. Perhaps because of this change, the Masoretic and Septuagint traditions differ in their assumptions about who is speaking in the verse. The MT seems to assume that Jeremiah is the speaker, as in the surrounding verses. The LXX, on the other hand, seems to assume that God is the speaker. Because of these problems, many commentators omit this part of the verse; see note 4.a-a. Those who delete the first part of the verse feel the different emphasis does not fit. Reventlow (*Liturgie,* 244–51) came to a different conclusion. He concluded that the mention of the drought indicated that this was a communal lament, because droughts were often the subject of communal laments.

If this and the previous laments only concerned the fortunes of Jeremiah, then perhaps the deletion of the first part of this verse would be justified. The evidence, however, argues for a link between the fortunes of Jeremiah and the people. If we accept the MT, which assumes that Jeremiah is the speaker, then this verse acknowledges the link between the fortunes of Jeremiah and the people. The people plotted against Jeremiah because they opposed God. Jeremiah mourns not only because of the plot against him but also because of the sin of his people, revealed in the plot.

5   The Lord's response to Jeremiah's complaint is very uncharacteristic. Instead of assuring Jeremiah that he will vanquish his enemies, through two parallel and perhaps ironic images, he tells him that the worst is yet to come. Jeremiah's present and future troubles are compared to running a footrace with another man and a horse. Likening the future troubles to a horse could be an oblique reference to the enemy from the north. The second image compares the present to living in a safe land and the future to living in the wilderness of Jordan, perhaps an image of exile. This offered no reassurance to Jeremiah and could not comfort him. Baumgartner (59) suggested that the uncharacteristic nature of the answer argues for its authenticity. Recognizing that the fortunes of Jeremiah and the people are inextricably woven together could also explain this uncharacteristic answer.

6 This verse plainly features Jeremiah as its subject. Jeremiah's own family are named among the conspirators mentioned earlier in 11:18–23. The personal nature of this verse has caused many commentators to suggest various dislocations (see *Notes*). As with the previous verse, this is not the normal oracular response to a complaint; it offers little if any reassurance to Jeremiah. If the verse is understood as parallel to 11:21–23, then it can be suggested that the conspirators among Jeremiah's family will be subjected to the same fate as other conspirators—complete annihilation. However, once again this would offer little comfort to the prophet. As with the previous verse, this suggests a link between the fortunes of Jeremiah and his people.

Explanation

For the prophet Jeremiah, suffering formed part of his prophetic office. When he became aware of the plot against his life, he cried to the Lord, "to you I have committed my cause" (11:20). In response to his complaint about the plot against his life, he first received a rather traditional word from the Lord, "Behold I will punish them . . . " (1:21). In the context of this response, we find that his suffering was the result of his prophetic ministry (11:21). When he complained further about the injustice of the situation, the answer he received was far from comforting. In essence, he was told that he would experience even more suffering (12:5–6). The plot against him and the injustice this represented was tied inextricably to the suffering and sin of the people. He was called to announce judgment upon the people. Being one of them caused him to suffer with them because of the Lord's judgment. As God's messenger, he suffered as a result of his prophetic ministry.

C. The Sorrow of God (12:7–17)

Bibliography

Driver, G. R. "1. Ben Sira, xxxiii.4; 2. Jeremiah 12:6." *JJS* 5 (1955) 177–8. **Emerton, J. A.** "Notes on Jeremiah 12:9 and on Some Suggestions of J. D. Michaelis about the Hebrew Words *nahā*, ʿ*aebrā*, and *jadă*." *ZAW* 81 (1969) 182–91. **McKane, W.** "Relations between Prose and Poetry in the Book of Jeremiah with Special Reference to Jeremiah iii 6–11 and xii 14–17." In *A Prophet to the Nations: Essays in Jeremiah Studies*. Ed. L. G. Perdue and B. W. Kovacs. Winona Lake, IN: Eisenbrauns, 1984. 269–85. **Müller, H.-P.** "«Der bunte Vogel» von Jer XII

9." *ZAW* 79 (1967) 225–6. **Seybold, K.** "Der 'Löwe' von Jeremia xii 8. Bermerkungen zu einem prophetischen Gedicht." *VT* 36 (1986) 93–104. **Soggin, J. A.** "Jeremias xii 10a: Eine Parallelstelle zu Deut. xxxii 8/LXX?" *VT* 8 (1958) 304–5.

Translation

7	*"I have forsaken my house,*	(2+2)
	I have abandoned my heritage;	
	I have given the beloved of my soul	(3+2)
	into the hands of her enemies.	
8	*My heritage has become to me*	(2+2)
	like a lion in the forest;	
	she has lifted her voice against me,	(3+2)
	therefore I hate her.	
9	*Has my heritage become a hyena's*[a] *lair*[b] *to*[c] *me?*	(4+3)
	Do the birds of prey[b] *surround her?*	
	Go gather[d] *all the wild beasts;*	(4+2)
	bring them[e] *to devour.*	
10	*Many shepherds have destroyed my vineyard,*	(4+2)
	they have trampled my portion,[a]	
	they have made my pleasant portion	(3+2)
	a desolate wilderness.	
11	*They*[a] *have made it a desolation;*[b]	(2+3)
	desolate, it mourns before me.[b]	
	The whole land is made desolate,	(2+5)
	[c]*but no one lays it to heart.*	
12	*Upon all the plains*[a] *in the wilderness*	(2+2)
	destroyers have come;	
	[b]*for the sword of the LORD devours*[b]	(4+3+3)
	[c]*from one end of the land to the other;*[c]	
	there is no peace for any flesh.	
13	*They sowed*[a] *wheat and reaped*[a] *thorns;*	(4+3)
	they have sifted[b] [c]*to no avail.*	
	They will be ashamed of [d]*their harvests*	(2+2)
	because of the anger of the Lord."[d]	

[14] *Thus says the LORD concerning all*[a] *my evil neighbors*[b] *who touch the heritage which I have made my people Israel inherit: "Behold I will pluck them from their land, but the house of Judah I will pluck from their midst.* [15] *And after I have plucked them, I will again have compassion on them, and I will bring them again each to his heritage and each to his land.* [16] *And if they diligently learn the way*[a] *of my people, to swear by my name, 'As the LORD lives,' as they have taught my people to swear by Baal, then they shall be built up in the midst of my people.* [17] *But if they will not listen,*[a] *then I will pluck up that nation, plucking it and destroying it," says the LORD.*

Notes

9.a. The meaning of this word is uncertain, occurring only here; compare BDB, 840, and KB, 741. The reading here follows the LXX ὑαίνης, "hyena"; see further J. A. Emerton, *ZAW* (1969) 182–91.

9.b. LXX reads σπήλαιον, "cave," in both places; the MT reads הָעַיִט, "bird of prey." Rudolph *(BHS)* suggested the second instance should be read with the article instead of the interrogative (הָעַיִט = הַעַיִט); it makes little difference. Holladay reads הָיֵעַט, "look greedily."

9.c. Rudolph *(BHS)* suggested reading כִּי, "for."

9.d. Reading the niph with the Vg הֶאָסְפוּ; so Volz, Rudolph, Holladay.

9.e. Some MSS and Vg read the qal אָתְיוּ, "come"; so Volz, Rudolph, Holladay. See GKC § 68i for the form.

10.a. Several MSS read נַחֲלָתִי, "my heritage." With no support from the versions, stay with the MT; see Soggin (*VT* [1958] 304–5), who argued that the MT is the most difficult reading and that on the basis of the MSS evidence, the reading should be retained.

11.a. Reading the pl (שָׂמֻהָ) for the MT sg (שָׂמָהּ) with the Syr, Tg, and Vg and all major commentators.

11.b-b. Holladay, following the lead of Rudolph, revocalized two words here (אָבְלָה = אֲבֵלָה, "dried-up"; שָׁמֵמָה = שָׁמְמָה, "she has become desolate"). With no support from the versions, remain with the MT.

11.c. Retaining the כִּי against Duhm, Rudolph; see McKane.

12.a. The meaning of this word is uncertain; see note 3:2.a. for discussion and bibliography.

12.b-b. Rudolph, following Duhm, suggested this was an eschatological gloss, mainly because of the reference to God in the third person.

12.c-c. Bright suggested this was an addition.

13.a. Some LXX read imperatives.

13.b. Repointing נְחֲלוּ = נָחֲלוּ with G. R. Driver, "Linguistic and Textual Problems: Jeremiah," *JQR* n.s. 28 (1937/8) 112; compare NEB.

13.c. Many MSS add a conj here, וְאַל; stay with MT.

13.d-d. Reading מִתְּבוּאֹתֵיהֶם for MT מִתְּבוּאֹתֵיכֶם. LXX reads ἀπὸ καυχήσεως ὑμῶν, ἀπό ὀνειδισμοῦ ἔναντι κυρίου, "of your boasting, because of reproach before the Lord," for the rest of this verse.

14.a. Rudolph *(BHS)* suggested omitting this word.

14.b. The LXX and Tg omit the suff, reading הַשְּׁכֵנִים, "the neighbors."

16.a. Reading sg דֶּרֶךְ with the LXX; cf. 10:2.

17.a. LXX reads ἐπιστρέψωσι = יָשׁוּבוּ, "repent."

Form/Structure/Setting

Jeremiah 12:7–13 is similar in form to the complaint portion of a lament; see C. Westermann, *Basic Forms of Prophetic Speech*, (Philadelphia: Westminster Press, 1967) 202–3. The oracle in 12:14–17 corresponds to the divine response portion of the lament. Most commentators agree that the speaker in the complaint is God. The complaint in vv 7–13 is poetry, and the divine response in vv 14–17 is prose.

The authenticity of vv 14–17 has often been questioned; so Duhm, Volz, McKane. On the other hand, its authenticity has often been upheld; so Weiser, Holladay, and Rudolph (v 14). It should not be assumed that just because vv 14–17 are prose they are a secondary expansion of the preceding lament. The first lament by Jeremiah establishes a similar pattern of poetry and prose; the divine response (11:21–23) is prose while the rest of the lament is poetry. Some commentators also consider part of the divine response (12:6) in the second lament to be prose, which would further establish the pattern; so Rudolph, McKane. In addition to this pattern of poetry and prose, other evidence argues for the authenticity of vv 14–17. The intrinsic connection between vv 7–13 and v 14 based upon the word "heritage" (נחלה) has been noted by many; see especially Rudolph. The thought and language of 15–17 corresponds to other genuine Jeremianic oracles; see 1:10; 18:1–12. The fact that the verses refer to exile and restoration is not sufficient reason to classify them as either exilic (so Thiel, *Die deuteronomistische Redaktion*, 162–68) or post-exilic (so Duhm and Volz). In short, there is no compelling reason to deny the authenticity of vv 14–17.

The location of 12:7–17 suggests that these verses describe the Lord's sorrow paralleling the sorrow Jeremiah expressed in the preceding laments. They express the anguish the Lord felt when confronted by the evil of the people, much as the preceding laments by Jeremiah (11:18–12:6) described his anguish over evil; compare Weiser. The preceding lament by Jeremiah was left uncharacteristically incomplete; the divine response seemed inadequate. These verses help explain this situation. God anguished over the evil of the people and the persecution of Jeremiah as his spokesman. The connection of this divine lament to Jeremiah's lament is confirmed by the common image of the land "mourning" or being "desolate" (אבל); see 12:4, 11.

The complaint portion of the passage (vv 7–13) portrays a period of invasion. The mention of Baal in v 16 suggests a Palestinian setting. These facts fit the period just prior to the Babylonian attack in 598/7, when Judah was being overrun by Chaldean, Aramean, Moabite and Ammonite marauding bands; so, e.g., Rudolph, Bright, Seybold (*VT* 36 [1986] 103–4).

Comment

7   In response to the evil of the people, the Lord forsakes and abandons them. It makes little difference whether we identify "house" (בית) with the temple (e.g., Kimchi, Carroll), the land (e.g., Duhm, Rudolph), or the people (e.g., McKane, Holladay). The image is the same; the Lord has withdrawn his presence and blessing. The description of his withdrawal is not an image of threat or judgment but of pathos. The Lord finds it necessary to abandon his "beloved" people.

8   The image of the lion is often used in the OT to describe the ascendency of Judah (e.g., Gen 49:8–10). In this verse Judah is again described as a lion, but here the analogy is not flattering. Judah, like a lion in the forest, roars against her God. Is this roar an act of defiance or an act of aggression? Given the plot against Jeremiah described in the preceding verse, the roar could very well be the roar of the lion as it leaps on its prey. Perhaps the most striking statement in this whole passage comes when the Lord declares that he "hates" his people, the very people who had earlier been described as his "beloved." Once again we catch a glimpse of the pathos of God (cf. 9:1–10).

9   This verse presents some tenacious translation problems; see H. P. Müller, *ZAW* 79 (1967) 225–28 and J. A. Emerton, *ZAW* 81 (1969) 182–91.

Two problems confront the translator. The word צבוע, translated here "hyena," occurs only here in the OT. The word עיט, "bird of prey," is translated by the LXX by σπήλαιον, "cave" or "lair." The traditional translation of העיט, reflected in the RSV, is "bird of prey." The translation followed ("cave" first, then "bird of prey") here makes good sense of the MT without resorting to emendation. Emerton, following Driver, suggested that the translation of העיט first as "cave" and then as "bird of prey" was intended as a play on words. The image presented is that of a hyena's lair, foul with its victim's carcasses, surrounded by hungry birds of prey. The verse describes Judah as corrupt within, like a hyena's lair, and surrounded by her enemies without, who are ready to pounce upon her.

10   Verse 10 envisions the destruction of agricultural prosperity by invaders. The shepherds of this verse are foreign rulers (cf. 6:3). The structure of this verse closely parallels that of v 7. The first two cola of both verses feature a double description of Judah. The last two cola describe God's giving up of his people to her enemies in v 7 and the destruction of Judah by her enemies in this verse.

11 The desolation of the land is further described in v 11. Rudolph proposed a different division of the words in the first half of the verse resulting in the translation "They have made her into a mournful wilderness, on my account she has become desolate," but with no support from the versions the change is unjustified (see also Holladay).

12 The invaders are pictured as rushing across the wilderness. The image is of the movement of armies throughout the land. The reference to no peace throughout the land may recall the promises of peace by the false prophets (see *Comment* on 8:10–12; cf. also 12:2).

The meaning of the word "plains," שְׁפָיִם in the first colon is uncertain (see note 12.a). Several exegetes, noting that this and the following verse speak of the Lord in the third person, whereas in the larger context he is the speaker, have proposed various deletions to resolve this difficulty (see e.g., notes 12.b. and 12.c.). In the OT, however, changes in person frequently occur within the same context.

13 This verse describes the destruction of crops by marauding armies. The people sowed grain, but because of the destruction of their crops, reaped only thorns; when they sifted their harvest they got nothing. The translation of נֶחְלוּ in the second cola as "sifted" fits the context better than the traditional translation of "tired themselves" (see note 13.b.). The Lord expressed his anger through the destruction of the people's crops.

14–17 The proclamation of judgment upon those nations which invaded and plundered Judah is expected, but his proclamation, like that of Amos 1–2, takes an unexpected turn: Judah will also experience exile (so Rudolph). Perhaps even more shocking is the promise to restore the other nations along with Judah, if they will learn the "way" of God's people (cf. 10:2).

Explanation

Jeremiah's complaint about the justice of God (11:18–12:6) presents Jeremiah as morally outraged at God over his fate. His outrage was heightened by God's answer, which offered no solace but informed him that he had only begun to suffer (12:5–6). The Lord is thus momentarily described as aloof from Jeremiah, as uncaring and unfeeling about his servant's fate. If the story of the injustice suffered by Jeremiah had ended here, Jeremiah could almost be perceived as morally superior to God. Normally, a complaint about God's justice would end with a description of the anguish one felt when confronted with the problem of evil (see Ps 73). But the account does not end with Jeremiah's lament; it is answered by a lament from God. The divine lament portrays God as also suffering because of evil, evil from the hand of his own people. This passage gives us a rare glimpse into the consternation and anguish that evil causes God. The anguish is especially acute for him when his own people are responsible for it. In these verses the Lord expresses both love and hate for his people, emotions we usually consider mutually exclusive, at least for God. When the Lord opened himself up to his people in love, he also opened himself to the possibility of hurt.

These verses present an image of God as passionately involved with his world and his people. It is amazing to think that evil can cause God the same anguish that it causes man. Passages such as this forever discredit the image of God as dispassionate and removed from his world.

D. Symbolism and Sin (13:1–27)

Bibliography

Andreasen, M.-E. "The Role of the Queen Mother in Israelite Society." *CBQ* 45 (1983) 179–94. **Baumann, E.** "Der Linnene Schurz Jer. 13:1–11." *ZAW* 65 (1953) 77–81. **Bourguet, D.** "La métaphore de la ceinture: Jérémie 13:1–11." *ETR* 62 (1987) 165–84. **Dahood, M.** "Two Textual Notes on Jeremiah." *CBQ* 23 (1961) 462–64. **Hermisson, H.-J.** "Jeremias Wort über Jojachin." In *Werden und Wirken des Alten Testaments, Festschrift für Claus Westermann zum 70 Geburtstag.* Ed. R. Albertz, et al. Göttingen: Vandenhoeck & Ruprecht, 1980. 266–68. **Long, B. O.** "The Effect of Divination upon Israelite Literature." *JBL* 92 (1973) 489–96. ———. "Two Question and Answer Schemata in the Prophets." *JBL* 90 (1971) 129–39. **McKane, W.** "Jeremiah 13:12–14: A Problematic Proverb." In *Israelite Wisdom: Theological and Literary Essays in Honor of Samuel Terrien.* Missoula, MT: Scholars Press, 1978. **Southwood, C. H.** "The Spoiling of Jeremiah's Girdle (Jer. xiii 1–11)." *VT* 29 (1979) 231–37. **Williamson, H. A.** "Jeremiah 13:21." *ET* 36 (1924/25) 45.

Translation

THE LINEN WAISTCLOTH

[1] *Thus said the LORD to me: "Go and buy a linen waistcloth for yourself, and put it upon your loins, but do not dip it in water."* [2] *And so I bought a waistcloth according to the word of the LORD, and put it on my loins.* [3] *And the word of the LORD came to me a second time,*[a] [4] *"Take the waistcloth which you bought, which is upon your loins, and arise, go to the Euphrates,*[a] *and hide it there in the cleft of the rock."* [5] *And so I* [a]*went and*[a] *hid it by the Euphrates, as the LORD had commanded me.* [6] *And after many days the LORD said to me: "Arise, go to the Euphrates, and take from there the waistcloth which I commanded you to hide there."* [7] *Then I went to the Euphrates, and I dug, and I took the waistcloth from the place where I had hidden it. And behold* [a]*the waistcloth*[a] *was spoiled;* [b]*it was good for nothing.* [8] *And the word of the LORD came to me:* [9] *Thus says the LORD, "Even so will I spoil*[a] *the pride of Judah and the great pride of Jerusalem.* [10] *This evil people who refuse to listen to my words,* [a]*who stubbornly follow their own heart*[a] *and go after other gods to serve them and worship them,* [b]*let them be like this waistcloth, which is good for nothing.* [11] *For as the waistcloth clings to the loins of a man, thus I made* [a] *the whole house of Israel and*[a] *the whole house of Judah cling to me," says the LORD, "that they might be to me a people, a name, a praise and a glory, but they would not listen.* [12] *You shall speak* [a]*to them this word."*

THE WINE JARS

Thus says the LORD, the God of Israel,[a] *"Every jar*[b] *shall be filled with wine. And if*[c] *they say to you, 'Do we not know that every jar shall be filled with wine?'* [13] *Then you shall* say to them: '*Thus says the* LORD, *behold I will fill with drunkenness all the inhabitants of this land,* ᵃ*the kings who sit upon the throne of David, the priests, the prophets,* ᵇ*and all the inhabitants of Jerusalem.* ¹⁴*And I will dash them one against another, the fathers and sons together, says the* LORD, *I will not spare or pity or have compassion, that I should not destroy them.*'

A FINAL WARNING

15	*Hear and give ear and do not be proud,*	(3+3)
	for the LORD *has spoken.*	
16	*Give glory to the* LORD *your God*	(4+2)
	before he brings darkness,	
	and before your feet stumble	(3+2)
	on the twilight mountains,	
	and you look for the light	(2+2+2)
	*and he makes it into gloom*ᵃ	
	*and makes*ᵇ *it deep darkness.*	
17	*But if you will not listen,*	(3+4)
	ᵃ*in secret*ᵃ *my*ᵇ *soul will weep for* ᶜ*your pride;*ᶜ	
	*my eyes will weep bitterly*ᵈ *and run down with tears,*	(4+4)
	because the LORD'S *flock has been* ᵉ*taken captive.*ᵉ	

A ROYAL WARNING

18	*Say*ᵃ *to the King and Queen mother:*ᵇ	(3+2)
	"Take a lowly seat,	
	for ᶜ*from your head*ᶜ *has come down,*	(3+2)
	your beautiful crown."	
19	*The store cities*ᵃ *are shut up,*	(3+2)
	with no one to open;	
	All of Judah is exiled,	(3+2)
	ᵇ*exiled completely.*ᵇ	

THE PEOPLE'S LOT

20	*"Lift up*ᵃ *your eyes*ᵇ *and see*ᶜ	(3+2)
	those coming from the north.	
	Where is the flock that was given to you,	(3+2)
	your beautiful flock?	
21	*What will you say when they*ᵃ *set*ᵇ*as head*ᵇ *over you,*	(3+3+3)
	those whom you have taught	
	to be your friends?	
	Will not pangs take hold of you,	(3+3)
	*like a woman in travail?*ᶜ	
22	*And if you say in your heart,*	(3+3)
	'Why have these things come upon me?'	
	Because of the greatness of your iniquity	(2+2+2)
	your skirts are lifted up,	
	and your heels suffer violence.	

23   *Can the Ethiopian*ᵃ *change his skin,*   (3+2)
      or the leopard his spots?
      Then neither can you do good   (3+2)
      who are trained to do evil.

24   *I will scatter you*ᵃ *like chaff driven*   (2+2)
      by the wind of the desert.

25   *This is your lot, your measured portion*ᵃ   (2+2)
      from me," says the LORD,
      "because you have forgotten me   (3+2)
      and trusted in the lie.

26   *I myself will lift up your skirts over your face,*   (4+2)
      and your shame will be seen.

27   *Your adulteries and your neighings,*   (2+2)
      your lewd harlotries,
      on the hills ᵃ*in the field*   (2+2)
      I have seen your abominations.
      *Woe to you, Jerusalem,*ᵇ   (3+2+3)
      you are not clean.
      How much longer yet?"

Notes

3.a. LXX lacks "a second time."
4.a. αʹ reads εἰς Φαραν, "to Pharan."
5.a-a. LXX omits; Janzen, *Studies*, 40, classified it as an expansion.
7.a-a. LXX reads simply "it"; see Janzen, *Studies*, 40.
7.b. Many MSS add the conj; cf. LXX and Syr.
9.a. Rudolph (*BHS*) suggested reading נשחת, "was spoiled," like v 7.
10.a-a. Missing from LXX.
10.b. Rudolph (*BHS*) suggested reading the form with the *waw*-consec, וְיהי.
11.a-a. This phrase is perhaps a later addition since the passage is about Judah and Jerusalem; its presence in LXX, however, argues for its authenticity.
12.a-a. For this phrase LXX reads πρὸς τὸν λαὸν τοῦτον = אל־העם הזה, "to this people." McKane suggested the LXX is original and MT resulted from an attempt to link this verse to preceding verses.
12.b. This can also be translated "skin"; see further A. M. Honeyman, "The Pottery Vessels of the Old Testament," *PEQ* (1939) 76–90; J. L. Kelso, *The Ceramic Vocabulary of the Old Testament* (BASORSup 5–6, New Haven: American School of Oriental Research, 1948) 25–26.
12.c. Reading with Rudolph (*BHS*) and supported by LXX ואם יאמרו, the אם omitted by haplogr.
13.a. Omitting ו, "and," with Rudolph (*BHS*).
13.b. LXX adds καὶ τὸν Ιουδαν, "and Judah."
16.a. The LXX reads καὶ ἐκεῖ σκιὰ θανάτου = ושם צלמות, "and there the shadow of death." G. R. Driver ("Linguistic and Textual Problems: Jeremiah," *JQR* n.s. 28 [1937/38] 112) understood the final ה as representing the masc suff.
16.b. Reading ושים.
17.a-a. Rudolph (*BHS*) suggested reading either במסררים, "in stubbornness," or במסרבים, "in rebellion," for MT במסתרים, "in secret," and placing it with the preceding line; compare NEB.
17.b. LXX and αʹ read 2 pl.
17.c-c. Rudolph, Volz, propose reading נלה, "captivity"; cf. second half of verse. Syr reads the equivalent of צרה, "distress."
17.d. Absent from LXX and omitted by many. Stay with MT.
17.e-e. LXX reads συνετρίβη = נשבר, "broken."
18.a. MT has sg; LXX and some Syriac MSS read the pl.
18.b. LXX and Syr read καὶ τοῖς δυναστέυουσι = ולגבורים, "and to the princes."
18.c-c. The MT is peculiar; most read מראשיכם, "from your heads," with LXX, Syr, and the Vg. Dahood (*CBQ* 23 [1961] 462) reached a similar translation without emending the MT consonantal text.

19.a. Often this is translated as the place name "Negeb." For this translation see Dahood, *Hebrew-Ugaritic Philology,* 66.

19.b-b. "Completely" (שׁלומים), is masc pl and "exiled" (הגלת) is fem sg; see GKC § 75m, 118g, 124d. The versions and Amos 1:6, 9 read גָּלוּת שְׁלֵמָה.

20.a. Reading the sg K; see GKC § 145m. Many MSS, Syr, Tg, and Vg read the sg. LXX reads sg and adds "Jerusalem"; so Volz, Bright. Rudolph, followed by Holladay, added "Zion."

20.b. MT reads pl. Rudolph (*BHS*) reads the sg to agree with K of previous note. Dahood (*Hebrew-Ugaritic Philology,* 50) retains the MT but reads the final *mem* as enclitic and the suff as sg.

20.c. Q reads pl, K sg.

21.a. Reading the pl יפקדו with the LXX; MT has sg (יפקד).

21.b-b. The first half of this verse is difficult, lit., "What will you say when he sets over you and you yourself have taught them, over your friends for a head." In MT b-b follows "friends." Rudolph (*BHS*) also transposed b-b but proposed reading it as an abbreviation of "Jerusalem" (ירוש); see also Williamson, *ET* 36 (1924/25) 45.

21.c. On this form see GKC § 128t.

23.a. Lit., "Cushite."

24.a. Reading ואפיצכם for MT ואפיצם, "I will scatter them."

25.a. LXX reads τοῦ ἀπειθεῖν ὑμᾶς = מריך, "your rebellion"; cf. NEB.

27.a. LXX adds "and."

27.b. LXX, *a´* add ὅτι=כי, "because."

Form/Structure/Setting

Chapter thirteen is an editorial unit consisting of at least five originally diverse passages united by the common themes of sin and judgment, and joined together by catchwords. The different units within the chapter can be distinguished from each other on the basis of form-critical criteria and changes in subject matter. The chapter is equally divided between poetry and prose (vv 1–14 are prose, and vv 15–27 are poetry). The different sections within the chapter can be outlined as follows.

> The Linen Waistcloth (13:1–12a)
> The Wine Jars (13:12b–14)
> A Final Warning (13:15–17)
> A Royal Warning (13:18–19)
> The People's Lot (13:20–27)

The first (vv 1–12a), third (vv 15–17), and fourth (vv 18–19) subsections share the ideas of judgment (see vv 9, 17, and 19) and pride (vv 9, 15, 17, and 18); compare Weiser. The catchword "spoil," שׁחת links the first two subsections (see vv 7, 9, and 14). "Listen," שׁמע, provides a link between the first and third sections (see vv 10–11, 15). The third and fourth subsections share the catchword "come down," ירד (vv 17, 18). The two final subsections contain the catchwords "beautiful," תפארת (vv 18, 20, also v 11), and "flock," עדר (17, 20). All of the sections share the idea of the pride or glory of the people being spoiled or shamed. The catchword "fill," מלא, connects this chapter to Jeremiah's laments; see 12:6; 13:12, 13. For the larger thematic connections of this chapter to this section see the introduction to chapters 11–13.

1–12a This first subsection, describing the spoiling of Jeremiah's loincloth, reports the first of many symbolic actions in this Book of Jeremiah; see also 16:1–4; 18:1–12; 19:1–2, 10–11; 27:1–28:17; 32:1–15; 43:8–13; 51:59–64 (see further J. Lindblom, *Prophecy in Ancient Israel* [London: Basil Blackwell, 1962] 137–48, 165–73;

G. Fohrer, *Die symbolische Handlungen der Propheten,* 2nd ed., ATANT 54 [Zurich: Zwingli Verlag, 1968] 33–55, 78–80). Commentators disagree about the exact nature of this symbolic act. The passage has been variously analyzed as a description of a normal symbolic action (Bright), a dream (Weiser), a vision (Rudolph), spoken parable (Volz), and an enacted parable similar to street theater (Carroll). The major obstacle to understanding the passage as an actual symbolic action is the mention of the Euphrates River. If Jeremiah had gone to the Euphrates River twice, as the passage indicated, this would have entailed two trips of about 700–800 miles. John Bright argued that Jeremiah did not actually go to the Euphrates, but to Parah, a short distance from Anathoth (see John 18:23). He believed that "Parah" was intended to stand symbolically for "Euphrates," heightened by similarity in sound and spelling between "Euphrates" (פְּרָת) and "Parah" (פָּרָה). He suggested the present text, which reads "Euphrates," resulted from later readers understanding and reading "Euphrates"; compare Thiel, *Die deuteronomistische Redaktion,* 170–74. Aquila's translation seems to assume "Parah" instead of "Euphrates"; see note 4.a.

The problem of the long trip to the Euphrates only exists if the passage is understood as referring to the exile. If we read "Parah" instead of "Euphrates," however, all reference to or suggestion of exile is removed. The explanation the passage gives for the spoiling of the waistcloth (vv 8–12a) is the idolatry of the people. Rudolph is perhaps correct in thus dating the passage to the early part of Jeremiah's ministry.

Following the Hebrew paragraph division we end this passage with the first phrase from v 12. Holladay noted that the phrase found in 12a, "And you shall speak to them this word," is found elsewhere in Jeremiah only at 14:17, where it likewise follows the passage to which it refers. This resolves the difficulty of the double rubric noted by many commentators (e.g., Rudolph and Bright).

12b–14 The basis of this passage is the quoting of a popular or even banal saying, "every jar shall be filled with wine." The provenance of the saying was perhaps a drinking bout associated with a pagan cultic occasion. B. O. Long (*JBL* 90 [1971] 134–39) analyzed that passage as an instance of the question-and-answer schema rooted in the practice of the people asking the prophet for an oracle; compare Ezek 21:1–10 and 37:15–19. The form of the passage, as we find it in Jeremiah, is a judgment oracle (cf. Holladay). The different images used in vv 13 and 14 (drunkenness and smashing) suggest that these verses were originally separate. This does not necessarily indicate, however, that v 14 is a later addition or not original to Jeremiah.

The passage reflects a time when the community was fragmented (see especially v 14) and could refer to the civil strife in the time of Zedekiah; so Rudolph, Weiser, and Weippert (*Die Prosareden,* 83).

15–17 Verses 15–17 are a brief poem in which Jeremiah calls for repentance. Verse 15 and the first colon of v 16 warn people to follow the Lord. The remainder of v 16 gives the consequences of not following him. The final verse reflects Jeremiah's grief over the people's fate. The passage can be understood as reflecting a future captivity, perhaps the period just before 597 B.C.; so Rudolph, Weiser.

18–19 Following the warning to the people comes a warning to the leaders. Most commentators feel the warning was addressed to Jehoiachin and the Queen mother, Nehusta (see 2 Kgs 24:8–17), just prior to the surrender in 597 (so, e.g.,

Bright). Since Jehoiachin was only eighteen years old when he reigned, many suppose that his mother counseled him; there is no concrete evidence to support this, however (see Andreasen, *CBQ* 45 [1983] 192). The warning could also have been addressed to Jehoiakim and his mother, Zebuddah (2 Kgs 23:36) (so Duhm).

Like the previous passage this passage in its present form is a judgment speech. It is structured like a lament and reflects the common lament meter, *qīnāh.*

20–27 Many commentators have questioned the unity of this passage; so Volz, Rudolph, McKane. The major difficulty in the passage is the change of voice: vv 20–22, 25–27 are second person feminine singular, and vv 23–24 are second person masculine plural. Rudolph classified vv 23–24 as secondary because in addition to the change of voice the exile is mentioned only in vv 23–24. It has been further recognized by many that vv 25–27 pick up the imagery of the shamed women from v 22. Other arguments can be marshalled in support of the unity of the passage. Against Rudolph, the exile is implied in the scattering of the flock by the enemy from the north in v 20. Weiser noted how "your lot" (גורלך) in v 25 picks up the threat of exile in v 24. The form of the passage is not monolithic, but the formal variation does not support the independent nature of vv 23–24. The passage is a mixture of accusation (vv 22, 23, 25b, 27) and announcement of judgment (vv 20–21, 24, 25a, 26), with no clear delineation between the two. The evidence both for and against the unity of the passage is inconclusive and its unity is maintained.

The passage is usually dated in the early period of Jeremiah's ministry; so Rudolph, Holladay.

Comment

1–7 The first seven verses of Jer 13 describe the symbolic action involving the linen waistcloth. The symbolic action involved three divine commands to Jeremiah. The first command (vv 1–2) instructs him to go, buy a linen waistcloth, and wear it but not wash it. Rashi, followed by many modern commentators, suggested that the reason for not washing the cloth was so that it would rot more easily since it was full of sweat. The reason the passage gives for not washing the cloth (see vv 8–12a below), however, does not agree with this. The possible significance of using linen for the waistcloth has also been noted by many (see e.g., Holladay, 397), but the explanation of the symbolic action in vv 8–12a gives no significance to the cloth used. Perhaps we should let the passage speak for itself. The second command to Jeremiah (vv 3–5) instructs him to go the Euphrates, to take the waistcloth off and hide it in the cleft of a rock (see *Form/Structure/Setting* on the Euphrates). In the final command (vv 6–7), Jeremiah is instructed to retrieve the waistcloth, but when he does he finds it spoiled, worthless.

8–12a Verses 8–12a explain the significance of this symbolic action. The majority of commentators understand this passage in relation to the exile. The passage itself, however, does not support such an interpretation. The explanation of the symbolic action likens the people to the loincloth. The constant wearing of loincloth symbolizes the Lord's continuous care of the people. As long as the people clung to the Lord and listened to him, they prospered, but when they abandoned him, they were spoiled (cf. Rudolph). The hiding of the girdle symbolizes the apostasy of the people. Verse 10 describes the people straying from God in terms of idolatry. The verse echoes the language and themes Deuteronomy, causing some to label the verse Deuteronomistic (so Nicholson, and Thiel, *Die deuteronomistische Redaktion*, 170–74; but see *Form/Structure/Setting* on 11:1–17 for a different assessment of a similar passage; cf. also *Comment* on 11:3–5). The similarity of v 10 to Deut 26:17–19 suggests that Jeremiah might have had this passage from Deuteronomy in mind.

12b–14 This brief oracle of judgment builds upon a popular, perhaps banal, saying. The passage was perhaps inserted after the preceding passage, because of the feeling that a further threat and description of judgment was needed (cf. Thiel, *Die deuteronomistische Redaktion*, 176–77). Jeremiah probably quoted this popular witticism to shock his hearers; we are not told how a prophet would know this drinking witticism if it came from a pagan cult. This understanding of the passage links it well with the preceding passage, particularly v 10, which speaks of the idolatrous practices of the people. Jeremiah builds upon this popular image and declares that the Lord will fill the people with drunkenness as the jars are filled with wine. The motif of drunkenness can also be found in Jer 25:15–29 and 48:26; see W. McKane, "Poison, Trial by Ordeal and the Cup of Wrath," *VT* 38 (1980) 474–92. The passage further describes judgment upon the people by the image of the shattering of the wine jars. The drunk people (full wine jars) totter around and stumble into one another, smashing one another. Verse 14 is thought by most to reflect intercommunity strife.

15–17 The people who would not listen to the Lord (vv 10–11) are now commanded to listen to a word of judgment from him. Nicholson has suggested the imagery in v 16 is that of shepherds guarding their flock (see v 17) upon a hillside, looking for the light of morning. Jeremiah warns the people that if they do not listen to the Lord, the darkness will never end, the dawn will not break forth. Verses 15–16 appear to be an oracle uttered by Jeremiah, while v 17 is Jeremiah's personal response to the oracle. Verse 17 expresses the anguish of the prophet over the impending exile of his people in terms similar to 8:21–23 [9:1].

18–19 This word of judgment to the rulers parallels the previous word of judgment directed to the people (vv 15–17). With most commentators (e.g., Weiser, McKane, and Holladay), we assume that the MT is correct and that Jeremiah received this word instructing him to declare judgment upon the king and queen mother; the LXX and Syriac assume that the people are the recipients of the message. The young king Jehoiachin (nineteen years old) and his mother are the most likely objects of this judgment speech (see *Form/Structure/Setting* for more on the role of the queen mother). The abdication of the throne symbolizes the defeat of the nation (cf. 22:24–30 for other words concerning Jehoiachin). The traditional translation of עָרֵי הַנֶּגֶב in v 19 has been "cities of the Negeb." This translation assumes that the Chaldean army or its allies had already cut off the cities to the south; see Rudolph. The general background for this passage is found in 2 Kgs 24:1–17. The translation of the phrase as "store cities" seems to fit the situation better. The store cities are shut up so that the king's armies could not be supplied. Defeat is unavoidable. Rudolph noted the "total" exile mentioned in v 19 and commented that Jeremiah either used poetic exaggeration or the exile was not as bad as he expected (cf. Jer. 52:28; 2 Kgs 24:12–16).

20–27 Jerusalem is the subject of this passage of accusation and announcement of judgment. In its present position the passage appears to give the reason for the exile threatened in the preceding verses, even though there is little direct connection. The first two verses of this passage (vv 20–21) announce the threat of the enemy from the north and condemn Jerusalem for failing to safeguard her flock. Verse 21 is difficult. The traditional understanding of the verse is perhaps still the best (cf. Kimchi); the verse alludes to the time when Ahaz appealed to Assyria for help (Isa 7). Ahaz thereby brought disaster upon the land by encouraging a foreign power to come and act as savior, opening the way for this power to come later as hostile invader. The people who "taught" (למד) themselves evil (see v 23), "taught" the foreign powers to be their friends and thereby sealed their doom (cf. 9:1–5 [9:2–6]). Jeremiah elsewhere used the image of birth pangs; see 4:31; 6:24; and 22:23. Verse 22 speaks of the reason for judgment and the resulting humiliation of Jerusalem. Many commentators, noting the euphemistic use of skirts and heels, perceive this humiliation as the rape of Jerusalem or the queen mother as would happen during invasion (cf. also v 27). Since v 27 speaks of the immoral practices of the pagan cults, the more likely image is that of public humiliation for adultery. The people are firmly entrenched in their evil (v 23); they can no more change their evil ways than an Ethiopian can change the color of his skin or a leopard change this spots. Jerusalem has trusted in "the lie," in Baal (v 25), and forgotten the Lord. Because of the sin of Jerusalem, the Lord will make her shame known (v 26). The people have readily participated in the immoral practices of the pagan cults, neighing like copulating horses (cf. 5:8). The adulteries of Jerusalem are evident to the Lord and because of them he brings invasion and captivity. The prophet cries, "Woe to you Jerusalem. How much longer can your uncleanness continue?"

Explanation

This chapter graphically illustrates sin and its effect. The evil of Jerusalem is portrayed first through the image of the linen waistcloth. The people are represented by the waistcloth (vv 1–12a). As long as the people clung to the Lord, they were preserved. When they sinned by abandoning the Lord and serving other gods, they became spoiled like the waistcloth; Jeremiah mockingly quotes to the sinful people a drinking witticism, "every jar shall be filled with wine" (vv 12b–14), perhaps what the people cried at the pagan festivals. They will be filled with wine and destroy themselves in their drunkenness. After these illustrations of sin and its effect, Jeremiah calls upon the people to repent before it is too late (vv 15–17), all the while knowing it is too late; exile is inevitable. Judgment and exile are coming, and the rulers will be removed from their thrones as the last act of subjugation (vv 18–19). The chapter ends with one last illustration of the people's sin. Jerusalem has committed adulteries with the pagan gods and will suffer the humiliation suitable for an adulteress (vv 20–27). The effects of sin are inevitable; the punishment fits the crime.

It is the nature of the sinner to deny the sin. After Jeremiah's graphic illustrations of their sin, how could his people deny their sin? Jeremiah's picture of judgment shows that it is a natural and inevitable result of sin. Because the people no longer clung to the Lord, they were spoiled like the waistcloth. Because they got drunk in the pagan rites, their drunkenness destroyed them. Because they defiled themselves through participation in pagan rites, their shame became evident for all to see.

VIII. Judgment and Ostracism (14:1–16:21)

Introduction

Laments by Jeremiah dominate this editorial unit. The first rather long section (14:1–15:9) contains two parallel laments that effectively proclaim God's judgment upon the people. The second section (15:10–21) uses two parallel laments to describe the social ostracism Jeremiah experienced as a result of his prophetic ministry. The final section further describes how Jeremiah's sufferings were the result of his prophetic ministry: the Lord commanded him to refrain from marriage and attending funerals and weddings to illustrate the severity of his message. The different sections originate from different times and dates and circumstances. They were probably compiled into this unit sometime after the fall of Jerusalem, perhaps by Jeremiah.

The major delimiter for this editorial unit is the superscription at 14:1 (compare 7:1; 11:1; and 18:1); so Rudolph; Hubmann, *Untersuchungen*, 109; Thiel, *Die deuteronomistische Redaktion*, 106–7. This unit is linked to the previous unit by the theme of drought (see 14:2–6; 12:4). The unit can be divided into three major sections, all of which are composed of subsections.

> 14:1–15:9 Drought and Destruction
> 15:10–21 Jeremiah's Ostracism
> 16:1–21 Jeremiah's Life and Related Sayings

The first two sections are both composed of two parallel laments and are relatively unified coherent sections. The final section contains several subsections more or less loosely joined together.

The first section contains both poetry and prose and is constructed as a counter-liturgy. The normal lament form is transformed in the first section into a vehicle for announcing God's judgment. The second section is composed entirely of poetry and contains two parallel laments similar in form to the first section. Jeremiah laments the social ostracism he experienced as a result of his prophetic ministry. The first section is perhaps an example of his words which precipitated his suffering. The final section more closely ties Jeremiah's suffering to his prophetic ministry. It relates how Jeremiah was commanded by the Lord to refrain from marriage and from attending funerals and weddings to symbolically illustrate the message of judgment he declared. In addition to the parallel form of the first two subsections and the development of theme throughout all three sections, the motif of the mother in all three sections (see 15:8–9; 15:10; 16:1–4; cf. Rudolph; Hubmann, *Untersuchungen*, 302–4) confirms the unity of the group. For further ties between the sections see *Form/Structure/Setting* on the individual sections.

A. Drought and Destruction (14:1–15:9)

Bibliography

Beuken, W. A. M., and **Grol, H. W. M. van.** "Jeremiah 14, 1–15, 9: A Situation of Distress and its Hermeneutics, Unity and Diversity of Form-Dramatic Development." In *Le Livre de Jérémie: le Prophète et son milieu, les oracles et leur transmission.* Ed. P.-M. Bogaert. BETL 54. Leuven: UP, 1981. 297–342. **Brueggemann, W.** "Jeremiah's Use of Rhetorical Questions." *JBL* 92 (1973) 358–74. **Castellino, G. R.** "Observations on the Literary Structure of Some Passages in Jeremiah." *VT* 30 (1980) 398–708. **Dahood, M.** "Emphatic Lamedh in Jer 14:21 and Ezek 34:29." *CBQ* 37 (1975) 341–2. **Fohrer, G.** "Abgewiesene Klage und untersagte Fürbitte in Jer 14, 2–15, 2." In *Künder des Wortes: Beiträge zur Theologie der Propheten.* Ed. L. Ruppert, P. Weimer, and E. Zenger. Würzburg: Echter Verlag, 1982. **Geus, C. H. J. de.** "The Importance of Archaelogical Research into Palestinian Agricultural Terraces with an Excursus on the Hebrew Word *gbī*." *PEQ* 107 (1975) 65–74. **Kessler, M.** "From Drought to Exile: A Morphological Study of Jer. 14:1–15:4." SBLASP (1972) 501–25. **Marenof, S. A.** "A Note on Jer. 14:4." *AJSL* 55 (1938) 198–200. **Meyer, I.** *Jeremia und die falschen Propheten.* OBO 13. Göttingen: Vandenhoeck & Ruprecht, 1977. **Polk, T.** *The Prophetic Persona: Jeremiah and the Language of the Self.* JSOTSup 32. Sheffield: JSOT Press, 1984. **Sisson, J. P.** "Jeremiah and the Jerusalem Conception of Peace." *JBL* 105 (1986) 429–42. **Thomas, D. W.** "A Note on וְלֹא יָדְעוּ in Jeremiah xiv 18." *JTS* 39 (1938) 273–74.

Translation

[1] *The word of the LORD* [a] *which came* [a] *to Jeremiah concerning the droughts:* [b]

2   *Judah mourns* [a]   (2+2)
   and her gates languish;
   they mourn on the ground   (2+3)
   and the cry of Jerusalem goes up.

3   *And her* [a] *nobles send their servants* [b] *for water;*   (4+2)
   they go to the cisterns, [c]
   [d] *they do not find water,*   (2+3)
   they return with their vessels empty;
   [e] *they are ashamed and confounded*   (2+2)
   and cover their heads. [e]

4   *Because the ground is dismayed,* [a]   (3+3)
   since there is no rain [b] *in the land,* [b]
   the farmers are ashamed, [c]   (2+2)
   [d] *they cover their heads.*

5   *Even a hind in the field*   (3+2+3)
   gives birth and forsakes, [a]
   because there is no grass.

6   *And the wild asses* [a] *stand on the heights,*   (3+3)
   they pant for air like jackals; [b]
   their eyes fail   (2+2)
   for there is no herbage.

7	*Though our iniquities testify against us,* (3+4)
	O LORD, act for your name's sake;
	For our backslidings are many, (2+2)
	against you we have sinned.
8	*O hope of Israel,*[a] (2+3)
	its savior in time of trouble,
	Why should you be like a stranger in the land, (4+3)
	and like a wayfarer[b] *who turns aside to spend the night?*
9	*Why should you be like a helpless*[a] *man,* (4+3)
	like a mighty man[b] *who is unable to save?*
	But you are in our midst, O LORD, (3+3+1?)
	and your name is called over us;
	Do not leave us!

[10] Thus says the LORD concerning this people: "Thus[a] they have loved to wander, they have not restrained their feet; [b]therefore the LORD does not accept them, now he will remember their iniquity [c]and punish their sins."[b,c]

[11] And the LORD said to me: "Do not pray again for the welfare of this people. [12] When they fast, I will not hear their cry; and when they offer burnt offering and cereal offering, I will not accept them; for by the sword, and by famine, and by pestilence I will consume them."

[13] Then I said: "Ah, Lord GOD, behold the prophets are saying to them, 'You shall not see the sword, nor shall there be famine, but[a] enduring peace[a] I will give you in this place.'"

[14] And the LORD said to me: "The prophets are prophesying falsehood in my name; I did not send them, and I did not command them, and I did not speak to them. A lying vision and divination, and worthlessness[a] and the deceit[b] of their own minds, they are prophesying to you."[c]

[15] Therefore thus says the LORD concerning the prophets who prophesy in my name[a] although I did not send them and who are saying, 'Sword and famine shall not come on this land': "By sword and famine those very prophets shall be consumed. [16] And the people to whom they are prophesying will be cast out into the streets of Jerusalem because of famine and sword; and there shall be none to bury them, neither them, their wives, their sons nor their daughters, for I will pour out upon them their wickedness." [17] And you shall speak to them this word:

	Let my eyes run down with tears, (3+3)
	night and day without ceasing.[a]
	For with a great[b] *wound the virgin*[c] *daughter* (3+2+3)
	of my people[d] *has been smitten,*
	struck by a fatal blow.
18	*When*[a] *I go out into the field,*[a] (2+2)
	I see those slain by the sword.
	And when[a] *I enter the city,*[a] (3+3)
	I see the ravages of famine.
	Yet both prophet and priest ply their trade[b] (3+3)
	in the land, [c]*and have no knowledge.*
19	*Have you completely rejected Judah,* (3+3)
	or does your soul loathe Zion?
	Why have you smitten us, (2+3)

> *so there is no healing for us?*
> ^a*We looked for peace and there was no good,* (4+4)
> *and*^b *for a time of healing, but behold terror.*^a

20 *We acknowledge our wickedness, O LORD,* (3+2+3)
    the iniquity of our fathers,
    for we have sinned against you.

21 *Do not spurn us,*^{a b} *for your name's sake,*^b (3+3+4)
    do not^c *dishonor*^d *your glorious throne,*
    remember, do not break your covenant with us.

22 *Are there among the false gods of the nations any that can cause rain?* (4+3)
    Or can the heavens themselves send showers?
    Is it not rather you, ^a*O LORD our God,*^a (3+2+3)
    ^b*in whom we set our hope?*
    For it is you who have done all these things.

15:1 *Then the LORD said to me: "Though Moses and Samuel*^a *stood before me, I would not be favorably disposed toward this people; send them*^b *out of my presence and let them go.* ²*And if they ask you, 'Where are we to go?' you shall say to them, 'Thus says the LORD:*

> *Those who are for death, to death;* (3+3)
> *and those who are for the sword, to the sword;*
> *and those who are for famine, to famine;* (3+3)
> *and those who are for captivity, to captivity.'*

³ *"And I will appoint over them four destroyers," says the LORD: "the sword to slay, and the dogs to tear, and the birds of the heavens and the beasts of the earth to devour and to destroy.* ⁴*And I will make them a terror*^a *to all the kingdoms of the earth, because of what*^b *Manasseh, the son of Hezekiah, king of Judah, did in Jerusalem.*

5 *"For*^a *who will pity you, O Jerusalem?* (4+3)
    Or who will bemoan you?
    And who will turn aside to inquire^b (3+2)
    about your welfare?

6 *You have rejected me," says the LORD,* (3+2)
    "you keep going backward;
    so I stretched out my hand against you and destroyed you, (4+2)
    ^a*and I have grown weary of relenting.*^a

7 *And I have winnowed them with a winnowing fork,* (2+2)
    in the gates of the land.
    I have made them childless, I have destroyed my people; (3+2)
    ^a*they did not turn from their ways.*^a

8 ^a*I have made their widows*^b *more in number* (2+2)
    than the sand of the seas.^a
    I have brought ^c*against the mothers of the young men*^c (4+2)
    a destroyer at noonday.
    I have made fall upon them,^d *suddenly,* (3+2)
    anguish and terror.

9 *She who bore seven has languished;* (3+2)
    her life has swooned away.
    Her sun went^a *down while it was still day;* (4+2)

> *she was shamed and disgraced.*
> *And the rest of them I will give to the sword*   (3+2)
> *before their enemies, "*
>
>

says the LORD.

Notes

1.a-a. The LXX reads καὶ ἐγένετο, suggesting the more regular form ויהי, "and was"; see GKC § 138e n. 2. This unusual heading also occurs in 46:1; 47:1; 49:34.

1.b. LXX has sg here. On this unusual pl, see GKC § 124e and König, *Syntax*, 259c; an abstract sg or a pl of extension?

2.a. Rudolph suggested that על־הבצרת, "Concerning the drought," was omitted by haplogr. This would make the meter of the verse more regular: 3+2, 2+3. With no support from MSS or the versions, stay with MT.

3.a. Reading ואדריה with the LXX. MT reads "their." Perhaps the MT arose in parallel with the following צעוריהם, "their servants." The two words are unusual and were perhaps used for their assonance.

3.b. The Q reads the more common form צעיריהם; cf. 48:4, which has the same Q-K.

3.c. On this word see C. H. J. de Geus, *PEQ* 107 (1975) 65–74.

3.d. Many MSS and versions add "and."

3.e-e. Absent from LXX: deleted by Duhm, Rudolph, Weiser, and NEB; see Janzen, *Studies*, 12; perhaps added because of v 4.

4.a. This whole phrase makes little sense. Rudolph suggested reading החרה, "parched," for this word, an adjectival form of חרר; cf. 17:6. Bright, following the LXX, translates it "Tilling the soil has stopped." Volz transferred "farmers" here and read "Because of the soil the farmers are dismayed"; see further S. Marenof, *AJSL* 55 (1938), 198–200.

4.b-b. Absent from LXX; Janzen (*Studies*, 40) suggested it was added from 1 Kgs 17:7.

4.c. Rudolph suggests inserting וחכלמו, "they are confounded"; see v 3b.

4.d. Many MSS, Syr, and Tg add the conj, reading וחפו; cf. v 3.

5.a. An inf abs used for a finite verb; see GKC § 113y, z.

6.a. Also translated "Zebra."

6.b. Absent from LXX.

8.a. LXX and some MSS add יהוה, "The Lord"; cf. 17:13.

8.b. LXX reads καὶ ὡς αὐτόχθων = וכאזרח, "native." Perhaps after the exile a "native" was the equivalent of a גר, "alien." MT best here.

9.a. LXX reads ὑπνῶν = נרדם, "sleeping"; see further J. Naveh, "A Hebrew Letter from the Seventh Century B.C.," *IEJ* (1960) 131–35.

9.b. LXX reads ὡς ἀνήρ= כגבר (?), "man."

10.a. Omitted from LXX.

10.b-b. This phrase is paralleled exactly by Hos 8:13; a quote, or more probably, a liturgical formula.

10.c-c. Omitted from LXX; Janzen (*Studies*, 40) suggested it was added from Hos 8:13.

13.a-a. Some MSS, with support from the versions, read שלום ואמת, "peace and assurance"; cf. 33:6.

14.a. Reading with the Q the normal form ואיל; an idol?

14.b. Reading with the Q the normal form ותרמית.

14.c. Some MSS and Tg read "them," להם.

15.a. LXX adds ψευδῆ, "falsely"; cf. v 14 and 23:25.

17.a. Omitting ו, "and," as a copyist's error.

17.b. Absent from LXX; cf. 4:6; 6:1.

17.c. Absent from LXX; probably should be deleted here.

17.d. Lit., "daughter of my people"; cf. 8:11.

18.a-a. Both of these are conditional clauses introduced by אם. The perfects, however, indicate that the situations are already fulfilled; see GKC § 159b.

18.b. According to E. A. Speiser ("The Word SHR in Genesis and Early Hebrew Movements," *BASOR* 164 [1962] 23–28), "travel about." See contra C. H. Gordon, "Abraham and the Merchants

of Ura," *JNES* 17 (1958) 29; W. F. Albright, "Abram the Hebrew, A New Archaeological Interpretation," *BASOR* 163 (1961) 44. Rudolph (following Condamin) proposed reading נסחבו,
"be dragged off," or "be taken captive," or reading את for the following אל. Giesebrecht proposed reading either שחרו, "they wear black clothes in mourning," or שחחו, "they are bowed
down."

18.c. Omitting the conj with many MSS, LXX, Tg, and Vg; see GKC § 155h. D. Winton Thomas
(*JTS* 39 [1938] 273–74) proposed retaining the *waw* and understanding the following word (ידעו)
as coming from a root meaning "to be still, quiet, at rest," resulting in the translation "both prophet
and priest travel about the land and have no rest."

19.a-a. Paralleled by 8:15; on the inf abs construction, see GKC § 113ff. Rudolph accepts the
words as original here and secondary in 8:15. Bright accepts them as original in both places.
Holladay and Berridge (*Prophet, People,* 104) consider them secondary here.

19.b. Many MSS, LXX, and Tg omit "and" as in 8:15.

21.a. LXX reads κόπασον, "refrain, desist."

21.b-b. M. Dahood (*CBQ* 37 [1975] 341–42) proposed reading for this phrase "the very abode
of your name."

21.c. Many MSS, LXX, and Tg add "and," reading ואל.

21.d. LXX reads ἀπολέσῃς = תחבל, "destroy."

22.a-a. Absent from LXX.

22.b. Omitting ו, "and," with LXX[51] and Bohairica; so Volz, Rudolph, Holladay.

15:1.a. LXX[A] and Arabic read "Aaron."

1.b. Reading שלחם, "send them," in place of MT שלח, "send"; the ם lost by haplogr; so Rudolph
(*BHS*) and most ET.

4.a. Reading the K. The Q לוערה is a transposition; cf. 24:9; 19:18; 34:17; see BDB, 266.

4.b. Some MSS, LXX, Syr, and Vg add כל־, "all that."

5.a. LXX and Syr omit; cf. Volz and Rudolph.

5.b. LXX omits; by homoioarcton with following word?

6.a-a. LXX (compare Syr) read καὶ οὐκέτι ἀνήσω αὐτούς = נלאיתי הנחם, "and I will no longer
spare them."

7.a-a. LXX reads διὰ τάς κακίας αὐτῶν, "because of their iniquities."

8.a-a. Rudolph (*BHS*) proposed transposing this phrase to the end of the verse.

8.b. Reading אלמנתם with Rudolph (*BHS*) cf. LXX, Syr, and Tg; the ם dropped by haplogr, but
see GKC § 91n.

8.c-c. Deleting להם with the LXX. This phrase presents several problems. The MT reads "I
brought to them, upon the mothers of the young men." LXX lacks "to them." Rudolph (*BHS*)
proposed reading "a destroying people" (לאם מחריב) for "upon the mothers of the young men."
Syr reads "upon the mothers and upon the young men."

8.d. Reading עליהם, "upon them, with a few MSS, Syr, and Tg. MT is preferred by Holladay and
Bright.

9.a. Reading the Q בא; the K באה is 3 fem sg; either form would be correct.

Form/Structure/Setting

Most commentators consider this long section an editorial unit. The only major disagreement about the extent of the passage concerns the inclusion of 15:5–9.
Apart from the oracular introduction (14:1), the passage consists of two parallel
laments (14:2–17a; 14:17b–15:4), followed by a divine lament (15:5–9); it can be
outlined as follows;

A 14:2–6	Drought	A' 14:17b–18	Defeat
B 14:7–9	Petition	B' 14:19–22	Petition
C 14:10–17a	Divine Response	C' 14:1–4	Divine Response
	D 15:5–9	Divine Lament	

The first lament generally concerns a drought, while the second lament generally concerns the ravages of war. The two laments, however, cannot easily be separated on a thematic basis. The theme of war can be found in the first lament (e.g., 14:12–13) and that of drought in the second lament (e.g., 14:22). Even though the highly structured nature of the section is not debated, the exact nature of the structure has been questioned. Bright recognized the editorial unity of the passage but concluded that it was composed (perhaps by Jeremiah) of originally independent units. Other commentators recognize the highly parallel structure of the two laments and feel the entire passage was composed for a specific purpose; so Rudolph and Holladay. The form of the passage has received considerable study, with the general lament structure recognized by most commentators. The description of distress (A 14:2–6; A' 14:17b–18) is characteristic of a communal lament; both of these passages also apparently feature Jeremiah as the speaker. The petitions (B 14:7–9; B' 14:19–22) are plainly communal, but they contain admissions of guilt, characteristic of individual laments. The divine responses (C 14:10–17a; C' 15:1–4) are judgment speeches rather than the expected *Heilsorakal*. This yields an uncharacteristic form for a communal lament: A—a description of distress by the cultic spokesman; B—a petition to the Lord for help, with confession of sin; C—a divine response of judgment. Recognizing these differences from a normal communal lament, many scholars have proposed that this passage is an imitation liturgy or counter-liturgy expressing the judgment of the Lord rather than his blessing; see for example Rudolph; Holladay; W. A. M. Beuken and H. W. M. van Grol ("Jeremiah 14, 1–15,9," in *Le livre de Jérémie*, 297–342). Thus when Jeremiah intercedes on behalf of the people, the opposite of the expected occurs. Instead of blessing, the Lord pronounces judgment. Jeremiah's intercession mocks the intercession and the promises of false prophets who interceded on behalf of the people and promised divine blessing as a result of their intercession. The divine lament in 15:5–9 expresses God's sorrow over the necessity of this judgment.

This section parallels the similar passage 8:4–9:10 [9:11]. The rhetorical form, peculiar to Jeremiah, מדוע, אם, ה, is found in 14:19a and 8:18, 22. The last half of 14:19 parallels almost word for word 8:15. The injunction to weep in 14:17 is similar to that in 8:23. The corruption of the prophet and priest is a concern in both passages: 14:13–16, 18 and 8:10–12. The divine laments, in response to the preceding declarations of judgment (15:5–9 and 9:1–10 [9:2–11]), are also similar; compare for example 9:5 [6], "They refuse to know me, the LORD'S oracle, therefore . . ." and 15:6 "You have rejected me, the LORD'S oracle, you are going back, therefore . . . ." The two passages seem to be in chronological order; the divine lament in 9:1–10 anticipates judgment in the future, "I will refine them and assay them" (9:6 [7]), while the divine lament in 15:5–9 sees judgment as past, "I have winnowed them . . . I have bereaved, I have destroyed my people" (15:7).

This passage describes the past judgment of sword and famine (e.g. 15:7) and anticipates further death and destruction (15:9). A probable date and setting would be during or after the first deportation and before the second deportation, thus during the reign of Jehoiachin or perhaps Zedekiah, about 597 B.C. (cf. Weiser and Rudolph).

Comment

1 The unusual superscription of this verse signals the start of a new section; see also 46:1; 47:1; 49:34. The immediate reference of the superscription is the following section on drought and destruction. The unusual form of the superscription caused Thiel (*Die deuteronomistische Redaktion*, 180–93) to classify the verse as a late addition. The presence of other similar superscriptions argues against this. The unusual word "drought" (הבצרות) has perplexed grammarians; see note 14:1.b.

2 Verse 2 begins the mournful description of a drought which afflicts the city. The words "mourn" (אבל) and "languish" (אמל) also describe drought (compare Isa 24:4; Joel 1:10), making their use especially poignant here; see Reventlow, *Liturgie*, 156–59, for a mythological connection between drought and mourning. The reference to "her gates" personifies the city; compare 12:4 where the land itself mourns because of drought. The "they" of the second bicolon refers back to "her gates." The word used for "mourn" (קדר) means "wear funeral clothes." The "cry" (צוחת) is the cry of distress and not a plea for help (צעקה).

3 As a result of the drought, even the nobles are unable to obtain water. Because of their weakness in the face of drought and the withdrawal of the Lord's blessing which the drought signals, the nobles are ashamed. The last bicolon of the verse, which describes their shame, is absent from the LXX and deleted by many commentators (see note 3.e-e). This description of the nobles covering their heads, like the farmhands do in the next verse, provides a good parallel and should be retained (so Holladay).

4 The farmers (אכרים) are the lowest persons on the social scale. They suffer from the drought just as the nobles do. Everyone from noble to peasant suffers because of the drought.

5 The "hind", who is normally very devoted to her young, gives birth and abandons her young for lack of grass.

6 Kimchi noted that the wild asses are described as panting for air in 2:24 also, but there they pant from lust; here they pant because of the heat and dryness. The lack of adequate grass causes the wild animals to go blind because grass provides needed nutrition; see J. V. K. Wilson, "Medicine in the Land and Times of the Old Testament," in *Studies in the Period of David and Solomon and Other Essays*, ed. T. Ishida, [Yamakawa-Shuppansha, 1982] 362.

7 Verse 7 begins the plea for help in the first lament. The cultic intercessor, on behalf of the community, confesses the guilt of the people and pleads to the Lord for help. The difficulty of understanding this passage as simply a confession of guilt and plea for help has long been recognized; see for example Baumgartner, *Die Klagegedichte*, 77–79. When the entire passage is perceived as a counter-liturgy, then the irony and pathos of these verses come through. Jeremiah pleaded for the people, all the while knowing that the divine response would be judgment rather than salvation. This passage perhaps also reflects Jeremiah's ambivalence concerning his prophetic role, similar to previous sections (see for example 11:18–12:6). How it must have caused him sorrow to declare judgment upon his people. The uncharacteristic confession of sin, usually found in individual laments, also signals that this is not a normal communal lament.

8–9   The plea for help in vv 8–9 contrasts the ideal with reality: what the Lord should be to the people and what he actually is. Kessler ("From Drought to Exile," 506) noted the a-b-b'-a' scheme in this short poem.

a   O hope of Israel,
            its savior in time of trouble,
b   Why should you be like a stranger in the land?
            and like a wayfarer who turns aside to spend the night?
b'   Why should you be like a helpless man,
            like a mighty man who is unable to save?
a'   But you are in our midst, O Lord,
            and your name is called over us;
        Do not leave us!

The ideal image of the Lord's relationship to the people begins and ends the poem (a, a'). The two middle bicola describe the reality of the situation (b, b'). Further, section a corresponds to section b' (the savior is unable to save) and section a' corresponds to section b (the one who dwells with them is like a stranger). The word "hope" (מקוה) in the first bicolon can also be translated "pool of water," particularly applicable in time of drought (cf. v 22 and see M. Dahood, "The Metaphor in Jeremiah 17, 13," *Bib* 48 [1967] 430). The expression "your name is called over us" in the final bicolon means "we are thine."

10   The divine response to the preceding lament begins with v 10. A declaration of judgment replaces the expected *Heilsorakal,* or declaration of salvation, negating the preceding confession of sin and plea for help. The description of the people as the ones who wandered negates the description of the Lord as the one who wandered off in v 8. Instead of declaring the people's sin forgiven in response to the confession of guilt in v 7, the Lord declared that he could not forget sin, further negating the plea for help. Holladay noted use of the preposition ל instead of the expected על. The preposition ל normally introduces direct speech, but the people are spoken about in third person, as if the Lord can no longer stand to address them directly.

11–12   In the preceding confession and plea for help (vv 7–9), Jeremiah acted as the cultic spokesman. The ironic nature of this cultic role is underscored by the prohibition to intercede in vv 11–12. This prohibition has many affinities to 11:9–17 concerning Jeremiah and the covenant. Both passages prohibit Jeremiah from interceding on behalf of the people (11:14; 14:11), and both describe how the Lord will not hear the prayers of the people or accept their offerings (11:11; 14:12); note also the similarity of 11:10 to 14:10. The judgment upon the people is described with the triad common in Jeremiah: "sword, famine, pestilence" (see Weippert, *Die Prosareden,* 148–91, for a detailed study of these words). The repeated usage of these words together in Jeremiah (thirteen times) and Ezekiel is striking. J. W. Miller (*Das Verhältnis Jeremias und Hesekiels,* 86) suggested that these words constituted a slogan which arose during this time (in connection with the "false" prophets?); compare vv 15–16.

13–16   The preceding verses concerned the nation; the attention now turns to the false prophets (cf. 6:13–15//8:10–12). In response to the prohibition of intercession, Jeremiah complained that the other prophets were promising the people freedom from war and peace (see further T. W. Overholt, *The Threat of*

Falsehood [London: SCM Press, 1970] 86–104). The preceding plea (vv 7–9) certainly would not foster hope in the people; instead of salvation, the result of Jeremiah's intercession on behalf of the people was judgment (v 10). The prohibition to intercede accomplishes the same end, contrasting with the false prophets' words of hope. Weiser noted how "place" (מקום) in the words of the false prophets (v 13) probably means "temple." The Lord denied the validity of the prophet's words through two triads: "I did not send . . . command . . . speak," and "a lying vision and divination . . . worthlessness . . . deceit." The prophets had promised that "sword and famine" would not come (cf. v 12). Now they and the people who listened to them will be consumed by famine and sword and their own wickedness. This "wickedness" can be either moral evil or disaster. The superscription in v 17a should properly conclude this section (cf. 13:12).

17–18 The second lament begins with v 17. Through words of lament, vv 17 and 18 describe the horror of defeat in war. The passage begins with a description of weeping similar to the conclusion of Jeremiah's lament in chap. 8 (see 8:23 [9:1]). As in the previous lament, Jeremiah appears to be the speaker. Because of defeat in battle the nation is seriously wounded. The fields are littered with the dead. The cities are filled with the victims of the famine accompanying the siege. The final colon is difficult if not impossible to translate. The problem concerns what the prophet and priest do not know. If they do not know the land, then the verse would refer to exile. If they have no knowledge and are wandering around in a daze, the verse could have in mind the results of invasion and defeat. The passage as a whole seems to picture a time after invasion but before the final deportation.

19 As in the previous lament, the description of distress is followed by a confession of sin and plea for help. This section begins with a rhetorical form peculiar to Jeremiah: מדוע, אם, ה (see further 2:14, 19; 8:19, 22; 22:28; 49:1; cf. v 22). The form implies a negative answer to the questions; thus the Lord has not completely rejected Judah nor does his soul loathe Zion. If this is so, then Jeremiah, as the cultic spokesman, asks why the nation is made to suffer so. The first part of v 19 contains ideas paralleled elsewhere: on the idea of the soul loathing or abhorring something compare Lev 26; Isa 6:10 and Lev 3:22 also present healing as the goal of repentance. The reference here, as in 8:15, which parallels the last part of the verse, is to the false prophets who preach "peace" (cf. vv 13–16).

20 Implied in the confession of guilt is the plea for the Lord to forgive (cf. vv 7, 10). How can Jeremiah, as the cultic spokesman, intercede on behalf of the people when he had earlier been commanded not to intercede (vv 11–12)? We need to be mindful that this passage has the opposite result of what is normally expected. Instead of a message of salvation, this plea for forgiveness results in a message of judgment. The seriousness of the situation becomes painfully clear.

21 The plea for help now changes direction; instead of the Lord being asked to act on behalf of the people, he is asked to act for his own sake. If he were to allow the temple and cult to suffer, it would cast bad reflections on him. "The glorious throne" means the temple and cult in Jerusalem (cf. 17:12). The Lord should remember his throne and not break the covenant (a covenant of protection?). The Lord is not the one who breaks convenants; the people do.

22   The plea for help ends with a rhetorical form (הֲלֹא אִם, ה) similar to the one with which it began (cf. v 19). Once again a negative answer is expected; none of the false gods can cause rain, but the Lord can. On the relationship of water and "hope" see v 8.

15:1   Once again the divine response to Jeremiah's intercession is negative. Now we learn that not only will the Lord not listen to the plea of Jeremiah, acting as the cultic intercessor, but he would not even listen if Moses and Samuel interceded for the people. Moses and Samuel are legendary intercessors; see Exod 32:11–32; Num 14:13–19; 1 Sam 7:8f; 12:19–23. The "peace" promised by the false prophets was declared false (vv 11–16), Jeremiah's intercession resulted in judgment, and not even the great intercessors of the past could avert judgment.

2   Where can the people turn? When they ask, Jeremiah has the ready-made answer (on this question-and-answer scheme see B. O. Long, *JBL* 90 [1971] 129–39). Many commentators have questioned the originality of the last colon, but there is no MS support for deletion. On the use of "pestilence," "sword," and "famine," see 14:15–16.

3–4   The word of judgment continues with the threat of four destroyers. The word translated "destroyers" (מִשְׁפָּחוֹת) is usually translated "clans." Giesebrecht and Volz suggested a play on 1:5 where the "clans" of earth are called to destroy Judah. Manasseh was considered the epitome of the wicked king; see 2 Kgs 21:10–15; 23:26; 24:3.

5   This brief word of lament by Jeremiah, in *qînāh* form, is communicated through three questions. The answer to all three questions is "no one": no one will pity Jerusalem; no one will bemoan her; no one will inquire about her welfare. The occurrence of "Jerusalem" and "peace" (שָׁלוֹם translated here "welfare") in the same verse has suggested to some commentators a connection to Ps 122:6–8; compare Berridge, *Prophet, People,* 177–78.

6   This divine lament, similar to previous divine laments (compare 9:1–10 and 12:7–17), expresses the sorrow of God over the necessity of judgment. The lament meter, *qînāh*, dominates these verses. The people who had accused God of rejecting them (v 21) are charged with rejecting God, thus assuring judgment; compare vv 6–7 with 9:7 and 12:7–8. Perhaps ironically, the Lord declared he was weary of "returning" (הִנָּחֵם) to a people who implored him not to "leave" them (14:9). The Lord was "weary" (לָאִיתִי) of relenting or leaving off his judgment on the people who have grown "weary" of repenting (9:4).

7   The "gates of the land" in v 7 probably means "the outlying towns"; the LXX reads "the gates of my people." The last phrase is open to multiple interpretation. The translation adopted here and by most recent translations is supported by a similar phrase throughout the prose of Jeremiah ("turn, each from his evil way"); see Weippert, *Prosareden,* 137–39.

8   Verses 7–8 negate the promise to Abraham to make his offspring more numerous than the stars in the sky (Gen 15:5) or the sand of the sea (Gen 22:17). The Lord made the people childless (v 7) and made their widows more numerous than the sand of the sea.

9   The expression "mother of seven" proverbially describes the fulfilled or complete mother; compare 1 Sam 2:5 and Ruth 4:15. The shame of the woman is comparable to the shame of the nobles and farmhands in 14:3–4.

Explanation

When the prophet of the Lord stands up and pleads for God's mercy on his people, we normally expect the Lord to answer with words of forgiveness and hope. In this passage Jeremiah used the form of the communal lament, normally the vehicle of hope, to give tragic expression to God's judgment upon the people. The communal lament was usually uttered on behalf of the people by a cultic intercessor, a prophet or priest. Through the lament the people expressed their sorrow and disappointment over the uncertainties of life. The cultic prophets of Jeremiah's day had also been supplying the divine responses. According to these prophets, God was about to deliver the people, and they promised "peace" and restoration. Jeremiah negated these promises. He uttered his own communal laments and even expanded them to include a confession of the people's sin. Instead of the divine response to Jeremiah's plea being an oracle of salvation, it was a word of judgment. And what a powerful word of judgment it is. When even the normal vehicle of blessing is transformed into a vehicle of judgment, from where can blessing come? What sorrow it must have caused both Jeremiah and the Lord to be brought to such a necessity. Through a litany of judgment, the Lord described the horrible deeds forced upon him by the people's actions. The people had rejected him for the last time; the time of judgment had come.

Jeremiah's role as intercessor is stressed throughout the book (see 7:16; 11:14; 14:11; 37:3; 42:2, 4, 20). The surprising note is that he is told repeatedly that he must not continue to intercede on behalf of such a sinful people. This only underscores the fact that intercessory prayer was a vital and natural part of his ministry and that only a restraining word from the Lord could have dissuaded him from continuing. Would that God's ministers were always so persistent in praying for others!

B. A Second Confession: Jeremiah's Ostracism (15:10–21)

Bibliography

Bracke, J. M. "Jeremia 15:15–21 (Expository Article)." *Int* 37 (1983) 174–78. **Bright, J.** "A Prophet's Lament and Its Answer: Jeremiah 15:10–21." *Int* 28 (1974) 59–74. [Repr. in *A Prophet to the Nations: Essays in Jeremiah Studies*. Ed. L. G. Perdue and B. W. Kovacs. Winona Lake, IN: Eisenbrauns, 1984. 325–38]. **Diamond, A. R.** *The Confessions of Jeremiah.* 52–78. **Gerstenberger, E.** "Jeremiah's Complaints: Observations on Jer 15:10–21." *JBL* 82 (1963) 393–408. **Holladay, W. L.** "The Background of Jeremiah's Self-Understanding: Moses, Samuel, and Psalm 22." In *A Prophet to the Nations: Essays in Jeremiah Studies.* Ed. L. G. Perdue and B. W. Kovacs. Winona Lake, IN: Eisenbrauns, 1984. 313–24. ———. "Jeremiah and Moses: Further Observations." *JBL* 85 (1966) 17–27. **Hubmann, F. D.** *Untersuchungen zu den Konfessionen Jer. 11, 18–12, und Jer. 15, 10–21.* Forschung zur Bible 30. Zurich: Echter Verlag, 1978. **Jungling, H. W.** "Ich mache dich zu einer Mauer: Literarkritische Uberlengungen zum Verhaltnis von Jer. 1, 18–19 zu Jer. 15, 20–21." *Bib* 54 (1973) 1–24. **Muilenburg, J.** "A

Confession of Jeremiah (Jer. 15:10–12, 15–21)." *USQR* 4 (1949) 15–18. **Patterson, R. M.** "Reinterpretation in the Book of Jeremiah." *JSOT* 28 (1984) 37–46. **Rad, G. von.** "The Confessions of Jeremiah." [Repr. in *A Prophet to the Nations: Essays in Jeremiah Studies.* Ed. L. G. Perdue and B. W. Kovacs. Winona Lake, IN: Eisenbrauns, 1984. 339–48.] **Schreiner, J.** *Von Gottes Wort Gefordert; Aus der Verkündigung des Propheten Jeremias.* Düsseldorf: Patmos Verlag, 1967. ———. "Ja sagen zu Gott—Der Prophet Jeremia." *TLZ* 90 (1981) 29–40. **Smith, G. V.** "The Use of Quotations in Jer. xv 11–14." *VT* 29 (1979) 229–31.

Translation

10   *Woe is me, my mother, that*[a] *you bore me,*   (4+5)
        a man of strife and contention[b] *to the whole land.*
    I have not lent and they have not lent to me,   (2+2)
        [c]*all of them curse me.*[c]

11 *The LORD answered,*[a]
    "Have I not strengthened[b] *you for good,*   (3+3)
        have I not intervened for you,
    in the time of trouble[c] *and the time of distress,*[c]   (3+1)
        because[d] *of the enemy?*

12   [a]*Can one break iron,*
        iron from the north and bronze?[a]

13   *Your wealth and your treasures*   (2+2)
        I will give as spoil,
    as[a] *the price,* [b]*for all your sins*   (2+2)
        [b]*throughout all your territory.*

14   [a]*I will make you serve*[a] *your enemies,*   (2+3)
        in a land[b] *you do not know,*
    for in my anger a fire is kindled,   (3+2)
        which shall burn forever."[c]

15   [a]*You know,*[a] *O LORD,*   (2+3+3)
        remember me and come to me,
        and take vengeance for me on my persecutors.
    [b]*In your forbearance*[c] *do not take me away,*[b]   (3+4)
        know that for your sake I bear reproach.

16   [a]*Your words were found, and I ate them,*   (3+4+2)
        and your words[b] *became to me the joy*
        and delight of my heart.[a]
    For your name is called over me,   (3+3)
        O LORD, God of Hosts.

17   *I did not sit in the company of merrymakers nor rejoice,*[a]   (3+4+2)
        because of thy hand on me, I sat alone,
        for you have filled me with indignation.[b]

18   [a]*Why is my pain unceasing,*[a]   (4+4)
        and my wound incurable, [b]*refusing to be healed?*[b]
    You are[c] *to me*   (3+2+3)
        like a dry wadi,[d]
        whose waters have failed.

19 *Therefore thus says the LORD,*

> *"If you return, I will restore you,* (2+2)
> *so that you may stand before me.*
> *And if you will utter what is precious rather than what is worthless,* (3+2)
> *you will be as my mouth.*
> *They shall turn to you,* (3+3)
> *but you shall not turn to them.*

20 *And I will make you to this people,* (3+3)
> *a fortified bronze wall;*
> *They will fight against you,* (2+2)
> *but they will not prevail over you.*
> *For I am with you,* (2+2)
> *to save you and to deliver you,"*
> ᵃ*says the LORD.*

21 *And I will deliver you*ᵃ *from the hand of the wicked,* (3+3)
> *and redeem you from the grasp of the ruthless.*

Notes

10.a. LXX reads ὡς τίνα = מִי, "who."

10.b. Omitting אִישׁ, "man," with some MSS, σ´, and LXX; cf. Holladay. Perhaps it was inserted to parallel the two occurrences of "time" (עֵת) in the following verse.

10.c-c. Reading כֻלָּהם מקללוני for MT כֻּלֹּה מקללוני; so GKC § 61h, Duhm, Rudolph, Weiser, Bright, Reventlow. LXX adds ἡ ἰσχύς μου ἐξέλιπεν, "my strength has failed." Rudolph *(BHS)* adds כִּי, "yet," lost by haplogr.

11.a. It has been proposed (so Rudolph and many ET), on the basis of the LXX, to read אָמֵן, "Amen," for the MT אָמַר, "answered." This emendation presupposes that Jeremiah is the speaker.

11.b. Many emendations of this word have been offered (see *BHS*, Carroll); the MT is followed here; cf. the differing ET.

11.c. Rudolph *(BHS)* suggested reading רעתו and צרתו, "its trouble" and "its distress"; compare LXX "their trouble," "their distress."

11.d. Rudolph *(BHS)* suggested reading אֶל, "to," for MT אֶת; cf. LXX and Vg. Rudolph also suggested transposing אֶל־הָאֹיֵב with the Syr after בְךָ: "have I not intervened for you because of the enemy?" Syr adds מִצָּפוֹן (v 12), "from the north."

12.a-a. LXX reads "Will iron be known? But your strength is a brazen covering."

13.a. Deleting לֹא, "without" (so Rudolph [*BHS*], McKane), on the basis of the LXX, Syr, and 17:3, but the same sense can be had by retaining it. Many translators consider vv 13, 14 as an intrusion from 17:3–4; so Bright, Volz, Weiser, Rudolph *(BHS)*; see NEB.

13.b. MT reads וּבְכֹל, "and . . . ," twice; Rudolph *(BHS)* omits "and" in both places on the basis of MSS evidence and 17:4.

14.a-a. Reading וְהַעֲבַדְתִּיךָ, with some MSS, LXX, Syr, and 17:4, for the MT וְהַעֲבַרְתִּי, "I will make to pass over"; so Rudolph *(BHS)*, McKane, Carroll, RSV.

14.b. Many MSS and 17:4 add אֲשֶׁר, "which."

14.c. Reading עַד־עוֹלָם with a few MSS and 17:4 for MT עֲלֵיכֶם, "over you"; so Rudolph *(BHS)*, McKane, Carroll, RSV.

15.a-a. LXX omits; Rudolph *(BHS)* suggested transposing these words to the end of v 11.

15.b-b. LXX reads μὴ εἰς μακροθυμίαν, "do not bear long with them."

15.c. Reading, with Rudolph *(BHS)*, לְאַרֶךְ.

16.a-a. LXX reads "from those who despise your words; consume them and your word shall be to me for the joy and delight of my heart. . . ."

16.b. Reading the K with many MSS and versions; the Q reads the sg and is a possibility. Duhm, Bright omit this word as dittogr from previous colon.

17.a. LXX reads εὐλαβούμην, "I was cautious, fearful."

17.b. LXX reads πικρίας, "bitterness."

18.a-a. LXX reads "Why do those who distress me prevail over me?" Rudolph *(BHS)* suggested the LXX understood נצח in the Aram. sense.

18.b-b. LXX reads πόθεν ἰαθήσομαι = מֵאַיִן אֵרָפֵא (so *BHS*), "whence shall I be healed?"
18.c. Some read הוֹי, "woe," for הָיוֹ; so Volz, Rudolph.
18.d. This word is not in MT but is derived from the following phrase.
20.a.-21.a. Absent from some LXX MSS. Janzen (*Studies*, 117) explained it on the basis of haplogr.

Form/Structure/Setting

This material appears to have been placed in this position for several reasons. The motif of the mother provides a direct link between this section (see v 10) and the previous one (see vv 8–9). The idea of drought (see v 18) probably echoes the concern in the previous section (see 14:1–16). The basic structure of the two units is also parallel: both consist of two laments with corresponding divine replies.

Several interrelated issues control the interpretation of the structure of this passage. Some scholars have noted that vv 13–14 parallel 17:3–4 and have thus classified vv 13–14 as secondary or have omitted them; see for example NEB, Giesbrecht, Rudolph, Carroll. Following earlier commentators, Rudolph noted that v 12 echoes 17:1 and likewise omitted v 12; compare Bright. Since vv 13–14 are included in the earliest MSS and versions and are not a simple parallel to 17:3–4, they are retained here; so also Weiser, Reventlow (*Liturgie*, 210–29), Hubmann (*Untersuchungen*, 233), Holladay. Difficulties also arise when determining the speaker in vv 11–14. God appears to be the speaker in vv 13–14. This is not so clear, however, in vv 11–12, as the differences between the MT and LXX show; see *Notes*. The clearest indication of the confusion is found in the first words of v 11. The MT has "The LORD *said*" (אָמַר), while the LXX has "*Amen*, LORD" (אָמֵן). The MT has been retained here with the understanding that the Lord is the speaker in vv 11–14; so, for example, Carroll, against Rudolph.

The inclusion or exclusion of vv 12–14 and the decision about the speaker largely determine the structure seen in this passage. Those who understand this passage as one lament, with vv 10–18 as the complaint portion and vv 19–21 the divine reply, usually omit vv 12–14 and consider Jeremiah the speaker in vv 11–14 (so e.g., Rudolph, Bright). If, however, God is considered the speaker, then the passage can be analyzed as two parallel laments, both consisting of a complaint and a divine response (see especially J. Vermeylen, "Essai de redactionsgeschichte des « Confessions des Jérémie »," in *Le Livre de Jérémie*, Ed. P.-M. Bogaert, 239–70, following Baumgartner, *Klagegedichte*). This passage is similar in structure to Jeremiah's first lament (11:18–12:6), having two parallel laments. The structure of the passage can be outlined as follows:

Complaint	v 10	vv 15–18
Response	vv 11–14	vv 19–21

The allusions to Jeremiah's call narrative found in the complaint portion of the first lament (v 10) and the response portion of the final lament (vv 19–21) enhance the parallelism. The connection between the first complaint (v 10) and the second response (vv 19–21) is much stronger than the connection of second complaint (vv 15–18) and the corresponding response (vv 19–21), thus causing many commentators to treat vv 15–18 and vv 19–21 separately. Hubmann (*Untersuchungen*, 254–57) noted a possible parallel between the divine responses.

The first response begins in v 11 with אִם־לֹא . . . אִם־לֹא, and the second response begins in v 19 with וְאִם . . . אִם .

As with the previous "confession" (11:18–12:6), commentators disagree about whether these are individual or communal laments (see *Excursus:* "Confessions" for the general discussion and *Comment* below for the particular issues of this passage). With this passage, as with the first "confession" (11:18–12:6), strong arguments can be made for classifying this lament as either individual or communal, and it is best not to press either classification too far. Jeremiah suffered persecution and rejection by the people, because of his prophetic vocation. But he surely also suffered with the people as their prophetic representative. Because confessions can be understood equally well as individual and communal laments, we should be cautious about being too strict in our interpretation of them.

The picture of Jeremiah presented in these verses is unflattering and therefore probably original. A latter Deuteronomistic editor, attempting to present Jeremiah as God's designated prophet, would tend to glorify Jeremiah and not picture him as complaining about his lot and accusing God of failure. These verses contain few historical details which would allow us to date them securely. They seem to portray a time during the middle of Jeremiah's ministry, after the reform of Josiah and before the final deportation, perhaps during Jehoiakim's reign (cf. Bright and Holladay).

Comment

10 The first of the two laments in this section begins with the traditional lament exclamation "Woe is me" (אֽוֹי־לִי). The speaker in the lament then addresses his mother. If the lament is understood as communal, then the "mother" must be Jerusalem (cf. Carroll). If, however, as is likely, the speaker is Jeremiah, then this lament begins with the rejection of God's calling, while the final lament ends with the reaffirmation of this calling (see v 20). Jeremiah described himself as a man of "contention" (רִיב) and "strife" (מָדוֹן). The word "contention" (רִיב) is used often in a legal context. In Jeremiah it most often describes a conflict between man and God; it is used to describe the Lord's indictment against his people (see 2:9), the people's indictment against the Lord (see, e.g., 12:1), and the Lord's indictment against the nations (see, e.g., 25:31). "Strife" (מָדוֹן) is found most often in wisdom sayings (see Prov 15:18, 28; 17:14; 22:10; 26:20; 28:25; 29:22). The two closest parallels to this passage are found in Ps 80:7, "strife to our neighbors," and Hab 1:3, "contention and strife." Both of these passages lament the failure of the Lord's blessing. Here Jeremiah complains that his ministry has only resulted in strife and contention, both for him and the people. He has not even engaged in business dealings, which are most productive of strife (so McKane, Calvin, Rashi, Rudolph, Weiser), and yet the people curse him.

11 The Masoretic and LXX traditions understand v 11 differently. The first word in the MT is "he said" (אָמַר) while the first word in the LXX is "Amen" (γένοιτο = אָמֵן), with the result that the Lord speaks in the MT (so here) and Jeremiah in the LXX (so RSV). In the previous verse Jeremiah had complained that the people were cursing him; the Lord answers this complaint with an oath of his own; on the לֹא אָם oath formula see M. R. Lehmann, "Biblical Oaths," *ZAW* 81 (1969) 74–92. In effect the Lord said, "Let me be cursed, if I have not been faithful toward you."

12 The question in v 12 seems out of place at first glance, leading many commentators to delete this verse (so Volz, Weiser, Rudolph, Bright); there is a radically different LXX version (see *Notes*). A similar question in the first confession (12:5), however, argues for the authenticity of this verse. The difficulty of understanding this verse begins with uncertainty about the syntactic subject of the verse: is the subject impersonal (so here; cf. Rudolph, Carroll, RSV) or is the subject iron, "Can iron break iron from the north and bronze?" (cf. McKane, KJV, NEB). The reference to "iron from the north" has been understood from ancient times as a reference to the enemy from the north (so, e.g., Targum, Vulgate, Rabbinic commentators). Some commentators, however, have assumed the phrase refers to high quality iron or steel (so, e.g., Michaelis, Baumgartner, *Klagegedichte*). Recognizing the great difficulty of understanding this verse, the following interpretation is offered. In the preceding verse, the Lord assured Jeremiah of divine protection, while this and the following verses describe the defeat and exile of his enemies. This verse, then, speaks of the overwhelming threat of the enemy from the north. The following two verses detail the coming defeat and exile at the hands of the enemy from the north.

13–14 Because the text of vv 13–14 closely resembles the text of 17:3–4, most commentators from the time of Hitzig have classified vv 13–14 as secondary; compare Rudolph. The differences between the two texts, however, justified their inclusion in both places. The nature of the differences suggests that vv 13–14 are a deliberate reworking of 17:3–4 for this context (see Hubmann, *Untersuchungen*, 256–57). These verses declare the coming defeat and exile of the people at the hands of the enemy from the north. They serve a double purpose: they assure Jeremiah that those who persecute him will be punished, and they also reaffirm the message of judgment Jeremiah has been proclaiming. Jeremiah was surely ambivalent about the message of these verses. He could have rightly rejoiced that his enemies would be punished. At the same time, he must have mourned that his people would suffer so and he with them.

15 The second of this pair of laments begins with a cry for revenge on the enemies (so Rudolph, McKane). The cry for revenge begins with a familiar phrase from a protestation of innocence, "O Lord, thou knowest" (cf. 12:3). The enigmatic third colon, "In your forbearance do not take me away," probably means "Do not be so patient with my enemies, that they have time to destroy me" (so Bright).

16 The protestation of innocence and the cry for vengeance (v 15) lead to a lament about Jeremiah's calling (cf. v 10). In words similar to the account of Ezekiel's call (see Ezek 2:8–3:3; see also Deut 8:3), Jeremiah described how he had joyfully made the Lord's words a part of his life (cf. 1:9). The purpose of this description is obviously to protest the evil that has come upon him as a result of his call, but it also builds upon his protestation of innocence. Berridge (*Prophet, People*, 119–20) argued that the words the prophet ate were probably not just the inspired prophetic word, but also written words (Deuteronomy?); see also Holladay. This verse ends with a phrase that indicates divine ownership: "Your name is called over me." Many scholars (e.g., Baumgartner, *Klagegedichte*;

Reventlow, *Liturgie,* 220–21; Carroll) have noted that if Jeremiah is saying that he belongs to the Lord then this is the only place where the phrase is used of individuals. Usage in the book of Jeremiah is representative: in Jer 14:9 it refers to the people; Jer 7:10, 11, 14, 30; 32:34; 34:15 apply it to the temple; and Jer 25:29 speaks of Jerusalem. This does not mean, however, that Jeremiah could not have applied the phrase to himself, especially in reference to his prophetic duties to the nation. It should cause the exegete to exercise caution when applying a strictly individualistic interpretation to these words; the ambiguity of these words is stressed once again. They can equally well describe the call of Jeremiah and the call of the nation. It is difficult to speak of Jeremiah's fate separately from the fate of his people; perhaps the ambiguity is intentional.

17 Verse 17 can be understood as either a continuation of Jeremiah's lament about his calling or as a continuation of his protestation of innocence from v 15. Several scholars (e.g., Reventlow, *Liturgie,* 221–24; Carroll) have noted how avoidance of the wicked is often a mark of righteous (see Pss 1:1; 26:4–5). Other scholars (e.g., Baumgartner, *Klagedgedichte,* 36; McKane) comment that the prophetic vocation requires an unnatural way of life. Jeremiah cannot fulfill his prophetic office and also be a man among men. These two interpretations are not necessarily mutually exclusive. Jeremiah could have found that his prophetic vocation prevented him from being a normal man and in fact brought rejection by his people. He could have recognized these results of his calling as indicative of his innocence.

Jeremiah's complaint "I sat alone" brings to mind the requirement that lepers should sit (dwell) alone, outside the camp (Lev 13:46). Jeremiah had become a social leper, an outcast among his own people. He lived apart from his people not because he enjoyed doing so but because they excluded him from their company.

18 The complaint now moves from the protestation of innocence, and Jeremiah's lament about his calling, to direct lament about how the Lord has treated him. Using medical language, Jeremiah describes his situation as a wound that could not be healed. As the capstone of his lament, Jeremiah compares the Lord to a stream that goes dry in summer and cannot be depended upon to provide water; compare 2:13 where the Lord is called the fountain of living water. Could this be a reference to the drought of the preceding complaints (see 14:1–15:9)?

19 In response to the accusation of v 18, the Lord demands that Jeremiah repent of his complaints and recrimination before he can be restored to his prophetic office. He must purge his words of worthless and bitter elements before he can speak the divine words (so Rashi, Kimchi, Bright.) Jeremiah must stand firm and not change his message to appeal to the people; he must wait for them to turn to him. As with the previous description of Jeremiah's calling, this rebuke could be aimed not only at him but also at the community he represented. As the Lord would renew Jeremiah to his prophetic office so he would renew the people to their privileged status. If the people would return to the Lord and not bow to the ways of their enemies, then he would restore them.

20–21 In words reminiscent of his first call (compare v 20 to 1:8, 18–19), the Lord assures Jeremiah that he will be with him and deliver him from all attacks by his enemies. These verses continue the allusions to Jeremiah's call narrative, which dominated the previous verses, and expand the conditional assurance of the previous verse. Traditional language is used in v 12 to offer a promise of rescue.

Explanation

The prophet Jeremiah found himself in a situation of conflict, conflict with his people and conflict with his God. He was at conflict with his people because of the message of judgment he proclaimed to them. He was at conflict with his God because he considered it unjust that he should suffer as a result of proclaiming God's message. He consequently complained to the Lord about his situation.

He began by expressing regret that he had ever been born to live such a life (v 10). Jeremiah felt such a strong sense of call that he believed that his life had been determined since before birth (see 1:4–5). Consequently when he bemoans his birth, he is also bemoaning his calling as a prophet. He also recognized that it was this prophetic ministry and nothing he had done that was the reason for his suffering. In response to this complaint the Lord first assured Jeremiah that he did intend good for him and reminded him that he had helped him in the time of trouble (v 11). The the Lord declared that Jeremiah's enemies would be punished; they would be the victims of defeat and exile (vv 12–14).

This first lament is followed by a second building upon the themes of the first. Jeremiah begins his complaint with a cry for vengeance upon his enemies (v 15). This is followed by an expanded lament about his calling (v 16) and a protestation of innocence which gives his calling as the reason for his suffering (v 17). The complaint ends with the accusation that the Lord had failed him like a stream that goes dry in summer (v 18). The Lord replied to this lament and responded to the accusation by demanding that Jeremiah repent of his complaining and bitter words, for only then would the Lord restore him (v 19). In obvious reference to Jeremiah's calling (see 1:9, 18–19), the Lord reaffirmed that he would protect Jeremiah and deliver him from his enemies (vv 20–21).

Jeremiah responded to the persecution resulting from the prophetic ministry with confusion, bitterness, and recriminations. The Lord responded to Jeremiah's confusion, bitterness, and recriminations with a call for repentance and a reaffirmation of his call. This passage portrays a great friction between the prophet and his God, a conflict that almost breaks the relationship. Somehow this conflict was integral to Jeremiah's message to his day. Perhaps it echoes the conflict played out in the pious of Jeremiah's day. Surely those faithful to the Lord were confused, bitter, and full of recrimination, because they were not delivered from the suffering of the nation at large. The message to them would be the same as that to Jeremiah. They must abandon their rebellious attitude in order to be restored to their chosen status before the Lord.

This passage probably reflects the greatest depth of despair that Jeremiah experienced in his ministry. He had preached to others about the reality of God, but now this made no sense in his own experience. He accused God of becoming an unreliable source of strength to him, like a wadi whose waters had failed. God's response indicated that if anyone had failed it was the prophet himself. He needed to repent or his call to be a prophet would be invalidated.

C. Jeremiah's Life and Related Sayings (16:1–21)

Bibliography

Aalders, G.C. "Fishers and the Hunters (Jer. 16:16)." *EvQ* 30 (1958) 133–39. **Goldman, M. D.** "Was Jeremiah Married?" *AusBR* 2 (1952) 42–47. **Weinfield, M.** "Jeremiah and the Spiritual Metamorphosis of Israel." *ZAW* 88 (1976) 17–56.

Translation

[1a]*The word of the LORD came to me saying:* [a] [2] *"You shall not take a wife,*[b] *nor shall you have sons or daughters in this place."* [3]*For thus says the LORD concerning the sons and daughters in this place and concerning their mothers who bore them and concerning their fathers who begot them in this land:* [4] *"When they die of deadly diseases, they shall not be mourned and they shall not be buried; they shall be like dung on the face of the ground. When they perish by the sword or by famine, their corpses shall become food for birds of the heavens and for beasts of the earth."* [5]*For thus says the LORD: "Do not enter the house of mourning nor go to lament or bemoan them, for I have taken away my peace from this people,"* [a]*says the LORD,* *"even my*[b] *steadfast love and mercy.* [6]*Both great and small shall die in this land, but they shall not be buried;*[a] *no one shall lament for them, or cut himself,*[b] *or make himself*[b] *bald for them.* [7]*No one shall break bread*[a] *for the mourner*[b] *to console him for the dead, nor shall any give him*[c] *the cup of consolation for his father or his mother.* [8]*You shall not enter a house where there is feasting, to sit eating and drinking with them."*[a] [9]*For thus says the LORD* [a]*of Hosts,*[a] *the God of Israel: "Behold I will cause to cease from this place, before your eyes and in your days, the voice of mirth and the voice of gladness, the voice of the bridegroom and the voice of the bride.*

[10]*"And it shall be when you tell this people all these things and they ask you, 'Why has the LORD spoken against us all this great evil? What is our iniquity, and what is our sin that we have sinned against the LORD our God?'* [11]*then you shall say to them: 'Because your fathers forsook me, says the LORD, and went after other gods and served and worshiped them, but forsook me and did not keep my law,* [12]*and because you have done worse than your fathers, for behold, every one of you follows his stubborn evil heart, refusing to listen to me;* [13]*therefore I will hurl you out of this land into a land which neither you nor your fathers have known, and there you shall serve other gods* [a]*day and night,*[a] *for I*[b] *will not show you favor.'*

[14a]*"Therefore behold the days are coming," says the Lord, "when it*[b] *shall no longer be said, 'As the LORD lives, who brought up the people of Israel out of the land of Egypt,'* [15]*but, 'As the LORD lives, who brought up the people*[a] *of Israel out of the north country and from all the countries where he had driven them.'*[b] *For I will bring them back to their own land which I gave to their fathers.*

[16]*"Behold I am sending for many fishers,"*[a] *says the LORD, "and they shall catch them;*[b] *and afterwards I will send for many hunters and they shall hunt them out from every mountain and every hill and from the crevices of the rocks.* [17]*For my eyes are upon all their ways;*[a] *they are not hid from me,*[a] *nor is their iniquity concealed from eyes.* [18]*And I will first* [a] *recompense them double for their iniquity and their sin, because*[b] *they have polluted my*

land, and have filled my inheritance with the carcasses of their detestable idols and abominations."[b]

19   O LORD, my strength and my stronghold,   (3+3)
         my refuge in the day of trouble,

      to you shall the nations come   (3+3)
         from the ends of the earth and say:

      "Surely our fathers have inherited lies,   (3+3)
         worthless things in which there is no profit.

20   Can man make for himself gods?   (3+3)
         such are no gods!

21   "Therefore, behold, I will make them know,   (3+3)
         this once I will make them know

      my power and my might,   (2+3)
         and they shall know that my name is the LORD."

Notes

1.a-a. Absent from LXX.

2.b. LXX adds λέγει κύριος ὁ θεὸς Ἰσραηλ, "Says the Lord the God of Israel."

5/6.a-a. Absent from LXX; Janzen, (*Studies*, 98) says MT original.

5.b. The poss is carried from "my peace"; compare ET.

6.b. The versions have pl in agreement with the preceding verb יספדו.

7.a. Reading לָהֶם with some MSS and LXX and Vg, for the MT לָהֶם, "for them."

7.b. Reading אֵבֶל for the MT אֲבֵל, "mourning"; cf. Rudolph *(BHS)*.

7.c. Reading אותו with the LXX for MT אותם, "them."

8.a. Reading אתם with some MSS and LXX for MT אותם, "them." Cf. previous note.

9.a-a. LXX, Syr omit.

13.a-a. LXX omits.

13.b. LXX and Vg read 3 pl = יתנו, "they," with the intention that the other gods will not show mercy.

14.a. Vv 14–15 parallel 23:7–8.

14.b. LXX reads ἐροῦσιν= יאמרו, "they"; compare Vg and 23:7.

15.a. LXX and Syr read "house"= בית; cf. 23:8.

15.b. Several MSS, Syr, Vg, and some Tgs read with 23:8 הדחתים, "I chased them."

16.a. Q reads לדיגים, probably under the influence of ציידים, "hunters"; both forms are found in MT.

16.b. The verbal form is disputed. GKC § 73b suggested piel; BDB, 185, suggested qal; others have suggested hiph.

17.a.a. Absent from LXX.

18.a. Absent from LXX.

18:b-b. This can be divided differently to give a slightly different sense (so, e.g., RSV, NEB), thus: "they have polluted my land with the carcasses of their detestable idols and have filled my inheritance with their abominations."

Form/Structure/Setting

Chap. 16 is composed of several independent subsections, some more closely than others. The first section (vv 1–9) appears to be primary with the other subsections secondarily attached to it. By general agreement (so Bright, Carroll, Holladay, McKane, Rudolph, Weiser) the chapter should be broken down into the following subsections for analysis:

vv 1–9   The Prohibition to Marry, etc.
vv 10–13   What to Tell the People
vv 14–15   Restoration
vv 16–18   Fishers and Hunters
vv 19–21   The Turning of the Nations

The first two subsections are closely related and treated together by some (so Bright, Rudolph). The major interpretive issue upon which most of the other interpretive decisions are based concerns the nature of vv 1–9. The traditional line of interpretation understands these verses as a description of Jeremiah's experience, a kind of symbolic action (cf. G. Fohrer, *Die symbolischen Handlungen der Propheten*, 2nd ed., ATANT 54 [1968] 66; so Rudolph; Weiser; Thiel, *Die deuteronmistische Redaktion*, 196; Bright; Holladay). Some recent commentators have questioned this understanding and have related the passage instead to the concerns of the people (so Carroll; cf. McKane). The traditional interpretation, however, best explains the passage and is still followed by the majority of commentators.

The connection of vv 1–9 to the preceding material, particularly 15:8–9, is acknowledged by nearly all commentators, even those with divergent interpretations. Two obvious points of connection are the mother motif (see 15:8–10 and 16:3), and Jeremiah's complaints about both the loneliness imposed upon him by his prophetic ministry (15:8–9) and the prohibitions against marriage and attendance at feasts (16:1–9). The internal connections among the various subsections are the result of the thematic development and growth of the material. The first subsection is a fairly straightforward description of a symbolic action similar to Hosea's command to marry a prostitute (see Hos 1:2–9). The second subsection (vv 10–13) was probably appended to the first when the symbolic action was proclaimed to the people as a word of judgment. The third subsection (vv 14–15) is a positive oracle meant to tone down the words of judgment inserted here secondarily from 23:7–8. The fourth subsection (vv 16–18) continues the theme of judgment. The theme of idols links the final subsection (vv 19–21) to the preceding subsection.

The forms of the various subsections differ widely. The poetic nature of vv 1–9 has been noted by several commentators: Volz and Thompson have analyzed the passage as poetry; Weippert (*Die Prosareden*, 166–69) and Holladay classify it as as *Kuntsprosa* (rhythmic prose); Bright speaks of the poetic background of vv 1–9. However, the poetic nature of the subsection is illusory and hard to define, and therefore the passage is better analyzed as prose. The disagreement concerning the form of the first subsection has been mention earlier. Those who deny that vv 1–9 describe a symbolic action in the part of the prophet usually base their denial upon the word of judgment on the people recorded in v 9. This obvious reference to the community, however, was probably added when the the symbolic action was proclaimed as a word of judgment to the people, like vv 10–13. Holladay has suggested that this passage reflects a supplementary call to Jeremiah. The second subsection (vv 10–13) is an example of the question and answer schemata analyzed by B. O. Long (*JBL* 90 [1971] 134–38), specifically his Type B; compare 5:19; 13:12–14; 15:1–4; 23:33. Subsection three (vv 14–15) is an example of one of many passages in Jeremiah which reinterpret an older tradition, in this case the Exodus tradition (see Weinfeld, *ZAW* 88 [1976] 17–56). The fourth subsection (vv 16–18) is an oracle of judgment building upon the previous proclamation of judgment. The final subsection (vv19–21) is a hymn, with elements of a lament, and concerns the nations' turning to the Lord.

Most commentators consider vv 1–9 original to Jeremiah (so Rudolph, Weiser, Weippert [*Die Prosareden*, 166–69], Bright, Holladay). The unusualness of the prohibition to marry argues for its authenticity: bachelorhood was almost unheard of at that time. The prohibition must have come early in Jeremiah's career, for men usually marry at an early age. The second subsection (vv 10–13) has been labeled as Deuteronomistic by Thiel (*Die deuteronomistische Redaktion*, 195–98), on the basis of the question and answer format (cf. Carroll). Weiser, however, argues for its originality on the basis of the same format and language. The ambiguous nature of the supposed Deuteronomistic language in vv 10–13 and the intrinsic connection to vv 1–9 suggest that vv 10–13 could be original to Jeremiah. The third subsection (vv 14–15) is secondary in this position but still probably original to Jeremiah (see on 23:7–8). Rudolph and Weiser classified vv 16–17 as original to Jeremiah and v 18 as a secondary comment on the preceding verses. The tradition of the double punishment (v 18) is old and probably also original (see Isa 40:2; cf. Holladay). The final subsection (vv 19–21), on the basis of Jeremianic language (so Weiser) and the ancient tradition of the conversation of the conversion of the nations (so Bright, Holladay), can be classified as original also.

Comment

1 The first subsection begins with a set formula similar to 1:4; see *Comment* there.

2 The command to Jeremiah to marry no one and to have no children contrasts with the command to Hosea, made over a century before, to take a wife and have children. Hosea married a harlot, illustrating the corruptness of the relationship between the people and the Lord, the children further illustrating the dissolution of the relationship. Jeremiah married no one, signifying the end of the relationship between the people and the Lord, and had no children, signifying the resulting destitution. Hosea's marriage to a prostitute is shocking, but not unheard of. Jeremiah's bachelorhood, however, is so unusual that the OT has no word for a bachelor (cf. Ludwig Köhler, *Hebrew Man* [London: SCM Press, 1956] 89).

3 The command to Jeremiah to refrain from marriage symbolically illustrates the sentence of judgment upon the people. Everyone (mother, father, and children) would be the recipients of judgment. The cultic associations of the word "place" מָקוֹם suggest that Jerusalem is intended by the phrase "this place" (cf. 7:3–20). For the concept of the death of the children compare 9:21.

4 The people shall die of "deadly diseases." The word for "disease" (תַּחֲלֻאִים) is used in 14:18 to describe the diseases associated with famine and invasion. The image of the corpses lying on the ground like dung and being food for the wild animals is also found in 7:33–8:3. Being left unburied was a terrible curse; see R. de Vaux, *Ancient Israel*, vol. 1 (New York: McGraw Hill, 1961) 56–59.

5 The word "mourning" (מַרְזֵחַ) used to describe the "house of mourning" is found elsewhere only at Amos 6:7. It probably describes a mourning feast similar to a wake; on the word and its usage see O. Eissfeldt, "מַרְזֵחַ und מַרְקְהָא 'Kultgenossenschaft' im spätjüdischen Schriftum," *Kleine Schriften* V (Tübingen: J. C. B. Mohr [Paul Siebeck], 1973) 136–42; O. Loretz, "ugaritisch-biblisch *mrzḥ*

« Kultmahl, Kultverein » in Jer 16,5 und Am 6,7," *Künder des Wortes: Beiträge zur Theologie der Propheten,* ed. L. Ruppert, P. Weimer, E. Zenger (Würzburg: Echter Verlag, 1982); P. D. Miller, Jr., "The *Marzh* Text," *The Claremont Ras Shamra Tablets,* ed. L. R. Fisher, AnOr 48 (Rome: Pontifical Biblical Institute, 1971) 37–48; M. H. Pope, "A Divine Banquet at Ugarit," in *The Use of the Old Testament in the New and Other Essays,* ed. J. M. Efird, (Durham, NC: Duke University Press, 1972) 170–203; B. Porten, *Archives from Elephantine: The Life of an Ancient Jewish Military Colony* (Berkeley and Los Angeles: University of California Press, 1968) 179–86. The command to refrain from mourning is similar to the command to Ezekiel to refrain from mourning his wife (cf. Ezek 24:15–27). The reason given for the cessation of mourning is that the Lord has taken away his "peace" (שׁלום), perhaps in repudiation of the false prophets who promised his "peace"; see 14:13.

6–7 Once again the threat that the people will not be buried is mentioned and the lack of mourners is added to it. The custom of gashing the body and shaving the head is mentioned here and, in spite of being forbidden in Lev 19:27–28, 21:5 and Deut 14:1, it is not disapproved of here (cf. also 41:5, 48:37; Amos 8:10; Isa 15:2–3; 22:12; Ezek 7:18). The food mentioned in v 7 has been variously described as food brought to mourners (Rudolph, Weiser) or brought to break mourning fast (Weiser); on funeral customs see further R. de Vaux, *Ancient Israel,* vol. 1 (New York: McGraw-Hill, 1961) 59–61.

8 Not only was Jeremiah forbidden to participate in funerals and mourning, here he is also forbidden to participate in weddings. The word "feasting" (משׁתה) used to describe the "house of feasting" can be found in Eccl 7:2, where it also contrasts with the "house of mourning."

9 As earlier, the command to refrain from participating in weddings indicates the coming judgment. The mention of "in your eyes and in your days," which obviously suggests a communal audience, reflects Jeremiah's explanation of his actions to the people. As at the beginning of this subsection (vv 2–3), "this place" probably refers to Jerusalem.

10 The second subsection is in the form of a question and answer (see *Form/Structure/Setting* on the form and parallels), predicated on the previous announcement of judgment; "these things" can only refer to what precedes. This passage arose at a later date as a result of Jeremiah's explanation of his refusal to get married or attend weddings and funerals. It is also linked to the previous passage by the use of "this people" (cf. vv 2–3).

11 The reason given for the coming judgment is first that the fathers of the people "forsook" (עזב) their God—the only place this indictment is found in Jeremiah, though the people are often accused of forsaking the Lord throughout the first half of the book of Jeremiah (cf. 1:16; 2:13, 17, 19; 5:7, 19; 17:13; 19:4; 22:9). The mention of the sin of the fathers is not uncommon, however (cf. 2:5; 7:26; 11:7–8; etc.). The people's forsaking the Lord is the second reason given for coming judgment.

12 Not only have the fathers sinned, but the people are even worse (cf. 7:26).

13 The judgment upon the people is that they will be "hurled" (טול) out of their land; this word occurs only here and at 22:26 in Jeremiah. Holladay used this in support of the passage's originality. The language used in this second subsection is conventional Jeremianic language as can be seen from the previous parallels.

14–15 This subsection is parallel to 23:7–8, with only slight variations, and seems more appropriate with the restoration material of that chapter (so also Duhm, Rudolph, Weiser, Thiel [*Die deuteronomistische Redaktion*, 201], Bright, Carroll, McKane, Holladay). It was inserted here to soften the threat; see 23:7–8 for *Comment*. Weinfeld, *ZAW* 88 (1976) 17–56, concluded that this material was original to Jeremiah.

16 The fourth subsection is a judgment oracle. Verse 16 announces the judgment. The passage has traditionally been understood as referring to deportation and exile (so e.g., Duhm, Volz, Rudolph, Thiel [*Die deuteronomistische Redaktion*, 200]). The fishers and the hunters are the Babylonian deportations in 597 and 586 B.C. Holladay's unconvincing attempt to identify the fishers and hunters with Egypt and Babylon is admittedly based on a "secondary" connection to Isa 19:8.

17 Because the Lord is mindful of all the iniquity of the people and their evil ways, he will bring judgment upon them. The "ways" are perhaps the pagan religious practices (cf. *Comment* on 10:2).

18 This verse summarizes the previous judgment and announces further judgment. Partly because of this, many commentators have classified this as a Deuteronomistic addition (e.g., Rudolph, Weiser). The absence of obvious Deuteronomistic language, however, suggests that it could be an authentic Jeremianic reflection on the previous oracle (so Holladay, McKane). The idea of "double" (משנה)punishment is unusual but not unique in the OT; compare Isa 40:2. M. Tsevat ("Alalakhiana," *HUCA* 29 [1958] 125–30) has argued that משנה means "equivalent" rather than "double" (cf. 17:18). The sense of the verse, however, is not altered and the change only makes God seem less severe. The "double" punishment should be related to the hunters and fishers of v 16.

19–20 The section ends with a short poetic fragment linked to the preceding verse by the reference to idols. In the first two bicola of v 19 the speaker pleads that the nations might one day turn to the Lord. The final bicolon of v 19 and the only bicolon of v 20 quote the nations as realizing their foolishness in worshiping idols. In context, this subsection links the turning of the gentiles to the return of Israel (so Rudolph, Carroll, Weiser).

21 In response to the request of v 19–20, the Lord affirms that he will make himself known to the gentiles. Note the threefold use of "know":

> Therefore, behold, I will make them *know*,
>   this once I will make them *know*
> my power and my might,
>   and they shall *know* that my name is the Lord.

Explanation

Jeremiah's call to be God's prophet was not only a call to speak in the name of the Lord, but also a call to announce the will of God through his life. In the previous chapter, Jeremiah complained that his life was a life of contention and strife as a result of his calling (see 15:10–12). Chap. 16 tells us how Jeremiah was forbidden to marry or even attend weddings or funerals, to illustrate the Lord's message to the people (16:1–13). These prohibitions struck at the center of Jeremiah's social life, causing untold heartache and loneliness. To be a bachelor, almost unheard of in his time, would have made him an object of derision and scorn. The failure to fulfill social obligations, such as attendance at weddings and funerals, has always been a social disgrace. The severity of the prohibitions illustrated the severity of the message of judgment he was commissioned to proclaim. The apostle Paul likewise suffered greatly for his ministry and like Jeremiah complained to his God about it (see 2 Cor 12:7–10).

The word of judgment proclaimed by Jeremiah's life was further emphasized by the image of "fishers" and "hunters" roving throughout the land to round up all the people for exile (16:16–18). When Jesus used the metaphor of fishermen to describe the mission of his disciples (see Mark 1:17; Matt 4:19), he was reversing its meaning from that intended by Jeremiah. Jeremiah's fishers caught men for judgment; Jesus' fishers caught them for salvation.

The chapter ends with a brief oracle relating the nations' turning to God with Israel's return from exile. This theme is mentioned in other prophetic books (see Isa 2:2–4; 18:7; 19:19–25; Zech 8:20–23; 14:16; Mal 1:11) but is rare in Jeremiah.

IX. Sin and Its Consequences (17:1–13)

The material in 17:1–13 is usually considered a loose collection of independent sayings, joined because of related themes. The material is usually classified as Mowinckel's "A" source, authentic Jeremianic material. The sayings may be identified as follows:

(1) vv 1–4   A judgment oracle giving an indictment of Judah and the sentence
(2) vv 5–8   A hymnic/wisdom saying concerning the Two Ways
(3) vv 9–10   Two proverbial/wisdom sayings concerning the nature of the heart and Yahweh's giving to each according to the deeds of each
(4) v 11   A proverbial/wisdom saying concerning unjust gain
(5) vv 12–13 A hymnic praise of Yahweh and judgment on those forsaking him.

While most commentaries have concluded that these oracles and sayings are unrelated to one another, there are elements that relate the separate sayings: the repeated reference (i) to the heart, לב (vv 1, 5, 9, 10) links sayings 1, 2, and 3; (ii) to giving, נתן (vv 4, 10) links sayings 1 and 3; (iii) to turning aside, סור (vv 5, 13) links 2 and 5; (iv) to forsaking, עזב (vv 11, 13) links 4 and 5; and (v) to writing, כתב (vv 1, 13) links 1 and 5. Indeed the two references to "writing" serve as an inclusio for the entire unit. Judah's sin is written on the tablet of her heart (v 1); she is one with those who turn away from Yahweh and are written in the earth (v 13). Several statements concerning Yahweh, almost epithets, serve to highlight the entire unit: (i) he is that blessed person's object of trust (v 7); (ii) he searches the mind and tests the inward parts (v 10); (iii) he is the hope/spring of Israel (v 13); and (iv) he is the fountain of living water (v 13). A rhetorical outline of the independent subunits showing their links may be constructed as follows:

A   Indictment of Judah for her sin—written on the heart—and judgment for Judah's sin (vv 1–4)
  B   The cursed man (v 5)
    C   The abode of the cursed man (v 6)
      D   The blessed man (v 7)
        E   The fruit of the blessed man (v 8)
          F   Heart deceitful above all (v 9)
          F' Yahweh searcher of heart/inward parts (v 10a)
        E' Yahweh gives to each according to fruit (v 10b)
      D' The one who gets riches unjustly will lose them and be a fool (v 11)
    C' The abode of Yahweh (v 12)
  B' Yahweh, the hope of Israel (v 13a)
A' Indictment on those forsaking Yahweh—written on earth—and judgment for forsaking Yahweh (v 13b–d)

AA', EE', and FF' show clear parallels, with AA' as a virtual inclusio and FF' as the rhetorical center of the chapter. BB', CC', and DD' show contrasts rather than synonymous parallels.

The center of the unit compares/contrasts the deceitful heart with Yahweh as the searcher of the heart (vv 9–10a). This passage serves as the focus of the larger unit showing the contrast between a holy Yahweh and a sinful humanity, but more to the point between a sinful Judah and a searching/testing Yahweh. Yahweh will give to Judah what her fruit calls for. The entire unit made up of independent sayings has been put together to focus on sin and its consequences. For an even closer link based on the speaker for these sayings, see below, *Afterword on 17:1–13: A Yahweh Speech*.

A. Judah's Sin and Its Consequences (17:1–4)

Bibliography

Allen, L. C. "More Cuckoos in the Textual Nest: At 2 Kings xxiii.5; Jeremiah xvii.3, 4; Micah iii.3; vi.16 (LXX); 2 Chronicles xx.25: (LXX)." *JTS* n.s. 24 (1973) 70–71. **Couroyer, B.** "La tablette du coeur." *RB* 90 (1983) 416–34. **Holladay, W. L.** "On Every High Hill and under Every Green Tree." *VT* 11 (1961) 170–76. **Hubmann, F. D.** "Textgraphik und Textkritik am Beispiel von Jer 17, 1–2." *BN* 14 (1981) 30–36. **Lattey, C.** "The Text of Jeremiah 17:1–2." *ExpTim* 60 (1948–49) 52–53. **Propp, W. H.** "On Hebrew SADE(H) 'Highland'." *VT* 37 (1987) 230–33. **Westermann, C.** *Basic Forms of Prophetic Speech.* Trans. H. C. White. Philadelphia: Westminster Press, 1967.

Translation

1   [a]*The sin*[b] *of Judah is written*   (3+2)
      with an iron stylus,
     engraved with a stylus point of hard stone   (3+2+2)
      upon the tablet[c] *of their heart*
      and at the horns of their[d] *altars.*

2   [a]*When their sons remember*[a,b]   (2+2+2)
      it is their altars and their Asherahs,
      beside[c] *green tree(s)*
     upon[d] *high hills*   (2+2)

3   *(or upon) my mountain*[a] *in the highland.*[b]
     Your wealth, all[c] *your treasures*   (3+2)
      I will give for plunder,
     Your high places[d] *for sin*[e]   (2+2)
      in all your borders.

4   *You have remitted it, now your inheritance [speaks] against you,*[a]   (3+3)
      which I gave to you.
     So, I will cause you to serve[b] *your enemies*   (2+2)
      in the land which[c] *you have not known,*
     For in my anger fire has been kindled:[d]   (3+2)
      it will burn forever!

Notes

1.a. Vv 1–4 are not present in the LXX; however, a variant form of these verses is found at Jer 15:12–14. Many commentaries take this reference to be primary and treat 15:12–14 as an addition (so Weiser, Volz, NEB).

1.b. Tg Jonathan reads, "the sins of the house of Judah."

1.c. θ´, Origen's Hex., the Lucianic version, and the OL read, "breasts of their heart."

1.d. The MT has מזבחותיכם, "your [pl] altars." This translation reads "their" with many MSS (de Rossi, III, 84) and the Syr and Vg, as well as most Eng. versions.

2.a-a. Lacking in Syr.

2.b. An alternate reading proposed by Rudolph (*BHS*) is לזכרון בהם, "for a remembrance against them." *BHS* would also move the *soph passuq* for v 1 to the end of this emended phrase for metrical reasons. This translation follows the MT.

2.c. Several MSS (de Rossi, III, 84) add כל, "every"; the Syr and Tg read "under every," apparently following the more common longer Deuteronomistic phrase, "on every high hill and under every green tree."

2.d. Many MSS (de Rossi, III, 84–85), θ´, the Arab., Tg, and Vg read "and upon"; the Syr reads "and upon every."

3.a. θ´ and the Tgs read pl, "mountains." *BHS* suggests reading הֲרָרִי; however, that emendation is unnecessary and gives a difficult const form followed by a prep phrase instead of an abs.

3.b. In this translation the phrase "my mountain in the highland" is added to the end of v 2 following the move of *soph passuq* suggested by *BHS*. The translation of שָׂדֶה as "highland" is suggested by Propp, *VT* 37 (1987) 231.

3.c. Many MSS (de Rossi, III, 85), θ´, Syr, Tg, and Vg read "and all."

3.d. This phrase is lacking in Syr and Tg. Rudolph (*BHS*) suggests reading במחיר, "with a price," as 15:13 has.

3.e. A few MSS (de Rossi, III, 85) read "in your sins"; σ´ reads "in all your sins," as does the related passage, Jer 15:13.

4.a. MT lit. reads, "and in you." LXX, Lucian, and Vg read "you alone." Cf. Deut 15:3 for this same verb with "your hand" as a number of commentaries read.

4.b. A few MSS (de Rossi, V, 65) read, "I caused your enemies to cross over"; cf. Jer 15:14.

4.c. "Which" is often omitted on the basis of 15:14 and for metrical reasons.

4.d. The Heb. lit. reads "you kindled"; the translation followed here follows an emendation based on MSS of Origen's Hex., Lucian, Tg, and 15:14.

Form/Structure/Setting

The meaning of this pericope is clear enough although the text is corrupt at a number of places. The passage is a poetic judgment oracle concerning the sin of Judah and its result. The passage is poetic, and the meter is primarily 3+2 and 2+2. The LXX may lack this passage because of haplography, perhaps because of the presence of the name Yahweh at the end of 16:21 and at the end of 17:5.

The passage has the elements of the oracle of judgment. Westermann (*Basic Forms,* 169–76) lists the elements of the "Announcement of Judgment against the Nation" as follows: (i) introduction, (ii) accusation, (iii) development, (iv) messenger formula, (v) intervention of God, (vi) results of the intervention. The indictment or accusation in vv 1–3a is followed by the judgment pronounced by Yahweh in vv 3b–4. More specifically, following Westermann, the accusation is v 1, the development is v 2–3a, the intervention by God is v 3b–4a, and the results of the intervention is v 4b–c. This translation has preserved the Hebrew text as much as possible. It shows in vv 2–3a the specifics or development of the indictment mentioned generally in v 1.

The dramatic shifts in person show well the oracle-of-judgment pattern rhetorically. The indictment is in third person; it is proclaimed for all—not just the defendant, Judah—to hear. The last line of the indictment switches to first person ("my mountain") showing clearly that the speaker is Yahweh. Yahweh is the one bringing the charge against Judah. The sentence, the consequences of Judah's sin, is given as a first- and second-person form: Yahweh is still the speaker and the sentence is addressed personally against Judah.

There is no indication of dating or setting for this oracle. The judgment could have been uttered at any point in Jeremiah's ministry. This material is often considered to be a part of the early preaching of Jeremiah perhaps included in the first scroll of chap. 36. Nothing within the material precludes that understanding.

Comment

1 The indictment begins with a reference to Judah's sin. The sin is written and engraved on the tablet of the people's heart as well as on the horns of the altars. The reference to a tablet being written upon was surely intended to call to mind Judah's covenantal relationship with Yahweh. At Sinai, Yahweh himself wrote the covenant stipulations upon tablets of stone (Exod 24:12; 31:18; Deut 4:13; 9:9; 9:10; etc.). The Book of Proverbs twice makes reference to the "tablet of the heart"; there חסד, "loving kindness," and אמת, "fidelity," are to be written upon the tablet of the heart (3:3), and Yahweh's words, commandments, and תורה, "torah," are to be written upon the heart (7:3). Both Proverbs passages have strong covenantal overtones. The contrast between Jeremiah and Proverbs is striking irony. Here it is Judah's sin, not her covenant love and faithfulness, that has been written upon the heart! The "horns of the altars" also brings covenantal relationships to mind. The horns of the altar were a place of sanctuary (1 Kgs 1:50, 51). The altar itself was the place of sacrifice, the place where sins could be confessed, sacrifices offered, and atonement effected. But instead, for Judah, the horns of the altar had become a place where sins were recorded but no atonement made. For a very strong contrast, compare Jer. 31:31ff. where, as stipulations of the new/renewed covenant, Yahweh will "put" (נתן) his "law" (תורה) within them and will "write" it (כתב) upon their heart (v 33a). There the consequences of Yahweh's action are that he will be their God and they will be his people. Further, he will "remember" (זכר) their "sin" (חטאתם) no more (vv 33b–34).

2 When the people came to the sanctuary to remember (also a strong covenant word: Deut 8:18; Num 15:39; Exod 20:8), their remembrance ("observance" or "commemoration") was not of their covenant with Yahweh; instead they worshiped their altars and Asherahs, together with their green trees and high places, all indicative of syncretistic Baal worship (Deut 12:2; Jer 2:20; 3:6, 13). The last phrase of the indictment, the first two words of v 3, returns to the first person. These trees or groves, high hills, and high places of Baal worship all belong not to Baal but to Yahweh! As so commonly occurs in Hosea, Jeremiah appropriates the marriage and fertility images to describe Yahweh and his covenant relationship with his people. Furthermore, this phrase contrasts again the syncretistic worship with that which should be given Yahweh on his "holy hill" (הר קדוש), Zion/Jerusalem (Pss 15:1; 48:2, etc.).

3 The language shifts to the judgment for Judah's sin. The images are those of warfare, invasion, and despoliation at the hand of an enemy army. The terminology is reminiscent of treaty curse language. The wealth and treasures Yahweh will give up to plunder (v 3) are more than the royal treasury stored in Jerusalem. It also includes precisely those fertility items Judah assumed came from Baal. As in Hosea where Yahweh threatens to remove the fertility of the land, so in this passage. It is the land itself, Judah's inheritance as Yahweh's chosen, that shall be taken from the people, for the land has become filled with "high places for sin" rather than covenant love for Yahweh.

4 Judah has remitted or dropped this inheritance which Yahweh had given her. The verb שׁמט basically means to let something drop; it is used of giving the land rest in the seventh year (Exod 23:11), where it is parallel to נטשׁ, "leave, forsake, let lie fallow." The verb is also used of remitting or forgiving a debt in the seventh year (Deut 15:2). In those other uses, the verb has positive covenantal overtones; here the connotation is negative. The irony is clear: Judah has forsaken or abandoned her covenantal inheritance. Therefore Yahweh will abandon Judah to her enemies, and she will find herself exiled from her inheritance in a land that she had not known. The judgment of Yahweh is to be a fire (cf. Amos 1–2) kindled against Judah that will burn forever.

Explanation

Judah based a relationship with God on covenant conditions. The covenant was inscribed on stone and at the same time hidden in the hearts of the people. Their sacrificial rites at the altar were intended to maintain that covenant by making atonement for their sins. The accusation is made that, instead of covenant fidelity, their sins were written on their heart. Instead of sacrifices to God to atone for their sins, the people's rites were dedicated to the pagan fertility gods. As a consequence, God is bringing to bear not the blessings of covenant but the curses for breaking covenant. Judah's wealth and treasures will be given over to plunder. Because she has broken covenant, Judah has given up her right to her inheritance. Now that inheritance, the land, will be taken from her, and she will serve her conquerors in a foreign land. How terrible are the consequences Judah has brought upon herself because of her sin!

B. The Two Ways (17:5–8)

Bibliography

Alonso Schökel, L. "'Tu eres la esperanza de Israel' (Jer 17:5–13)." In *Künder des Wortes, Beiträge zur Theologie der Propheten* Ed. L. Ruppert et al. Würzburg: Echter, 1982. 95–104. **Davidson, R.** "The Interpretation of Jeremiah xvii 5–8." *VT* 9 (1959) 202–5. **Holladay, W. L.** *Architecture.* 132, 151–58. ———. "Style, Irony, and Authenticity in Jeremiah." *JBL* 81 (1962) 44–54. **Lindblom, J.** "Wisdom in the OT Prophets." In *Wisdom in Israel and in the*

Ancient Near East Presented to Professor Harold Henry Rowley. Ed. M. Noth and D. W. Thomas. VTSup 3. Leiden: Brill, 1955. 192–204.

Translation:

^{5 a} *Thus says the LORD:*^a

Cursed is the strong man who trusts in humankind,	(4+3+3)
and makes flesh his strength;	
and from the LORD he turns aside his heart.	
⁶ *He will be like a scrub bush*^a *in the Arabah,*	(3+4)
he will not see when anything good comes;	
he will settle in the scorching wilderness,	(3+4)
[in] an uninhabited salt land.	
⁷ *Blessed is the strong man who trusts in the LORD;*	(4+3)
The LORD will be his [object of] trust.	
⁸ *He will be like a tree planted near water*	(4+3)
which sends its roots unto the stream.	
He will not fear^a *when scorching heat comes,*	(4+3)
for his leaves will be luxuriant green over him.	
Nor will he be anxious in the year of severe drought,	(4+4)
for he will not cease producing fruit.	

Notes

5.a-a. This phrase is lacking in LXX.

6.a. Alternatively, read "like one stripped (naked)"; that image would indicate the deadly threat to one trying to survive in the heat of the Arabah without water or protection. The translation chosen gives a better parallel to v 8 and gives a similar image of lacking water and, therefore, life.

8.a. The K, LXX, and Syr read "fear" as translated here. The Q, Codex Cairensis, and Tg read "see," a direct parallel to v 6.

Form/Structure/Setting

A new pericope is indicated by the introductory messenger formula in v 5. Although missing in the LXX, this formula serves to mark the transition. It does, however, fall outside the meter of the section, and that which follows is not a prophetic oracle, but instead an explication of the "Two Ways" somewhat similar to Ps 1. Thus McKane omits the phrase, and Bright and Holladay put it in brackets as an insertion. Many commentaries note the parallels with Ps 1 and assume this passage is dependent on Ps 1, is a wisdom psalm, and is, therefore, late. However, Ps 1 could be dependent on this passage, or the two might be independent. Recent research has argued that Ps 1 may not be late.

Others (e.g., Lindblom, "Wisdom," 200) argue that the passage must be late because of its wisdom content. That also need not be the case. Certainly wisdom traditions both in the ancient Near East in general and in Israel specifically were quite ancient.

The content of vv 5–8 is contrastive parallelism between the one blessed and the one cursed. Verses 7–8 are strongly reminiscent of Ps 1, though the metaphor is more tightly enunciated in this passage.

The unit is poetic, with the primary meter of 4+3 and 3+3. Verses 5–6 present the curse portion in three lines, whereas vv 7–8 give the blessing portion in four lines.

Comment

The placement of this pericope immediately after vv 1–4 produces a specific effect: Judah has been like a man who trusts in humanity and in his own strength rather than in Yahweh. His end will be that of the cursed one of vv 5–6. The implicit call to response in vv 7–8 is to be like the blessed one, enjoying the fruit of Yahweh's blessing even in severe times.

Perhaps this pericope begins with the curse because of the judgment just announced on Judah; Judah is like one cursed. The reference to the scorched places (חררים, v 6) certainly picks up the allusion to Yahweh's eternal anger (v 4). So likewise do "Arabah" and "an uninhabited salty land." Even in the second half of the pericope, the mention of "scorching heat," חם, and "severe drought," בצרת (both in v 8), carry through the image. These hot images may depict metaphorically Yahweh's hot anger. The images may also relate to treaty curses, since a salty land implies a lack of fertility and life.

The one cursed is the "strong man" (גבר) who trusts in "humankind" (אדם), either in terms of political treaties and alliances or in terms of his own personal strength rather than in Yahweh. Indeed, this person deliberately turns away from Yahweh (5b). This is precisely the sin of which Judah is accused. The consequences of such action are devastating. The scrub bush is constantly exposed to the sun and heat of the Arabah. There is little or no water to sustain growth, if sufficient to sustain life itself. The image is one of barrenness and unproductiveness. The words themselves have notable assonance: כערער, (karʿ ār,"like a scrub brush"), בערבה (bᶜᵃrābā, "in the Arabah"). The alternative translation offered in the Notes would indicate one stripped naked, one who also has no protection against the unrelenting sun and scorching heat of the Arabah. The implication is that he could not survive. So he will not be alive to see when something good comes. The place he has chosen is a wilderness place, uninhabited—without life.

By contrast, the blessed man trusts in Yahweh and Yahweh is the object of his trust. This double occurrence of a word root, here בטח "trust," is a typical example of Jeremiah's style (Holladay, JBL 81 [1962] 46). Because he trusts in Yahweh, he will receive blessing. He will flourish like a well-watered tree. Even when drought comes to the land, he will continue to flourish because he has the source of water nearby.

These verses have a word play on the Hebrew words "see" (ראה) and "fear" (ירא). The cursed man will not see the good when it comes (i.e., the end of the curse), apparently because he will be dead. The blessed man doesn't fear the drought (the curse); even if drought comes he has the source of water at hand. The contrast of these two situations is intensified by the use of similar-sounding words in Hebrew. The Q reading of v 8 would have "see" in the latter place. Then the passage would affirm that the tree would not see scorching heat because of his supply of water and his canopy of luxuriant leaves. Such word plays are common to Jeremiah (Holladay, JBL 81 [1962] 45–46).

Explanation

The OT often presents the two ways, the way of blessing and the way of curse. Here, the two ways are presented as a speech of the Lord unlike the usual wisdom setting of two ways, which would tend to have the wise man uttering such words. The unit is presented as though God picks up a familiar wisdom theme and speaks it in response to the accusation and sentence given in vv 1–4. Judah is now under God's curse and can expect the fruits of God's anger. Perhaps a bit of hope can be seen in vv 7–8: even now if Judah would trust in God, then maybe she might enjoy the fruits of God's blessing.

C. The Deceitful Heart (17:9–10)

Translation

9	*More deceitful*[a] *is the heart than all,*	(3+2+2)
	it is incurable;[b]	
	who can know it?	
10	*I am the LORD, the one searching the heart,*	(4+2)
	[a] *the one testing the inner parts,*	
	and[b] *thus giving to each person according to his way,*[c]	(3+2)
	[d] *according to the fruit of his deeds.*	

Notes

9.a. The LXX has βαθεῖα, "deep," while the Lucianic text and OL have "heavy, weighty," and the Syr has "hard, difficult."

9.b. The LXX reads "man" (i.e., אֱנוֹשׁ instead of אָנֻשׁ), as does the Syr. The Tgs have "strong." The possible double meaning of אנשׁ, of which MT uses one meaning and LXX uses the other, is a typical word play of Jeremiah's.

10.a. Many MSS (de Rossi, III, 86–87) and versions add the conj to the beginning of this line.

10.b. Many MSS (de Rossi, III, 87) and versions omit the conj. Cf. Jer. 32:19.

10.c. Reading the K also supported by 4QJer[a] (Janzen, *Studies*, 178). Codex Cairensis, many MSS (de Rossi, III, 87), the versions, and Q read the pl, "his ways," as does 32:19.

10.d. Many MSS (de Rossi, III, 87) and versions add the conj, as does 32:19.

Comment

These two verses, though expressing different ideas, belong together. Taken together they form the center of the entire unit from v 1 through v 13. The contrast these two verses speak are the very contrast of the entire unit: deceitful, sinful humanity in contrast to a holy and just God. Verse 9 is probably a proverbial saying or riddle that looks back to the previous unit, to v 5, the one cursed who turns his heart from Yahweh. It also looks further back to v 1, where Judah's sin is inscribed on her heart. Indeed, the heart is deceitful and incurably sick. (On the sick heart, cf. Jer. 8:18, where the reference is to heartsickness from grief over Judah's sin.) Because it is so deceitful, the poet wonders who may know it? From human perspective it may seem that no one can know the inscrutable heart of a person who is deliberately deceitful. Yet the answer is swift in coming. Yahweh knows! Yahweh is the one who searches the heart and tests the inward parts of humankind (cf. ובחנת לבי, Jer. 12:3). He knows the heart and gives to each according to the fruit of his/her deeds. This reference to fruit again links this passage with the preceding one (v 8). Another link with the first section of this unit may be seen in the repetition of the word "give." Yahweh who had *given* the inheritance to his people (v 4) will now *give* to each according to his way, according to the fruit of his/her deeds (v 10). A link is also provided within this passage for the confession in vv 14–18. Although the heart is incurable (v 9), a source of healing is available, Yahweh himself (v 14). In one sense, the hope of healing in v 14 answers the incurable nature of the heart's sickness precisely as Yahweh's searching of the heart (v 10) answers the question of its unknowable qualities (v 9).

D. The Partridge and the One Gaining Wealth Unjustly (17:11)

Bibliography

Driver, G. R. "Birds in the Old Testament: II. Birds in Life." *PEQ* 87 (1955) 132–33. **Sawyer, J. F. A.** "A Note on the Brooding Partridge in Jeremiah xvii 11." *VT* 28 (1978) 324–29.

Translation

11   A partridge[a] broods but he will not hatch,   (4+4)
       one making wealth but not by justice:
     in half his days[b] it forsakes him   (3+3)
       and at his end he will be a fool/carcass.

Notes

11.a. LXX reads קרא twice, once as "partridge," secondly as "calling."
11.b. The K reads "his day" (sg); this translation follows the Q and Codex Cairensis.

Comment

This single verse is another proverbial saying. The form is a simple comparison quite common to Proverbs (e.g., Prov 25:11–14). The English seems awkward, but the parallelism of the Hebrew is striking. The meaning is clear. Following the adopted translation, the partridge broods the eggs but they will not hatch. That proverb would suggest that some tragedy strikes the eggs: a predator or infertile eggs. (The alternative translation followed by many English versions suggests the partridge gathers a brood not its own, whether stealing eggs as some suggest, or following the pronouns, the male sitting on a nest and hatching the young. In any event, the partridge cannot keep the young. In due course the young will leave.) Similarly for that one acquiring wealth by unjust means, the wealth too will be lost (or leave him). The last line probably hides a powerful word play, so common to Jeremiah. The clear intention is that this unjust man will become a "fool" (נבל). However a closely related word נבלה, meaning "corpse" or "carcass" is used a number of times by Jeremiah (e.g., Jer 19:7). The implied word play would be most powerful. The end of all, humans and birds alike, is death, the corpse. The proverb begins on a note of birth, but a frustrated attempt at giving birth, and ends on an implicit mention of death. The partridge and the unjust one alike will end as carcasses. Wealth cannot go beyond death and will not help that unjust one when he has become a corpse/fool. So the one seeking after wealth by unjust means is doubly a fool!

E. Judgment on Those Forsaking God (17:12–13)

Bibliography

Baumgartner, W. *Jeremiah's Poems of Lament.* **Berridge, J. M.** *Prophet. People.* **Dahood, M.** "The Metaphor in Jeremiah 17, 13." *Bib* 48 (1967) 109–10. **Reventlow, H. G.** *Liturgie* .

Translation

12 A throne, glorious,
   exalted[a] [b]from the first   (2+2+2)
   is the place of[b] his[c] sanctuary.
13 The hope/spring[a] of Israel is the LORD;   (3+2)
   all those forsaking you will be shamed.
  The ones turning me aside[b] will be written in the earth[c] (3+3)
   for they have forsaken the source of living water, [d]the LORD.[d]

Notes

12.a. LXX reads ὑψωμένος, "being raised, lifted."
12.b-b. This phrase is lacking in the LXX.
12.c. The suff could also be translated "our."
13.a. Another word play is evident in the use of מקוה, which can mean both "hope" and "collection of water, spring."
13.b. Following the Q וסורי; the K has יסורי.

13.c. Baumgartner, Dahood, and others suggest אֶרֶץ should be translated here as "underworld, Sheol" (see BDB, 76a).

13.d-d. This phrase is perhaps an addition, according to Rudolph (*BHS*). It does lie outside the metrical structure of the verses. Furthermore, the sign of the direct object, אֵת, is not common in poetic passages. It would seem that the phrase deliberately disrupts the metrical structure for emphasis and to mark the end of the Yahweh speech (see below). In addition, the phrase indicates the correctness of the translation of the phrase "the ones turning me aside," contra RSV and other translations.

Form/Structure/Setting

Baumgartner (*Jeremiah's Poems*), Berridge (*Prophet, People*), and Reventlow (*Liturgie*) have suggested that this section forms the introduction to the confession which follows in vv 14–18. They present the evidence that often the Individual Lament began with an introductory invocation. Holladay cautions that the shift from first person plural (v 12, reading "our sanctuary") to first person singular (v 14 . "Heal me") creates problems in accepting that position. However, if v 12 is read "his sanctuary," as rendered here, the difficulty is averted. More to the point is the matter of determining the speaker for these verses. If the reconstruction given below is followed, this unit is tied to what precedes rather than to what follows. However, noting the possibility of this section being a part of an Individual Lament does indicate that it might serve as a transition section. Originally it may have served as the introduction to the confession/lament which follows. Now it serves to close out the preceding section of vv 1–13.

As already mentioned in the introduction to the unit (vv 1–13), there are numerous connections between this last section and the unit as a whole. Further mention should be made to the relation between this section and vv 5–8. In both the contrast is made between the blessed and the cursed/shamed. In both the parallel is made on the basis of water for the blessed. Here the image of the fountain of living water from 2:13 is repeated. Holladay has noted Jeremiah's frequent use of assonance (*JBL* 81 [1962] 46). Four assonant words are a key to these verses: מָרוֹם, "exalted,: מָקוֹם, "place," מִקְוֵה, "hope/spring," and מָקוֹר, "source."

The root עזב appears twice in verse 13, picking up on its usage in verse 11. There it referred to wealth which would forsake the unjust. In this verse the reference is to those who forsake Yahweh, another clear reference to 2:13. Such double use of a word root is quite common in Jeremiah (Holladay, *JBL* 81 [1962] 46).

Comment

Verses 12–13a are words of the congregation, hymnic words of praise. But the metrical structure indicates a line of *qīnāh* rhythm, the rhythm of the funeral dirge or lament within the hymn. The *qīnāh* rhythm comes precisely where the tone of the passage shifts from the praise to a word of judgment on those forsaking Yahweh.

Baumgartner and Dahood have suggested that "earth" in v 13 should be understood as the underworld, Sheol. This suggestion is attractive and would give a striking antithetical parallelism in the three lines:

A   the sanctuary, an exalted (raised) throne
  B   the hope/spring, Yahweh, whoever forsakes him will be shamed
A' ones turning me (Yahweh) aside will be written in underworld
  B' they have forsaken Yahweh, source of living water

Dahood has also suggested that the word יֵבֹשׁוּ should be emended to יִבָשׁוּ, reading "will wither" for "will be shamed." While this suggestion is attractive, it is not compelling in view of the occurrences of the root בוש in vv 14–18. It is quite possible that Jeremiah chose the term deliberately because of the ambiguity in image the two roots create.

There is a significant change of speaker in these two verses. Verses 12–13a is clearly a congregational praise statement. Yahweh is addressed in third person (13a and 12b). Verse 13b shifts to a second person address to Yahweh. Such shifts are not uncommon in hymns addressed to Yahweh and do not indicate a major break in the flow of the hymn. However, the second half of v 13 does have a major shift in speaker. Here Yahweh takes up the hymn and turns it into a judgment oracle.

Afterword on 17:1–13: A Yahweh Speech

A comment needs to be made concerning the speaker(s) throughout this passage. It has been argued above that the passage exhibits a continuity beyond what most commentators have suggested. The rhetorical outline indicated that continuity. At this point, the speaker(s) need(s) to be identified. As argued above, the chapter begins with an indictment in vv 1–3a. The speaker is not indicated until v 3a. There the reference to "my mountain in the countryside" indicates that Yahweh is the speaker, even if one assumes that the prophet is his spokesman, uttering Yahweh's indictment. The sentence is given in vv 3b–4. Here again Yahweh is the speaker, this time more obviously: "Your wealth . . . I will give for plunder. . . . I will cause you to serve your enemies. . . ." Verses 5–8 are a clear unit. The blessing and curse balance one another well. The speaker is identified at the beginning of the unit: "Thus says Yahweh." Obviously that phrase indicates that someone else, probably the prophet himself, uttered the introductory phrase. But the speaker of the unit is understood to be Yahweh. The unit has a wisdom emphasis on the two ways. Although spoken to Yahweh, it is not contradictory to say that these verses were in this context spoken by Yahweh. Yahweh takes up a familiar hymnic theme and speaks the words to contrast the rewards the people themselves spoke (or sang) for the faithful as opposed to those who turn aside from him. Throughout this unit, Yahweh takes up the songs and proverbs of the people to speak his message to them. Verses 9–10 are also a unit. No speaker is indicated specifically for v 9. However, since 9 and 10 belong together, they have the same speaker. In v 9 Yahweh speaks what was probably a well-known proverb-riddle to the people. In v 10, he answers the proverb-riddle and clearly identifies himself as speaker. Verse 11 is the only verse in the whole unit that has no clear speaker. It, like v 9, is a proverb. Since it has vocabulary ties with vv 12–13, it will be assumed that the same speaker is indicated. Verses 12–13a are a short hymn of praise addressed to Yahweh. Verse 13b is a response of Yahweh to the hymn. In v 13b Yahweh is the "me" from whom the others turn aside. It is possible that vv 12–13a are spoken by the people, but, in keeping with the unit, it seems more likely that Yahweh is the speaker. He again takes up a well-known hymn, one often sung by the people, and responds to it. With this understanding, Yahweh would also be the speaker of the proverb in v 11. As he takes up a proverb in v 9 and responds to it, so here in vv 11–13a he takes up a proverb and a hymn and then responds to it. One link between the proverb of v 11 and the hymn fragment of vv 12–13a is the verb עזב, "abandon." Thus Yahweh can be understood as speaking the entire pericope, at times taking up words used by the people in their hymns and proverbs, but speaking an extended judgment oracle on the people for their sins .

X. Oracles (17:14–20:20)

A. A Third Confession of Jeremiah: Heal Me, Destroy Them (17:14–18)

Introduction

If vv 1–13 are seen as a series of Yahweh speeches, then vv 14–18, another of the "confessions" of Jeremiah now has a suitable literary context. The first verse of this confession clearly responds to the previous speeches. It has a certain ambiguity, for it could well be the prayer of the people, using "I" to refer to the entire community corporately. But the succeeding verses indicate that the speaker is Jeremiah. Perhaps he began this confession with an intercession for the people, but remembering the relationship of the confessions to the Individual Psalm of Lament, it seems more likely that this passage simply contains the elements of an Individual Lament.

Bibliography

Baumgartner, W. *Jeremiah's Poems.* **Berridge, J. M.** *Prophet, People.* **Diamond, A. R.** *The Confessions of Jeremiah.* **Kelly, F. T.** "The Imperfect with Simple *Waw* in Hebrew." *JBL* 29 (1920) 1–23. **Lundbom, J. R.** *Jeremiah: A Study in Ancient Hebrew Rhetoric.* SBLDS 18. Missoula, MT: Scholars Press, 1975. **O'Connor, K. M.** *The Confessions of Jeremiah.* **Orlinsky, H. M.** "On the Cohortative and Jussive after an Imperative and Interjection in Biblical Hebrew." *JQR* n.s. 31 (1940–41) 371–82; 32 (1941–42) 191–205, 273–77. **Polk, T.** *The Prophetic Persona.* Sheffield: JSOT Press, 1984. **Smith, M. S.** *The Laments of Jeremiah and Their Contexts : A Literary and Redactional Study of Jeremiah 11–20.* SBLMS 42. Atlanta: Scholars Press, 1990.

Translation

14	*Heal me, O LORD, let me be healed,*	(3+2+2)
	Deliver me, let me be delivered,	
	For you are my (object of) praise! [a]	
15	*Behold, they for their part are the ones saying to me,*	(3+2+2)
	"Where is the word of the LORD?	
	Pray, let it come!"	
16	*But I for my part, did I not press*	(2+2)
	after you away from evil? [a]	
	The day of incurable sickness	(2+2)

       I did not desire.[b]

       You for your part know that which came forth from my lips;   (4+3)

         it was before your presence.

17   *Do not be to me as a terror,*   (2+3)

         A shelter/refuge are you in an evil day.

18   *Let the ones pursuing me be shamed,*   (2+2)

         but do not let me for my part be shamed.

       Let them for their part be terrorized,   (2+2)

         but do not let me for my part be terrorized.

       Bring upon them an evil day,   (4+3)

         and with double destruction destroy them!

Notes

14.a. Rudolph (100), following Duhm (148), suggests reading תֶחָלָתִי, "trust." However, the MT reading fits the context equally well without emending the text.

16.a. The Heb. has מרעה, lit., "from shepherding," and is followed by the Tg. That wording could be understood in the sense that Jeremiah did not press or hasten to stop shepherding (prophesying) for Yahweh. See further under *Comments*. The LXX has ἐγὼ δὲ οὐκ ἐκοπίασα κατακολουθῶν ὀπίσω σου, "I have not wearied following after you." Bright (116), following Skinner, suggests reading לֹא אַצְתִּי (ל) יוֹם רָעָה, which would parallel יוֹם אֲנוּשׁ in the next line and match the two occurrences of יוֹם רָעָה in vv 17–18. The reading adopted here follows that of a´ and σ´, who have ἀπὸ κακίας, "from evil," apparently emending the vowels of the Heb. to מֵרָעָה. If the phrase is understood as a question rather than a statement, the emendation often suggested (as in *BHS* for example), לְרָעָה, is unnecessary.

16.b. Following the suggestion of *BHS*, Baumgartner, and others, the *athnah* is moved to the word הִתְאַוֵּיתִי from the word יָדַעְתָ.

Form/Structure/Setting

Baumgartner considers vv 12–18 to be the third of the confessions. Verses 12–13 he calls "a festive, hymnic introduction" (52), which although many consider inauthentic, Baumgartner feels may indeed be authentic (53). Verses 14–18 compose an individual lament with the same elements so common in Psalms: a petition (v 14), the lament itself (v 15), protestation of innocence (v 16), additional petition (v 17a), confession of trust (v 17b), further petition (v 18) (cf. Baumgartner's outline, p. 55). As noted in the previous pericope, vv 12–13 fit better there than as an introduction to this pericope. The material of this confession, along with the other laments, is usually ascribed to Mowinckel's "A" source, the authentic Jeremianic material.

Comment

In v 14, the verb רפא "to heal," is parallel to ישׁע "to deliver, save." Healing is the more specific term. It can imply healing from illness, but it can mean more than simply curing illness. At times רפא means "to make whole," or "repair" (see 1 Kgs 18:30; 2 Kgs 2:21 for the active meaning [both piel] and Jer 19:11 for the passive meaning [niph]). ישׁע describes the "delivering" or "liberating" or "giving victory" or "saving" of one. The appearance of these two words in parallel provides a stronger picture image than either word alone. Healing is more of an internal concept, whereas delivering is more external. The petition of v 14 is for wholeness within and liberation from external troubles. The speaker is not identified within this verse. The people of Israel who have forsaken Yahweh (v 13) could be speaking this petition as confession and entreaty, or Jeremiah might be praying this prayer as intercessor, or he might be praying the prayer on his own behalf. Only the additional verses of the pericope make clear the speaker is Jeremiah.

The second half of the first two lines of v 14 may be translated as a faith assertion in an indicative mood:

> "Heal me, O LORD, and I will be healed"

as a purpose clause:

> "Heal me, O LORD, so that I may be healed"

or as a further petition:

> "Heal me, O LORD, let me be healed."

The first option is the traditional translation and has a number of recent adherents (Bright, Carroll, McKane); the second is the choice of Holladay. Nevertheless, the context of Jeremiah's prayer and petition seems to give preference to the latter alternative. The grammatical construction in each line with an imperative followed by a conjunction favors a continuation of mood closely related to the imperative. The cohortative ה on, וְאִוָּשֵׁעָה further indicates the voluntative mood of the third choice.

The last phrase of v 14 has been emended by many to read, "You are my hope." (See *Notes* above.) Following either that reading or the MT as accepted here, the phrase is another epithet of Yahweh. (Cf. v 7, "Yahweh will be his [object of] trust"; v 10, "I am Yahweh, the one searching the heart, the one testing the inner parts"; v 13a, "The hope/spring of Israel is Yahweh"; v 13b, "the source of living water, Yahweh.") This epithet is made even more personal by the use of the second person masculine singular independent personal pronoun אתה, "you."

Verses 15 and 16 are characterized by the emphatic use of independent personal pronouns. These pronouns have been translated to show their emphatic character by the addition of the phrase "for my/their/your part." The two verses clearly belong together because of this rhetorical feature. Further, these two verses form the center of the lament/confession, and they alone lack any element of petition. Rhetorically one might structure the entire pericope as:

A   Petition (v 14a–b)
   B   Epithet (using 2ms pronoun) (v 14c)
      C   Lament, protestation (vv 15–16) (using one each 3mp, 1cs, and
          2ms pronouns)
A'   Petition (v 17a)
   B'   Epithet (using 2ms pronoun) (v 17b)
A"   Petition (v 18) (using 2 1cs pronouns and a 3mp pronoun)

Lundbom (*Jeremiah*, 88–89) presents a different chiasmus for vv 13–16a. However, his chiasmus does not cover the entire lament, and fragments v 12 from v 13. This chiastic pattern is faithful to the pericope.

The lament in 15–16 is introduced by the demonstrative הנה, "behold," and has three emphatic elements, the first referring to the ones causing trouble, "they," an otherwise undefined group in this section. The second emphatic element is the speaker, "I." And the final emphatic element is directed to Yahweh, "you." The trouble which precipitates the lament is indicated by the mocking words of the troublers, "Where is Yahweh's word? Pray, let it come!" This report probably indicates the scorn of the troublers, that Jeremiah always brought strong messages of judgment, messages that had not come to pass. So the lament reflects some of Jeremiah's personal frustration that his messages had not brought about repentance, nor had they brought about the judgment indicated.

Verse 16 can be understood in several different ways. The translation adopted above results from a change in pointing the MT as indicated in the *Notes*. The major part of line 1 is taken to be a question rather than a statement, "For my part, did I not press you to turn away from evil?" In response to the people's mocking words, Jeremiah affirms again that he has been intercessor for his people. Even though they have refused to repent, still he has interceded on their behalf. He has not desired the destruction of his people. He has only proclaimed what Yahweh had first heard or uttered. The third of the emphatic pronouns speaks of Yahweh who knows what has been spoken because it was first heard by him or came from his presence. On the phrase אתה ידעת, "you know," cf. Jer 12:3: ואתה יהוה ידעתני, "and you, Yahweh, know me."

Verse 16 also is a protestation of innocence. Jeremiah has done nothing wrong; indeed he has only interceded for his people and proclaimed Yahweh's word to them. Yet he has not been vindicated.

Verse 17 has both a petition and a confession of faith. The confession of faith gives another epithet of Yahweh. Jeremiah makes use of a word play between מחתה, "terror," and מחסי, "shelter/refuge." "Terror" is a favorite word of Jeremiah's, whether referring to the actions of others directed against him or to God's judgment on others for their sins. "Shelter/refuge" is found most frequently in the Psalms, often in laments and trust psalms.

Verse 18 turns to the other side of v 17. Whereas v 17 petitioned Yahweh not to terrorize Jeremiah, v 18 asks that shame and terror be brought on those pursuing him, but not on him. Two key words from v 17 are picked up and used in v 18. "Terror" appears twice in v 18 as a verb, and "and evil day" also appears. The last phrase of v 18 may refer to a double destruction or a second destruction. In either image, the thoroughness of destruction is being emphasized. Jeremiah, who in v 16 protests that he has not pressed Yahweh to send evil, here does precisely that! The contrast is clear in vv 15–18 between what "they" have done and what Jeremiah has done (vv 15–16), and between what Jeremiah prays for himself (vv 17, 18b, 18d) and what he prays for them (18a, c, e–f).

Explanation

Verses 14–18 are set over against vv 1–13. In the former the sins of Judah are emphasized; in this passage Jeremiah's innocence is indicated. Jeremiah prays for healing and deliverance on the one hand and for vindication on the other. Is this healing from and deliverance from *them,* from the enemy, from those who mock at Jeremiah's/Yahweh's word? If so, then the vindication parallels the petition of v 14.

Often in Psalms the lament is answered with an oracle of assurance (Brueggemann, *Jeremiah 1–25,* 157). Here no assurance is given. Indeed, there is no response from God at all, only silence. God's silence to Jeremiah's prayer matches his silence to his people. We hear Jeremiah's complaint and his pain and then . . . nothing.

B. Sabbath Observance (17:19–27)

Bibliography

Andreasen, N.-E. A. *The Old Testament Sabbath.* SBLDS 7. Missoula, MT: Scholars Press, 1972. **Barnes, W. E.** "Prophecy and the Sabbath (A Note on the Teaching of Jeremiah)." *JTS* 29 (1927–28) 386–90. **Nicholson, E. W.** *Preaching to the Exiles.* Oxford: Basil Blackwell, 1970. **Stuhlman, L.** *The Prose Sermons of the Book of Jeremiah.* SBLDS 83. Atlanta: Scholars Press, 1986. **Thiel, W.** *Die deuteronomische Redaktion von Jeremia 1–25.* WMANT 41. Neukirchen-Vluyn: Neukirchener Verlag, 1973.

Translation

[19] *Thus has the* LORD *said* [a]*to me,*[a] *"Go, stand in the gate of the people*[b] *through which the kings of Judah come in and go out, (stand) in all the gates of Jerusalem,* [20]*and say unto them 'Hear the word of the* LORD, *O kings of Judah, and all Judah and all inhabitants of Jerusalem who come in these gates.* [21] *"Thus has the* LORD *said, 'Watch out for the sake of your lives, and do not carry a burden on the Sabbath day, nor bring one within the gates of Jerusalem.* [22]*Furthermore, do not carry out any burden from your houses on the Sabbath day, nor do any work, but instead, sanctify the Sabbath day just as I commanded your fathers.* [23]*Nevertheless, they did not listen nor incline their ear; instead, they stiffened their neck/back*[a] *so as not to hear*[b] *and so as not to accept correction.* [24]*Now it will happen if you will really listen to me,' an oracle of the* LORD, *'so as not to bring a burden within the gates of this city on the Sabbath day, and to sanctify the Sabbath day so as not to do any work* [a]*on it,*[a] [25]*then they will continue to come into the gates of this city, kings* [a]*and officials,*[a] *the ones who sit on the throne of David, the ones who ride on the chariot and on the horses, they and their officials, the men*[b] *of Judah and inhabitants of Jerusalem; and this city will endure forever.* [26]*They will come from the cities of Judah and from the environs of Jerusalem, from the land of Benjamin and from the Shephelah, from the hill country and from the Negev, ones bringing a burnt offering and a sacrifice, a grain offering and incense,* [a]*ones bringing a thank offering*[a] *(to) the house of the* LORD. [27]*But if you will not listen to me to sanctify the Sabbath day so as not to lift a burden on the Sabbath day and enter within the gates of Jerusalem on the Sabbath day, then I will*

kindle a fire in her gates and I will devour the fortifications of Jerusalem and it will not be extinguished.'"

Notes

19.a-a. This phrase is not present in the LXX and some MSS of the Tg.

19.b. The reading followed is that of the Q; the K omits the definite article. Furthermore, the phrase בְנֵי־הָעָם is taken to refer to the people as a group. Rather than a specific gate, this would refer to any gate through which the people might enter the temple.

23.a. The LXX adds at this point the phrase "greater than their fathers." The reading of the LXX would imply that v 23 is speaking of the sins of the current generation rather than the sin of the fathers.

23.b. Following the Q rather than the untranslatable K.

24.a-a. The K, בה, may be understood as the regular pre-exilic 3 masc sg suff attached to the prep, as occurs occasionally in the MT (e.g., Gen 12:8). Thus the Q correction is not necessary. The word is lacking in the LXX.

25.a-a. Many commentaries omit these words as a dittogr from the next line, arguing that officials would not sit on the throne of David. While that is quite true, the kings would sit on the throne of David and the officials would ride on chariots as the next phrase states. Therefore the Heb. is intelligible as it stands.

25.b. Lit., "man," sg, in MT.

26.a-a. Many commentaries omit this phrase as an insertion, perhaps from 33:11.

Form/Structure/Setting

The final pericope of chap. 17 is one that seems unconnected with the previous units in the chapter. The pericope is clearly a unit and deals with Sabbath observance. There is also a shift from the poetic-oracular material of vv 1–18 to prose.

Verse 19 begins ostensibly with the typical messenger formula כֹּה־אָמַר יהוה, "thus says the LORD." However, the formula has an additional word here: אֵלַי, "to me." What might otherwise be expected as Yahweh's response to Jeremiah's lament/confession is seen in reality as the beginning of a new unrelated pericope. Indeed few suggestions to relate this pericope to the previous unit have been offered. Holladay (509) suggests that the threefold appearance of יום, "day," in vv 14–18 may have attracted this pericope with its sevenfold occurrence of "(Sabbath) day" here. Another possibility is that breaking Sabbath observance was one of the sins of Judah that Jeremiah includes under forsaking Yahweh in vv 1–13. The passage is clearly prose, often designated as a "prose sermon" (Nicholson, Stuhlman).

There are strong covenantal overtones in the passage. The stipulations for both keeping covenant and breaking covenant are specified. The imperatives and negative commands (vv 20–22, 27) heighten the hortatory sermonic element.

The unit is usually considered part of Mowinckel's "C" material, and, therefore, considered to be post-exilic. However, as will be noted in the following *Comment*, nothing within the unit precludes its being from the time of Jeremiah.

Comment

The unit has a single theme, that of keeping Sabbath observance, specifically of carrying no burden on the Sabbath either into the gates of the city nor out of their houses. The oracle is addressed to the kings and officials on the one hand and to all the people on the other. If the people faithfully keep Sabbath observance, then the city and its leaders and the regular round of offerings will continue for ever. If, however, the people continue to break Sabbath observance as did their ancestors, then Yahweh himself will destroy Jerusalem. The terminology Jeremiah uses to describe the destruction of Jerusalem is precisely what Amos uses in chaps. 1–2 for the destruction of the nations surrounding Israel and Judah (Amos 1:4, 7, 10, 12, 14, 2:2; 2:5; cf. Amos 1:14 for "kindle"). The only difference is that Jeremiah speaks of the fire against the gate, while Amos speaks of the fire against the wall. The imagery is that of siege warfare that results in the destruction of the capital city and, by extension, the kingdom. Fire was often used in a siege to reduce the defenses around the gates and gate towers. Often such fires would spread throughout the city bringing catastrophic destruction.

It is possible that this pericope hides an ironic word play. The word משא means both "burden" and "oracle." Jeremiah uses the word both ways, meaning "oracle" in 23:33 (2x), 34, 36 and 38 (3x). There might well be a bitter irony in that the people are breaking Sabbath observance by carrying burdens into the city and out of their houses, but simultaneously refuse to lift up or carry—or even hear—Yahweh's oracle. Such a word play would be typical of Jeremiah's style.

Some commentaries argue that this passage does not belong to Jeremiah's time but is a product of the post-exilic community, perhaps at the time of Nehemiah or Ezra (e.g., Carroll). The emphasis on Sabbath would well fit post-exilic concerns, as would the legalism of the passage. However, the references to temple and kings do fit well into a pre-exilic context, and nothing in the passage precludes its being Jeremianic.

The mention of "stiffening of their neck" in v 23 provides a link with 19:15. Both passages refer to the stiffening of the back and refusal to hear God's word as a cause of judgment.

In v 25, many commentaries argue that the reference to riding chariots and horses does not mean actually "riding" the horse, that horseback riding was not known in the region at the time of Jeremiah. However, Assyrian reliefs from the mid-600's B.C. show mounted troops. Further, the references to riding an ass (1 Sam 25:20; 25:42) and a mule (2 Sam 13:29; 18:9) apparently refer to mounted riders. In addition, 2 Kgs 18:23=Isa 36:8 apparently refers to mounted troops. There is no reason to doubt horse riders in this passage.

Explanation

Sabbath observance is but one of the covenant concerns expressed by Jeremiah. Why the keeping of Sabbath was of such great concern to Jeremiah is unclear. Perhaps Jeremiah saw Sabbath observance as one of the unique features of Israel's religion. Since the whole chapter is concerned with fidelity to Yahweh versus forsaking Yahweh, Sabbath observance would be one sign of fidelity. The implication is that even concerning this feature of covenant, Israel is now being unfaithful as had her ancestors. The strong declaration of judgment upon Sabbath breakers in this passage matches the judgment in the rest of the chapter on those who forsake Yahweh.

C. The Potter's Shop (18:1–12)

Introduction: Some Literary Connectives

In several ways chaps. 18 through 20 are connected literarily. On the level of theme, the potter theme as the basis for the message of chap. 18 is closely related to the potter's decanter which serves as the thematic center of chap. 19. These two themes are both similar and contrastive. In chap. 18 the vessel is remade according to the potter's wishes. But in chap. 19 the vessel is destroyed. While still plastic, clay can easily be remolded and shaped; once fired it becomes fixed and brittle. It can no longer be reshaped as the potter might wish, but it can be destroyed at its owner's hand!

Then the last two verses of chap. 19, which record Jeremiah's message proclaimed in the temple (from the context, probably a repetition of many of the words spoken at Topheth), provide a direct link to chap. 20, which records the response of Pashhur, the chief officer of the temple, to Jeremiah's words.

In addition to this thematic linkage, there are structural links between chaps. 18, 19, and 20. The three chapters may be outlined in terms of Yahweh's word and response to it (or action called upon by it) as follows:

18   Word of Yahweh: Instruction (vv 1–2)
    Action: Response of Jeremiah and results (vv 3–4)
  Word of Yahweh: Interpretation (vv 5–11)
    Response of Judah/Jerusalem (v 12)
  Word of Yahweh: Judgment (vv 13–17)
    Response of Jeremiah: Confession (vv 18–23)
      (His acceptance of Judgment on Judah)
19   Word of Yahweh: Instruction, Judgment (vv 1–13)
      Within vv 1–13 there is both action called for and Yahweh's word of
      instruction/judgment:
        1–2   Word of instruction calling for action
        3–9   Word of judgment concerning the place
        10   Word of instruction calling for action
        11–13 Word of judgment: interpreting the action
    Action of Jeremiah (v 14)
  Word of Yahweh: Judgment (v 15)
20   Action/Response: Pashhur (vv 1–3)
  Word of Yahweh: Response to Pashhur and judgment (vv 4–6)
    Response of Jeremiah: Confession (vv 7–12)
    Response of Jeremiah II: Lament (vv 13–18)
      (Lament that he must be the one to speak judgment)

Following this outline, one notes the pattern of Yahweh's word and a response to it. Each word of Yahweh has a response, some in terms of verbal response, others in terms of action. The double response of Jeremiah at the end of chap. 20 serves to bring closure to the larger unit.

Also from this outline, the larger unit falls into two halves, chap. 18 and chap. 19–20. Each half opens with a word from Yahweh to Jeremiah calling for a symbolic action; each has interpretation of the symbolic action in terms of judgment oracles; each has a response that involves plots or action against Jeremiah; each closes with a confession of Jeremiah.

Bibliography

Blank, S. *Jeremiah, Man and Prophet.* Cincinnati: HUC, 1961. **Brekelmans, C.** "Jeremiah 18,1–12 and Its Redaction." In *Le Livre de Jérémie Le prophète et son milieu. les oracles et leur transmission.* Ed. P.M. Bogaert. BETL 54. Leuven: Leuven UP, 1981. 343–50. **Fretheim, T. E.** "The Repentance of God: A Study in Jeremiah 18:7–10." HAR 11 (1987) 81–92. **Johnston, R. H.** "The Biblical Potter." *BA* 37 (1974) 86–106. **Mize, R.** "The Patient God." *Lexington Theological Quarterly* 7 (1972) 86–92. **Stinespring, W. F.** "The Participle of the Immediate Future and Other Matters Pertaining to Correct Translation of the Old Testament." In *Translating and Understanding the Old Testament.* Ed. H.T. Frank and W. L. Reed. Nashville: Abingdon, 1970. 64–70. **Wanke, G.** "Jeremias Besuch beim Töpfer, Eine motivkritische Untersuchung zu Jer 18." In *Prophecy, Essays presented to Georg Fohrer . . . .* Ed. J. A. Emerton. BZAW 150. Berlin: de Gruyter, 1980. 151–62. **Weippert, H.** *Die Prosareden.* 48–62, 191–209.

Translation

[1] *The word which came to Jeremiah from the LORD, saying,* [2] *"Get up, go down to the potter's house, and there I will cause you to hear my words."* [3] *So I went down to the potter's house, and,* [a]*behold, he*[a] *was making a work upon the potter's wheel.*[b] [4] *But the vessel which he was making was blemished in the clay*[a] *at the potter's*[b] *hand; so he remade*[c] *it*[d] *another vessel just as it was pleasing in the potter's eyes to do.*

[5] *Then the word of the LORD came to me, saying,* [6] *"Like the potter, am I not able to do to you, O house of Israel?"* [a]*An oracle of the LORD.*[a] *"Behold like the clay in the potter's hand, thus are you in my hand, O house of Israel.* [7] *If at any moment I speak against a nation and against a kingdom to pluck up, to break down and to destroy,* [8] *and then that nation turns from its evil*[a]*which I have spoken against it,*[a] *then I will repent concerning the evil which I had proposed to do to it.* [9] *Furthermore, if at another moment I speak concerning a nation and concerning a kingdom to build and to plant,* [10] *and it does the evil*[a] *in my sight so as not to listen to my voice, then I will repent concerning the good which I had spoken to do good to it.* [11] *So now, pray, say to the men of Judah and concerning the inhabitants of Jerusalem,* [a]*saying, 'Thus says the LORD,*[a] *"Behold, I am about to form (out of clay) against you evil and about to propose against you a plan. Pray, turn, each from his evil way, and make good your ways and your deeds"'"* [12][a]*Then they said,*[a] *"It's hopeless!"*[b] *because we continue to go after our thoughts, and we continue to do each the stubbornness of his/her own evil heart."*

Notes

3.a-a. The K has the otherwise unattested form וְהִנֵּהוּ (assuming the pointing would be the same for both forms); the Q has the more common form והנה הוא.
3.b. The Heb. reads lit., "upon the two wheels or stones," על־האבנים in the dual. The reference is to the two stones which made up a potter's wheel, see *Comment* below.
4.a. For MT בחמר, several MSS (de Rossi, III, 88) read כחמר; lacking in LXX.
4.b. LXX omits "potter's," reading "in his hands."
4.c. The Heb. reads lit., "he returned and made"; שוב + another verb is used often for remaking or redoing an action (BDB, 998a).

4.d. The Heb. can also be translated "he (re)made himself another vessel."

6.a-a. Omitted in LXX.

8.a-a. Lacking in LXX and Syr.

10.a.The K is הרעה; the Q is הרע. The meaning of the two is virtually identical. רעה appears elsewhere in this section four times (vv 8 [twice]; v 11 [twice, once an adjective]) and once רע (v 12 [an adjective]).

11.a-a. Lacking in LXX.

12.a-a. Following the Tg, Syr, and LXX, which understand a *waw*-consec with an impf, ויאמרו.

12.b. The force of the niph ptcp נואש is "there is no hope, its hopeless!" (BDB, 384b).

Form/Structure/Setting

This section of chap. 18 is clearly prose. It is one of the so-called prose sermons and is usually classified as part of the "C" material. It is related to the symbolic acts we find elsewhere in Jeremiah (chap. 13, chap. 19, etc.). The major distinction from the symbolic actions is that here Jeremiah observes rather than acting. The action of another serves as the basis for the message Jeremiah will receive and communicate.

The division of the section into short paragraphs indicates some of the shifts within the section:

vv 1–2	Word of Yahweh—Instruction
vv 3–4	Response of Jeremiah and the results
vv 5–11	Word of Yahweh—Interpretation
v 12	Response of Judah/Jerusalem

Even within this outline, vv 5–11 may be further divided:

v 5	Introduction
v 6	Yahweh is like potter to Israel
vv 7–10	The principle of antithetical possibilities: turning from evil will bring good, but turning from good will bring evil.
v 11	Application of the principle to Judah/Jerusalem

Verse 6 has a kind of double chiastic structure, one in each half of the verse:

```
A    Like the potter, am I (not able to do)
   B    to you
   B'   O house of Israel
A'   an oracle of the LORD

A    Like the clay
   B    in the potter's hand
A'   thus are you
   B'   in my hand
A"   O house of Israel
```

Verses 7–10 present possible conditional scenarios, not unlike that presented in Jonah 3. Verses 7–8 are balanced exactly by vv 9–10. In each the pattern is: (i) a condition introduced by רגע followed by an imperfect אדבר; (ii) another condition introduced by a perfect with *waw*; (iii) a result introduced by the perfect with *waw* וְנִחַמְתִּי. In each case the reversal of Yahweh's original plan is brought about by a change in the nation addressed. But the application is not found primarily within vv 7–10. These verses present only the possibilities. The application is found in v 11, where the word וְעַתָּה, "so now," indicates a transition to the specific application.

Verse 12 is taken as the response of Judah/Jerusalem to the message. Usually commentators have understood the response to be defiant, "We will go after our own thoughts and we will each do the stubbornness of his/her evil heart." Instead the mood may be that of despair and hopelessness: "Its hopeless! (We can't help it!) We continue going after our thoughts . . ."

Either the entire unit (Carroll, Duhm, Mowinckel) or vv 7–10, and 11b–12 are often considered to be a later addition to the original Jeremianic material (Nicholson, 155, and *Preaching*, 80–81; cf. Thiel, 210–17). However, Bright and Holladay (cf. also Weippert) argue for the unit being basically Jeremianic. If the entire unit is not Jeremianic, the author has certainly used the language of Jeremiah to create the message (see further in *Comment*, below). Although there are clear rhetorical shifts in the passage at v 7 and again at v 12, the potter metaphor is carried through the unit. The participle יוֹצֵר, "form," in v 11 follows the twofold occurrence of that form in v 6 and its fourfold occurrence in vv 1–4. Although the word has a participial meaning in v 11 and a nominal meaning elsewhere, such shifts of usage of a root form are typical of Jeremiah's style (Holladay, *Style*). Also the words וְלִנְתוֹץ, "to break down," לִנְתוֹשׁ, "to pluck up," וּלְהַאֲבִיד, "to destroy," in v 7 and the words לִבְנֹת וְלִנְטֹעַ, "to build and to plant," in v 9 are typical Jeremianic vocabulary (cf. 1:6, etc.). Also typical of Jeremiah's style is the use of a participle followed by one or more occurrences of a noun from the same root, וְחֹשֵׁב, "propose," מַחֲשָׁבָה, "plan," and מַחְשְׁבוֹתֵינוּ, "our thoughts," in vv 11–12.

The setting of the unit would appear to be before the fall of Jerusalem in 587/6 B.C.E. The context would indicate an impending judgment, but one that might yet be averted (vv 7–8, 11). At this point, Jeremiah and Yahweh still offer the hope that repentance (שׁוּב) might prevent the judgment indicated. Two factors within the passage might indicate that judgment is inevitable: v 4 speaks of making another vessel (or remaking the vessel), a likely reference to the exilic devastation of the nation with a hope of restoration; and v 12 speaks of a hopeless situation because a stubborn people either refuses to change or cannot change its ways. On the whole, a pre-exilic setting seems preferable, and likely one prior to Zedekiah's reign when the message of coming national collapse was inevitable.

Comment

1   Verse 1 is entirely introductory. It sets the context for the scene which follows. The formulaic wording is identical with 7:1 and 11:1; cf. 21:1.

2   While the syntax of an imperative followed by a perfect with a *waw* (קוּם וְיָרַדְתָּ) is not rare, one more normally expects an imperfect to follow the imperative and carry the force of a command. The meaning is clear, "Get up, go down . . . "

The use of the article on "potter" (הַיּוֹצֵר) indicates some specificity, but certainly not that Jerusalem had only one potter. The word for "potter," יוֹצֵר, is the participle; the root primarily means "to form, shape, or fashion." The root is used extensively of Yahweh's work, especially in creation, and often appears in parallelism with ברא, "create": Yahweh shapes humankind (אדם) from clods of clay (borrowing Speiser's terminology; he specifically says "clods in the soil," Gen 2:7–8 [*Genesis*, AB, 14–16]); the use of clay clods for עפר fits well the pot-making context. Similarly Yahweh shapes every beast of the field and the birds (Gen 2: 19), even Leviathan (Ps 104:26); the earth (Isa 45:18), dry land (Ps 95:5), mountains (Amos 4:13); light (Isa 45:7); indeed Yahweh shapes all, הכל (Jer 10:16; 51:19). So the image of Yahweh as potter is a well-known metaphor for Jeremiah to use.

3 Jeremiah follows Yahweh's directive and goes to the potter's house. There he watches the potter making a vessel, specifically a "work" (מלאכה), upon the "two wheels/stones." Potters in the ancient Near East used either a slow or fast wheel. A slow wheel was composed of two stones, the lower with a concave area and the upper with a convex projection that fit into the concave opening to give a pivot. When oil was used as a lubricant, the upper wheel could be spun so that its mass would give a number of slow revolutions, during which time the potter could shape the vessel on the wheel. On a fast wheel, the two stones would be connected by an axle and the potter would use his feet to rotate the lower wheel. This would keep the wheel turning continuously, permitting him to use both hands on the vessel much more effectively. Johnston suggests that Jeremiah referred to a fast wheel.

4 The reference to a blemish "in the clay at the hand of the potter" is ambiguous. Is the blemish in the clay itself? Is there foreign matter, too large an inclusion or grit? Is the clay too wet or too dry to work properly? In the shaping was the clay left too heavy so that it began to sag under the weight? Or was the blemish in the design and shaping? Did the potter have a particular vessel in mind and not make the vessel just as he desired so that he had to remake it? The text doesn't give any specifics; it merely states that for whatever reason the potter remade the vessel into one pleasing in his eyes.

6 The explanation given in v 6 is also nonspecific. An interpretation of judgment comes from the further development found in vv 7–11. Indeed this is why many commentaries consider 7–11 to be an expansion of an originally oblique, ambiguous message. Granted, v 6 only specifies that Israel is like clay in the potter's hand, that Yahweh can fashion Israel as he pleases. Yet even the idea of remaking from v 5 implies a change for Israel. And knowing Jeremiah's message regularly included judgment for sins, the development in 7–11 fits his proclamation well.

7–10 There is a repetition of Jeremiah's beautifully assonant phrase from the call experience (1:10) in v 7 (לנתוש ולנתוץ, "to pluck up and break down") (cf. also 31:28). That assonance continues in the call narrative with the word ולנטוע, "to plant," (1:10) which also occurs in this passage in v 9. Indeed five of the verbs from that call passage occur here in vv 7 and 9.

The interpretation of the scene at the potter's house is now given in terms of two general principles set forth as possibilities. The context suggests a conditional sentence structure. If God proposes evil for a nation because of its evil ways and that nation turns from its evil, then God will turn from the evil he had proposed. The reverse is also true: if God proposes good for a nation because of its good ways and that nation turns from its good ways, then God will turn from the good he had planned to do. The principle is simply the working out of covenant stipulations. Treaties and covenants regularly included conditions of the covenant. For the keeping of covenant, the lord promises blessings on the vassal; but for breaking covenant, the lord promises punishment for the vassal. What was true in the political arena was also true for God and his relationship with his creation. The closest biblical parallel to a working out of this principle is the case of the Ninevites in the Book of Jonah.

11 The general principles of vv 7–10 are applied specifically to Judah/Jerusalem in v 11. And the specifics are given in terms of judgment. Israel had been the nation concerning whom God had proposed to do good. They were his covenant people, enjoying the benefit of covenants with Abraham and the other ancestors, as well as the Sinaitic covenant. But now because Israel had broken covenant, God was bringing judgment on them. Yet still v 11 offers hope. If Israel will "turn," "return," "repent" (all translations of שׁוב) from its evil ways, perhaps God will turn from the evil he has proposed.

שׁוב occurs quite frequently in the prophets as the word for repentance. Jeremiah is especially fond of using the root with a variety of meanings (cf. chap. 3 where he uses the root sixteen times in twenty-two verses).

Verse 11 returns to the metaphor of the potter. The same participial form יוצר is used; however here Jeremiah uses it with a verbal thrust rather than a nominal thrust. Following Stinespring, that participle and the succeeding one are translated with the sense of an immediate future, indicating what Yahweh is about to do.

12 Verse 12 gives the response of the people. The emendation and translation adopted here suggest that these words are a response of the people in which they despair over their inability to change. The words "It's hopeless!" do not indicate stubborn refusal to repent. Instead they indicate a lack of power to change. Perhaps the people reflect a fatalism or determinism that says in effect, "I am clay in God's hand. He is shaping me and I have no control over the outcome." That reading of vv 1–6 is a possible one. However, vv 7–10 do not allow that interpretation to stand. Their response is not adequate. The result is the same as if they refused to repent.

Explanation

Jeremiah sees a parable acted out at the potter's house. He then receives an interpretation of the parable. The parable is general: a potter making a vessel finds a flaw in it, and so remakes it into another vessel pleasing to him. The interpretation first applies the parable to the broad category of nations and kingdoms: nations and kingdoms are like clay in Yahweh's hands; they are a part of his creation for him to form and shape as he will. But more specifically, Yahweh as creator is guided in part by the response of nations and kingdoms. As they respond to him, so he responds to them. (Yes, even the potter responds to the clay, in that different mixtures of clay are necessary for different vessels.)

Then application is made. Judah and Jerusalem are clay in Yahweh's hand. Because of their negative response to him, Yahweh is forming evil against them. But, the clay is still plastic; change is still possible. So the people are called on to turn from their evil ways, to repent, and to do good.

In response the people despair that they cannot (or will not) change; they will continue with their stubborn, evil ways.

D. A Horrifying Thing (18:13–17)

Bibliography

Albright, W. F. "A Catalogue of Early Hebrew Lyric Poems (Psalm LXVIII)." *HUCA* 23 (1950/51) 23–24. **Brueggemann, W.** "Jeremiah's Use of Rhetorical Questions." *JBL* 92 (1973) 358–74. **Dahood, M.** "Philological Notes on Jer 18,14–15. " *ZAW* 74 (1962) 207 – 209 . **Driver, G. R.** "Things Old and New in the Old Testament." *MUSJ* 45 (1969) 467–69. **Fitzgerald, A.** "BTWLT and BT as Titles for Capital Cities." *CBQ* 37 (1975) 167–83. **Gordis, R.** "The Biblical Root SDY-SD: Notes on 2 Sam. i.21; Jer. xviii.14; Ps. xci.6; Job v.21; Isa. xiii.6." *JTS* 41 (1940) 37–39. **Loretz, O.** "Jeremia 18,14: Stichometrie und Parallelismus Membrorum." *UF* 4 (1972) 170–71. **Propp, W. H.** "On Hebrew SADE(H) 'Highland.'" *VT* 37 (1987) 230–33.

Translation

13 *Therefore, thus says the LORD:*
　　"*Pray ask among the nations,* (2+2)
　　　who has heard (words) like these?[a]
　　An exceedingly [b]*horrible thing*[b] *she has done,* (3+2)
　　　the virgin, Israel.[c]
14 　*Has rock departed*[a] *from*[b] *[the] highland*[c] (3+2)
　　　or snow from Lebanon?
　　Do gushing[d] *waters dry up,*[e] (3+2)
　　　cool[f] *flowing (waters)?*
15 　*Yet*[a] *my people have forgotten me,* (2+2)
　　　to the No-thing[b] *they burn incense.*
　　They stumbled[c] *on their ways,* (2+2)
　　　on their old paths,
　　(and) to go (on) pathways,[d] (2+3)
　　　a way that was not a highway;
16 　*so as to*[a] *make their land a horror,* (3+2)
　　　(a place of) shrieks[b] *forever.*
　　Everyone passing by opposite her will be horrified[c] (4+2)
　　　and will shake his/her head.
17 　*Like*[a] *an east wind* [b]*I will scatter them* (2+2)
　　　before an enemy;[c]
　　back and not face I will show[d] *them* (3+2)
　　　on the day of their calamity."

Notes

This section is quite corrupt in Heb. A number of emendations have been necessary to make sense of the text. The procedure followed is to maintain the consonantal text where possible, making as few emendations as possible. In the emendations the evidence of the versions has been followed when possible.

13.a. Holladay suggests reading אָלָה, "curse," instead of אֵלֶּה "these."

13.b.b. The Tg read "bewildering thing."

13.c. A few MSS (de Rossi, III, 88) read "Jerusalem."

14.a. *BHS* suggests היעבר, "Has it crossed over . . .," instead of היעזב, "Has it departed . . .," but this emendation isn't necessary.

14.b. This translation moves the prep מ from צור "rock," to שׂדי and assumes it governs the next phrase as well.

14.c. LXX reads *mastoi*, "breasts" (=Heb. שׁד instead of שׂדה). *BHS* suggests reading שׂריון, "Sirion," another name for Mount Hermon. This translation follows MT and accepts Propp's suggestion that שׂדה should here be translated as "highland."

14.d. Reading זבים for the MT זרים "foreign."

14.e. Transposing two consonants and reading ינשׁתו, "they dry up," for the MT ינתשׁו, "they were plucked up."

14.f. Reading MT. *BHS* suggests reading מקרים, "springs," instead of קרים, "cool."

15.a. Reading כי as an adversative, GKC § 163.

15.b. Translating שׁוא, "emptiness, vanity," as referring to an idol, an idol that is nothing ("Nothing").

15.c. Reading as *BHS* suggests, וִיכָשְׁלוּ, instead of MT וַיַכְשִׁלוּם "They caused them to stumble." LXX reads καὶ ἀσθενήσουσιν, "and they weakened."

15.d. *BHS* suggests that תהו be inserted, perhaps having fallen out because of haplogr.

16.a. Translating the prep ל as indicating a result.

16.b. The translations offered for שׁריקת (the Q, for the K שׂרוקת) indicate that the word was onomatopoetic; thus I have translated it as "shrieks."

16.c. The Tgs have "will shout."

17.a. Many MSS (de Rossi, III, 88) and printed eds. have ברוח "with an (east) wind."

17.b. The Tgs add "so."

17.c. The Tgs and LXX read, "their enemies."

17.d. Reading with LXX, Vg, Tgs, and Syr a hiph, אַראֵם, for the MT qal, אֶרְאֵם, "I will see them."

Form/Structure/Setting

The word לכן serves as a transition word. It ties this unit with the preceding one, but at the same time indicates a move to a new unit. The previous unit ended with Yahweh's call to Judah to "turn," "repent," שׁוב, and Judah's seeming inability to change. Yahweh now responds to Judah.

This unit begins with the messenger formula, כה אמר יהוה again indicative of a new section. This unit is poetic and predominately 3+2 and 2+2 meter. The five-fold recurrence of the *qīnāh* rhythm indicates something of the lament structure and content of the unit.

The unit may be outlined rhetorically as follows:

A   Announcement: Israel has done horrible things (v 13)
   B   Three rhetorical questions: Do unnatural things happen in nature? (implied answer, no) (v 14)
   B'   But Israel has done horrible, unnatural things (vv 15–16)
A'   Announcement: Yahweh about to do a horrible thing—show Israel his back on day of calamity (v 17)

This section has numerous vocabulary and sense parallels with chap. 2, especially vv 10–13. A few of the more significant are indicated below:

Jeremiah 2	Jeremiah 18
Cross to the coasts of Cyprus and look, send to Kedar and examine with care; see if there has ever been such a thing (v 10)	Ask among the nations (v 13b)
	who has heard (words) like these? (v 13b)
Has a nation ever changed its gods, even though they are no gods? (v 11a)	to the No-thing they burn incense (v 15b)
Be appalled, . . . be shocked, be utterly desolate (v 12a)	Everyone passing by her will be horrified (v 16b)
	An exceedingly horrible thing you have done (v 13c)
for my people have committed two evils: they have forsaken me,	Yet my people. . .(v 15a) have forgotten me(v 15a)
the fountain of living water, . . .(v 13a)	Do gushing waters dry up, cool flowing (waters)? (v 14b)
Yet my people have forgotten me . . . (v 32)	Yet my people have forgotten me (v 15a)

The unit is a judgment oracle. The indictment is given in v 13 with expansion in vv 14–16. The sentence is pronounced in v 17. The indictment begins in third person singular ("Israel"), then switches to third person plural in vv 15–16 ("my people. . .they"). The sentence is pronounced in first person.

Verse 13 has a rhetorical question introduced by the pronoun מִי, "who." This question expects a negative answer. It is then followed in v 14 by what Brueggemann calls a double rhetorical question, but as reconstructed here a triple rhetorical question. The question in v 13 is not related to the three questions in v 14 beyond being rhetorical and expecting a negative answer. Verse 13 does in a sense prepare one for the three questions in v 14. The triple rhetorical question form in v 14 has the pattern אִם . . . ה (Brueggemann, 358), the ה of the second question being understood from the context. The three questions are followed by a development introduced with an adversative כִּי. The negative answers expected to the questions lead one further to expect the adversative following.

The two infinitives in 15c and 16a also mark a part of the structure; however, the second infinitive is understood as a result, "so as to make, in order to make, as a result to make."

This unit is considered to be Jeremianic. Although nothing within the unit suggests a specific date, it is noteworthy that there is no call to repentance nor offer of mercy. Such may indicate a date shortly before 597 B.C. or between 597 and 587 B.C.

Comment

13 The indictment of Israel/Judah in v 13 is quite general. The specifics are reserved for the following verses. The prosecutor, Yahweh, presents the case. "Ask among the גּוֹיִם, the nations, the pagan foreigners, who has ever heard anything like this?" The implied answer is "No one." Yet the details are not yet given. No horrible thing has yet been described. The style is intended to build anticipation. The covenant name of the community, Israel, is used in the passage, reminding one again of the covenantal context. Israel is described further as virgin, a common personification of lands and cities. In addition the metaphor would suggest purity, innocence, and helplessness. Yet Israel is anything but pure and innocent.

The exceedingly "horrible thing," שַׁעֲרֻרִת, is assonant with שְׁרִרוּת, "stubbornness," of v 12 and may serve to link the two sections.

14 The rhetorical questions of v 14 as reconstructed here deal with natural phenomena. Does one ever remove all the rock from the highlands? Does the snow depart from Lebanon? Do the gushing spring waters, cool flowing waters, dry up? These questions expect a negative response. Nature is predictable and unchanging. The reference to waters is reminiscent of the metaphor in 2:13 of the fountain of living waters and of Jeremiah's complaint in 15:18, "will you be to me like waters that fail," like a dry wadi in mid-summer? Brueggemann has indicated the wisdom background of these rhetorical questions. indeed he sees in them a didactic purpose. An appeal is made to nature to show how unnatural is Israel's behavior.

15 Since nature doesn't change but is faithful to its Creator, surely one can expect no less from Israel, Yahweh's covenant people. Yet that is precisely Jeremiah's point! The people have been faithless to their Creator. The particle כִּי carries forth the force of the rhetorical questions and provides the resolution in the form of an adversative. Although not following the same pattern precisely, chap. 2 uses rhetorical questions and brings the resolution in a clause introduced by כִּי. There, however, כִּי is a causal particle.

In the related passage in chap. 2, the people are said to have forsaken Yahweh, עזב. That same root occurs in v 14 above. In this verse the verb used is שׁכח, "forget." In chap. 2 the verb שׁכח appears twice in v 32, once in a virtually identical phrase.

The Hebrew שָׁוְא is usually translated "emptiness, vanity." In passages such as this where the reference is likely to idols, it is often translated as vain thing. The word "No-thing" captures the impact of the Hebrew as well as the thrust that idols lack real existence; they are not living beings, they are nothing. The fact that the people were burning incense to these objects further identifies them as idols or symbols of the pagan deities.

As a result of their behavior, the people stumble on their way (cf. Jer 12:5, "If you fall down in a safe land, how will you fare in the thickets of the Jordan?"), and end up on the wrong road, on a pathway rather than a highway. The word for "highway," סְלֻלָה, depicts a raised road, somewhat comparable to the image of an interstate highway.

16 The infinitive לָשׂוּם at the beginning of v 16 indicates a result. It picks up the stumbling and going on pathways from v 15, but also goes back to the beginning of v 15 for its referent: because they have forgotten Yahweh, so they make their land a horror. Mention has been made in the *Notes* that שְׁרוּקַת is probably onomatopoetic. All the uses of the root שׁרק indicate a loud cry, often an outcry in parallel with the word שַׁמָּה, "horror." The word "shriek" conveys the proper sense of horror and astonishment.

17   The east wind is the desert wind, the hot sirocco wind that can be so devastating to humans and vegetation alike. Yahweh, who would be like the cool
gushing waters (v 14) or the fountain of living waters (2:13), now will be like a
hot, parching desert wind (cf. 17:6). But the metaphor is not here primarily the
heat; instead it is the strong force of the wind that scatters. So will the people be
scattered before an enemy.

The worst is yet to come. When the day of calamity comes, when the people
cry to Yahweh for help and deliverance, he will turn his back on them. Rather
than seeing his face, usually a sign of blessing, they will see only his back. No
blessing, no forgiveness for this people in their distress.

Explanation

A judgment oracle now indicts the people. If a parable and its interpretation
fail (vv 1–12), perhaps a direct accusation will succeed. The accusation mentions observations from nature. Does nature change? No, comes the reply, nature
is constant. But Israel, God's covenant people, does change. They are not constant
in their covenant fidelity. They have forgotten Yahweh, making offerings to idols
that are No-thing and leaving the paths of following Yahweh. The results are
horrifying to all who see. The people will be scattered before their enemy, and
worst of all, Yahweh will turn his back on them at the time of calamity.

E. Jeremiah's Fourth Confession (18:18–23)

Bibliography

Baumgartner, W. *Jeremiah's Poems.* 56–59. **Berridge, J. M.** *Prophet, People.* **Diamond, A. R.**
The Confessions of Jeremiah. **Hubmann, F. D.** "Jer 18,18–23 im Zusammenhang der
Konfessionen." In *Le Livre de Jérémie.* Ed. P.-M. Bogaert. BETL 54. Leuven: Leuven UP, 1981.
271–96. **Kelly, F. T.** "The Imperfect with Simple *Waw* in Hebrew." *JBL* 29 (1920) 1–23.
Lundbom, J. R. *Jeremiah: A Study in Ancient Hebrew Rhetoric.* SBLDS 18. Missoula, MT:
Scholars Press, 1975. **O'Connor, K. M.** *The Confessions of Jeremiah.* **Orlinsky, H. M.** "On the
Cohortative and Jussive after an Imperative or Interjection in Biblical Hebrew." *JQR* n.s. 31
(1940–41) 371–82; 32 (1941–42) 191–205, 273–77. **Polk, T.** *The Prophetic Persona.* JSOTSup 32.
Sheffield: JSOT Press, 1984. **Seitz, C. R.** "The Prophet Moses and the Canonical Shape of
Jeremiah." *ZAW* 101 (1989) 3–27. **Smith, M. S.** *The Laments of Jeremiah and Their Contexts: A
Literary and Redactional Study of Jeremiah 11–20.* SBLMS 42. Atlanta: Scholars Press, 1990.

Translation

[18] *Now they said,*
　　"Come, let us [a]*plot against Jeremiah plots,*[a]   (4+4+4)
　　　　for 'it cannot vanish: Torah from priest,
　　　　nor counsel from sage, [b]*nor word from prophet.'*[b]

> *Come, let us smite him* ᶜ*with the tongue,*ᶜ   (3+2)
> *let us not*ᵈ *pay attention to any of his words.* "

19   *Pray, pay attention to me,* LORD,   (3+3)
> *listen to the voice of my adversaries.*ᵃ

20   *Is evil being repaid instead of good?*   (3+3)
> ᵃ*Yet they have dug a pit*ᵇ *for me.*ᵃ

> *Remember my standing in your presence*   (3+3+3)
> *to speak good about them*
> *and to cause your anger to turn from them.*

21   *Therefore, give their children to famine*   (4+2)
> *and deliver them over to the hand of the sword;*

> *let their wives become childless and widows,*   (4+4+3)
> *and let their men be slain dead,*
> *their youths smitten by sword in the battle.*

22   *Let a cry be heard from their houses*   (3+4)
> *indeed,*ᵃ *bring against them suddenly a marauding band.*

> *For they have dug a pit*ᵇ *to capture me*   (3+3)
> *and they have hidden snares for my feet.*

23   *But you, O* LORD, *you know*   (3+3)
> *all their counsel against me to the death.*

> *Do not*ᵃ*continue to*ᵃ *cover over their iniquity;*   (2+3)
> *do not*ᵃ*continue to*ᵃ ᵇ*wipe away*ᵇ *their sin from your presence.*

> *Let them be*ᶜ ᵈ*ones who have stumbled*ᵈ *in your presence;*   (3+4)
> *in the time of your anger act against them.*

Notes

18.a-a. This infelicitous Eng. is an attempt to show Jer's double use of the root חשׁב as a verb and a noun. The RSV "make plans" or NASV "devise plans" is better Eng.; "devise plots" catches the force of the Heb. better. But none of those indicate Jer's style of using a root repeatedly as an emphatic word play.

18.b-b. The Tgs have "nor instruction from the scribe."

18.c-c. *BHS* suggests reading בלשׁונו, "with his tongue." The final *waw* would be moved from the beginning of the next word, or would be assumed to have fallen out by haplogr.

18.d. LXX omits MT ‐ ואל, "not." The implication of the LXX then is "let's pay close attention to his words, so we can trap him with what he says."

19.a. The Tgs, Syr, and LXX read "my plea," apparently understanding a Heb. ריבי.

20.a-a. The LXX has here ὅτι συνελάλησαν ῥήματα κατὰ τῆς ψυχῆς μου καὶ τὴν κόλασιν αὐτῶν ἔκρυψάν μου, "for they have spoken words against me and have concealed their punishment from me."

20.b. One Tg MS has "snares"; cf. v 22.

22.a. Reading כי as an emphatic particle.

22.b. Many MSS (de Rossi, V, 66) and Q have שׁוחה, as does v 20; K has שׁיחה, an alternate form of "pit" (BDB, 1001b). LXX λόγον apparently understands Heb. שׁיחה, "complaint." One Tg MS has "snares"; cf. v 20.

23.a-a. On the addition of the phrase "continue to" see *Comment.*

23.b-b. MT תֶּמְחִי is an unusual form of the hiph impf. GKC § 75ii suggests תֶּמַח as the correct form. *BHS* suggests either that form or a qal form תֶּמַח. The MT orthography may be an archaic form indicating a *lamed he/yod* root.

23.c. The K is יהיו; the Q, followed in this translation, is ויהיו.

23.d-d. One MS reads מֻשְׁלָכִים, "ones being cast out," cf. Syr. LXX reads ἡ ἀσθένεια αὐτῶν, "their weakness." *BHS* suggests מֻכְשָׁלָם, "their stumbling." MT gives a reasonable translation without emendation.

Form/Structure/Setting

This section is another of the "confessions" of Jeremiah. It has many of the typical elements of the Individual Lament form and may be outlined as follows:

> lament (plan of the ungodly) (v 18; following Baumgartner, *Jeremiah's Poems*, 59)
> petition (v 19)
> lament (v 20a–b)
> confession of innocence (v 20c–e)
> petition, curse (vv 21–22b)
> lament (v 22c–d)
> confession of trust, lament (v 23a–b)
> petition, curse (v 23c–f)

Verse 18 is usually treated as prose and is often considered to be an addition (see Hubmann, O'Connor, Diamond). Carroll even makes it into a separate section. Yet its many ties with the confession makes such an understanding questionable. Here v 18 is considered to be poetry and an integral part of the confession. Only the introductory phrase, "Now they said," lies outside the meter of the verse.

Verse 18 exhibits a tight structure:

> imperative לכו followed by a cohortative, action directed against Jeremiah (1st line)
> proverbial saying introduced by כי (2nd–3rd lines)
> imperative לכו followed by a cohortative, action directed against Jeremiah (4th line)

Furthermore v 18 has close ties with material earlier in the chapter, ties that serve to link the three units. Hubmann has argued for a pattern of:

> prophetic prose sermon (vv 1–11)
>   response of people introduced by ואמרו (v 12)
> prophetic speech (vv 13–17)
>   response of people introduced by ויאמרו (v 18)

Both the message and the messenger have been rejected; thus the most harsh judgment can be called for in this confession/speech.

The Hebrew root חשב, "plot," appears several times within the first and last units of the chapter (vv 8, 11, 12, 18) and serves to link the material. Also assonance and word play seem to occur between the roots חשב and קשב, "pay attention," in v 18, and the root קשב in vv 18 and 19. These serve to link vv 18 and 19.

Verses 18–23 fall into two strophes, 18–20 and 21–23. Verses 18 and 21 parallel one another nicely: v 18 gives the plots against Jeremiah and the refusal to heed his words (and therefore Yahweh's words); v 21 gives the results for refusing to heed Yahweh's words. O'Connor has noted structural parallels between vv 19–20 and 22–23 (*Confessions*, 55–56). This chart is more complete than hers:

(19) ושמע	"listen"	תשמע (22)
(20) כי־כרו שוחה	"for they have dug a pit"	כי־כרו שיחה (22)
(20) לנפשי	"for me" "to capture me"	ללכדני (22)
(20) לפניך	"in your presence"	לפניך (23)
	"from your presence"	מלפניך (23)

(20) לדבר עליהם טובה   (23) עצתם עלי למות
"to speak concerning them good"   "their counsel against me to the death"
(20) להשיב את־חמתך מהם   (23) בעת אפך עשה בהם
"to cause to turn your anger from them"   "in the time of your anger act against them"

There are numerous parallels between this passage and others in Jeremiah, especially 6:11–12, 14:12–18, 15:2, etc.

Although no specific historical setting within the ministry can be associated with this confession (or the others), it is assumed to come from the period of his ministry, and could have well been included in the material of the scroll mentioned in chap. 36.

Comment

18 The identity of "they" is never clarified within this passage. It is possible that "they" are the specific enemies of Jeremiah who have been attacking him. This view would identify them with the adversaries of v 19. However, it is more likely, in light of the entire unit, that "they" refers to the people as a whole. In this way, ויאמרו here would parallel precisely the form in v 12.

The people quote a proverbial saying as their rationale for attacking Jeremiah. Since torah cannot vanish from priests, nor counsel from sages, nor a word from prophets, the only possible action for the people is to fight him back in kind, to smite him with the tongue. The proverb suggests that nothing can shut up a prophet—he always has a word (the last word?). Not only will they attack Jeremiah with words, they will simply not heed his words. Interestingly, the LXX translation suggests just the opposite: that the people will carefully scrutinize all his words, in order to trap him with his own words (cf. v 22d).

19 Jeremiah begins his complaint proper by picking up the words the people are saying. "But you, O Yahweh, pay attention to me, and listen to what they are saying." The emendation of יריבי, "my adversaries," to ריבי, "my complaint, plea," fits the context well and would give v 19 good synonymous parallelism. But MT also fits well without emendation and ties v 18 with v 19 well. The force of the hiphil imperative, הַקְשִׁיבָה, is weakened by the addition of the cohortative הָ.

20 The rhetorical question at the beginning of v 20 has brought considerable discussion in the commentaries. The issue is primarily whether Jeremiah speaks these words, as is usually accepted, or the people (Holladay). If one assumes these words are those of the people, then the words become the voice of Jeremiah's adversaries mentioned in v 19. I prefer to take v 18 as the words of the people mentioned in 19b. Then these words are Jeremiah's and preface his complaint in the rest of this verse. The complaint then deals, not with Yahweh's treatment of Jeremiah, but with the people's treatment. Further, the complaint is not merely Jeremiah's concern for the treatment he has received, but of the treatment Yahweh has received. In their refusal to heed Jeremiah's words, the people reject Yahweh's words. Thus the coming words of condemnation in vv 21–23 may be seen not merely as Jeremiah's cry for vengeance but as the retribution or payment (שלם as a verb) the people bring upon themselves.

21–22 There is no glee or comfort to Jeremiah in these words. It is the people's actions, not Jeremiah's words, that cause these inevitable actions. Already Yahweh had indicated these actions were coming (14:10ff) and had even

told Jeremiah not to intercede on their behalf. But Jeremiah had interceded any-
way (18:19). Now even Jeremiah understands that the people will not heed and
repent. The word לכן, "therefore," marks the transition to judgment. Rather than
bitter denunciation, these words are Jeremiah's sorrowful acknowledgemnt that
the people will not change and judgment is inevitable.

23 The first two lines of v 23 continue the complaint of the end of v 22. The
final words of judgment come in the last four lines of the verse. The translation
of these verses suggests that Jeremiah again acknowledges the correctness and
necessity of judgment. He recognizes that intercession for his people no longer
has a place; he puts them in Yahweh's hands. The translation "do not continue to" emphasizes the shift from intercession to an acceptance of judgment.
The word מכשלים "ones who have stumbled," retains the MT reading. It picks
up the same verb as in v 15 and emphasizes that the people's fall is their own
doing.

Explanation

Jeremiah's confession dwells on evil being repaid for good (v 20). He has
only tried to proclaim Yahweh's message, but has been attacked for doing so.
More than that, Jeremiah recognizes that Yahweh has only tried to do good for
his people. But *they* have responded to his good with evil. Even when Jeremiah
has interceded for them, still the people have not responded—or have responded
only with additional attacks on him and Yahweh. Now Jeremiah recognizes that
judgment must come, and that Yahweh was right when he told Jeremiah not to
intercede for the people. Still Jeremiah has no comfort, no joy, in pronouncing
condemnation on the people.

F. The Broken Decanter (19:1–13)

Bibliography

Crawford, T. G. *Blessing and Curse in Syro-Palestinian Inscriptions of the Iron Age.* Ph.D. diss., The
Southern Baptist Theological Seminary, 1990. **Hillers, D. R.** *Treaty-Curses and the Old Tes-
tament Prophets.* BibOr 16. Rome: Pontifical Biblical Institute, 1964. **Janzen, J. G.** *Studies.* **Kelly,
F. T.** "The Imperfect with Simple *Waw* in Hebrew." *JBL* 29 (1920) 1–23. **Kelso, J. L.** *The
Ceramic Vocabulary of the Old Testament.* BASORSup 5–6. New Haven: ASOR, 1948. **March, W.
E.** "Prophecy." In *Old Testament Form Criticism.* Ed. J. Hayes. San Antonio: Trinity University
Press, 1974. 141–77. **Stinespring, W. F.** "The Participle of the Immediate Future and Other
Matters Pertaining to Correct Translation of the Old Testament." In *Translating and Un-
derstanding the Old Testament.* Ed. H. T. Frank and W. L. Reed. Nashville: Abingdon Press,
1970. **Thiel W.** *Die deuteronomistische Redaktion.* 219–26. **Wanke, G.** *Untersuchungen zur
sogenannten Baruchschrift.* BZAW 122. Berlin: de Gruyter, 1971.

Translation

[1] *Thus said the LORD,*[a] *"Go, buy a potter's*[b] *earthenware*[c] *decanter,*[d] [e]*and [gather] from the elders of*[e] *the people*[f] *and from the elders of the priests,*[f] [2]*and go out*[a]*to the valley of the son of Hinnom*[a] *which is (at) the entrance of the gate of potsherds,*[b] *and there proclaim the words*[c] *which I speak to you.* [3]*Say, 'Hear the word of the LORD, O kings of Judah*[a] *and inhabitants of Jerusalem. Thus says the LORD of armies, the God of Israel, "Behold, I am about to bring evil upon this place such that the ears of everyone hearing it will tingle:* [4]*because they have forsaken me, they have treated as foreign this place, they have burned in it incense to other gods which they had not known, they and their fathers and the kings of Judah,* [a]*and they have filled*[a] *this place (with) innocent blood.* [5]*They have built*[a] *the high places*[b] *of the Baal to burn their sons in the fire,* [c]*burnt offerings for the Baal,*[c] *which I had not commanded*[d]*and I had not spoken*[d] *and it (the fire?) did not come up unto my heart.*

[6]*"Therefore, behold, days are coming," an oracle of the LORD, "when this place will no longer be called (the) Topheth and the valley of (the son of) Hinnom, but instead the valley of slaughter.*[a] [7]*I will empty*[a] *the counsel of Judah and Jerusalem in this place; I will make them fall by the sword before their enemies and by the hand of the ones seeking their life; I will give their corpses for food to the birds of the heavens and to the beasts of the earth.* [8]*I will make this city a horror and a shriek: everyone passing by her will be horrified and will shriek at all her wounds.*[a] [9]*I will make them eat the flesh of their sons and the flesh of their daughters. Everyone will eat the flesh of their fellows in the siege and in the distress with which their enemies,* [a]*the ones seeking their lives,*[a] *cause them distress.'"* [10]*Then break in pieces the decanter in the sight of the men who went with you,* [11]*and say to them, 'Thus says the LORD of armies, like this I will break in pieces this people and this city, just as he broke in pieces the potter's vessel and cannot*[a]*restore it*[a] *again;* [b]*and they will bury in Topheth from absence of a place to bury.*[b] [12]*Thus I will do to this place,' an oracle of the LORD,* [a]*'and to its inhabitants,*[a] *and*[b] *make this city like Topheth.*[c] [13]*Then the houses of Jerusalem and the houses of the kings of Judah will be like the place of Topheth, defiled,*[a] *namely*[b] *all the houses where they burned upon their roofs to all the host of heaven and poured out drink offerings to other gods.'"*

Notes

1.a. Several MSS (de Rossi, III, 89), LXX, Syr, and Tg eds. add "to me." *BHS* suggests perhaps adding "to Jeremiah"; cf. v 14.

1.b. LXX reads in place of the noun "potter's," the adjective "formed."

1.c. Lacking in the Syr.

1.d. The Heb. בַּקְבֻּק is undoubtedly onomatopoetic, descriptive of the sound of pouring a rather thick liquid such as an oil from a decanter. Compare with the modern name בַּלְבָּל for a narrow, long-necked vessel for pouring thin liquids such as water.

1.e-e. A few MSS (de Rossi, III, 89) omit the *waw*. Syr, Tgs, and LXX read "and take with you from the elders of the people."

1.f-f. LXX omits "the elders of." For the full phrase in Heb., see 2 Kgs 19:2.

2.a-a. LXX has "to the burial place of the sons of their children."

2.b. Q has הַחַרְסִית; cf. LXX χαρσιθ; K has הַחַרְסוּת. Although translated "potsherds" here, the translation could just as well be "Potsherd Gate." On this gate see further under *Comment*.

2.c. A few MSS (de Rossi, III, 89) add הָאֵלֶּה , "these"; LXX reads "all the words."

3.a. LXX adds here, "and men of Judah."

4.a-a. *BHS* suggests omitting the *waw* and transposing the *athnah* to the word "fathers" on the previous line. *BHS* would thus understand the sentence meaning that the inhabitants and their ancestors had burned incense here to other gods, but that the kings of Judah had filled it with innocent blood (the human sacrifice of the next verse).

5.a. *BHS* suggests emending to an impf.

5.b. LXX, Tgs have a sg.

5.c-c. Not in LXX or the parallel passage of 7:31.

5.d-d. Not in LXX^S and LXX^B.

6.a. Tgs and Syr read "the slain," as they and LXX read at 7:32.

7.a. The Heb. word וּבַקֹּתִי is from the same root as בַקְבֻּק in v 1 (and v 11 below) and is an obvious word play.

8.a. One MS (de Rossi, III, 89), LXX, and Vg have the sg.

9.a-a. Lacking in LXX.

11.a-a. For MT לְהֶרְפֵּה , codex fragments from C and many MSS (de Rossi, III, 89) have לְהֹרְפֵּא; the two are understood as variants of the same Heb. root.

11.b-b. Lacking in LXX.

12.a-a. *BHS* suggests this is an addition; the phrase certainly does not flow smoothly following the phrase, "the LORD's oracle."

12.b. One MS (de Rossi, III, 89) and LXX omit the conj, "and."

12.c. LXX reads, "like the fallen one, the one who has perished."

13.a. LXX reads the longer phrase as "will be like a fallen/perished/ruined place [LXX^B and LXX^A add "from"] uncleanness." *BHS* suggests omitting the prep "from" or reading the form as a pual ptcp plural, following the Syr.

13.b. On this use of the prep לְ, see BDB, 514b 5.e.(d) and GKC, 458, 3 § 143e.

Form/Structure/Setting

A major issue concerning chap. 19 is its character. Most commentators have assumed much of the chapter comes from secondary or redactional hands. The general argument is that vv 1–2a and 10–11a only are original (the verses that call for a specific action) and that the judgment speeches (vv 2b–9 and 11b–13) are later, reflecting a Deuteronomistic redaction of Jeremiah (the specific argument and verses are those given by Nicholson [138], Nicholson, *Jer 1–25* [163]. Others holding similar arguments, but not necessarily having precisely the same verses or arguing for Deuteronomistic redaction include: earlier, Cornill, Giesebrecht, Volz, Rudolph [109], Nötscher [152]; more recently, Bright [131], Carroll [386]). Thus the material is usually classified as a prose sermon belonging to Mowinckel's "C" source.

By this redactional breakdown, v 10 follows directly after v 2a. The result is a passage structurally similar to 13:1–11, the linen loincloth episode. In that instance, Jeremiah is commanded several times by Yahweh to perform an action: buy a loincloth and wear it, hide the loincloth near the Euphrates, go and find the loincloth. Each time Jeremiah does as he is told. Finally an interpretation of his actions and of the results is given. Here Jeremiah was given the instruction to buy a decanter, go out to the valley of Hinnom, and shatter the decanter. He does so and the interpretation is given,

If the unit of v 2b–9 is redactional, then the redactor has created several deliberate links to material in vv 1–2a and 10–11 and in chap. 18. The first and major link may be noted with the word בַקְבֻּק, "decanter," in v 1 and its recurrence in v 11, and the same root in v 7. Jeremiah is especially fond of word plays of this sort (Holladay, *JBL* 81 [1962] 44–54). It is noteworthy that although the two occurrences of בַקְבֻּק are in the material considered by all to be Jeremianic, the occurrence of the root בקק, "empty," as a verb in v 7 is in the material considered to be an expansion or redactional. (See further under *Comment* on the way in which the pottery image is carried through the judgment oracle of vv 2–9.) Another link may be noted in the recurrence of the root שמם, "horror," and שׁרק, "shriek," in v 8, both of which also occur in 18:16. That linkage matches the obvious one with the word יוצר, "potter," in v 1 and in chap. 18 (2, 3, 4[2x], 6[2x], 11). This same word occurs again in 19:11. It is evident that, whether it is considered to come from an early oral or literary stage (Wanke, *Baruchschrift*) or a later redactional stage (Nicholson, etc.), clear and deliberate linkages occur within this pericope which also relate this pericope to chap. 18.

Kuenen has noted the parallels between this chapter and 7:30–34. He argues that they have the same relationship as do chap. 26 and 7:1–15 (the Temple Sermon). Both chaps. 19 and 26 are, in his view, the expanded narrative accounts of two events; 7:1–15 and 7:30–34 give only the spoken words of those events. His parallel is even more interesting when one notes that 19:14–15 record another Temple Sermon! (See next section where those verses are treated with 20:1–6.)

19: 1–13 may be outlined as follows:

Yahweh word: commanding a prophetic action (vv 1–2)
Yahweh word: a judgment oracle (vv 3–9)
    general announcement of judgment (v 3)
    the indictment itself (vv 4–5)
        (יען אשר introduces the reason for judgment)
    pronouncement of the sentence (vv 6–9)
        (לכן introduces the sentence)
        general announcement of sentence (v 6)
        sentence explained by a series of 1st common
            singular perfect verbs:
                ובקתי, "I will empty" (v 7)
                והפלתים, "I will make them fall" (v 7)
                ונתתי, "I will give" (v 7)
                ושמתי, "I will make" (v 8)
                והאכלתים, "I will make them eat" (v 9)
Yahweh word: commanding a prophetic action (v 10)
Yahweh word: a judgment oracle (vv 11–13)
    pronouncement of the sentence (vv 11–13a)
        premise for the sentence (v 11)
            (introduced by כאשר)
        the sentence announced (v 12)
            (introduced by כֵּן)
        result (v 13a)
            (*waw* introducing the result)
    reason for the indictment (v 13b)
        (introduced by preposition ל, "in regard to")

The material in this section is prose. From the outline above, it may be seen that the entire pericope is set as a series of Yahweh speeches, both calling for symbolic actions and giving judgment oracles. There are four messenger formulae in the first section (vv 1–9) and two in the second (vv 10–13).

The section includes both calls for symbolic action (compare chap. 13 and chap. 17) and messages related to the action (the so-called prose sermon). The form of the prose sermons, vv 3–9 and vv 11–13, is that of the judgment oracle. The first prose sermon in vv 3–9 has the fuller form beginning with the announcement of coming judgment (v 3). The verbal form is a participle preceded by הנני, "behold." Following Stinespring's suggestion, this pattern is translated as an immediate future. Following the introductory word, there is the indictment itself in v 4; it is introduced by יען אשר, "because." The accusation is developed in v 5. Verse 6 includes both a messenger formula and the results of Yahweh's intervention. The shift to the sentencing part of the judgment oracle is indicated by the word לכן, "therefore." The results of Yahweh's intervention are expressed even before the intervention is mentioned, in order to heighten the anticipation of the extremely harsh intervention, vv 7–9. There is clear relationship between the material, especially vv 5–6, and 7:30–32.

The second judgment oracle, vv 11–13, is not only shorter but also has several elements omitted and others inverted. The oracle is closely related to the symbolic action commanded and grows out of that action. Jeremiah is to break the decanter and then speak the judgment oracle as an interpretation of his action. The beginning of the oracle cannot be understood apart from the symbolic action. The oracle begins with a messenger formula (v 11a) and is followed by a description of Yahweh's intervention (v 11b). The use of כאשר, "just as," to introduce the intervention links it directly to the symbolic action of the previous verse. Some brief results of this intervention are also given (11c). V 12 has another messenger formula and another description of Yahweh's intervention; here כן, "thus" introduces the intervention. Verse 13a again reports the results of Yahweh's intervention. Finally, v 13b gives the accusation or indictment that has caused the judgment, introduced by the preposition ל here "namely," (see *Notes* above for more on the use of the preposition).

Throughout the pericope the first person forms are highlighted. Although Jeremiah is addressed often in second person, and the people are addressed in third person, the first person forms carry the bulk of the development. Jeremiah's actions, given as second person perfects (translated here as imperatives from the context) only provide the backdrop for the action Yahweh expresses in first person. There are at least eleven first-person references in the first oracle and two in the second. Yahweh will personally carry out the sentence, and the results will be most horrifying to experience. Even though Jeremiah is commanded to carry out a symbolic action, it remains just that—symbolic. Yahweh's actions will complete what Jeremiah's only symbolized.

Nothing within the unit precludes its belonging to the period of Jeremiah's ministry. No indication of setting or date is present. The harsh words of judgment with no mention of grace could indicate a time during the reign of Jehoiakim shortly prior to 597 B.C., or just prior to 587 B.C.

Comment

1   The messenger formula that opens this chapter has been emended by many of the versions because what follows directly is not an oracle but directions to the prophet. Thus the words "to me" or "to Jeremiah" are often inserted. Typical formulae are found at 13:1, 16:1, and 18:1. All have some reference to the prophet. The first verbal form is an infinitive absolute of הלך; it is followed by a second

person masculine singular perfect verb. This construction is a favorite of Jeremiah's, occurring nine times with no intervening words and once with an intervening phrase. GKC § 113bb indicates this use as an emphatic imperative.

The verse needs a verb before the words "from the elders of the people"; possible verbs include אָסְפָה, "gather," or הָבִיאת, "bring," or לְקַחְת, "take."

The phrase "elders of the priests" is often deleted on the basis of the LXX, as an expansion; however the phrase does occur at 2 Kgs 19:2 and Isa 37:2, where it is translated by RSV as "senior priests."

2 The location of the "valley of the son of Hinnom" is widely debated in the commentaries. Most follow Dalman and identify it with the valley just south of the walls of Jerusalem, which forms west of the city, turns south forming the southern boundary for the biblical city (and also the border between Benjamin and Judah), and then merges with the Kidron valley just southeast of Jerusalem and descends to the Dead Sea. Assuming that the NT references to Gehenna referred to the same place, the southern location seems most probable. The valley was notorious for its pagan cults and cult practices.

Likewise uncertain is the location of the Potsherd Gate. The Targums identify the gate with the Dung Gate mentioned in Neh 2:13; 3:13–14, etc. If the implication concerning the identification of the Hinnom Valley is that of the NT, that the area was the garbage dump, then the gate may well have been called either. It would then have been a gate south of the temple mount, leading out to the valley southward. (On the call to go and proclaim a message at a gate, cf. 7:2; 17:19; 36:10.)

3 The NEB "I will bring" and RSV "I am going to bring" both lack the thrust of the participle following הִנֵּה. As Stinespring has shown, the phrase indicates an immediate future, here a most ominous future, "I am about to bring."

The phrase "this place" could refer either to Jerusalem, the city as a whole, or specifically to Topheth, the site of the pagan cult practices described below. Since v 6 specifies "this place" as Topheth probably the same identification holds here.

4 The phrase "because they have forsaken me" introduces the indictment against the people because of what they have done. It is similar to phrases in 2:13,32; 17:13; 18:15, and is explained here in reference to the cult practiced at Topheth; see v 5 below and 7:31–32.

For נכר in the piel, BDB (649b) suggests a sense of profaning or defiling. Certainly the place was profaned and defiled by the presence of a foreign cult. More to the point, the place, a part of Yahweh's chosen land, was being treated as foreign by the introduction of foreign cult practices. The same root appears in 5:19 ("foreign gods") and 8:19 ("foreign worthless things [הבל], idols").

The specifics of the indictment include burning incense to other gods and filling the place with innocent blood. The word describing the burning of incense (piel of קטר) is often used of the worship of other gods or illegal worship. As such the same stem appeared in 18:15. The recurrence of this verb may well mark another link between the two chapters. The mention of innocent blood is made specific in the next verse. The emendation suggested by *BHS*, omitting the initial *waw* on ומלאו and moving the *athnaḥ* to "their fathers," gives a better balance to the verse. However, the emendation is not necessary. The emendation would have the people guilty of burning incense to foreign gods and the kings guilty of burning their sons (v 6). However, in the closely parallel section in

7:30–32, it is the people of Judah (v 30) who are accused of burning their sons and daughters (v 31).

5 This verse is quite similar to 7:31. The comments made there hold for this passage. There are slight differences in the present passage; here only the sons are mentioned (in 7:31 it is both sons and daughters). Furthermore, this passage adds the phrase "burnt offerings [עֹלוֹת] for Baal" after the word "fire." The explanation that these offerings had not been commanded by Yahweh nor desired by him raises the question whether they were performed in Yahweh's name. Was this a cult site and were the cult practices dedicated to Yahweh or to Baal-Yahweh in a syncretistic manner? The wording of the text seems to indicate an affirmative answer. Yahweh seems to be disavowing any association with the practices, suggesting that the people were making such associations.

6 Compare 7:32 and *Comment* there. If Topheth is understood as a form indicating a fireplace or a place of burning (so possibly, BDB, 1075, KB, 1038), then the identity with the valley of Hinnom and the garbage dump all give similar indications. In 2 Kgs 23:10, the Topheth (with the definite article) is defiled by Josiah as a part of his reform. It is there understood as a place of Molech-sacrifice where children were "made to pass through the fire." Compare this with the Punic practice of Molk-sacrifice at Carthage and from Punic inscriptions.

The act of renaming is another symbolic action throughout the Book of Jeremiah. Whether the renaming was hopeful as was the case of Jerusalem to be named "throne of Yahweh" (3:17) or judgmental as in the case of Pashhur (20:3) and here, the new name expressed some symbolic characteristic of the person or place. The valley of Hinnom would become known as the Valley of Slaughter. The child sacrifices had already made it such, but Yahweh's judgment will turn it into a valley of slaughter recognized by all.

7 The word "empty" is from the root בקק, the same root of the word "decanter" (בקבק) of vv 1 and 10. The word is surely onomatopoetic, just as is the word for the vessel. It gives the sound of a vessel being emptied of its liquid. Yahweh is going to "empty out, pour out" the counsel of Judah and Jerusalem here. The symbolic action has begun. It is not merely the breaking of the decanter that is symbolic; already here the decanter is identified with Judah and Jerusalem and an action is described. If the location is the garbage dump, then the counsel, or plans, of the people is seen as garbage, poured out on the dump.

"Counsel" is the same word as found in 18:23. There it referred to the people's plans against Jeremiah; here it seems to refer to the nation's plans. To pick up on the imagery of 18:11, Yahweh has his own plans which he will carry out.

Yahweh's sentence is death; the people will fall to an enemy. Even worse is the judgment that they will have no one to bury them; their bodies will be scavenged by carrion eaters. Proper burial was a major concern of the Hebrews and exposure of the corpse or exhumation of the remains was the ultimate indignity (1 Sam 31:8–13; 1 Kgs 14:10–11, etc.). Hillers (*Treaty-Curses*, 68–69) has shown this was often a curse stipulated for those breaking a treaty. Furthermore, the visible presence of bones would defile the area. Their corpses would now defile their "sacred" cult site, just as Yahweh said their pagan cult practices had already defiled it (v 4). On the use of bones to defile an area, see Josiah's reforms and the defiling of cult sites with human bones (2 Kgs 23:13–16, 19–20).

8 The references to making the city a horror and a shriek are quite similar to those in 18:16. Furthermore, the repetition of a Hebrew root as a noun and a verb in the same verse is a favorite stylistic device of Jeremiah (Holladay, *JBL* 81 [1962] 44–54). That occurs twice here with the roots שׁמם, "be horrified," and שׁרק, "shriek." The language is similar to treaty curses.

9 Cannibalism portrays graphically one of the horrors of siege warfare. Hillers (62–63) has shown that this too is a curse often found in ancient Near Eastern treaties. This reference to a typical treaty curse, along with the one in v 7 above, suggests strongly a covenantal context for this judgment oracle. Because the people have broken covenant by forsaking Yahweh (v 4), he will now bring upon them curses typical for treaty-breakers.

The second part of the verse has two of Jeremiah's favorite stylistic features: (i) assonance between the words מָצוֹר, "siege," and מָצוֹק, "distress," and (ii) double use of the same root צוק, as a noun "distress" and as a verb "cause distress."

10 Verse 10 moves again to a call for action. After the judgment oracle is pronounced, the judgment is portrayed symbolically: Jeremiah is commanded to break the decanter in full view of those who had accompanied him. If v 7 is seen as a symbolic act, emptying the vessel (=Judah) of its plans, this act carries the image even further. The vessel had been made according to the potter's desire (chap. 18); it was emptied of its contents according to its owner's wishes (19:1, 7); now it will be destroyed according to its owner's wishes. (Compare with this the action mentioned in some treaty curses of burning wax figures to enact the curses of a treaty [Hillers, 20–21].)

Since the verb קנה, "acquire, buy," can also be used of creation (Gen 14:19, 22; Deut 32:6), the owner motif complements the potter motif of chap. 18 and depicts Yahweh ultimately as both the one forming and the one owning this people.

11 The links between v 10 and v 11 are unmistakable. The verb שׁבר, "break," referring to the action commanded of Jeremiah in v 10, is repeated as an action Yahweh will do in v 11 and then is repeated in an indefinite form referring back to Jeremiah's action. Also the words ככה, "like this," and כאשׁר, "just as," provide links with the previous verse.

The image of the shattered vessel that cannot be repaired is striking. It carries the potter image to another level. As long as the clay was plastic, the potter could remake the vessel as he desired. However, once the vessel has been fired, it cannot be remade. Whereas Judah the vessel in chap. 18 still had the opportunity for repentance and change at the potter's hand, now she faces unmistakable destruction. Even if every sherd of the broken vessel were recovered, the vessel could not be repaired (רפא, "heal, repair"); the broken sherds would be left where they fell, outside the Potsherd Gate at the garbage dump. The root רפא, and its variant רפה, occurs often in Jeremiah (3:22; 8:22; 17:14[2x]; 30:17, etc.) with the sense of healing or restoring.

The burying in this verse contrasts with the exposure mentioned in v 7 above. The results are the same in both cases—death of the people and defilement of the area because of the presence of corpses, bones, and burials. Turning the area into a cemetery would defile it, just as surely as unburied bones.

12 Verse 12 begins with כן־אעשׂה, "thus I will do," linking it back to the action of v 10. However, the judgment spoken refers back not only to the breaking of the decanter, but to the defilement of Topheth (vv 6, 11). Clearly these two judgments are closely tied. To make the city like Topheth could refer either to the burials there (v 11), making the whole city one immense cemetery, or to Topheth being the garbage dump and the whole city becoming a refuse pit (see *Comment* on v 2).

13 More specifics of the syncretistic cult practices are given in this verse. These practices included incense offerings to the "Host of Heaven," a reference to astral worship. Making such offerings from the rooftops may indicate an attempt to be as close as possible to the objects of worship. The other practice mentioned is pouring out a drink offering to other gods (again using both the verb and noun from the same root, נסך, "pour out"); compare 7:18.

All the houses where these practices occur will also become like Topheth. Topheth serves as the focal point of yet another judgment. First, the city was to become like Topheth (v 12). Now the houses of the people and of the king will become like Topheth, defiled. There is a multiple play on Topheth and defilement here. There is the defilement from the corpses, defilement from the pagan cult practices, and probably defilement from the garbage dump.

The pericope ends at this point. The narrative that opens the next section does not mention that Jeremiah actually did as he was instructed in these verses. With the symbolic actions of chaps. 13 and 18, his carrying out of the actions is recorded. However, neither chap. 7 nor chap. 26 specifically records that Jeremiah went to the temple as instructed to deliver the message. In chap. 26 such action is implicit in the response of the people to his words. One may assume that Jeremiah did indeed carry out this symbolic act. It will be argued below that Pashhur's response in 20:1–3 was to more than Jeremiah's words of 19:15, probably including the words of this pericope.

Explanation

In this section Jeremiah is passive. He is the recipient of the instructions and the interpretation, but no actual movement is mentioned. Yet the passage also indicates symbolic actions expected of the prophet. Indeed, the focus of the passage is on the symbolic actions involving the potter's decanter. Chap. 18 has already set forth the identity of the people as pottery vessels and Yahweh as the potter, able to make and remake as he pleases.

Picking up on that identity, this chapter moves to other images involving the decanter. First there is the contrast between a whole, useful, and probably filled decanter and the broken sherds implied in the name of the gate. The image is even more striking if the site is equated with the garbage dump.

The first judgment oracle condemns the pagan cult activities practiced at the site. The symbolic action related to this oracle is the emptying of the decanter (v 7), indicating that Yahweh was emptying out the plans of Judah; he has his own plans, plans of judgment and death. A most horrifying depiction of the destruction of Judah and Jerusalem with death abounding is the curse pronounced by Yahweh.

Then the symbolic destruction of the decanter is described. This shattering enacts the destruction/death of the first oracle. The place was a place of broken sherds and a place of broken covenants, because the people had forsaken Yahweh for their syncretistic pagan worship. Thus Yahweh would bring the covenant curses upon the people; they would become like broken sherds. Unlike some earlier passages in Jeremiah (e.g., 3:22), where healing/restoration was still possible if the people would repent, this oracle offers no such hope. Indeed this destroyed vessel cannot be repaired again (v 11). The passage offers only unmitigated judgment.

G. Another Temple Sermon and Its Results (19:14–20:6)

Bibliography

Ahituv, S. "Pashhur." *IEJ* 20 (1970) 95–96. **Christensen, D. L.** "Terror on Every Side." *JBL* 92 (1973) 498–502. **Clines, D. J. A.** and **Gunn, D. M.** "Form, Occasion and Redaction in Jeremiah 20." *ZAW* 88 (1976) 390–409. **Görg, M.** "Pashur and Pisanhuru." *BN* 20 (1983) 29–33. **Holladay, W. L.** "The Covenant with the Patriarchs Overturned: Jeremiah's Intention in 'Terror on Every Side' (Jer 20:1–6)." *JBL* 91 (1972) 305–20. **Honeyman, A. M.** "*Magor missabib* and Jeremiah's Pun." *VT* 4 (1954) 424–26. **Martin, D. C.** "Pashhur." *Mercer Dictionary of the Bible.* 647. **Nicholson, E. W.** "Blood-spattered Altars?" *VT* 27 (1977) 113–16. **Stinespring, W. F.** "The Participle of the Immediate Future and Other Matters Pertaining to Correct Translation of the Old Testament." In *Translating and Understanding the Old Testament.* Ed. H. T. Frank and W. L. Reed. Nashville: Abingdon, 1970. 64–70. **Wächter, L.** "Überlegungen zur Umnennung von Pašhūr in Māgôr Missābīb in Jeremia 20,3." *ZAW* 74 (1962) 57–62. **Wanke, G.** *Untersuchungen zur sogenannten Baruchschrift.* BZAW 122. Berlin: de Gruyter, 1971.

Translation

[14] *Then Jeremiah came from Topheth*[a] *where the LORD had sent him to prophesy, and stood in the court of the house of the LORD, and said to all the people,* [15] *"Thus says the LORD of armies, the God of Israel,* [a] *'Behold I am about to bring*[a] *unto this city and* [b]*upon all its towns*[b] *all the evil which I have spoken against her because they have stiffened their back so as not to hear*[c] *my words.'"*
[20:1] *Now when Pashhur, the son of Immer,*[a] *the priest*[b] *heard (he was* [c]*overseer-leader*[c] *in the house of the LORD) Jeremiah had prophesied these words,* [2a]*Pashhur struck Jeremiah the prophet*[a] *and put him in the stocks*[b] *which were in the* [c]*upper Benjamin Gate*[c] *which was at the house of the LORD.*
[3a]*The next morning*[a] *Pashhur brought Jeremiah out from the stocks; Jeremiah said to him, "The LORD has not named you Pashhur, but 'Terror*[b] [c]*on every side.'*[c] [4]*For thus says the LORD, 'Behold, I am about to make you a terror*[a] [b]*to yourself and*[b] *to all your loved ones: they will fall by the sword of their enemies and your eyes will see it;* [c]*and all*[d] *Judah I will give into the hand of the king of Babylon and he will take them into exile to Babylon and strike them with the sword.* [5]*And I will give all the wealth of this city*[a] *and all her produce* [b]*and all her precious things,*[b] *and all the treasures of the kings of Judah* [c]*I will [also] give,*[c] *into the hand of their enemies* [d]*and they will plunder them and they will take them*[d] *and they will bring them to Babylon.* [6]*But you, Pashhur,*[a] *and all the inhabitants of your house, will go into captivity;* [b]*you will go*[b] *to Babylon,* [b]*and there*[b] *you will die, and there you will be buried, you and all your loved ones to whom you prophesied with a lie.'"*

Notes

14.a. *BHS* suggests reading "from the entrance" or "from the entrance of the gate" to fit better with v 2.

15.a-a. Q has מביא; K lacked the א due to haplogr. This translation follows Stinespring's suggestion that participles may often be understood as immediate futures.

15.b-b. Heb. lit. reads "this city and its cities"; LXX reads, "and its villages."

15.c. Tgs read "receive."

20:1.a. Syr has "Amariah."

1.b. LXX minuscules have "false prophet" instead of "priest"; cf. v 6.

1.c-c. Tgs have "prefect of the priests." The pl of "overseer," פקדים, occurs in 29:26.

2.a-a. LXX simply has, "He struck him."

2.b. Tgs read "prison."

2.c-c. LXX has "upper house set apart."

3.a-a. Lacking in LXX.

3.b. LXX and θ´ have "exile."

3.c-c. Not in LXX. Tgs have for the full name "Those who kill with the sword shall be gathered together against you round about."

4.a. LXX has "exile"; Tgs, "misfortune."

4.b-b. Lacking in LXX.

4.c. LXX adds "and you."

4.d. Tgs add "the men of the house of."

5.a. Some Tg MSS read, "this land."

5.b-b. Lacking in LXX.

5.c-c. Lacking in LXX.

5.d-d. Lacking in LXX.

6.a. Not in LXX.

6.b-b. Not in LXX.

Form/Structure/Setting

The section is a prose account of another Temple Sermon (19:14–15) and the results of this proclamation (20:1–6) (cf. 7:1–12 and chap 26). However, it seems quite likely that the message proclaimed in the temple was not merely the single verse but more likely a repetition or summary of the fuller judgment oracles in 19:3–9 and chaps. 11–13. The repeated occurrences of the phrase "this place" (vv 3, 4[2x], 6, 7, 12) and "this city" (vv 8, 11, 12) from the previous section provide a link to this section. Further, the mention of Topheth in v 14 links with the previous section literarily as well as temporally. The "evil which I have spoken" of v 15 most naturally refers back to the judgment oracles of the previous section.

Perhaps the single most important link is the phrase in 20:4, "they will fall by the sword of their enemies," in reference to Pashhur's loved ones. This phrase is quite similar to the phrase of the first judgment oracle of the previous section, 19:7, "I will make them fall by the sword before their enemies." The repetition of "kings of Judah," in 19:3, 4, 13 and 20:5, also links the sections.

Additionally, the comment that Pashhur "heard . . . Jeremiah had prophesied these words" (20:1) most naturally includes the full judgment oracles of chap. 19 rather than the single verse 19:15.

The function of vv 14–15, then, is to bring the judgment oracles, first spoken to only a few, to the whole people. More than just the select ones from the elders, now priests, and judicial and religious leaders, hear the word. The action of Pashhur may well be related specifically to the proclamation to all the people of these oracles.

The narrative continues in 20:1–6. Pashhur strikes Jeremiah and puts him in stocks (public humiliation?) overnight. Upon his release, Jeremiah announces a judgment oracle against Pashhur and his family. With all possible irony, the man in charge, Pashhur, is told that he is not in charge. He can beat and humiliate Jeremiah, but ultimately he and his family will be humiliated! The judgment oracle against Pashhur has a symbolic renaming (perhaps like a slave name; end of v 3), a messenger formula (v 4a), an interjection introducing the sentence (4b), Yahweh's intervention (4c), and the results of that intervention (4d–6). The intervention is twofold: personal (involving Pashhur and his loved ones) and national.

This judgment oracle has several parallels to the oracles in 15:13–14 and 17:3–4. All three have the verb form אֶתֵּן, "I will give," the noun אוֹצְרוֹת, "treasures," and a form of the root בֹּז, "plunder"; similarly, all three speak of the "enemies," אֹיְבֵי.

Likewise, there is also a word play with a twist on עֹרֶף, "back"; in 19:15, the people have stiffened their backs so as not to hear Yahweh's words, but in 18:17, Yahweh will show the people his back and not his face on the day of calamity.

In terms of an outline, the section has the following elements:

Action of Jeremiah: he goes to the temple and proclaims the message (v 14)
Message of Yahweh (v 15)
Action of Pashhur: he strikes Jeremiah and puts him in stocks (20:1–2)
Message of Yahweh (vv 3–6)
    Renaming (v 3)
    Messenger formula (v 4a)
    Judgment based on word play of Pashhur's name
    (=Intervention of Yahweh) (v 4b–d)
        judgment on Pashhur and loved ones (v 4c)
        judgment on nation (v 4d)
    Development of judgment
    (=Results of Yahweh's intervention) (vv 5–6)
        to the nation (v 5)
        to Pashhur and his family (v 6)

Two features are evident from this outline. There is a balance and movement from action to message and from human actor to divine word. As noted above (*Introduction:* "Some Literary Connectives," 18:1–12 [p240]), this balance is part of the fuller pattern noted throughout chaps. 18–20. The second pattern is a chiastic structure within the judgment oracle directed against Pashhur:

A word against Pashhur and loved ones (v 4c)
  B word against all Judah (v 4d)
  B' word against Jerusalem and Judah (v 5)
A' word against Pashhur and loved ones (v 6)

The material of this unit is often called biographical prose; Jeremiah is referred to in the third person. It is Mowinckel's "B" material and is often said to come from the hand of Baruch (Wanke).

Comment

14 Verse 14 forms the transition between the two judgment oracles spoken outside the city gate and this section. It moves Jeremiah geographically from outside the city into the city and into the temple. It also moves the message from being directed to a select group of the leaders to all the people. The reference to Topheth links this section with the prose message of the two oracles (vv 6, 11, 12, 13).

The movement of Jeremiah to the temple seems significant. It indicates that Jeremiah had access to the temple still (or again). Chap. 36 is dated by the text to the fourth year of Jehoiakim (=605/4 B.C.; v 1). There Jeremiah sends Baruch to read the scroll in the temple because he is "prevented [עָצוּר] from entering the house of the LORD" (v 5). Bright (174–75) argues that this section preceded that temple sermon of 605–604 B.C. He would date this incident to the period between 609 and 605 B.C. The content of the oracles of chap. 19, however, offer no call for repentance and no hope of forgiveness. The judgment is unalterable, unlike the temple sermon of chaps. 7 and 26 and even unlike chap. 36 which also still has some hope of repentance (vv 3, 7). Therefore the dating of the event to the period after 605–604 B.C. but before 597 B.C. seems best. Holladay (539) prefers a date of 601–600 B.C. for the incident.

15 The message proclaimed in the temple was undoubtedly more than the single verse indicated here. As argued above, it seems probable that at least the content of the judgment oracles of vv 3–9 and 11–13 were proclaimed. Just as chap. 26 includes only a brief account of the temple sermon also found in chap. 7 in somewhat fuller form, so here we find only an abbreviated portion of a larger message found in 19:3–13. And even accepting the fuller form would not suggest that the entire message proclaimed to the people was so short.

The phrase "unto this city and upon all its towns" has had considerable discussion. Clearly the phrase refers to Jerusalem and the cities or towns surrounding. Often the phrase "daughters [i.e., daughter-cities]" will be used in this connection (e.g., Josh 17:11[6x]; 17:16, Jer 49:2). The specific phrase "against Jerusalem and against all her cities" occurs in Jer 34:1. LXX clearly has that understanding in its translation "this city and her villages." NEB, following a suggestion of Driver and Gaster, translates עָרִים as "blood-spattered altars," based on a Ugaritic word. Nicholson has shown convincingly that there is no compelling evidence for the existence of a Hebrew word meaning blood-spattered altar, and even the Ugaritic word probably meant something else.

20:1 The name Pashhur occurs in biblical Hebrew as the name of at least three different individuals, two in Jeremiah: Pashhur ben Immer in this chapter and Pashhur ben Malchiah in chaps. 21 and 38. (The Pashhur of Neh. 10:4 [3] is the third definite individual; the other occurrences could refer to one of the above or to different individuals.) The name also has been found on two Hebrew seals and on an ostracon from Arad. The name itself probably derives from the Egyptian meaning "son or portion of Horus." On the word play involved in the changed name given Pashhur, see under v 3 below.

Pashhur was פְּקִיד נָגִיד, translated here "overseer-leader." Keil argued that נָגִיד was the official term and פְּקִיד was attached to it as an explanation (743). Cornill, on the other hand, argued that פְּקִיד was primary and נָגִיד an addition, on the evidence of Jer 29:26, where the phrase פְּקִיד בֵּית יהוה occurs (233). In both passages, the function of the official is to maintain order or handle disturbances in the temple. Cornill, Rudolph, and others see the office as temple police. Perhaps in our setting we would say chief of security. The assonance of the two words may indicate their originality. Perhaps even a bit of sarcasm is indicated by the double term. Here the priest and overseer-leader strikes and puts in stocks the prophet who in his call had been appointed Yahweh's overseer (הפקדתיך, 1:10). Read in the context of 29:26, Jeremiah would easily be seen as a madman in both situations by his actions and words against the status quo.

The word נבא may be either a perfect or a participle. In this translation it has been understood as a perfect. The point is not that Pashhur necessarily heard Jeremiah proclaiming the oracle, but that he heard the event had taken place.

The meaning of the word המהפכת is uncertain. It is assumed to be stocks or a similar confining and, perhaps, torturing instrument. The word used by the Tg to translate the Hebrew can be understood as either "prison" or "collar." LXX has "trap-door," perhaps understanding a dungeon. As suggested above, perhaps the idea is confinement together with public humiliation. Interestingly, the three times this word occurs in biblical Hebrew, it is used of action against a prophet/seer because of displeasure at the prophet's words. The location of the confinement, "in/at the upper Benjamin Gate by the house of the Lord," could indicate confinement within the guard rooms often found at a gate complex or could indicate stocks found at a public place such as a gate. The gate is specified as being "by the house of the LORD." As such the gate could be one that gave entry either into the temple or into the city. Burrows has suggested that the word "Upper" indicates a temple gate, being on higher ground, and the corresponding "Lower" Benjamin Gate would be the city gate, referred to simply as the Benjamin Gate in 37:13 and 38:7 (*IDB*, 853).

3 Verse 3 records the change of name Jeremiah gives Pashhur. That Jeremiah intends a word play on the name is clear (contra Keil, 744–45). In all likelihood, since the name change introduces a judgment oracle, the change should be a reversal from a positive name to a negative. The word play need not, however, be based on the actual etymology of the name. Biblical Hebrew has numerous examples of word play based on assonance or homonyms. Holladay (*JBL* 91 [1972] 305–20) has the most convincing explanation for the word play. He suggests Pashhur is by assonance taken to be from two Aramiac words, פש, a participle of פוש meaning "fruitful," and סחור, "round about." The word play then would be a reversal from "fruitful all around" to "terror/destruction on every side."

The new name מגור מסביב is almost universally understood to mean "Terror on every side" or something comparable. מגור is from גור III (BDB, 159–60), meaning either terror itself or the cause of terror. The fact that the LXX apparently translates only מגור leads some commentators to see מסביב as an addition. Further, the LXX translation for מגור, "exile, foreigner," understands a different root, גור I (BDB, 157), rather than גור III. Holladay has argued that Jeremiah may have deliberately played on all three root meanings of גור in the oracle against Pashhur. Certainly the probability of a double meaning of גור is likely with the reference to exile in v 4 and the LXX, though Holladay's triple entendre seems forced. The full name appears five times in Jeremiah (apart from here, at 6:25; 20:10; 46:5; 49:25) and twice elsewhere (Ps 31:14; Lam 2:22 in a slightly different form); the full form as MT has fits well the context here.

4–5 These verses explicate the name change of the previous verse. Indeed they explain especially the word מסביב: Pashhur will become a terror or a symbol of terror not just to himself, but to all those who are around him, from loved ones to "all Judah." The terror will come to all who are around Pashhur. Not only will Pashhur symbolize that terror in what happens to his loved ones, but he will have to witness it himself. Likewise, all Judah will both symbolize the terror and experience it.

Most important is the mention of the king of Babylon in v 4. This is the first explicit reference to the place of exile in the book. Prior to this, the threat has been an unnamed foe from the north (1:13), or a land which you have not known (15:14). Now the judgment has been given specificity, and historicity, in a word, reality.

6 Verse 6 returns specifically to Pashhur. Not only will those around him become a terror, but Pashhur too. Specifically he and his household will go to exile to Babylon, there to die and be buried. Pashhur, who would terrorize Jeremiah for the message he proclaimed, will be terrorized and will become a terror for all to witness, as will all Judah (vv 4–5). Just as the people of Jerusalem and Judah would die at the hands of their enemies (19:7), so Pashhur would die. Only he would die and be buried in a foreign land.

Explanation

Following the destruction of the earthenware decanter (19:10), Jeremiah went into the temple court and again proclaimed a message of judgment and destruction. Pashhur, a temple official, arrested Jeremiah, struck him, and put him in stocks overnight. The next day, when Pashhur brought Jeremiah out of the stocks, Jeremiah announced a judgment against Pashhur and all his loved ones, based on a word play on Pashhur's name. His new name would be "Terror on every side." In one sense Pashhur would be "Terror on every side" to those who knew him, for evil would befall all of them. In another sense, Pashhur would himself experience "terror on every side" at the loss of family and loved ones, and even his own life in exile. Not only Pashhur, but all the exiles from Judah, would suffer this terror at the hand of the Babylonians.

H. A Final Confession (20:7–13)

Bibliography

Baumgartner, W. *Jeremiah's Poems.* 59–62, 73–78. **Berridge, P. E.** *Prophet, People.* 151–55. **Clines, D. J. A.** and **Gunn, D. M.** "Form, Occasion and Redaction in Jeremiah 20." *ZAW* 88 (1976) 390–409. ———. "'You Tried to Persuade Me' and 'Violence! Outrage!' in Jeremiah XX 7–8." *VT* 28 (1978) 20–27. **Diamond, A. R.** *Confessions.* 101–13. **Fishbane, M. A.** *Text and Texture.* New York: Schocken, 1979. 91–102. **Held, M.** "The Action-Result (Factitive-Passive)

Sequence of Identical Verbs in Biblical Hebrew and Ugaritic." *JBL* 84 (1965) 272–82.
Holladay, W. L. *Architecture.* **Hubmann, F. D.** "Anders als er wollte: Jer 20, 7–13." *BLit* 54
(1981) 179–88. **Janzen, J. G.** "Jeremiah 20:7–18." *Int* 37 (1983) 179–83. **Kelly, F. T.** "The
Imperfect with Simple *Waw* in Hebrew." *JBL* 29 (1920) 1–23. **Levenson, J. D.** "Some Un-
noticed Connotations in Jeremiah 20:9." *CBQ* 46 (1984) 223–26. **Lewin, E. D.** "Arguing for
Authority: A Rhetorical Study of Jeremiah 1.4–19 and 20.7–18." *JSOT* 32 (1985) 105–19.
Marrow, S. "Hamas ("violentia") in Jer 20, 8." *VD* 43 (1965) 241–55. **O'Connor, K. M.**
Confessions. 66–80, 130–46. **Pitard, W. T.** "Amarna *ekemu* and Hebrew *naqam*." *MAARAV* 3
(1982) 5–25. **Seitz, C. R.** "The Prophet Moses and the Canonical Shape of Jeremiah." *ZAW*
101 (1989) 3–27. **Smith, M. S.** *The Laments of Jeremiah.*

Translation

7   *You persuaded[a] me, O LORD, and I was persuaded;* (3+2)
    You overpowered me, and you overcame.
    I have become (an object of) derision [b]all the time,[b] (3+3)
    everyone mocking me.
8   *[a]For as often as I speak,[b] I utter outcries;[a]* (3+3)
    violence and devastation I proclaim.
    For the word of the LORD is to me (3+3)
    a reproach and a derision all the time.
9   *I have said, "I refuse to mention him,* (2+3)
    I refuse to speak in his name";
    but it is [a]in my heart[a] like a burning fire (4+2)
    [b]being shut up[b] in my bones,
    I am exhausted from holding it in, (2+2)
    I cannot overcome.
10 *Indeed, I have heard many slanders:* (4+2+2)
    "'Terror[a] on every side!'
    [b]Inform! Let us inform on him!"
    Everyone who wishes me well (3+2)
    is watching for my stumbling.[b]
    "Perhaps he can be persuaded and we can overcome him, (4+3)
    then let us take our vengeance on him."
11 *But[a] the LORD is with me* (2+2)
    like an awe-inspiring hero.
    [b]Therefore, the ones pursuing me will stumble, (3+2)
    they will not overcome.[b]
    They will be shamed greatly; (2+2)
    surely they will not succeed.
    [c]Eternal ignominy, (2+2)
    it will never be forgotten.[c]
12 *[a]O LORD of armies, the one testing the righteous,[b]* (4+3)
    the one seeing inner parts and heart,
    let me see your vengeance on them (3+4)
    for unto you I have revealed[c] my case/complaint.[d]
13 *Sing to the LORD!* (2+2)
    Praise the LORD!

> *For he has delivered the poor person*   (4+2)
> *from the hand of evil ones.*

Notes

7.a. The verb פתה can have the connotations of "seduce," "entice," or "persuade." See further under *Comment.*

7.b-b. LXX reads "continuously."

8.a-a. LXX has "for I will laugh because of my bitter speech."

8.b. Tgs insert "weeping."

9.a-a. Not in LXX.

9.b-b. LXX reads "flaming" in parallel with the previous line. The Tgs have "washing my bones clean."

10.a. Tgs and LXX have "gathering around," understanding מגור to be derived from גור I, "assemble, gather, sojourn." See above, *Comment* on 20:3. The Heb. preserves exactly the same phrase as 20:3.

10.b-b. LXX has a different understanding of this section, reading "Conspire, let us conspire against him. All his friends watch for his intention."

11.a. Translating the *waw* as an adversative.

11.b-b. LXX has "they persecuted but they could not perceive."

11.c-c. The Tgs have "eternal humiliation shall cover them which shall not end."

12.a. *BHS* suggests that the entire verse is an addition here from 11:20, with which it is quite similar.

12.b. A few MSS (de Rossi, V, 66) have צדק instead of צדיק, as does 11:20.

12.c. *BHS* suggests reading a piel inf instead of a piel pf.

12.d. The Tgs have "my humiliation."

Form/Structure/Setting

A major portion of the discussion on this passage has involved its extent. Rudolph and Janzen have treated the entire passage as a unit. But most scholars have divided 20:7–18 into at least two units, 7–13 and 14–18 (including Baumgartner, Berridge, Hyatt, Weiser, Bright, Cornill, Carroll, Clements, McKane, Holladay, Ewald, Keil, etc.) Quite a number of these scholars have further divided 7–13 into two units, 7–9 and 10–13 (Baumgartner, Berridge, Condamin, Cornill, Carroll, Nötscher, McKane, etc.) or 7–10 and 11–13 (Laetsch, Condamin, Lundbom). Others have suggested that v 12 is an addition based on 11:20 (Baumgartner, Duhm, Rudolph, Hyatt, etc.) or that v 13 is secondary (Duhm, Cornill, Giesebrecht, Holladay, Lewin, Fishbane [possibly], etc.); Cornill even suggests that vv 11–13 are all additions.

Lundbom (following Condamin) would divide the unit after v 10 on the basis of an inclusio, the repetition of the two Hebrew roots פתה and יכל in vv 7 and 10. Certainly there is a transition beginning at v 11 from lament to confession of trust. But this transition and the inclusio do not mark the end of the pericope.

The arguments of Clines and Gunn (*ZAW* 88 [1976] 390–409), O'Connor, and others concerning the form-critical (see below, the Individual Lament form) and literary (chiastic structure, below) unity of vv 7–13 seem compelling; this section will be treated as a unit, the final of Jeremiah's so-called confessions.

The unit is poetic, but lacking in a dominant meter. Of the eighteen lines/ stichs, eight have a *qīnāh*-type meter [the first half-line is longer than second— 3+2, 4+3, 4+2, 4+2+2] and eight have the same meter in both halves [3+3, 2+2].

In terms of form, the unit is an Individual Lament, although it does not have all the constituent elements (Polk, 152):

invocation of Yahweh (v 7)
lament (vv 7–10)
confession of trust/certainty of a hearing (v 11)
petition (v 12)
praise (v 13)

Westermann (*Praise and Lament,* 182) has suggested that the Individual Lament is characterized by a trichotomous structure based on the three subjects of these laments: subject I = Thou, God; subject II = I (the speaker); subject III = the enemy. In that regard, Jer 20:7–11 may be divided as follows: subject I = v 7a; subject II = vv 7b–9; subject III = vv 7f, 10.

Fishbane (93) has discovered a chiastic structure of five stanzas within vv 7–12:

A   stanza 1: direct speech to God, "You" (v 7)
  B   stanza 2: self-reflection, indirect reference to God, "He" (vv 8–9)
    C   stanza 3: recollection of enemies' plots against "him" (v 10)
  B'   stanza 4: self-reflection, indirect reference to God, "He" (v 11)
A'   stanza 5: direct speech to God, "You" (v 12)

He also notes that stanzas 2 and 3 develop the claims of stanza 1, and stanzas 4 and 5, expressing exuberant hope, differ markedly from stanzas 1 through 3 in mood, theme, and tense. This outline clearly separates v 13 from the rest of the unit. Fishbane calls that verse a hymn, either added by Jeremiah or the words of another (102).

Nevertheless, it is possible to understand 13 as a part of the unit literarily. The double reference to Yahweh in vv 7–8 forms an inclusio with the double mention in v 13. The center of the unit literarily then becomes the additional two references to Yahweh in vv 11a and 12a, both the strong trust statements. With this understanding we have the contrast between the complaint against Yahweh in v 7 and praise of Yahweh in v 13. The trust statements in vv 11a and 12a provide the focal point of the unit, which explains the turn to praise in v 13. Sandwiched between these references to Yahweh are three mentions of the "enemies": their plots (v 10), their certain fall (v 11b–d), and a call for Yahweh's vengeance on them (v 12b). The following chiastic structure is offered as a way of understanding this entire confession from a rhetorical sense to match its form-critical extent:

A   Complaint against Yahweh (vv 7–9)
  B   Complaint against "enemies" (v 10)
    C   Assurance: Yahweh is with me (v 11a)
  B'   Fall of the "enemies" (v 11b–d)
    C'   Assurance: Yahweh sees the heart (v 12a)
  B"   Vengeance on "enemies" (v 12b)
A'   Praise of Yahweh for deliverance (v 13)

In addition there are several words that recur within the unit. The verb פתה occurs twice in v 7 as a piel/niphal pair, the so-called action-result or factitive-passive sequence (Held), and again in v 10. It appears first in a complaint against Yahweh (Yahweh is the active one persuading Jeremiah, and he is persuaded). Then it appears in a complaint against the "enemies" as a niphal as they hope Jeremiah can be persuaded.

Paired closely with פתה is the verb יכל, "overcome." This verb occurs in vv 7 and 10: Yahweh persuades, overpowers (חזק), and overcomes; the enemies hope Jeremiah is persuaded so they can overcome. But this verb also occurs twice more, in vv 9 and 11. In v 9, Jeremiah, who has tried not to proclaim Yahweh's word, admits that he cannot overcome (Yahweh). In v 11, Jeremiah speaks with confidence that his enemies also cannot overcome (him or Yahweh). Clines and Gunn (VT 28 [1978] 23) argue that יכל is the key word of the passage.

One other repeated word within this unit bears mention. The noun נקמה, "vengeance," is spoken first by the enemies and directed against Jeremiah in v 10; in v 12 it is spoken by Jeremiah to Yahweh against those enemies. In both cases the mood appears to be cohortative.

The sixfold repetition of כי within the unit is significant. But somewhat surprisingly כי does not have the rhetorical force at the center of the unit as is often the case. The two occurrences in v 8 at the beginnings of the two lines serve to set v 8 apart from vv 7 and 9. Verse 8 then becomes the transition from 7 to 9, with the two כי's being causal. The כי at the beginning of v 10 marks the transition from complaint against Yahweh to complaint against enemies and is emphatic. Likewise its occurrence in third line of v 11 is emphatic. In the last line of v 12, כי introduces a motive clause, as it also does in v 13.

At the rhetorical center of this passage are two occurrences of the word "Yahweh," each with a *waw*. In v 11, the *waw*-adversative marks the transition from complaint to confidence and is the turning point in the confession. The *waw* introducing v 12 links 11a and 12a and carries forth the assurance of v 11. The latter part of v 11, describing the certain fall of the enemies based on the assurance of 11a, is introduced with the strong linking phrase על־כן, "therefore."

In terms of connectives with other units, the most striking is the repetition of מגור מסביב from the previous section (20:3) in v 10. The "enemies" are depicted as picking up that phrase, "Terror on every side," and using it, either in mocking or in reference to his actions (i.e., Jeremiah was the "terror on every side"). Bright (134) has suggested the repetition of this catchword is the reason for the placement of this confession here. However, since most scholars assume the poetic material to be earlier than the prose, this would then be the earlier block. Nevertheless, the repeated phrase may be a redactional link for the present placement.

Additional links are evident between this section and other confessions. Verse 12 is quite similar to 11:20, also in a confession. However, those who would remove v 12 here as a gloss from that passage or addition (*BHS*, Rudolph, Hyatt, etc.) must explain the divergencies from 11:20. It does fit well in this context as both form-critical and rhetorical analyses show (contra Hyatt). This verse also provides several parallels to 17:10 ("the one testing," "heart," "inner parts"), which, although not itself a part of a confession, is in a Yahweh speech preliminary to a confession. Within the confessions proper are repetitions of בוש, "shame" (17:18 [2x]; 20:11), רדף, "ones pursuing me" (15:15; 17:18; 20:11), זכר, "remember" (11:19; 15:15; 18:20; 20:9), and, in striking contrast, עריץ, "awe-inspiring/ruthless" (20:11; 15:21; referring to Yahweh and the wicked, respectively). A final link which needs to be mentioned relates both to confessions and to the call experience. The promise made in that call, "I will be with you" (1:8, 19), is repeated in confessions as a word of assurance (15:20; 20:11).

Comment

7   The verb פתה is variously translated as "deceive, seduce, persuade." Heschel (I, 113) has emphasized the sexual connotation of seduction, arguing that פתה and חזק used together imply seduction and rape. Although it is possible for the words to have those connotations, especially when brought together, in neither case is the sexual connotation the most common. Furthermore, despite the common English translation of פתה as deceive (KJV, RSV), the context does not indicate that Yahweh has in any way deceived Jeremiah: from his call experience on, Yahweh has warned Jeremiah of the opposition he would encounter. The context rather suggests the meaning of persuasion (Clines and Gunn, *VT* 28 [1978] 20–27). Clines and Gunn suggest that the word פתה deals especially with attempts, not necessarily success, in persuading, hence the title of their article, "You Tried to Persuade Me. . . ." However, in this passage, the context makes clear that Yahweh was quite successful: Yahweh persuaded and Jeremiah was fully, completely persuaded. Yahweh's persuasion overpowered (חזק) Jeremiah, and Yahweh overcame (יכל).

Jeremiah's complaint here is directed against Yahweh. Yahweh is the one who has called him to be a prophet, who formed him from the womb for this task (1:5). Perhaps the persuasion he speaks of here relates to that call. When Jeremiah demurred (1:6), Yahweh persuaded, overpowered, and overcame him. The result is that Jeremiah has become an object of derision and mocking.

8   That which Jeremiah speaks is זעק, "outcries," often used in the sense of one crying in despair for help, but in this instance indicating a cry of horror from the parallel half-line. The message is one of violence and devastation, a horror for Jeremiah to have to proclaim. Scholars are divided concerning the referent of violence and devastation. It could refer to the message Jeremiah brings: violence and devastation are imminent for Judah and Jerusalem (Blank, [*Jeremiah*], Hyatt, Thompson), to the sins of the people (Keil, Nötscher), to attacks on Jeremiah by his enemies (Baumgartner, Rudolph), or even to a charge by Jeremiah that Yahweh had attacked him (Marrow [*VD* 43 (1965) 241–55], Berridge [*Prophet, People*], Clines and Gunn, [*VT* 28 (1978) 20–27], Carroll). Although the text is somewhat ambiguous, and the ambiguity may have been deliberate permitting all four interpretations (so Holladay), the preponderance of evidence favors the first interpretation. The message Jeremiah proclaims is chiefly one of violence and devastation against Judah for the sins of the people.

Because he is the one who must proclaim it, the word of Yahweh has become an object of reproach and derision for Jeremiah. The first half of this verse deals with the content of Yahweh's word; the second half explains the results to Jeremiah for proclaiming that word.

9   As a result of the derision and mocking (v 7) and the reproach and derision (a different word than v 7) (v 8), Jeremiah had decided no longer to proclaim the word. "I have said" is a Hebrew phrase that can also mean "I have decided, I have made up my mind." The word זכר, here translated "mention," most often means to "remember," "recall," or even "commemorate" (17:4). Certainly Jeremiah

is not proposing to disremember Yahweh, to forget, as do the people. In this instance, the verb must have the connotation of mentioning. That connotation fits well with the parallel half-line, refusing to speak in Yahweh's name.

Verses 8 and 9 have a threefold repetition of the root דבר, once as a noun, "word" of Yahweh, and twice as a verb. When Jeremiah speaks, it is a message of violence; therefore, he determines not to speak.

Even this ploy will not work for Jeremiah as the latter part of v 9 explains. "Heart" is parallel to "bones" in the second line of v 9. Both words refer to that which is within Jeremiah. Although some (Holladay, following Kutsch) would emend עָצֻר, "being shut in," to עֹצֶר, "pressure," the MT is quite understandable and gives a more vivid image. The last line of v 9 speaks of Jeremiah's exhaustion from trying to hold in Yahweh's word. The task is impossible. Whereas Yahweh overcame Jeremiah (v 7), Jeremiah cannot overcome Yahweh's word or purpose. Again Jeremiah is overcome by Yahweh!

10 Verse 10 moves from a complaint chiefly against Yahweh (vv 7–9) to a complaint against "enemies." The particle כִּי used in an emphatic manner marks this shift. The slanders that Jeremiah has heard could relate back to vv 7–8. The slanders could well be directed against Jeremiah, or against God. A report of the slanders follows. The enemies or slanderers pick up the phrase "Terror on every side" that spoke Yahweh's judgment on Pashhur (vv 3ff.). Their response is to try and find some way to inform on Jeremiah— some word or action to bring charges against him.

The phrase אֱנוֹשׁ שְׁלוֹמִי, "ones who wish me well," may indicate that even his friends have turned against him. Alternatively, Jeremiah may be using the phrase sarcastically of his enemies. The latter seems more likely.

In the last line of the verse, the enemies use precisely the same vocabulary as did Jeremiah in reference to Yahweh in v 7. Now the enemies try to persuade and overcome Jeremiah. Their purpose is to take their vengeance on him.

11 The *waw*-adversative marks the rhetorical center of the unit and also the transition. From lament and complaint, the confession shifts to the strongest words of trust and confidence. Despite the fact that Yahweh has overcome him, and that enemies have tried to do the same, Jeremiah has assurance that they will fail. Furthermore, he also has the assurance that Yahweh is not his enemy! The promise of Yahweh's abiding presence from the call experience (1:8, 19) and from other laments (15:20) reassures him: "But Yahweh (is) with me!"

The next phrase, גִּבּוֹר עָרִיץ, has been traditionally translated as "dread warrior, dread champion." Particularly noteworthy is the fact that elsewhere עָרִיץ is used of enemies or the wicked. This is the only passage in the OT where it is used in reference to Yahweh. Perhaps Jeremiah has deliberately chosen an ambiguous term because of his own ambiguity here. Yahweh has been almost like an enemy to him. Yet clearly Jeremiah sees this force now as directed not against him but against his enemies. A series of reversals has begun with the *waw*-adversative and word of confidence.

Further evidence is gained from the remainder of the verse, which describes the results on the enemies, specifically their downfall. The phrase עַל־כֵן indicates another transition, this time from the strong trust statement to a hoped-for result. The enemies have been watching for Jeremiah's "stumbling," צָלַע (v 10), but instead will themselves "stumble," כשל. They had hoped to overcome Jeremiah, but will not overcome. They will succeed only in getting shame and ignominy.

12   Verse 12 again opens with a word of confidence expressed as a compound epithet of Yahweh. Yahweh is "Yahweh of armies," a common epithet and one quite similar to "awe-inspiring hero." The additional epithets, as mentioned above (*Form/Structure/Setting*), have links with 11:20 and to a lesser extent 17:10.

The second line of the verse moves to petition. Whereas the enemies had sought to take their vengeance on Jeremiah, he now asks to see Yahweh's vengeance on them. The reversals continue as the enemies' words fall upon them.

13   The confidence of vv 11a and 12a continues in the hymnic conclusion of this verse. The plural imperatives שירו and הללו, "Sing! Praise!" present no difficulty, nor does typical hymnic language. Perhaps Jeremiah is quoting a verse of a well-known hymn to express his praise. It is possible, though not necessary, to equate the "poor person" with Jeremiah himself, who is confident of deliverance from "evil ones." It is more likely that Jeremiah has used a typical hymn to praise Yahweh for deliverance.

Explanation

In this confession, Jeremiah begins with a complaint against God. God has both persuaded and overpowered Jeremiah. He has become God's prophet in part willingly (though under persuasion), and in part under compulsion (being overpowered). As a result Jeremiah has become an object of scorn and mocking. His message is always "violence and devastation," ambiguous whether it is a threat of judgment, the content of the people's mocking, a report of the people's sins, or a report of what he has received from their hands (or even from God's hands).

When he determines no longer to speak his message, he is unable to hold it in. Even with this message, Jeremiah cannot overcome and have his way; he is again overcome. He hears the slanders of the people, mocking his words, "Terror on every side." Perhaps they consider Jeremiah to be the terror on every side; all he can preach is doom and gloom. They watch for his fall and, in an ironic twist, take up Jeremiah's words describing how God overpowered him: "maybe he can be persuaded and we can overcome him."

But Jeremiah will not be overcome by these enemies. God may have overpowered him, but he has the assurance God will not be the enemy. God is his heroic warrior, his champion to defend him and take on all enemies. Therefore, the enemies are the ones who will stumble, not Jeremiah. They will be overcome and shamed.

Jeremiah closes this confession with a hymn of praise. Perhaps he depicts himself as the poor one of this hymn who is delivered by the Lord from the hand of evil ones. Note the change that has occurred. He began with a complaint against God. But when he shifted to a complaint against his enemies he had the assurance that they, not God, were the real enemy. God was his mighty warrior-defender.

I. Cursed Was the Day (20:14–18)

Bibliography

Baumgartner, W. *Jeremiah's Poems.* **Blank, S.** "The Curse, Blasphemy, the Spell, and the Oath." *HUCA* 23/1 (1950–51) 73–95. **Bright, J.** "Jeremiah's Complaints: Liturgy, or Expressions of Personal Distress?" In *Proclamation and Presence.* Ed. J. I. Durham and J. R. Porter. London: SCM Press, 1970, 189–214. **Clines, D. J. A.,** and **Gunn, D. M.** "Form, Occasion and Redaction in Jeremiah 20." *ZAW* 88 (1976) 390–409. **Condamin, A.** *Le Livre de Jérémie.* 3rd ed. Paris: J. Gabalda, 1936. **Dahood, M. J.** "Denominative *rihham,* 'to conceive, enwomb.'" *Bibl* 44 (1963) 204–5. **Diamond, A. R.** *Confessions.* **Hillers, D. R.** "A Convention in Hebrew Literature: The Reaction to Bad News." *ZAW* 77 (1965) 86–90. **Holladay, W. L.** *Jeremiah: A Fresh Reading.* New York: Pilgrim Press, 1990. **Hubmann, F. D.** "Anders als er wollte: Jer 20, 7–13." *BLit* 54 (1981) 179–88. **Ittmann, N.** *Die Konfessionen Jeremias.* WMANT 54. Neukirchen-Vluyn: Neukirchener Verlag, 1981. **Janzen, J. G.** "Jeremiah 20:7–18." *Int* 37 (1983) 178–83. **O'Connor, K. M.** *Confessions.* **Polk, T.** *The Prophetic Persona.* **Prijs, L.** "Jeremia xx 14ff.: Versuch einer neuen Deutung." *VT* 14 (1964) 104–8. **Schottroff, W.** *Der altisraelitische Fluchspruch.* WMANT 30. Neukirchen-Vluyn: Neukirchener Verlag, 1969. **Smith, M. S.** *The Laments of Jeremiah.* **Westermann, C.** *Jeremia.* Stuttgart: Calwer, 1967.

Translation

14	*Cursed was the day*	(2+3)
	on which I was born,	
	the day on which my mother gave birth to me	(3+2)
	it could never be blessed.	
15	*Cursed was the man who brought news*	(4+2)
	to my father, saying:	
	"A son has been born to you, a boy!"	(3+2)
	who caused him to rejoice greatly.	
16	*Surely that man*[a] *was*[b]	(3+3+2)
	like cities which the LORD overthrew[c]	
	without pity;	
	he heard[d] *a distress call in the morning,*	(3+2)
	a battle alarm at noon-time,	
17	*because*[a] *he did not kill me in*[b] *the womb*	(3+3+3)
	and let my mother be for me my grave,	
	her womb forever pregnant.	
18	*Why did I come forth from the womb*	(4+3+3)
	to see trouble and sorrow	
	and my days end in shame?	

Notes

16.a. *BHS* suggests reading הַיּוֹם, "the day," instead of הָאִישׁ, "the man." However, there is no MS or versional evidence for such an emendation.

16.b. *BHS* suggests יְהִי with the versions; this translation follows MT וְהָיָה.
16.c. LXX adds "in anger."
16.d. *BHS* suggests יִשְׁמַע; this translation follows MT וְשָׁמַע.
17.a. Taking אֲשֶׁר as a causal form.
17.b. Reading the MT מֵרֶחֶם with a temporal sense, "from the time I was in the womb"="in the womb." *BHS* suggests בְרחם; Dahood has proposed a denominative verb and would read מְרֻחָם, "enwombed."

Form/Structure/Setting

This last section of chap. 20 has caused considerable discussion because of its sudden, dramatic caesura from hymnic praise in v 13 to the depths of despair that issue in a curse on the day of Jeremiah's birth. One possible solution, though accepted by only a few scholars, is to move vv 14–18 prior to vv 7–13 (Ewald).

More generally, the section has been understood as a separate section, either lament or self-curse (Baumgartner, *Jeremiah's Poems;* Blank, *HUCA* 23/1 [1950–51] 73–95; Bright, "Complaints"), reflecting originally an entirely different situation in the life of Jeremiah (Keil). More correctly the section is a curse of the prophet's birth-day and the messenger who announced his birth. Its placement here is usually considered to be redactional, either to close this major block of material (for a discussion of the extent of the block, see *Afterword* below), or to introduce the next block, chaps. 21–24 (Clines and Gunn, *ZAW* 88 [1976] 390–409; Lewin, *JSOT* 32 [1985] 105–19). Emphasis then is not placed on the shift in mood and tone, though such a solution overlooks the deliberate juxtaposition and is not completely satisfactory.

Clearly, the section is a curse poem. A form of *qīnāh* meter predominates (six of the eight lines have more stresses on the first half-line than on the second (or third). Many scholars have emphasized the fact that Jeremiah is using conventional or stereotypical language (Schottroff, *Fluchsprüch;* Hubmann, *BLit* 54 [1981] 179–88; Ittmann, *Die Konfessionen;* Clines and Gunn, *ZAW* 88 [1976] 390–409); there are numerous parallels to Job 3:

> Job 3:1, 3, 4, 8   reference to day of birth   Jer 20:14
>   use of specific words for curse
>   Job 3:8   אָרַר   Jer 20:14, 15
>   Job 3:1   קלל
>   Job 3:8   קבב
> Job 3:3   birth announced, specifically of a male   Jer 20:15
> Job 3:10   reference to remaining in womb   Jer 20:17, 18
> Job 3:11   reference to death "from" the womb   Jer 20:17
>   Job 3:20ff.   the question why   Jer 20:18

From parallels such as these in Job, it has been suggested that this was conventional language accompanying a judgment oracle rather than expressing the emotions of the prophet at personal calamity (Clines and Gunn). However, it seems impossible to separate completely the feelings of the prophet from the intensity of these words (Polk, *Prophetic Persona*).

An attractive proposal has been made by Prijs (*VT* 14 [1964] 104–8), who suggests, at least for v 15, that we have not the typical optative or wish construction (see Blank, *HUCA* 23/1 [1950–51] 76), but a statement of fact, indicative

mood (already suggested for some curses, though not in reference to this passage by Pedersen, *Der Eid bei den Semiten,* 86; and Blank, 77, n. 17). If, as Holladay
suggests, the statement includes v 14 as well, the poem has a slightly different
thrust. Rather than desiring a curse, Jeremiah is stating a fact: the day was cursed
because of his birth and the man was cursed for relating the news of his birth.

Parallels between this pericope and other confessions, especially chap. 15 are
noteworthy: the reference to his mother, the presence of a curse on Jeremiah,
the trouble and distress, the question "why?" Thus, although the language of this
section is very striking, the thought is not uncommon to Jeremiah.

The material of the unit may be outlined as follows:

> Curse on day of birth (v 14)
> Curse on messenger of birth (v 15)
> Development and further curses on messenger (v 16)
> Motivation for curses: because he didn't kill me (v 17)
> Lament: Why was I born? (v 18)

Rhetorically, this material can be put in a chiastic structure:

> A   Curse on day of birth (v 14)
>   B   Curse on messenger (vv 15–16)
>   B'   Motivation directed against messenger (v 17)
> A'   Lament on birth (v 18)

As Lundbom has noticed (and Condamin already earlier, though not calling
it an inclusio), there is an inclusio for this pericope; היום at the beginning of v
14 is matched by ימי at the end of 18. Likewise the reference to the day of birth
in 14 is matched with the question "Why did I come forth from the womb?" in
18.

In addition there is a very clear chiastic structure within v 14 itself; even the
meter is balanced chiastically, 2+3 and 3+2:

> A   Cursed was the day (v 14a)   (2+3)
>   B   on which I was born (v 14b)
>   B'   the day on which my mother gave birth to me (v 14c)   (3+2)
> A'   it could never be blessed (v 14d)

The setting for this pericope is ambiguous if it is to be treated apart from its
Sitz im Buch. Lundbom would relate it to the situation around 605–4 B.C., after the
Temple Sermon when Jehoiakim was threatening Jeremiah's life. It is often related
to the aftermath of the fall of Jerusalem/Judah in 587 B.C. because of the reference to the "cities overthrown without mercy" (v 16), which alludes to the
destruction of Sodom and Gomorrah and the cities of the plain (Gen 19; Carroll).
The pericope might even relate to the last days of Jeremiah's life in forced exile
in Egypt (v 18, "my days end in shame"). Of course, it is quite possible to understand the pericope as a part of the Pashhur incident, the prophet's response to
his humiliation. That is clearly one intent of its present placement. Nevertheless,
attempts to relate undated material to specific events in the life of the prophet
can only be tentative at best.

Comment

14   The implication of the statement of fact ("Cursed was the day . . .") is that the day was cursed because Jeremiah was born on it. He is not retroactively wishing that curse or calling for it; he is stating its reality.

What (or who) is *not* cursed in the poem is as remarkable as that which is cursed. Jeremiah says the day of his birth and the messenger who brings the news of the birth are cursed. But Jeremiah does *not* say his parents nor God are cursed, nor even himself directly. Admittedly, the implication of self-curse is present in the motivation for the messenger being cursed ("because he did not kill me in the womb," v 17).

15   The messenger seems to have received unusually harsh treatment as commentators note (Thompson, Brueggemann, Laetsch, etc.). Holladay emends the text so that the messenger is removed and "the man" of vv 15–16 is Jeremiah himself; however, his proposal seems forced. Prijs (*VT* 14 [1964] 104–8) has suggested that the messenger is cursed because he announced Jeremiah's birth and Jeremiah is the prophet of doom. The messenger shares the fate of all Judah. The curse he endures is the curse of the whole people, and the messenger becomes an anonymous representative of them all. Jeremiah may well have understood himself as being like that messenger but, rather than bearing good news of God's deliverance, his message has been one of distress and battle cries (v 16).

16   The reference to overthrowing cities is an allusion to Sodom and Gomorrah in Gen 19. The same root הפך is used in various inscriptions as a part of a curse (Sefire, Zakir, Ahiram) in reference to overthrowing persons (or their rule) who break the treaty or deface the inscription.

17   The MT has מרחם, literally, "from the womb." The logical difficulty of the MT is that if Jeremiah is killed after he emerges from the womb, then the womb would not be his grave, nor his mother forever pregnant. The LXX ἐν μήτρα avoids this dilemma, as does the emendation often proposed to read בְּרֶחֶם. But to expect such precision of poetry is unnecessary; further, the preposition מן can have a temporal meaning, thus "from the womb" could mean "from the time I was in the womb"="in the womb." In an interesting curse, Deir Alla Combination II, line 13, speaks of death taking away a child still in the womb. Baumgartner refers to examples of everlasting pregnancy in folklore.

18   The question "Why?" moves from the statements about Jeremiah's birth back to the present. The mention of coming forth from the womb relates this verse back to the previous ones, but carries the thought forward. Just as vv 14–17 had juxtaposed birth with death, so does this verse, at least by implication ("my days end").

The despair within this pericope is not so complete and bitter as a curse understanding would have it. Taken by itself, this verse is much less bitter than, for example, 15:18. The question blunts some of the force of the curse statements. The unit becomes more of a lament. Indeed, the question "why?" is common in personal laments (Baumgartner). If Jeremiah speaks of the judgment against Judah and Jerusalem in v 16, then the trouble, sorrow, and shame here are the outgrowth of national disaster as much as personal trouble. Like the typical question in the individual lament, this one remains unanswered. Indeed this pericope and larger unit closes with the unanswered question (see *Afterword* below).

The corporate or national aspects of this section serve as a transition to chaps. 21–24, which follow (Clines and Gunn, *ZAW* 88 [1976] 390–409; Lewin). Those chapters are a collection of judgment oracles against Judah.

To whom was the question addressed? Was it just a question raised in general, with no expectation of answer? Or could the question and the entire unit be addressed to God, just as was the confession before it. Certainly the *Sitz im Buch* would permit such. If the poem is addressed to God, then we note Jeremiah's despair is not complete. Even if it is unanswered, Jeremiah still looks to God and addresses God—not with the same confidence and assurance of vv 11–13 above, but still addressing God as the only possible source of an answer or solution or vindication.

Explanation

Jeremiah gives a statement of fact: the day of his birth was a day cursed— cursed because he was God's messenger to announce the doom and destruction of the nation and cursed because he would himself have to experience it. Yet the tone of the pericope is not primarily self-curse, or even self-pity. There is despair to be sure, the despair of trouble and sorrow, personal and national. But closure comes with an unanswered question, unanswered but addressed to God. Still Jeremiah has a glimmer of hope/trust.

Afterword for 11:1–20:18

Some brief word must be given concerning the larger units to which this pericope belongs. It has been argued above (18:1–12, "Introduction: Some Literary Connectives," p 240) that at least chaps. 18–20 form a larger unit on the basis of content. In addition, the opening words of chap. 18 and chap. 21 seem to mark new units ["The word which came to Jeremiah from the LORD"] (Thiel, Diamond), meaning that chaps. 18–20 form a single unit. Certainly thematic connections are present: the potter/pottery image in chaps. 18 and 19, the Pashhur incident as an apparent outgrowth of the broken pottery connecting chaps. 19 and 20.

But what of other units? Several suggestions have been made concerning chaps. 11–20 as a larger compositional unit. Thiel, Westermann, Holladay (*Architecture*), and Smith all posit this larger unit. But the most satisfactory proposal is that of O'Connor (*Confessions*, 130–31) who outlines the unit as follows:

REJECTION AND TRIUMPH OF THE PROPHETIC WORD

1. Chaps. 11–12
   Curse
   Collection of material on the theme of Yahweh's chosen
                                             Confession
2. Chap. 13
   Symbolic Action
     Appeal for Repentance
   Collection of material on the destruction of the proud

3. Chaps. 14–16
   Collection of Materials on the End of Life in the Land
      Chap. 14: End of Physical Life
      Chaps. 15–16: End of Social Life
                                                      Confession
4. Chap. 17
   Collection of Materials on the Heart which Yahweh will Judge
                                                      Confession
5. Chaps. 18–20
   Climax and Conclusion
      Appeal for Repentance

                                                      Confession
   Symbolic Action
   Imprisonment of the Prophet

                                                      Confession
Curse

These chapters definitely have structural connections. Beyond the inclusio formed by the curses of 11:1–14 and 20:14–18, this section contains the entire corpus of confessions as customarily designated. More specifically, the curse of chap. 11, a curse on covenant breakers, is about to be carried out against the people because they have broken covenant. The final curse statements point to that judgment.

The question still remains whether the larger unit should consist of chaps. 11–20 or a yet larger body. Rudolph had argued (xvii) that chaps. 1–20 make up a major unit with chaps. 21–25 added later. Many modern scholars have followed that suggestion. Lundbom indicates a major inclusio in 1:5, "before *you came forth from the womb* I consecrated you," and 20:18, "why *from the womb did I come forth.*" He also notes that these two passages and 15:10 are the only places Jeremiah refers to his birth. Chap. 20 also ends with a reference to the end of his days (v 18) which contrasts as a kind of inclusio with the reference to his birth in 1:5. Thus he argues these markers indicate the compositional unity of chaps. 1–20 (though he does call for some insertions to have occurred later). Much of the argument concerning a large unit such as 1–20 has centered around the composition of the *urrolle* of chap. 36. That question aside, the argument for some larger unit, certainly including chaps. 11–20 and probably including most of 1–20 is persuasive.

XI. Oracles against Zedekiah and Jerusalem (21:1–10)

Bibliography

Balentine, S. E. "The Prophet as Intercessor: A Reassessment." *JBL* 103 (1984) 161–73. **Berridge, J.M.** *Prophet, People.* **Boecker, H. J.** *Law and the Administration of Justice in the Old Testament and Ancient Near East.* London: SPCK, 1980. **Driver, G. R.** "Hebrew Notes." *VT* 1 (1951) 241–50. **Malamat, A.** "The Twilight of Judah." In *Congess Volume Edinburgh 1974.* VTSup 28. Leiden: Brill, 1975. 123–45. **McKane, W.** "The Construction of Jeremiah Chapter xxi." *VT* 32 (1982) 59–73. **Overholt, T. W.** "King Nebuchadnezzar in the Jeremia Tradition." *CBQ* 30 (1968) 39–48. **Pohlmann, K. F.** *Studien zum Jeremiabuch.* 31–47. **Reventlow, H. G.** *Liturgie.* 143–49. **Selms, A. van.** "The Name Nebuchadnezzar." In *Travels in the World of the Old Testament.* Ed. M. S. H. G. Heerma van Voss et al. Assen: Van Gorcum, 1974. 223–29. **Smith, M. S.** *The Laments of Jeremiah.* **Stade, B.** "Bemerkungen zum Buche Jeremia." *ZAW* 12 (1892) 276–308. **Wanke. G.** *Baruchschrift.* **Weippert, H.** "Jahwekrieg und Bundesfluch in Jer 21,1–7." *ZAW* 82 (1970) 396–409. ———. *Die Prosareden.*

Translation

[1] *The word which came to Jeremiah from the LORD when King Zedekiah sent to him Pashhur ben Malchiah and Zephaniah ben Ma^{c}aseaiah, the priest, saying,* [2] *"Pray, seek*[a] *on our behalf the LORD, for Nebuchadrezzar,*[b] *the king of Babylon, is about to wage war against us; perhaps the LORD will do*[c]*with us*[c] *according to all his wondrous deeds,* [d]*and he will go up*[d] *from against us."* [3]*Then Jeremiah said unto them, "Thus say to Zedekiah:*[a] [4] *'Thus says the LORD,* [a]*the God of Israel,*[a] *"Behold I am about to turn back the weapons of warfare* [b]*which are in your hands,*[b] *with which you are about to fight* [c]*the king of Babylon and*[c] *the Chaldeans, the ones who are about to besiege you from outside the wall.* [d]*I will gather them*[d] *to the midst of this city.* [5]*Now I myself will fight with you, with an outstretched hand and a strong arm, in anger and in rage and in great wrath.* [6]*I will smite the inhabitants of this city, both human and beast; in a great pestilence*[a]*they will die.* [7]*Afterwards,"* *an oracle of the LORD,* *"I will give Zedekiah, the king of Judah, and his servants, and the people* [a]*who remain*[a] *in this city from the pestilence,* [b]*from the sword, and from the famine,* [c]*into the hand of Nebuchadrezzar, the king of Babylon,*[c] *and into the hand of their enemies,* [d]*and into the hand of*[d] *the ones seeking their life; and he*[e] *will smite them with the edge of the sword; he*[f] *will not have pity on them,* [g]*nor spare,*[g] *nor*[h]*have compassion."'*

[8]*"To this people say, 'Thus says the LORD, "Behold I am about to put before you the way of life and the way of death.* [9]*The one staying in this city will die by the sword and*[a] *by famine*[b]*and by pestilence;*[b] *the one who goes forth* [c]*and falls down*[c] *unto the Chaldeans who are about to besiege you will live,*[d] *his life will be his for the spoil of war*[e] [10]*Surely I have put my face against this city for evil and not for good,"* *an oracle of the LORD;* *"into the hand of the king of Babylon it has been given and he will burn it with fire."'"*

Notes

2.a. Tg reads "pray on our behalf."
2.b. Not in LXX. On the spelling of the name, here Nebuchadrezzar, see *Comment.*
2.c-c. Not in LXX.
2.d-d. Tg has "and he will be taken away."
3.a. LXX adds "the king of Judah."
4.a-a. Not in LXX.
4.b-b. Not in LXX.
4.c-c. Not in LXX.
4.d-d. Not in LXX; Tgs read "I will gather you."
6.a. LXX reads "and they will die" (i.e., "I will smite the inhabitants . . . in a great pestilence, and they will die.")
7.a-a. This translation follows a few MSS (de Rossi, III, 90), LXX, Syr, and Tg, which omit the conj and sign of direct obj וְאֵת; thus "and the people remaining . . . ," rather than MT, "and the people and the ones remaining" (see *Comment* below).
7.b. Many MSS (de Rossi, III, 90) and the versions add the conj וּ, "and from the sword."
7.c-c. Not in LXX.
7.d-d. Not in LXX.
7.e. LXX has the pl, "and *they* will smite them."
7.f. LXX has lcs, "I will not have pity."
7.g-g. Not in LXX.
7.h. LXX has lcs, "I will not have compassion."
9.a. Many MSS (de Rossi, III, 90) omit the conj וּ, as does the parallel passage in 38:2.
9.b-b. Not in LXX.
9.c-c. Not in Syr, also not in the parallel passage 38:2.
9.d. K יְחֶיֶה, Q וְחָיָה.
9.e. A few MSS (de Rossi, III, 90) and LXX add "and live."

Form/Structure/Setting

Chaps. 21–24(25) are generally recognized as a separate unit, something of an appendix to chaps. 1–20 (Holladay, *Architecture;* O'Connor, *Confessions;* etc.). Specifically, O'Connor has suggested that chaps. 21–25 reflect the aftermath of the fall of the nation. Although set as predicting the fall in chap. 21, O'Connor argues that the fall is taken as a *fait accompli* (146) throughout the entire section.

Whether one accepts her position or not, clearly chap. 21 starts a new section. The opening words, "The words which came to Jeremiah from the LORD," indicate a new section comparable to similar words at 7:1; 11:1; 18:1; 30:1; 34:1; 35:1.

The section has one or two prose sermons, "C" material, describing a meeting between Jeremiah and representatives of King Zedekiah and the oracles from that meeting. This marks the first dated material in the book (although here the date formula is not specific as to the year of the king's reign). The context is set by v 2 and is that of the Babylonian siege of Jerusalem, understood in this translation as that which is about to occur. The date of this oracle then would be c. 588 B.C. The outcome is an oracle of judgment against the city and the king.

The extent of the smaller units are debated as are the larger. Verses 1–7 fit that speech pattern well. However, v 8 seems to begin a new oracle, not addressed to the king's representatives ("Thus you [pl] say to Zedekiah," v 3) but to Jeremiah to be delivered to the people ("To this people you [sg] say," v 8). The content of the two oracles is, nevertheless, quite similar.

It has been argued at least since Michaelis *(Observationes)* that chap. 21 is juxtaposed to chap. 20 on the basis of the occurrence of the name Pashhur, even admitting that different individuals are referred to (Pashhur ben Immer in chap. 20, Pashhur ben Malchiah in chap. 21). Rudolph has noted that link but also notes a strong contrast in the position of the prophet in the two passages, from one persecuted by priest to one sought out by king and priest. He feels that this contrast may also be part of the reason for the placement of chap. 21. Smith has noted the contrast in terms of Yahweh's repeated directives that Jeremiah not intercede on behalf of the people in chaps. 11–20 and the request for intercession by the leaders in chap. 21. He further notes that chaps. 21–25 identify the enemies who are primarily unidentified in chaps. 11–20.

Several other passages are often referred to in comparison with the content of chap. 21, especially 34:1–7 and 37:3–10, but also 52:4–16, 39:1–10, and 2 Kgs 25:1–12. Ewald argued that chap. 37 was a sequel to 21:1–7. Stade (*ZAW* 12 [1892] 276–308) thought that the present passage and 37:3–10 referred to the same event, and when properly combined would give a more complete account of the event. Duhm and Erbt both take chap. 37 to be the primary account and chap. 21 to be a later editorial rewriting of chap. 37. Hyatt (977) says 21:1–10 is a Deuteronomic editor's rewrite of the event of 37:3–10, which has no independent historical value. Cornill, Giesebrecht, and Volz see the two chapters as describing two different events, a position accepted here. Chap. 21 indicates a context prior to the beginning of the siege of Jerusalem; chap. 37 specifically refers to a brief release from siege when the Egyptian army approached the frontier of Judah and the Babylonian army left to face the Egyptians.

McKane (*VT* 32 [1982] 59–73) has argued that this present passage has been edited to give a rough approximation of the threefold description of those latter passages: (i) the siege, famine, and pestilence; (ii) Zedekiah's attempted escape and capture; (iii) the capture and destruction of the city. That all these passages refer to the same events surrounding the final siege of Jerusalem is clear. But to suggest any historical reconstruction of 21:1–10 on the basis of any of the other passages seems highly speculative. As Bright has suggested, this passage seems to indicate a time before the siege is actually begun when troops are still in the field, and the context of the other passages indicates the siege was underway or temporarily lifted.

Many commentators have noted that the LXX is considerably shorter than the MT in this passage. The consensus of scholars is that the MT represents an expansionist text in most of these places.

The material of 21:1–10 may be outlined as follows:

Introduction (v 1)
Request for oracle/intercession (v 2)
Report of the oracle to Zedekiah (vv 3–7)
An oracle addressed to the people (vv 8–10)

Comment

1   The contrast between 20:1–2 and 21:1–2 is striking as Rudolph and others have noted. In the one the prophet is arrested, beaten, and humiliated by a priest

overseer-leader; in the other, two officials of the king, one of them a priest, come to Jeremiah at the king's request, seeking intercession. Perhaps the historical context has caused this contrast; *in extremis* one turns to any possible source of aid, even a prophet of doom and gloom. Keil describes this verse and the following as the heading specifying the occasion for the following prediction.

Pashhur ben Malchiah appears again in 38:1 and his descendants in Neh 11:12 and 1 Chr 9:12. In 38:1ff. Pashhur is among those who throw Jeremiah in a cistern and leave him to die. Zephaniah is mentioned again in 29:25, 29; 37:3; 52:24; 2 Kgs 25:18. In chap. 29, chronologically set before this chapter, Zephaniah receives a letter from Shemaiah, who is among the exiles of 597 B.C. in Babylon, rebuking him for not denouncing Jeremiah. In chap. 37, Zephaniah is again part of a group that approaches Jeremiah for Zedekiah seeking intercession. Chap. 52 (=2 Kings 25) records the death of Zephaniah and others at the hands of the Babylonians.

2 The reason these officials of the king come is to seek Jeremiah's intercession with Yahweh. Although the prophet's role as intercessor is widely viewed as a major role, Balentine (*JBL* 103 [1984] 161–73) has shown that it has specific reference only a few times in the OT, and there chiefly of Jeremiah. Although the word דרש נא, "pray, seek," might imply an oracle rather than intercession, the following explanation clearly indicates intercession, "perhaps the LORD will do with us (=for us) according to all his wondrous deeds." The deeds for which the king hoped could refer to the mighty acts of God during the Wilderness-Wandering period or the Conquest but are probably associated with Yahweh's intervention during the invasion of Sennacherib just over a hundred years earlier (2 Kgs 19; Isa 37).

The reference to Nebuchadrezzar in this verse is the first specific reference by name to this Babylonian king in Jeremiah. The spelling of the name in this passage follows the Babylonian form of the name, usually normalized as Nabu-kudurru-usur. The name means "May (the god) Nabu protect the boundary-stone" or "May Nabu protect the son/crown prince" (van Selms, in *Travels*). In an interesting article, van Selms has argued that the better-known form, Nebuchadnezzar, came from a nickname, probably with negative connotations, "May Nabu protect the mule." The name Nebuchadrezzar occurs thirty-three times in the OT, twenty-nine of those in Jeremiah and four in Ezekiel. By comparison Nebuchadnezzar occurs fifty-seven times, eight times in Jeremiah. There are at least seven (van Selms says eight) variants in the spelling of the name. All the occurrences of Nebuchadnezzar in Jeremiah occur between chaps. 27 and 29, though no satisfactory explanation for this variation within Jeremiah has been offered.

This translation understands the context of the oracle to be just prior to the beginning of the siege of Jerusalem (so Bright); thus the translation "Nebuchadrezzar . . . is about to wage war against us." It may be argued that the war has already begun, and certainly that is true. But the point is that Jerusalem has not yet come under siege; Nebuchadrezzar is about to bring the war directly to the city and its inhabitants.

The last phrase of the verse, "and he will go up from us," refers to Nebuchadrezzar. A certain irony is expressed in the very choice of words here, for often עלה על has the connotation of "going up against" one in battle. Here עלה מעל indicates "going up from" or "departing." Alternatively, the Hebrew could be understood as a true causative "He (Yahweh) will cause to depart."

Perhaps a comparison with Ezekiel should also be noted; there the כבוד יהוה "glory of God" "departs from" (עלה מעל) the city before it falls (Ezek 11:23). It is possible that a similar referent is intended here, certainly not that these officials are desiring Yahweh to depart, but perhaps that they wish him to go out to do battle with the Babylonians. And the author may have a double entendre in mind, that in reality Yahweh is about to depart because of the people's sins. This possibility is all the more likely when one realizes the word for the people's deeds, מעלל, in vv 12 and 14 preserves the same consonants as "depart from."

3–4   The oracle which proceeds is directed specifically to Zedekiah (in contrast to the one below, vv 11–12, which is addressed to an unnamed king). The words "Thus say to Zedekiah" (v 3) are second person masculine plural form, spoken to the two messengers to deliver to the king. The preposition אל most commonly has the connotation of "to, toward"; it indicates here the one to whom the word is directed (cf. vv 1, 8, 13; ל v 11). However, the preposition can also have the meaning "against," and these oracles might be spoken against, as well as to, the person(s). This is certainly the case in v 13 below.

It is quite possible that the opening of the oracle to Zedekiah has a deliberate ambiguity, that it might be interpreted positively or negatively, precisely as the preposition אל could indicate that it was spoken "to" or "against" Zedekiah. In seeking an oracle, Zedekiah is hoping that Yahweh will rise up as the Divine Warrior to defend his people. The oracle does depict Yahweh as that Divine Warrior, but first ambiguously as to whom he is fighting, then clearly fighting against his people.

The first phrase of the oracle indicates that Yahweh is about to do something to the weapons the soldiers of Zedekiah are using. Bright prefers understanding this phrase by metonymy referring to the troops themselves. Surely Bright's suggestion is possible, though the vivid imagery of one's own weapons being turned against one seems the more powerful image. מסב, from the root סבב, can mean "turn, change, turn around, turn back, surround, encompass." The ideas expressed by this word in contexts of war are usually threefold: (i) surrounding an enemy (or being surrounded); (ii) turning around or back, and avoiding battle; and (iii) turning back or reversing weapons. In another stem the root has the idea of surrounding protectively. The ambiguity is therefore whether Yahweh is "surrounding" the weapons to protect them and the soldiers, or to blunt them; whether Yahweh is "reversing, turning back" the weapons because the enemy has been defeated, or turning the defenders' own weapons against them.

The ambiguity continues in the last phrase of the verse. Who or what is being gathered into the midst of the city? Is it the weapons (so Vg, Rashi, Rudolph, etc.)? If so, does this mean that siege is underway and all the soldiers must retreat into the city, or that the soldiers' weapons are being used against the city (did they flee in such chaos that they dropped their own weapons?), or is the war won and the soldiers returning their weapons now unneeded? Is it the soldiers that are gathered into the city, with similar options as with the weapons? Or is it the Babylonians who are gathered into the midst of the city (Kimchi, Volz, etc.)? And even if the Babylonians, are they entering as conquering plunderers, or are they gathered by Yahweh and the soldiers in defeat and placed on public display? Clearly Divine Warrior imagery abounds. But the remainder of the verse is tantalizingly ambiguous. The preponderance of evidence would suggest an oracle of judgment, for which Jeremiah was well known. But for a king seeking any possible hope *in extremis*, perhaps the ambiguity of the words could be grasped momentarily as the desired deliverance oracle.

5 Verse 5 continues the Divine Warrior image. In fact, the imagery becomes more intense. Now Yahweh is in the midst of the fray, fighting with his mighty power. The descriptive phrase "with an outstretched hand and a strong arm" uses vocabulary found frequently in holy war descriptions of Yahweh. In holy war, Yahweh fights on behalf of his people against the enemy. Interestingly, the phrase is switched here from its common form "with a strong hand and an outstretched arm." Some commentaries (Holladay; Berridge, *Prophet, People*) have suggested this switch is deliberate to indicate that Yahweh is fighting against rather than for his people.

Is there any way to interpret this verse in the same ambiguous manner as suggested for the previous one? Regularly the two prepositions translated "with," עם and את, when used with לחם, "fight," have the connotation of fighting with, i.e., against. Similarly the prepositions ב, על, and אל with לחם all regularly mean "fight against." When Hebrew writers wanted to express "fight for (i.e., on behalf of), the preposition ל was used; however, על could also be used in the same manner (Judg 9:17; 2 Kgs 10:3). 2 Chr 32:8 uses עם in a positive manner, though the phrase is slightly different ("Yahweh our God is with us to help us and to fight our battles"). Furthermore in this verse the preposition ב does not have its usual connotation following לחם; instead of "against," it means "with," indicating instrumentality. So another use of את here, one indicating help or support, is not too far-fetched. The ambiguity would be precisely that of the English, "I am going to fight with you." And since the vocabulary is strongly that of Divine Warrior, one might well expect the ambiguity of a possible positive meaning.

The intensity of Yahweh's involvement is indicated, not only by the phrase "with an outstretched hand and a strong arm," but also by the emphatic use of the first person pronoun אני.

6 Any possible ambiguity is resolved in this verse. The intention of the oracle all along is to bring the message of judgment to Zedekiah. The ambiguity of vv 4–5 would keep him listening, and perhaps hook him until the clear condemnation of this verse is spoken. Now the unclear is made clear with the reference to "this city," obviously Jerusalem. Yahweh is indeed the Divine Warrior, but he is fighting against his people rather than for them.

The judgment mentioned in this verse is being struck with pestilence (דֶּבֶר) like that with which the Egyptians were struck (Exod 5:3; 9:15; cf. Num 14:12), a common occurrence in the confined situation of siege warfare. Note that, like Exodus, the pestilence strikes both human and animal. The LXX understands this verse "I will smite the inhabitants of this city, human and beast, in a great pestilence, and they will die." The language of pestilence is reminiscent of treaty curses.

On a first reading of this verse, the judgment seems clear and total: man and beast will all die in the pestilence. From this reading, v 7 seems contradictory and unnecessarily redundant. Such a reading places too much rigidity on the oracular form. Totality of death is not the intention. The judgment is pestilence and death, undoubtedly widespread, but by no means complete. Verse 7 then explains and expands the judgment, almost as an example of parallelism, completing the incomplete picture given first.

7 The transition word "afterwards" and the repetition of a messenger formula ("the LORD's oracle") have led many to assume this verse is a later addition, expanding the judgment of v 6. McKane has suggested that the verse may be dependent on 52:4–16 and that a redactor has attempted to bring this oracle into closer harmony with chap. 52. If so, the redactor has done a clumsy job and has still left many difficulties in harmonizing the two. Nowhere does this passage indicate the attempted flight of Zedekiah as chap. 52 does. It seems more likely that this verse is parallel to and explicative of the previous verse.

Clearly the verse is wordy and, at places, cumbersome. The juxtaposed phrases of the MT "and the people, and the ones remaining" are redundant. This translation follows the versions which remove this difficulty by reading "and the people remaining. . . ." Some commentators feel these phrases are also redundant: "into the hand of Nebuchadrezzar, . . . and into the hand of their enemies, and into the hand of the ones seeking their life." Again LXX remedies this redundancy by omitting the reference to Nebuchadrezzar and reading "into the hand of their enemies, the ones seeking their life." Nevertheless, the MT may well represent a piling up of judgment and enemies for emphasis to indicate the gravity of the oracle. The verse thus clarifies the variegated judgment Judah can anticipate.

The piling up of judgment is emphasized by the use of triads. Whereas v 6 spoke only of pestilence as the means of judgment, v 7 lists a triad: pestilence, sword, and famine. Similarly, when speaking of the human agent to bring about this judgment, a triad is given: Nebuchadrezzar, their enemies, and those seeking their life. Also, the final phrases describe Nebuchadrezzar's lack of mercy as a triad: he will not have pity, nor spare, nor have compassion. In each case, the triad serves to magnify the full extent of the judgment. This repeated use of triads is a part of the justification for the emendation at the beginning of the verse. With the emendation, we have another triad: Zedekiah, his servants, and the people remaining. The thrust of this triad would also be on the extent of judgment; it reaches all the people.

The LXX has one other significant difference from MT in this verse. The last two phrases in LXX have first person common singular verb forms, "I will not have pity . . . , I will not have compassion." In the MT, those same verbs appear in 13:14 as first person common singular forms. The difference is whether Yahweh or Nebuchadrezzar is refusing to show mercy. With all the Divine Warrior imagery in this oracle, and with the clear parallel at 13:14, the LXX reading would represent a most fitting climax to the oracle, though the result on the people would be the same in either case. The translation here follows MT to complete another triad.

8 This verse introduces the second oracle of the section. This oracle is directed toward the people. The second person masculine singular form of the verb ([you] say) contrasts with the second person masculine plural form of the previous oracle. Clearly the one to deliver this oracle is different from the two royal officials who deliver the first one. Probably Jeremiah is addressed by Yahweh and is to deliver the oracle. The oracle begins with a presentation of the two ways, the way of life and the way of death (cf. Jer 17:5–8, 18:7–10). The oracle seems to begin with a clear choice, and one might expect clear-cut positive or negative outcomes. But this expectation is dashed in v 9.

9 The negative result is given first. It basically recapitulates vv 6–7. The triad of sword, famine, and pestilence recurs. The positive outcome is only positive by comparison. It requires one to go out and fall down (=surrender) before the Chaldeans. All this one is promised is his life, but at least he will not die.

10 Verse 10 explains the reason for the harsh alternatives presented in the oracle. Both Yahweh as Divine Warrior and his human agent, the king of Babylon, are mentioned in the verse.

The additional feature of this oracle is the mention of burning the city with fire.

Explanation

Zedekiah, facing an imminent siege at the hands of Nebuchadrezzar, sent envoys to Jeremiah to request intercession with God. Jeremiah responds with an oracle using the familiar language of the Divine Warrior. But whereas God the Divine Warrior had always historically fought on behalf of his covenant people, Jeremiah proclaims that God will fight as Divine Warrior *against* his people. The oracle begins ambiguously, but moves quickly to unmistakable judgment brought by God against the king and people. There is a piling up of description to show that the whole people are about to undergo extreme suffering and even death from all their enemies. In this oracle no mitigation is offered; there will be no pity, no sparing, no compassion.

The second oracle is directed to the people and does at least offer a slight "out." If the people stay in the city, they will die. But if the people will go out and surrender to the Babylonians, they will live. They will be captives, but they will have their lives.

XII. Oracles against the Kings of Judah (21:11–23:8)

This unit is made up of a number of oracles, mostly independent, addressed to the last kings of Judah. Several of these oracles are addressed to unnamed kings; others are addressed by name to Shallum (Jehoahaz), Jehoiakim, and Coniah (Jehoiachin). The oracles are all relatively short, five verses being the longest, and are each independent, although there are linkages between several of the independent oracles, and several are addressed to the same king.

Verse 11 marks the transition to this section with the phrase וּלְבֵית מֶלֶךְ יְהוּדָה, "to/concerning the house of the king of Judah." This introductory phrase parallels a similar transition word at 23:9, לַנְּבִאִים, "to/concerning the prophets," which introduces a unit addressed to the prophets, 23:9–40.

The first seven oracles alternate between poetry and prose, as do oracles 8–13. Only oracles 7 and 8 juxtapose poetic oracles. The oracles will be treated separately in this unit.

A. Oracle against a King and Jerusalem (21:11–14)

Bibliography

Boecker, H. J. *Law and the Administration of Justice in the Old Testament and Ancient East.* London: SPCK, 1980. **Dahood, M.** "The Value of Ugaritic for Textual Criticism." *Bib* 40 (1959) 164–68. **Davies, G. H.** "Psalm 95." *ZAW* 85 (1973) 183–95. **Humbert, P.** "Die Herausforderungsformel 'hinneni eleka.'" *ZAW* 51 (1933) 101–8. **McKane, W.** "The Construction of Jeremiah Chapter xxi." *VT* 32 (1982) 59–73. **Weiser, A.** *Das Buch Jeremia.*

Translation

11	[a] *Now, to the house of* [a] *the king of Judah,*	(3+2)
	Hear the word of the LORD	
12	*O house of David,*	(2+3)
	thus says the LORD:	
	"Execute justice [a] *every morning,* [a]	(3+4)
	deliver the one robbed from the hand [b] *of the extortioner,* [b]	
	lest my rage go out like the fire	(3+3+3)
	and burn and no [c] *one extinguishing it* [c]	
	[d] *because of the evil of their* [e] *deeds.* [d]	
13	*Behold I am against you, O* [a] *one enthroned above* [a] *the valley,* [b]	(4+3)
	O rock [c] *of the plain,"* [d] *an oracle of the LORD,*	
	"the ones saying, 'Who will descend [e] *against us*	(3+3)
	and who will come into our dwelling places?'	

14a   ᵃ*I will visit against you*   (2+2+2)
        according to the fruit of your deeds,
        *an utterance of the LORD;*ᵃ
    *I will kindle a fire*ᵇ *in her forest*ᵇ   (3+3)
        *and it will consume everything*ᶜ *around her.*"ᶜ

Notes

11.a-a. LXX omits the conj and prep, making this phrase more nearly parallel to 12a, "O house of the king of Judah."

12.a-a. *BHS* suggests reading לבקרים, a pl meaning "continually." However, Amos 4:4 uses the same phrase as MT has here for a similar meaning, "Bring sacrifices every morning [=daily]."

12.b-b. *BHS* suggests reading "his extortioner," as do LXX, Syr, and the Tgs.

12.c-c. Tgs have "protection."

12.d-d. Not in LXX.

12.e. K חם-ֹ, "*their* deeds," Q כם-ֹ, "*your* deeds."

13.a-a. The Heb. ישבת, a fem sg qal act ptcp means lit., "one sitting." The word is often translated "inhabited" as many EVV do here. Weiser has argued that it should have here the connotation of sitting enthroned, as it does in the phrase "enthroned above the cherubim" in reference to Yahweh. See further under *Comment.*

13.b. *BHS* suggests possibly reading עפל, "hill, Ophel." Such emendation is not necessary.

13.c. LXX transliterates as *Sor,* "Tyre."

13.d. *BHS* suggests perhaps reading המשגב, "height, retreat."

13.e. LXX reads "alarm, frighten," apparently understanding the Heb. root as חתת. The Heb. יחת actually comes from the root נחת.

14.a-a. Not in LXX.

14.b-b. *BHS* notes proposals to read בערה, "burning," but prefers the MT.

14.c-c. For MT סביביה, *BHS* suggests a probable reading of סבכה, "her thicket."

Form/Structure/Setting

Verse 11 introduces this entire unit with the phrase ולבית מלך יהודה, "to/concerning the house of the king of Judah." This introduction is parallel to the phrase לנבאים, "to/concerning the prophets," in 23:9. The latter phrase introduces the next major block, a unit addressed to the prophets, 23:9–40. The material of this pericope is a poetic oracle directed to or concerning the house of the king of Judah. It is usually assigned to the "A" material. Although vv 13–14 are often separated from 11–12 and treated as another oracle because the verses are addressed to another object, Jerusalem, rather than the household of the king, they will here be treated together with vv 11–12. The parallels between these verses are too strong to ignore: royal language (king [v 11] and house of David [v 12], cf. enthroned over [v 13]), fire and burning imagery (v 12d–e cf. v 14d–e), and reference to evil deeds in vv 12f and 14b (מעלל, qualified by "evil" and "fruit of," respectively).

In terms of the setting and context for this oracle, it seems clear that the thrust of vv 1–10 is similar to that of 11–14. Yet vv 11–14 do not identify a fixed context. The context for these verses comes only from its *Sitz im Buch,* its juxtaposition with vv 1–10. There are clear links between the two units, however. The object spoken to in vv 13–14 is the city, Jerusalem, referred to as "that city" in v 10. The feminine singular form of the participle ישבת (v 13), "one enthroned over," presupposes

עִיר, "city," as the antecedent. In addition the references to burning in vv 12 and 14 pick up the references to burning the city in v 10. The original context and setting of the oracle cannot be determined. Only its redactional placement following 21:1–10 suggests a setting.

The material may be outlined as follows:

> An oracle to the (unnamed) king of Judah (vv 11–12)
> An oracle to (unnamed) Jerusalem (vv 13–14)

Comment

11–12 Verse 11 marks the transition to a new oracle, and from prose to poetry. The introductory phrase "To the house of the king of Judah" marks the ones to whom this entire section is addressed. As has been noted above, this introductory phrase has a parallel at 23:9, "To the prophets." Most commentators assume that 21:11–23:8 should therefore be considered as a single large unit. It should be noted that this short oracle (vv 11–12) is not addressed to a specific king. Only from its juxtaposition with vv 1–10 is it associated with Zedekiah. Indeed, the mood and tenor of this oracle is not that of absolute judgment as found in vv 1–10. Also here, there is a call to positive action, which, if followed, might avert the judgment.

Verse 11 is entirely introductory. It parallels exactly the first two lines of v 12. The three imperatives of vv 11 and 12 ("hear," "execute," "deliver") are all masculine plural forms, addressed not just to a specific king, or only to the king, but to the royal administration. The use of triads, in this case of imperatives, is characteristic of Jeremiah's style (see, e.g., 21: 5–7).

The concern of v 12 is with dispensing justice, first in general terms, "execute justice every morning," then in a specific instance, "deliver the one robbed from the hand of the extortioner." These social concerns are reminiscent of Amos and Isaiah. The word לַבֹּקֶר, literally, "to the morning," clearly has the meaning of "each day, each morning" or even "continually." Amos 4:4 has a similar usage of the word in reference to sacrifices which are brought daily. Isa 10:2 uses much of the vocabulary of this verse with a similar meaning.

These concerns are with the legal system but are also covenantal; much of the covenant was concerned with law. Maintaining justice was one part of maintaining covenant. Although the relationship between the king and the justice system has been much discussed (see especially Boecker, *Law*), there seems no doubt that the king was ultimately to maintain justice for all the people.

The transition to threat or judgment is provided with the word פֶּן, "lest." The threat of this oracle is that Yahweh's rage go out like fire and burn with no extinguishing. The repetition of the word "fire" from v 10 and the image of burning (though using different words) provide a link between this oracle and the previous one. It seems almost as though this oracle is being presented as one of the reasons for the judgment of 21:1–10. Because this oracle and ones like it were not heeded, the judgment spoken in this oracle has come about as 21:1–10 makes clear.

Also the word "deeds" of v 12 provides a link to the oracle in vv 13–14 along with the word "fire" and the burning image.

The last three lines of v 12 are identical with the last three lines of 4:4.

13–14   These verses form a short oracle against an unnamed city, though the context clearly identifies it with Jerusalem. The opening phrase, "Behold I am against you," has been called a "challenge formula" *(herausforderungsformel)* by Humbert; it was a formula whereby one challenged another to individual combat. A slightly different form of the expression occurs in the challenge (or response to the challenge) of David to Goliath in 1 Sam 17:44–45 ("The Philistine said, 'Come against me. . . .' David said, 'You come against me with a sword . . . , but I come against you in the name of Yahweh of armies, the God of the army-ranks of Israel"). Clearly the language is battle imagery and relates to the Divine Warrior image. Just as in the previous oracles, Yahweh is declaring himself to be fighting against his people. The challenge is set against an unnamed feminine object ("you," 2 fem sg), an anticipatory pronoun referring to the feminine singular "one enthroned" of the next phrase.

The unnamed city is called "one sitting enthroned above the valley." This translation, offered by Weiser (*Das Buch,* 182), and followed here sees a parallel in the royal terminology of the king "sitting", יֹשֵׁב, on his throne, and the royal capital seen as "sitting" enthroned in its position. Likewise, the phrase parallels those descriptions of Yahweh "sitting enthroned" (i.e, "Yahweh of armies, who sits enthroned above the cherubim"). This city is also called "rock of the plain." At least by the time of the LXX, the city was thought to be Tyre, probably on the reading of צוֹר for the MT צוּר. Carroll notes that some of the elements in this oracle are also found in the oracles against Moab and may be conventional terms for denouncing a foreign city-state. If so, this becomes just another of the reversals in which Yahweh fights against rather than for his people.

Since Jerusalem is surrounded on three sides by valleys, the phrase "enthroned above the valley" would be quite appropriate for the city. Furthermore, it is possible there is a deliberate play between this phrase and chap. 19 with its references to the pagan worship practices in the Valley of Hinnom just outside the walls of Jerusalem.

An additional double entendre may also be involved in the phrase. Dahood has shown a number of instances where עמק means "strength" as its cognate *ʿmq* does in Ugaritic. So the phrase might mean something like "enthroned in strength," and parallel the strength denoted by "rock of the plain."

"Rock" is a designation often used of Yahweh, especially in the Psalms. Davies (*ZAW* 85 [1973] 189) has argued that in at least several of these instances, "rock" might also refer to the temple mount. If this is so, the association of rock-Yahweh-Zion and Jerusalem would be a well-known motif.

The last two lines of the verse present the words of the inhabitants of this city. They are secure, even invulnerable, and ask the rhetorical questions, "who will descend against us, who will enter our dwelling places?" The implication is that no one can. Their position above the valley and plain makes them feel perfectly safe and impregnable. The kind of "inviolability of Zion" tradition that arose after the deliverance from the Assyrians under Sennacherib may lie behind the allusions in these two verses. Yet, as the next verse will make clear, Yahweh, who is against the city, will bring devastation upon her.

The words מעון and מעונה, "dwelling place," have three connotations in MT: (i) the den or lair of wild beasts (and especially jackals), (ii) the dwelling place of Yahweh, either in heaven or in his temple, and (iii) figuratively of Yahweh as the dwelling place of his people. It seems that Jeremiah is using another of the cultic metaphors of the people against them. Not only will the Divine Warrior fight against them, but also their Dwelling Place will destroy their dwelling places! An alternative image might be that of Yahweh the hunter, tracking his people as though they were wild beasts, even to their den.

Verse 14 provides the answer to the rhetorical questions of v 13. Who can descend against the city and enter the dwelling places? Yahweh can and will. Yahweh will "visit" them, but not graciously (see Jer 15:15); he will visit in judgment on the basis of their deeds (cf. v 12). The judgment is described in terms of "kindling" (יצת) a fire which "consumes" (אכל) everything around. That which is burned is her "forest," יער, a somewhat unusual reference to the city of Jerusalem. If the royal imagery of v 13 still holds, the reference may be to the palace; Solomon's palace (or a portion of it) was called "the house of the forest of Lebanon" (1 Kgs 7:2).

The last word of the verse, סביביה, "around her," may provide additional links to chap. 20. There the new name given to Pashhur was "terror round about." This description of fire consuming all round about the city may well echo the judgment spoken against Pashhur.

Explanation

The oracle of vv 11–12 seems to belong to an earlier context. There the implication is made that if the king executes justice even to the oppressed, then God's anger might be turned aside. But vv 13–14 speak of God's judgment on an overly self-secured city; the fruit of her deeds will be repaid her.

B. Oracle against an Unnamed King (22:1–5)

Bibliography

Blank, S. "The Curse, Blasphemy, the Spell and the Oath." *HUCA* 23/1 (1950–51) 73–95. Krapf, T. "Traditionsgeschichtliches zum deuteronomischen Fremdling-Waise-Witwe-Gebot." *VT* 34 (1984) 87–91. Michaelis, J. D. *Observationes Philologicae et Criticae in Jeremiae Vaticinia et Therenos.* Mowinckel, S. *Zur Komposition des Buches Jeremia.* Muilenburg, J. "The Form and Structure of Covenantal Formulations." *VT* 9 (1959) 347–65. Nicholson, E. W. *Preaching to the Exiles.*

Translation

¹*Thus says the LORD, "Go down to the house of the king of Judah and speak*[a] *there this word.* ²*Say, 'Hear*[a] *the word of the LORD, O king of Judah, who sits on the throne of David, you and* [b]*your servants*[b] *and your people who enter these gates.* ³ *"Thus says the LORD, 'Do justice and righteousness, and deliver the one robbed from the hand of the extortioner.* [a] *Also sojourner,*[b] [c]*orphan and widow do not oppress,* [d]*do not treat violently; nor innocent*

blood shed in this place. [4]*For if you will surely do this word then kings sitting on the throne of David will enter the gates of this house, ones riding on the chariot and on the horses,* [a]*he*[b] *and* [c]*his servants*[a,c] *and* [d]*his people.*[d] [5]*But if you will not hear*[a] *these words, by myself I have sworn,' an oracle of the LORD, 'that this house will become a desolate waste.'"*

Notes

1.a. Tgs have "prophesy."
2.a. Tgs have "receive."
2.b-b. LXX has "your house."
3.a. *BHS* suggests reading "his extortioner"; cf. LXX, Tgs, Syr, and 21:12 notes.
3.b. LXX and Tgs read "proselyte."
3.c. A few MSS (de Rossi, III, 90) and the versions add the conj "and."
3.d. Many MSS (de Rossi, III, 90–91) and the versions add the conj "and."
4.a-a. *BHS* suggests this phrase is an addition, probably from the second half of v 2.
4.b. LXX and Vg read "they."
4.c-c. Following the Q and fragments from C; the K has "his servant." LXX has "their servants."
4.d-d. LXX and Vg have "their people."
5.a. LXX has "hear"; Tgs have "heed."

Form/Structure/Setting

The form of the speech is a prose oracle directed to an unnamed king and the people concerning covenant responsibility. Because the king is unnamed, the oracle cannot be dated explicitly. Many commentators take the oracle to be from the "C" source (Mowinckel) and a part of a Deuteronomistic redaction (Rudolph; Nicholson, *Preaching*, 87).

Verses 1 and 2 are introductory: a messenger formula and direction to the prophet to go and speak the oracle (v 1) followed by more directions ("speak") to the prophet and those addressed (the king, his servants and his people, along with directions to the king and people ("hear the word of Yahweh"). The oracle itself begins in v 3, prefaced by another messenger formula. Muilenburg calls oracles of this type covenant speech. He finds the elements to include: presence of a covenant mediator, witness motif, I-Thou style, recital of mighty acts, emphatic call to obedience, inclusion of apodictic requirements, conditional sentence structure, and the transitional "and now" phrase (*VT* 9 [1959] 355). While not all these elements are present in this oracle, enough are present to show its kinship with the covenant speech form. The prophet has the role of covenant mediator here. The I-Thou style is clear, as is the emphatic call to obedience (v 3). The call to obedience is set in the form of apodictic commands, positive and negative (v 3). Finally, both positive and negative conditions are given, based on obedience or disobedience to the covenant commands (vv 4–5).

The setting of the passage is difficult to determine. Clearly the passage has much in common with 21:11–12 as has been noted at least since the time of Duhm. At least four locations may be indicated by the text of the passage: the temple, the palace, the city gates/court, or the larger entity Jerusalem. The words "Go down" (v 1) imply Jeremiah was in the temple when he received the oracle and directions (cf. 36:5–12; 26:10; Michaelis had already noted this in the late eighteenth century). So a temple context must be considered as the reference for "this place" (v 3), "this house" (vv 4, 5), and "these gates" (vv 2, 4). However, Jeremiah is directed to go to the king's house (v 2). So it is also possible that the references are all to the royal palace. Furthermore, since the covenant commands deal with dispensing justice (v 3) and there are two references to the gates (vv 2 and 4), a court or judicial context may be presupposed. In the discussion of 21:11–12, the responsibility of the royal house in the administration of justice was noted. Finally, "this place" could also refer to the larger entity of Jerusalem. In chap. 19, the phrase "this place" is used several times of Topheth, the place of child sacrifice in the Valley of Hinnom just outside the walls of Jerusalem. The shedding of innocent blood is mentioned there (19:4) as well. Topheth becomes the image for the destruction all Jerusalem will suffer in that passage (19:10–12). So all four locations are possible referents for these terms. Indeed, it is not necessary for all the place references to mean the same location.

From the statements in this passage and 21:11–12, I would argue that the references are to the temple. I would argue that in many places where "this place" or "house" is used in a context that refers to judgment or blessing, temple may be in the foreground or background of the motif. Temple was both *the* house and *the* place *par excellence.* So it is only natural that the temple would become the most important symbol of blessing or judgment.

The gates mentioned then would be those connecting the palace area to the temple, through which the king and his officials would enter the temple. And if current reconstructions of pre-exilic Jerusalem are correct, which suggest Ophel was an administrative area filled with public buildings separating the lower city from the palace and temple area, then these same gates would be the ones many, if not most, of the people would use. (Note the architecturally and archaeologically similar plaza and major entrances to the Herodian Temple at the southern end of the Temple Mount.)

One must also wonder if a similar temple location is indicated in other passages where Jeremiah is told to "go down," for example in 18:1 when he is to go down to the potter's house. If so, the implication would be that Jeremiah received a number of his oracles in the temple and was more closely associated with the temple than might have been thought. Furthermore, his being barred from the temple (chap. 36) might have had implications for his receiving oracles: the priests and other temple officials barred him so he could not receive additional oracles. Their attempts were, however, unsuccessful, for even when barred, he received another oracle instructing him to write down all the oracles he had received up to that day (36:1–8).

The present location of the oracle in the book is undoubtedly influenced by its proximity to 21:11–12, with only two verses intervening. The kinship between the oracles is striking. Both have an initial reference to "the house of the king of Judah" (21:11a; 22:1b) and are prefaced with the command "Hear the word of Yahweh" (21:11b; 22:2a). Both have the full messenger formula, "Thus says Yahweh" (21:12a; 22:3a). Both command dispensing justice (מִשְׁפָּט, 21:12b; 22:3b). Both include the identical phrase "and deliver the one robbed from the hand of the extortioner" (21:12c; 22:3c). Nevertheless, some differences also exist. The "house" of 21:11–12 seems to refer more to the household, the king and his family, whereas in 22:1 the "house" is apparently the palace itself. Elsewhere in the oracle of chap. 22 "house" probably refers to temple as noted above. Also the judgment in the two oracles differs: fire in chap. 21, becoming a desolate waste in chap. 22. Still, the similarities are more striking than the differences and likely reflect variants on a judgment-against-king motif. The placement of this prose oracle between related poetic oracles (see *Form/Structure/Setting* of 22:6–7 below), is probably because of these similarities.

The unit may be outlined as follows:

Introduction: Command to Jeremiah and Directions (v 1)
Command to the king and people (v 2)
Oracle Itself: Covenant speech vv (3–5)
    Apodictic commands, positive and negative (v 3)
    Continued blessing as consequence of doing God's word (v 4)
    Judgment as consequence of disobedience (v 5)

As was the case in chap. 19, no mention is made of Jeremiah's actually going and delivering this oracle. Certainly such a delivery is expected, but it is not reported in the text. One most naturally assumes that the author/editor felt it unnecessary to report the action following the reception of the message. Furthermore, the multiple introduction probably indicates multiple editing or layering of the tradition which may give a present context differing from an original context. That may explain the ambiguity of "house" and "this place" in the oracle.

The similarities of this oracle with the Temple Sermon of chap. 7 are also quite striking. Chap. 7 is addressed to the people as a whole rather than the king specifically, but the addresses have many similar expressions: (i) "Proclaim there this word" (7:2) and "Speak there this word" (22:1); (ii) "You say, 'Hear the word of the LORD'" (7:2=22:2); (iii) "If you will indeed do justice" (7:5) and "Do justice" (22:3); (iv) "Sojourner, orphan, and widow do not oppress" (7:6; 22:3; a different verb for "oppress" is used, and different ways of expressing negative prohibitions are used, but the meanings are virtually identical); (v) "Nor innocent blood shed in this place" (7:6=22:3). In addition, both oracles give the positive and negative consequences for obedience and disobedience.

While some of these similarities may be simply because of the use of some of Jeremiah's stock expressions, another explanation also seems possible. Perhaps this oracle in 22:1–5 is a variant of the Temple Sermon delivered to the king either prior to or just subsequent to the Temple Sermon. If that were so, the king would be Jehoiakim, and the date c. 609 B.C. Also, the possibility of repentance and avoiding judgment evident in this oracle fits best with the earlier period of Jeremiah's ministry.

Comments

1–2 The material in these two verses is introductory. Notice the multiple layers of command (extending into v 3), at least five levels occur:

1 "Thus says the LORD"
  2 "Go down . . . and speak there this word"
   "Say"
    3 "Hear the word of the LORD"
     4 "Thus says the LORD"
      5 "Do justice and righteousness"

Jeremiah is told to go to the king's house, the palace, to deliver the message. As noted above, the fact of going down to the palace implies Jeremiah received this oracle in the temple.

However, a location within the palace doesn't fit very well with the words "you and your servants and your people who enter these gates." It may be that v 1 has been added as a new introduction to the oracle to make it more nearly parallel 21:11. Just as the Sabbath oracle of chap. 17 was spoken at a gate and directed to the kings and people (17:19–20) and the action-message of the broken decanter was spoken at a gate and directed to the kings and people (19:2–3), so also is this oracle. The gates would be those linking palace and temple and would be the ones used by the king with his entourage, and also by many of the people.

3 The message is clearly that of covenant responsibility in the judicial area and emphasizes the administration of true justice on those whose rights were so easily disregarded, the poor one who has been robbed, the orphan, the widow, the sojourner. These were the very ones who had no one to plead their case for them, and probably no resources to get such assistance. Further, these would be the very ones who knew little about how to get justice.

The last phrase of v 3 does not quite fit the tenor of the other apodictic commands. Where the others dealt with injustice, this one deals with death. Does it mean those who have been wrongly judged and sentenced to death by the royal-judicial system (like Naboth, 1 Kgs 21)? Or does it refer to cultic practices such as Topheth and the slaughter of innocent children (Jer 19)? Or could it refer to sacrifices Yahweh does not desire, preferring right living (Amos 5:21–24; Hos 6:6; Isa 1:12–17, etc.)? Any of the suggestions are possible, and the ambiguity of specific reference may be a part of Jeremiah's style and choice of stock phraseology.

4–5 The positive condition expressed in v 4 is parallel to 17:24–25. There keeping Sabbath laws would result in kings who sit on the throne of David, officials and the people continuing to enter the gates of the city, i.e., inhabiting the city. Here the reference is to entering the temple, i.e., the temple will remain. The phrase "who sits on the throne of David" seems to be a Jeremianic phrase; the Deuteronomist prefers "who sits on the throne of Israel" and uses the former only twice, both of Solomon in 2 Kgs 2.

The negative condition of v 5 is parallel to the negative in 17:27. There the image was fire destroying the city in judgment; here the temple will become a desolate waste from unnamed cause. But compare 21:11–12, which definitely uses the fire motif in a similar judgment sense and likewise has similarities to the present oracle.

Within v 5, the negative condition is the reference to Yahweh swearing by himself. When humans swear, it is by that which is of greatest importance, often by Yahweh (Josh 2:12; Judg 21:7; 1 Sam 24:22, etc.) or by Yahweh's name (Isa 48:1; Jer 12:16; Zech 5:4). A very common oath formula included the words "As Yahweh lives" (Judg 8:19; 1 Sam 14:39; and often). But by what does Yahweh swear? He swears by himself (בִּי, 5x), by his being (נַפְשׁ, 2x), by his holiness (קֹדֶשׁ, 2x), by his name (שֵׁם, once), and by his right hand (יָמִין, once). In addition, Yahweh often uses the oath formula, "As I live" (חַי אָנִי). Although not occurring in a majority of these instances, the phrase "an oracle of Yahweh," נְאֻם יהוה, often accompanies the oath or swearing. (See further, Blank, *HUCA* 23/1 [1950–51] 73–95.)

Explanation

The call to the unnamed king is to practice justice. The implication is that practicing true justice for all, even the helpless of society, would result in God's continuing blessing and the continuation of their life as they were experiencing it. However, failure to practice justice would bring about God's judgment and the desolation of society as represented by temple/palace. The further implication of the judgment aspect is that the kings, officials and people were not practicing justice in the manner God expected, else there would be no need for the threat of judgment.

Who within our society are represented by the ones robbed by extortioners or by the sojourner, orphan, and widow? Is it the poor, the migrant, the alien? Is it the Third World worker who provides delicacies for our table, or cheap products for our market, but barely ekes out an existence for himself and his family? Is our concern for justice limited to ourselves and those like us? Or do we practice justice even toward those who have no advocate?

C. Another Oracle against an Unnamed King (22:6–7)

Bibliography

Fleming, D. "Lebanon, Mount." In *Mercer Dictionary of the Bible.* Ed. W. E. Mills. Macon, GA: Mercer UP, 1990. **Lindström, F.** *God and the Origin of Evil.* Coniectanea Biblica, OT ser. 21. C. W. K. Gleerup, 1983. **Mattingly, G. L.** "Gilead." In *Mercer Dictionary of the Bible.* Ed. W. E. Mills. Macon, GA: Mercer UP, 1990. **Soggin, J. A.** "The Prophets on Holy War as Judgment against Israel." In *Old Testament and Oriental Studies.* BibOr 29. Rome: Biblical Institute Press, 1975. 67–71. **Weippert, H.** "Jahwekrieg und Bundesfluch in Jer 21:1–7." *ZAW* 83 (1971) 396–409. **Weiser, A.** *Das Buch des Propheten Jeremia.*

Translation

6	*For thus says the LORD*	(3+3)
	concerning the house of ᵃ*the king of* ᵃ *Judah:*	
	ᵇ *"Gilead are you to me*	(3+2)
	the head of the Lebanon.	
	*[I swear] if I do not make you a wilderness,*ᵇ	(3+3)
	cities not ᶜ*being inhabited.*ᶜ	
7	*Surely I have consecrated*ᵃ *against you destroyers,*ᵇ	(3+2)
	*a man and his weapons;*ᶜ	
	*they will cut from the choicest of your cedars*ᵈ	(3+2)
	and throw them upon the fire."	

Notes

6.a-a. Not in the MS fragments from C.

6.b-b. The Tgs have a paraphrase, "Should you be as beloved before me as the house of the sanctuary, which is high on the tops of the mountains, even then would I not make you a wilderness. . . ."

6.c-c. K is sg; Q is pl. The sg fits the 2 masc sg pronouns and the sg noun "wilderness" better; the pl fits the pl noun "cities" better.

7.a. The Heb. verb קדשׁתי lit. means "consecrate, set apart." It is often used of preparation for Holy War (see *Comment*). Both the Tgs and LXX take a nonmilitary sense of "appoint."

7.b. The Tgs have "stumbling blocks."

7.c. The LXX has sg "ax, weapon."

7.d. The Tgs have "strong men."

Form/Structure/Setting

This short oracle is poetic. The phrase "concerning the house of the king of Judah" picks up the nearly identical phrase in 21:11, "Now to the house of the king of Judah." Similarly, the reference to fire and cedars in this unit parallels the images of fire and forests in 21:11–14. So this unit has clear links with 21:11–14. Perhaps the prose section of 22:1–5 has been inserted at a later stage of composition between 21:14 and this unit.

In terms of form, this short section is a judgment oracle directed against the royal house, though the specific king is unnamed. Holladay has pointed out the chiastic structure of the unit. Beyond the introductory line, v 6a (which may or may not be considered a part of the poetic oracle), the unit has four bicola or lines. Lines 1 and 4 refer to Lebanon and cedars, an obvious parallel. Lines 2 and 3 speak of actions of Yahweh against "you" in first common singular form.

The oracle may be outlined as follows:

Introductory word: messenger formula, directed against the royal house (v 6a)
Positive word of Yahweh's choice (v 6b)
Oath of what Yahweh is about to do (v 6c–7)

The language of the oracle is allegorical, using the images of cedar and Lebanon to represent the royal house. Using the language of Holy War, the allegory states that the cedars will be cut down and burned, the royal house will become like a wilderness, uninhabited.

Comment

6 The introduction to the oracle is quite similar to the introduction in 21:11. The image of trees and forests is in the forefront of this section; forest is mentioned specifically in 21:14. Both Gilead and Lebanon were noted in antiquity for their forests. The cedars of Lebanon were especially well known and prized for their strength and beauty. But Gilead is also noted for its oak and pine forests (Mattingly, "Gilead"). The other image of this verse is that of mountain. Both Lebanon and Gilead were mountainous regions. The image is that of a tree-covered mountainous region, an image of strength and stately beauty. Yahweh describes the royal house of Judah with that image. As so often is the case, the judgment oracle begins with a very positive image, but one that quickly changes.

As was noted in 21:14, one part of the royal palace in Jerusalem was known as the House of the Forest of Lebanon, probably because that was the source of the timber used in its construction and paneling. So there would be some logic to use the image of mountainous forests to describe the royal family.

In this judgment oracle, no specific charge or sin is specified. The oracle moves directly from the positive image to an oath describing judgment.

The oath is introduced with the formula אִם־לֹא. The general explanation of the oath is that the speaker swears some curse upon himself unless the conditions of the oath are met. In effect, for a human speaker, the equivalent would be "May God do so to me, if I do not do this," i.e., "I will surely do so!" A difficulty arises when Yahweh is the speaker. Blank and Gesenius (GKC § 149) both argue that Yahweh would not use a self-imprecation. But that misses the point. Yahweh simply uses the same strong oath language as do humans to emphasize the seriousness of this judgment. This translation includes the oath idea with the words "I swear" added in brackets. The negative of the Hebrew, and this translation, imply that Yahweh will surely make the royal house an uninhabited wilderness.

This judgment of becoming a wilderness is a common OT metaphor (Hos 2:5). Unlike the mountainous forests, filled with trees, the wilderness is at times depicted as being uninhabited by humans (Job 38:26) and often as desert land (Deut 32:10; Judg 1:22). Primarily it is an area of little vegetation, of seasonal pasturage but few trees, and the habitation of wild animals. It presents quite a negative contrast to the massive trees of the mountains.

The phrase "cities without inhabitant" may refer to the wilderness area. Even in the wilderness, some cities exist, along important trade routes and near water sources. The judgment would imply that even these cities will be destroyed. Alternatively, the phrase may refer to Judah's cities: just like the mountainous forests are to become a wilderness, so Judah's cities are to be left uninhabited.

7 Verse 7 continues the metaphor of destruction and devastation. Picking up on the language of Holy War ("I have consecrated," קִדַּשְׁתִּי), the oracle again turns a positive image against the royal house. Holy War was that war Yahweh waged on Israel's behalf against her enemies. Although Israel had to field the army, it was Yahweh who fought the battle and won the victory. Soldiers were to be consecrated before Holy War in recognition of the sacred nature of the undertaking. But in this instance, Yahweh has consecrated destroyers to come and fight Holy War against Judah. Another metaphor Judah knew so well is turned against her by this oracle. Each man has his weapons, but the weapons and the warriors are turned against Judah, not to fight for her. (Note Weippert's article [*ZAW* 83 (1971) 396–409] concerning the reversals of Holy War ideology in reference to chap. 21. The same reversal holds here.)

The image then returns to that of forest land. (The LXX understands the last phrase of 7a to refer also to forests, for it translates "a man and his ax." But the Holy War image makes "weapons" more likely.) The destroyers Yahweh has consecrated will cut down the choicest of the cedars and burn them as so much firewood. Normally the choice wood would be used for special building purposes. But here the land is simply devastated. Trees are cut and burned in a scorched-earth policy. The judgment is harsher than permitted under Holy War conditions (Deut 20); there the trees were to be spared, except for ones used to make siege works. Here they are cut and burned. Total devastation is the judgment on Judah. And certainly the fact that a part of the palace was called the House of the Forest of Lebanon was not forgotten. The destruction of the palace by burning is probably in the background of this image. The foreground, however, is the royal household, the king and his family, who will suffer devastation.

Explanation

This oracle employs an oath formula and the language of Holy War to indicate that God has turned his judgment, usually reserved for foreign nations, against Judah. Judah will now experience the consequences of Holy War, and of God's wrath described in terms of burning fire.

D. Why Was This City Destroyed? (22:8–9)

Bibliography

Hillers, D. R. *Treaty-Curses and the Old Testament Prophets.* BibOr 16. Rome: Pontifical Biblical Institute, 1964. **Long, B. O.** "Two Question and Answer Schemata in the Prophets." *JBL* 90 (1971) 129–39. **Skweres, D.** "Das Motiv der Strafgrunderfragung in biblischen und neuassyrischen Texten." *BZ* 14 (1970) 181–97.

Translation

[8] *Great* [a] *nations will cross over against this city, and they will say, each to his fellow, "For what reason has the LORD done thus to this great city?"* [9] *And they will say, "Because they have forsaken the covenant of the LORD* [a] *their God,* [a] *and they have worshiped other gods and they have served them."*

Notes

8.a. Not in LXX.
9.a-a. Several MSS (de Rossi, III, 91) have "the God of their fathers."

Form/Structure/Setting

This short pericope seems at first to be a continuation of the previous one, although it is prose and the previous one was poetic. However, upon closer examination, differences emerge, chiefly that the former unit addressed the house of the king and its devastation whereas this section speaks of the destruction of the city, unnamed, though certainly intending Jerusalem. Further, this pericope specifies the cause of the judgment, but none was mentioned in the previous one. Nevertheless, the two pericopes flow quite well from the one to the other, probably accounting for their juxtaposition.

The form of this pericope is question and answer. Long has noted this specific form and passage, and has isolated three elements of the form: (i) a setting for the question, including the ones who ask it; (ii) the question itself, given as a direct quotation; and (iii) the answer, also given as a direct quotation. Long argues that the form is a literary convention rather than a speech form and belonged to a post-exilic group such as the Deuteronomistic Historian. The three elements are all present in this passage: setting and ones asking the question (v 8a); the question itself (v 8b); and the answer (v 9).

Remarkably similar parallels have been noted in the Assyrian annals of Ashurbanipal:

> "Whenever the inhabitants of Arabia asked each other: 'On account of what have these calamities befallen Arabia?' (they answered themselves:) 'Because we did not keep the solemn oaths (sworn by) Ashur, because we offended the friendliness of Ashurbanipal, the king, beloved by Enlil!'" (Pritchard, *ANET* 3 [1969] 300).

The annalistic nature of this report suggests it being a literary convention among Assyrian historiographers. The form is clearly related to treaty curses. In the Assyrian example, the people ask themselves why this calamity has befallen them and answer the question themselves. The answer is cast in terms of breaking a treaty with Ashurbanipal, so Ashurbanipal has invaded and defeated them. In the Jeremiah example, it is foreigners who ask the question, and the answer is cast in terms of breaking a covenant with Yahweh.

Comment

8 As this passage is cast, and in comparison with the Assyrian example above, it is noteworthy that foreigners are the ones asking why this city has been so devastated. The reference to passersby is similar to a reference in 19:8. There the context was clearly the siege and resulting famine in the city, but the passersby were not specifically designated as foreigners. Their response is horror and shrieking at the devastation.

Though not stated explicitly, one might assume that the foreigners here asking the question are the very soldiers who are causing the destruction. Such an assumption is reinforced by the terminology "cross over against." The verb עבר is used in a military sense of crossing over to or against an enemy (see 1 Sam 14:1, 4, 6, 8). The addition of the preposition על reinforces the idea of an invasion against one (cf. 1 Sam 14:4).

If that is the case, it is quite ironic that foreigners, one would assume pagans, themselves have the answer. The answer is twofold. First, they acknowledge that it is Yahweh who has devastated the city, rather than the invading army. Second (v 9), Yahweh has done so because the people of the city have forsaken the covenant with Yahweh. Clearly, such language is intended as a literary convention and not an actual conversation between some soldiers.

The city that is devastated is unnamed in this pericope. Yet clearly Jerusalem is intended from the context. It is *the* city, just as the temple is *the* house.

9 The specific reason is given for the devastation of the city: because they have forsaken the covenant with Yahweh. Elsewhere in Jeremiah, the people are often accused of forsaking Yahweh (that phrase is a stock expression for Jeremiah), once of forsaking his torah-instruction (9:12), but only here of forsaking his covenant.

As is often the case, the general charge is made first, forsaking the covenant, and then specifics are added, worshiping and serving other gods. The mention of other gods again recalls 19:4–8. In both passages Yahweh is forsaken, in both the worship of other gods is mentioned, and in both passersby respond to the devastation.

Explanation

This brief dialogue repeats images from 19: 4–8 in a question-and-answer format. The destruction of Jerusalem is assumed. The question is asked, "Why?" The response is cast in covenantal terms: "Because the people have broken their covenant with God." Although the devastation was brought by enemy invasion and siege, the ultimate source is God, who brought it because of the people's sins.

E. Weeping for the Dead or the Living? (22:10)

Bibliography

Roach, C. C. "Notes and Comments." *ATR* 23 (1941) 347–48.

Translation

¹⁰ Do not weep ^a for the one who is dead,^a   (3+2)
        do not lament for him;
     weep indeed for the one about to go [into exile]^b   (3+4+3)
        for he will not return again
        nor see the land of his birth [again].^c

Notes

10.a-a. LXX, Tgs, and Syr have "for the dead."
10.b. The phrase in brackets is not represented in Heb. However, the verb הלך does have the connotation of going into exile within itself (BDB, 230, I1b).
10.c. The word "again" is not present in this line, but the idea is carried by the parallelism from the previous line.

Form/Structure/Setting

This single verse of poetry is often joined to the following pericope as referring to Shallum-Jehoahaz (see v 11). However, as this verse stands independently, it does not refer to a specific king, or even necessarily to royalty (see Roach, *ATR* 23 [1941] 347–48).

Roach suggests an original setting for this lament at a funeral; it is appropriate for any funeral in Judah's last years. The meaning would be: don't weep for this one who has died, but instead weep for those who remain who will go into exile and never again see their homeland. A further implication is that these exiles, when they die, will be buried in a foreign land, considered to be a terrible tragedy—worse perhaps than death itself.

The lament has a negative and a positive command, "do not weep, indeed weep." The words "weep" and "lament" keep the funereal mood heightened.

Most scholars argue that the setting of this verse should be related to the death of Josiah and the brief rule and exile of Shallum-Jehoahaz. Holladay, who relates the oracle to Jehoahaz, does note that the oracle might have had ironic reuse when Jehoiachin succeeded Jehoiakim. However, he argues Jeremiah would have had no sadness over Jehoiakim's death as this verse implies. I feel Holladay is overstating the case for sadness here. The command not to weep or lament parallels precisely the language of v 18 below. Thus the lament could have been uttered for either Josiah or Jehoiakim. But Roach's argument for no specific individual's death, for any death, seems the most likely original setting. The *Sitz im Buch* does relate to a royal funeral, and specifically to Jehoahaz, on the basis of v 11 below. The specific repetition of שוב, "return," and a word parallel to הלך, in this case יצא, "go out," strengthens the linkage with vv 11–12. Likewise v 12 speaks of not seeing this place again, a parallel to not seeing again the land of his birth.

In terms of the structure, this verse has five lines, a bicolon and a tricolon. Lines 1 and 5 have a contrastive parallelism between death and birth that serves also as an inclusio. Also lines 3 and 4 have contrastive/synonymous parallelism between going into exile and not returning again. Finally there is the contrastive parallelism between the commands "do not weep/do not lament" and "weep indeed" in lines 1 through 3. There is a synonymous parallelism between the one who is dead and the one who goes into exile. Both are cut off; the one is dead, the other is perhaps worse than dead, for at death he will not even be buried in his homeland.

Comments

10 The use of the participle להלך as an immediate future intensifies the poignancy of this lament. One has died; others are facing imminent exile but may not even realize it. Jeremiah remarks that the weeping and lamenting should be reserved for those facing the exile, separation, and death in a foreign land.

F. An Oracle against Shallum (22:11–12)

Bibliography

Honeyman, A. M. "The Evidence for Regnal Names among the Hebrews." *JBL* 67 (1948) 13–25. **Wildberger, H.** "Die Thronnamen des Messias, Jes. 9, 5b." *TZ* 6 (1960) 314–32.

Translation

[11]*For thus says the LORD to Shallum,*[a] *the son of Josiah,* [b]*the king of Judah,*[b] *the one reigning after Josiah his father, who* [c]*went out*[c] *from this place; he will not return there again.* [12]*For*[a] *in the*[b] *place where they*[c] *took him captive, there he will die, and this land he will not see again.*

Notes

11.a. The Lucianic recension of the LXX has "Jehoahaz" for the MT "Shallum" and LXX "Sellem."
11.b-b. Lacking in the LXX and Syr.
11.c-c. The Tgs have "went into exile."
12.a. The fragments from C, several other MSS (de Rossi, III, 91), and the versions read כִּי־אִם, "But. . . ."
12.b. MT lacks the definite article; LXX has "in that place." According to GKC § 130c, מְקוֹם is a const and אֲשֶׁר serves as the abs (or better, the clause introduced by אֲשֶׁר serves as the abs), thus no article is needed.
12.c. LXX and Vg read 1cs, "where I took."

Form/Structure/Setting

This short prose oracle is the first within this chapter, and the first in these oracles addressed to the royal house beginning at 21:11 that addresses a specific king by name. It is often interpreted as a prose equivalent to or comment on v 10. However, that unit is addressed to an unnamed person, not necessarily a royal figure. Only the juxtaposition of the two units makes this an equivalent to or comment on v 10. If that is to be assumed, then these two verses must be later than v 10. Further the context presupposed by these two verses need not be that originally addressed by v 10. But if the two did originally belong together, v 10 was spoken prior to the exile of Shallum and vv 11–12 after his exile, confirming the permanence of the exile.

The messenger formula of v 11 is followed by the identity of the king as Shallum, the son of Josiah. The judgment spoken in the oracle is that he has gone forth (a perfect; cf. the participle in v 10) and will not return again. He will die in exile and not see his land again. No reason for the judgment is given, nor are conditions mentioned.

Comment

11–12 The identity of Shallum with Jehoahaz seems certain. Honeyman has argued that Jehoahaz was the regnal name and Shallum the given name of this individual, a position accepted by Rudolph, Bright, and most other commentaries. On the basis of 1 Chr 3:15, it would seem that Jehoahaz was the regnal name and Shallum the given name. That Yahweh would speak an oracle through Jeremiah to Jehoahaz when he is already in exile might seem strange. One solution would be to assume that the oracle is "concerning Jehoahaz" rather than "to Jehoahaz." However, since the other oracles in this larger section are spoken to the kings as well as "concerning" them, one would assume the same here. From a historical perspective, there is no need to assume that communication between exiles in Egypt and Judah was lacking; we know communication existed with the Babylonian exiles just a few years later, and we know of communication between colonies in Egypt and Judah in the next century (the Elephantine materials). So such communication was quite possible, and an oracle delivered in Jerusalem might well have been sent to Egypt.

Jeremiah probably uses considerable irony in his choice of vocabulary to speak of Jehoahaz's exile. The verb יָצָא regularly has the idea of going out or going forth.

Although it is used a few times of exile, as here, I am aware of no other passage where this word refers to an exile into Egypt. Normally ירד or בוא are used in reference to journeys to Egypt. However, יצא is the primary word used of the Exodus *from* Egypt. Ironically then, the most common word used in describing Israel's departure from Egypt is here used to describe the king's exile *to* Egypt.

The specific location where this oracle was given is not mentioned in the text. One might assume that it was given in the royal palace or its courts, for the benefit of the succeeding king. Or the oracle may have been given before an assembly of the people within Jerusalem. On the other hand, the double appearance of מקום may well suggest a temple setting. מקום is frequently used in reference to the temple, and such a location for both the reception and delivery of an oracle is quite appropriate. There too it could have had a royal audience, or the broader audience of the people present.

Explanation

This oracle, directed specifically to Shallum, the king who has been taken exile to Egypt, repeats the thrust of the previous lament to an unnamed person. Shallum, who has already been taken captive, will not return, but will die in that foreign land.

G. An Oracle against Jehoiakim (22:13–19)

Bibliography

Dahood, M. "Two Textual Problems in Jeremiah." *CBQ* 23 (1961) 462–64. **Joüon, P.** "Un Parallèle à la 'Sépulture d'un Ane' de Jérémie." *RSR* 27 (1937) 335–36. **Köhler, L.** "Archäologisches." *ZAW* 34 (1914) 146–49. **Westermann, C.** *Basic Forms of Prophetic Speech.*

Translation

13	*"Woe to the one building his house without righteousness*	(4+3)
	and his upper rooms without justice;	
	he causes his neighbor to work for nothing	(3+3)
	and does not give him his wage.	
14	*ᵃ The one saying, 'I will build for myself ᵃ*	(2+2+2)
	a house of stature	
	with spaciousᵇ upper rooms.'	
	He cutᶜ for it its windows,ᵈ	(3+2+2)
	panelingᵉ with cedar,	
	painting with scarlet.	
15	*ᵃ Do you reign,ᵃ even you,*	(3+2)
	contendingᵇin cedar?ᵇ	

> *Your father, did he not eat and drink*   (4+3+3)
> *and do justice and righteousness?*
> ^c*That being so, it was good came to him.*^c

16 *He pled the cause of the afflicted and the needy;*   (3+2)
>   ^a*that being so, it was good.*^a
> *Is not this the knowledge*^b*of me?"*^b   (3+2)
> *an oracle of the LORD.*

17 *"But you have no eyes nor heart*   (4+2)
>   *except upon your unjust gain*
> *and upon pouring out the*^a*innocent blood*   (3+3)
>   *and upon extorting and upon doing oppression."*^b

18 *Therefore, thus says the LORD*   (3+2+2)
>   *to Jehoiakim, the son of Josiah,*
>   *the king of Judah:*
> ^a*"They will not lament over him,*   (3+2+2)
>   *'alas,* ^b*my brother,'*^b
>   ^c*'alas, (my)*^d *sister';*^{c,e}
> *they will not lament*^f *over him,*   (3+2+2)
>   *'alas, lord,'*
>   ^g*'alas,* ^h*his majesty.'*^{g,h}

19 *The burial of an ass, he will be buried,*   (3+2+3)
>   *dragged and thrown down*
>   *outside the gates of Jerusalem. "*

Notes

14.a-a. LXX has "You built for yourself."

14.b. MT has an unusual form, a masc pl pual ptcp, but the three nouns immediately preceding are fem pl ("upper rooms," and "sizes," translated here as "stature") and masc sg ("house"). Rudolph revocalizes the form as an otherwise unattested piel ptcp. This translation takes the form as MT and puts it in apposition with "upper rooms," lit., "with upper rooms, (with) ones being spacious," i.e., "with spacious upper rooms."

14.c. The Tgs read "he frames windows."

14.d. MT has "my windows"; *BHS* suggests reading the sg. GKC § 87g suggests moving the *waw* from the beginning of the next word, thus giving חלוניו ספון, "his/its windows, being paneled."

14.e. This translation follows the emendation suggested by *BHS* of an act form, סָפֹן, "paneling," for the MT pass form סָפוּן "being paneled." The act form gives a better parallel to the next phrase, though the MT is not impossible.

15.a-a. Instead of the MT, Duhm, followed by *BHS*, suggests reading a hithp, הֲתִתְמֲלֵךְ, "Do you (play-) act as king"; see GKC § 54e for the hithp having the nuance of acting, or playing a role. The Tgs have, "Do you imagine to be like the former king, your father, . . . ?"

15.b-b. LXX translates this phrase differently and restructures the flow of the sentence, "that you are provoked with Achaz your father." LXX^A has "Achaab" instead of "Achaz."

15.c-c. LXX transposes these words prior to "do justice" and relates them to the doing of justice: "it is better for you to do justice and righteousness. . . ."

16.a-a. *BHS* suggests deleting this phrase as an addition from v 15. It is also lacking from LXX, which understands v 16 differently: "They do not know, they do not judge the case of the lowly and the case of the poor; is this not that you do not know me?"

16.b-b. Tg has "knowledge in which I take pleasure."

17.a. The fragments from C omit the definite article.

17.b. MT is from the root רצץ; Tg takes the root as רוץ and translates "and what is your soul's good pleasure to do."

18.a. LXX adds before this line the phrase "Woe unto this man."

18.b-b. Origen's recension of the LXX simply had "brother," omitting the pronoun "my," as did the Vg. The Lucianic recension has "lord."

18.c-c. Lacking in the LXX.

18.d. The 1cs suff from "brother" probably carries its force to this line as well.

18.e. Origen's recension and the Lucianic recension of the LXX have "brother," a repetition of the previous line; Syr has "my brother," likewise a repetition. *BHS* suggests perhaps reading "his sister."

18.f. LXX has "weep." Holladay suggests reading שׂרֹף, "burning," instead of MT סְפֹד, "lament," on the basis of 34:5. However, the next two lines argue against his emendation.

18.g-g. Lacking in LXX.

18.h-h. Origen's recension and the Lucianic recension of the LXX read "brother" from the previous lines. Syr has "lord." *BHS* suggests perhaps reading "lady" or "beloved." The Tg has "his kingdom." Dahood suggests the pair here should be "his father" and "his mother" (see further under *Comment*).

Form/Structure/Setting

This poetic oracle has primarily the *qînāh* meter, with variations (3+2, 3+2+2, 4+3+3, 4+2), of a lament. It begins with the Hebrew הוֹי, "Woe!" Although woe-oracles are fairly common in the prophetic materials, especially in Isaiah and Amos, they appear infrequently in Jeremiah.

In terms of form, this oracle is a judgment speech to an individual. In its basic form, the judgment speech to individuals has a summons to hear, an accusation, the introduction to the announcement of judgment by a messenger formula, and the announcement of judgment. This passage has all the elements except the summons to hear. Verses 13–17 present the accusation. Verse 18a–c is the transition to an announcement of judgment; it has both the transition word לָכֵן, "therefore," and the messenger formula "Thus says the LORD." Verses 18d–19 give the announcement of judgment.

Westermann has noted the similarity between the judgment speech to individuals and the woe cry forms. It is therefore not surprising to find a woe cry within this judgment speech, forming a part of the accusation. The "woe cry" is introduced by הוֹי, "woe," and is usually followed by a participle (as here) relating some specific action of the one addressed. Usually the ones addressed in a woe cry are anonymous but are the ones practicing the action which is denounced. The woe cry is closely related to the curse formula, "Cursed is the one who. . . ." The parallel with a woe cry would be "Woe to the one who. . . ." The word הוֹי seems to have served two major functions in Hebrew, one to introduce the woe cry and the other to introduce a funeral lament or mourning cry. Within this pericope both uses of הוֹי are found.

Although the one to whom this oracle is addressed is not specified at the beginning of the pericope, the recipient is identified at the point of transition to announcement of judgment. Perhaps the omission of the name at the beginning is deliberate, another case of ambiguity deliberately intended to heighten tension and focus on the climax when the one to whom the oracle is addressed is named. (Nathan's parable to David [2 Sam 12] would have had little impact if David had been identified as the rich man with many flocks initially. The tension and climax are built by the person remaining unnamed.)

There is clear movement through the sections of the speech. In the first half of the accusation (vv 13–14) the third-person forms dominate. In the second part of the accusation (vv 15–17), there is a shift to second person and an identity with a royal person. In this section a comparison is made between the present unrighteous ruler (spoken to in second person masculine singular forms) and his just father. Then the announcement of judgment (vv 18–19) returns to the third-person form with the identity of Jehoiakim as the subject.

Within this oracle at least two chiastic structures can be isolated. In the accusation section as a whole, one chiastic pattern emerges:

A   Jehoiakim's injustice (vv 13–15a)
   B   His father's righteousness (vv 15b–16)
A'   Jehoiakim's injustice (v 17)

A more intricate chiastic pattern can be found within the second part of the accusation, the "you" section:

A   Jehoiakim's reign of contention (v 15a)
   B   His father's righteousness (v 15b)
      C   Result: good for father (v 15c)
   B'   Further righteousness of father (16a)
      C'   Result: good for all (v 16b)
         D   Right actions = knowledge of God (v 16c)
   B"   Contrast: Jehoiakim has no eyes and heart (v 17a)
A'   Jehoiakim's injustice (v 17b)

Linkages within the sections of the pericope are provided by the contrastive repetition of justice and righteousness (contrastive because in reference to Jehoiakim it is lack of justice and righteousness) in the two parts of the accusation. Also the twofold בלא, "without," of v 13 links with the twofold הלוא, "Is not?" in vv 15 and 16 and with the two occurrences of לא in v 18, providing a connection between the two parts of the accusation and the announcement of sentence. In addition, the mention of cedar in vv 14 and 15 serves to connect the two parts of the accusation. The repetition of הוי in v 13 and twice in v 18 forms a kind of inclusio for the whole pericope as well as indicating the two functions of הוי, woe cry and mourning cry.

Comment

13   As is typical of a woe cry, this oracle opens with an anonymous "Woe to the one who. . . ." Furthermore, there is considerable ambiguity at first. No mention is made of a royal building; the woe cry could well be addressed to any one who builds his house with unrighteousness. Even the word "house" is ambiguous: does the writer mean his house, or his family, or, assuming a royal person, his dynasty? Some ambiguity is quickly removed. The mention of the upper rooms certainly indicates the primary image is that of a building.

The specific injustice is mentioned within this first verse: making his neighbor/fellow work for nothing. It is not clear why the neighbor agreed to do so, and this ambiguity remains for the moment.

14   Further description of the house is given in this verse. The house is one of stature, with spacious upper rooms and windows. The image of a mansion is emerging; this is no ordinary house, nor even the house of just any well-to-do person. This is a house that is quite elaborate, both in its dimensions and in its decor: cedar paneling and scarlet paint.

Note the contrast between what this unnamed person says and the reality already reported. He says "I will build for myself. . . ." The reality is that he is using his neighbors/ fellows to do the labor and then not paying them.

The phrase "The one saying" is a typical way for Hebrew to express one's inner thoughts. Hebrew had no direct word for "thought" or thinking. So thoughts were expressed in terms of words spoken.

15 Finally more of the ambiguity is removed. The question of reigning tells us that a king is involved. The building must refer to a palace. The unpaid labor may well involve corvée workers, forced to give their time without compensation for royal-state building projects.

Carroll interprets the passage as not referring to a royal building project, the rhetorical question asking: "Do you think you are a king, competing in cedar?" According to his view, the builder is not a king but is building like one. While his view has some merit, it does not deal with the issues raised by this person's unjust ways. How could he get away with such corrupt practices? Only a king could do so without expecting legal repercussions.

Already in v 15, the woe cry has made one abrupt change, from third person to second person. It now makes another dramatic change. Now the emphasis of the accusation is shifted to a contrast in this individual king's actions and the actions of his father. His father ate and drank (probably a hendiadys meaning he lived his life, he went about his routine life; compare Eccl 2:24; 3:13; 5:18; 8:15; Luke 17:26–30), nothing extraordinary, but he did justice and righteousness! The result was that good came to him.

16 Some of the specifics of the father's justice and righteousness are now enumerated. The language is definitely that of covenant terminology. The father faithfully executed the covenant, even for those who were often helpless. Though the specific vocabulary differs, the impact is quite similar to that of 22:3 and 21:12 in the nearby context, and numerous other passages in Jeremiah. Nevertheless, the terms mentioned here, pleading the case of the afflicted and the needy, are not common in Jeremiah. עני appears only here in Jeremiah and אביון occurs only three other times in the book.

Again the result was good. The lack of the prepositional phrase "to him" following "good" may indicate a broader scope for "good." Perhaps the implication is that the whole nation enjoyed the good brought about by the justice and righteousness of the king.

As the chiastic structure of the second half of the accusation depicted above indicates, the center falls in the phrase "'Is not this the knowledge of me?' an oracle of the LORD." The rhetorical question, like the one just above, implies an affirmative answer, "Yes, doing righteously and helping the needy is knowing Yahweh." The verb ידע, "to know," communicates much more than knowledge in the sense of information. It implies relationship, to know Yahweh is to have a relationship with him, and as this passage indicates, that relationship is based on covenant and keeping covenant. The heart of the accusation against this as yet unnamed king is that he has not kept covenant; he therefore has no real knowledge of Yahweh, no relationship with him. His father did enjoy that positive relationship, and the results are twice called good.

Surely Jeremiah was aware of the death Josiah had died, killed in battle at the still youthful age of thirty-nine or forty. How could Jeremiah pronounce the results of Josiah's life good? The Deuteronomistic historian has a struggle with that one. But Jeremiah may well have had some of the positive effects in mind. Judah did regain some of the territory lost to the Assyrians during Josiah's reign. The cult was reformed, and many of the syncretistic practices were removed. The sole worship of Yahweh was practiced, at least in the temple. In this passage Jeremiah also commends Josiah for his keeping covenant. Yes, the death was tragic; but the life Josiah lived was good and his relationship with Yahweh was good. He was a good king, and he brought good to his people.

17 The particle כִּי has the adversative sense "but" following the twofold הֲלוֹא (BDB, 474, כִּי 3e; GKC § 163a). The reference to eyes and heart speaks of both an inner and an outer reality. With the eyes this one sees what he wants; with his heart-mind, he knows what he wants. The combination suggests the total energy of this individual being focused on a single goal. Unlike his father, who directed his energies toward justice, this one's desire is for unjust gain, pouring out innocent blood, extorting, and oppression. In a word, he has no concern who is hurt while he seeks to achieve his goals.

The spilling of innocent blood and oppression relate back to 22:3, as did justice and righteousness in v 15. Here, though, the contrast is clear. The message of 22:3 called for justice and righteousness and not spilling innocent blood nor oppressing; this king is committing those very acts. Relating further to the oracle in 22:1–5, it is clear that the accusation here anticipates the same type of judgment as specified in 22:5. Because this king has not been obedient, has not kept covenant, then the judgment of 22:5, which Yahweh has sworn by his self, becomes operative.

18 The shift to an announcement of judgment is indicated by the transition word לָכֵן, "Therefore." It connects the judgment with the accusation and implies that the truthfulness of the accusations is the reason for the judgment. Immediately after the transition word, the messenger formula occurs. As is typical, the judgment is introduced by the messenger formula, assuring an awareness that the judgment is not being spoken by a mere messenger but is from the one who has sent the messenger: Yahweh is the source of this judgment. Another shift occurs in v 18, as the pronouns used return again to third-person forms.

The messenger formula is followed by the identity of the one who is accused and now judged, Jehoiakim, the son of Josiah. If, as suggested above, the king's name has been deliberately left out until now, it is included here to make unmistakable the one to whom the harsh judgment is spoken. The heightening of tension and concern caused by the anonymity of the subject and the piling up of accusations lead to a climax at the announcement of judgment. It is appropriate and expected from a form-critical perspective that the name be included at the beginning of the announcement of judgment.

The judgment itself speaks of the death of Jehoiakim and is twofold. The remainder of this verse deals with one aspect of the death, that Jehoiakim will not be mourned at his death. The next verse covers the other aspect, that his burial will be like that of an animal: his dead body will be dragged out and thrown outside the gates, without proper burial.

The remainder of this verse records the lament which will not be uttered at this king's death. The words of the lament are probably conventional. "Alas my brother; alas (my) sister" would be words of grief/consolation for the mourners. These would be the words the mourners would speak to one another. Probably the first common singular suffix on "brother" carries over to "sister" as well.

The repetition of the phrase "they shall not lament over him" requires no emendation. Repetition often serves an emphatic purpose, and that is the case here. Further, a different lament follows: "Alas lord, alas his majesty." Dahood has suggested understanding אֲדוֹן as "father," and emending הֹדֹה to הָרָה, "she who conceives, mother." Such an emendation would give four familial terms in the laments. Holladay then argues that these four terms could all apply to Jehoiakim, mentioning several ancient Near Eastern inscriptions where the king is said to be both father and mother to some of his people. That suggestion, while attractive, is not compelling. Instead, it is preferable to see the first two terms of the lament referring to the mourners. These two terms, taken as "lord" and "his majesty" refer to the king.

19 Not only will Jehoiakim lack laments at his death, but the judgment continues that he will lack a proper burial. The description here is that of the disposal of a large animal. The carcass of the king, like an ass, will be dragged outside the city and dumped quite unceremoniously. Note the contrast with the grandiose building plans of this king. A proper burial was a major concern for the Hebrews; lack of proper burial was among the most serious of curses. See further on 19:7.

Explanation

Jehoiakim in this judgment speech is compared with his father. The results are most unfavorable to Jehoiakim. Whereas Josiah lived justly and practiced righteousness, all that has concerned Jehoiakim has been his personal building projects without regard for the oppression he caused. But Jehoiakim will receive retribution from God. When he dies he will not be mourned, nor will he receive proper burial, a dire curse-judgment.

H. Oracle against Jerusalem (22:20–23)

Bibliography

Dahood, M. *Ugaritic-Hebrew Philology.* BibOr 17. Rome: Pontifical Biblical Institute, 1965. **Daiches, S.** "Exegetical Notes." *PEFQS* 59 (1927) 162–63.

Translation

20   "Go up the Lebanon[a] and cry out,   (3+3)
      on Bashan[b] *give your voice;*
   cry out from Abarim[c]   (2+3)
      for they have been broken, all your lovers.

21   ªI spoke against you in your (time of) security;ª,ᵇ   (3+3)
        you said, 'I will not listen.'ᶜ

        This is your way from your youth   (3+3)
        becauseᵈ you would not listen to my voice.

22   All your shepherds, ªthe wind will shepherd,ª   (2+3)
        and your lovers, into the captivity they will go.

        For at that time you will be ashamed and humiliated   (4+2)
        from all your evil.ᵇ

23   ªO one enthronedª in the Lebanon,ᵇ   (2+2)
        ᶜ,ᵈone being nestedᶜ in the cedars,ᵈ

        how you will bellowᵉ when birth-pangs come upon you,   (3+2)
        anguish like one giving birth."

Notes

20.a. The Tg has "the house of the sanctuary."
20.b. The Tg has "in the gates of the mountain of the house."
20.c. Syr has "from across the sea"; the Tg has "at the fords"; cf. LXX, "to the other side of the sea."
21.a-a. The Tg has "I sent to you all my servants the prophets when you were dwelling in safety."
21.b. LXX reads "transgression."
21.c. The Tg has "I will not receive instruction."
21.d. Lacking in LXX.
22.a-a. Tg has "will be scattered to every wind."
22.b. LXX reads "all your lovers."
23.a-a. The K is identified by GKC § 90.3a as an old case ending. An identical form occurs at 10:17. The Q gives the normal form יֹשֶׁבְתְּ.
23.b. The Tg has "in the house of the sanctuary."
23.c-c. See note 23.a. This form has the same old case ending for the K. The Q is מְקֻנַנְתְּ.
23.d-d. The Tg has "among kings, bringing up her children."
23.e. The MT נֵחַנְתְּ is apparently from the root חנן, "be pitied." LXX, Syr, and Vg all read as though the word were from אנח "groan, sigh," with the MT form being a result of metathesis. However, Dahood has argued for a Heb. root חנן, "groan," on the basis of Ug. parallels. In one Ug. passage, the word is parallel to a heifer lowing for her calf. This translation picks up the Ug. parallel and suggests "bellow" as appropriate.

Form/Structure/Setting

The two imperatives at the beginning of v 20 are both feminine singular. The feminine singular forms separate this unit from both the preceding and the next one. The one addressed is a personified city or locale. The phrase יֹשַׁבְתְּ בַּלְּבָנוֹן, "O one enthroned in the Lebanon," would seem to indicate one of the city-states such as Tyre, Sidon, or Byblos. Thus some commentaries take the form to be an Oracle against Foreign Nations (Carroll).

However, because similar imagery is used in v 6–7 in reference to the house of the king of Judah, and because all the other oracles within this section of chaps. 21–24 are directed against Judah, Jerusalem, and her leaders, it seems better to understand this oracle as referring to Jerusalem personified, as was the situation in 21:13–14. A strong link with 21:13–14 is found in the vocative (יֹ)שַׁבְתְּ, "O one enthroned" (21:13; 22:23). The descriptive location following "enthroned one" shows contrastive parallelism; in 21:13 it is the one enthroned above the valley, in 22:23 it is the one enthroned in the Lebanon (mountains). Likewise connecting the two units is the idea of Yahweh being against the city. In 21:13 it was a direct discourse statement הנני אליך, "Behold I am against you." In this passage, the words are a report דברתי אליך, "I spoke against you . . ." (22:21). A final connection, though not as definite, is the mention of forest in 21:14 and the references to Lebanon and cedars in this passage.

The specific references to Lebanon and cedars provides links with 22:6–7, although there the oracle is decreed against the house of the king rather than the city. However, 22:6 does make a reference to an uninhabited city, perhaps a further link to this pericope.

The reference to the wind shepherding the shepherds (v 22) provides a link with 23:1–4, a passage concerned with the shepherds (leaders) who have not properly discharged their responsibility.

Other ties with the immediate context are evident as v 20 begins with a lament for the dead and vv 18–19 have just spoken of the death Jehoiakim will face. Also v 22 speaks of the captivity as does v 12 and earlier v 10 (though the word "captivity" doesn't occur in v 10).

This pericope is poetic, like the previous one. The bicola which make up the unit have mixed meter, though 3+3 is most common.

The form of the pericope is a judgment oracle. It begins with the introduction that sounds much like a typical lament, with the imperatives צעקי, "cry out," and תני קולך, "give your voice" (v 20). The introduction moves quickly to the accusation of the judgment oracle (v 21). Verse 22 then gives the announcement of judgment but lacks the usual transition word and messenger formula. Verse 23 forms a conclusion, in part paralleling the introduction, but also carrying forth the judgment by speaking of the pain the city will suffer from its judgment.

The unit itself has a couple of features serving as inclusios. "Lebanon," from the first line of v 20, is repeated in v 23. Also words expressing outcries appear in vv 20 and 23 to form a kind of inclusio. In v 20 the cries come from lament language; in v 23 the cries come from the pain of childbirth. It is ironic that the unit begins with a death image and ends with a birth image, especially since the judgment concerns the destruction of the city.

The pericope may be outlined as follows:

Lament over loss (v 20)
Accusation, cause for loss (v 21)
Sentence, describing loss (v 22)
Results: anguish like childbirth (v 23)

Comments

20 The identity of the feminine referent of the imperatives of this verse has been discussed above. Although it may be that the original referent was other than Jerusalem, in its present context Jerusalem must clearly be the referent.

The mention of the three places, Lebanon, Bashan, and Abarim, should be compared with the mention of Gilead and Lebanon in v 6. The three are all noted as mountainous regions, Lebanon to the north, Bashan to the northeast, and Abarim to the southeast.

The call to go up these mountains (assuming the imperative עֲלִי carries forward to each of the three place names) may be compared to the call in Isa 40:9 to climb a high mountain in order to proclaim good news. Here the news is that of tragedy and mourning.

The reason for all this mourning is given in the last line of v 20: all the city's lovers have been broken. Who are the lovers? In the covenant terminology, Israel-Judah was the wife of Yahweh; clearly Yahweh should have been her only lover. Yet Hosea and Jeremiah both use the marriage metaphor often to depict Israel's/Judah's unfaithfulness. Israel/Judah forsakes Yahweh and runs after other gods, especially the Baalim. In a couple of passages, the lovers are the foreign nations with whom Israel-Judah allies herself. But now these lovers have been destroyed. If the reference is to foreign nations, the word speaks their destruction; if the reference is to other deities, then these deities (images, and probably also sanctuaries) have been destroyed.

21 The preposition אֶל can be understood either as Yahweh speaking "to" or "against" the city. Because of the clear judgmental tone to the oracle, and the parallel in 21:13, אֶל is understood as "against" here.

The word שַׁלְוָה is understood variously. Some take it to mean "prosperity" (KJV, RSV); others take it to mean "complacency" (Holladay). BDB gives the primary meaning as "quietness, ease" (1017), but also gives a meaning of "security." The latter meaning seems best to fit the context: Yahweh had warned Judah, even in her days of security, but she would not listen; now security is gone and judgment is upon her.

The reference to "youth" calls to mind the passage in 2:2ff., which speaks of the "covenant-love" (חֶסֶד) of Israel's youth, and the contrast in chap. 3, where from their youth they have sinned against Yahweh (3:24–25). The present passage picks up the words of 3:24–25, words of confession, and turns them into an accusation here. This city has not listened, has not confessed, has not changed its behavior.

22 Shepherds are supposed actively to shepherd the flock. In this judgment a reversal takes place and the shepherds are themselves shepherded by the wind. There is the image of reversal here, and more, for the shepherds are usually identified with the leaders (see 23:1–4). The leaders are going to be led. Even more than that, these shepherds, the strong ones protecting the flock, are shepherded by the wind; they are so weak that they are blown to and fro by the wind.

There are at least two word plays in this verse. The word for "shepherd," both the noun and verb, is the Hebrew root רָעָה. That forms a word play in terms of assonance with רוּחַ, "wind." A second word play is evident in the last line of the verse where רָעָה, "evil" (root רעע), occurs. It is also possible that additional word plays are present. LXX translates the last phrase as "your lovers" and may have understood רֵעַ (from the root רעה, II), "fellow, companion, lover." While this translation does not adopt the reading of the LXX, that meaning may have been a deliberate double entendre, especially since "lovers" (root אהב) occurs in the second line of the verse.

23 The double description "enthroned in the Lebanon" and "nested in the cedars" certainly presents an image of a city in the mountain heights. As such, the image would complement the word in v 21 about the security of the city. The image might also speak of the timber from Lebanon's cedars that was used in building projects in Jerusalem. But the last two lines of the verse give a quite different image. This city, so lofty and secure, will be brought low by Yahweh's judgment. She will be in anguish like a woman giving birth—only instead of birth pangs, the irony is that the judgment more accurately describes her death throes.

This oracle began with a lament; it ends with birth pangs. But in another reversal, new life is not promised from the birth pangs. Only the pain and anguish are described. The lament implies that the pain is more nearly the last gasps before death.

Explanation

Jerusalem, the royal city, the capital, symbol of the nation, is accused and judged. In the opening verse the city is depicted as lamenting over the loss of her lovers. Then she is judged and sentenced. In the closing verse she is suffering desperate pain, described as birth pangs, but more likely intending death throes.

I. Oracle against Coniah (22:24–27)

Bibliography

Hermisson, H.-J. "Jeremias Wort über Jojachin." In *Werden und Wirken des Alten Testaments.* Ed. R. Albertz et al. Göttingen: Vandenhoeck & Ruprecht, 1980, 252–70. **Honeyman, A. M.** "The Evidence for Regnal Names among the Hebrews." *JBL* 67 (1948) 13–25. **Malamat, A.** "Twilight of Judah." *Congress Volume, Edinburgh 1974.* VTSup 28. Leiden: Brill, 1975, 123–45.

Translation

[24] *"As I myself live," an oracle of the LORD, "even though Coniah, the son of Jehoiakim, the king of Judah, was a signet ring on my right hand, surely from there*[a] *I have torn you away.*[a] [25] *Furthermore, I have given you into the hand of the ones seeking your life,* [a] *and into the hand of*[a] *ones whom you yourself feared from their presence,* [b] *even into the hand of Nebuchadrezzar, the king of Babylon,*[b] *and into the hand of the Chaldeans.* [26] *I have hurled you and your mother who gave you birth to another*[a] *land,*[b] *where you were not born, and there you will die.* [27] *But unto the land which they are* [a] *desiring with their beings*[a] *to return* [b] *there, surely there*[b] *they will never return."*

Notes

24.a-a. Vg: "I will tear him off"; Tg: "I would exile you."
25.a-a. Not in LXX.
25.b-b. Not in LXX.
26.a. Not in LXX.
26.b. *BHS* suggests omitting the article on הארץ.
27.a-a. MT has מנשאים את־נפשם, lit., "lifting up their beings." Tg has "deceiving themselves."

27.b-b. MT has שָׁם שָׁמָּה. This translation follows MT and translates the second occurrence as an emphatic. *BHS* suggests omitting the first word (which has the *athnaḥ*) and moving the *athnaḥ* to the second.

Form/Structure/Setting

This prose oracle gives the judgment against Coniah. It is virtually an oath or curse. The opening words "As I live" set the tone of the oath. The implication is that Coniah has broken covenant with Yahweh, therefore Yahweh is now speaking the oath or curse for disobedience against him. Holladay calls this a judgment-speech without a reason, following Westermann's categories. While that is possible, it seems better to understand this particular judgment oracle as an oath or curse form.

The second-person format sets this oracle off from the one which follows, both of which are directed against Coniah. The oath form appeared above in v 6. Here the oath is fuller, including the phrase "As I live" and the messenger formula "an oracle of The LORD."

As translated here, this oracle speaks primarily of accomplished deeds. The perspective seems to be set by v 27. That verse speaks of Judah as the land to which Coniah and his mother desire to return. The implication is that they are already in exile, seeking to return to their homeland. Therefore, the pericope is translated in a past tense, except for the references to the king's death. Such a translation enhances the oath form: Yahweh's curse against Coniah has already come to pass. Yet those who hope the results are only temporary, and desire a quick return for the exiles, are going to be disappointed. Coniah and his family will die in exile.

There are links between this passage and others. The reference to giving Coniah into the hand of the ones seeking his life, into the hand of the ones he fears, into the hand of Nebuchadrezzar, king of Babylon, into the hand of the Chaldeans (v 25) is very similar to 21:7. Also the mention of being sent to a land where he was not born (v 26) parallels the mention of the land of one's birth in 22:10, as does the reference to dying in a foreign land (v 26; cf. 22:10, 12). Following the same image is the parallel reference to never seeing or returning to the land of one's birth again (v 27; cf. 22:10, 12).

The connections with the pericope which follows are numerous. Indeed, the two oracles seem quite similar; perhaps the next one may be considered as a poetic oracle paralleling this prose one. In addition to the name Coniah in both (vv 24, 28), there is the verb טול, "hurl," which only appears in Jeremiah in these two pericopes (v 26 and v 28) and in an oracle against the people (16:13). Both pericopes also refer to two lands, the land of Judah (vv 27 and 29) and the land of the exile (vv 26 and 28) using the word אֶרֶץ. Another link, this one somewhat contrastive, is the mention in each pericope of two generations: in this pericope it is Coniah and his mother who are hurled into captivity (v 26); in the next pericope it is Coniah and his descendants (seed) who are hurled into exile (v 28).

The setting of the oracle is sometime shortly after Jehoiachin-Coniah has been taken into exile in 597 B.C. Perhaps this oracle was spoken during those optimistic days after Zedekiah came to the throne, when some thought the exile would be of short duration (see chaps. 27–28, Hananiah's words) and the exiles would return to Judah and to their former positions. Jeremiah's words consistently speak of the lengthy duration of the exile (in addition to the present passage, compare chaps. 27–29). That Jehoiachin had a long life in exile and was ultimately released from imprisonment is stated in 2 Kgs 25:27–30. The tone of that latter passage may suggest some (the Deuteronomists?) still considered Jehoiachin as the legitimate ruler of Judah.

The contents of the pericope are an oath describing judgment that has already befallen Coniah and a word about his death in exile.

Comment

24 Coniah is identified as the son of Jehoiakim. Clearly the reference is to Jehoiachin, Jehoiakim's son who succeeded him for only three months in 597 B.C. Jerusalem was under siege by Nebuchadrezzar at the time, and Jehoiachin was forced to surrender. He and his family were exiled to Babylon, and his uncle Zedekiah was placed on the throne by the Babylonians. According to Honeyman, Coniah is the given name, and Jehoiachin is the throne name of this individual. The two names have virtually the same meaning, with the name elements simply being reversed. The former means Yahweh is firm, enduring; the latter means Yahweh has established.

The crux for interpretation within this pericope concerns the dating of the oracle: was it delivered prior to Jehoiachin's exile or after it began? Most translations assume it was delivered before Jehoiachin was taken captive to Babylon. But I see this pericope as parallel to the oracle to Shallum-Jehoahaz in vv 11–12. The thrust of the oracle is not that Yahweh is about to remove Jehoiachin for some unspecified reason; instead the oracle reports that Yahweh has removed him. The major point of the oracle is the length of exile. Exile will not be short; things will not return to be the way they were. This king and his mother will live out their lives in exile and die in that foreign land of their captivity.

Following that understanding, there need be no debate as to the meaning of Jehoiachin being Yahweh's signet ring. Most English versions have "Even if (though) Coniah were a signet ring . . ." implying that he is *not* the signet ring. This causes some difficulty because the signet ring implies authority vested by Yahweh (Hag 2:23). Since Jehoiachin was king, though only for a short time, he was in the very position of authority the signet ring image implies. Surely the oracle doesn't imply that Jehoiachin was the wrong person to be king. The translation offered here removes all question concerning Jehoiachin as signet ring. It affirms that he was the signet, but that Yahweh tore him away (that suggests tearing away something very precious to Yahweh).

25 The redundancy within this verse, a fourfold description of the captivity, does not necessarily indicate glosses, but just a way of heightening the calamity of the situation by means of parallelism or repetition.

26 The word טול, "hurl," depicts a violent throwing, as in hurling a spear (1 Sam 18:11; 20:33), or Yahweh hurling the storm wind on the ship in Jonah (1:4). The exile was a violent experience, picking up and displacing persons to foreign lands.

This verse also brings together images of birth and death. Birth is pictured by reference to Jehoiachin's mother, and the repetition for emphasis "who gave you birth," as well as by the land of exile "another land, where you were not born." These three birth images are counterbalanced tersely with the words "there you will die." This word of judgment yet to be accomplished was even harsher than exile itself. To die and be buried in a foreign land was a terrible curse; a good death and proper burial to the Hebrews meant to be gathered to one's ancestors, i.e., to be buried where they were buried.

27 This verse repeats the judgment of v 26. The king and his mother will never return to their native land. Just as birth and death images are used effectively in this pericope, so also are land images used. Verse 26 emphasizes the foreignness of the land where the king has been exiled ("another land" and "where you were not born"). This verse speaks of the homeland, "the land which they are desiring with their beings to return there," and then tersely states "there they will never return." Again the severity of the judgment and the duration of the exile are emphasized.

Explanation

This pericope concerns Jehoiachin, the young son of Jehoiakim who succeeded his father while Jerusalem was under siege. Jehoiachin was soon captured and taken exile to Babylon. This oracle pictures the anguish Yahweh felt at the exile of the young king (the signet ring Yahweh himself tore away), even though it was necessary. At the same time, hopes of a quick return are dashed in this oracle. Jehoiachin will die and be buried in the land of his exile; he will never return to his homeland.

J. Another Oracle against Coniah (22:28–30)

Bibliography

Herrmann, J. "Jer 22, 29; 7, 4." *ZAW* 62 (1949–50) 321–22. **Tawil, H.** "Hebrew צלח/הצלח, Akkadian *eseru/susuru*: A Lexicographical Note." *JBL* 95 (1976) 405–13.

Translation

28	ᵃ"Was he a vessel ᵃ despised, shattered,ᵇ	(3+3+4)
	ᶜthis man ᶜ Coniah,	
	or a utensil no one desired?	
	Why were theyᵈ hurled,	(2+2)
	ᵉhe and his descendants,ᵉ	
	and thrownᶠ unto theᵍ land	(2+2)
	which theyʰ had not known?	
29	ᵃO land, land, land,ᵃ	(3+3)
	hear the word of the LORD.	
30	ᵃThus says the LORD,ᵃ	(3+4+3)
	'Write this man, "Childless."ᵇ	

> ^c*No man will succeed in his days.*^c
> *Indeed, no one will succeed,*   (3+4+3)
> *none sitting upon the throne of David*
> *nor* ^d *ruling again in Judah.'"*

Notes

28.a-a. Lacking in LXX.

28.b. Lacking in LXX; *BHS* suggests the form is possibly corrupted from אֶין חֵפֶּץ in the next line. However, MT can be understood without emendation. "Vessel" could easily refer to a pottery vessel which is both despised and shattered. Hurling this vessel (next line) could well shatter it.

28.c-c. Lacking in LXX; *BHS* suggests deleting as a gloss from v 30.

28.d. LXX has a sg verb, as does Syr. *BHS* suggests reading a sg. This translation follows MT.

28.e-e. Lacking in LXX; *BHS* suggests deleting.

28.f. LXX has a sg, "he was thrown," as does Syr.

28.g. *BHS* suggests deleting the definite article; cf. the LXX.

28.h. LXX has a sg verb, as does Syr.

29.a-a. Tg has "From his land I will exile him to another land. O land of Israel, listen to. . . ."

30.a-a. Lacking in LXX; *BHS* suggests deleting the phrase.

30.b. MT lit. means "stripped," but is taken to mean "stripped of children, childless" (*BHS*, 792). LXX has "proclaimed by a herald," i.e., banished.

30.c-c. Lacking in LXX; *BHS* suggests deleting.

30.d. LXX omits the conj.

Form/Structure/Setting

This poetic oracle of judgment is spoken against Coniah just as the previous prose one was. As noted there, many similarities serve to link the two oracles. They are probably juxtaposed to provide a deliberate prose-poetic double oracle against Jehoiachin. However, the two do have a somewhat different emphasis. The previous oracle is more concerned with the extent of the exile; this oracle is concerned with Jehoiachin's descendants: no descendant of his will occupy the throne of David.

The pericope has three tricola and three bicola. There is one small chiastic pattern in the first half of v 28:

A Vessel despised, shattered
  B this man Coniah
A' utensil no one desires

Verse 28 asks two rhetorical questions introduced by הַ and אִם. Usually such a pattern suggests alternatives (BDB, 50, 2a[b]). The implication in this verse is that both expect a negative answer. Then the verse asks another question, introduced by מַדּוּעַ. The latter question is never answered.

Verse 29 addresses the personified land, which has been one focal point of both this and the previous oracle. V 30 then gives the judgment speech of Yahweh, announcing that Jehoiachin would have no descendant to rule over Judah.

The poem has most of the elements of a judgment oracle and thus fits that form. It lacks the accusation, replacing it with the questions as an introduction to the sentence. The messenger formula introduces the sentence itself. The judgment sentence is clear and severe: Coniah-Jehoiachin will have no heir to rule over Judah.

The questions in v 28 may reflect questions raised by the people in response to Jehoiachin's exile. Why was Jehoiachin taken away when it was his father who rebelled against the Babylonians? The questions are not answered nor even addressed. But understanding the exile of Jehoiachin as an accomplished event (as in the previous pericope) may help us interpret. The first two questions imply a negative response. No, Coniah was not despised above other rulers; no, he was not a utensil that no one desired (i.e., yes, some did desire him). Nevertheless, judgment has become inevitable. Even though some cared for this man, even though he was only a youth when captured, judgment has come and will continue to come on him. He will not return to his homeland, nor will he have descendants to occupy the throne.

The setting for this oracle is probably just after the exile of Jehoiachin, the same time as the previous oracle. The strong message of judgment is intended to quash the hopes for a quick return from exile and a return to the prior status quo.

Comment

28 The image of this verse is that of a useless, perhaps cracked, pottery vessel that is flung away, as one might throw trash on the garbage dump. The question is put: Is Coniah such a despised, undesirable utensil? The implied answer is: No, he is not. Then the next question follows: Why then was he hurled into exile? No answer to that question is forthcoming.

Notice that in this verse it is Jehoiachin and his descendants that are exiled. Compare this with the previous pericope where it is Jehoiachin and his mother who are exiled. The implication is that Jehoiachin and all his immediate family are exiled.

Who poses these questions? Is it the supporters of Jehoiachin remaining in the land? Or is it Jeremiah raising the question? Even this remains ambiguous. Nevertheless, the next two verses, especially v 30, do expand the judgment against Jehoiachin.

29 The threefold repetition of אֶרֶץ need not be considered an addition. Compare other threefold phrases: Jeremiah's "Temple of Yahweh, Temple of Yahweh, Temple of Yahweh" in 7:4; Isaiah's "Holy, Holy, Holy" in 6:3; and Ezekiel's "Ruin, Ruin, Ruin" in 21:32[27]. Repetitions are rather common in MT, but a threefold repetition is rare and probably intended as a striking emphasis.

Land is addressed with the threefold vocative and is the subject of the imperative that follows. Even the inverted word order adds further emphasis to the sentence.

30 The image in v 30 shifts to that of a scribe, whether a census taker (as Holladay suggests) or land register (as Carroll suggests) or a scribe tallying prisoners of war to be taken to Babylon. The official in charge says of Jehoiachin, "Write (register) this man, 'Stripped' (perhaps dishonored, disgraced) or 'Childless.'" A register of those taken captive would logically include the head of the family followed by a listing of dependents. It might also include comments such as disgraced, banished (as LXX implies), or stripped (of power). Such is to remain the condition of Jehoiachin. The fact that children are apparently included in v 28, and sons are listed in 1 Chr 3:17-18, should not diminish the thrust of the oracle. The sense of "childless" or "stripped" is that Jehoiachin will have no descendant ruling upon the throne of David.

The word צלח occurs twice in this verse. Often the word is translated with the sense of "prosper." However, here a better sense seems to be that of "succeed." No man will succeed during Jehoiachin's days; indeed none will succeed. The implication might be that of prosperity: that no man would prosper during his days. But the full intent of that phrase is shown in the two parallel lines, "none sitting on the throne of David, nor ruling again in Judah." Jehoiachin will have no descendant to advance or succeed to the throne.

Carroll has a lengthy suggestion that this pericope might have originally been used to justify Zedekiah's reign against those who supported the exiled king Jehoiachin. Then later it could have been used as an anti-Zerubbabel oracle in the post-exilic period. That certainly is possible, but is not its original function.

Explanation

The pericope describes Jehoiachin, asking if he is a broken, despised vessel, and implying that he is not. So Jehoiachin is a person of value. Then why was he so cruelly cast into exile? The question isn't answered.

The judgment is repeated. Jehoiachin will have no descendant to occupy the throne of David. The exile will be long and the occupation complete.

We still have the question concerning the severity of judgment on this youthful king who just ascended to the throne. Perhaps this poem knows of the fate of Zedekiah, whether only prophesied or actually accomplished. The historical description of the fall of Jerusalem in 586 B.C. includes the attempted flight of Zedekiah and his family, their capture, the slaughter of his sons before his eyes, and his own blinding and captivity (2 Kgs 25:1–7). If the poem knows of Zedekiah's fate, it is then placing the severity of judgment on the only royal figure remaining. The sins of Judah fall upon her chief royal representative, Jehoiachin. His suffering symbolizes the suffering of all the people. In one sense Zedekiah as last king suffered as a representative; but in another sense, Jehoiachin, because he survived Zedekiah and had surviving sons, was the representative sufferer. The pericope says that kingship was lost and would not be reestablished by a descendant of Jehoiachin. Judah will suffer the full consequences of her sins in the full loss of independence and monarchy. The everlasting covenant with David has been broken, not by Yahweh but by the kings and the people themselves. The judgment is most severe, depicted as Yahweh tearing off his signet ring from his right hand (v 24 in previous pericope).

K. Judgment on Present and Future Shepherds and a Blessing (23:1–4)

Bibliography

Holladay, W. L. "The Recovery of Poetic Passages of Jeremiah." *JBL* 85 (1966) 401–35. **Klein, R. W.** "Jeremiah 23:1–8." *Int* 34 (1980) 167–72.

Translation

[1] *"Woe shepherds destroying and scattering the flock of my* [a] *pasture,"* [b] *an oracle of the LORD.* [b] [2] *Therefore thus says the LORD, the God of Israel against the shepherds, the ones shepherding my people, "You yourselves have scattered my flock and thrust them out and you have not taken care of them. Behold, I am about to take care of you with the evil of your deeds,"* [a] *an oracle of the LORD.* [a] [3a] *"Furthermore, I myself will gather together the remnant of my flock from all the lands* [b] *where I thrust them. Then I will cause them to return unto their abode/meadow/habitation, and they will be fruitful and multiply.* [4] *Further, I will raise up over them shepherds, and they will shepherd them. They will no longer fear, nor be dismayed,* [a] *nor be visited/lacking,"* [a] *an oracle of the LORD.*

Notes

1.a. LXX has "their pasture." Cf. 10:21 ("their [the shepherds'] flock") and 13:17 ("the LORD's flock"); both readings are possible, but there is no reason to emend the MT.
1.b-b. Lacking in LXX.
2.a-a. Lacking in LXX.
3.a. *BHS* suggests the entire verse may be a gloss; see Rudolph (125).
3.b. LXX has sg "from every land," or better, "from all the earth" (so Rudolph, 124).
4.a-a. Not in LXX. Giesebrecht (127), following Grätz, reads פחד, "nor be afraid," instead of פקד, "nor be visited/lacking."

Form/Structure/Setting

There are questions concerning both the extent and form of this unit. Keil (347), Rudolph (125), Nötscher (174), and Thompson (485–86) suggest the unit extends through v 8. Cornill (262) suggests the unit includes only vv 1–6. Bright (145), Carroll (443), and Holladay (613) argue that the unit should include only vv 1–4, the position held by this translation.

The further question concerns whether the unit is poetry or prose. Holladay (*JBL* 85 [1966] 420–24) originally took the passage to be poetic, followed by Thompson (485–86); Holladay has since changed his position and now holds that the passage is "a carefully crafted sequence of structured prose" (613). Most other commentators have argued that the passage was prose, though perhaps with some poetic elements. It is understood here as prose.

The precise form of the pericope is difficult to decide. It begins with the word "Woe" and could be a woe speech; however, that form only extends through v 1. V 2 has several elements of a judgment speech: the transition word לכן, "therefore," the messenger formula (here in an amplified form, "thus says the LORD, the God of Israel"), the ones accused (shepherds shepherding my people), the accusation ("You yourselves have scattered my flock . . ."), and a first-person speech by God announcing judgment ("Behold I am about to take care of you . . ."). One might naturally expect the judgment to continue in the following verses. However, vv 3 and 4 move beyond the judgment oracle to an announcement of deliverance. After an additional messenger formula (end of v 2), the tone shifts to what Yahweh is going to do for the remnant of his people. The tone is entirely positive. The flock-shepherd image is carried forward first by depicting how Yahweh will provide for the flock, then by the word that Yahweh will raise up good shepherds who will care for the flock. The typical formula "do not fear" becomes a part of the narrative report: "They will no longer fear, nor be dismayed . . ." (v 4).

The unit as a whole has a chiastic structure as follows:

A   Woe to shepherds destroying the flock (v 1)
  B   You yourselves scattered, thrust out, have not taken care of my flock (v 2)
    C   Behold I take care of you (v 3a)
  B'   I myself will gather, bring back my flock (v 3b)
A'   I will raise up shepherds who will shepherd (v 4)

The whole pericope shows the distinction between what the evil shepherds have done and what Yahweh will do.

The unit does have some ties with the previous chapter, especially to 22:22, with its reference to shepherds. Chap. 22 dealt primarily with Judah's kings, some unnamed, others specified, and secondarily with Jerusalem and the people of Judah. One would assume that the shepherd reference in 22:22 spoke of Judah's leaders, especially her kings. The same certainly is true for the shepherd imagery here. Beyond this specific reference, the sheep-shepherd image is common in the OT in such passages as Ezek 34; Ps 23; Pss 95:7; 100:3; Isa 40:10–11, etc.

A further link with the previous chapter is the first word of v 1, הוי, "Woe." This same word introduced the oracle of 22:13–19 and occurred twice in v 19 as an inclusio. Interestingly, there are several other stylistic features the two oracles have in common: (i) "Woe" followed by a participle describing the subject (22:13; 23:1); (ii) transition to judgment statement indicated by לכן, "therefore" (22:18; 23:2); (iii) judgment itself introduced by messenger formula כה אמר יהוה, "Thus says the LORD" (22:18; 23:2).

There is a triple word play with the root פקד in this section. The shepherds "have not taken care of" (qal stem, פקד) the flock, so Yahweh will "take care of" (qal stem, פקד) the shepherds (both in v 2)! Then Yahweh will raise up good shepherds so that none of the flock will be visited/lacking (niphal stem, פקד). The last occurrence could imply that with good leaders Yahweh will no longer visit or take care of (in the negative sense!) the sheep or shepherds. The meaning might just as well be that with good shepherds not any of the sheep will be lacking or missing. This type of ambiguous word play is quite common in Jeremiah.

Comment

1   The responsibility of the shepherds was to protect the flock. It was the wild animals who would destroy or scatter the flock. But here the shepherds are accused of being like the wild animals and destroying what they were to protect. Although the term "shepherd" might refer to any of Judah's leaders, the context seems to refer specifically to the kings—especially in light of the next pericope.

Note especially that the flock is here designated "the 'flock of my (Yahweh's) pasture," a reference found several times in the Psalms (74:1; 79:13; 95:7; 100:3).

2   The "woe" serves as a kind of accusation. It is followed by the typical transition to an announcement of judgment found in the judgment speech against individuals. (By form this is unexpected, because the woe was addressed to a group, "the ones shepherding.") There is further confusion with the typical judgment speech form; the judgment is not announced immediately. Instead, the accusation is repeated and expanded, using a typical Jeremianic word play that involves a kind of reversal. The shepherds have not "visited/taken care of " the flock in a positive sense; therefore, in judgment Yahweh will "visit/take care of " the shepherds in a very negative sense. One interpretation is that Yahweh will visit upon them the evil of their deeds: he will turn their own deeds back upon them. Alternatively, Yahweh may visit against them/take care of them because of their evil deeds.

Verse 2 also has the first half of a contrastive pair, completed in v 3. The contrast is made between the shepherds, addressed in a second person masculine plural emphatic form, "You yourselves/you for your part" and Yahweh speaking in a first common singular emphatic form, "I myself/I for my part." For a similar contrastive pattern see 17:15–16.

3   The judgment oracle ends abruptly with the messenger formula at the end of v 2. Verse 3 begins a salvation oracle. The conjunction *waw* serves as the connective between the two. It has been translated here as "furthermore"; it seems not to be completely adversative, "but," nor even the temporal "then." The conjunction has elements of both a temporal quality, marking a shift between what the shepherds *had been doing* and what Yahweh *would do* (past-present and future), and a contrast between the shepherds and Yahweh. "Furthermore" seems the best word to capture both elements.

Another shift occurs in this verse. Whereas in v 2 Yahweh had accused the shepherds of thrusting out the flock, here Yahweh claims to have thrust the flock to diverse lands. However, the two are not necessarily contradictory. Yahweh exiled the people because of their sins and the sins of their leaders. The prophet could express that truth either in terms of Yahweh as the active one exiling the people, or by saying that their sins caused their exile. The real contrast expressed in the verse is twofold. First there is the contrast between the shepherds and Yahweh. Then there is the contrast expressed in the verbs: the shepherds' actions resulted in the flock being thrust out, but Yahweh's actions are to gather together the ones scattered. His further action is expressed by the word phrase "I will cause them to return." The contrastive parallelism is similar to that found in poetry:

    A   You (shepherds) scattered my flock
        B   and thrust out them
            C   and did not take care of them
            C'   I (Yahweh) will take care of you
    A'   I will gather together the remnant of my flock
        B'   I will cause them to return.

When they return, it will be to their נוה, "dwelling place, habitation, abode." The common dwelling place of sheep is the sheepfold, so many English versions translate as "fold(s)" (KJV, RSV, NRSV).

The last two words of v 3, ופרו ורבו, "and they will be fruitful and multiply," goes back to Genesis and creation terminology. These very words are a part of the blessing/command to the sea creatures and birds (Gen 1:22), but also, more to the point, the blessing/command to humankind (Gen 1:28). After the flood, the blessing/command was reaffirmed (Gen 9:1). In a sense, this return will mark the same kind of new beginning as did creation and as did the post-flood era. Interestingly Exodus opens with the same description of the Hebrews: they are fruitful and swarm/teem and multiply, so that the land is full of them (Exod 1:7). Exodus and creation terminology intermingle, and this new exodus/return will also use both types of language.

4 In place of the shepherds who have scattered and thrust out Yahweh's flock, Yahweh will raise up shepherds who will shepherd them (רעים ורעום). In this picture, Yahweh first serves as shepherd (v 3) by gathering and returning the flock; then he raises up other shepherds (leaders, kings) over the flock who will properly care for them.

Like many of the oracles of salvation, this pericope includes a statement about not fearing. Unlike the usual imperative/jussive form of the statement, "Do not fear," introducing the oracle of salvation/deliverance, the statement is here set as a narrative statement. Because of the changed situation, because Yahweh will already have brought about deliverance, they will not fear, not be dismayed, nor be visited/lacking. The combination "not fearing" and "not being dismayed" occurs at least fifteen times in the OT; of those, three are in Jeremiah. Six of the fifteen give as the reason not to fear that Yahweh is with the ones addressed (עם four times, את twice). In most of the other occurrences, the presence of Yahweh is assumed if not stated, as is the case here. The phrase is a typical promise of deliverance based on Yahweh's presence.

The additional phrase ולא יפקדו, "and not be visited/lacking," may be interpreted in a couple of ways. פקד may be understood negatively as in its second occurrence in v 2: Yahweh will "visit" in judgment, he will "take care of" the shepherds. Such a negative sense is then itself negated by this phrase: Yahweh will *not* (לא) visit in judgment. Alternatively, this niphal form of פקד may have the sense of "lacking, missing." In that case, the final phrase would have the meaning that none of the flock would be missing; when Yahweh gathers the flock and returns them to their fold and raises new shepherds, they will have nothing to fear, and Yahweh will not miss a single one of the flock.

Explanation

Although the pericope begins as a woe speech and then becomes a judgment oracle against the shepherds/leaders, it then shifts in tone and content and becomes a deliverance oracle for the people. Judgment is coming, and/or has already come on the flock as well as the shepherds. But there is hope for the future. Yahweh is about to deal with his shepherds. After that he will gather and bring back his flock to their home. Under the guidance of new shepherds, the flock will no longer have anything to fear; not even one of the flock will be missing.

L. A Future King (23:5–6)

Bibliography

Baldwin, J. G. "*Semah* as a Technical Term in the Prophets." *VT* 16 (1964) 93–97. **Gibson, J. C. L.** *Textbook of Syrian Semitic Inscriptions: Volume III Phoenician Inscriptions.* Oxford: Clarendon Press, 1982. 134–41. **Honeyman, A. M.** "Observations on a Phoenician Inscription of Ptolemaic Date." *JEA* 26 (1940) 57–67. **Lipinski, E.** "Études sur des textes «messianiques» de l'Ancien Testament." *Sem* 20 (1970) 41–57. **Swetnam, J.** "Some Observations on the Background of צדיק in Jeremias 23, 5a." *Bib* 46 (1965) 29–40.

Translation

5	*"Behold days are about to come,"*	(3+2+2)
	[a] *an oracle of the LORD,*[a]	
	"when I will raise up for David	
	a rightful/righteous[b] *sprout;*[c]	
	then a king will rule and act prudently/have success	(3+2+2)
	and he will bring about justice	
	and righteousness in the land.	
6	*In his days Judah will be delivered/liberated*	(3+3)
	and Israel[a] *will dwell securely;*	
	and this is his name which [b]*he will call him*[b]	(2+2)
	'The LORD is [c]*our righteousness.'"*[c]	

Notes

5.a-a. The placement here indicates the phrase falls outside the metrical structure indicated; however, there is no MS or versional evidence to delete the phrase. MT is accepted.

5.b. Syr and Tg have "righteousness," thus Syr, "a rod/shining one of righteousness," and Tg, "an Anointed One/Messiah of righteousness."

5.c. See the Syr and Tg rendering of צמח in 5.b. LXX ἀνατολήν has both the meaning "growing" and "rising" (as of the sun).

6.a. LXX^S, "Jerusalem."

6.b-b. For the unusual MT form, a few MSS (de Rossi, III, 92; V, 66) have יקראו, "they will call." Syr, Tg, and Vg all have "they will call him."

6.c-c. LXX transliterates the name as Ἰωσεδὲκ and reduplicates the name Yahweh, "The Lord will call his name Iōsedek [i.e., Yah is righteous]." Tg has the name as "Righteous deeds shall be done for us before the Lord in his days." σ´ and Vg have "our righteous one."

Form/Structure/Setting

The passage is poetic and has two tricola followed by two bicola. The passage is an oracle of deliverance like the last two verses of the previous pericope. In addition to the deliverance of the people, there is also the announcement of a royal figure whom Yahweh will raise up, comparable to the shepherds of the previous pericope. There is a prose parallel to this pericope in 33:14–16.

The major contrast between this passage and the previous pericope is in the emphasis. This pericope emphasizes the royal figure; the previous one emphasized the people/flock being delivered. The passage is similar to Isa 11:1–9: both speak of a growth from the family of David (Isa 11:1; Jer 23:5); both speak of Yahweh's hand upon the ruler (Isa 11:2; Jer 23:5); both speak of his wise and righteous and just rule (Isa 11:2–5; Jer 23:5); both speak of the deliverance/return of the people (Isa 11:11; Jer 23:6); both speak of the security of the people during his rule (Isa 11:6–9; Jer 23:6). One additional feature of this pericope is the naming of this king, which is similar to the naming in Isa 9:5.

The pericope can be outlined in a chiastic pattern as follows:

A   Yahweh will raise up a legitimate/righteous ruler (v 5a–c)
   B   This king will rule prudently/have success (v 5d)
      C   He will bring justice and righteousness (v 5e–f)
   B'   In his days Judah will be delivered and be secure (v 6a–b)
A'   Yahweh will name him "Yahweh our righteousness" (v 6c–d)

Several features of the pericope stand out in this outline. The center of the pericope deals with the king's rule of justice and righteousness. And the root צדק, "righteous," appears as an inclusio in 5c and in 6d as well as in the center 5f. Yahweh serves as the subject of A/A', while the king is the subject of B/B' and C.

The clear interest in צדק, "righteous(ness)," and the word play in naming the king both point to a comparison with Zedekiah. This pericope apparently is intended to give a reversal of Zedekiah's reign and fate. Whereas Zedekiah had sought some miraculous intervention from Yahweh but was told only defeat and death would follow (21:1–10; cf. chap. 34), this new king will have success and will see the deliverance of the people from their captivity. The name of this new king reverses the elements of Zedekiah's name (צדקיהו, "Zedekiah"; יהוה צדקנו, "Yahweh is our righteousness"), indicative perhaps that all the aspects of Zedekiah are here reversed. The implication is that even the righteousness of this new king contrasts with Zedekiah; his name said "Yahweh is righteousness/my righteousness," but the king himself was anything but righteous.

The date and setting of this pericope have been much debated. Duhm, Volz, Erbt, Skinner (*Prophecy and Religion*), Nicholson, and Carroll (though he also offers the alternative that the oracle might refer to Zedekiah) feel the passage is late. Keil gives the passage a distinctly messianic interpretation, saying that this "branch" could not even refer to Zerubbabel (who is also called a branch , Zech 3 : 8 , 6 : 12), but only to *the* Messiah as the Targum interprets. Cornill, Giesebrecht, Peake, Rudolph, Hyatt, Bright, and Holladay all affirm the passage as Jeremianic.

A further question concerns the referent of this particular king. Does the oracle speak of Zedekiah as the rightful/legitimate ruler and, therefore, come from early in his reign? If so, this oracle might serve to legitimate a pro-Babylonian ruler instead of a deposed and captive Jehoiachin (Swetnam, *Bib* 46 [1965] 29–40). Lipiński (*Sem* 20 [1970] 41–57) has even argued that the pericope was read/delivered as an official proclamation rite for the new name of the new king, Zedekiah, in 597 B.C. And Bright prefers a date early in Zedekiah's reign, if not at his coronation. However, Holladay prefers a date at the end of Zedekiah's reign, just before Jerusalem fell. I tend to agree with the dating proposed by Holladay, or even a date after the fall of Jerusalem. The word of hope and positive view of kingship are clearly a contrast to the rule of Judah's last kings. The phrase "Behold days are coming" probably is intended to contrast with present days and may indicate the fall has already occurred. But I would take the words to be Jeremianic and not later exilic or post-exilic.

Comment

5   Several studies have been made on the phrase צמח צדיק. A Phoenician inscription of the third century B.C. from Cyprus contains the same phrase (Gibson, *Textbook*, 134–41), and there the context indicates "rightful scion" (Swetnam, *Bib* 46 [1965] 29–40). Such a double meaning of words from the same root (צדק="rightful" here and "righteousness" at the end of this verse and in the next verse) would be quite typical of Jeremiah. Nevertheless, the meaning "righteous" is just as plausible, and Jeremiah just as frequently uses repetitions of the same root with the same meaning, to build toward a climax. Both meanings may have been in Jeremiah's mind as a deliberate ambiguity.

The word השׂכיל likewise has a possible double meaning. It can refer to success; thus this king would be contrasted with the shepherds/kings who suffered defeat and failure. Alternatively, the word can speak of prudence as a positive aspect of this king's rule in contrast to former kings. The positive characterization of the next two lines (he will bring justice and righteousness) would supplement either interpretation.

ארץ, "land," has major significance in regards to the return. It is another of those refrains from earliest theologies. The promise of the land is repeated throughout the narratives of the Ancestors/Patriarchs in Genesis. It is the goal of the Exodus, finally achieved in Joshua-Judges. One of the great judgments of the prophets was the loss of land. Here Jeremiah's promise of the future for this king includes a specific mention of the land.

6   Judah is promised liberation or deliverance, though it is not stated whether this king would bring about the liberation or Yahweh. In the parallel line Israel is said to dwell securely. Probably Israel and Judah are being used as synonyms; the liberation would mean that the people could then dwell securely.

The word יקראו is somewhat ambiguous. Is it an impersonal subject "One will call him"? More likely Yahweh is the implied subject as the LXX understands, "Yahweh will call him. . . ." The formula here is that of naming or renaming one. Several kings are known to have taken/been given throne names at the time of their coronation. Mattaniah was the given name of Zedekiah (the throne name). Similarly Coniah was the given name of Jehoiachin and Shallum the given name of Jehoahaz. This king's given name is not mentioned, although some assume Zedekiah is intended. It seems more likely that, since the reference is future,

Zedekiah may serve as the foil, but some later king is intended. The play on Zedekiah's name has been discussed in the *Form/Structure/Setting* section above. The use of the full form "Yahweh" as a name element is striking because of its rarity (all other cases occur in place names).

Explanation

Yahweh is about to raise up a new king, either a *rightful* (=legitimate) descendant of David, or a *righteous* one. This king will bring the covenant conditions to the people: righteousness and justice. Liberation will come and the people will dwell securely in their own land. This king will be named "Yahweh is our righteousness."

M. The Return (23:7–8)

Bibliography

Greenberg, M. "Hebrew Oath Principle *Ḥay-Ḥē*." *JBL* 76 (1957) 34–39. **Weinfeld, M.** "Jeremiah and the Spiritual Metamorphosis of Israel." *ZAW* 88 (1976) 17–56.

Translation

> [7a] *"Therefore, behold days are about to come,"* an oracle of the LORD, *"when they will no longer say, 'As the LORD lives who brought up the children* [b] *of Israel from the land of Egypt!'* [8] *Instead, 'As the LORD lives who* [a]*brought up and who*[a] *brought back* [b]*the descendants*[c] *of the house* [d] *of Israel from a north land and from all the lands where*[e] *he thrust them.'*[e] [f]*Then they will dwell*[f] *in their land."*

Notes

7.a. In the LXX, vv 7 and 8 are found after 23:40.
7.b. LXX reads "house," reading בֵּית instead of בְּנֵי.
8.a-a. Lacking in the LXX.
8.b. LXX adds "all."
8.c. Lacking in Syr and some Tg editions.
8.d. Lacking in LXX; the Syr of Walton's Polyglot and one edition of the Tg has והשבתים "children."
8.e-e. MT has "I [i.e., Yahweh] thrust them." This translation follows LXX, "he thrust them," which also is the reading of the parallel passage in 16:15.
8.f-f. LXX has, "And he has restored them"; 16:15 has, והשבתים " Then I will bring them back."

Form/Structure/Setting

This short unit begins similarly to the previous one. The word "Therefore" serves to link the two units, though each was originally independent. The previous unit emphasized the future king; this one emphasizes the return from exile.

The unit is prose and, like the two previous ones, has a positive message of what will come after the judgment/exile. Perhaps the similar opening "Behold, days are about to come" serves as a catchword to bring both together here. Or perhaps their similar content, dealing with the kings and the people following judgment, is the reason for their juxtaposition.

In form, the oracle is another deliverance oracle, promising a return to their land. Within the oracle are embedded two examples of oath formulas, each introduced with the stock oath phrase חַי־יְהוָה, "As the LORD lives!" As discussed above (see under 22:5), the Hebrews often spoke their oaths upon Yahweh's life. In this oracle the prophet gives two extended oath formulas to show the changed situation. The oath one would use up to the time indicated in this oracle is "As the LORD lives who brought up the children of Israel from the land of Egypt." That oath touched on the great deliverance activity of Yahweh in the OT, the Exodus. But that oath will no longer be spoken; instead the new oath formula will be "As the LORD lives who brought up and brought back the descendants of the house of Israel from exile." The new oath formula will include Exodus, אֲשֶׁר הֶעֱלָה, "who brought up," but also includes a word about a new exodus, a return from exile, . . . וַאֲשֶׁר הֵבִיא, "and who brought back. . . ."

Beyond the immediate links with the previous two oracles, this pericope has closest ties with the parallel section in 16:14–16.

Weinfeld (ZAW [1976] 18) has shown that the phrase that introduces this pericope (as well as the previous one), הִנֵּה־יָמִים בָּאִים, is particularly Jeremianic: it occurs fifteen times in Jeremiah and only six times outside of Jeremiah (Samuel one time, Kings one time, Isaiah one time, Amos three times). He has further indicated that most of these occurrences introduce oracles concerning return from exile, rebuilding Jerusalem, the "Sprout" of David, or vengeance to be brought against Israel's enemies. Apparently the formula was a favorite of Jeremiah's for introducing positive words concerning future hope.

The pericope may be outlined as follows:

An oath no longer quoted: Yahweh brought up from Egypt (v 7)
A new oath: Yahweh brought up and brought back from exile (v 8a)
Again they dwell in their land (v 8b)

Comment

7–8 For specific comments on these verses, see the comments on 16:14–15. The major difference between the two passages is the very end. 16:15 ends with "Then I will cause them to return [root שׁוב] to their land which I had given to their ancestors"; here the root ישׁב occurs ("they will dwell") and the last phrase is missing.

Explanation

The words וְלֹא־יֹאמְרוּ עוֹד . . . כִּי אִם, "they will no longer say. . . . Instead," mark a change of practice based on changed circumstances. Jeremiah speaks of a new hope that will be as significant as the Exodus. Future Hebrews who lived after the return would put it alongside the Exodus as indicative of Yahweh's mightiest of acts.

Afterword for 21:11–23:8

The lengthy section 21:11 through 23:8 has dealt primarily with oracles against kings. The last three oracles, 23:1–8, exhibited a change of tone, moving in 23:1–4 from woe cry to judgment against an individual to oracle of deliverance. The last two oracles, 23:5–6, 7–8, were both oracles of deliverance. Their placement may serve as a concluding corrective to the judgment speeches, indicating that Jeremiah also had messages of hope. The hope, however, is realized only in a future time after the judgment spoken in the earlier oracles of this section.

XIII. Oracles concerning Prophets and Prophecy (23:9–24:10)

A. An Oracle concerning the Prophets (23:9–12)

Bibliography

DeVries, S. J. *Prophet against Prophet.* Grand Rapids, MI: Eerdmans, 1978. **Meyer, I.** *Jeremia und die falschen Propheten.* Freiburg: Universitätsverlag, 1977. **Overholt, T. W.** *The Threat of Falsehood.* SBT, 2nd ser. 16. Naperville, IL: Allenson, 1970.

Translation

9 ᵃ*To the prophets:* ᵃ
    Broken is my heart within me,   (3+2)
      shaking are all my bones;
    *I have become like a drunk*ᵇ *man,*   (3+3)
      like a male passed out/overcome from wine,
    from the presence of the LORD   (2+3)
      *and from the presence of*ᶜ*his holy words.*ᶜ

10   ᵃ*"Indeed,*ᵇ *the land is full of adulterers,*ᵃ   (4+4+3)
      ᶜ*indeed, from the presence of curse*ᵈ *the land dries up;*ᶜ
      pastures of (the) wilderness wither.
    ᵉ*Their course (of life) is evil,*   (3+2)
      *their strength is not right.*ᵉ

11   *Indeed, both prophet*ᵃ *and priest are profane,*ᵇ   (3+3)
      even in my house I have found their evil,"
                an oracle of the LORD.

12   *"Therefore, their way will be to them*   (4+3+2)
      like slipperiness in the darkness; ᵃ*they stumble*ᵃ
      and they fall in it.
    Indeed, I will bring against them evil,   (3+2)
      the year of their visitation,"
                an oracle of the LORD.

Notes

9.a-a. This phrase is a superscription to the unit that follows. See 21:11 for a similar form. LXX places vv 7 and 8 at the end of the chap. after v 40; this phrase can be taken either as the conclusion of v 6 (as does Göttingen LXX) or as the beginning of v 9 (Rahlfs). The Tg has "My heart is broken in my inward parts before the prophets of falsehood," bringing the superscription into the flow of the verse and interpreting the prophets as "false prophets."

9.b. LXX has "broken," perhaps understanding שָׁבוּר.

9.c-c. LXX has "the beauty of his glory," perhaps suggesting הדר כבודו.

10.a-a. Lacking in LXX.

10.b. *BHS* suggests probably inserting ו מרעים, thus reading, with כי indicating the beginning of Yahweh' s words, "his words, 'the land is full of evildoers and adulterers. . . . '"

10.c-c. *BHS* suggests the phrase is probably an addition.

10.d. A few MSS (de Rossi, V, 66), LXX, and Syr have אֵלֶּה, "these," instead of אָלָה, "curse." The Tg has "oaths of falsehood."

10.e-e. The Tg has "and because they increase in the desire of their souls, evil shall come upon them, and their mighty men shall not prosper."

11.a. The Tg has "scribe."

11.b. The Tg has "have stolen their ways."

12.a-a. MT is apparently from the root דחח; a few MSS and editions read ידחו, from the root דחה. Also quite similar is the root נדה, which has occurred three times in this chapter already. All three roots have the same general meaning of being cast or thrust down. KB gives a derivative of דחח as meaning "stumbling," the translation adopted here. The Tg also has "they shall stumble."

Form/Structure/Setting

A new section of materials is clearly indicated by the superscription, which stands apart from the poetic meter of the rest of the pericope. The superscription is similar to the one found at 21:11. That "To the prophets" is an appropriate superscription for the section is indicated by some twenty-three occurrences of the root נבא "to prophesy, a prophet," within vv 9–40. The only individual pericope lacking an occurrence of the root is vv 23–24.

Holladay (624) has noted that this collection of material (vv 9–40) may have originally been attached to the end of the "confessions." In that case, the material from 21:11–23:8 would have been inserted at a later time. He notes that the words לבי, "my heart," and עצמותי, "my bones," both appear in 20:9 near the beginning of the last confession and may serve as a connective to this section.

However, there are also links with the closer context as well. In v 12 the rare root דחח, "thrust out, stumble" occurs, which is both assonant with and nearly identical in form and meaning to נדה, "thrust out," which occurs three times previously in this chapter, in vv 2, 3, and 8. Also in v 10 the word נאות, "pasture," occurs; this word is from the root נוה and is nearly identical in form and meaning with the word נוהן, "their pasture," in v 3, which is also from that same root. Furthermore, the root פקד, here "visitation," in v 12 recalls the threefold occurrence of the same root in vv 1–4 above. Such use of assonance and similar or identical roots is quite common to Jeremiah and may indicate that this is the original location of this pericope.

The passage begins with words of Jeremiah, almost a lament, in v 9. This is followed by a judgment oracle in vv 10–12. In a real sense the last words of v 9, "from the presence of his holy words," serve to introduce the Yahweh speech of v 10. The first part of the judgment oracle is the accusation, vv 10–11. The last verse has immediately before it a messenger formula; the verse begins with the transition word לכן, "Therefore," followed by the announcement of judgment. The announcement of judgment and accusation both have first person elements indicating Yahweh himself is speaking directly, in addition to the double messenger formula, "an oracle of the LORD," at the end of vv 11 and 12.

Comment

9 The first phrase is taken as a superscription introducing the larger section of vv 9–40. The word (ים)נביא, "prophet(s)," or a verbal form of the root occurs twenty-three times in the section from v 9 to v 40. The superscription is set off from the poetic structure of the remainder of this pericope.

The meaning of bones "shaking," root רחף, is taken from KB. BDB suggests "grow soft," but since the word is a *hapax legomenon,* one cannot be absolutely certain of the meaning. KB does have the advantage of relating the qal and niphal stems to one root rather than two as does BDB. This is certainly the meaning understood by LXX and Vg.

The meaning of the previous phrase, "Broken is my heart," is both simpler and more complicated. The words are both known well enough, שבר means in the niphal stem "to be broken, crushed, shattered," and לב is "heart, mind." Most English commentaries make the point that the prophet here is not heartbroken so much as distressed in his mind. Bright offers "My reason is staggered," and Thompson, "My heart is deeply disturbed." It seems that this is precisely the mental/emotional trauma both the Hebrew and the English "heartbroken" denote. More than his reason is involved; his whole being has been shaken and shattered by his experience described here.

The second bicolon of the verse describes the prophet as one drunk. The meaning could refer to physical symptoms of an ecstatic state, matching the trembling of the first bicolon, or the meaning could be "overcome," related to the third bicolon, overcome from Yahweh's words just like a drunk one is overcome from wine. The best interpretation probably admits both meanings.

The verse as a whole describes the prophet's reaction to Yahweh's presence and words. The language is similar to several of the confessions of Jeremiah (15:16–18; 20:8–9).

10 This verse moves from the reaction of the prophet to the judgment speech Yahweh utters. The כי at the beginning may indicate the beginning of Yahweh's words, or may have the emphatic sense. The verse is difficult as it stands, and most modern commentators have emended the text. One common proposal, that of Duhm, accepted more or less by Giesebrecht, Cornill, Volz, Condamin, Bright, and Holladay, is to move the first line of the verse after the third line. Granted, that would improve the flow of thought from the first half of the verse to the second half. The emended verse would then read, picking up in v 9: "and from the presence of his holy words— / for from the presence of these the land is dried up / pastures of (the) wilderness wither." This understanding does require another emendation, reading MT אָלָה, "curse," as אֵלֶּה, "these." With the emendation, one finds a parallel in Amos 1:2.

However, the present text is understandable without resorting to such drastic emendation and rearranging. The first line gives an accusation, "the land is full of adulterers." The next two lines give the result of the sin "because of curse, the land/pastures dry up/wither." The verse then returns to the adulterers in the last two lines. A similar passage to the first three lines is found at 12:4.

The last two lines clearly refer back to the adulterers. Their course of life, their way, is evil; and their strength is not right—it too is evil. Who are the adulterers? Is the reference to those actually committing adultery, or is Jeremiah here using the metaphor of the worship of other gods as adultery, as he does in other passages? Either is possible, though I expect the metaphorical usage is utmost in the prophet's mind, especially since the next verse moves to the profane or godless ways of priest and prophet.

11 KB understands the word חנף to mean "inclined away from the right relation to God." (The word is assonant with נאף, "adulterers," of the previous verse.) Notice that priest and prophet are linked with the sinful actions of the people. The image from vv 10 and 11 are focusing increasingly on a point. The accusation starts very broadly: the land is full of adulterers. Then it narrows: prophet and priest are profane. Finally it focuses at a climax: even in my house I have found their evil. The first-person forms pointing to Yahweh only appear in the climactic accusation, and it is immediately followed by a messenger formula, reinforcing its importance.

12 Verse 12 moves to the announcement of judgment, though partial judgment has been indicated in v 10 as a result of the evil. Following the pattern of the accusation, the announcement of judgment begins in third person and switches to first person only at the climax.

The image in the tricolon comprising the first three lines is that of stumbling and falling in the dark on a slippery path. The word דרכם, "their way," parallels closely מרוצתם, "their course," of v 10, suggesting that the judgment is announced against all the people, rather than just prophet and priest of v 11. Likewise, the threefold repetition of רעה, "evil," in vv 10, 11, and 12 would tend to indicate that the judgment falls upon all.

The bicolon at the end of v 12 (the messenger formula at the very end lies outside the metric structure, but serves as an appropriate indication of the end of the pericope) brings a direct word of judgment in first-person form. Because of their evil described in vv 10 and 11, Yahweh will bring evil against them. The specific judgment mentioned is the year=time of their visitation=their being visited=their punishment. The intent is not to say that Yahweh would bring evil on them *in* the year of their punishment (NRSV) but that the time of their punishment itself is the judgment.

Explanation

The prophet himself is heartbroken from Yahweh's words, because of the strong judgment spoken against the people and the leaders (specifically the prophets in this section). Nevertheless, he must speak the words. The judgment of this pericope is that Yahweh's year=time of visitation=punishment is announced. He will bring evil on the people for their evil.

B. Samaria's Prophets and Jerusalem's Prophets
(23:13–15)

Bibliography

McKane, W. "Poison, Trial by Ordeal and the Cup or Wrath." *VT* 30 (1980), 474–92.

Translation

13	*"Now among the prophets of Samaria*	(2+2)
	I have seen an immoral thing:	
	they prophesied by Baal	(2+3)
	and misled my people, Israel.	
14	*But among the prophets of Jerusalem*	(2+2)
	I have seen a horrifying thing:	
	adultery and walking in falsehood,	(3+3)
	they strengthen the hands of evil doers	
	so that they do not turn,[a]	(2+2)
	a man from his evil.	
	They are to me, all of them, like Sodom,	(3+2)
	[b]*her inhabitants,*[b] *like Gomorrah."*	

15 *[Therefore, thus says the LORD of armies against the prophets]*

"Behold I am about to feed them with wormwood	(3+2)
and make them drink poison water,	
For from the prophets of Jerusalem	(4+3)
has gone out profaneness to all the land."	

Notes

14.a. MT שבו, 3 masc pl pf, does not properly follow לבלתי; see GKC § 152x. *BHS* suggests either the inf שוב or the impf ישבו; this translation presupposes the 3 masc pl impf.

14.b-b. MT וישביה has no clear antecedent in the verse. *BHS* suggests perhaps reading ויחד(ו), "all together, all alike." However, with the mention of Jerusalem in the first line of the verse, it seems likely that the form is correct and refers to the inhabitants of Jerusalem, paralleling "my people, Israel" in v 13.

Form/Structure/Setting

Verse 12 ended with a messenger formula, marking the end of the pericope. Verse 16 begins with a messenger formula, indicating the beginning of another new pericope. Thus, vv 13–15 are set off from what precedes and follows.

Verses 13–15 form a separate judgment speech directed against the prophets, specifically against the prophets of Jerusalem. Vv 13–14 mark the accusation and have an interesting parallel between the sins of the prophets of Samaria and the sins of the prophets of Jerusalem. The implication seems to be that the prophets of Samaria have already brought about the loss of the Northern Kingdom, Israel; and now the prophets of Jerusalem are doing even worse! Verse 15 marks the transition to an announcement of judgment indicated by the word לכן and the messenger formula. The sentence itself is given in the first half of v 15; the last half of the verse returns again to accusation.

There are several links between this passage and the previous one: (i) the reference to prophets (which, as noted above, links all but one of the pericopes in this section), (ii) the word root נאף, "adultery," which appears in v 14 and v 10 above, and (iii) the root חנפה, "profane," which occurs in v 15 and v 11 above. In a sense, this pericope might be seen as an explanation of the previous one; more specifics are given here in terms of both accusation and judgment.

The pericope may be outlined as follows, primarily in a parallel structure:

A   Samaria's prophets: immoral (v 13a–b)
  B   Prophesied by Baal: action (v 13c)
    C   Led Israel astray: result (v 13d)
A'   Jerusalem's prophets: more horrifying (v 14a–b)
  B'   Adultery, falsehood, encouraging evildoers: action (v 14 c–d)
    C'   No one turns from their evil: result (v 14e–f
      D   They are all like Sodom and Gomorrah (v 14g–h)
A"   Yahweh speaks (messenger formula) (v 15a)
  B"   I will feed them poison: action (v 15b–c)
    C"   Profaneness to whole land: motivation (v 15d–e)

Comment

13   The *waw* on ובנביאי seems unnecessary. It could serve to link this pericope with the previous one. But as Naegelsbach, followed by Rudolph, noted, the *waw* parallels perfectly the one at the beginning of v 14. And since the two verses are so closely parallel, the *waw* fits quite well.

The word תפלה has been variously understood. The Vulgate, followed by Calvin and more recently by Holladay, has understood the word as "fatuous." RSV translates it as "unsavory"; Bright, Thompson, NRSV have the connotation of "disgusting." Using the passages in Lam 2:14 and Job 1:22 along with this verse, the connotation is more nearly "immoral." Clearly that which is evil or wrong is being indicated in these three passages. The point of the text is not to diminish the sinfulness of the prophets of Samaria; instead, it is to condemn Jerusalem's prophets even more. Samaria was bad; Jerusalem is even worse!

The sin of Samaria's prophets is prophesying by Baal. Elsewhere Jeremiah will use terminology of adultery, of forsaking Yahweh, of breaking covenant, all with dire consequences for turning to Baal. Certainly *prophesying* by Baal would have been no slight wrong!

The word הנבאו, "they prophesied," is a hithpael perfect, third person masculine plural; the ת has assimilated with the נ (GKC § 54c; BDB incorrectly calls the form an imperative).

The word ויתעו is a hiphil from תעה and means "cause to wander, lead astray, mislead." It is used several times of sheep going astray (Isa 53:6) or being led astray (Jer 50:6). The latter meaning fits the context here and again brings the shepherd-sheep image of vv 1–4 to mind.

14 The sin of Jerusalem's prophets is even more horrifying than that of Samaria's. Every one would have known the fate of Samaria and her inhabitants; thus this statement portends the direst possible consequences for Jerusalem.

The sins mentioned are נָאוֹף, qal infinitive absolute, "committing adultery," הלך בשקר, qal infinitive absolute, "walking, going" + "in falsehood" and "strengthening the hands of evildoers." Whether the prophets are accused of the sexual sin of adultery or of adulterous worship practices is not clear; either would have been considered gross immorality. In parallel with the preceding verse concerning Samaria's prophets, the sin may well have been the worship of other gods.

Likewise, "walking in falsehood" may refer simply to lying; but because Jeremiah uses שֶׁקֶר so frequently of prophesying falsely, that may be its thrust here. The prophets live by the lies they are prophesying.

Further, rather than aiding all those who belong to the covenant community, these prophets are helping the evildoers. Is this charge that the prophets actually help the wicked? Or is it that by their false prophesying, they are promoting the cause of the wicked? Regardless, the result is that the evildoers do not שׁוב, "turn, repent," from their evil. To Yahweh, all of them have become like Sodom and Gomorrah, wicked and ripe for destruction. One must assume that "all of them" refers not just to the prophets but to all the people, who are to suffer the judgment. This interpretation is supported by "her inhabitants," which apparently refers to the inhabitants of Jerusalem (so Bright).

15 The sentence is indicated both by the transition word לכֵן and the messenger formula. The sentence involves the image of a banquet Yahweh hosts (Rudolph; McKane, *VT* 30 [1980] 474–92), perhaps symbolized by the communion meal shared by worshipers and priests in the temple. But here the food and drink are poison, another of the reversals Jeremiah is so fond of using. There is a likely word play involving assonance among מרעים, "evildoers" (v 14d), מרעתו, "his evil" (v 14f), and מי־ראשׁ, "poison water" (v 15c).

Does the judgment fall only on the prophets? The first line of v 15 addresses the judgment specifically against the prophets. But the last line of the verse speaks of the profaneness, godlessness that has gone out to all the land. It would seem that, as in v 14, the judgment is to fall upon the entire population.

Explanation

Jerusalem's prophets are compared with Samaria's. Samaria's prophets had committed immorality, serious immorality, but Jerusalem's have done even more horrifying things. Adultery, falsehood, and strengthening evildoers are among the charges (the first two probably indicating the worship of false gods and living by their own false prophecies). The result of these sins is that all the people have become to Yahweh like the inhabitants of Sodom and Gomorrah. Thus he is about to bring judgment upon them in the form of an anti-banquet where the participants are fed poison rather than nourishing food.

C. Further Words against False Prophets (23:16–22)

Bibliography

Fleming, D. *The Divine Council as Type Scene in the Hebrew Bible.* Ph.D. diss., Southern Baptist Theological Seminary, 1989. **Lipiński, E.** "באחרית הימים dans les textes preexiliques." *VT* 20 (1970) 445–450.

Translation

16 *Thus says the LORD of armies:*
"*Do not listen to the words of the prophets,*   (3+2+3)
  [a]the ones prophesying to you;[a]
  they fill you[b] with empty hopes.
The vision of their heart they speak,   (3+2)
  not from the mouth of the LORD.
17 *They [a]keep on[a] saying*   (2+3+3)
  [b]to the ones spurning the word of[b] the LORD,
  'Peace/well-being will come to you.'
  [c]To[d] everyone going   (2+3+3)
  in the stubbornness of his own heart[c] [e]they say,[e]
  'Evil will not come against you.'
18 *For*
Who[a] has stood in the council of the LORD   (4+3+3)
  [b]that he might see[b][c] and hear[c] his word?
  Who has paid attention to [d]his word[d] [e]that he might hear?[e]
19 *Behold the storm-wind of the LORD,*   (3+2)
  wrath[a] has gone forth;
  a tempest[b] whirling,   (2+4)
  upon the head of the wicked it whirls.
20 *The anger of the LORD will not turn aside*   (3+2+2)
  until he has done and until he has carried out
  the purposes of his heart.
  [a]In the days afterwards[a]   (2+3)
  you will fully[b] understand it.
21 *I did not send the prophets,*   (2+2)
  yet they ran;
I did not speak to them,   (2+2)
  yet they prophesied.
22 *But if they had stood in my council,*   (2+3)
  [a]then they would have made [b]my people[b] listen to[a] my word,
  [c]and they would have made them turn[c] [d]from their evil way   (3+2)
  and[d] from the evil of their deeds."

Notes

16.a-a. Lacking in LXX.

16.b. Lacking in LXX. LXX understands slightly differently: "because they are seeing for themselves a vain (vision)."

17.a-a. The versions lack the inf abs אָמוֹר, "keep on (saying)"; *BHS* suggests deleting it.

17.b-b. Instead of MT לִמְנַאֲצַי דִּבֶּר, "to the ones spurning me, (Yahweh) has said, '…'", *BHS* suggests reading לִמְנַאֲצֵי דְּבַר, "to the ones spurning the word of Yahweh." That emendation is accepted in the present translation.

17.c–c. LXX has this phrase repeated twice: "to the ones walking after their own will, every one who walks in the error of his own heart, they say. . . ."

17.d. For MT וְכֹל, *BHS* suggests perhaps reading וּלְכֹל, "and to all." LXX and Vg so understand, as does this translation.

17.e-e. Not in some LXX MSS (Alexandrinus and Sinaiticus), nor OL nor Arab.

18.a. *BHS* suggests perhaps adding מֵהֶם, "from them." RSV and NEB accept that addition. However, such an addition would overload the line in terms of meter.

18.b-b. MT, which is followed in this translation, has a juss form; the versions apparently presuppose וַיַּרְא, "and seen." *BHS* suggests possibly reading וִירָאֵהוּ, "that he might see him."

18.c-c. Lacking in LXX; Syr, Vg, and Tg apparently presuppose וַיִּשְׁמַע, "and heard."

18.d-d. Lacking in LXX; many MSS (de Rossi, III, 92) and editions as well as Q read דְּבָרוֹ, "his word." That is the reading adopted by this translation. K has דְּבָרִי, "my word."

18.e-e. *BHS* suggests reading for MT qal a hiph, וְיַשְׁמִעַ, "that he might cause to hear." A hiph form of the verb appears in v 22.

19.a. *BHS* suggests the word is a gloss. Nevertheless, it does fit the metrical structure quite well. MT is accepted in this translation.

19.b. *BHS* deletes the conj; it is lacking from the parallel phrase in 30:23. From a syntactical position, either MT or the emendation is possible with no difference in translation.

20.a-a. While MT has a fut sense as translated here, "in the days afterwards" (i.e., after the judgment referred to), Tg is explicitly eschatological in its meaning, "at the end of the days."

20.b. MT has בִּינָה, "understanding," taken here as adding emphasis to the verb בִּין, thus "fully understand." The word is lacking in LXX, Syr, and the parallel passage, 30:24.

22.a-a. LXX has "and if they had heard."

22.b-b. LXX adds a conj and takes this phrase with the next clause, "and my people they would have made to turn."

22.c-c. LXX omits the conj and adds the previous phrase to this clause (see note 22.b-b.).

22.d-d. Lacking in LXX.

Form/Structure/Setting

There is some debate concerning the extent of this pericope. Some commentators and translations end it with v 20, taking 21–22 as a separate unit. However, the many ties between vv 21–22 and 16–20 seem best understood if it is treated as one pericope.

Also there is variation among the translations as to whether the passage is poetry or prose. RSV, for example, takes vv 16–17 to be prose and the remainder to be poetry. This translation assumes the whole is poetry, with only two elements standing outside the poetic meter.

The passage is hortatory, largely an attack on the false prophets. But it is primarily an appeal to the people not to give heed to false prophets, rather than judgment addressed to the prophets. The speaker is set by the beginning of v 16 as Yahweh, and the first-person forms in vv 21–22 follow that understanding. However, the third-person references to Yahweh in vv 17–20 show that the prophet has switched character and is himself speaking in those verses, nevertheless, speaking Yahweh's words. This shift in person is not sufficient to indicate that 21–22 form a separate pericope.

The setting for this pericope is a period of optimism. One possibility would be during the reign of Jehoiakim, perhaps about the time of the Temple Sermon (Chaps. 7, 26). A similar view of sin and optimism seems apparent in that context. Another possibility would be during the reign of Zedekiah about the same time as that set in chaps. 27–29, the confrontation with Hananiah and the letters from (and to) the exiles. Again there was optimism then that the exile would be temporary, and that Yahweh's judgment had already been experienced. Verse 19 might well address those who have experienced some judgment and feel that now Yahweh's anger has been soothed.

The entire pericope may be outlined as a parallel structure, with references to the prophets, followed by a reference to their actions or words. In the center are two references to Yahweh's actions/words:

A   Don't listen to the prophets (v 16b–d)
  B   They speak their vision, not Yahweh's (v 16e–f)
A'   They keep on saying (v 17a–b)
  B'   "Peace, no evil will come" (v 17c–f)
A"   Who has stood in council of Yahweh? (v 18a)
  B"   in order to see and hear his word (v 18b–d)
    C   Storm wind of Yahweh, wrath gone forth (v 19)
    C'   Anger of Yahweh will not turn aside (v 20a–c)
      D   Afterwards, you will understand (v 20d–e)
A'''   If they had stood in Yahweh's council (v 21a)
  B'''   they would have made people listen and turn (v 21b–d)

Comment

16 The first phrase probably stands outside the poetic structure though it could be scanned as a 2+2 unit:

Thus says
Yahweh of armies:

The word מהבלים from the root הבל, basically means "to cause to become empty, vain." Because the words of the prophets are "empty," they give the people who listen empty hopes, hence the translation offered here (so BDB).

That which the prophets have been prophesying is "the vision of their own heart"; it is *their* vision and word, not Yahweh's. Bright translates this phrase as "self-induced vision," which seems to connote a self-induced state, a trance, in which a vision occurs. While that is possible, the Hebrew emphasizes that the vision is of the prophets, not of Yahweh.

17 This verse deals with the words of these prophets, words that did not address the evil of the people. The message of the prophets was שלום, "Peace, all's well" (cf. 6:14; 8:11). Apparently for all circumstances, even to those who spurned Yahweh and followed their own heart, the message was still: "Don't worry, no evil will come your way."

The root נאץ, "spurn," is a strong word for rejecting Yahweh, one of its noun derivatives being understood as "blasphemy." The use here probably involves a word play involving assonance with the root נאף, "adultery," in vv 10 and 14 . The seriousness of this sin may be noted in that the most frequent object being spurned is Yahweh, his name, or his word.

18 The question raised in v 18 may be a rhetorical question expecting a negative answer: "Who has stood in Yahweh's council? No one." But v 22 seems to imply that the prophets should have been there, and other passages from the OT, especially 1 Kgs 22 (Micaiah ben Imlah), indicate the true prophet did indeed stand in Yahweh's council (cf. also Jer 28:20; 15:19). In this passage, too, the contrast seems to be between the true prophet, such as Jeremiah, who does stand in Yahweh's council, and the false prophet who does not but merely speaks his own words.

This verse has in parallel "standing in Yahweh's council" and "paying attention to his word." The implication is that however the word/vision of Yahweh is received it has come directly from him. The contrast with the word taken from the prophet's own heart (v 16) is obvious.

19 Verses 19–20 are a general statement of judgment based on Yahweh's word as opposed to the message of the false prophets (v 17). The reality is that Yahweh is like a terrifying storm directed against the wicked. He will not cease until he has completed all his purposes. The contrast between the purposes of Yahweh's heart (מזמות לבו) on the one hand and the vision of the false prophets' heart (חזון לבם, v 16) and the evil following the stubbornness of their heart (הלך בשררות לבו, v 17) on the other is clear and is strikingly Jeremianic.

The Hebrew root סער, "to storm, rage" (verb) / "a storm, tempest" (noun), is used here of Yahweh's wrath. The same root appears four times in Jonah 1 of the storm Yahweh brought against the boat in which Jonah was fleeing. It is used most often as a symbol of Yahweh's wrath.

The phrase באחרית הימים, "in the days afterward," (v 20) simply indicates a future time here. It refers to the days about to come when Yahweh would bring full judgment on his people (perhaps implying that partial judgment has already come). When those days come, then the people will understand the severity of Yahweh's wrath. This use of the phrase does not have the eschatological meaning that it later came to have (e.g., Dan 10:14, where the phrase refers to end times).

21 The prophet switches to first-person forms in speaking for Yahweh in vv 21–22. Some commentators would make these two verses a separate pericope, but clearly they seem to conclude this one instead.

This verse indicates two functions of the prophet as Yahweh's messenger. When Yahweh sent his messenger, the messenger was to go, bearing the message. These prophets have gone, indeed they have run, *but* Yahweh never sent them. They also prophesied, proclaimed their message; however, Yahweh never spoke a message to them. Clearly this verse picks up on v 16 and repeats its message.

22 Verse 22 reiterates v 18 from a contrastive point of view. In v 18, it is clear that the false prophets have not stood in Yahweh's council. This verse states that they should have stood there, so they would have heard and caused the people to repent. The implication of this verse is that if the false prophets had proclaimed Yahweh's message, then perhaps the judgment about to come (vv 19–20) might have been averted.

Explanation

How could a prophet confuse his own word with God's word? How could a prophet fail to speak condemnation to the sinful, covenant-breaking situation? Perhaps part of the answer was political and economic. The prophets were often part of the establishment; as such they were concerned with the maintenance of the establishment for their own security and well-being. Another part of the issue may have been purely rationalistic: Yes, some of our folks are sinful, but look at the pagans around us; they don't even worship God, and they practice the grossest of sins; by comparison, we're good folk and surely God will take that into account. "Our" sins are acceptable, but "their" sins are not. Besides, who wants to hear judgment preached all the time; just preach on the love of God.

According to this pericope, the true prophet is one who first stands in Yahweh's council so that he/she might see and hear Yahweh's word. Then the prophet proclaims that word so that those who hear might turn from their evil ways. The further implication is that, at least for this specific context, God's word is one of judgment rather than commendation and well-being.

D. The Preeminence of God (23:23–24)

Bibliography

Herrmann, W. "Jeremia 23,23f als Zeugnis der Gotteserfahrung im babylonischen Zeitalter." *BZ* 27 (1983) 155–66. **Lemke, W. E.** "The Near and Distant God: A Study of Jer 23:23–24 in Its Biblical Theological Context." *JBL* 100 (1981) 541–55.

Translation

23   "ᵃAm I a God of nearness,"ᵃ   (3+3)
                an oracle of the LORD,
    "and not a God of distance?
24   *If a man is hidden in the hiding-places,*   (3+2)
    will I not see him?"
               ᵃ*an oracle of the LORD.*ᵃ
    "The heavens and the earth,   (3+2)
    do I not fill them?"
            an oracle of the LORD.

Notes

23.a-a. LXX has a statement rather than the MT question: "I am a God nearby, says the LORD, and not . . . ."

24.a-a. Lacking in LXX.

Form/Structure/Setting

The three rhetorical questions are easily translated; there are relatively few textual concerns. The major variant occurs in the LXX, which makes the first question into a statement, reversing its impact.

The three questions are taken as poetry in this translation, although the threefold occurrence of "an oracle of the LORD" is understood to lie outside the poetic structure.

The three most recent commentaries on Jeremiah (Holladay, Carroll, McKane) all take this unit to be a separate pericope with no direct connection to what precedes or follows. Yet Holladay and Carroll, and especially Lemke (*JBL* 100 [1981] 541–55) assume the three questions can only be interpreted in their broader context, that is, within their present setting.

We will take the unit as a separate pericope, and will propose two readings of the passage, one an independent reading, the other a reading related to the *Sitz im Buch*.

No setting is indicated by the unit itself; it only gains a setting as a part of its present context.

Comment

23 The first rhetorical question is unlike the other two in at least two ways. First, the two halves of the question are interrupted by the messenger formula, which stands outside the poetic structure. Second, the question has two parts that involve a contrast: "Am I a God of nearness and not a God of distance?" The question can receive no single simple answer. Yes, Yahweh is a God of nearness; he is regularly depicted as being near his people (in at least spatial, temporal, cultic, and salvific senses [Lemke, *JBL* 100 (1981) 541–55). But the contrast is also true; Yahweh is also a God of distance: he comes from distant Sinai, he sees from afar, and is God from of old. This question may be answered yes and no. The rhetorical question affirms both the immanence and transcendence of Yahweh. As it stands independently, it affirms both aspects equally.

24 The two rhetorical questions in this verse are each concluded with a messenger formula. They both expect a positive response to the negative question. Yes, Yahweh will see the one hiding; and yes, Yahweh fills the heavens and the earth. These two questions likewise affirm the immanence and transcendence of Yahweh. Even one deliberately hiding cannot hide from him; yet in his transcendence, he fills the whole of his creation.

The interpretation given of these two verses thus far treats them independently of their *Sitz im Buch*. Understanding the verses within their present context gives some additional possibilities for their interpretation.

The false prophets (addressed in the previous and the following pericopes) apparently considered Yahweh a distant God, one who did not see the actions of the people (or the prophets). He was near only to receive their cultic offerings and to defend them from their enemies. Not so, says Jeremiah. Every hiding place is seen by Yahweh; every secret sin is observed by him. This transcendent one who fills the universe sees and knows every action and every person. Moreover, Yahweh sees the prophets: they have not stood in his council, nor spoken for

him, but he knows where they stand and what they say! Following this understanding, these two verses serve as the basis for judgment against the people and/
or the prophets.

E. Dreamers of Dreams and Yahweh's Word (23:25–32)

Bibliography

Werblowsky, R. J. Z. "Stealing the Word." *VT* 6 (1956) 105–6.

Translation

[25] *"I have heard what the prophets said, the ones prophesying in my name falsehood,
saying, 'I have dreamed, I have dreamed.'* [26a] *How long?* [a] [b] *Will the heart of the prophets
turn,* [b] *the ones prophesying the falsehood* [c] *and the ones prophesying* [c] *the deceitfulness of
their heart?* [27] *The ones planning* [a] *to make my people forget my name* [a] *in their dreams
which they recount each to his fellow, just as their fathers forgot my name for Baal.*

[28]   *The prophet who has a dream,*   (3+2)
        let him recount a dream, [a]
        and (the one) who has my word,   (3+3+2)
        let him speak my word faithfully.
        [b] *What (value) has the straw in comparison with the grain?"* [b]
            an oracle of the LORD.

[29]   *"Is not my word thus* [a] *like fire,"*   (4+3)
            an oracle of the LORD,
        "and like a forge-hammer it shatters rock?

[30] *Therefore, behold, I am against the prophets,"* *an oracle of the LORD,* *"the ones stealing away my words, each from his fellow.* [31] *Behold, I am against the prophets,"* *an oracle
of the LORD,* [a] *"the ones taking their tongue* [a] [b] *and uttering an oracle.* [b] [32] *Behold, I am
against* [a] *the ones prophesying* [a] *false dreams,"* *an oracle of the LORD.* *"They recount them
and cause my people to err in their falsehoods and in their recklessness. But I for my part
have not sent them, nor have I commanded them; they have surely been of no benefit to
this people,"* *an oracle of the LORD.*

Notes

26.a-a. *BHS* suggests perhaps reading חלמתי and adding it to the end of v 25 instead of MT עד־מתי.
26.b-b. For MT היש בלב, which lacks a subj, this translation accepts the proposal first made by
Giesebrecht (though later dismissed by him), and followed by Duhm, Cornill, and more recently
Holladay, to move the ב to the previous word, creating an impf of the verb שוב.
26.c-c. *BHS* suggests probably reading a niph ptcp ונבא, "and the ones prophesying, " for the MT
noun const ונביאי, "and the prophets of." This translation follows the emendation suggested by *BHS*.
27.a-a. LXX reads "to forget my name," omitting "people" and reading the verb as a simple stem
rather than a causative. Syr has "to cause my people to err in my name."

28.a. *BHS* suggests reading "his dream," as does LXX.

28.b-b. The Tg has "Behold, just as a man separates the straw from the grain, so one separates the righteous from the wicked, says the LORD."

29.a. Lacking in Syr and Vg. The LXX has a double use of the word, "Those are my words, says the LORD. Are not my words a blazing fire?" The Tg reads "all." *BHS* suggests reading כוה, "burning."

31.a-a. LXX has "who cast out prophecies of the tongue." The Tg has "who prophesy according to the good pleasure of their heart."

31.b-b. For MT וינאמו נאם, a few MSS (de Rossi, III, 92–93) have נאם יהוה, as is suggested by Syr and Vg. LXX has "and sleep their sleep," apparently understanding the Heb. root נום, "slumber."

32.a-a. MT נבאי, lit., "the prophesyings of . . ." or "the ones prophesying of . . . ." Many MSS (de Rossi, III, 93) have נביאי, "prophets of"; LXX has "the prophets who prophesy. . . ." BHS suggests inserting הנביאים, "the prophets [who prophesy dreams]."

Form/Structure/Setting

This pericope has both prose and poetry, the poetry confined to v 28 and 29. The pericope has a sort of inclusio formed by the words "prophesy," "falsehood," and "dream" in vv 25 and 32. The reference to dreams carries through the entire pericope, being mentioned again in vv 27 and 28.

The unit as a whole is a judgment speech in the first person. It begins with the accusation in vv 25–27. Verses 28–29, the poetic section, seem almost to interrupt the flow of the pericope. The two verses set forth Yahweh's expectations for a prophet, expectations that these false prophets have not met. In setting the context of Yahweh's expectations, these two verses then provide a contrast between true prophet and false prophet, which serves as a partial basis for the announcement of judgment in vv 30–32. Seen in this manner, the poetic section does fit into the form-critical structure of the pericope as a whole.

Verses 30–32 do provide the announcement of judgment, introduced by the typical transition word לכן, "Therefore," and followed with only an intervening phrase identifying the ones against whom judgment is addressed, by a messenger formula. The judgment itself has three parts, each introduced by the virtually identical words, "'Behold I am against the prophets (ones prophesying) . . . ,' an oracle of the LORD." The last of these judgments is the most complete, and includes the words forming an inclusio with the first verse of the accusation.

Comment

25 That dreams were a major means of legitimate divine revelation is well established in the OT. Some biblical materials express a great interest in dreams and their interpretation (Gen 28, Jacob; Gen 37, 41, Joseph; 1 Kgs 3, Solomon; Dan 2, 4, 7). Num 12:6–8 declares that dreams are a means by which Yahweh makes himself and his word known to the prophets. In this instance, the accusation is that these false prophets are wrongly interpreting their dreams, or wrongly ascribing the dreams to Yahweh.

26 The verse contains two rhetorical questions. The first "How long?" is more of an interjection and often appears in laments.

The second question raised in this verse (if the emendation proposed under *Notes* is accepted) implies a negative response. "Will the heart of the false prophets turn, return, repent? No, it will not." A part of the answer comes in the later description within the verse. It is as though Jeremiah deliberately builds his rhetorical question to intensify the accusation with each successive phrase. "Will it turn?" The question is completely ambiguous and the answer is open. "Will it turn, the heart of the prophets?" The ambiguity is lessened; the subject is now known, but the answer is still indefinite. "Will it turn, the heart of the prophets, the ones prophesying the falsehood?" Now both the subject and a part of the accusation is clear. The prophets have been prophesying falsehood, but is it deliberate falsehood? Could they turn? "Will it turn, the heart of the prophets, the ones prophesying falsehood and prophesying the deceitfulness of their heart?" Now all ambiguity is removed. Not only are these false prophets, but they are deliberately prophesying deceitfully. The accusations intensify and the clear negative answer becomes obvious in this skillfully crafted rhetorical question.

27 The accusations continue and also intensify yet again. Not only do these false prophets speak deceitfully in Yahweh's name, but they also plan (חשׁב, "think, plan, devise") to *make* the people forget (hiphil of שׁכח) Yahweh's name. The deliberate nature of the false prophets' actions is striking. How far removed the prophets, those supposedly Yahweh's spokesmen, are from the covenant.

28 Verse 28 begins a brief poetic section within the pericope. This verse and the next one serve as a transition to the announcement of judgment that follows. Rather than accusation, this section presents instructions for prophets to follow. It is Torah, instruction. The first four lines are synonymous parallelism, with "dream" parallel to "my word." Dream and Yahweh's word may be taken as separate forms of revelation, or as parallel ways of expressing Yahweh's revelation. The word אמת, "faithfully," should be taken with each part of the parallel expression. Thus the instruction to the prophet is, if you dream a dream, recount that dream faithfully, and if you receive a word, speak that word faithfully. In addition, the conjunction joining the two halves of the parallelism may be taken as the conjunction "and" or as the adversative "but." In the latter case speaking Yahweh's word would be set apart from dreaming a dream. Jeremiah does seem to deprecate dreamers, using the term always for false prophets. In that sense, while dreams were understood by Jeremiah to be a legitimate form of divine revelation, his personal experience led him to see that the "dreamers" of his time were misusing that form of revelation to espouse their own personal agenda. (Although BDB [321] suggests dreams were the lowest form of prophetic revelation, the OT itself does not as a whole view dreams so negatively, e.g., Joel 3:1.)

The rhetorical question at the end of the verse probably reflects a well-known proverb. "What value has straw in comparison with grain? None." Grain is the food, that which is kept. Straw is the leavings; it may be mixed with mud to make bricks but is basically trash. The meaning of the proverb is surely tied to the word אמת. Faithfully recounting a dream or speaking Yahweh's word equates with grain. Anything else equates with straw, trash. Although the same language is not used, there may be some association here with Yahweh's word to Jeremiah in 15:19. In that passage a comparison is made between what is worthless and what is precious, precisely the same comparison as here. When related to the next verse which speaks about the power of Yahweh's word, it is also possible that this proverb may speak negatively about dreams—not so much in and of themselves but as the false prophets are (mis)using them.

The messenger formula at the end of the verse marks off this poetic section from the one that follows. The two are independent oracles placed together to form the transition from accusation to judgment.

29 Like v 28, this verse exhibits synonymous parallelism. A messenger formula breaks the two parallel lines. The connection with the previous verse is clear. That verse spoke of a comparison between dreams and Yahweh's words as means of divine revelation. This verse amplifies the comparison by dealing with the power of Yahweh's words. Both lines of the verse speak of the great power of Yahweh's word using similes: it is like fire and like a forge-hammer. Fire bears the image of destruction, but also of refining. Likewise, the hammer may shatter, break in pieces, or may be used to cut that which is being forged, therefore being sharp, incisive. The hammer may also be used in refining to beat out the base material. Alternatively, hammer may refer to the stone-mason's craft and depict the cutting of blocks, or the final shaping of blocks.

Both images (fire and hammer) show the relationship between destruction and refining; they are clearly judgment images. While Yahweh's word does refine, it burns away the straw, it shatters and removes the common rock while leaving the ore, it cuts and shapes the stone into a useful architectural unit.

30 The judgment speech itself consists of three separate first-person statements. Like the accusation above, the judgment speech involves a great deal of repetition and has an intensifying of the characterization of the false prophets. None of the judgments gives specifics of the sentence. The first judgment merely states that Yahweh is against the prophets and includes a characterization of the prophets. They are ones who steal Yahweh's words from one another. This charge may mean that these false prophets are taking and using as their own the genuine oracles of other prophets [so Johnson, 47–49] or taking the words of earlier prophets [so Berridge, *Prophet, People,* 32ff.] or stealing the words of other false prophets. In either case, they are claiming for themselves that which was another's revelation (or that which was never revelation).

31 The second part of the judgment again declares Yahweh's opposition to the prophets without specifics of the judgment. Again there is additional characterization of the prophets: they take their tongue; that is, they speak their own words rather than speaking Yahweh's words. Then they utter an oracle. Clearly this last phrase involves a word play on the phrase "Yahweh's oracle." The verb וַיִּנְאֲמוּ is the only occurrence of a verbal form of נְאֻם in the OT. The implication of this phrase is that although these prophets utter an oracle, it is not Yahweh's oracle.

32 The final part of the judgment begins with a slightly different formula, "Behold, I am against the ones prophesying. . . ." These prophets are characterized as prophesying false dreams. The accusation of earlier verses is made more specific here. The dreams are called false dreams. Further, as the prophets recount these false dreams, they make the people err due to the falsehoods of the prophets and their recklessness. Here is another case of the shepherds leading the sheep astray (cf. 23:1–4).

An emphatic personal pronoun with an adversative conjuction introduces the next part of the characterization, וְאָנֹכִי, "But I for my part. . . . " Yahweh asserts that he has neither sent nor commanded these prophets, another way of saying their words are their own, not Yahweh's. Further, Yahweh asserts that these prophets have surely (infinitive absolute of the following verb) not benefited (hiphil of יעל) the people. The hiphil of the same verb appears in reference to the Baalim in 2:8.

Explanation

This pericope is primarily an attack on the false prophets and their misuse of dreams as a means of divine revelation. The prophets are accused of speaking their own words and fabricating revelations from dreams. Yahweh's instruction to the prophets is simple: faithfully recount dreams and speak his words. Yahweh's words themselves will do the rest because of their power.

But Yahweh is against the false prophets because they have been speaking their own words. Three times Yahweh says he is against them, matching the threefold reference to "the ones prophesying" in vv 25–26. The strongest denunciation is that Yahweh has neither sent (commissioned) nor commanded (spoken to) the false prophets, and they have been of no benefit to the people .

F. The "Burden" of the Lord (23:33–40)

Bibliography

Boer, P. A. H. de. "An Inquiry into the Meaning of the Term משא." *OTS* 5 (1948) 209–13. **Gehman, H. S.** "The 'Burden' of the Prophets." *JQR* n.s. 31 (1940–41) 107–21. **McKane, W.** "משא in Jeremiah 23. 33–40." In *Prophecy: Essays Presented to Georg Fohrer.* Ed. J A. Emerton. BZAW 150. Berlin: de Gruyter, 1980. 35–54. **Walker, N.** "The Masoretic Pointing of Jeremiah's Pun." *VT* 7 (1957) 413. **Weil, H. M.** "Exégèse de Jérémie 23, 33–40 et de Job 34,28–33 (Jérémie 44, 9) ." *RHR* 118 (1938) 201–8 . **Wernberg-Møller, P.** "The Pronoun אתמה and Jeremiah's Pun." *VT* 6 (1956) 315–16.

Translation

[33] *"Now when this people,* [a]*or the prophet or a priest,*[a] *will ask you, saying, 'What is the "oracle/burden" of the LORD?' then you will say unto them,* [b] *'You are the "burden."*"[b] *And I will abandon you,'"* *an oracle of the LORD.*

[34] *"The prophet, and the priest and the people who say 'the "burden/oracle" of the LORD,' I will take care of that man and his house.* [35] *Thus you will say, each to his fellow and each to his brothers, 'What has the LORD answered and what has the LORD spoken?'* [36] *But 'the "burden/oracle" of the LORD' you will not remember/mention*[a] *again, because the*[b] *'burden/oracle' will be for each his (own) word,* [c]*but you have overturned/perverted the words of the living God, the LORD of armies, our God.* [37] *Thus you will say to the prophet, 'What has the LORD answered you*[c] *or what has the LORD spoken?'* [38a]*"But if you say 'The "burden/oracle" of the LORD,'"*[a] *therefore thus says the LORD, "Because you say this word 'the burden/oracle of the LORD' and I sent to you saying, 'do*

not say "the burden/oracle of the LORD," '[39]*therefore, behold,* [a]*I will forget*[a b]*you surely*[b,c]
*and I will abandon you and the city which I gave to you and to your fathers out of my
presence.* [40]*I have placed against/upon you an everlasting reproach and an everlasting
ignominy which never* [a]*will be forgotten.* "[a]

Notes

33.a-a. *BHS* suggests these words are added from v 34.

33.b-b. For MT אֶת־מַה־מַשָּׂא, "What burden/oracle?" *BHS* says, following LXX and Vg, אַתֶּם הַמַּשָּׂא,
"You are the burden/oracle." The emendation is accepted in this translation. For a discussion of the
translation of מַשָּׂא as "burden" or "oracle," see below under *Comment*.

36.a. LXX has "you will name," apparently understanding a hiph form of זכר, "mention." However, BDB does suggest a like meaning for the qal.

36.b. *BHS* suggests for the MT הַמַּשָּׂא, "the burden," reading הֲמַשָּׂא, a question, "Is his word a burden for one?"

36–37.c-c. Lacking in LXX .

38.a-a. Lacking in LXX .

39.a-a. *BHS* suggests for MT וְנָשִׁיתִי, "I will forget," reading with a few MSS (de Rossi, III, 93) and
the versions וְנָשִׂיתִי = וְנָשָׂאתִי, "I will lift up, bear, carry." Although the word play on the root נשא with the
various nuances of מַשָּׂא is an attractive suggestion, the assonance involving נשה is equally plausible.

39.b-b. Lacking in LXX .

39.c. *BHS* suggests for MT נָשׁא (inf abs, emphasizing the action of the verb), reading נָשׂא (likewise
an inf abs). See note 39.a-a. above.

40.a-a. In the LXX, vv 7–8 are placed at the end of this verse.

Form/Structure/Setting

This pericope has a number of difficulties of translation and interpretation.
Not the least of these difficulties is the determination of the one(s) addressed.
The "you" of v 33 is masculine singular. The masculine singular forms appear in
vv 33–34. Then in vv 35–36 the ones addressed are masculine plural. In v 37 the
one addressed is masculine singular. In vv 38–40 the ones addressed are masculine
plural. Many commentaries assume that Jeremiah is the one addressed in the
masculine singular forms and that the false prophets, leaders, and even people
as a whole are addressed in the masculine plural forms. However, nothing in the
pericope identifies the masculine singular individual.

The pericope begins with a question and the response given to it. This particular
form of question and answer, "when they ask you . . . , you say to them . . . "
matches Long's "type B" form and is found a number of times in Jeremiah (5:19;
13:12–14; 15:1–4; 16:10–13).

The remainder of the pericope develops a word play on מַשָּׂא based on the
question and response in v 33. Verse 34 continues the judgment announced in v
33, but with a different nuance. In vv 34ff. the judgment comes especially on
those who speak the words "the מַשָּׂא of the LORD." The instruction given here is
that those words are not to be uttered. This speech form is unusual in Jeremiah;
normally his judgment speeches are based on the actions of the people, not the
use/misuse of formulaic phrases.

Verses 38b–40 do form a fairly typical judgment speech. The accusation is given,
"Because you (continue to) say . . . , after I had sent to you saying, 'do not say. . . .'"
Even prior to the accusation is a messenger formula and the word לָכֵן, "there-
fore," introducing the judgment announcement. The particle כִּי has a causal force

and introduces the accusatory basis for the judgment speech. The announcement of judgment follows in vv 39–40. It is introduced by a second לכן. It also has the first person format, here הנני, "Behold, I will. . . ."

Comment

33 The unnamed person is asked the question, "What is the משא of Yahweh?" The question is ambiguous due to the existence of two different meanings for משא: "burden" and "oracle, utterance." McKane has argued that the two are homonyms, though BDB lists both from a single root, נשא. If both meanings are from one root, how are the two different meanings related? "Burden" is obvious enough from the root נשא, "lift, bear, carry"; the thing carried is the burden. But "oracle" is less obvious. One line of reasoning has argued that the oracle was a harsh, judgmental message and was therefore a burden for the prophet to bear. Another line of reasoning is that the prophet lifted up his voice in delivering the oracle, hence the relationship to the root meaning. Regardless of these alternatives, it is clear that the word play throughout this pericope revolves around the double meaning of משא as burden and oracle.

The word play becomes clear in the question and answer given in this verse. To the question, surely having as its primary meaning "What is the oracle of Yahweh?" the response is "You are the burden." This double meaning will continue throughout the pericope.

Yahweh then charges that he will abandon those who are the burden. It must be noted that prophet, priest, and the people were brought together in asking the question and are all included in the judgmental response.

34 This verse reinforces the judgment announced in the previous verse. All, including prophet and priest and people, will come under the judgment. The judgment announced is that Yahweh will פקד, "visit" or "take care of," those individuals. The verb פקד can have either a positive or a negative connotation; the visitation can be either for blessing or for judgment. Only the context determines which meaning is appropriate. Here the implication is a negative "visitation" and "taking care of" the people.

35 The instructional part of this pericope begins with this verse. The correct response is given here: You (plural) say to one another, "What has Yahweh answered/responded or what has Yahweh spoken?" This response to be made suggests that the other, perhaps traditional, one is going to be changed.

36 Now the other response is given, as a negative: Don't remember/mention the words "oracle/burden of Yahweh" again. Alternatively, the sentence could mean : You won't remember the "oracle of Yahweh" any more. A similar meaning is found in reference to the ark of the covenant in 3:16. This would imply that the phrase would be forgotten, paralleling Yahweh's threat to abandon them in v 34.

The second part of the verse is more difficult. This translation has assumed that the משא should be understood as "burden," and that the burden is for each one his own word. What the people perceive to be an oracle is only their own word, not Yahweh's. Further, the word play probably means that this word is no oracle; it will be a burden for each one.

That interpretation seems most likely because of the last part of the verse; the charge is that the people have perverted Yahweh's words.

37 This verse parallels and repeats much of v 35. However, the distinction is the ones addressed: one's fellow and brother in v 35, the prophet here.

38 In this verse, the word play with משא continues, although the meaning in each case is clearly "oracle" of Yahweh. This verse begins a judgment speech, with the word לכן, "therefore," marking the introduction to the words of judgment. A messenger formula follows. The initial word of the sentence, ואם, "and if," indicates a conditional setting. The judgment speech is conditional upon the continued use of the forbidden words. Note also that the people using the words have no excuse: Yahweh had sent word to them to cease using the words. The form leads one to expect the judgment to be announced immediately. However, the rest of this verse merely restates the accusation.

39 The word לכן at the beginning of this verse overloads the introduction to a judgment speech, repeating the form from v 38. The form fits more naturally in v 38 with the messenger formula; however, this verse as the apodosis follows better from the protasis in the first part of v 38.

The word ונשיתי, "I (will) forget," is followed by an infinitive absolute, נשא, "to forget." The interpretive question is whether both these forms derive from the same root, and if so, from what root. Many commentaries follow the versions in understanding the root to be נשא, "lift up," and to involve another word play with משא, "burden." However, such an understanding does involve a textual emendation. The MT can be accepted and a word play still understood, involving assonance between the two roots, נשה and נשא. The unusual spelling of the infinitive absolute has surely led to part of the confusion of roots.

The word play involving assonance continues in the remaining two verb forms of the verse. Yahweh will also נטש, "abandon," them, a word repeated from v 33. Further, נתתי, "I gave," is assonant with נטש.

The abandoning involves both the people addressed and the city. נטש can involve persons abandoning Yahweh (Deut 32:15; Jer 15:6). Here Yahweh turns the tables on the people as he abandons them. Yahweh's abandoning the city brings to mind his departure from the city (Ezek 8–11 and the departure of the כבוד, "glory"). In abandoning them, Yahweh leaves the people and the city to their own resources.

Both the repetition of משא יהוה "burden/oracle of Yahweh," and the root נטש "abandon," from v 33 in vv 38–39 serve as a kind of inclusio for the pericope.

40 The unremitting nature of the judgment is indicated in this verse. Yahweh has put on/against the city and people an "everlasting reproach" (חרפת עולם) and "ignominy" (וכלמות עולם), a clear reference to the coming judgment of devastation and exile. So complete will be the destruction that it will never be forgotten. It will bring everlasting shame. The phrase here is quite similar to 20:11: "Eternal ignominy [כלמת עולם], it will never be forgotten."

The mention of this judgment not being forgotten stands starkly alongside the previous reference to the prophets making the people forget Yahweh's name (23:27). The people may forget Yahweh's name, but they will never forget the coming judgment.

Explanation

The pericope begins with a question and answer that include a statement of judgment. A word play on משא, "oracle" and "burden" is introduced, which is carried throughout the pericope. The people ask, "What is Yahweh's oracle?" They are told, "You are Yahweh's burden! You will be abandoned."

The pericope then instructs that the words "oracle/burden of Yahweh" no longer be used, because the people have perverted Yahweh's words (perhaps a reference to the previous pericope where the prophets have spoken their own words as Yahweh's). Anyone who does speak the words "the oracle of Yahweh" will come under Yahweh's judgment. They will be abandoned and will be an everlasting reproach and ignominy that will never be forgotten.

XIV. A Vision and Judgment Oracles (24:1–25:38)

A. Two Baskets of Figs (24:1–10)

Bibliography

Berridge, J. M. *Prophet, People.* **Bright, J.** *Jeremiah.* **Long, B. O.** "Reports of Visions among the Prophets." *JBL* 95 (1976) 353–65. **Niditch, S.** *The Symbolic Vision in Biblical Tradition.* HSM 30. Chico, CA: Scholars Press, 1983. **Pohlmann, K.-F.** *Studien.* **Raitt, T. M.** "Jeremiah's Deliverance Message to Judah." In *Rhetorical Criticism, Essays in Honor of James Muilenburg.* Ed. J. J. Jackson and M. Kessler. Pittsburgh Theological Monograph Series 1. Pittsburgh: Pickwick Press, 1974. 166–85. **Reventlow, H. G.** *Liturgie.* **Thiel, W.** *Die deuteronomistische Redaktion.* **Weinfeld, M.** *Deuteronomy and the Deuteronomic School.* Oxford: Oxford University Press, 1972. **Zimmerli, W.** "Visionary Experience in Jeremiah." In *Israel's Prophetic Tradition: Essays in Honour of Peter Ackroyd.* Ed. R. Coggins, A. Phillips and M. Knibb. Cambridge: Cambridge UP, 1982. 95–118.

Translation

[1a] *The LORD showed me, and behold two baskets of figs* [b] *being set* [b] *before the temple of the LORD after Nebuchadrezzar, king of Babylon, took into exile Jeconiah, the son of Jehoiakim, the king of Judah, and the princes of Judah, and the skilled craftsmen,* [c] *and the smiths* [c] *from Jerusalem, and brought them to Babylon.* [2] *The one basket had very good figs, like first-ripe figs, and the other basket had very bad figs that could not be eaten from badness (rottenness).*

[3] *Then the LORD said to me, "What do you see, Jeremiah?" Then I said, "Figs, the good figs are very good, but the bad are very bad, which cannot be eaten from badness."*

[4] *Then the word of the LORD came to me, saying,* [5a] *"Thus says the LORD, the God of Israel,* [a] *'Like these good figs, I will regard for good the captivity of Judah whom I sent from this place to the land of the Chaldeans.* [6] *Further, I will put my eye* [a] *upon them for good and I will cause them to return to this land. I will build them and not break down; I will plant and not pull up.* [7] *I will give them a heart to know me, for I am the LORD; they will be to me a people and I will be to them God, if they will return to me with all their heart.*

[8] *'But like the bad figs which cannot be eaten from badness,'* [a] *indeed, thus says the LORD,* [a] *'thus I will make Zedekiah, the king of Judah, and his princes, and the remnant of Jerusalem, the ones remaining in this land and the ones dwelling in the land of Egypt.* [9] *I have made them* [a] *for a terror* [a] [b] *for evil* [b] *to all the kingdoms of the earth, for a reproach, and for a by-word,* [c] *for a taunt and for a curse* [d] *in all the places where I banish them there.* [d] [10] *I will send against them the sword,* [a] *the famine, and the pestilence until they are destroyed from upon the ground that I gave to them* [b] *and to their fathers.'"* [b]

Notes

1.a. LXX^A, the Lucianic recension, and minuscules add "And." *BHS* suggests reading כֹּה, "Thus," which could have fallen out by haplogr following כֹּה at the end of 23:40.

1.b-b. The hoph ptcp occurs only here and at Ezek 21:21 [16]. *BHS* suggests possibly emending to עֹמְדִים or מְעָמְדִים, or even מוּדָעִים.

1.c-c. LXX has "and the prisoners." The word הַמַּסְגֵּר may imply locksmiths, or goldsmiths. LXX "prisoners" does indicate the root סגר. Driver has argued that the term referred to the harem. LXX also adds "and the rich," following this phrase.

5.a-a. *BHS* labels this phrase as an addition.

6.a. A few MSS, LXX, and Vg have the pl, "eyes."

8.a-a. *BHS* labels this phrase as an addition.

9.a-a. Q לְזַעֲוָה, "for a terror," as translated here; K לִזְוָעָה, "an object of trembling, quaking, fright."

9.b-b. Lacking in LXX. Syr, Tg editions, and Vg add a conj. *BHS* suggests either deleting the form as dittogr, or transposing to the end of v 8 to parallel לְטוֹבָה, "for good," of v 5.

9.c. The fragments from C, many MSS, LXX, Syr, and one Tg MS add a conj.

9.d-d. *BHS* suggests this phrase is an addition taken from Deut 28:37. Rudolph notes that this phrase is inconsistent with v 10.

10.a. Many MSS, LXX, Syr, and Tg Codex Reuchlinianus add the conj ו.

10.b-b. Lacking in LXX.

Form/Structure/Setting

The chapter has the form of a prose vision report. Although prose, Mowinckel placed it with his "A" material. Although some commentators have assumed that the passage is Deuteronomistic (Nicholson and Hyatt), and others put it as later (Duhm and May), many take it to be largely Jeremianic (Rudolph, Bright, Holladay). The passage appears to have several later expansions.

In terms of form, the passage has a similarity with chap. 18. Although that passage is not specified as a vision but is instead an action, the elements are quite similar. Long (*JBL* 95 [1976] 353–65) has suggested the elements of a vision report as follows (the verse breakdown is supplied for Jer 24 with parallel verses from Jer 18 in brackets):

(i) announcement of vision (24:1a) [18:1–3a]
(ii) transition (24:1b, הִנֵּה) [18:3b]
(iii) vision sequence (24:1c–10) [18:3c–11]
    (a) the image (24:1d–2) [18:3c–4]
    (b) Yahweh's question (24:3a) [lacking]
    (c) prophet's answer (24:3b) [lacking]
    (d) Yahweh's oracle (24:4–10) [18:5–11]

The formal similarity between the two passages is evident. Even closer formal similarities exist between Jer 24 and Amos 7–8.

The oracle falls into two nearly balanced halves, the good figs being identified in the first half with exiles and the bad figs in the second half with Zedekiah and the ones remaining in the land.

The historical context is indicated by the references to the exile of Jeconiah-Jehoiachin and the reign of Zedekiah. That setting gives a date for the vision between 597 and 587 B.C.

Comment

1 The vision context is set with the phrase "The LORD showed me," as found also in Amos 7 and 8.

The content of the visions is two fig baskets that were set before the temple. Whether the vision had a physical basis or was only visionary (perhaps a dream?) cannot be determined.

The location "before the temple" suggests the figs were an offering brought to the temple. In this verse no differentiation is made for the two baskets.

A context and a time are given. In addition to the location, the vision is set after Jeconiah (=Jehoiachin), the son of Jehoiakim, and many of the leaders and skilled craftsmen were taken exile to Babylon in 597 B.C.

2 Verse 2 continues the description of the baskets. Differentiation is made in terms of extremes: one basket has very good figs, the other very bad ones. The "first-ripe figs" (הבכרות) were considered a special delicacy (BDB, 114). Closely related to that word is "first-fruits" (בכורים), a ritual offering given to Yahweh (Lev 2:14; 23:17, 20; etc.). Perhaps the very choice of words by Jeremiah is intended to suggest the figs were an offering.

The "badness" of the second basket is not completely clear; probably the intention is rottenness, rather than wild, sour, or blemished figs. In a comparable image 2 Kgs 2:19 speaks of "bad" water. If that water was undrinkable, these figs are inedible.

3 The vision does not within itself readily provide an interpretation. The interpretation belongs to God. The question-and-answer motif that follows is relatively common in the prophets (Amos 7 and 8; Zech 5:1–4; Jer 1:11–14). Typically the answer of the prophet reiterates the statement describing the vision. Such repetition should not be understood as unnecessary; instead it indicates that the prophet has seen the vision correctly. It is comparable to the messenger correctly repeating the message entrusted to him. It further indicates that the source of interpretation is God, not the prophet—the interpretation is not evident from the vision.

4 The entire verse is an introductory formula. It is identical with 16:1. It serves to move from the vision to the oracle interpreting that vision. Verses 5–10 provide the interpretation.

5–7 The messenger formula is considered an addition by Rudolph, Holladay, and others. Rudolph states that a messenger formula is inappropriate for a private visionary experience. However, the oracles Jeremiah received were delivered to the people and often introduced by a messenger formula. So also this vision could well be followed by a messenger formula to interpret it for the people. The vision is not given just for the prophet's edification, nor even intended primarily for the prophet. The vision provides the basis for the oracle which follows; they are directed to the king and the people.

The meaning of the oracle is clear, if unexpected by its original hearers. The theology of many who remained in Judah and Jerusalem following the exile of 597 B.C. interpreted themselves as the ones blessed and the exiles as the ones under judgment. This oracle stated just the reverse. The ones taken "captive" (גלות) are the ones who may receive blessing.

Yahweh is emphatically the actor in this oracle. Nine verbs in these verses are first common singular, "I," and two additional first common singular personal pronouns occur. In each instance, Yahweh is the subject. He is the one who sent the captives to the land of the Chaldeans (v 5), but he will regard for good (v 5), put his eye on them for good (v 6), and cause them to return (v 6), if they will return to him.

Portions of the language in the oracle are reminiscent of Jeremiah's call experience, "I will build them [בניתים]," "I will not break down [לא אהרס]," "I will plant them [נטעתים]," "I will not pull up [לא אתוש]," but here Yahweh is the subject rather than the prophet as in the call (see 1:10). These same verbs plus one more occur in 18:7–9 as part of the oracle using the figure of the potter and the vessel, and are another indication of the similarity between chap. 18 and the present chapter.

The phrase "I will give them a heart to know me" in v 7 is similar to the phrase "I will give them one heart and one way to fear me" in 32:39. In both instances the change of heart will draw people to God. As in other passages, "heart" implies the inner person, the will or the mind. Whereas most references to the heart in Jeremiah speak of a stubborn, rebellious, or evil heart (3:17; 5:23; 11:8, etc.) and the judgment it brings, this passage refers to a change of heart and offers hope to the exiles. Yet the hope is conditional as the final phrase of this verse indicates.

The words "to know me" are found in Jeremiah, in addition to this passage, at 22:16 and 31:34, and with closely related words at 5:5. The negation, that the people did *not* know Yahweh, also occurs (2:8; 4:22; 5:4 [in a slightly different phrase]; 9:3, 6). This terminology is common in Hosea, with which Jeremiah has numerous points of contact. One may find the phrase or closely related ones at Hosea 2:8; 2:20; 4:1; 5:4; 6:3; 6:6; 8:2; 13:4.

The phrase כי אני יהוה may be understood as a causal, "for I am the LORD," or as a result, "that I am the LORD." The latter would then function as a double accusative, the fuller phrase being "that they may know me, [that is] that I am the LORD." Such a translation would be closely related to the common phrase in Ezekiel "and you (they) shall know that I am the LORD" (Ezek 6:7; 6:10, etc.). The former translation seems better in this context and avoids the double accusative. The causal phrase emphasizes the active role of Yahweh. An example from Hosea provides a close, though not perfect, parallel. Hos 11:8–9 has first-person verbs with Yahweh as subject, offering mercy and hope to Israel. The causal clause providing the reason for such mercy states כי אל אנכי, "because i am God."

The series of first-person verbs beginning in v 5 is coming to a climax; the phrase "for I am the LORD" serves as a preliminary climax. Yahweh will work positively for these exiles *because* he is Yahweh.

A fuller climax of the verse now follows. The strong covenantal language is clear: "they will be to me a people and I will be to them God." Similar terminology is part of the Exodus event-Sinaitic covenant (Exod 6:7; Lev 26:12; Deut 29:12[13]). Weinfeld (*Deuteronomy*, 80) mentions the similar terminology in the Abrahamic covenant (Gen. 17: 7–8), "to be unto you God." The phrase occurs six additional times in Jeremiah (7:23; 11:4; 30:22; 31:1; 31:33; 32:38). It should be noted that the other occurrences in Jeremiah either stipulate conditions (7:23; 11:4) or are found in a restoration context (occurrences in chaps. 30–32). This passage bridges both contexts; it is a restoration oracle, but it is also conditional as the next phrase indicates. Again similarity with the language and theology of Hosea is evident. Hos 1:9 gives the negative sense: "Call his name Not my people, for you are not my people and I am not your God" (RSV). The positive is given in Hos 2:25[23]: "And I will say to Not my people, 'You are my people'; and he shall say, 'Thou art my God'" (RSV).

The phrase כי־ישבו אלי בכל־לבם is often taken as causal, "*for* they will return to me with all their heart." Such a statement seems to run counter to Jeremiah's theological understanding and would represent an unconditional promise of God. It is much more likely that the clause should be understood as conditional: "*if* they will return to me with all their heart." The strong disjunctive accent just before this phrase (*athnah*) lends support to the conditional nature of the phrase. Further, this condition serves as the focal point of the entire verse and oracle, rather than just the last half of this verse. One hearing the oracle would be led to assume the statements in vv 5–7 are all unconditional until reaching this last phrase. But this conditional phrase governs the whole oracle. The blessings God promises are contingent upon repentance (שוב, here translated "return") by the people.

8–10 The last half of the oracle parallels the first part relatively closely. The twist in the original hearers' expectations is continued. Those remaining in the land are not the good figs; they are the bad/rotten figs. Two of the same verbs recur, נתן and שלח. The first-person verbs again predominate.

The *waw* on כתאנים at the beginning of v 8 is an adversative conjunction. It serves to mark the contrastive parallelism with v 5ff. The messenger formula, here with כי understood as an emphatic, is considered by many as secondary or redactional (Rudolph, Volz, Holladay, Carroll, Niditch [*Symbolic Vision*]). However, by understanding כי as an emphatic rather than causal particle, MT does make sense. The messenger formula might then simply parallel the one in v 5. The phrase is nonetheless cumbersome in the Hebrew.

The reference to "ones dwelling in the land of Egypt" would seem anachronistic if it referred to those who fled to Egypt after 587 B.C. or after the assassination of Gedaliah. Therefore many commentators assume the entire passage is late (Carroll) or that this phrase is a later addition (Holladay, Volz, Niditch). However, the latter years of Judah's independence prior to the exile witnessed continued maneuverings between pro-Egypt and pro-Babylon elements of the royal court. It is not unreasonable to expect that some of the pro-Egypt party may have fled to Egypt at the time of the deportation of Jehoiachin in 597 B.C. (so Bright). Although Holladay argues that rhetorically the phrase is expansionist, it is no more so than the previous phrase, "the ones remaining in this land." Furthermore, the rhetoric of both phrases fits Jeremiah's point precisely. The ones remaining in the land are the bad figs. The ones exiled are the good figs. But those who fled from the land to escape the exile are also part of the bad figs. Jeremiah's message had long been one of submission to the yoke of the Babylonians. Any attempt to avoid that yoke was an effort to avoid Yahweh's chastisement, which would ultimately result in inevitable judgment.

9 The language of v 9 is closely related to that of treaty curses. The words here are reminiscent of 19:8, where the context is similar. The horrors of siege warfare and its aftermath are being described in both instances.

10   The triad sword, famine, and pestilence is a favorite of Jeremiah's. It appears often in the siege warfare contexts to describe the totality of destruction (see 21:7 and further comment there).

The major difference between vv 5–7 and vv 8–10 is the lack of any condition or hope within these latter verses. The former offer hope conditional on the people's repentance; but the latter declare unrelenting judgment on Zedekiah and those remaining in the land.

Yet this unrelenting judgment is no different from other oracles against Jehoiakim (22:18–23; 25:1–14) or Zedekiah (21:1–7; 34). The judgment against Jehoiakim was certain, and it came in 597 B.C. The present judgment spoken against Zedekiah is just as certain, and it too would come (in 587 B.C.). However, just as blessing could come even to the exiles who bore the onus of judgment in 597 B.C. if they would repent (24:5–7), so the potential for mercy is still present. Judgment would surely come; it could not be averted. But mercy might be possible beyond judgment if the people repented. In that sense, vv 5–7 have the final word.

Explanation

In common with many of the prophets, God shows Jeremiah a vision. He interprets the vision by means of an oracle. The oracle presents a twist in that the exiles, the ones who have borne the brunt of judgment already (in 597 B.C.), are to be the recipients of blessing, if they repent. Further, those who perhaps considered themselves righteous or blessed by God because they remained in the land are promised unrelenting judgment. That word offers only the strongest judgment on the self-righteous of any age.

Despite the unrelenting judgment of the last three verses, the oracle as a whole does offer a message of hope. *If* the people will repent, then God may turn his eye upon them for good. Even a Zedekiah, even the most hardened sinner, can take heart—if that person will only repent.

B. Judgment on Judah (25:1–11)

Bibliography

Ackroyd, P. R. "Two Old Testament Historical Problems of the Early Persian Period." *JNES* 17 (1958) 23–27. **Borger, R.** "An Additional Remark on P. R. Ackroyd, *JNES* XVII, 23–27." *JNES* 18 (1959) 74. **Bright, J.** *Jeremiah.* **Christensen, D. L.** *Transformations of the War Oracle in Old Testament Prophecy.* HDR 3. Missoula, MT: Scholars Press, 1975. **Fensham, F. C.** "Maledictions and Benedictions in Ancient Near Eastern Vassal-Treaties and the Old Testament." *ZAW* 74 (1962) 1–9. **Fishbane, M.** "Revelation and Tradition: Aspects of Inner-Biblical Exegesis." *JBL* 99 (1980) 356–59. **Hillers, D.** *Treaty-Curse.* **Holladay, W. L.** "Style." *JBL* 81 [1962]

44–54. **Lemke, W. E.** "Nebuchadrezzar, my Servant." *CBQ* 28 (1966) 45-50. **Nicholson, E. W.** *Jeremiah 26–52.* **O'Connor, K. M.** *The Confessions of Jeremiah* . **Orr, A.** "The Seventy Years of Babylon." *VT* 6 (1956) 304–6. **Plöger, O.** "Siebzig Jahre." In *Festschrift, Friedrich Baumgartel zum 70. Geburtstag.* Ed. J. Hermann. Erlangen: Universitatsbund Erlangen, 1959. 124–30. **Schenker, A.** "Nebukadnezzars Metamorphose—vom Unterjocher zum Gottesknecht." *RB* 89 (1982) 498–529. **Stinespring, W. F.** "The Participle of the Immediate Future and Other Matters Pertaining to Correct Translation of the Old Testament." In *Translating and Understanding the Old Testament.* Ed. H. T. Frank and W. L. Reed. Nashville: Abingdon, 1970. **Vogt, E.** "70 anni exsilii." *Bib* 38 (1957) 236. **Westermann, C.** *Basic Forms of Prophetic Speech.* Trans. H. C. White. Philadelphia: Westminster, 1967. **Whitley, C. F.** "The Term Seventy Years Captivity." *VT* 4 (1954) 60–72. ———. "The Seventy Years Desolation—A Rejoinder." *VT* 7 (1957) 416–18. **Zevit, Z.** "The Use of עֶבֶד as a Diplomatic Term in Jeremiah." *JBL* 88 (1969) 74–77.

Translation

[1] *The word which came unto* [a] *Jeremiah concerning all the people of Judah in the fourth year of Jehoiakim, the son of Josiah, the king of Judah* [b] *(it was the first year of Nebuchadrezzar, the king of Babylon),* [b] [2] *which* [a] *Jeremiah the prophet* [a] *spoke concerning all the people of Judah and to all the inhabitants of Jerusalem, saying,* [3] *"From* [a] *the thirteenth year of Josiah, the son of Amon, the king of Judah and unto this day, these twenty-three years* [b] *the word of the LORD has come to me,* [b] *and I have spoken to you* [c] *repeatedly,* [c] [d] *but you have not listened* . [d] [4a,b] *Yet the LORD has repeatedly sent* [b] *to you* [c] *all his servants* [c] *the prophets, but you have not listened nor have you inclined your ears* [d] *to listen.* [d] [5] *They have said, 'Pray turn each from his evil way and from your evil deeds and you will remain upon the land which* [a] *the LORD* [a] *gave to you and to your fathers from of old even unto eternity.* [6a] *Do not go after other gods to serve them or to worship them; you shall not provoke me to anger with the work of your hands* [b] *so that I will not bring evil* [b] *against you.'* [7] *Yet you have not listened to me,"* [a] *an oracle of the LORD,* [b] *"in order to provoke me to anger* [b] *with the work of your hands to bring evil against you."* [a]

[8] *Therefore, thus says the LORD of armies, "Because* [a] *you have not listened to* [a] *my words,* [9] *behold, I am about to send and take* [a] *all the families of the north,"* [a] [b] *an oracle of the LORD,* "and *Nebuchadrezzar, the king of Babylon, my servant,* [b] *and I will bring them against this land and against her inhabitants* [c] *and against all these* [d] *nations around,* [c,e] *and I will put them under the ban, and I will make them for a horror and for a shriek and for desolations* [f] *forever.* [10] *And I will destroy the sound of exultation and the sound of rejoicing, the sound of bridegroom and the sound of bride,* [a] *the sound of (two) millstones* [a] *and light of lamp.* [11] *Then all* [a] *this land will be a desolation,* [a] *a* [b] *horror; and* [c] *these nations will serve the king of Babylon* [c] *seventy years."*

Notes

1.a. Several MSS (de Rossi, III, 94) have אֶל instead of עַל.
1.b-b. Lacking in LXX.
2.a-a. Lacking in LXX.
3.a. LXX has "*In* the thirteenth year," for MT "*From* the thirteenth year."
3.b-b. Lacking in LXX.
3.c-c. Reading הַשְׁכֵּם, "repeatedly," in an adv sense (see KB, 970) with the fragments from C and several MSS (de Rossi, III, 94) rather than MT אַשְׁכִּם, "I rose early."

3.d-d. Lacking in LXX.
4.a. *BHS* suggests deleting all of v 4 as a later addition.
4.b-b. LXX has "And I sent," with Yahweh as the speaker.
4.c-c. LXX has "my servants," maintaining consistently Yahweh as speaker as in 4.b-b.
4.d-d. Lacking in LXX.
5.a-a. LXX and one Tg MS have "I gave"; see note 4.b-b.
6.a. *BHS* suggests deleting the entire verse as a later addition.
6.b-b. LXX has "to bring you harm."
7.a-a. Lacking in LXX; *BHS* suggests deleting.
7.b-b. Reading with Q and the fragments from C הכעיסיני, "to provoke me"; K has הכעסוני, "they provoked me."
8.a-a. LXX has "you did not believe."
9.a-a. LXX has "a family from the north."
9.b-b. Lacking in LXX; *BHS* suggests deleting.
9.c-c. *BHS* suggests this passage is an addition anticipating vv 15ff.
9.d. Lacking in LXX and Vg.
9.e. Several MSS (de Rossi, III, 95) have מסביב, "from round about."
9.f. LXX has "and an everlasting reproach."
10.a-a. LXX has "the scent of myrrh."
11.a-a. Lacking in LXX; *BHS* suggests deleting.
11.b. Many MSS (de Rossi, III, 95) and versions add the conj "and."
11.c-c. LXX has "And they will serve among the nations seventy years," lacking any reference to the king of Babylon.

Form/Structure/Setting

This passage is a prose section, as is most of the chapter. Scholars differ as to the extent of the unit, or the best place to divide it. Many would divide the passage at the end of v 8 and/or at the end of v 14. I have chosen to divide the passage after v 11 because of the shift from judgment against Judah and Jerusalem in 1–11 to judgment against Babylon and the nations in v 12 and following.

The pericope has many of the common elements of a judgment oracle against the nation (see Westermann, *Basic Forms,* 169–76). Although cast as a prophetic speech by vv 4 and 5, the remainder of the pericope is actually a first-person speech of Yahweh. It has the following outline:

Messenger formula (vv 4–5)
Call to repent (vv 5–6)
Response of people (v 7)
Transition to judgment "therefore" (v 8)
Repeated messenger formula introducing judgment (v 8)
Judgment, introduced by הנה, "behold" (vv 9–11)

Two general comments about the LXX of this chapter are important to note. The LXX is significantly shorter than the MT, omitting numerous phrases and even several complete verses. Many of the LXX omissions are phrases specifically identifying Babylon or Nebuchadrezzar. More importantly, the LXX places most of the Oracles against Foreign Nations of MT chaps. 46–51 after v 13 (and omits v 14).

Following the superscription which gives the date, the remainder of the pericope gives the message, basically a summary of Jeremiah's preaching, which called for repentance and then threatened judgment because the people have not listened.

No setting is indicated by the pericope; however, a date formula is given in the superscription, the fourth year of Jehoiakim. This date is c. 605 B.C. It is further specified as the first year of Nebuchadrezzar. This was also the year that Nebuchadrezzar defeated Egyptian forces in the battle of Carchemish. This battle marked a turning point in ancient Near Eastern history. After this, Babylon was clearly the dominant force in the entire region. From this time on, Babylon, rather than Egypt, would be the major force in Syria-Palestine. It should be mentioned that some commentators, such as O'Connor (*Confessions*, 146), argue that chaps. 21–25 presuppose the fall of Judah has already taken place.

This unit has some literary connections, especially with chap. 1. Verse 3 speaks of the beginning of Jeremiah's ministry in the thirteenth year of Josiah's reign. This repeats the date given in 1:2 and might be an inclusio marking the beginning and end of one section of the book of Jeremiah. (That chaps. 1–25 compose one of the major sections is widely accepted by scholars; see, e.g., Bright, 163; and Nicholson, 14–15.) A similar inclusio might be indicated in the call of Jeremiah to be "a prophet to the nations" (1:5), the judgment spoken against the nations in 25:31–32, and the listing of numerous nations in 25:18–26. These passages mark the major references to judgment against foreign nations in Jeremiah 1–25.

Additional connections with chap. 1 include the words "The word of the LORD has come to me" (25:3; cf. 1:1); "I have spoken to you, repeatedly" (25:3; cf. 1:6–9); the verb "send" (25:4, 9; cf. 1:7); and the mention of the "families of the north" (25:8; cf. 1:14–15).

There are also clear connections between this chapter and chap. 35, especially 25:5–7 and 35:12–17.

Comment

1 The pericope begins with a superscription that includes a date formula. Several other chapters in Jeremiah also have date formulas; among them are 1:1–3; 26:1; 27:1; 28:1; 32:1; 36:1; etc. The date itself is c. 605 B.C., a portentous year in ancient Near Eastern history. The text mentions parenthetically that the year was Nebuchadrezzar's first as ruler of Babylon. It was also the year the Babylonians under Nebuchadrezzar defeated the Egyptian forces at Carchemish, establishing Babylonian power as supreme in the entire Fertile Crescent. Politically, the Babylonians will now be the chief power to reckon with in Syria-Palestine. Such a word was ominous, for now Babylon in general and Nebuchadrezzar specifically could be identified as the foe from the north who would serve as Yahweh's instrument of judgment. Such a reminder at the beginning of this pericope intensifies the mood of gloom and doom.

3 The date reference to the beginning of Jeremiah's ministry here matches that of 1:2. Jeremiah states that the word of Yahweh had come to him, and as a consequence he had spoken to the people, "repeatedly" (הַשְׁכֵּם, following the emendation proposed in *Notes* above), not just occasionally. However, the people have not listened or responded.

4 A further part of the indictment is that Yahweh had not just sent Jeremiah but had repeatedly sent all the prophets; nevertheless, the people had refused to heed any of them.

5–6 The message Jeremiah has been delivering (and the other prophets as well) is given in summary fashion here. The first part of the message, "Pray, turn each from his evil way," is found several additional times in Jeremiah (18:11; 26:3; 35:15; 36:3, 7). The context is set with a plural imperative, weakened slightly with the particle נא, "Please turn, please repent."

There is a shift of person from that first call to repentance to the next phrase, "and from your evil deeds," a shift from third person masculine singular to second person masculine plural. This phrase also occurs several times in Jeremiah (4:4; 21:14 [cf. 21:12]; 23:2 [cf. 23:22; 26:3]; 44:22).

The consequence of the call to repentance is expressed in the imperative that follows, "and remain (ישׁב)," i.e., "turn, and you will remain" [GKC § 110f] The word play involving the two roots שׁוב, "turn," and ישׁב, "remain," is another example of the assonance frequently found in Jeremiah (Holladay, *JBL* 81 [1962] 46).

The positive call for repentance is followed by two negatives in v 6. The first, "Do not go after other gods," has the negative אל followed by the jussive. The second negative has the strong prohibition formed by לא and the imperfect, "you shall not. . . ." The consequence of that second negative is expressed by an additional לא with an imperfect, linked to the previous one with a *waw*-conjunction. Like the positive imperatives, these two prohibitions give command and result: "you shall not provoke me . . . and I will not bring evil" has the implication "you shall not provoke me . . . so that I will not bring evil." The two verbs, the hiphil of כעס, "provoke," and the hiphil of רעע, "bring evil," are each found most frequently in the book of Jeremiah, and seem to indicate his vocabulary (כעס is also common in the Deuteronomistic history, though רעע is much less so).

7 This verse is quite repetitious of the previous verse, describing the refusal of the people to hear Yahweh's words, and thus justifying the coming message of judgment. The messenger formula ("an oracle of the LORD") indicates again that Yahweh, not Jeremiah, is the speaker. The close parallels between vv 6 and 7 do not necessarily indicate verbosity but instead emphasize as strongly as possible the people's repeated rejection of Yahweh's word and call to repentance. The word "to listen," שׁמע, has the triple meaning of hearing, listening, and heeding/obeying. All three are implied in the current passage. The people have not heard the words, they have not listened to the message, and they clearly have not heeded or obeyed the call to repentance.

8 Verse 8 clearly marks the transition to judgment. The reappearance of the full messenger formula ("thus says the LORD of armies") indicates a formal sentence as well as providing absolute certainty as to the speaker, Yahweh. The judgment is based on the refusal of the people to listen (hear, heed, obey) as indicated in the previous verse. Again the language leaves no doubt about the people's sinfulness.

9 The judgment itself begins with the phrase "behold, I am about to send and take." The construction has the particle הנה, "behold," with the first common singular suffix followed by a participle. Following Stinespring's suggestion, the participle is understood here as an immediate future. The perfects following, each linked with a *waw*, are translated as continuing the immediate future context.

The language of "sending" picks up the description of Yahweh's previous action in sending the prophets repeatedly to the people. Since they refused to respond to the prophets, now Yahweh will send another sort of messenger.

The reference to "all the families of the north" recalls the similar phrase "all the families of the kingdoms of the north" in Jeremiah's call experience, 1:15. Here, however, the identity of the northern families or tribes is clarified; specifically among those sent for is Nebuchadrezzar, king of Babylon. Nebuchadrezzar is further identified as "my servant," the same term used to describe the prophets in v 4. The implication is that since Yahweh had sent one group of servants who had been ignored, he would now send another messenger, one of a different sort who could not be ignored. For the third time in as many verses, a messenger formula occurs reminding all that Yahweh is the speaker and the one acting.

The description of the judgment against the land and inhabitants is typical of language Jeremiah uses (שׁמה, "horror," occurs twenty-four times in Jeremiah; שׁרקה and related forms, "shriek," occur nine times; and חרבות and related terms, "desolations" occur nineteen times), with the addition of the verb חרם, "I will put them under the ban." The relationship of these terms with treaty curses has been mentioned above (see *Notes* and *Comment* on 18:16 and 19:8).

10   The result of the judgments of v 9 is that all occasions of joy will cease in the land, which is itself a treaty curse (Hillers, *Treaty-Curse*, 57–58; Fensham, *ZAW* 74 [1962] 5–6). Not only will rejoicing cease, but in addition the sounds and sights of everyday activity will cease: "the sound of the two millstones" (i.e., the sound of grain being ground will cease as a result of famine or depopulation), and the "light of lamp" (i.e., it will cease from lack of oil or depopulation).

11   The summary statement of v 11 repeats two of the key words of v 9, desolation and horror. In addition there is the reference to the length of oppression, seventy years. The time reference has attracted considerable interest. Attempts to fit a precise seventy-year period have not been fully successful, whether 627/26–539/38 or 536, or 586–516 (see Whitley, *VT* 7 [1957] 416–18). The number may indicate a full lifespan (as in Ps 90:10) in comparison to forty years indicating a generation, and thus indicate a long period of servitude to Babylon. Clearly the seventy-year figure became important in later OT writings. In Dan 9, the seventy years of Jeremiah is mentioned as the basis for a new prophetic word referring to seventy *weeks* of years.

Explanation

For over twenty-three years Jeremiah has proclaimed God's call to Judah to repent. Repeatedly through his prophets God had urged the people to repent, but they had not heeded the warnings. Now the judgment is imminent; God will use a different kind of messenger to deliver a different kind of message. Nebuchadrezzar will become God's servant delivering his message, one of devastation and destruction. Judah will pay a terrible price for her sins. All signs of joy, even signs of everyday life will cease from the land. And the judgment will be long lasting.

C. Judgment on Babylon (25:12–14)

Bibliography

Orr, A. "The Seventy Years of Babylon." *VT* 6 (1956) 304–6. **Plöger, O.** "Siebzig Jahre." In *Festschrift, Friedrich Baumgartel zum 70. Geburtstag.* Ed. J. Hermann. Erlangen: Universitats-bund Erlangen, 1959. 124–30. **Vogt, E.** "70 anni exsilii." *Bib* 38 (1957) 236. **Whitley, C. F.** "The Term Seventy Years Captivity." *VT* 4 (1954) 60–72. ———. "The Seventy Years Deso-lation—A Rejoinder." *VT* 7 (1957) 416–18.

Translation

[12a] *"And it will be, when seventy years are completed, I will visit [b]against the king of Babylon and [b] against that nation," [c]an oracle of the LORD, "their iniquity, and against the land of the Chaldeans, [c] and I will make it horrors forever.* [13]*And I will bring [a] against that [b] land all my words which I have spoken against her, every thing which is written in this book [c]which Jeremiah prophesied against all the nations. [c]* [14a]*For even they [Babylon] will serve [b] (as slaves) many nations and great kings; I will requite them [Babylon] ac-cording to their work and according to the deed of their hands." [c]*

Notes

12.a. *BHS* suggests the verse may be an addition.
12.b-b. Lacking in LXX.
12.c-c. Lacking in LXX.
13.a. Following Q וַהֲבֵאתִי; K has וְהֵבֵאתִי.
13.b. *BHS* suggests reading הַזֹּאת, "this," instead of MT הַהִיא, "that."
13.c-c. *BHS* suggests this is added because of vv 15ff. and should be deleted (cf. LXX).
14.a. Lacking in LXX; *BHS* suggests it is perhaps an addition joined with v 12.
14.b. *BHS* suggests reading an impf rather than a pf.
14.c. In LXX after v 13 is inserted many of the oracles against the nations of chaps. 46–51.

Form/Structure/Setting

Verses 12–14 form a semi-independent oracle against Babylon. It is linked with 25:1–11 by וְהָיָה, "And it will be." Additional linkage is provided by the repetition of "seventy years." However, unlike the previous pericope, this oracle speaks judgment against Babylon. In that sense it provides a transition between vv 1–11 with judgment against Judah and Jerusalem, and vv 15–29, which speak of judg-ment against Judah and all the nations surrounding.

I haven chosen to treat this oracle independently as a preface to the oracles against the nations, although I recognize that it could also be placed at the end of the previous pericope. The rationale for placing it independently is that it addresses Babylon, a foreign nation, and foreign nations are neither the focus nor even addressed in the previous section. In addition, although Babylon is among the nations addressed in the next pericope (as is Judah), Babylon is not mentioned until the very end as a climax. In that sense, these two units are paral-lel, each indicating God's judgment on Babylon.

This oracle is set as a first-person speech of Yahweh speaking generally of judgment against Babylon for her sins. No context or date formula is given for the oracle. As noted in the previous pericope (25:1–11), the date of 605 B.C. is mentioned there, though O'Connor (*Confessions,* 146) argues that chaps. 21–25 reflect the aftermath of the fall of Jerusalem/Judah in 587/86 B.C. Such judgment on Babylon would fit an exilic context well.

Comment

12 For comments on seventy years, see v 11 above. The oracle is set as a Yahweh speech by the messenger formula and the first-person pronouns. The word "visit" in the sense of judgment occurs relatively frequently in Jeremiah (cf. 23:2), in reference to Yahweh "visiting" both Judah and other nations.

The same kind of devastation that has been spoken against Judah will be visited against Babylon: she will become שַׁמָּה, "horrors, horrifying."

13 This verse, which speaks of all the words spoken against Babylon, seems to presuppose the oracles against the nations of chaps. 45–51. Likewise, the reference to every thing written in this book seems to make the same presupposition. Further, the mention of a book or scroll, סֵפֶר, may refer to the scroll of chap. 36. The mention of such oracles may be the reason LXX placed the majority of the oracles against the nations following this verse. In such a case, the MT placement could well be the original, with LXX trying to eliminate a textual difficulty. That aside, the passage does indicate that oracles against the nations were included in some book/scroll of Jeremianic material, quite possibly that of chap. 36.

14 Verse 14 is difficult in terms of antecedents for the many pronouns. The first "they" apparently refers to the Babylonians, who will serve unspecified nations ("them"). The second clause ("for I will requite them") parallels the first and refers to the Babylonians as object. The shift from subject to object and from unspecified oppressors to Yahweh as judge/active agent is typical of Jeremiah's parallelism.

Explanation

In this transition oracle, still a Yahweh speech, the judgment shifts from Judah and Jerusalem to Babylon, the nation Yahweh has used to bring judgment on his covenant people. As the old saying goes, "What goes around comes around." God will in due course bring the same measure of his judgment on Babylon that he has brought on Judah. Babylon will pay for her sins just as Judah does. Each nation will be requited for her deeds (v 14).

D. Judgment on the Nations (25:15–29)

Bibliography

Bardtke, H. "Jeremia der Fremdvolkerprophet." *ZAW* 53 (1935) 220–27. **Brongers, H. A.** "Der Zornesbrecher." *OTS* 15 (1969) 177–92. **Carroll, R. P.** *Jeremiah.* **McKane, W.** "Poison,

Trial by Ordeal and the Cup of Wrath." *VT* 30 (1980) 474–92. ————. *A Critical and Ex-egetical Commentary on Jeremiah.* **Nicholson, E. W.** *The Book of the Prophet Jeremiah Chapters 26–52.* **O'Connor, K. M.** *The Confessions of Jeremiah.* **Roche, M. de.** "Is Jeremiah 25:15–19a a Piece of Reworked Jeremianic Poetry?" *JSOT* 10 (1978) 58–69.

Translation

[15]*For*[a] *thus says the* LORD, *the God of Israel,* [b]*to me*[b]: *"Take this cup of* [c]*raging [wrathful] wine*[c] *from my hand and make drink it all the nations to whom I am sending you.* [16a]*They will drink and reel [shake]*[a] *and behave insanely*[b]*from the sword which I am sending in their midst.* "[b] [17]*Then I took the cup from the* LORD*'s hand and I made all the nations to whom the* LORD *sent me drink:* [18a]*Jerusalem and the cities of Judah, her kings and*[b] *her officials, to make them a desolation, a horror, a shriek*[c]*and a[n object of] curse as at this day;*[c] [19]*Pharaoh, the king of Egypt, his servants and his officials, and all his people,* [20a]*and all the mixed company;*[a,b] [c]*all the kings of the land of Uz,*[c] *all the kings of the land of the Philistines:* [d]*Ashkelon, and Gaza, and Ekron, and the remnant of Ashdod;* [21]*Edom and Moab and the Ammonites;* [22]*all the kings of Tyre and all the kings of Sidon, and* [a]*the kings of the coast*[a] *which is across the sea;* [23]*Dedan and Tema and Buz*[a] *and all the ones whose corners (of hair) are cut off;* [24a]*all the kings of Arabia,*[a] [b]*and all the kings of the mixed company,*[b] *the ones dwelling in the desert-wilderness;* [25]*all the kings of Zimri,*[a] *all the kings of Elam, and all the kings of Media;* [26]*all the kings of the north, the ones near and the ones distant, each to his brother; all the kingdoms*[a]*of the earth*[a] *which are upon the surface of the ground;* [b]*and the king of Sheshak*[c] *will drink after them.*[b]

[27]*And you say to them, "Thus says the* LORD *of armies, the God of Israel, 'Drink, and get drunk, and vomit,*[a] *and fall, and you shall not rise because of the sword which I am sending in your midst.'"* [28]*And it will be, if they refuse to take the cup from your hand to drink, then you will say to them, "Thus says the* LORD *of armies: 'You shall surely drink!'* [29]*For behold, against the city upon which my name is called, I am about to bring evil, and you, shall you be exempt from punishment? You will not be exempt for I am about to call sword against all the inhabitants of the land,* [a]*an oracle of the* LORD *of armies.* "[a]

Notes

15.a. Lacking in LXX.
15.b-b. Lacking in LXX, Syr, and one Tg MS.
15.c-c. LXX has "unmixed wine."
16.a-a. LXX has "and vomit."
16.b-b. *BHS* suggests an addition from v 27b.
18.a. *BHS* suggests this verse is an addition.
18.b. This translation follows *BHS* suggestion, adding the conj "and" with many MSS (de Rossi, III, 95) and versions.
18.c-c. Lacking in LXX.
20.a-a. *BHS* suggests joining with v 19; cf. LXX and Syr.
20.b. עֶרֶב refers to a mixed company, probably ones of various ethnic backgrounds living among, but not fully assimilated into, the majority population.
20.c-c. Lacking in LXX.
20.d. LXX omits the *waw*-conjunction; the *waw* is not translated here (nor in several places in nearby verses) to give a smoother Eng. rendering.
22.a-a. LXX has "and the kings," omitting "of the coast."
23.a. LXX has "Rōs."

24.a-a. Lacking in LXX.

24.b-b. *BHS* suggests deleting as dittogr.

25.a. *BHS* suggests perhaps reading זמכי, which would be interpreted as *atbash*, for עלם, "Elam" (for a discussion of *atbash*, see *Comment* on vv 19–26 below). In that case either this phrase or the phrase following should be deleted as dittogr. LXX lacks the phrase "all the kings of Zimri." Others have suggested emending the text to גמרי, "the Cimmerians."

26.a-a. Lacking in LXX and Syr; *BHS* suggests deleting.

26.b-b. Lacking in LXX.

26.c. Tg has "which is Babylon."

27.a. MT has וקין; the K of several MSS (de Rossi, III, 96–97) and fragments from C have וקון; *BHS* suggests, and this translation follows, reading וקיי, which is understood as an alternate form of וקיאו.

29.a-a. Lacking in LXX.

Form/Structure/Setting

This pericope is a report of a symbolic action against the nations. Jeremiah is told by Yahweh to take a cup from Yahweh's hand and make the nations drink from it (vv 15–16), which he does (vv 17–26). He then is to speak a word of explanation and judgment concerning the cup which they have drunk (vv 27–29).

The symbolic action recalls others in Jeremiah, for example, chaps. 13 and 19. Here Jeremiah is to take a cup of raging wine and give it to all the nations starting with Judah and ending climactically with Babylon. For a full discussion of the possible interpretations of the cup of raging wine, see the excursus by Smothers in volume 2 of this commentary. Whatever the origin of the metaphor, clearly in this context the cup of raging wine is a metaphor of judgment (see McKane, *VT* 30 [1980] 490–91). The last part of v 16 and vv 27 and 29 show that judgment is the outcome of drinking from the cup.

The unit may be outlined as follows:

Yahweh's word: commanding an action (v 15)
Yahweh's word: announcing judgment (v 16)
   Prophet's action: fulfilling the command (vv 17–26)
Yahweh's word: commanding an action (v 27a)
Yahweh's word: announcing judgment (v 27b)
Yahweh's word: restating the command for an action (v 28)
Yahweh's word: announcing judgment again (v 29)

No indication of date is given in the pericope. However, with the clear understanding that Babylon is to be the destroyer of Judah, certainly a date after 605 B.C. is appropriate. O'Connor (*Confessions*, 146) argues that the entire section of chaps. 21–25 presupposes the exile. That dating is quite possible for this pericope with its judgment on the nations, but it is not necessary.

Comment

15 A full messenger formula introduces the symbolic action of Jeremiah against the nations. On the metaphor of the cup, see *Form/Structure/Setting* and the excursus by Smothers in volume 2. This verse marks a shift from Yahweh speech to prophetic action. Although Jeremiah is not identified as the person spoken to ("thus says the LORD . . . to me"), the identity seems evident from the context and on the basis of vv 1–4 and 13 above.

16 The result of drinking from the raging cup is either drunkenness or sickness. Some would understand the cup to be a cup of poison, since the word חמה, "raging," is used of a snake's venom in some passages (Deut 32:24, 33; Pss 58:5; 140:4 [3]; see Brongers, *OTS* 15 [1969] 177–92; McKane, ICC, 634–35; the Targum "cup of cursing" may also imply poison). The image shifts to that of sword briefly, indicative of a second metaphor of the manner in which Yahweh will bring about his judgment.

17–18 Verse 17 reports that Jeremiah did as Yahweh had commanded him. Verse 18 gives Jerusalem and Judah as the first of the nations to drink from the cup. Jerusalem and Judah represent the first of the nations to receive God's judgment, probably because of the unique covenant relationship they enjoyed with God. The words "desolation, horror, and shriek" have previously been used of the judgment Judah would suffer; here they link this judgment prophecy with previous ones (e.g., chaps. 18 and 19). The additional description, that Judah has become an object of curse, reminds one further of the covenant context; curse is a part of broken covenant as surely as blessing is a part of obeyed covenant.

The phrase "as at this day" implies that judgment has already come upon Judah and Jerusalem. Possibly this pericope is to be dated after 597 B.C. rather than 605 B.C. of the previous pericope. A date after 597 B.C. would provide an appropriate context for the destruction of much of Judah and Jerusalem.

19–25 A listing of rulers and nations is given in these verses. Various suggestions have been made concerning the list of nations included in the judgment. In general, it seems that the list begins with Egypt to the south (and west) of Judah and moves northward, listing those nations/groups that border Israel, and then moves to more distant countries, skipping Babylon until the very end. A couple of the entries do not quite fit this pattern, specifically Uz, if it is understood as an Arabian region, and Buz and Zimri, which are otherwise unknown.

Such a listing moves generally from south to north (the opposite direction of the "foe from the north" oracles). The list also moves from neighboring nations to more distant nations, with Babylon being the climax of the oracle. Thus the list progresses from Egypt on the southwestern border of Judah to Philistia along the southwestern coastal plain, then to the southeastern and eastern border with Edom, Moab, and Ammon. Then the list moves to the northwestern border with Phoenicia and more distant northwestern areas ("the coast across the sea," perhaps Phoenician colonies or Cyprus or the coastal regions of Turkey). Next the list moves again to the eastern regions, this time to those places more distant than Edom, Moab, and Ammon: Arabia and the desert dwellers. Then the list moves to the distant lands beyond the Babylonian homeland: Elam and Media (and presumably the otherwise unknown Zimri). A summary statement follows: all the kings of the north, near and far, and all the kingdoms of the earth drink from the cup. Finally, as the climactic focus of the pericope, the king of Sheshak (*atbash* for Babylon) drinks from the cup.

The use of *atbash*, the substitution of ת for א, שׁ for ב, etc., is found in several places in the OT. Often such substitutions were deliberate codes to obscure the identity of a person/place. Nicholson (*Jeremiah 26–52*, 222–23) suggests that the Babylonians themselves may have employed the name Sheshak in reference to Babylon. Carroll suggests the code may have served a magical purpose in incantations (500). If the magical nature of the *atbash* is accurate, and if the Babylonians themselves used the name Sheshak, then the terse mention of Babylon would heighten the climactic effect.

27–29 This final paragraph of the pericope has an explanation of the symbolic action. A full messenger formula introduces the Yahweh speech. The drinking and drunkenness/sickness is clarified. All who drink will fall and not rise. The metaphor of drunkenness is then changed in midverse to that of military defeat: "fall, and you shall not rise because of the sword which I am sending" (v 27).

Should any refuse to drink of the cup, a specific word is given, "You *shall* surely drink!" Verse 29 provides a rationale for the universal judgment. If God will bring judgment and devastation against the city that bears his name, can any city or land expect to be exempt? Obviously, the answer is no. All nations will come under God's judgment.

Explanation

In a symbolic action, Jeremiah is commanded to take a cup of raging wine and give it to all nations, beginning with Judah, and ending with Babylon, and he does so. All who drink of it become drunk/sick. The metaphorical judgment is then explained in terms of another metaphor, a sword, symbolic of military defeat. The thrust of this symbolic action/message is that no nation is exempt from God's judgment.

E. Oracles against the Nations (25:30–38)

Bibliography

Bardtke, H. "Jeremia der Fremdvolkerprophet." *ZAW* 53 (1935) 227–30. **Castellino, G. R.** "Observations on the Literary Structure of Some Passages in Jeremiah." *VT* 30 (1980) 398–408. **Hillers, D.** *Treaty-Curse.* **Holladay, W. L.** *Jeremiah 1.* **Kaiser, W. C.** "מלא." *TWOT*, 505.

Translation

> [30] *And you, for your part, prophesy to them all these words, and you say to them:*
>   *"The LORD roars from a height,*   (3+4)
>   *from [a] the dwelling of [a] his holiness, he gives his voice;*
>   *he roars loudly against his habitation,*   (3+3+3)
>   *shouting[b] like the ones treading he will respond*
>   [c] *against all the inhabitants of the land.* [c]
> [31]   *An uproar comes to the ends of the earth*   (4+4)
>   *for the LORD has a controversy with the nations;*

> He will enter into litigation with all flesh: (4+3)
>> the wicked ªhe will giveª to the sword,"
>>> an oracle of the LORD.

³² Thus says the LORD of armies,
>> "Behold evil is about to go out   (3+2)
>> from nation to nation
>> and a great storm is stirred up   (3+2)
>> from the remote parts of the earth.

³³ The ones slain by the LORD ªin that dayª will be from (one) end of the earth unto the (other) end of the earth; ᵇthey will not be bewailed, nor be gathered,ᵇ nor buried; dung upon the face of the earth they will be.

³⁴   Howl, O shepherds, and cry out,   (3+3)
>> mourn, O nobles of the flock.
>
> For your days have come for slaughter ªand your dispersions,ª   (4+3)
>> you will fall ᵇ like a precious vessel.ᵇ,ᶜ
>
³⁵   Flight will perish from the shepherds,   (3+3)
>> and escape from the nobles of the flock.
>
³⁶   The sound of the shepherds' cry!   (3+3+3)
>> the howling of the nobles of the flock!
>> for the LORD is devastating their pasture.
>
³⁷   The meadows of peace are silent   (3+3)
>> from the heat of the LORD's anger.
>
³⁸   He has abandoned his lair likeª the young lion,   (3+3)
>> forᵇ their land will become a horror
>
> from ᶜ the heat ofᶜ the oppressionᵈ   (3+3)
>> ᵉand from the heat of his anger."ᵉ

Notes

30.a-a. LXX omits "the dwelling of."
30.b. LXX, Origen, and *a'* transliterate the Heb.
30.c-c. *BHS* suggests joining with v 31; cf. LXX.
31.a-a. MT has "he will give them"; LXX has "they are given"; Vg has "I have given."
33.a-a. LXX has "on the day of the Lord."
33.b-b. Lacking in LXX.
34.a-a. Not in LXX.
34.b-b. *BHS* includes a suggestion of Ehrlich (1912, 309) to read בבלי חמלה, "without mercy."
34.c. LXX has "like choice rams."
38.a. *BHS* suggests deleting as dittogr.
38.b. *BHS* suggests possibly deleting.
38.c-c. Several MSS (de Rossi, III, 97), LXX, and Tg have חרב. *BHS* suggests reading חרבו.
38.d. LXX has "great," reading "before the great sword."
38.e-e. Lacking in LXX.

Form/Structure/Setting

This last unit of the chapter and in this section of the Book of Jeremiah is primarily poetic. The unit is composed of two separate poetic oracles, the second one having a single verse of prose within. The thrust of both oracles is Yahweh's judgment, which is reaching to the ends of the earth.

The first oracle has elements both of the oracle of judgment against the nation and of the *rib* or lawsuit pattern. The Hebrew root ריב, "controversy," appears as a noun in v 31; so also does the niphal of the root שפט, here translated "enter into litigation." In both oracles, the focus is on the results of judgment, or to use Westermann's elements (see *Form/Structure/Setting* for 17:1–4), the intervention by God and the results of that intervention.

Holladay (678) has noted that v 34 is a call to communal lament, with its commands to howl, cry out, and mourn. Certainly a lament is appropriate in the context of the unrelenting judgment of these oracles.

The implication of these two oracles is that the time of indictment or accusation with any possibility of repentance is past. Only judgment is now possible.

Because the judgment is expressed against the nations, it is possible, though not necessary, that the oracles should be dated after the fall of the kingdom (so O'Connor, *Confessions,* 146).

Comment

30   The emphatic use of the personal pronoun brings into the forefront the prophet's role. He is the messenger delivering Yahweh's message. Both the messenger and the one sending him have clearly defined positions. The phrase "and you say to them" links this oracle with the last part of the previous pericope (v 27) which begins with the same phrase. The introductory words of v 30 stand outside the poetic meter.

The triple occurrence of the root שאג, "roar," emphasizes the loud voice of Yahweh. שאג occurs often in the metaphor of a lion roaring when it has found prey. The image could be that of Yahweh about to bring judgment on the nation, like a lion taking its prey. Alternatively, the metaphor could be that of Yahweh's voice roaring like the thunder, loudly proclaiming the imminent judgment.

The two parallel lines, "The LORD from a height roars, / from the dwelling of his holiness he gives his voice," are reminiscent of the similar opening to the book of Amos: "The LORD from Zion roars, / from Jerusalem he gives his voice" (Amos 1:2). Words identical to Amos 1:2 appear at Joel 4:16. It would seem that this phrase was a common one introducing judgment, and one the people would know well. Jeremiah then would be taking a common phrase and changing it slightly by omitting the direct reference to Zion-Jerusalem, but having the same implication, מעון קדשו, "dwelling of his holiness," is used several times of Yahweh's dwelling place, whether the temple on Zion or in heaven (Ps 68:6[5]; Zech 2:17[13]; Deut 26:15). Likewise מרום, "height," is used at times of Zion-Jerusalem (Jer 17:12). Jeremiah uses the same image concerning judgment as is mentioned in Amos and Joel; it represents Yahweh's roaring as originating from Zion. Jeremiah deliberately does not mention Zion-Jerusalem in the opening lines because that is to be the beginning point of the judgment, as the next line makes clear.

Yahweh's roaring is directed not just *from* Zion-Jerusalem, but also *against* (על) Zion-Jerusalem, here designated נוהו, "his habitation." Elsewhere Zion-Jerusalem is called a habitation only in Isa 33:20. But Zion is only the beginning point of

Yahweh's response; it is a roar against all the inhabitants of the land. The phrase "inhabitants of the land" could indicate all the people of Judah; but it could also mean all the "earth," the wider implication of אֶרֶץ. I would suggest that this verse limits the judgment to Jerusalem and Judah, and the next verse, by way of parallelism, extends the judgment to all nations.

31 שָׁאוֹן, "uproar," is a synonym for שָׁאַג, "roar," of v 30. This verse is parallel to the previous one, with the roaring of judgment now extended to the ends of the earth (using the same word אֶרֶץ, translated "land" above).

The legal connotations are evident from the word רִיב, "controversy," and the verb שׁפט, "enter litigation." This lawsuit-type judgment is more common in the prophets in reference to Israel and Judah, but here refers to the nations. The first oracle is concluded with a messenger formula, which stands outside the metric structure.

32 The second oracle of the unit is also introduced by a messenger formula. In this oracle the focus is upon the judgment on all nations; Judah and Jerusalem are not mentioned specifically. The metaphor employed in the opening of this oracle is evil depicted in terms of a great storm.

33 This prose verse in the midst of the poetic oracle describes the results of the storm judgment. The phrase בַּיּוֹם הַהוּא, "on that day," gives a somewhat eschatological impression to the oracle. The judgment results in mass death, so great a judgment that they will not be mourned nor buried. Similar terminology has previously been applied to the dead in Judah and Jerusalem from impending judgment (8:2; 12:12; 16:4); now the same results will come to the nations. The judgment is closely related to treaty curses (Hillers, *Treaty-Curse*, 68–69).

34 The metaphor shifts for the remainder of the oracle to that of shepherds and the destruction of both the shepherds and the pasture. The shepherds are the rulers of the nations (cf. 2:8; 23:1, 2). אַדִּירֵי הַצֹּאן, "the nobles of the flock," occurs only in this pericope. The word אַדִּיר, can refer to chiefs and kings, giving good parallel to the use of shepherds here. The leaders are commanded to cry out (from distress) and mourn. The word "mourn" is a hithpael of פלשׁ and refers to mourning acts, perhaps "rolling" in ashes or dust.

The leaders are to cry out because of impending slaughter. One might expect the metaphor to continue in reference to the sheep being led to slaughter, as in Jer 11:19 and Isa 53:7. Here slaughter is coming, but, paradoxically, it is the shepherds rather than the sheep who are to be slaughtered.

The phrase "your days have come" is literally in Hebrew "your days are full." That phrase (or the substitution of years for days) appears frequently in the OT to mark the completion of a time span (Kaiser, *TWOT*, 505). One cannot but compare the NT passage in Gal 4:4, "Now when the time was fully come" (RSV). Here the time for judgment on the shepherds has come.

The phrase "your dispersions" seems to interrupt the flow of the poetry. It is not present in LXX, and most commentators consider it to be corrupt and unintelligible. However, the phrase is understandable as it stands. Usually the sheep are the ones slaughtered; and should the shepherd be lost, the sheep are usually scattered "like sheep without a shepherd" (1 Kgs 22:17; cf. Ezek 34:5; Jer 10:21; 23:1–2). Here paradoxically the shepherds are going to face slaughter and/or dispersions instead of the sheep. "Dispersion" could also be a description of the aftermath of warfare: displacement and exile.

The last phrase of the verse, "you will fall like a precious vessel," concentrates not on the fact of falling but on the result. A precious vessel, especially if of costly ceramic, would shatter upon falling; a common vessel might be heavy enough to survive such a fall. The image is again that of destruction.

35 The image of flight perishing, of unsuccessful attempts to flee from impending judgment, is found in other prophetic works (Amos 2:14) and in laments (Ps 142:5[4]; Job 11:20). There will be no refuge (an alternate meaning of מָנוֹס) for those seeking to escape Yahweh's judgment.

36 Verse 36 is not a complete sentence; it is an exclamation concerning what is heard: the sound of the shepherds' cry of distress, howling in despair. The reason for this outcry is Yahweh's devastation of their pastures.

37 As a result of Yahweh's actions, the peaceful meadows are silent. No sheep are there; nor are there shepherds. After the howling cries only deadly silence remains—silence and devastation.

38 Like the image that opened the previous oracle (v 30), this oracle closes with the depiction of Yahweh as a lion. In the previous oracle, it was the lion's roar that was emphasized. In this oracle, the lion's roar is replaced by the howls of the shepherds as disaster overtakes them. In the previous oracle Yahweh was roaring against his habitation, Zion-Jerusalem, and then against all nations. Here he has abandoned his lair (סֻכּוֹ); is it possible that lair is a metaphor for Yahweh's dwelling, Zion? The land that becomes a horror could refer to Judah or to the nations more broadly. The cause of the horror is the heat of the oppression (or oppressors [BDB, 413, taking the form as a collective])—the enemies Yahweh uses to overthrow the nations—and the heat of Yahweh's anger. As Jeremiah often does, the parallel lines indicate both the external force Yahweh uses and Yahweh himself as the active force.

Explanation

This pericope speaks only judgment. The judgment will come upon God's habitation—Zion-Jerusalem—and upon the nations as well. The message is unremitting devastation and destruction. And the final picture, after all has been said and done, is the image of a battlefield littered with unburied corpses and silence. The messenger has brought God's message; the people have not heeded; the result is devastation and deadly silence.

Index of Authors Cited

Aalders, G. C. 213
Aberbach, D. 135,137
Achtemeier, E. xxiv
Ackroyd, P. R. xxvi, 154, 157, 158, 361
Aeschimann, A. xxiv
Aharoni, Y. xvi, xlv, 100
Ahituv, S. 263
Ahius, F. 165, 172, 173
Ahuvija, A. 6
Albertz, R. 19, 20
Albright, W. F. 199, 246
Allen, L. C. 221
Alonso Shökel, L. 224
Althann, R. xli, xliv, 66, 67, 69, 70, 74, 75, 76, 91
Anderson, F. I. xxv
Andreasen, M.-E. 186, 191
Andreasen, N.-E. A. 237
Andrew, M. E. 154
Aquinas, T. xxiii
Arama xxiii
Ari-Yonah, M. xvi
Astour, M. C. 50
Augustin, F. xxvi, xxxi
Avishur, Y. 135

Bach, R. 6
Bailey, K. E. 34, 38
Baldwin, J. G. 328
Ballentine, S. E. 113, 282
Baly, D. 74
Balzer, K. 6
Bardtke, H. 368, 372
Barker, K. L. xxvii
Barnes, W. E. 237
Barrois, A.-G. 107
Barstad, H. M. 25, 28
Baumann, E. 186
Baumgartner, W. xv, xvi, 137, 165, 172, 173, 181, 201, 208, 210, 211, 229, 230, 233, 234, 250, 252, 268, 270, 273, 276, 277, 279
Beek, G. W. Van 159
Beer, G. 83
Behler, G. M. 172
Ben-Corre, A. D. 135, 140
Ben-Reuven, S. 140
Berger, K. xxvii
Bergman, J. 39
Berkovitz, E. 85, 86
Berridge, J. M. xxv, xxvii, 6, 13, 66, 70, 78, 80, 85, 97, 101, 104, 130, 132, 133, 135, 141, 143, 161, 163, 172, 230, 233, 241, 250, 268, 270, 272, 273, 276, 277, 282, 287, 350, 356
Bertholet, A. xv
Beuken, W. A. M. 195, 200
Bewer, J. A. 6
Black, M. xvii
Blackwood, A. W. xxiv
Blank, S. H. xxv, xxvii, 172, 241, 273, 276, 277, 278, 294, 298, 301
Boadt, L. xxiv
Bode, E. L. 13
Boecher, H. J. 282, 290, 292
Boer, P. A. H. de 6, 70, 74, 113, 351
Bogaert, P.-M. xxv, 154
Bonnard, P. E. xxv
La Bonnardière, A. M. xxv
Borger, R. 361

Botterweck, G. J. xix
Bourguet, D. 186
Bracke, J. M. 205
Brekelmans, C. 241
Briend, J. xxv
Briggs, C. R. xxvii
Bright, J. xxiv, xxv, xxvii, xxxv, xlv, xlvii, 23, 27, 31, 35, 42, 47, 58,72, 75, 78,105, 108, 109, 117, 132, 134, 137, 138, 153, 157, 162, 163, 170, 175, 176, 183, 184, 189, 190, 191, 198, 199, 200, 205, 207, 208, 209, 210, 211, 214, 215, 216, 218, 225, 234, 235, 243, 256, 266, 270, 272, 276, 277, 284, 285, 286, 306, 324, 329, 330, 336, 339, 343, 356, 357, 358, 361, 364
Brockington, L. H. xli, 43, 75, 90
Brodie, L. 6, 10
Bromiley, G. W. xv
Brongers, H. A. 368, 371
Bronznick, N. M. 145, 147
Broughton, P. E. xxvii, 6
Brown, F., S. R. Driver, and C. A. Briggs xiii, 14, 31, 86, 98, 105, 116, 137, 150, 157, 182, 199, 214,230, 241, 242, 251, 256,259, 260, 267, 304, 312, 316, 321, 335, 338, 342, 348, 351, 352, 356, 375
Brown, R. E. xv
Brueggemann, W. A. xxiv, xxvii, 130, 133, 135, 141, 144, 151, 152, 153, 195, 237, 246, 248, 249, 279
Buchanan, G. W. xxvii
Burkitt, F. C. 174
Busch, R. J. Vanden xxvii
Buttery, A. 109
Buttrick, G. A. xv

Calvin, J. xxiv, 132, 144, 209, 339
Capella, A. xxiv
Caquot, A. 36, 50, 95
Carlson, E. L. xxvii
Carmignac, J. 154, 157
Carroll, R. P. xxiv, xxv, xxxi, xxxvii, xxxviii, xl, 8, 9, 19, 85, 132, 138, 139, 145, 153, 157, 158, 159, 162, 163, 176, 177, 184, 190, 207, 208, 209, 210, 211, 214, 215, 216, 218, 235, 239, 243, 252, 256, 270, 273, 278, 293, 311, 314, 322, 323, 324, 329, 346, 360, 368, 371
Caspari, W. 113
Cassuto, U. xxvii, 148
Castellino, G. R. 69, 70, 145, 146, 148, 195, 372
Cazelles, H. 13, 56, 58, 130, 146, 166
Cereskő, A. R. 34, 36
Charles, R. H. xii
Cheyne, J. K. xxiv
Childs, B. S. xxvii, 6, 13, 139
Christensen, D. L. 70, 97, 263, 361
Christoph a Castro xxiv
Chrysostom xxiii
Clements, R. E. xxiv, 6, 270
Clines, D. J. A. 263, 268, 270, 272, 273, 276, 277, 280
Cogan, M. 13, 113
Condamin, A. xxiv, 149, 270, 276, 278, 336
Cornill, C. H. xxiv, 6, 175, 256, 266, 267, 270, 284, 324, 329, 336, 347
Corré, A. D. xxvii, 93, 94, 113, 116
Couroyer, B. 221

Craigie, P. C. xxiv, 9, 26, 29, 32, 35, 51, 64, 71, 73, 120, 125
Crawford, T. G. 254
Crenshaw, J. L. xxvii, 172, 180
Cross, F. M. xli, xlii, xliv
Cross, F. M. and D. N. Freedman xviii
Culican, W. 113, 123
Cummins, P. xxvii
Cunliffe-Jones, H. xxiv
Cyrill of Alexandria xxiii

Dahlberg, B. T. 6, 12
Dahood, M. J. xxvii, xli, 7, 31, 85, 86, 89, 90, 93, 95, 107, 108, 113, 132, 135, 137, 139, 154, 156, 159,162, 174, 175, 186,188, 189, 195, 199, 202, 229, 230, 231, 246, 276, 277, 290, 293, 307, 309, 313, 314
Daiches, S. 313
Dalglish, E. R. xxiv
Dalmam, G. 259
Davidson, R. xxiv, xxvii, 155, 224
Davies, G. H. 290, 293
Day, J. 113
Déaut, R. le 66
Deist, F. E. 156, 157
Delcor, M. 113
De Vries, C. E. 2
De Vries, S. J. 334
Diamond, A. R. xxv, 172, 174, 177, 205, 233, 250, 252, 268, 276, 280
Dick, M. B. 155
Dietrich, M., O. Lozetz, and J. Sammartin xvi, 108
Dobbie, R. xxvii
Donner, H. xvi
Dossin, G. 98
Driver, G. R. xiv, 36, 50, 107, 131, 157, 159, 163, 174, 181, 183, 184, 188, 228, 246, 266, 282, 355
Driver, S. R. xiii, xxiv, xxvii, 162
Duhm, B. xxiv, xxxii, 132, 134, 138, 139, 149, 152, 157, 158, 160, 183, 184, 191, 198, 207, 218, 234, 243, 270, 284, 295, 308, 329, 336, 347, 357
Durham, J. I. xxv

Efird, J. M. xxvi
Efros, I. 83
Ehrlich A. B. xli, 373
Ehrman, A. 174
Eichler, U. xxvii, 172
Eichrodt, W. 113
Eissfeldt, O. xxvii, 216
Elliger, K. 75
Ellison, H. L. xxvii, 62
Elliot, R. H. xxvii
Emerton, J. A. 93, 94, 107, 108, 182, 184, 351
Ephraim of Syria xxiii
Eppstein, V. 80
Erbt, W. 284, 329
Erlandson, S. 53
Ewald, H. 270, 277, 284

Feinberg, C. L. xxiv, 87
Fensham, F. C. 361, 366
Fishbane, M. A. 34, 42, 48, 80, 81, 268, 270, 271, 361
Fisher, L. R. xviii
Fitzgerald, A. 246

Fleming, D. 299, 341
Fohrer, G. xxiv, 89, 91, 113, 190, 195, 215
Forbes, A. D. xxv
Forbes, R. J. 107
Fox, M. V. 22, 24
France, R. T. xxvii
Frank, R. M. xxvii
Freedman, H. xxiv, xviii
Freehof, S. B. xxiv
Fretheim, T. 172, 241

Gailey, G. G., Jr. 70
Gale, N. H. 107
Garbini, G. 83
Garcia Moreno, A. 6, 8
Gaster, T. H. 93, 266
Gehman, H. S. 351
Gelio, R. 107, 108, 161, 162
Gemser, B. 25
Gerstenberger, E. xxvii, 174, 205
Gesenius, W., E. Kautzsch, and G.
   Bergstrasser xiv
Gesenius, W., E. Kautzsch, and A. E.
   Cowley xv, 22, 131, 137, 142, 157, 163,
   167, 168, 183, 189, 198, 199, 207, 214,
   247, 251, 256, 259, 301, 306, 308, 312,
   314, 337, 338, 363
Geus, C. H. J. de 195, 198
Gevirty, S. 135
Ghislerius, M. xxiv
Gibson, J. C. L. xiv, 36, 50, 95, 131, 328,
   330
Giesebrecht, F. xxiv, 199, 204, 208, 256,
   270, 284, 324, 329, 336, 347
Gilula, M. 6
Glueck, N. 22
Goldman, M. D. 213
Gordis, R. 246
Gordon, C. H. xix, 95, 108, 159, 198
Gordon, T. C. xxvii
Görg, M. 113, 116, 263
Gouders, K. 6, 8
Graf, K. H. 157
Granild, S. xxvii, 166
Gray, J. 44, 95, 113, 169
Grech, P. 58, 60
Green, A. R. W. 125
Green, J. L. xxv
Greenberg, M. 331
Grelot, P. xxvii
Grol, H. W. M. van 195, 200
Grover, M. 89, 90
Gunkel, H. xviii
Gunn, D. M. 263, 268, 270, 272, 273, 276,
   277, 280
Gunneweg, A. H. J. 6, 174

Haag, E. xxv
Habel, N. C. xxvii, 6
Hacohen, D. B. 135, 137
Hadey, J. 113
Hall, G. H. 19
Haran, M. 58, 61
Harmand, J. 113
Harris, J. R. 33
Harris, R. L. xix
Harris, S. L. 13, 14
Harrison, R. K. xxv
Harvey, J. 25
Hayes, J. H. xlv
Healey, J. E. 74, 75
Held, M. 116, 130, 135, 137, 138, 268, 272
Heltzer, M. 108
Henry, M.-L. 6
Herdner, A. xiv, 50

Hermission, H.-J. 186, 317
Herrmann, J. 113, 320
Herrmann, S. xxvii, xxxi, xlv, 172
Herrmann, W. 345
Hertzberg, H. W. 113
Heschel, A. J. xxv, 273
Hillers, D. R. xxvi, 254, 260, 261, 276, 302,
   361, 366, 372, 375
Hitzig, H. F. 210
Hobbs, T. R. xxvii, xxxi, 49, 50
Höffken, P. xxvii
Hoffmann, Y. 39, 40
Hoftijzer, J. xiv
Holladay, W. L. xxv, xxvi, xxvii, xxxi,
   xxxvii, 6, 7, 19, 31, 34, 38, 42, 46, 53,
   54, 55, 59, 75, 76, 80, 85, 93, 97, 101,
   104, 107, 120, 132, 133, 135, 137, 138,
   139, 140, 142, 143, 144, 145, 147, 149,
   150, 152, 153, 160, 162, 166, 172, 176,
   178, 179, 183, 184, 185, 189, 190, 191,
   192, 199, 200, 201, 202, 205, 207, 208,
   209, 210, 214, 215, 216, 217, 218, 221,
   224, 225, 226, 230, 235, 238, 243, 247,
   253, 256, 261, 263, 266, 267, 269, 270,
   273, 274, 276, 278, 279, 280, 283, 287,
   300, 305, 309, 313, 316, 318, 322, 324,
   329, 330, 335, 336, 339, 346, 347, 357,
   358, 361, 365, 372, 374
Honeycutt, R. L. xxviii
Honeyman, A. M. 188, 263, 305, 306, 317,
   319, 328
Horst, F. 13
Horwitz, W. J. xxviii
Houberg, R. 174
Hubmann, F. D. 165, 172, 173, 174, 176,
   178, 194, 205, 208, 210, 221, 250, 252,
   269, 276, 277
Huffman, H. B. 25, 27
Humbert, P. 290, 293
Hvidberg, F. F. 123
Hyatt, J. P. xxv, xxvi, xxviii, xxxvii, 130, 138,
   140, 166, 167, 172, 176, 270, 273, 284,
   329, 357

Irwin, W. A. 13
Isbell, C. D. 113
Ittmann, N. 172, 173, 276, 277

Jackson, M. 113
Jacob, E. 150
Janzen, J. G. xxviii, xli, xlii, xliii, xliv, 7, 14,
   132, 147, 167, 188, 198, 208, 214, 227,
   254, 269, 270, 276
Jastrow, M. 85
Jean, C.-F. xiv
Jeremias, J. xxviii
Jerome xxiii, 160
Jobling, D. K. xxviii, xxxvii, xxxviii, 46, 47,
   57, 172
Johnson, A. R. xxvi, 350
Johnston, R. H. 241. 244
Jones, A. xv
Jong, C. de 6, 11
Jongeling, B. 135, 138, 141, 144
Jöuon, P. 49, 307
Jungling, H. W. 15, 205
Jungling, J.-W. 13

Kahler, L. 39
Kaiser, W. C. 372, 375
Kautzsche, E. xiv, xv
Keil, C. F. xxiv, 266, 267, 270, 273, 277,
   285, 324, 329
Keller, B. xxviii
Kelley, P. H. xxviii

Kelly, F. T. 233, 250, 254, 269
Kelso, J. L. 188, 254
Kepelrud, A. S. xxviii
Kessler, M. 195, 202
Kilian, R. 6
Kimchi, D. xxiii, 133, 139, 144, 152, 153,
   160, 184, 193, 201, 211, 286
Kirk, H. E. 174
Kissane, E. J. 155, 157
Kittel, R. xiii
Klein, R. W. 324
Klein, W. C. xxviii
Klopfenstein, M. A. 130, 132
Köehler, L. and W. Baumgartner xvi 182,
   260, 334, 335
Köhler, L. 216, 307
König, E. xxvi, 113, 156, 198
Kovacs, B. W. xxvi
Krapf, T. 294
Kraus, H.-J. 6, 113
Kraus, J. P. xxvi
Kuenen, A. 257
Kuist, H. T. xxv, xxviii
Kumaki, F. K. 78, 113, 161
Kurichianil, J. xxviii
Kutsch, E. xxviii, 151, 152, 153, 274

Laberge, L. xxviii
Labuschagne, C. J. 155, 157
Laetsch, T. 270, 279
Lamparter, H. xxv
Lattey, C. 221
Lauha, A. 13, 73
Lehmann, M. R. 210
Lemke, W. E. 345, 346, 362
Leslie, E. A. xxv
Levenson, J. D. 269
Levin, C. 1
Levitan, I. S. 83
Levy, A. J. 166
Lewin, E. D. 6, 269, 270, 277, 280
Liddell, H. G., R. Scott, and H. S. Jones
   xvi
Limburg, J. 25, 27
Lindblom, J. 13, 80, 130, 135, 189, 224, 225
Lindström, F. 299
Lipinski, E. 328, 330, 341
Loewenclau, I. von 39
Long, B. O. xxviii, 13, 49, 50, 89, 91, 146,
   186, 190, 204, 215, 302, 356, 357
Lörcher, H. xxviii, xxxi, xxxvi
Lorenz, R. 113, 126
Loretz, O. 13, 107, 135, 217, 246
Lowth, W. xxiv
Ludwig, T. M. xxviii
Lundbom, J. R. xxvi, 85, 89, 97, 233, 236,
   250, 270, 278, 281

Maag, V. 2
Macholz, G. C. 113
Maimonides, M. 18
Malamat, A. xxviii, xlv, 78, 282, 317
Maldonatus, J. xxiv
Manahan, R. E. xxviii
Marböck, J. xxviii
March, W. E. 254
Marenof, S. A. 195, 198
Margaliot, M. 155, 157, 158, 159
Marks, J. 6
Marrow, S. 269, 273
Martens, E. A. xxv
Martin, D. C. 263
Martin, J. D. 49
Martin-Achard, R. xxviii
Marx, A. 13, 15

Mattingly, G. L. 299, 300
Maurus xxiii
May, H. C. 85
May, H. G. xxviii, 357
McCarthy, D. J. 170
McKane, W. xxv, xxvi, 34, 49, 53, 54, 78, 130, 132, 134, 135, 137, 138, 139, 140, 143, 144, 146, 147, 152, 153, 157, 158, 159, 161, 162, 163, 164, 174, 176, 181, 183, 184, 186, 188, 191, 192, 207, 209, 210, 211, 214, 215, 218, 225, 235, 282, 284, 288, 290, 338, 340, 346, 351, 353, 368, 370, 371
Medico, H. E. del 27
Mehl, L. 6
Melanchthon, P. xxiv
Melchert, J. xxvi
Mendenhall, G. 170
Meyer, I. xxvi, 75, 89, 93, 101, 195, 334
Michaelis, J. D. xxiv, 210, 284, 294, 295
Michalowski, K. 45, 96
Michaud, H. 6
Migne, J. xvii
Mihelic, J. L. 172
Milgrom, J. xxviii, 25, 113, 124
Miller, J. M. xlv
Miller, J. W. xxvi, 202
Miller, P. D., Jr. 217
Mize, R. 241
Moor, J. C. de 50
Moot, J. C. de 135
Mosis, R. 6
Mottu, H. 6
Mowinckel, S. xxxii, 176, 177, 220, 234, 238, 243, 256, 265, 294, 295, 357
Muffs, Y. 70, 74
Muilenburg, J. xxviii, xxxvii, 6, 46, 205, 294, 295
Müller, H.-P. 181, 184

Naef, H.-D. 25
Naegelsbach, C. W. E. xxiv, 339
Naveh, J. 198
Neher, A. xxvi, xxxvii
Neil, W. xxv
Neilsen, K. 25
Nicholson, E. W. xxv, xxvi, xxxv, xxxvi, 9, 34, 36, 53, 81, 91, 192, 237, 238, 243, 256, 257, 263, 266, 294, 295, 329, 357, 364, 369, 371
Niditch, S. 13, 356, 360
Noth, M. xlv, 17
Nötscher, F. xxv, 141, 142, 256, 270, 273, 324,

O'Connor, K. M. xxvi, 233, 250, 252, 269, 270, 276, 280, 283, 364, 366, 370, 374
Odajima, T. 70
Olmo Lete, G. del 5, 6, 8,
Olyan, S. M. 34
Oosteroff, B. J. 146, 147
Origen xxiii
Orlinsky, H. M. xxviii, 233, 250
Orr, A. 362, 367
Overholt, T. W. xxvi, xxviii, xxxi, 1, 6, 25, 36, 93, 101, 134, 141, 144, 155, 157, 158, 160, 202, 282, 334

Pákozdy, L. M. von 113
Paterson, R. M. 19, 206
Paul, S. M. 62, 148, 150
Peake, A. S. 175, 176, 329
Pearce, R. A. 113
Pedersen, J. 278
Perdue, L. G. xxvi

Petersen, D. L. 56
Petrie, W. M. F. 33
Pilch, J. J. xxviii
Pitard, W. T. 269
Plataroti, D. 113
Plöger, J. G. 6
Plöger, O. 362, 367
Pohl, A. 148
Pohlmann, K.-F. xxvi, xxxi, xxxv, 282, 356
Polk, T. xxvi, 172, 195, 233, 250, 271, 276, 277
Pope, M. H. 148, 217
Porten, B. 217
Porter, J. R. xxv
Prewitt, J. F. 100
Press, R. 135
Prijs, L. 276, 279
Pritchard, J. B. xii, xlv, xlvi, xlvii, 98, 126, 303
Propp, W. H. 221, 222, 246, 247

Rabin, C. 75
Rad, G. von 135, 160, 172, 174, 206
Rahlfs, A. 334
Raitt, T. M. xxvi, 46, 356
Ramsey, G. W. 25
Rashi (Solomon ben Isaac) xxiii, 133, 138, 152, 160, 191, 209
Rast, W. E. 113
Reicke, B. xiii
Reid, D. P. xxviii
Rendsburg, G. 93, 94
Reventlow, H. G. xxvi, xxxvii, 6, 13, 70, 72, 113, 119, 135, 137, 138, 139, 161, 162, 163, 172, 173, 175, 176, 177, 180, 201, 207, 208, 211, 229, 230, 182, 356
Reymond, P. 113
Rhodes, A. B. 113
Richter, W. 6
Ridouard, A. xxvi
Ringgren, H. xix, 39
Rizzi, G. 70
Roach, C. C. 304, 305
Robinson, G. 113, 123
Robinson, T. H. 75, 107
Roche, M. de. xxviii, 22, 25, 29, 135, 137, 369
Röllig, W. xvi
Ross, J. E. 7
Rossi, G. B. de xli, 22, 26, 31, 35, 43, 53, 59, 63, 78, 81, 86, 90, 105, 108, 137, 222, 227, 241, 247, 251, 255, 256, 270, 283, 295, 302, 306, 328, 334, 342, 348, 352, 362, 363, 369, 370, 373
Rost, L. xiii
Rowley, H. H. xvii, xviii, xxviii, 53, 54, 166, 174, 176
Rudolph, W. xxv, xli, 7, 131, 137, 139, 140, 143, 144, 146, 147, 153, 156, 157, 158, 160, 161, 162, 163, 164, 165, 167, 168, 175, 176, 183, 184, 185, 188, 189, 190, 191, 192, 194, 198, 199, 200, 207, 208, 209, 210, 214, 215, 216, 217, 218, 222, 234, 256, 267, 270, 272, 273, 281, 284, 286, 295, 306, 308, 324, 329, 339, 340, 357, 358, 360
Rupert of Deutz xxiii
Rusche, H. 151, 153

Sakenfeld, K. D. 22
Sanctius (Sanchez), G. xxiv
Sasson, J. M. 153
Sauer, G. 13
Sawyer, J. F. A. 228
Schenker, A. 362

Schmuttermayr, G. 89
Schneider, D. xxvi
Schottroff, W. 22, 276, 277
Schreiner, J. xxv, xxviii, 7, 113, 151, 153, 174, 206
Schulz, H. 113
Schürer, E. 153
Schutzinger, H. xxviii
Seebass, H. 62, 65
Seierstad, I. P. xxvi
Seitz, C. R. xxvi, 250, 269
Sekine, M. xxv, 113, 124
Sellin, E. xvi
Selms, A. van xxv, 130, 133, 135, 282, 285
Seybold, K. 182, 184
Shehr, T. xxviii
Shultes, J. L. xxvi, 7
Sisson, J. P. 130, 134, 195
Skinner, J. xxvi, xxxvii, xxxviii, 151, 172, 173, 234, 329
Skweres, D. E. 89, 91, 302
Smith, E. J. 113
Smith, G. A.
Smith, G. V. 206
Smith, M. A. 141, 143, 145
Smith, M. S. xxvi, 233, 250, 269, 276, 280, 282, 284
Smothers, T. 370
Snaith, H. 141, 143
Soden, W. von xii, xiv
Soggin, J. A. 34, 38, 42, 58, 61, 75, 80, 90, 98, 107, 113, 141, 142, 182, 183, 299
Southwood, C. H. 186
Speiser, E. A. 198, 244
Spencer, A. B. 58, 59, 116
Sprank, K. 135
Stade, B. 7, 114, 282, 284
Stager, L. E. 114, 125
Stinespring, W. F. 241, 245, 254, 258, 259, 263, 264, 362, 364
Stoebe, H.-J. 22, 114
Strobel, A. xxv, 42, 114
Stuhlman, L. xxvi, xli, 237, 238
Sturdy, J. V. M. xxviii, xxxi, xxxv, 114
Suganuma, E. 25
Sutcliffe, E. F. 85, 89
Swetnam, J. 328, 330

Talmon, S. xli, 13, 14
Tambasco, A. xxviii
Tawil, H. 93, 320
Telcs, G. xxviii
Theodoret of Cyrene xxiii
Thiel W. xxvi, xxxi, xxxv, 19, 137, 146, 147, 165, 176, 178, 183, 190, 192, 194, 201, 215, 216, 218, 237, 243, 254, 280, 356
Thomas, D. W. xiv, 26, 70, 93, 195, 199
Thompson, J. A. xxv, 3, 16, 27, 31, 35, 41, 44, 59, 61, 65, 91, 109, 116, 215, 273, 279, 324, 336, 339
Thompson, J. G. S. S. xxvi
Toll, C. 114, 116
Tov, E. xli, xlii, xliv
Tsevat, M. 218
Tsevat, T. 39
Tucker, G. M. 1
Turner, P. D. M. 56

Urbock, W. J. xxviii

Vaggione, R. P. 17
Vaux, R. de 60, 114, 216, 217
Vawter, B. xliii
Vermeylen, J. xxviii, 7, 8, 172, 208
Virolleaud, C. 50

Vischer, W. 7
Voeglin, E. 7
Vogels, W. 7
Vogt, E. xvi, 1, 7, 362, 367
Volz, P. xxv, 7, 132, 134, 137, 139, 143, 144,
    149, 152, 153, 157, 158, 167, 176, 183,
    188, 189, 190, 191, 198, 199, 204, 207,
    208, 210, 215, 218, 222, 256, 284, 286,
    329, 336, 360

Wachter, L. 263
Waldman, N. 107, 109
Walker, N. 351
Wambacq, B. N. xxv, 155
Wanke, G. xxvi, 241, 254, 257, 263, 265,
    282
Watson, W. G. E. 22, 23
Weften, P. xxix, 172
Weil, H. M. 351
Weinfeld, M. xxviii, 58, 60, 61, 114, 124,
    213, 215, 218, 331, 332, 356, 359
Weippert, H. xxvi, xxxi, xxxv, xxxvi, 7, 80,
    81, 114, 119, 190, 202, 204, 215, 216,
    241, 243, 282, 299, 301

Weiser, A. xxv, 157, 183, 184, 189, 190, 191,
    192, 198, 200, 203, 207, 208, 209, 210,
    214, 215, 216, 217, 218, 222, 270, 290,
    291, 293, 299
Weisman, Z. xxix
Werblowsky, R. J. Z. 347
Wernberg-Møller, P. 351
Westermann, C. 89, 183, 221, 222, 271,
    276, 280, 307, 309, 318, 363, 374
Whitley, C. F. xxix, 114, 362, 366, 367
Wiener, C. 22
Wilcoxen, J. A. 114
Wildberger, H. 305
Wilhelmi, G. 166, 167
Williams, P. 25
Williams, W. G. 13
Williamson, H. A. 186, 189
Wilson, J. V. K. 201
Wiseman, D. J. xlv, xlvi, xlvii
Wisser, L. xxvi, 85
Wissowa, G. xvii
Wittstruck, T. 85, 88
Wolf, C. xxvi, xxxix

Wolff, S. R. 114, 125
Wood, P. S. 13
Woods, J. xxv
Wright, G. E. xii, 114
Wurz, H. 49
Wyk, W. C. 114

Xella, P. 50

Yadin, Y. 109
Young, D. W. 114, 116

Zakowitch, Y. 49
Zevit, Z. 362
Ziegler, J. xli
Zimmerli, W. 7, 13, 356
Zlotowitz, B. M. xli
Zobel, H.-J. 22
Zofia, S.-G. 107
Zwingli, U. D. xxiv

Index of Principal Subjects

Anathoth 2, 3, 179
Antanaclasis 36
Apostasy 45, 55, 123, 134, 140, 171
Aramaic 160
Ark of the covenant 61
Assonance 99, 261, 353
Atbash 370

Baal worship 37, 38, 39, 45, 52
Beth-Hacherem 100
Birth-imagery 84, 320

Call (vocation) narrative 7, 8
Canaanite (fertility) worship 52, 54, 88, 259
Chiastic structure 143, 202, 220, 271, 278, 300, 310, 311, 321, 325, 329
Child sacrifice 125, 126, 259
Circumcision 154, 155
Confessions of Jeremiah 79, 81, 165, 172, 173, 233, 252, 275, 281
Court of law 97
Covenant 24, 44, 45, 46, 51, 55, 170, 224, 238, 245, 292, 298, 303, 316, 359
Creation terminology 327

Deuteronomic influence xxxv, 53, 54, 91, 117, 118, 147, 168, 169, 192, 256
Deuteronomy 134
Divine judgment 109
Divine Warrior 287, 289
Dreams 347, 348
Dwelling place 293, 294

Enemy from the north 109, 139
Early love 24

False love 43
False prophets 350
Foolish/ignorant 96

Gedaliah xlvii
God's sovereignty 112

"Heal"/"deliver, save" parallel 234, 235

Idolatry 161, 171, 259
Indictment of spiritual leaders 135
Intercessor 74, 165, 205

Jehoahaz (Shallum) 306
Jehoiachin (Coniah) 319
Jehoiakim 3
Jeremiad xxx
Jeremiah, the book (anthology) xxx–xxxiii, xxxvi, xl
Jeremiah, the man xxx, xxxvii–xl, xlv, 3, 185, 209

Jeremianic language 117–18
Josiah xlv, xlvi, 3
Judgment 72, 73, 79, 82, 92, 111, 112, 218, 339, 365, 375, 376
Judgment speech 309, 310, 315, 337, 338, 348, 350
Justice 292, 299, 312

Lament 79, 100, 120, 139, 140, 163, 176, 177, 191, 194, 204, 205, 209
Lawsuit 21, 27, 29, 38, 40, 44, 209, 374
LXX xlii, xliii, xliv, xlv, 362, 363

Marriage, divorce, remarriage 51, 55
Memphis 33
Metaphors:
    assayer 110
    camel 38
    circumcised heart 68
    hardness of soil 67, 68
    land, harvest 24
    love, marriage 24, 64
    stain 37, 38
    vine 37
    vineyard 92
    wild ass 38
    wilderness 301
    wind/whirlwind 76, 77
    wounded beast 32
"Mock liturgy" 106
Mode of language xxxiii, xxxiv, xxxv
Mourning 216
Mourning women 151

Nebuchadrezzar (Nebuchadnezzar) xlvi, xlvii, 285, 288
New covenant xxx, xxxi

Oracle of judgment 222, 248, 258, 264
Order/chaos 81, 82

Parallel structure 339, 343
Partridge 228, 229
Pashhur 264, 265, 266, 267, 268, 284, 285
Potter 243, 244, 245, 261
Prehistory of text xli–xlv
Prophetic elegy 151
Prose discourses xxxiv, xxxv

Qīnāh rhythm 230, 277, 309
"Queen of Heaven" 122, 123
Question and answer form 302
Qumran xlii, xliii

Repentance 45, 48, 57, 59, 60, 64, 68, 69, 245, 365
Rhetorical question 41, 203, 248, 249, 253, 343, 346, 347, 348, 349

Roaring lion
    (Yahweh) 374, 376
    (Judah) 184

Sabbath observance 239
Sacrifices (burnt-offerings) 124
Shepherds 375–76
Shiloh 121, 122
Similes
    Bedouin 52
    fowler 96
    rampaging lion 41
    vineyard/grape harvest 103
Stubbornness 148
Suffering of God 145, 146, 165, 171, 183, 184, 185, 186, 204
Symbolic action 189, 191, 215, 216, 240, 241, 256, 258, 260, 261, 262, 267, 370, 372
Syncretism 52, 127, 262

Tahpanhes 33
Tarshish 160
Tekoa 100
Temple 120, 121
Temple sermon 120, 264, 297
Theodicy 88, 89, 180
Trees/forests 300
Topheth 260, 261, 262

Valley of Hinnom (Valley of Hinnon, ben-Hinnom) 125, 128, 259, 38

Warning oracle 99
Word plays
    "almond"/"watching" 16
    "burden"/"oracle" 239, 353, 354
    "empty"/"decanter" 260
    "fool"/"corpse" 229
    "fruitful all around"/"terror on every side" 267
    "have not taken care of"/"take care of"/"will be 'visited' or 'lacking'" 325
    "plot"/"pay attention" 252
    "see"/"fear" 226
    "slave"/"treaty" 32
    "wind"/"spirit" 92
    "Zedekiah"/"Yahweh is our righteousness" 329

Yahweh speech 231, 232

Zedekiah xlvii, 3, 286, 329, 330, 331
Zephaniah 285

Index of Biblical Texts

A. Old Testament

Genesis

1	81
1:1–2:4a	81
1:22	327
1:28	327
2:4b	81
2:7–8	244
2:19	244
9:1	327
12:6–7	135
12:8	238
14:19, 22	261
15:5	204
17:7–8	359
17:10–14	68
18:23–33	87
19	278, 279
22:17	204
28	348
27	144
27:35	144
35:5	156
37	348
34:13	144
41	348
49:8–10	184

Exodus

1:7	327
3:11–4:12	11
5:3	287
5:24–26	154
6:3	170
6:7	170, 359
9:15	287
13:5	168
15:14–16	106, 109
19:5	170
19:5–6	61, 66
20:8	223
22:1 (Heb)	42
22:2–3 (EVV)	43
22:29	125, 126
23:11	224
24:12	223
25:22	170
31:18	223
32:11–32	204
35:3	123

Leviticus

2:14	358
3:22	203
13:46	211
17:8	124
19:27–28	217
21:5	217
22:17–25	124
23:17	358
23:20	358
26	203
26:12	359

Numbers

5:11–31	139
12:6–8	348
14:12	287
14:13–19	204
15:32–35	123
15:39	223
18:20	160

Deuteronomy

1:31	64
4:13	168, 223
4:20	168
4:26	29
4:30	170
5:9	40
5:15	82
6:3	168, 170
6:4	168
7	65
7:8	168
8	28
8:3	210
8:5	64
8:18	168, 223
8:19	168
9:5	168
9:9	223
9:10	223
10:16	154
11:9	168
12:2	223
14:1	217
15:2	224
15:3	222
18:9–22	xxvii
18:15–22	9
18:18	9
20	301
24:1	53
24:1–4	49, 50, 51, 54
26:9, 15	168
26:15	374
26:17–19	192
27:3	168
27:15	168
27:15–26	170, 171
27:26	168
28:14	168
28:37	357
28:59	9
29	147
29:1 [MT 28:69]	168
29:9 [MT 8]	168
29:12 [MT 13]	359
29:17	147
29:18	117, 147
29:22–28	91
30:1–20	106
30:6	66, 67, 154
30:19	106
31:5	170
31:20	168
32:1–2	106
32:6	261
32:8 [LXX]	182
32:10	301
32:15	354
32:24, 33	371
34:10–12	9

Joshua

2:12	298
5:6	168, 170
17:11	266
17:16	266

Judges

1:22	301
8:19	298
9:17	287
21:7	298

Ruth

4:15	204

1 Samuel

1–4	121
2:5	204
2:18	9
7:8	204
12:19–23	204
14:1, 4, 6, 8	303
14:4	303
14:39	298
17:44–45	293
18:11	319
20:33	319
24:22	298
25:20	239
25:42	239
31:8–13	260

2 Samuel

1:21	246
13:19	44
13:29	239
15:12	170
18:9	239
23:7	155

1 Kings

1:50, 51	223
3	348
7:2	294
7:6	83
8:51	168
9:8–9	91
14:10–11	260
16:4	126
16:20	170
17:7	198
18:30	234
21	298

22 — 344
22:1 — xlv
22:17 — 375
22:23 — 169

2 Kings

2 — 298
2:19 — 358
2:21 — 234
8:51 — 168
9:37 — 116, 149
10:3 — 287
11:14 — 170
16:3 — 125
18:23 — 239
19 — 285
19:2 — 255, 259
21:6 — 125
21:10–15 — 204
22:3–23:5 — xlvi
23:5 — 221
23:10 — 38, 125, 260
23:13–16, 19–20 — 260
23:15–20 — 57
23:26 — 204
23:29–30 — xlvi
23:30–37 — xlvi
23:36 — 191
24:1 — xlvi
24:1–17 — 192
24:3 — 204
24:8–17 — 190
24:10–16 — xlvi
24:10–17 — xlvi
24:12–16 — 192
25 — 285
25:1 — xlvi
25:1–7 — 323
25:1–12 — 284
25:5–7 — xlvi
25:18 — 285
25:22–23 — xlvi
25:23–25 — xlvi
25:24 — xlvi
25:26 — xlvi
25:27–30 — 319

1 Chronicles

3:15 — 306
3:17–18 — 322
9:12 — 285

2 Chronicles

20:25 [LXX] — 221
32:8 — 287
34:1 — xlv
34:3–7 — xlvi
34:8–35:19 — xlvi
35:20–24 — xlvi
36:9–10 — xlvi
36:15 — 117

Ezra

2:23 — 179

Nehemiah

2:13 — 259
3:13–14 — 259
7:27 — 179
10:4 [EVV 3] — 266
11:12 — 285

Job

1:22 — 339
3 — 277
3:1, 3, 4, 8 — 277
3:1 — 277
3:3 — 277
3:3–13 — 80, 81
3:8 — 277
3:10 — 277
3:11 — 277
3:20 — 277
5:21 — 246
11:20 — 376
20:19 — 146
34:28–33 — 350
38:26 — 301

Psalms

1 — 58, 106, 225
1–50 — xxiv
1:1 — 211
13:1 — 177
15 — 119, 120
15:1 — 223
15:2–5 — 120
16:5 — 160
22 — 205
23 — 325
24 — 119, 120
24:3–4 — 120
26:4–5 — 211
28 — 177, 178
31:14 — 267
34:11 — 32
48:2 — 73, 223
58:5 — 371
65:6–8 — 160
68:6 [MT 5] — 373
73 — 185
74:1 — 326
77:3 — 7
77:18 — 160
79:6 — 163
79:6–7 — 162, 163, 164
79:7 — 163
79:13 — 326
80:7 — 209
80:8–11 — 37
81:13 — 147, 168
83:11 — 116
89:11 — 160
90:10 — 366
91:6 — 245
95 — 290
95:5 — 244
95:7 — 325, 326
100:3 — 325, 326
104:26 — 244
107:43 — 147
122:6–8 — 204
140:4 [MT 3] — 371
142:5 [MT 4] — 376

Proverbs

1:7 — 96
3:3 — 223
7:3 — 223
5:15–18 — 30
8:22–30 — 10
15:18, 28 — 209
16:9 — 164
17:14 — 209
22:10 — 209
25:11–14 — 228
26:20 — 209
28:25 — 209
29:22 — 209

Ecclesiastes

2:24 — 311
3:13 — 311
5:18 — 311
7:2 — 217
7:6 — 14
8:15 — 311

Isaiah

1:1 — 2
1:12–17 — 298
1:25 — 110
2:2–4 — 61, 219
6:1–13 — 8
6:3 — 322
6:6–7 — 11
6:8 — 11
6:10 — 203
7 — 193
8:6 — 246
9:5 — 329
9:5b — 305
10:2 — 292
11:1 — 329
11:1–9 — 329
11:2 — 329
11:2–5 — 329
11:11 — 329
18:7 — 219
19:8 — 218
19:19–25 — 219
24:4 — 201
33:17 — 137
33:20 — 374
36:8 — 239
37 — 285
37:2 — 259
38:14 — 132
40–48 — 157, 158
40:2 — 216, 218
40:9 — 316
40:10–11 — 325
40:18–20 — 160
41:6–7 — 160
41:8 — 49
44:9–20 — 160
44:12 — 156
45:7 — 244
45:18 — 244
46:5–7 — 160
48:1 — 298
49:1 — 7
49:9 — 49
53:6 — 339
53:7 — 375

Jeremiah

1 — 18, 24, 364
1–20 — xxiii, xxxi, 281, 283
1–25 — xxv, xxvi, xxxi, xxxii, xxxv, 364
1:1–25:13 — 9, 11
1–25:14 — xxv
1–28 [LXX] — xlii
1–32 — xxiii

1:1	178, 362	2:32	248, 249
1:1–3	xli, 364	2:33–37	25, 30, 31, 34, 39, 41
1:2	362, 364	3	245, 316
1:4	3, 216	3:1–4:2	67
1:4–5	212	3:1–4:4	45, 50, 53, 56, 59, 60, 63, 66, 68, 70, 109, 110
1:4–10	2, 14, 15, 17	3:1	54, 55, 60, 64, 70
1:4–19	14, 15, 269	3:1–5	55, 64, 158
1:5	204, 273, 281, 364	3:2	54, 57, 63, 183
1:6	243, 273	3:2–5	54
1:6–9	364	3:2, 9	50
1:7	17, 170, 364	3:2, 13	63
1:8	17	3:3	54, 63, 64, 95
1:8, 18–19	211	3:4	63
1:8, 19	273, 274	3:5	57
1:9	210	3:6	56, 57, 223
1:9, 18–19	212	3:6–11	57, 59, 181
1:10	109, 183, 244, 267, 357	3:6, 8, 11	57
1:11–14	358	3:7, 8, 11	63
1:13	109, 268	3:8	50
1:13–15	72	3:10	63
1:14–15	364	3:11	57
1:15	366	3:12	59
1:16	179, 217	3:12b	60
1:17 [LXX]	xli	3:12–13	59, 60
1:18	108	3:13	63, 169, 170, 223
1:18–19	205	3:14	63
2	30, 33, 47, 48, 51, 68, 70, 110, 249	3:14–18	54, 57
2:1–4:4	72	3:15	50, 164
2–6	25, 27, 45, 46, 48, 67, 70, 72	3:16	353
2:1–6:30	71	3:17	148, 168, 260, 359
2:1	9, 50, 70	3:18	63
2:1–3	27, 28, 31, 32	3:18, 19	50
2:1–19	23	3:19	59, 60
2:1–37	45	3:19 59	
2:2	30, 36, 41, 43, 52, 63	3:20	55
2:2	316	3:21	49, 50
2:2–3	31, 47	3:22	59, 64, 261, 263
2:3	32	3:24–25	316
2:4	22	4	130, 139
2:4–13	23, 36, 40	4–6	xli, xliv, 76, 91, 111
2:5	217	4:1	55, 67
2:5, 8	36	4:2	69
2:6	40, 41	4:3–4	52, 56, 58, 61, 66
2:6, 8	36	4:4	109, 154, 292, 365
2:7, 23	36	4:5–6:30	45, 47, 71, 109, 129, 130
2:8	38, 41, 60, 134, 351, 359, 375	4:5	64
2:8, 23	36	4:5–6	99
2:8–13, 26–28	158	4:5–8	99
2:9	31, 40, 209	4:5–10	99
2:9–18	23	4:5–18, 23–28	109
2:10	248	4:6	77, 99, 198
2:10–13	248	4:10	130
2:11a	248	4:11	49, 50
2:12a	248	4:12	14, 179
2:13	211, 230, 249	4:19–21	81
2:13a	248	4:19–22	162
2:13, 17, 19	217	4:20	164
2:13, 27, 28	36	4:22	144, 359
2:13, 32	259	4:23–28	112
2:14–19	23, 28, 30, 36, 203	4:24–26	145
2:14, 31	133, 137	4:31	7, 193
2:18–19	23	5:1–9	95, 96, 102, 103, 133, 134
2:20	223	5:2	102
2:20–28	43	5:3	130, 133, 144
2:21	139	5:4	359
2:23	43	5:4, 5	133
2:23–26	43	5:5	102, 359
2:24	43, 201	5:7–9	144
2:25	43	5:7, 19	217
2:26	43	5:8	193
2:27	53, 55	5:9	95, 97, 102
2:28	43, 167	5:9, 29	95, 130, 142, 143
2:29	179	5:10	103, 139
2:29–32	27, 43	5:10a	80
2:30	60		

5:12–13	95		
5:18b	80		
5:19	147, 215, 259, 352		
5:20–25	158		
5:20–29	144		
5:22–23	133		
5:23	359		
5:31	103		
6	132		
6:1	198		
6:1–8	109		
6:3	184		
6:7	144		
6:9	103, 130, 139		
6:9–15	102, 103, 133		
6:10	106, 154		
6:11	102		
6:11–12	253		
6:12–15	130, 132, 134, 138, 139		
6:13	102		
6:13–14	74		
6:13–15	202		
6:14	130, 343		
6:15	102, 157		
6:22–30	70, 74, 77, 80, 82, 84, 88, 93, 97, 101, 103, 107, 137, 193		
6:24	137, 193		
6:25	106, 267		
6:27	130		
6:27–30	144		
6:28	144		
7	171, 262, 266, 297, 343		
7:1–8:3	168, 169		
7:1	165, 194, 243, 283		
7:1–15	257		
7:2	259, 297		
7:3–20	216		
7:4	320, 322		
7:5	297		
7:6	297		
7:10, 11, 14, 30	211		
7:13, 25	168		
7:16	165, 167, 205		
7:16a	167		
7:17	169		
7:18	262		
7:19	259		
7:22	170		
7:23	169, 170, 357, 359		
7:24	148, 168, 170		
7:26	217		
7:29	49		
7:30	260		
7:30–32	258, 260		
7:30–34	257		
7:31	260		
7:31–32	259		
7:32	256, 260		
7:33–8:3	216		
8	203		
8:2	375		
8:3	144		
8:4–9:25	70		
8:4–9:10 [MT 11]	200		
8:4–5, 19, 22	137		
8:7	152		
8:8	147		
8:8–9	152		
8:9	147		
8:10–12	138, 185, 200, 202		
8:10–13	102		
8:11	198, 343		
8:11, 15	144		
8:12	102, 152		
8:13–9:23	135, 141		

Reference	Pages
8:14	147
8:15	199, 200, 203
8:18	228
8:18, 22	200
8:19	144, 150, 259
8:19, 22	133, 203
8:21–23 [MT 9:1]	192
8:22	261
8:23 [MT 9:1]	144, 150, 200, 203
9:1–5 [MT 2–6]	193
9:1–10 [MT 2–11]	184, 200, 204
9:2	152
9:3	357
9:4	204
9:5 [MT 6]	200
9:6 [MT 7]	200, 357
9:7 [MT 8]	180, 204
9:9	148
9:9–21	147
9:11	152
9:12	151, 170, 303
9:13	168
9:16–21	144
9:21 [MT 22]	116, 164, 216
9:22–10:18 [LXX, 4QJer^b]	xlii, 157
10–11	189
10:2	183, 185
10:4	xlii
10:5	xlii
10:6–8	xlii
10:9	xlii
10:16	244
10:17	314
10:19–21	78
10:21	324, 375
10:25	152
11–13	189, 264
11–20	xxvi, 284
11:1	194, 243, 283
11:1–17	178, 192
11:2, 3, 6	168
11:3	65
11:4	357, 359
11:7–8	217
11:8	148, 359
11:9–17	202
11:10	202
11:11	202
11:14	202, 205
11:16	178, 178
11:18–23	78
11:18	172
11:18–12:2	172, 205
11:18–12:6	172, 184, 185, 201, 208, 209
11:19	270, 272, 375
11:20	272, 275
11:21–23	183
12:1	14, 209
12:2	185
12:3	210, 228, 236
12:4	194, 201, 336
12:5	210, 249
12:5–6	185
12:6	181, 183, 189
12:7–8	204
12:7–9	160
12:7–13	143
12:7–17	178, 204
12:12	49, 50, 375
12:14–17	11
12:16	147, 298
13	242, 257, 262
13, 19	368
13:1–11	256
13:1, 16	258
13:10	148, 168
13:12	203
13:12, 13	189
13:12–14	215, 352
13:14 [MT]	288
13:17	168, 324
13:19	179
14	179
14:1–15:9	211
14:1	165
14:1–16	208
14:6	49
14:9	211
14:10	253
14:11–12	165
14:12–18	253
14:13	71, 217
14:17	190
14:18	216
14:19	133, 137
14:19b	137
14:22	158
15	278
15:1–4	215, 352
15:2	253
15:2–3	217
15:5–9	143
15:6	354
15:8–9	208, 215
15:8–10	215
15:10–12	218
15:10–21	165, 172, 174
15:12–14	222
15:13	222
15:13–14	265
15:14	222, 268
15:15	272, 294
15:16–18	336
15:18	249, 279
15:19	344, 349
15:20	15, 273, 274
16:1	358
16:1–4	189
16:4	116, 375
16:10	169
16:10–13	352
16:11	147
16:12	148, 168
16:14–15	332
16:14–16	332
16:15	331, 332
16:21	222
17	257, 298
17:1	208, 227
17:1–4	226, 227, 374
17:1–13	227, 230, 233, 236, 238
17:1–18	238
17:3	207
17:3–4	207, 208, 210, 265
17:4	207, 226, 228, 273
17:5	222, 227
17:5–8	230, 288
17:5–13	224
17:6	198, 250
17:7	235
17:8	228
17:10	235, 272, 275
17:11	230
17:12–13	229, 234
17:12–18	172, 234
17:12	203, 236, 374
17:13	xli, 198, 202, 217, 235, 236, 259
17:13a	235
17:13b	235
17:13–16a	236
17:14	228, 230, 261
17:14–18	228, 230, 231, 238
17:15–16	326
17:18	218
17:19–20	298
17:19–27	238
17:24–25	298
17:27	298
18	240, 257, 261, 262, 359
18, 19	371
18–20	240, 265
18:1	165, 194, 258, 283, 296
18:1–3a	355
18:1–11	252
18:1–12	183, 189, 265
18:2	257
18:3	257
18:3a	355
18:3c–4	355
18:3c–11	355
18:4	257
18:5–11	355
18:6	257
18:7, 9	7
18:7–9	11, 359
18:7–10	288
18:8	252
18:10–11	256
18:11	252, 257, 260, 365
18:12	148, 168, 170, 252, 253
18:12a	256
18:13–17	240, 252
18:14–15	xli
18:15	253, 259
18:16	257, 261, 366
18:17	265
18:18–23	172, 240
18:20	272
18:23	260
19	240, 242, 264, 266, 293, 296, 297, 298
19–20	240
19:1–2	189, 240
19:1–13	240
19:2	264
19:2–3	298
19:3, 4, 6, 7, 12	264
19:3–9	240, 258, 264, 266
19:3–13	266
19:3, 13, 14	264
19:4	217, 296
19:4–8	303, 304
19:5	125
19:6, 11, 12, 13	266
19:7	229, 264, 268, 313
19:8	303, 360, 366
19:8, 11, 12	264
19:10	240, 268
19:10–12	296
19:11	234
19:11–13	240, 258, 266
19:14	240
19:14–15	240, 257
19:15	169, 239, 240, 262
19:18	199
20	240, 263, 268, 276, 277, 284, 294
20:1–2	284
20:1–3	240, 262
20:1–6	257
20:3	260, 270, 272
20:3	274
20:4–6	240
20:7–12	240
20:7–13	172, 277
20:7–18	269, 276
20:8–9	336

20:9	272, 335	23:11	338	31:33	170, 359
20:10	267	23:12	179, 337	31:33a	223
20:11	273, 354	23:14	343	31:33b–34	223
20:11–13	280	23:15	146, 147	31:34	359
20:13–18	240	23:16	337	31:35–36	135
20:14–18	172	23:17	118, 148, 168	32	179
20:14	276	23:22	365	32:1	364
21	179, 266, 280, 282, 283,	23:23–24	335	32:1–15	189
	284, 290, 296, 301	23:25	198	32:19	227
21–24	277, 280, 283, 314	23:27	354	32:22	168
21–25	281, 283, 284, 364, 368, 370	23:33	215	32:33	168
21:1	243	23:33, 34, 36, 38	239	32:34	211
21:1–7	299, 361	23:40	331, 334, 357	32:35	125
21:1–10	291, 292, 329	24	179	32:38	359
21:5–7	292	24:6	11, 56	32:39	359
21:7	318, 361	24:9	199	33:6	198
21:10	56, 292	25:1–4	369	33:10	169
21:11–23:8	292, 335	25:1–11	367, 368	33:11	238
21:11	286, 298, 300, 306, 335	25:1–13	9	33:14–16	329
21:11a	296	25:1–14	xxxii, 361	33:14–26	xlii
21:11b	296	25:11	366	33:20–21, 25–26	135
21:11–12	286, 295, 296, 298	25:13 [LXX]	xlii, 362, 366, 369	34	179, 329, 361
21:11–14	300	25:14	168, 361, 362	34:1	266, 283
21:12	295, 311, 365	25:15	139, 168	34:1–7	284
21:12a	296	25:15–29	366	34:5	309
21:12b	296	25:15	361, 366	34:13	170
21:12c	296	25:18–26	364	34:15	211
21:13	286, 314, 315, 316	25:19	168	34:17	199
21:13–14	314	25:23	153	35	364
21:14	300, 315, 365	25:27	373	35:1	283
22	296, 325	25:29	211	35:12–17	364
22:1–5	300, 312	25:31	209	35:15	365
22:3	311, 312	25:31–32	364	35:17	169
22:5	312, 332	25:33	116	36	xxxii, xxxiii, xxxiv, xl, 9, 19, 20, 21,
22:6	315, 318	26	113, 120, 122, 257, 262, 266, 343		23, 223, 253, 266, 281, 296, 368
22:6–7	297, 314, 315	26–45	xxvi, xxxi, xxxv	36:1	364
22:7	163	26–52	xxiv, 360, 363	36:1–8	296
22:9	147, 217	26:1	364	36:3, 7	266, 365
22:10	306, 315, 318	26:1–6	113, 119	36:5	266
22:10, 12	318	26:1–19	113	36:5–12	295
22:11	304, 305	26:3	365	36:10	259
22:11–12	305, 319	26:10	295	36:29	9, 11
22:12	217, 315	26:19	169	36:31	169
22:13	325	26:20–23	41	36:32	xxxii
22:13–19	xlvi, 100, 325	27 [LXX 34]	xli, 171, 179	37	177, 284, 285
22:14	137	27–28	318, 319	37:3	205, 285
22:15–16	153	27:1–28:17	189	37:3–10	284
22:16	359	27–29	285, 343	37:5	xlvi
22:18	305, 325	27:1	364	37:13	267
22:18–19	315	27:1–3	xlvi	38	266
22:18–23	361	28:1	363	38:1	285
22:19	325	28:20	344	38:1	285
22:21	169, 170	29	179, 285	38:2	283
22:22	325	29–52 [LXX]	xli, xlii	38:7	267
22:23	193	29:1–32	160	38:28 [LXX]	7
22:24	323	29:18	168	39:1–10	284
22:24–30	192	29:19	168	39:4–13	xlii
22:26	217	29:25, 29	285	39:5	14, 179
22:28	133, 137, 203, 318	29:26	264, 266, 267	39:16	169
22:29	113, 116, 118	30–32	359	40:2	169
23:1–2	375	30–33	xxxii	40:5	xlvi
23:1–4	315, 316, 335, 338, 350	30:1	283	40:7–41:15	xlvi
23:1–6	324	30:1–2	xxxii	40:11–12	xlvi
23:1–8	324	30:17	261	41:5	217
23:2	365, 368	30:18	164	42:1–43:7	xlvi
23:2, 3, 8	335	30:22	170, 359	42–44	4
23:3	335	30:23	342	42:2, 4, 20	205
23:5	153	30:24	342	43:6–7	xl
23:6	334	31–34	170	43:7–9	33
23:7	214	31:1	359	43:8–13	189
23:7–8	214, 215, 216, 218, 334, 351	31:15	151	44:6, 17, 21	169
23:8	214	31:28	7, 244	44:9	350
23:9	290, 291, 292	31:31	xxxi	44:17–19, 25	113
23:9–40	290, 291, 335, 336	31:31	223	44:22	365
23:10	334, 338, 343	31:31–34	61	45–51	368

46	xlvi
46–51	xxxii, xlii, 11, 363, 366
46:1	xxxii, 198, 201
46:5	267
47:1	198, 201
48:4	198
48:15	163
48:37	217
48:44	179
49:1	137, 203
49:2	266
49:25	267
49:32	153
49:34	198, 201
49:41	133
50:6	339
50:42	107, 108
51:15–19 [LXX 28:15–19]	157
51:16 [LXX 28:16]	157
51:19	244
51:37	143
51:59–64	189
52	285, 288
52:4–16	284, 288
52:9	179
52:19	14
52:24	285
52:28	192
52:30	xlvi

Lamentations

2:6	94
2:14	339
2:22	267
3:24	160

Ezekiel

1–3	8
2:8–3:3	210
3:1–3	11
3:16–21	106
6:7	359
6:10	359
7:18	217
8–11	354
11:23	286
14:1–5	92
15:1–8	37
16	24
20:25	124
20:25–26	125
21:1–10	190

21:21 [MT 16]	357
21:32 [MT 27]	322
22:17–22	107
22:18–22	110
23	55
33:1–20	106
34	325
34:5	375
34:29	195
37:15–19	190

Daniel

2, 4, 7	348
7	85
9	366
9:2, 24–27	xxxix
10:5	155
10:14	344

Hosea

1–3	24, 51
1:2–9	215
1:9	360
2:5	301
2:8	359
2:18–25	124
2:20	359
2:25 [MT 23]	360
4:1	359
5:4	359
6:3	359
6:6	298, 359
8:2	359
8:13	198
10:12	68
11:5	130
11:8–9	357
13:4	359
13:7–8	88
14:10	147

Joel

3:1	349
4:16	374

Amos

1–2	185, 224, 239
1:1	2
1:2	336, 374
1:4, 7, 10, 12, 14	239

1:6, 9	189
1:14	239
2:2	239
2:5	239
2:14	376
4:4	291, 292
4:13	244
5:21–24	298
5:25	124
5:26	123
6:7	216, 217
7–8	357, 358
8:10	217

Jonah

1	344
1:4	319

Micah

3:3	221
4:1–4	61
4:16 [LXX]	221

Habakkuk

1:3	208
1:6	137
3:12	162

Zephaniah

1:2, 3	137

Haggai

2:23	319

Zechariah

2:17 [MT 13]	374
3:8	329
5:1–4	358
5:4	298
6:12	329
8:20–23	219
13:9	110
14:16	219

Malachi

1:11	219
3:3	110

B. New Testament

Matthew

4:19	219
11:17	150
16:13–19	12
21:13	128

Mark

1:17	219
4:1-9	68
10:5	xxvii

Luke

13:6-9	139
17:26-30	311
19:41-44	140

John

18:23	190

Romans

2:25-29	154

1 Corinthians

1:31	153

2 Corinthians

10:17	153
12:7-10	219

Galatians

1:15-16	12
4:4	374

James

1:9153

C. Apocrypha, Pseudepigrapha, and Other Ancient Texts

Baruch

1:1-3:8xli

Sirach

33:4181

Dead Sea Scrolls

4QJer131, 142, 156, 157, 227

1 Clement

13:1153

Index of Key Hebrew Words

All indexed words appear in their lexical forms. Significant variations from that root form which occur in the text appear in parentheses after the root: e.g. צדק (צדיק). Variant spellings are indicated by brackets: e.g. רפא [רפה]. Proposed examples of word plays and assonances are divided by virgules: e.g. שָׁקֵד/שֹׁקֵד.

אבד	8, 243
אבל	184, 201
איה יהוה	21, 27
אכל	91, 92, 294
אם־לא	209, 301
אמת	351, 352, 353
אסף	137, 138, 259
ארץ [ארע, ארק]	158, 230, 318, 322, 330, 373
בגד	55–56, 63
בוש	36, 43, 231, 272
בוש/יבש	36
בנה	243, 357
גור	267, 270
דָּבָר	179, 287
דרך	43, 57–58, 63, 159, 336
ה...אם...הלא	204, 248
ה...אם...מדוע	133, 137, 200, 203, 248, 321
הבל	28, 259, 342
הוי	309, 310, 325
הלך אחרי	21, 27, 36
הנה (הנני)	50, 236, 258, 259, 352, 355, 364
הנה־ימים באים	332
זכר	223, 272, 273–74
זנה	54
חזק	272, 273
הי־יהוה	298, 332
חנף	50, 54, 336, 338
חסד (חסיד)	57, 153, 316
חשב	243, 252, 348
טול	217, 318, 319
ידע	152, 218, 236, 311
יכל	270, 272, 273
יצא	144, 305, 306–7
יצר (יוצר)	7, 243–44, 245, 257
ירא/ראה	226
ישב	291, 314, 332, 363
ישב/שוב	363
ישע	234
כה אמר יהוה	220, 335, 343
כשל	254, 275
לב	220, 335, 343
לכן	247, 254, 258, 309, 312, 325, 335, 338, 339, 347, 351–52, 353
מדבר	40, 143
מדוע	21, 133, 137, 200, 203, 248
מגור מסביב	267, 268, 270, 272
מהתה/מחסי	236
מי־ראש	138, 139–40, 339
מצא/מצמאה	36
מקוה	202, 229, 230
מקום	120, 202, 203, 216, 230, 307
משא	239, 351, 352, 353
משפט	88, 132, 133, 134–35, 179
נאף	336, 338, 339, 343
נבא (נביא)	267, 290, 291, 334, 335, 338, 347
נבל/נבלה	229
נטע	243, 244, 357
נטש	353
נשא/נשה	353
נתן	59, 220, 223, 265, 353, 358
נתץ	243, 244
נתש	243, 244, 357
סבב	286, 294
סיר	14, 67
עבד	21, 32, 36, 37
עזב	148, 150, 217, 220, 230, 232, 249
ערים	36, 266
עריץ	272, 274
פקד (פקיד)	102, 266, 267, 325, 327, 334
פרת/פרה	190
פתה	270, 271, 272, 273
צדק (צדיק)	179, 329, 330
צלח	166, 323
צמח צדיק	330
צעק	201, 315
צפון/צפענים	139
קדש (קדוש)	223, 298, 300, 301, 373
קשב	106, 252, 253
ראה/ירא	226
רוח	92, 160, 316
ריב	27, 40, 179, 209, 253, 372, 373
רעה	99, 316, 327
רעה/רעע	99
רפא [רפה]	63, 234, 261
שוב	47, 48, 50, 51, 54, 55, 57, 59, 63, 66, 87, 130, 132, 133, 243, 245, 247, 305, 332, 339, 358, 363
שו/ישב	363
שחת	166, 189
שכח	249, 348
שלוח	316
שלום	130, 204, 217, 342
שמה	249, 364
שמם (שממה)	257, 261, 366
שמע	63, 138, 169, 170, 189, 252, 364
שפים [שפיים]	49–50, 75, 185
שָׁקֵד/שֹׁקֵר	16
שקר	63, 102, 144, 339
שרק (שרוקה)	249, 257, 261, 364
שררות [שרירות]	59, 117, 118, 148, 249, 343
תפלה	338
תקע/תקוע	99